Eyewitness Accounts of the American Revolution

Letters
of William Lee
1766-1783

Edited by Worthington Chauncey Ford

The New York Times & Arno Press

973.3
L 5'1L
7 7353
Jan. 1972

Reprint Edition 1971 by Arno Press Inc.

*

LC# 70-140863
ISBN 0-405-01254-3

*

Eyewitness Accounts of the American Revolution, Series III
ISBN for complete set: 0-405-01187-3

*

Manufactured in the United States of America

LETTERS

OF

WILLIAM LEE

William Lee

LETTERS

OF

WILLIAM LEE,

SHERIFF AND ALDERMAN OF LONDON; COMMERCIAL AGENT
OF THE CONTINENTAL CONGRESS IN FRANCE; AND MIN-
ISTER TO THE COURTS OF VIENNA AND BERLIN.

———

1766=1783.

COLLECTED AND EDITED BY

WORTHINGTON CHAUNCEY FORD

VOL. I.

BROOKLYN, N. Y.:
HISTORICAL PRINTING CLUB.
1891.

TO

MY FATHER,

WHOSE LIBRARY OF AMERICANA,

THE FRUIT OF A HALF CENTURY'S DEVOTION,

HAS RENDERED THESE VOLUMES

POSSIBLE.

CONTENTS OF VOL. I.

(v)

INTRODUCTION.

In 1641, a Lee emigrated from England to Virginia and settled in Northumberland. From him descended many who occupied prominent positions in the colony of Virginia, and in the State when it had thrown aside the control of the mother country; as tobacco planters, as politicians, as merchants and as diplomatists, the name constantly recurs in Virginian history, and as constantly with reputation. Like most Virginian families, their connections with the leading gentry by marriage were numerous, and not a little contributed to their influence. After Bacon's rebellion it was an aristocracy of planters that controlled affairs in the colony, and not until the revolution and the democratic movement that accompanied it, were the offices of honor and profit in the administration thrown open to the "common born." The favor of the king appointed the governor, and all minor appointments in the executive were bestowed to increase the influence of the king, and, it may be added, the governor. The plums of patronage were thus naturally bestowed upon the leading spirits of the colony, either as rewards for services rendered, or to secure a somewhat factious agitator to the royal cause. Landed property carried with it influence, and by this means the larger planters commanded not only the favor of the governor, but also the suffrage of the electors. The Council of the governor, the high offices of State, and the House of Burgesses were controlled, if not monopolized, by the "aristocrats" of the colony. They might be heavily mortgaged to their English or Scotch factors, but they were politically supreme, and the same names run through generations in the respective offices.

Richard Lee, the emigrant, described himself as "lately of Stratford-Langton, in the county of Essex," and research in the English records has shown that there was a family of Lees settled at Quarrendon, Stratford-Langton, Ditchley, etc., in that county. It was to this family, therefore, that the emigrant belonged, and not to the Shropshire Lees, to which some would give him. Fancy and fiction have woven a a pretty tale about the loyalty of the Lees to the house of Stuart;* but cold fact has shown the fancy to be misdirected. A Lee may have invited the fugitive loyalists to come to Virginia, and even suggested that Charles II. come out as the ruler of the colony; he may have visited Charles at Breda to learn if he would protect the colony, did it declare its allegiance to him; and a proclamation "on the death of Cromwell," may have been issued, proclaiming in Virginia Charles II. King of Great Britain, two years before the restoration. "The King, had he no other subject in England, should dispose at will of those of the house of Lee." † Governor Berkeley, no doubt, was a royalist at heart, and not only opened his house and purse to the fugi-

---

* Lee's Memoirs of the War. Edited by Robert E. Lee. The Cyclopedia of American Biography has taken its sketch of the emigrant from the work.

† Walter Scott's *Woodstock*, ch. xxxvii.

tive royalists who came to Virginia to escape persecution in England, but also wrote to Charles, "almost in-
viting him to America." * But he did not proclaim
him king either after the death of Cromwell, or after
the retirement of Richard Cromwell, and he accepted
his re-election to the governorship at the hands of the
Assembly, before the Assembly had recognized the
position of Charles. It was not until the restoration
of Charles had been accomplished that Virginia dis-
played her loyalty, and reinstated the king as the
sovereign of the colony.

While much that has been asserted about Richard
Lee, the emigrant, must be set aside as fiction, enough
remains to show that he was a man of some prominence
in the colony. In association with Thomas Ludwell,
John Carter, Robert Smith and Henry Corbin, he was
on a commission appointed by Governor Berkeley, in
1663, by royal command, to devise means of improving
the staple of tobacco.† He must have died soon after,
as a subsequent commission, appointed for much the
same purpose, named Thomas Ludwell, Secretary of
the colony, and Major-General Robert Smith, but Lee
was omitted. As such commissions were usually
composed of members of the Governor's Council, or the
House of Burgesses, it is likely that Lee was in one of
those bodies. He left a family of eight children, six
sons and two daughters.‡

---

* 1 Bancroft, 162.

† Campbell, *History of Virginia*, 264.

‡ I use the valuable *"Record of the descendants of Col. Richard Lee,"* prepared by C. F. Lee, Jr., and J. Packard, Jr., published in the *New England Genealogical Register*, 1872.

Richard, of Westmoreland, the son of the emigrant, married a daughter of Henry Corbin, who had emigrated from Warwickshire, England, nine years after Richard Lee, and settled in Middlesex County, Virginia. This Richard was a member of the governor's Council, resigned at the time of Bacon's rebellion, upon a scruple of taking the oaths, but was later reinstated with his former rank at the Board.* Governor Spottswood describes him as "a gentleman of as fair character as any in the country for his exact justice, honesty and unexceptionable loyalty. In all the stations wherein he has served in this government, he has behaved himself with great integrity and sufficiency; and when his advanced age would no longer permit him to execute to his own satisfaction the duty of Naval Officer of the same district [North Potomack], I thought I could not better reward his merit than by bestowing that employment on his son."† Richard Lee died in 1714, and one of his sons, Philip, removed to Maryland, causing a split in the family.

A younger son, Thomas, married Hannah Ludwell, a connection that greatly strengthened his position in the colony, for this lady was a connection of Frances, Lady Berkeley, the wife of Sir William Berkeley.‡ He was member of the general court, and in 1741 he

---

* II Spottswood, 38.

† I Spottswood, 178. He had been appointed by Berkeley.

‡ This lady was married three times: 1. Captain Samuel Stephens, of Warwick county, Virginia; 2. Sir William Berkeley; and 3. Philip Ludwell, of Rich Neck; but she retained the title of Lady Berkeley. She was a sister of Alexander Culpeper.

acted with William Beverley, of Blandfield, as one of the commissioners on the part of Virginia to treat with the Indians at Lancaster, Pa.; and it may have been his experiences on that mission that led him to join in forming the Ohio Company in 1748, which had for its object the settlement of a large tract of country on the Ohio. As president of the Council, he became the acting Governor of the colony in the interim between the departure of Sir William Gooch (1749), and the arrival of Governor Dinwiddie; succeeding John Robinson in that position; and in his will, made at that time, he styled himself "President, and commander-in-chief," of Virginia. He died in 1751, leaving a large family, which gave an unusual number of prominent characters to the exciting period of the Revolution that was now approaching. The fourth son, Thomas Ludwell Lee, was a member of the governor's council from 1758–1775, served in the House of Burgesses, was a delegate to the colonial conventions of 1774 and 1775, and a member of the committee of safety. He took an active part in the convention of 1776 that gave the first constitution under which Virginia became a State, and was one of the five revisers of the law acting under that constitution. At the time of his death, in April, 1778, he was a judge in the general court. Of his brothers Richard Henry, Francis Lightfoot (Loudon), William and Arthur, it will be unnecessary to give full sketches in this place.* William is the subject of these volumes.

---

* I am about to publish a collection of letters of Richard Henry Lee, and my brother, Paul Leicester Ford, is collecting

William Lee, the tenth child of Thomas and Hannah
(Ludwell) Lee, was born in Stratford in August, 31st,
1739. Of his earlier years nothing is known, not even
traditions coming down in the family to give a glimpse
of what his training and experience may have been.
His position appears to have been overshadowed by
that of his elder brothers, and it is not until the indignant protests of the colony called forth by the stamp
act were framed, that his name is found. He is then
enrolled among those who were active against those
acts, and this was the index of his subsequent political
career. Late in 1766, or early in 1767, he accompanied
his brother, Arthur, to England, to engage in mercantile pursuits.

The Lees arrived in London at an important period,
for it was one of political transition, or experiment,
due to the increasing leaven of democracy. The king
was intent upon having a voice in the disputes of the
day, and upon laying down a policy that was to control. But in seeking to carry this idea of a personal
government of the sovereign into effect, he was obliged
for the time to depend upon the support of a number
of factions, quarreling among themselves, and apparently incapable of so combining as to constitute a party
willing and ready to co-operate with him. His close
advisers were extremely unpopular, and with reason
too; for Bute had not the character required to make
a prime minister of the necessary vigor and honesty,
and Chatham, the one man in whom the people had

the writings of Arthur Lee. Both of these brothers have suffered greatly at the hands of their biographer.

unbounded confidence, shook their faith by accepting
honors from the king at a crisis; and when he did
reach power, was spell-bound by that strange malady
that destroyed his capacity for directing the affairs of
State, and still further removed him from those whose
intimacy should have strengthened his position. Ministry succeeded ministry with little power of cohesion,
and with many points of difference among themselves.
The Rockingham ministry was ousted in 1766, the
year in which the Lees are said to have reached England, and Pitt sought to dissipate faction by calling
around him a heterogeneous collection of subordinates,
to be dominated by his own personality. Wilkes, a
source of uneasiness to the ministers, seized the opportunity to seek for a reversal of his outlawry, but failed,
and returning to Paris, eased his feelings in a letter to
the Duke of Grafton that contributed much to place him
before the people as a martyr to popular liberty, and
led the way to his subsequent agitation and preferment
in municipal politics. His election by Middlesex,
arrest and committment under a charge that appeared
to the people "cruel, malignant and indefensible,"
the ready use he made of the riot in St. George's Field,
and the letter of Lord Weymouth, and the subsequent
expulsion from Parliament, raised him at once to a
popular idol, and the democracy became aggressive—
even riotous. The expulsion of Wilkes from the
House of Commons gave a common ground on which
the opposition could stand together,—the defence of
the rights and liberties of the subject.

The ministry, taken from the Bedford party, was

embroiled by the rising opposition of America to any form of taxation, and change of individual members seemed incapable of producing any unity of policy, or singleness of action. Lord Shelburne was crowded out, and his known American sympathies pointed him out as a leader of that part of the opposition that favored the colonies, though he was no friend to Wilkes and his faction. The retirement of Chatham gave the king and the king's friends an opportunity which they were not slow to act upon. In Lord North the king found his desired minister, and under North the influence of the opposition began to wane.

In a period of turmoil the agitator has his opportunity : and when the movement extends to the lowest basis of society, the demagogue comes to the front. Wilkes was in every way a demagogue, but he was shrewd in the use of the chances that an obstinate and autocratic king threw in his way. It is now generally conceded that Wilkes was a true "martyr" to the lawlessness of a House of Commons, guided by the Crown ; and so far as he combatted that lawlessness, and demonstrated the right of his conduct, he rendered a real and lasting service to constitutional liberty. As an agitator, he held London, a very important factor in English politics, under his complete sway, and from 1768 to 1774, he was the point around which the city agitation surged. More than this, he "had done more than any other single man to unite a divided and powerless opposition, and to mark out the lines of political parties."* The means he made use of were danger-

---

* III Lecky, 143.

ous to an extreme, as through disaffection, want and distress, the city was subject to mob outbreaks involving a serious menace to life and property. Juries partial to the lawless would not find a true bill against rioters, and would not do justice to soldiers under prosecution for obeying orders in quelling riots. The government was distinctly unpopular, openly opposed to the popular views, and in every respect was little more than a provisional administration, bridging over the passage from the old control of a ministry, alone responsible for its acts, to a rule of the king and the king's friends.

Arthur Lee was in close relations with Wilkes from the first. He drew up the preamble and resolutions which embodied the political activity of the Bill of Rights party; it was Lee who wrote the address of thanks to Aldermen Crosby and Oliver for their opposition to the acts of the Commons; it was he who first introduced the American grievances into the Wilkes movement, and added them to the arraignment of the ministry. He was from the beginning of his English stay thrown in with the Chatham-Shelburne party, whose waning influence and subsequent impotency soon threw it into an ineffectual opposition. He himself had parliamentary aspirations as early as 1767, and as a step to securing that advancement, he desired the agency of Virginia.* As *Junius Americanus* he argued the cause of America before the people of London, and he always deemed the cause of America the cause of Middlesex. His associations with Wilkes and

---

* I Arthur Lee, 192.

the "bill of rights" party gave him a compact, earnest and powerful instrument of agitation, and he undoubtedly used it to advance his own views, as well as to advance the political fortunes of his brother.

While Arthur Lee was a politician from his first entrance into London life, and was assiduously cultivating acquaintances and connections that could be useful to him in the near future, William was more inclined to a commercial career. It has not been possible to trace the steps he took to establish himself in a commercial line, for the records are wanting. In 1769 he meditated a voyage to India, but abandoned the idea, and married on 7 March, 1769, Hannah Philippa Ludwell, eldest daughter of Philip Ludwell, of Green Spring, James County, Virginia.* The ceremony was performed in the Parish Church of St. Clement's Dane, in the county of Middlesex, London. This marriage may have brought him the capital necessary to enter a mercantile firm, for in 1769 or early in 1770 he is found in partnership with Dennis DeBerdt, whose daughter married Joseph Reed, of Pennsylvania; and with Stephen Sayre, an adventurer from America. He was engaged in the Virginia tobacco trade in 1769, but whether on his individual account, or as a member of a firm, I have been unable to determine. He made his first venture in that trade in that year, and in January 1770 the following circular letter was issued, written by Lee to his Virginian acquaintances:

---

* The lands at Greenspring, near Jamestown, had been settled on Sir William Berkeley, for his great services to the colony and to the Stuarts. Philip Ludwell died 27 March, 1767.

LONDON, JAN. 27, 1770.

Dear Sir: According to the advices of our W. Lee, we now send out Capt James Walker in the new Ship Liberty, to load for us in Potomack. We have purchased her, that our friends may be upon a certainty of a regular annual ship to bring home their tobacco, & carry out their goods.

We shall think ourselves extremely happy to be favor'd with your consignments & interest, for which purposes, if the plan will be agreeable to you, we will endeavor to prevent your former connections from being any objection. On this head, we should wish you to write us explicitly, that we may be fully acquainted with what you desire; tho' for the present we hope Capt W. will receive some of your favors. As we conclude our Mr. L. has mentioned our plan fully to you, we think it needless to say any thing more here, only with our best respects to y^r Lady & Family, we remain with the highest esteem, Dear Sir,

Your mo: Ob: Hble Servt,

DEBERDT'S, LEE & SAYRE.
DENNYS DEBERDT,
DENNIS DEBERDT, JUN.,
WILLIAM LEE
STEPHEN SAYRE

Richard Henry Lee, Esq., Chantilly, }
Potomack River, Virginia. }

Among the letters of Richard Henry Lee to his brother William, are found many references to these tobacco ventures, and to the affairs of the plantation at Greenspring, but it is unnecessary to repeat them here, and the commercial career of William may be passed over.

As William Lee, before he left England to take office under an American appointment, was candidate for more than one of the high offices under the corporation of London, we may give a glance at the political institutions of the metropolis. In many respects they were unique, survivals from the Middle Ages, and entirely anomalous when compared with that of other cities in the kingdom. The municipality was governed by a Lord Mayor, a Court of Aldermen, a Court of Common Council, two Sheriffs, and other executive and judicial officers. The freemen of the city elected the Aldermen and Common Council; but the freeman to be an elector must have a certain property qualification in the city. Citizenship was confined to members of the sixty-nine livery companies of London— the Livery of London—and it was the Livery that elected the chief officers of the city and the Members of Parliament. The Livery, assembled in Court of Common Hall, would nominate two of the Aldermen, who had served as Sheriffs, and one of these two was elected Lord Mayor by the Aldermen. An Alderman was chosen for life from one of the wards into which the city was divided, and acted as magistrate for the city of London, formed a part of Common Council, and presided over the assemblies in his own ward—the Ward mote. The Sheriffs were chosen by the Livery annually, and had certain judicial functions to perform in the Sheriff's Court. So that the man who served as Sheriff stood a fair chance of becoming Lord Mayor, by passing through an election to the Court of Aldermen.

In the middle of June, 1773, a number of the Livery of London met at the Half Moon Tavern to consider

the proper nominations for the Shrievalty. Mr. Hun-
ford, a name to be met with often on such occasions,
nominated two Aldermen—Kirkman and Plomer; upon
which Dr. Arthur Lee nominated Mr. Stephen Sayre,
Citizen and Framework-Knitter, and made a warm and
sensible speech, unfortunately not reported, but was
said to "reflect much honor on the Doctor's head and
heart." Objection was made that Sayre was little
known, and certain offensive remarks were made upon
Mock-Patriotism, clearly an indication of the existence
of some differences of opinion, not tempered by the
spirit of Wilkes. Plomer was a favorite in the race,
and the meeting proceeded to canvass between Kirkman and Sayre, and the latter won. Why, the bare
outline of the proceedings fail to show. On the 24th,
the election was officially completed, and Sayre pledged
himself to "have a watchful eye upon every step
taken to advance the power of the Crown, and against
the inroads of despotism and corruption from entering
the city." He was a Patriot, a Wilkesite, and a demagogue.

Plomer held his office for a few days only, having, as
he afterwards explained, a "misunderstanding with
some gentlemen, who, I hope, (as they profess themselves to be) are still the friends of the public."* A
new election was ordered to fill his place, and the Livery assembled at Common Hall on July 3d. Each of
the Aldermen, who had not served as Sheriff, was placed
in nomination; but no enthusiasm was shown save
when Kirkman was named. Then William Lee, citi-

* *London Chronicle*, 7 June, 1774.

zen and Haberdasher, was suggested, "a known and approved friend of liberty," and an almost unanimous approval shown. He was declared elected, and spoke as follows:

Gentlemen of the Livery and Fellow Citizens:
I return you my warmest thanks for the honour you have this day conferred upon me, in chusing me one of your Sheriffs for this great city and the county of Middlesex. The office I chearfully undertake, as it is an undoubted proof of your approbation of those public principles in which I have lived, and which I shall most assuredly carry to my grave. As neither the terrors of a tyrannical Court, nor its allurements, will ever have any influence over my conduct, so I shall always esteem it the most distinguished honour of my life to obtain the confidence and applause of the independent Livery of London. The trust which you have reposed in me shall, on all occasions, be exerted, with its utmost honour, in opposition to the arbitrary encroachments which are daily making on our rights and privileges. It shall not be my fault if we do not transmit to our posterity undiminished, and even untainted, those glorious privileges and immunities which our ancestors have so nobly handed down to us."*

Stephen Sayre was a native of New York, had been

---

*The new Sheriffs did not take office until September 29th, when they were sworn in with the usual solemnities. They "went immediately from Guildhall to the several prisons, and gave many humane directions about the treatment of the prisoners, who have a good hot dinner provided at their expence. The private friends of the new sheriffs were elegantly entertained at the London Tavern." *London Chronicle*, 30 September, 1773. They afterwards went to Westminster, where they were approved of the king, and counted the horse-shoes and hobnails, "according to antient custom."

a classmate of Joseph Reed at Princeton, and later appears to have acted in some land transactions, in which Charles Townshend, Chancellor of the Exchequer, was interested. Removing to London, he had engaged in the American trade, and failing in that, had married a lady of fortune, turned banker, and dabbled in politics, the turmoil of Wilkes' agitation affording a fertile ground for such a restless nature as Sayre's.

The attitude of Sayre is more distinctly marked than that of Lee in these political events, for Sayre was somewhat eccentric, dashing, ambitious, and, it must be added, unscrupulous in his methods. He afterwards said he "was brought into office upon public principles, and as a partizan with a set of men who were of a decided character," and both decision of character and partizanship were needed in the elections. For the meetings of the Livery of London were not marked by the decorum and soberness of judgment that should mark a deliberative assembly, and cuffs and kicks were administered under party feeling as readily as epithets, more forcible than polite, were bandied among the different factions. The past history of the metropolis, in contrast with the existing situation under Wilkes' domination, afforded much thought to the spectators, and occasioned comparisons by no means complimentary to the ruling spirits. Courage of conviction, as well as energy of action, was needed in the public officers, for the spirit of democracy was inclined to assume strange shapes, and required a strong hand to keep it within reasonable bounds. A revolution was in the air, and only men influenced by "true revolution principles" were put in office. Although a necessary part of their duty, it required some courage on the part of the sheriff to issue summonses to John Wilkes and Serjeant Glynn to attend their places in Parliament,—a measure that invited the hostility of the Court.

It was not a period of squeamishness in politics, for bribery controlled Parliament, and loud-mouthed vituperation and scandalous abuse of opponents marked the discussions, so called, of political questions. Wilkes did not hesitate to insert a paragraph in the *Public Advertiser*, that "all parties in the city look forward with pleasure to the conclusion of a Mayoralty, in which violence, tyranny, neglect of public business, a contempt of all order and decorum, with the most sordid parsimony, have prevailed."* And at the coffee-houses was circulated a paper announcing that on Wednesday the 29th of September, would be run for over Groaning Common, a purse of four thousand guineas and a gilt state coach :

BY LORD NORTH'S STUDD.

The famous horse Rosy Wine, Shakespeare, in claret. The little horse Economy, Esdaile, in green.

BY SHELBURNE'S STUDD.

The powerful horse Spavin, Sawbridge, with a gold collar. The American horse Drubwell, Oliver, in red.

THE BILL OF RIGHTS STUDD.

The famous horse British Liberty, Wilkes, in blue,

---

*John Townshend had been Lord Mayor, through whom Lord Shelburne hoped to destroy Wilkes' influence in the city

and the much-admired horse Ready Money, Bull, in white.

Stephen Sayre, Esq ; ⎫
William Lee, Esq ; ⎬ Stewards. *

It was an electioneering skit, the contest for the Lord Mayoralty coming off on the day named, and the Ministerial, Opposition, and popular candidates being thus described.

In November occurred an election for a member of Parliament, in which the contest of faction ran high. The "ministerial" candidate was John Roberts, and against him Wilkes pitted the Lord Mayor, Frederick Bull, whose advancement had been due entirely to his wealth and his unbounded admiration for "Squinting Jack," as the political "boss" of the city was familiarly called. Poor Roberts was unmercifully treated during the poll, and his descent from the hustings was marked by an outbreak in which he was jostled, trod on, his shins broken, and he was generally ill-treated. That the election was an honest one can hardly be asserted with confidence, for tricks that are still employed in political elections were fully resorted to—charges of bribery, scurrilous paragraphs, forged utterances, personal intimidation, and colonization of voters. The Sheriffs presided, and were supposed to preserve order, but in this case their partisanship appeared to have got the better of their discretion. One Hunt, who claimed to be a member of the Armourers and Braziers' Company, had cast his vote for Bull, when he was charged with being no livery-man.—a charge that was true.

---

* *London Chronicle,* 11 September, 1773.

Sheriff Lee, however, settled the matter by seizing the challenger by the collar, putting him in charge of the constables, and detaining him for some hours, while the dishonest voter went free. The injured freeholder advertised Lee in the papers as one "whose personal capacity I despise and hold in the utmost contempt."

Although Bull received a majority of the votes of the livery-men, Roberts demanded a scrutiny, or re-canvass, and six scrutineers were appointed in behalf of each candidate. Among those named on the side of Bull were Wilkes and Arthur Lee. Before the scrutiny was completed, Roberts demanded to be represented by counsel, a demand that the sheriffs saw fit to deny, for the reasons given in their address to the livery-men. * Roberts thereupon withdrew from the contest, and Bull was declared elected.

Of Lee's services as sheriff, I find little record apart from this election incident. He attended the usual city feasts, was present at executions, "on horseback, dressed in black and carrying a white wand," and on the whole bore the dignities of his office as conscientiously as he performed its duties. With such a plutocrat as Bull in the Mayor's chair, dispensing hospitality with a lavish hand, as he had pledged himself to do, the sheriffs erred on the other side, and many a sly hit was made on their parsimonious habits, and their omission to entertain as had been the custom. For twelve months he and Sayre were in office; his coach and livery "trimmed with green, with cuffs and collars elegantly trimmed," were familiar objects in the city,

---

* Printed *Post*.

and his political record maintained by his devotion to the Patriot. In September, 1774, he resigned his gown and chain to his successor, and with Sayre, gave "a hot dinner for the poor prisoners in the Compters and Ludgate prison; and also an entertainment for the serjeants and yeomen of the county."

At the installation of his successor in September, 1774, Mr. Lee made an address to the Livery.

"*Gentlemen of the Livery:*

"'To a heart like mine, that beats high with affection and zeal for liberty and the public good, and particularly for the welfare and happiness of the honest and independent Livery of London, your liberal thanks are one of the highest gratifications.

"In the execution of the high and important office with which you entrusted your late Sheriffs, they made the laws and constitution of this country, together with the rights and franchises of the Citizens of London, their only rule of conduct, and in every instance they have endeavored to discharge their duty as became honest and upright men. They have studied to reform the various abuses that have from time to time crept into the office; but it is impossible in one year to rectify all those which, perhaps, have been growing for ages; however, it is to be hoped your present worthy Sheriffs will continue the work of reformation that is now begun for them. We have been particularly careful to prevent every imposition on the unhappy persons who have been from various causes and misfortunes put under our care. We have made out a new special jury book for the city of London, in preparing which we used all the care and caution possible to make it correct. Were I not from principle most firmly and immoveably attached to the prosperity and happiness of the Livery of London, your generous and noble conduct this day would bind me to you forever."

Lee, now a private citizen, was politically ambitious, and while declining to stand for the aldermanship from the Cordwainers' Ward in July, 1774, he was spoken of as a candidate for Parliament from Southwark,* and did stand, the vote at the end of each day standing:

	Mon.	Tues.	Wed.	Thurs.	Total.
Mr. Polhill	185	384	605	14	1195
Mr. Thrale	165	329	522	10	1026
Mr. Lee	123	195	417	12	741
Sir Abraham Hume . .	55	167	232	3	457 †

However gratifying this result was to him, he seems convinced that he had aimed too high, for almost two weeks later he was one of the candidates for the aldermanship of Bridge Ward within,‡ but apparently not of his own free will, as he declined a poll. The resignation of Barlow Trecothick, because of ill health, left a vacancy in the court a few days later, and Lee at once set out on a canvass of Vintry Ward. Trecothick is doubtless one of the few merchants named by Lee as favorable to the American cause, and this may have determined him to take up the fight, his opponent being Nathaniel Newnham, of Botolph-lane.§ At the Ward Mote, the show of hands was in favor of Newnham, and on a poll which was open for two hours, Newnham was elected by a majority of thirteen votes, securing 59 against Lee's 46.‖

---

* *London Chronicle*, 4 October, 1774.

† Do., 15 October, 1774.

‡ Do., October 27.

§ Do., November 3d.

‖ *London Chronicle*, 5 November, 1774.

Meanwhile political matters were drawing to a crisis, forced upon the ministry by the course of events in America. Parliament had adjourned late in December, to meet again on January 19th. "By his majesty's command" Lord North submitted the papers relating to the Disturbances in North America, and the contest opened. What was done in Parliament has only a secondary interest for us, as it is the city of London that concerned William Lee. Parliament determined to stand by the king, and produced the bill to prohibit New England from participating in the Newfoundland fisheries, and restraining the trade of the same. The merchants and traders had already acted. On Wednesday morning, 4 January 1775, between three and four hundred merchants engaged in the American trade met at the King's Arms Tavern, Cornhill, to take into consideration "the present unhappy disputes between the mother country and her colonies." Mr. Thomas Lane was chosen chairman, and Mr. Barclay opened the discussion by asserting that the meeting was not a manœuvre of government, as had been charged, and proposed the following resolutions:

"That it is the opinion of this meeting, that the alarming state of the trade to North America makes it expedient to petition to Parliament for redress.

"That a committee be appointed to prepare a petition to the House of Commons, and lay the same before a general meeting, to be held at this place this day se'nnight."

Mr. Bacon (member for Aylesbury) thought the

mode of petitioning rather premature, as the king had already said he would lay the petition from America before Parliament, and the action taken upon that should be awaited. Mr. David Barclay urged action, as the silence of the merchants in the year previous had been made a handle of last session by the minister. Mr. Baker put in a word for an "extremely guarded" expression in pointing out the particulars of redress, as "in case of any one thing demanded or omitted, which may be afterwards found necessary to add or expunge, the Parliament may hold the petitioners to the direct letter, which perhaps would be inefficient to their general purposes." The West India merchants of Bristol offered their coöperation in the objects of the meeting through Mr. Samuel Vaughan, and Mr. Hayley said the traders of Liverpool, Manchester, Leeds, and other places, were awaiting the results of the London conference. After some further discussion, a committee of twenty-three—three to each province and two over— nine of whom were to make a quorum—was appointed to draw up a petition. William Lee was named a member of this committee.

The next week the petition was laid before the merchants, and on the suggestion of Mr. Watson, mention of the Quebec bill was added as a grievance, and three members for the province of Quebec were added to the committee—Mr. Strettell, Mr. Watson, and Mr. Hunter. The petition was then completed, approved by the meeting, and ordered to be prepared for signing and submission to Parliament. The petition rehearsed the acts that had disturbed the Colonies, checked commerce with them, and were reacting on the trade and manufactures of the kingdom, and asked that the matter might be thoroughly examined, and that they might be heard in support of their petition.*

This paper was presented to the House by Alderman Hayley, who asked that it be considered in the Committee of the Whole House, to which the other American papers were referred, and that the Petitioners be heard upon it. Sir W. Meredith thought a separate committee more expedient, and after a spirited discussion, this proposition was adopted.† The merchants were displeased at such a course of conduct, and some even proposed to withdraw the petition, to show their sense of its reception. At the suggestion of Alderman Kirkman a second petition was drawn, praying that the House would take no action on the American papers laid before it, until the merchants had been heard on their petitions. Parliament promptly rejected the request contained in this petition, and Mr. Wooldridge, one of the merchants' committee, appearing at the bar, stated that the merchants would waive appearing before the committee—the Coventry committee, as it was called. The merchants then decided to petition the Lords, and after considering a proposition to prepare one to the king, decided against it for the present. The passage of the bill to restrain the New England fisheries by both houses convinced them of the

---

* The Petition is printed in Force, *American Archives*, Fourth Series, I., 1513.

† Force, *American Archives*, Fourth Series, vol. I., 1513, where the debate is given.

futility of looking to Parliament for reddress, and they determined to approach the king (March 22d). On the following Thursday, Mr. Lane, Mr. Molleson and Mr. Bridgen, representing the merchants, waited on his majesty at St. James, and presented their petition, "which his majesty received very graciously."

Lee from the first warned his Virginia correspondents against putting much faith in the merchants of England, for interest guided their sympathies, and the administration was able to work upon their fears. He wrote to America to persevere in maintaining the recommendations of Congress. To his mind no success could follow such a measure unless the English merchants and manufacturers should combine in their opposition to the measures of the Ministry, and combination was, under the circumstances, difficult. "Nothing but a cloud of petitions well supported can save the American commerce, and with it every American merchant and trader, from speedy and total ruin." *

The Boston port bill convinced him there was a "settled plan to subvert the liberties and constitution of this country as well as of America;" the king was obstinately bent upon this; his advisers, the ministry, were supporting him; Parliament was their submissive instrument; and the people, sunk in luxury and dissipation, would acquiesce in any proposal that should be laid before them. The principal actors were almost brutally characterized: Lord North, "a tyrant from principle, cunning, treacherous and persevering; a perfect adept in Sir R. Walpole's plan of corrupting;"

---

* William Lee to William Hicks, 23 January, 1775.

Dartmouth, "who will whine, preach and cry, while he is preparing to stab you to the heart." The first act of violence on the part of England, he thought, would absolve their allegiance to the Crown, dissolve the government, and do away with the compact between king and people. Rebellion was justified, and the colonies united in a federal union, governed by a Congress, would escape the shackles of slavery that were being forged for them.

The Livery of London now took up the question, and at a meeting held on the 5th of April, unanimously agreed to make an address and remonstrance to the throne on the American measures, and ostentatiously voted their thanks to the Lords and Commoners who had opposed the restraining act. Whether Lee was active in calling the meeting and forcing a conclusion is not determined, and it is more than likely that the ruling spirit was Wilkes himself; for he had a score of long standing to settle with the king, and he was not a man to hesitate about using so convenient an instrument for teasing his majesty as this meeting and its objects presented. In this he was eminently successful. Could the reception be avoided? asked the monarch: for he was well aware of the animus that this apparently regular proceeding was intended to convey, recognizing it as a "new dish of insolence from the shop that has fabricated so many," and characterizing the paper as an "insolent production." Custom compelled the king to receive the deputation, but Wilkes was informed by the chamberlain that he was not to speak to his majesty, and was to be accompanied by only a certain number of the Livery.* So the petition was presented, and called out a rebuke from the king for "encouraging the rebellious disposition which unhappily exists in some of my colonies," but his majesty afterwards admitted, "he had never seen so well bred a mayor."† Lee was one of those who went to the foot of the throne with Wilkes.

In May, 1775, the alderman of Aldgate ward, John Shakespeare, died, and a ward-mote was held at Iron-mongers' Hall to elect a successor. The candidates were William Baker, citizen and weaver; Mr. Townsend, a wine merchant; Mr. De Sante, citizen and cloth worker, and William Lee, citizen and haberdasher. Lee was put in nomination by Mr. Deputy Partridge, and seconded by Mr. Von Thorpe, one of the Common Council of the ward. Mr. Lee was elected, and made a "spirited speech" to the electors, summarized by the *London Chronicle* as follows:—

"He assured them, that though he was elected for life, he should always think himself accountable to them for the discharge of the trust reposed in him. That as a public magistrate, he should attend the dispensation of justice with care and assiduity; and as their particular magistrate, he should endeavor to promote and maintain harmony, peace, and good order in the ward.

"He said that as to his public principles, he held the free constitution of this country sacred and inestimable, which, as the source and security of all our happiness, it was the duty of every honest man to defend from

---

* *Annual Register*, xviii., 106.

† Walpole's *Last Journal*, I., 484.

violation; that therefore it should ever be his care, by every exertion and at every hazard, to resist the arbitrary encroachments of the Crown and its Ministers, upon the rights of the citizens, and the liberties of the people.

"As an American, he declared it his wish that the union between Great Britain and the colonies might be re-established, and remain forever, but that constitutional liberty might be the sacred bond of that union.

"He considered the attempts of the present administration against American liberty, as a plain prelude to the invasion of freedom in this country; but he trusted, that the virtue of the Americans, aided by the friends of freedom here, would teach the Tories of this day, as their ancestors had been happily taught, how vain a thing it is to attempt wresting their liberties from a people determined to defend them."

He was sworn in on the 14th of June, and after the meeting was over "went in the state coach with the Lord Mayor to the Mansion House, where he was elegantly entertained by his Lordship, with a number of other guests."*

This propensity of the city to elect foreigners to its highest offices was not a little curious. Neither as a merchant nor a statesman, had Wilkes an immediate interest in the colonies, and indeed he had little interest in London, where his ambition for office had placed him in the highest post of honor. Sayre as sheriff was a foreigner, and so was Lee. "The Livery, etc., of London, are unceasing in their endeavors to destroy the importance of the metropolis, by their choice of aliens and improper people to offices, that were filled

---

London Chronicle, 14 June, 1775.

once with Gentlemen only of acknowledged worth and fortune."*

"Colonel Onslow sneered at the city's going to 'the west end of the town, and other parts of the kingdom, to find Patriots qualified to preside over them as magistrates, and represent them in the city senate. Instead of the fat, inactive, commercial aldermen, they have chosen 'Patriots,' as Shakespeare says, not 'sleek-headed men, and such as sleep o' nights.' They have discarded the fat, sleek, well-carcased black dock-tails, and have substituted the long-tailed, patriotic aldermen, animals which champ the bit, and prance and curvet; but I doubt whether these blood bays will draw as well as the old nags."

The honor thus conferred upon Lee was a great one, and, as he said in after years, it was the first time it had been conferred upon an American. It was a life-position, respectable and much sought for; he could now look with complacency on the future, for what he held satisfied his political ambitions. Events were tending to destroy his contentment, for he viewed with ever-increasing alarm the efforts of the king and ministry to force the colonies to submission. He again and again impresses upon his correspondents the expediency and necessity of meeting these efforts, and a merchant himself, he calls for non-intercourse. In this recommendation, it must be admitted, he was influenced by an "enlightened self-interest." The experiences under similar non-importation agreements by the colonies in 1765 and 1769, had led to a well-founded conviction among the English traders that the colonists could not

---

* *London Chronicle*, 27 May, 1775.

live up to them, and must break through any association from sheer necessity. On the London exchange
the suggestion of non-intercourse aroused no fears, and
this apathy was mistaken for hostility to the claims of
America. "The merchants are almost universally your
enemies; therefore, instead of doing you any good, their
whole influence will be against you, unless you force
them thro' interest to take an active part in your
favor." Lee could name but three merchants, besides
himself, who were actively favorable to America:—Mr.
Trecothick, Mr. Bromfield, of Boston, and Mr. Johnson, of Maryland. He was in a good position to understand the feeling on Change, for he was one of the
framers of the petition of the merchants and traders to
the Commons, a petition that was to go thence to the
throne, and even to the people. "There is nothing
very serious in this business," he wrote, "therefore,
do not expect any great good from it." The most
ministerial merchants were the busiest in the matter.
"I cannot too much urge you to pay no attention
to the proceedings of the merchants;" the petition
is "only a blind to recover their lost reputation in
America."

As a partisan, he had drawn upon himself some criticism, and doubtless incurred danger on account of his
known and freely-expressed sympathies. It is in this
that his interest was shown, for he skilfully availed
himself of it to urge his claims to recognition. "Why
give your trade," he asked, "to merchants who are
your enemies? Why play into the hands of those who
will persecute you? I am an American, and am risking

my property, interests, and even life, in your cause; is it asking too much to claim your patronage? Send your tobacco to your friends, of whom I am one of the first."

The period is full of interest to the student of the Revolution, and Lee must have taken a prominent part in the agitation of the day. The Lord Mayor, Aldermen and Livery, determined to again approach the king, having received no reply to the petition handed to him in April. The king gave notice that he would receive the new petition at the Levee on Friday; but the Livery had resolved not to present their address unless the king was sitting on his throne, a demand not warranted by custom, or justified by law. His majesty replied "I am ever ready to receive Addresses and Petitions, but I am the judge where."* The error into which the petitioners had been drawn was recognized, for the Livery did not have the right to petition as a body, much less to force the king to receive it as it should dictate. The "Lord Mayor, Aldermen and Livery, assembled in common hall," were not cognizable to king or Parliament; and it was not until the change was made into the "Lord Mayor, Aldermen and Commons of the City of London, in Common Council assembled," that the address could be received.

---

* *London Chronicle*, 29 June, 1775. The Livery returned a message that at the next meeting of Parliament the city would instruct its members to ask who advised the king to refuse to the citizens leave to present a petition to him seated on the throne, that they might be impeached and punished.

The controversy was timely, as the London Council had before it a letter from the Committee of New York, detailing the grievances of the colonies, asserting their determination to defend their rights with their blood, and asking the vigorous exertions of the city of London to "restore union, mutual confidence, and peace to the whole empire." * On the 5th of July a Court of Common Council met to consider what should be done in the matter. As the debates are buried in the files of the newepapers of the day, and were not recovered by Mr. Force for his collection, they are given in full:—

After the usual formalities of opening the court, Mr. Deputy Poole began the debate.—He observed that the dispute was between Administration and America, consequently that the court had very little right to interfere, and the more particularly, as it was only an association of the people of New York; that it was an opposition of the Americans to all order and good government; that it was wholly with the Americans to relieve themselves, by complying with the just and reasonable demands of government. "With what propriety (said he) can we approach his Majesty in behalf of people who are averse to all order and good government, who aim at nothing less than independence from the parent state, and who exult over the distress of their mother country?" The Deputy declared, that, "respecting himself, he ever was a friend to public liberty; but that he was also a friend to Majesty. That we had nothing to fear from the present king on that score, as he had ten tender pledges, which might be considered as so many supports to the constitution. That in the midst of all this hurry many talked pompously respecting

---

*The letter is dated '5 May, 1775, and was laid before the Common Council 23 June, 1775.

liberty, but *few* ACTED upon liberal principles." The Deputy concluded with this remarkable expression: "It is liberty that makes all nature look gay; but the moment we desert the honor of our sovereign, or the dignity of our laws, then will both liberty and property be endangered." He was followed by

Mr. Hurford, who declared, that the business was of so much importance, that he durst not trust to his memory, and therefore had committed his thoughts to paper; which with leave of the court he read. It contained a copious disquisition of American grievances, wherein he descanted on the several unpopular bills. He declared that he had given his opinion fairly, which he would justify before God and man; and that, advanced in years as he was, he was ready to, and actually would, if necessity required, take up arms in defence of his liberty and religion; and that he would not wish to exist one moment longer, than they were preserved to him; he said that the measures of administration, respecting America, evidently tended to despotism, and that the whole empire was by such baneful councils, shaken to its foundation. He moved for a committee to consider and report the proper measures to be adopted on this important business.

Mr. Deputy Jones.—As the last gentleman has given us, for once, his real sentiments, I move that his speech may be printed.

This occasioned a laugh at Mr. Hurford's expense; as some gentlemen give themselves the liberty of doubting the steadiness of his political conduct.

Mr. Maynard objected to a committee, because the last Court had not thought fit to adopt that measure.

Mr. Stavely entirely joined with Mr. Hurford in his sentiments, and in order to lay the groundwork of the business, he had drawn up some resolves, which he submitted to the court.—He read his resolves, which did not contain anything new upon the subject; although the language, in the opinion of many, was rather too severe.

Alderman Harley desired, before any resolves were entered into, that an act, made by the approved friends of liberty who are *now out of place*, and consequently at the head of opposition, be first read.—The Act of 6 Geo. III. (during the administration of the Lord Rockingham) was read, which recognizes and expressly confirms the authority of Parliament over all the colonies.

The Alderman said, he brought forward this act to show what was the opinion of the men who now so strenuously oppose government and parliamentary authority, and that only Mr. Beckford was against that act. He entered into a detail of the several ways and methods that opposition had used to inflame the Americans, and the basest falsehoods had been circulated to answer insidious purposes; that the Americans had been told that the people of England would join them, and that they would be supported, etc., and he prayed the court that, together with our zeal for America, we should consider the distresses of poor old England.

Alderman Kirkman observed, notwithstanding the act just read, that the Americans had frankly in their assemblies opposed the Act, and had never acknowleded the legality of it. He recommended the greatest care and caution in the proceedings, and to act with temper, moderation and firmness.

Mr. Alderman Lee took a very copious view of the argument respecting the Act of Parliament; he contended "that the act cited could not give a right which did not exist; that Parliament had no right *then*, nor had they *now*, to make such an act. That the Americans had not acknowledged such authority, and that as the spirit of the Act was done away, so should the letter likewise. He recapitulated the Ministry's many oppressions of the unoffending Americans, such as depriving them of their charters, unheard and untried, establishing unconstitutional Admiralty powers, seizing their property violently, sending an armed force to command obedience by the sword, etc. These proceedings, he said, were *too much* for human *nature to bear.*" He therefore seconded Mr. Stavely's set of resolves, as a groundwork to proceed on.

Mr. Sawbridge observed that Alderman Harley had given a very different state of the Americans than he was taught to believe, for that a very intelligent gentleman, Dr. Rush, who resides in America, by his letters asserted, that the Americans supposed a great majority of the people of this country were against them. He paid a compliment to Mr. Beckford's memory, declaring that he always revered it, but now more than ever, as he found that great man had seen through the fatal effects that would attend the putting into execution that act of Parliament which was meant to subjugate the Americans; he lamented the unhappy state of affairs, and concluded by approving of Mr. Stavely's resolves.

The question was now called for, when the argument was unexpectedly taken up.

Mr. Stone.—He noted, with his usual precision of method, that there were three ways which appeared to him, in which the business before the Court might be transacted:

First. Entering into the resolves. Secondly, writing a letter to the Committee of New York by way of answer, and, Thirdly, to petition his Majesty.

That it was the business of the Court to adopt the most eligible. With respect to the first, he declared, that he conceived it a very improper period to widen the breach, by publishing irritating resolves.—That such a proceeding would actually weaken any application either to King or Parliament, and by that method destroy the means by which the Corporation might be serviceable.

As to the second mode, he thought the court could not think of answering the letter, until every method had been tried to serve the cause both of America and England; that the Committee of New York expected such conduct, and that to answer the letter before every step had been taken that carried even a probability of success, would be to evince the imbecility of the proceedings; that the resolves would carry neither weight nor consequence; and perha[j]s at present, they might be dangerous, and even hurtful to the cause they were meant to serve.

Respecting the last mode, viz.: Petitioning the King; he submitted the mode to the court, whether to petition to withdraw the troops from Boston, or humbly to pray that his Majesty would call the Parliament. That in short, we must take Parliament as it was, and not as we could wish it to be; he recommended impartiality and patience; and said, that the matter was of the utmost importance, and as such ought to be considered.

The debate now took a new turn.

Mr. Sharpe took up the matter in behalf of the Americans; he said he had as much respect for his Majesty as any man living, and that it was regard for his Majesty's safety which induced him to be so warm; he asked, can they be rebels (alluding to the Provincials) who support the law? No man *who fears God* CAN OR OUGHT to obey the late cruel acts of Parliament establishing popery, etc.

Alderman Harley argued for Parliamentary authority; and *Mr. Hurford* taxed him with promulgating the old doctrine of passive obedience and non-resistance, and declared that he would deprive that man of his being who would dare presume to sport with his liberty or religion.

A general debate ensued, wherein Alderman Kirkman, Sir Watkin Lewis, Mr. Maynard, and Mr. Stone, were against the resolves offered by Mr. Stavely; Mr. Sharpe, Alderman Lee and Deputy Piper were in favor of them; others were for a petition to withdraw the troops. To this Alderman Harley objected, alleging that it could not be done; some were for desiring the King to call the Parliament together; and the question was going to be put, when

Mr. Merry observed, that hitherto the advocates for America had dealt only in assertions; he desired proof; he wanted to know whether there were no claims in the charters, which submitted them ultimately to the power of the British legislators; he declared that all the Acts of Parliament heretofore made might be considered; as he apprehended sufficient proof might be brought, that the Americans were bound to obey. Mr. Sharpe said it was impossible to enter into that business in this court, and Mr. Merry answered, that it would be highly improper to resolve on any measures, until the dispute had been sifted to the bottom.

Mr. Stavely said, that the right of taxation could not be entered into, the subject was too wide and diffusive.

Mr. Stone very aptly replied, that it would be leading the court into absurdity to make resolves tending to inflame, when even Mr. Stavely, the very member who framed them, acknowledged he was not complete master of the right of taxation.

This seemed to finish the resolves; for several little parties were immediately formed, and Mr. Stavely was much pressed to withdraw his motion, which, after some reluctance, he agreed to. Thus ended the court, after having sat four hours in close debate, endeavoring to form a plan of operation; and another court was summoned for Friday.

PROCEEDINGS ON FRIDAY.

The letter from the Committee of General Association* being read, Mr. Hurford rose with a string of resolves in his hands, which in the end proved to be his own resolves only, for the Court threw every one of them out. Mr. White expressed his opinion that Mr. Hurford was rather premature in reading his already fabricated resolves, for he conceived the first business

---

* Of New York.

should be to consider whether the Corporation of the City of London should or should not take into consideration a letter from a set of gentlemen, who (however respectable as individuals) were not known to the Court as a lawfully associated body. This observation was followed by Mr. Merry, who spoke well on the subject, but was not attended to with that decency which for the honor of the Corporation of London might have been expected.

The argument then took rather an unexpected turn, one of the court stating the question, "Whether the Americans were or were not in an actual state of rebellion." This argument Mr. Merry strongly supported in the affirmative, and it was as strongly confuted on the other hand by Mr. Sharpe, who was very warm on the side of the Americans. In the course of this part of the debate, Mr. Merry frequently called on the Recorder for his opinion, as to the law construction of the present state of the Americans' opposition to government. The Recorder could not refuse speaking, when plainly called upon; but gave such an opinion as left the Court as uninformed as they were before the question was put.

At length a motion was framed by Mr. Hunt, and seconded by Mr. Selby, for an address to his Majesty, praying him to suspend hostilities against the Americans, etc. The question being put, the Lord Mayor declared his opinion, that the question was carried in the affirmative; a division was then moved, when there appeared for the question: 6 Aldermen, 66 Commons, and 2 tellers, in all 74; against it: 6 Aldermen, 51 Commons, 2 tellers, in all, 59; so that it was carried by a majority of 15 ONLY.

It is necessary to observe, that the Court in general had no objection to framing and presenting an humble address, but the Alderman and Commoners in the minority did not chuse to adopt any line of conduct which wore the face of dictating to the throne; they conceived that the favorite term of the majority, "suspend hostilities," tacitly implied that his Majesty had commenced hostilities; whereas the truth evidently is, the King's troops have acted merely on the defensive.

Mr. Hurford's* motion was, "That an humble address and petition be presented to his Majesty, praying that his Majesty will be pleased to suspend hostilities against our fellow-subjects in America, and adopt such measures as may restore union, confidence and peace."

The speakers were Aldermen Sawbridge, Kirkman, Harley, Lee, and Lewis; Commoners, D. Jones, D. Leeky, Hurford, White, Merry, Stavely, Sharp, Parish, Hunt, and Dunnage.

The Aldermen for the motion were Bull, Kirkman, Lewis, Newnham, Lee, and Plomer; against it, Aldermen Harley, Esdaile, Plumb, Kennet, Hopkins, and Hart.

The Sheriffs were ordered to go up to St. James' next Wednesday, to know his Majesty's pleasure when he will permit the Lord Mayor, Aldermen and Common Council to wait on him with the said address. †

The King had been an interested spectator of these proceedings, and he did not anticipate any serious results from the two meetings. "If," he wrote to Lord North, on the 5th, "the Common Council can on Friday be prevented from taking any step with regard to the rebellion in America, it would be desirable; but the comfort is, by the many absurd steps taken by that body, if they act otherwise, it will not be of much effect. I have no doubt but the nation at large sees the conduct of America in its true light, and, I am certain,

---

* Probably an error for *Hunt*.

† *London Chronicle*, 8 July, 1775.

any other conduct but compelling obedience would be ruinous and culpable; therefore, no consideration could bring me to swerve from the present path which I think myself in duty bound to follow." He received the Sheriffs graciously and appointed the 14th for the presentation. The Lord Mayor, accompanied by Aldermen Bull, Lewis, Hayley, and Lee, the two sheriffs, and about sixty common councilmen, with other city officers, went to St. James at the time appointed, and presented an "humble address and petition," praying for a suspension of "operations of force" against the Americans. The King replied, that while the Americans openly resisted the constitutional authority of the kingdom, he owed it to the rest of his people to "continue and enforce those measures by which alone their rights and interests can be asserted and maintained." *

The reply of the King seems to have exercised some restraining influence on the Common Council; for when that body convened on Friday, the 21st, and the King's words were laid before it, a motion to transmit a copy to New York with the petition of the corporation was lost by a vote of 64 against 50. And with this, the matter appears to have rested.

The merchants, traders and manufacturers were petitioning Parliament and the King, and agitating for or against the measures of the Ministry—petitions prepared in the usual way, and for the most part signed with so little real conviction that the writers would

---

* The address and reply may be found in the *Annual Register*, xviii, 255; and in Force, *American Archives, Fourth Series*, ii, 1602.

have added their names on either side of the question with a little urging. The enthusiasm was fictitious, forced by a few partisans, and carried on for effect. The London petition was regarded as a remarkably tame and submissive "protest," considering the noise made in its preparation; and the public smiled to see the ardor of mechanics and merchants as voiced in the columns of the press.

> "How blest are we in this bright age!
> When each Mechanic is a sage
> In ev'ry kind of knowledge.
> Statesmen, Casuists, Rhetoricians,
> *Grand Resolvers*, Politicians,
> As from Court and College."

A meeting of merchants in London on October 4, at which Lee was present, produced another "humble petition," but the matter excited no comment. As an engine for influencing King or Parliament, paper remonstrances were now useless.*

In 1776, when a new Chamberlain was to be chosen for London, Wilkes determined to capture this rich office, and entered into a canvass, his opponent being

---

* "Mr. Alderman Lee preferred a complaint before the Lord-Mayor against Captain Ross, of the Yankee privateer, for running his fist in his face on the Royal-Exchange, and uttering words at the same time amounting to a challenge; on which his Lordship issued his warrant to bring Captain Ross before him, when it appeared that the quarrel originated on board the Yankee; but the offence complained of being a breach of the peace, the Captain was bound over to answer it, himself in £1,000, and two sureties in £500 each."—*Gentleman's Magazine*, 1776, p. 383.

Benjamin Hopkins. On the day of election Wilkes came out far behind Hopkins, receiving only 1673 votes against 2869 votes cast for his rival, a clear evidence to him that the liverymen had sold and surrendered the capital to the Ministry. "No longer worthy the name of freemen, they are sunk into tame, mean vassals, ignominiously courting, and bowing their necks to the ministerial yoke." The empire was ripe for destruction, and ruin and slavery were advancing with giant strides upon it. "If we are saved, it will be almost solely by the courage and noble spirit of our American brethren, whom neither the luxuries of a court, nor the sordid lust of avarice in a rapacious and venal metropolis, have hitherto corrupted. Yet with some chosen friends, however few, I will, while I live, dare to oppose the alarming fatal progress of this deluge of corruption and court influence, and to protract at least the impending ruin by continuing firm and intrepid in the cause of public virtue, and the independency of the capital." *

Alderman Lee, doubtless one of these "chosen friends," was not willing to concede the defeat of Wilkes without a contest. With about twenty of the liverymen, he presented a protest against the installation of Hopkins as Chamberlain, based upon a by-law of the Court of Common Council made in 1572, which prohibited the corporation from conferring any office of honor or emolument in the city, on any person whatever who is not a freeman by birth or servitude. This musty regulation of more than two hundred years'

---

* *Annual Register*, 1776, 154.

standing would, as was pointed out, have militated as strongly against the election of Wilkes as of Hopkins; but Lee urged its validity, seconded by Sir Watkin Lewis.

"Very warm debates commenced. Sir Watkin and Mr. Lee were the principal speakers, except a new Alderman, Mr. Wooldridge, who took up the argument very fairly, objected to Mr. Lee's motion in terms that will ever do him great honour; and in the course of the debate, fairly refuted the objection made by Mr. Alderman Lee; and shewed, that the by-law upon which the objection was founded was made merely to prevent the Lord Mayor and Court of Aldermen from giving away the offices of the city, which the livery of London alone had a right to bestow.—Upon this, Mr. Lee founded another objection; and attempted to prove that the livery of London did not meet in common-hall for the purpose of elections prior to the year 1572. But in this he was also mistaken; the Recorder declared, that the livery did elect all their officers before that time. Mr. Wooldridge then gave it as his opinion, that Mr. Hopkins would be entitled to such damages as he could prove to have suffered by the refusal of the Court of Aldermen to swear him in, when he had been declared by the presiding officer of the court duly elected; that the court were highly censurable if they did not; and that, although he should always wish to act with those who were the real friends of the constitution, yet he would never vote against his conscience for any man living. The whole court seemed to approve his principles; and when the question was put, Aldermen Alsop, Kennet, Plumbe, Rawlinson, Thomas, Peckham, Plomer, Bull, Hayley, Newnham, and Clark, voted with Mr. Wooldridge, for swearing Mr. Hopkins into his office; and only Sir Watkin Lewis and Mr. Lee opposed it."

In all this time, Arthur Lee was active in obtaining

intelligence from his friends and forwarding it by way
of Paris to the Secret Committee in Philadelphia.
William was no less active, though not recognized by
any notice from the Committee; and that the English
government was aware of this correspondence is proved
by some intercepted letters from the brothers in the
Public Records. He was looking forward to some employment in the cause, and the commercial experience
he had gained in London pointed him out as fit to
undertake the commercial agency of Congress in some
part of France. That he suggested such an appointment is shown by one of his letters, and some time
early in 1777 he was, with Thomas Morris, a half
brother of Robert Morris, appointed commercial agent.
He received notice of this appointment in April, 1777,
and closing up his commercial affairs as far as he could,
he set out for Paris, where he arrived on the 11th of
June.

II.

THE beginning of the American Revolution thus found William Lee in a high office in the London corporation, with affiliations that drew him strongly to the side of the colonies. His family were "rebels" to the authority of the King, and his mercantile connections were largely with Americans, for he was one of the best-known American merchants in London, who frequented "Virginia walk" on the Royal Exchange. His political relations had brought him into connection with those who from principle or interest were opposed to oppressing the colonies, bitterly opposed to reducing them by arms. His connections and his opinions were well known in the city and to the government, and he, and his brother Arthur, were soon objects of suspicion to the ministry. It was not surprising, therefore, to find in the English Records Office some letters from William to his brother in Virginia that administration had intercepted; and the contents of these missives fully justified the suspicion of the ministry of his disloyalty, and arouse in us a feeling of surprise that the writer was not seized or his usefulness as an agent of America repressed.* He, in the meantime, pursued his course as Alderman, attending regularly the court, certainly as late as March 24, 1777, and all the while active in the American cause. He was, with a num-

*Letters from Dumas to Arthur Lee were sent through William.

ber of others, on the committee appointed * to draw up
a petition from the Common Council against the bill
impowering his Majesty "to secure and detain persons
charged with, or suspected of, the crime of high treason,
committed in North America, or on the high seas, or
the crime of piracy." On March 31st, with the other
aldermen, he attended a church service, and later an
entertainment and ball given by the Lord Mayor.
Meanwhile he was obtaining and sending intelligence
to his friends, to Dumas, the American agent in Holland, and through his brother, Arthur, to Deane in
France.

In April, 1777, he received from Deane a notice of
his appointment as commercial agent for the Continental Congress at Nantes, an office to be held in conjunction with Thomas Morris, also an American. This
Morris was a step-brother of Robert Morris, who was a
leading merchant of Philadelphia, an active patriot, and
later the financier of the confederation. But Thomas
had none of the good qualities of his famous brother,
and, of weak purpose, had more than once become so
absorbed in dissipations as to be deprived of all utility
for the conduct of any business. When Lee received
notice of his appointment, Morris was already at
Nantes, nearly always stupid by drink, a besotted and
often rampant drunkard, and at odds with Deane,
Franklin and Arthur Lee, his superiors. Closing his
concerns in England as far as he could, Lee went to
Paris, arriving in June, and found the affairs of the

---

* 14 February, 1777.

Nantes agency at a dead-lock, Morris incapable of rendering accounts, and a Mr. John Ross, a Scotchman, sent down by the Commissioners to attempt a settlement. Pending this settlement Lee was advised to remain in Paris. In order that the subsequent events may be better understood, something of the previous history of the American Commissioners at Paris may be told.

In 1775 the French government sent to America a secret agent, by name Bonvouloir, charged with instructions to extend to the rebellious colonies the hope of obtaining supplies and aid from France. About the time of his arrival Congress constituted a committee to correspond with persons in Europe for advancing political and commercial matters, and in November this became the Committee of Secret Correspondence. Acting upon the guarded suggestions of Bonvouloir, Silas Deane, a merchant and late a member of Congress from Connecticut, was named as agent of the United Colonies in France, and sent abroad to work upon the sympathies of the French court and the commercial cupidity or interests of the people, and, in exchange for the trade of the Colonies, to obtain supplies for carrying on the contest against the mother country. In the same month two Frenchmen, Penet and Pliarne, from Nantes, landed in Rhode Island, prepared to enter into a contract with Congress for supplies. To France, then, were the attentions of Congress directed, and Deane set out on his mission with every circumstance apparently in his favor: certainly matters in France were in far better train for countenancing America than

Deane or Congress could have hoped; for the purpose of the court to aid the Colonies was already practically taken, and only the details remained to be mapped out. In Caron de Beaumarchais the ministry had an agent actively bent upon committing the French court on the side of the Colonies, and even now plying it with arguments for taking such a step.

Franklin had already laid a train for securing supplies, and in such a way as to involve the permission, if not the protection, of the French court. Availing himself of a friendship of some years' standing with M. Barbeu Dubourg, he had induced him to seek out manufacturers, or dealers, who would be willing to supply the Colonies with the necessaries of war. Having access to the court, Dubourg proved of great assistance, as he could hold out the idea of a toleration, at least, of the King's ministers to his undertakings, and did in fact enjoy the confidence of some of the ministers. He approached the firm of Montaudoin, ship-builders at Nantes, and had interested them in his schemes, when the treachery of the crew of a Continental vessel, by carrying her into a British port, gave to the English ministry a clue to Montaudoin's connection with America, the contract of Penet, Pliarne & Co. with the Secret Committee, and, by implication, the encouragement of the French court. This intelligence was obtained early in April, 1776, and was at once made the subject of a conversation between Lord Rochford and Beaumarchais, then in London, ostensibly to purchase coin for the French islands. The charge was skillfully turned by Beaumarchais, but he had become convinced that the time to act had come, and so informed Vergennes, basing his argument largely on the necessity of guarding the French possessions in America from Great Britain. He, the Count de Laureguais, who had been charged in London with the task of reporting on Beaumarchais' acts, and Garnier, the French *chargé d'affaires*, were influenced by the intelligence picked up by Arthur Lee among his Patriot friends, naturally bent upon exaggerating the strength and unanimity of the Colonies that they might be used against the ministry.

On May 2d, 1776, Vergennes took the important step and laid before the King a note authorizing the appropriation of one million livres for the service of the English colonies, to be so used that no suspicion could lie against the court as the source of it. The nature of this aid was clearly indicated; it was to be a loan, pure and simple,* and to be expended by a commercial house controlled by a merchant residing in one of the French ports. Would Spain contribute another million on the same terms? Vergennes was opening the governmen, arsenals to Dubourg, and on Beaumarchais' return to France late in May, he was placed at the head of the firm of *Roderigue, Hortalez et Cie*, with a credit from the court. Before operations were well begun the contribution of a million livres by Spain became available, and while Beaumarchais was seeking to unite the interests of Dubourg with his own operations, Silas

---

* "Sa majesté s'est determinée à leur faire avancer à titre de prêt un million de nos livres."—*Vergennes to Grimaldi*, 3 May, 1776.

Deane appeared in Paris, as an authorized agent from the Colonies.* Deane brought letters from Franklin to Dubourg and his co-worker Chaumont, and this, under the circumstances, placed him in a sort of competition with Beaumarchais and his then confidant, Lee, if not with Vergennes, who supplied the money. A short time convinced Deane that Dubourg, who was seeking to discredit Beaumarchais with Vergennes, in the hope of securing his own influence and interests, was not so essential to his aims as Franklin had represented; and the offer of the services of Hortalez & Co., with direct assurances in favor of this house from the ministry, determined him to contract with Beaumarchais, and before the end of July an agreement was reached. By dash, courage and unscrupulous acts, Figaro conquered and ousted the "*radoteur médecin*," intercepted his letters, and captured Deane. One person he overlooked—Edward Bancroft, whose interest Deane was instructed to seek, and who was informing the English cabinet of what the American agent was doing.

In this gradual shifting of power and influences, the American envoy found himself in a position that involved no little embarrassment. Dubourg still considered him under his influence; Vergennes by his conferences with him stamped him as a recognized agent; and ship builders, manufacturers of arms and military supplies, waited upon him for orders; while cargoes were made up from the royal arsenals and made subject to his orders. He was courted by merchants and overrun

* Deane arrived in Paris July 5th.

with offers of service from men of real military abilities as well as from mere adventurers. Burdened with work, he took* on the recommendation of Arthur Lee, a secretary to assist him—William Carmichael, from Maryland, whose name will occur often in these pages. In December he wrote, "Had I ten ships here I could fill them all with passengers for America." †

It was inevitable that in these changing relations Deane should make mistakes. He was obliged to depend upon others for his purposes, and his agents he could select only on the recommendation of others, as much strangers to him as were his immediate agents. The well-intended instructions of Franklin, it is now known, placed Deane in direct communication with the British cabinet; for Bancroft was an English spy, and reported to his employers what the American envoy was doing. More than this, there were a number of other spies, dogging his footsteps, prying into his correspondence, bribing his servants, and confusing his agents. Even when Franklin and Arthur Lee had come to Paris, the same system was continued, and the British ministry enjoyed a system of intelligence as secret as it was successful. Nor were Deane's schemes threatened from the enemy alone; he was cajoled, amused and deceived by those to whom he had given his confidence. The Du Coudray incident was only one of many, but it nearly ruined Deane's plans for that year, and was one of the reasons

---

* October, 1776.

† To Jay, 3 December, 1776.

for producing a strong resentment against Deane in Congress. There is now little question of Deane's ardent wish to carry out the purposes of his mission, of his activity and energy in meeting obstacles, and of his extensive schemes for aiding his employers. There is as little doubt of the difficulties that surrounded him, the malignity of his enemies, and the injustice of his treatment at the hands of Congress. His history is one of the blots on the history of the Revolution, and to this day remains as mysterious as ever.

In the meanwhile Arthur Lee had remained in London, collecting intelligence which was forwarded to Congress through Deane. His suspicious nature had full play, and he was so injudicious as to forward to Congress reflections upon certain members, and their agents, that could not but cause dissensions and bad feeling. Jay and Benjamin Harrison he said were unworthy of confidence; Reed and John Langdon were to be suspected. In August, 1776, he crossed to Paris, where his presence embarrassed Deane not a little. In December Franklin arrived in France, bearing a commission from Congress naming himself, Deane and Arthur Lee as Commissioners to the Court of France; and an express was at once sent to notify Lee. Certain vessels were already loaded with cargoes for America, ready to sail, and Franklin entered into the task of obtaining further supplies. By the beginning of March, ten vessels had been dispatched to America under the account of Beaumarchais, and the American privateers by their success were involving the commissioners in embarrassments, which were shared by the Court of France. The disposition of the prizes was entrusted to commercial agents, and the financial needs of the commissioners made a speedy realization of profits expedient, if not necessary. Such a block as Morris in the path was annoying and ruinous. The instructions of Congress to Morris and Lee were unknown, having been retained by Morris, and matters had reached such a pass that only the summary removal of Morris could improve the situation.

July 31, 1777, the Commissioners informed Mr. Lee by letter that as the hope of obtaining a clear state of Morris' transactions by Mr. Ross had vanished, "we think it prudent and right for you to proceed to Nantes as soon as possible, and there take such measures as to you shall appear most advantageous for the publick Interest, which we accordingly advise you to do." And on the same day wrote to Morris, notifying him of Lee's appointment and his intention of going to Nantes, and adding: "We make no doubt but you will immediately communicate to him a full and clear state of them, and proceed in your conducting them with that mutual good understanding and harmony which is so necessary to the Credit of your Employers and advantageous to the interest of the publick." But something had occured that gave offense to William Lee. Early in January, Jonathan Williams, a nephew of Franklin, had been sent to Nantes by the Commissioners, and to him had the sale of prizes been committed, as well as the care of fitting out some vessels for continental service. Upon reaching Nantes, Lee learned from Morris of this appointment, and the measures taken by Williams to carry out his instructions, and deeming them contrary to the instructions of the Continental Committee, asked the Commisioners to revoke the orders given to Williams. Lee asserted that no answer was ever received to this request, and he returns again and again to the slight implied, taking it as a direct insult to himself.

That the Commissioners were willing to do full justice to Lee's demand, is proven by the draft of a reply to his letter drawn up by Frankin:—

AUGUST, 1777.

Gentlemen:—We have received yours of the 16th Instant. We think Mr. Morris would have done well in communicating to us the Orders from the Committee when he received them: But had we been acquainted with them, he must be sensible that his Conduct has been such as to justify our Interfering for the safety of the Interest, under the general authority we had received to instruct Capt. Wickes in his Proceedings while in Europe; and as we have been called upon for considerable Sums in fitting out the vessels who have taken the Prizes, it seems the more necessary that they should be put into some hands on whose care & attention to Business we could place some Confidence for the Reimbursement. Had Mr. Lee been present at Nantes, or in France, when the Orders complained of were given by us, they would certainly not have been given. As the Case stands we think we had a Right to give them, and desiring to avoid Disputes shall withdraw them.

And as by the Committee's Letter to us of Oct. 24, '76, we are inform'd in the following Words, that Orders were given to Capt. Wickes to "send his Prizes into such of the French Ports as are most convenient, addressing them at Dunkirk to Messrs. Stival & Son, at Havre to M. Limozin, at Bordeaux to Messrs. Delap, at Nantes to Messrs. Pliarne, Penet & Co., *and at any other Ports in France to such other Persons as you may appoint:* and the Brigantine in question having been sent in to Port L'Orient, we, as far as the said Letter authorizes us, do desire that Mr. Lee alone may take the charge of disposing of her.

It is proper you should be informed that Mr. Morris, by his Letter of Feb. 4, acquainted us that he had remitted us 90,000 Livres, in part of the 10,000 £ sterling he was ordered to pay us, which sum of Livres we should find in the Hands of M. Sollier, who at the same time inform'd us that he had receiv'd it, and held it ready to be paid to us on our Order. We suffer'd it to remain in his Hands as a Deposit, drawing for Parts of it as we had occasion: But now he refuses to pay any more of our Drafts, and detains the money alleging that he has orders from Nantes for so doing. This Conduct towards us, must make us cautious how we advance hereafter for the armed Vessels, as we ought not to hazard the leaving ourselves destitute of cash, and will oblige us to write to the Congress to provide for our Expenses with greater Certainty.

We desire, Gentlemen, a full Copy of your Instructions with the Dates, that we may compare them with such as we have received & regulate ourselves accordingly, having not the least desire to impede the Operations of Mr. Lee, tho' we have abundant Reasons to be dissatisfied with the conduct of Mr. Morris.

We are Gentlemen,
Your most obed't &c.

To Morris & Lee.

Had this letter been sent, it would have quieted the complaint of Lee, for he had come to an arrangement with Morris, and did dispose of one prize—receiving from the sale the only recompense that accrued to him as commercial agent, during his service. But he claimed that Franklin was setting up Williams to oppose him. "Upon the death of Mr. Morris, my brother, having observed that Dr. Franklin's determination to provide for his nephew, Mr. Williams, and his suspicions that we were resolved to oppose him, prevented all harmony, and was greatly injurious to the public business, was in hopes, etc."* Exactly when these suspicions were first awakened does not clearly appear. Six months before Lee arrived in France, Williams was at Nantes, sent informally to superintend the shipment of supplies that the weakness of Thomas Morris jeopardized, and proving efficient, was continued at that place, but apparently acting without a definite appointment, and under the immediate directions of the Commissioners. The original mission of Williams was only a prudent business move, well calculated to save the concerns at Nantes from falling into inexplicable confusion. The sending of Ross to close Morris' accounts, was also a precaution which, had it been successful, would have been alike advantageous to the Congress, the Commissioners and to Lee; and with this advantage in view, it was wise to suggest that Lee await this settlement that he might not fall heir to the confusion that Morris had produced in his accounts. In the interim, Williams was an available agent, informed of the plans and wishes of the Commissioners, and capable to carry them into effect. Where then did the error lie? Lee himself took the remarkable step of

---

*Statement of Arthur Lee.

combining with the incapable Morris, and his brother Arthur Lee prevented the recall of Williams.

That Lee knowing how impracticable it was for Morris to undertake any transactions, should have been willing to join forces with him, can only be explained by his jealousy of Williams. He was fully aware that Morris had treated him with gross disrespect and submitted him to indignities that a sensitive man would have keenly resented; he knew that the Commissioners had practically superceded Morris, and appealed to Congress in justification; he seems to have set out from Paris for Nantes free from well-marked suspicions of the Commissioners' hostility to himself and his brother; and yet he tied his fate to this sinking and worthless individual. This surely was a mistake, but it was one that Arthur Lee rendered irrevocable. For he opposed the sending of the reply to the letter of Morris and Lee. "An answer was prepared to this letter and shown to me; it expressed a willingness to recall these powers and to vest them in Mr. Lee alone, with very strong expressions against Mr. Morris. I objected what was obvious, that this would destroy the harmony recommended, and without which the public business could not go on; that the right answer seemed to me plain and simple, which was to recall the powers complained of, without saying anything for or against either of the gentlemen, which it was manifest would be productive of bad consequences. My opinion was not approved. Neither that nor any other answer was ever sent to this or to any of the letters written to us by the agents, jointly or separately."*

*Arthur Lee's statement.

A second letter was prepared, of which not even the draft remains, but which caused much dispute among the Commissioners. Arthur Lee also prevented this letter being sent, representing that William would soon be in Paris to receive his commission. Thus, on a quibble raised by Arthur, no reply was sent, and William conceived a grievance against the "junto" at Paris, that under his brother's care rapidly ripened into a hatred that passes all understanding.

It must have been about the middle of August that the agents wrote to the commissioners about Williams, for Lee did not reach Nantes until the 4th of that month. Yet the impossible character of Morris was then well known to him. "I think it utterly out of the question to make anything of this strange unhappy man;" and yet he urges Arthur to do nothing that would throw the affairs of the agency into his sole conduct.* It was not until this period that he saw his instructions that Morris had kept from him. On the 19th arrived a cargo of rice consigned to the commissioners, which Morris placed in the hands of Gruel, against Lee's protest, who suspected the integrity of this real or fictitious firm.† He was then urging Robert Morris to write and consign to him alone, and had agreed that Williams acting under his orders should dispose of certain prizes that had just been brought into Nantes.‡ At the beginning of September, when

---

* *William Lee to Arthur Lee*, 12 August, 1777.

† See *William Lee to Robert Morris*, 21 August, 1777.

‡ *William Lee to Arthur Lee*, 21 August, 1777.

he had received from America a hint that he might be sent to Vienna or Prussia, his complaints were loud against Morris, against Penet and Gruel, and his suspicions of Carmichael were taking shape; but Williams had not yet fallen into disfavor, and the utterances against Dana and Franklin were so vague as to suggest a doubt whether he himself had conceived any dislike of them, or was merely reflecting dimly what his brother Arthur was already feeling strongly.

The origin of Arthur's dislike of Deane and of Franklin, a dislike that rapidly became an intense hatred, need not be detailed here, but dated from a period long anterior to the French mission. The almost malignity with which this hate was shown forms one of the dramatic elements of early American diplomacy in Europe, and when it is sifted down, will be found to be as unreasonable as it was unjust, and will redound to the injury only of Arthur Lee and those who shared his beliefs. He involved his three brothers, William, Francis Lightfoot, and Richard Henry; he ruined Deane without good cause, as is now generally admitted; he fanned party feeling in Congress to such a height that its action was paralyzed at a most important juncture, and its influence nearly destroyed. The result has been that he has gone into history as a marplot, and his better qualities, of which he had many, forgotten. But this belongs to his story. It was certain that he poured all his suspicions into his brother William's ears, and found a sympathetic listener. With Izard to furnish further fuel, the three indulged in an interchange of letters containing insinuations,

open charges and interpretations of actions, that do the
writers little credit, however assured they may have
been in the honesty of their convictions. Fortunate it
is that their correspondence did not come to light at
the time, for the little that was known did Americans
incalculable harm in Europe, and hindered operations
at home. While in power, their efforts were directed
against those whom they regarded as their opponents;
but once removed from office, their better judgments
convinced them of the inexpediency of continuing the
difficulty, and, posing as martyrs, they left it to history
to do them justice. Thanks to the extravagancies
of Arthur Lee's biographer, this justice has never been
meted out.

Early in October William went from Nantes to Paris,
to obtain the recall of the powers given to Williams.
He was there given his commission and instructions as
minister to the German courts, a change of office that
threatened to reduce his profits, as he confessed. But
the split among the commissioners had now become
well defined, and was widening daily. Lee doubted
the honesty of the contract for tobacco entered into
with the Farmers General. Deane had become an
"insolent meddler, contravening the orders and appointments of Congress," and the monopolizer of the
American business. Rumors were in the air of his
personal dishonesty, of his being engaged in private
ventures wherein he was to pocket the profit, if any,
and Congress the loss, should they so end. Lloyd,
whom Lee wanted to make commercial agent at Nantes,
wrote to Ralph Izard, the newly appointed minister to
Naples, on November 12th:—

" I have no doubt from what I discovered during my residence at Rouen, and Havre, that Mr. Deane has private, as well as publick pursuits; and I am more than ever convinced that he is a very improper person to be applied to, for advice or assistance relative to a Loan where he is not materially interested. I am confident your idea of the man is just, in every particular; but our opinions of and concerning him, as also others, it will be most prudent to reserve solely ourselves, for reasons which are sufficiently manifest.   *   *   *

" I am confident the [commercial] business cannot be conducted with any degree of propriety or satisfaction, except there is a most effectual removal of the present agent [Williams] who appears possessed of full and ample powers, and still continues his long accustomed course; for which reason until there was an absolute certainty of that step's being taken, I could not give my assent to an acceptance.   *   *   *   *

" I am extremely sorry that the acrimonious humor continues to prevail among the Controllers [Commissioners], as I think it cannot but produce effects, which must prove injurious to the business that they have to transact; besides rendering them objects of contempt to those with whom they ought to be respectable."

Of Carmichael, Lee had the "worst opinion" and could not trust himself to speak or write to him. The Commissioners were taken to task for supposed inaction with respect to certain American vessels seized at Nantes. These matters were freely discussed in Lee's letters to his European confidants, as well as to his American correspondents.

The new appointment of William Lee would naturally remove him from the cares of the commercial agency, and he asserted that he abandoned from that time any participation in those concerns.* But he carried into the diplomatic mission the same distrust of Deane that he had felt when agent. Congress had omitted to provide for the expenses of the missions of Lee and Izard, and the Commissioners did not think themselves authorized to advance money. This was regarded as an attempt to starve out the envoys, and so get rid of them. Lee applied to Franklin for a copy of the treaty proposed to the Court of France, as he was instructed to make that the basis of his own diplomacy; but no copy was given until January, 1778, some months after his first application for it. These two incidents appear to be the cause of his subsequent hatred of Franklin. In November, 1777, it was known that Deane's contracts with some of the French officers had been repudiated by Congress, and that Deane was recalled. To show further distrust of him would have been useless, but Franklin was now the obstacle to be overcome. The opportunity for attack soon came, and William Lee submitted to the wild charges and wilder suspicions of his brother Arther. Franklin had suppressed intelligence; he did not confer with Lee and Izard; he did not settle Deane's accounts before the latter went to America; he affronted a Mr. Stevenson; he kept a knowledge of the treaty with France from the other ministers; he had not answered their letters; he was a plotter and conspirator, aiming at monarchy; and became to the Lee faction the very quintessence of wickedness.

* This was not strictly true, for he again went to Nantes and still further entangled himself in the intrigues of that place.

The development, progress and results of this almost insane jealousy of Franklin are depicted in these letters of William Lee so fully that no summary can do them justice. It is impossible at this day to sympathize with their feelings, and it is almost impossible to give what credit is due, for the basis of the charges against Franklin is mere rumor and suspicion, and the *MS.* record is too incomplete to enable us to check or correct the multitude of little incidents that became such important matters when brooded over by disappointed ambition, or looked at through a medium so strongly colored by personal character. In footnotes a running comment is given, and we have William Lee's full statement for the first time. It is only just to credit him with the good that he accomplished, and with the patriotic intention that governed his desires. His treaty with the Dutch was important, and valuable merely as an expression of good will, for the moral effect of a treaty is often of far greater weight than the actual terms. He was sent upon a fool's errand to the Courts of Vienna and Berlin, for even had their views been favorable to America, they could have given little real aid. He was throughout his mission heavily handicapped by being so completely under the influence of Arthur Lee.

The measures that led to his recall belong properly to the history of Congress, and will be detailed in the volumes of the correspondence of Richard Henry Lee. That a complete change in the methods of conducting American affairs in Europe had become necessary is obvious, for the system of Commissioners had produced only difference and faction, that no explanations or concessions could heal. The sacrifice of Deane was not enough to restore harmony, and the Lees and Izards were set aside, leaving Franklin master of the situation. Here, practically, ended the public career of William Lee. He was without public employment, and had sacrificed his commercial prospects in undertaking to act with the colonies; the little circle of friends he had on the continent was in the same position, and nearly as incapable of aiding him as they were of supporting themselves. Nursing a sense of injury, and bitterly complaining of the neglect of Congress, he yet was able to sink his feelings in a dignified silence, and, when committed beyond recall to animosities which he expended every effort to sustain and foster, he was so patriotic as to submit his plea to Congress, and then remain inactive. He resided in Europe until about 1784, when he returned to America, and obscurity in Virginia, devoting himself to his plantation at Greenspring. Failing eyesight prevented him from taking an active part in public affairs, and almost total blindness had come upon him before his death, which happened 27 June, 1795.

He had four children by his wife: William Ludwell, born 23 January, 1775, died in 1802; Portia, born in 1777, married William Hodgson, of White Haven, England, and died in 1840; Brutus, born November, 1778, and died in the following year; and Cornelia, born in Brussels, 3 March, 1780, married John Hopkins in 1806, and died in 1817 or 1818.

The perfect frankness in which these letters were

written shows on their surface the merits and faults of the writer. That he was earnest, honest, and of strong prejudices, is not to be denied; that he was patriotic and sincerely attached to the American cause, is evident; that he used his best endeavors to advance that cause, and made heavy sacrifices to do it, all the proofs adduced show; that his abilities were not small, and that he shared some of his brother's political capacity, these pages will prove. But his career was a chequered one, and everything was against his accomplishing what would be of lasting service. His partisanship in the Wilkes agitation gave him a standing in London politics; but he was no sooner in a high position, than the American contest compelled him to sacrifice it. His training as a merchant made him eminently fit for the position of commercial agent at Nantes; but his intriguing with Morris ruined his usefulness, and placed him in a wrong attitude to his superiors. His diplomatic appointment would, under any circumstances, have proved an empty mission so far as it could advance the cause of the Colonies; but he rendered it worse than abortive by submitting to the plots of his brother, and made his own negotiations an instrument to discredit the American Commissioners. It was certainly a great misfortune for him to be ever on the point of accomplishing something, but ever to be thwarted by the prejudices that others so studiously fostered in him; and if he failed to accomplish what were the ends of his appointments, the blame should be shared with others.

While thus recording the failures of the man, his claims to be remembered must not be overshadowed.

He was the only American who has served as Alderman of London; his diplomatic career takes on interest from his connection with Franklin, perhaps the greatest diplomatist ever representing America in Europe; the reputation of his brothers lends an interest to his own life, and it is impossible to speak knowingly of Richard Henry Lee, without treating of William and Arthur, who so strongly influenced his conduct in Congress. Without the charm of Arthur's style, or the marked political ability of Richard Henry, his letters are important as a contribution to Revolutionary history, and solve many a question in the foreign relations of the young republic in its most trying period.

I have sought to give the letters as they were written, and have in notes added what I deemed of service in explanation of the text. The cyphers, four in number, have not been discovered in full, and can only be explained in part, no record of them being found among the papers that have passed through my hands. In conclusion, I must express my deep obligations to Mr. Cassius Francis Lee, of Alexandria, to whose generosity I owe the larger number of the letters contained in these volumes.

WORTHINGTON CHAUNCEY FORD.

Brooklyn, January, 1891.

LETTERS

OF

WILLIAM LEE.

TO HIS SISTER.

SAN——, Nov. 20, 1766.

My Dr Sister:

I wanted much to see you this week but am afraid it will not be in my power 'till next Monday or Tuesday. Vincent Rust has refused to repair Rust's warehouses. John Newton and his father, who were appointed by the court to view them, have reported that it is better to build new ones than to repair the old, and that Vincent Rust is willing they sh^{d.} be removed from his land; Dr. Flood has drawn up a petition to the assembly to remove the Warehouses to Kinsale; it was signed by himself and the two Newtons only, when I saw it, and had the order of Court of the above return annexed to it, but I believe John Newton got all the subscribers he could at Court. You no doubt see into this scheme, and as the 'Squire's Sam goes off to-morrow morning by Day break for W^{ms}burg, I think you will much neglect your own interest and that of y^r Daughter if you do not write pressingly about it by Sam to our Brother Richard Henry. If you will agree to build the Warehouses at y^r own expense, I think it will be easy to get a good subscription to have them removed to where Simpson lives. Mention that to

Col. Lee for I am sure it will be considerably more advantagious to the planters, and I think you have a better right to any private advantage than D^r· Flood.   I am sincerely

Y^r most Affectionate

WILLIAM LEE.

ISAAC WM. GIBERNE* TO WILLIAM LEE.

PELLEVILLE, 8th July, 1773.

My very dear and worthy Friend:

Capt. Rayson informing me after dinner this day

---

* Of the "Rev." Isaac William Giberne the commissary (William Robinson) wrote in 1766: "His mother is a milliner in the city of Westminster. He was not bred to the church, but was sometime a clerk in some office on Tower Hill. He obtained orders and came here under the countenance and protection of the present governor [Fauquier]. He purchased the disgust of the Clergy at his first coming by unsuccessful endeavors to reconcile them to an Act of which they had sent a complaint to England, boldly setting his Youth and Rawness in opposition to the past and present feelings of long experience. In imitation of the Governor he wrote a letter to the Treasurer and Trustees of a Fund here for the relief of poor clergymen's widdows and orphans, to withdraw his subscription and express his disapprobation of the design untill it should be amended to his humour. Many of the Laity think him too fond of cards and Gaming for one of his cloth. He has removed from one Parish to another two or three times. I believe there is no danger of injuring him when I incline to think forwardness and Levity distinguishing parts of his character."—*Papers relating to the History of the Church in Virginia,* 522.

at my House that he shall certainly sail on Saturday or Sunday, I am obliged to hurry a few Lines
to you, as well to inclose a bill of lading, as to
return my best thanks for your several favors, together with that of Mr. Arthur Lee—the politeness
of which claims every acknowledgment from me.
I beg my humble respects may be presented to him
in your agreeable manner, with an assurance that
I should have gratefully wrote to him myself, was
I not confin'd to my Bed by order of Dr. Jones, in
ease of my leg from a violent sprain I met with in
jumping out of my Phaeton, near a fortnight
since. I am obliged to write with a tablet over my
knees. As to the Commissary ship, I should not
have been so solicitous about, had not my Lord
Bishop† given me a full expectance of it, on vacancy. Nor should I now repine at the *Insincerity of
Lawn-sleeves*—was not my being inclined to *Meth-
odism*, made a *pretext* for the Injurious Disappointment! a Pretext *as false*, as 'tis unworthy the Bishop's character to espouse it, as he has been assur'd
from 3 different Persons, not only of my Orthodoxy,
but of yᵉ success of my endeavours in preventing the
settlement of such sectaries in my Parish; and for
which I have the publick acknowledgments of my
vestry. He could have no other Information of any
attachment to them, than what must arise from his

---

† Richard Osbaldiston, Bishop of London.

own Breast, from my Lord D[artmou]th's being suspected to be a follower of them. Poor Pretence, for ye forfeiture of his Honor! But here let it rest. Your Goodness in planning for a future vacancy, while it proves your friendship and Regard for my Interest, shall be ever remembered with the most respectful Gratitude;—but my dear Friend must excuse me, if I cannot prevail with myself ever to make another attempt against so cruel and inveterate a suspicion, and which is *nourish'd* by the B—p [Bishop] himself!*

I observed what you wrote about not receiving Letter of advice of Mortimer's Bill of £20. I should have been sorry it had been protested; (as it would have been the first to my Discredit) as I gave you advice of it, and always do of my Draughts; but miscarriages will happen.

---

* "Formerly Bishop Gibson was invested by a commission from the king with a power to exercise ecclesiastical jurisdiction in the Colonies, and to delegate this power to his Commissaries; which he did, and the offending brethren were sometimes brought before these Spiritual courts; and if not exemplarily punished, they were at least kept in some awe. Since the death of that Prelate, no Bishop of London hath thought fit to take out such a commission. It seems it is attended with considerable expense; and some B[ishop]s are fond of their money; and thus the flock in America is left in such hands as chance or necessity throw in their way, without ability to get rid of them, even though they should prove ravening wolves. As to sending us a Bishop, it means nothing, but the extension of the power of the Priesthood."—*Letter from Virginia*, 5 April, 1772. In *London Chronicle*, 25 June, 1772.

I must say I expected something more than my proceeds for yᵉ Tobaccos (£50, 18s, 2d) which went in Walker.   Mr. Russell far exceeded those sales. Nor can I understand the difference you mention of yᵉ nᵒ· side of Rapᵏ· Tobacco.   My overseers at Home and at the Glebe, are reckon'd neat Planters, and it is *generally* allow'd our Tobaccos are more valuable than the Potomack; and yet we get no better prices, or scarcely so good.   And as to Rappahanock, our merchant store-keepers here assure me, that yᵉ *sᵒ· side* Tobacco is not worth a farthing a hhd. more than ours, when equally handled.   So I must beg a *Truce* with such Distinctions.

The old ⸺ spent the day with me over last court.   He looks fresh and hearty; and is I am afraid as lewdly indulgent as ever from the appearance of his waiting maids, Bab and Henny.   If ever he marries, you may depend on it (as I told him the other day) it will be with some mopsqueezer who can satiate his filthy amours in his own way.   Col. C—r* your friendly Godfather, cannot be prevail'd on to ship you a pound of his Tobacco.   He is even outrageous (with an Oath in his mouth) when I solicited him on Rayson's arrival.   Entre nous, I should not desire his Consignment was I in your place without an *extra-*

---

* Carter?

ordinary commission for such a correspondence. Was you to read the letter he wrote to Mr. Mollison,* you would certainly be of my opinion. I send you nine Hhds of excellent stuff per your ship; which I know to be good and very neatly priz'd and well secur'd. I hope they will go to a good Market and sell before the latter ships land their Cargoes. I have also sent a couple of hhds. for a Gardener I bought from your ship, by y^e Recommendation of Col$^{o.}$ R$^{d.}$ H. Lee.

In yours of 25th Jan$^{y.}$ last, you say you can only promise me *Neighbour's Fare* for my Tobaccos last year. Pray remember my good Friend, that as Col$^{o.}$ Fras. Lee is literally and almost my next door neighbour, that my sales do not fall short of his; otherwise your promise fails, as I shall be content in y^e *Equality* of *his* price, let it be what it will. I hope my last Draught to Mortimer is paid. He told me it was for a chariot he had commission'd you to buy for him; so that as it was for your own payment I drew the more readily. I hear he has sold it to Mr. Spotswood on gaining the Harness clear. You know the Doctor's manœuvres where a Penny can be turn'd. Capt. Rayson is I really think industrious for your concern here. He neglected bringing my account this morning for about a hund^d w$^{t.}$ of single sugar, and 4 small

---

* W. & R. Molleson were merchants in London engaged in the American trade.

Glocester Cheeses, with a couple of Salt Sellers he brought me from London; I must therefore beg you will pay him his Demand, and return me his account, and which is all I shall trouble you with at present. I think there is now a fine Opening for you to enlarge your Trade here, if you are so inclin'd. Rayson says he expects to be in Virginia in ye Fall in a larger ship. I shall get ready for him, and you may depend on a larger Consignment from me; and every service in my power to render you, wherever I can solicit; as no one can be more deserving of my wishes.

Col^o. F. Lee's Lady* and Mr. Counsellor Wormly's† took a seat with me in my Phaeton lately to Stratford;‡ your Brother R^d. Henry and his Lady‖ met us, and we were very jovial for two days, in which your Health and Lady's were not forgot. In returning to Menokin,§ I was obliged to *Gully* the Ladies by Dick Parker's Mill in a terrible Road, in order to save our necks. That is, by my driving skill, I drove the whole carriage into a deep gully, to prevent the over-setting on either side which lay on an ascent, and by which means no other Acci-

---

* Rebecca, a daughter of John Tayloe, of Mt. Airy.

† Ralph Wormley married Sarah Berkley of Barn Elms.

‡ The residence of Philip Ludwell Lee.

‖ Mrs. Anne Pinkard, *nee* Gaskins.

§ The seat of Francis Lightfoot Lee.

dent happened than the loss of about 3 Tears from
ye bright eyes of ye Councillor's Lady. The uneasy posture in which I write, has obliged me to
lay down my Pen a Hundred times, since I began
my letter. Nor can I hold it any longer than to
beg a good Price for ye enclosed Bill of Lading, as
I am at present *very poor*, and in ye greatest need
of all your *pecuniary assistance*. Give ye enclosed
letter to my young friendly Correspondent as directed, and be always assured of every Esteem and
Respect dwelling in ye Breast, of, Dear Sir,

Your faithfull and obliged

I. W. GIBERNE.

P. S.   Paddy Maxwell is just arriv'd from Dublin with Convicts.

Another P. S.   If I can well manage my Finances in another year, I may perhaps pay a visit
to my *Natale Solum;* and as I breath'd my first air
in the Parish of *Allhallows Barking* (which I take
to be yours) I may very likely take a circuit round
Tower Hill. My respects wait on your Lady.
Had not my poor mistaken mother made so partial
a Distinction of her Children in her will (to ye ex-
clusion of her sons) I might have been in such a
state, as to have made my little Forest Plantation
here, the most rurally pleasant of any in the colony.
What improvements I have made, you would be
pleas'd with; but I shall put myself to no further

expense. Mrs. Giberne desires to be remembered to you and yours; but says she will never leave Virginia on this side her Grave.

THE ADDRESS OF THE SHERIFFS TO THE LIVERY OF LONDON.*

[DECEMBER, 1773.]

Gentlemen:

The address of Mr. Roberts, one of the late candidates to represent you in Parliament, makes it necessary that we should state to you the reasons on which we refused Counsel in the scrutiny which he demanded. The act of Parliament which appoints a scrutiny in elections by the Livery, and prescribes the mode in which it shall be conducted, directs, That six persons qualified to vote at such elections shall be allowed as Scrutineers for and on behalf of the Candidate or Candidates on each side, and ordains that the scrutiny shall be ended within fifteen days after its commencement.

Upon due consideration, therefore, of the words of the act, and of the time prescribed for finishing the scrutiny, it appeared to us that it was the intention of the Legislature to substitute Scrutineers in the place of Counsel; and that if Counsel were allowed, it would be almost impossible to go through the scrutiny in the time prescribed by

----

London Chronicle, 1 January, 1774.

law. We were confirmed in this opinion by finding
that there was no precedent of Counsel having ever
been allowed on such scrutinies for fifty years past;
and that though it was demanded, and refused by
the last Sheriffs, so far was it from being thought a
denial of justice, that, among all the exceptions
which were taken to their proceedings, this was
never mentioned.

In consequence of this opinion we gave notice to
the Candidates and their Scrutineers to meet us at
Guildhall on Monday the 20th instant preceding
the scrutiny, which was to commence on the 23d,
to hear the manner in which we intended the scrutiny should be conducted. We expected, that if
the mode we proposed were exceptionable, they
would then offer to us their objections, to which
we should have paid all due attention. The majority of the Scrutineers on both sides being present, we informed them, among other things, that
we had determined not to admit Counsel. No objection was made then, nor at any time after, till
on Thursday, when we attended at Guildhall to
proceed on the scrutiny. Mr. Roberts and his
Scrutineers, before the other Candidate and his
Scrutineers appeared, demanded, by the mouth of
Mr. Sergeant Davy, that the Counsel he had
brought might be admitted.

We stated to them the reasons on which our
former declaration was formed; and that as we

saw no cause for altering it, they could not be admitted. We observed too, that we might properly be charged with partiality and injustice, if we altered a resolution signified to both parties on an application by one party only; when, in all probability, the other Candidate would, in consequence of our declaration, come unprovided with similar assistance.

We were then told that notice had been sent of it to our office, and to the Mansion House the night before, which we found had been done, but so late in the night that it did not come to the hands even of the Secondaries till the very morning on which the scrutiny was to begin. Upon our asking Mr. Sergeant Davy whether he knew of any instance of counsel being allowed in scrutinies of this kind since the 11th of George the First, regulating particularly all elections in the City of London; or of any law that gave to the Candidate the right of demanding to be heard by counsel in this case; *he replied in the negative.* We have thus, Gentlemen, stated the facts for your judgment. Circumstanced as we were, and raised to this office by your free and popular suffrage, we did not expect to escape the censure of partiality; but we have been particularly cautious not to deserve it. We have always conceived that we should then most effectually answer the wishes of our Constituents, when we discharged our trust with strict impartiality, and held the scales of justice with an even, unbiased hand. It is the *preservation*, not the *perversion*, of the law, from which the people expect security and protection.

Mr. Roberts speaks of "*certain important questions of law* which his *counsel* were instructed to discuss before us, and adds that, without such learned assistance he could not make out his objections." We cannot conceive what important points of law could possibly have arisen in so simple a business as that of this scrutiny. The act of Parliament has specified particularly what shall be the objections. They consist of a few, and those the plainest, matters of fact, which the meanest capacity is competent to state and to determine. The only question that admits of the least latitude is, what shall be deemed receiving of alms within the act. This question has been agitated a thousand and a thousand times over at wardmotes, and the decisions upon it are known to every citizen who gives common attention to such business. We wish Mr. Roberts had been pleased to have stated to us at the time, or to you in his address, what were those *important questions of law*, that we might *then*, and you *now*, have judged whether they were relative to the question before us, or upon which we ought to have given judgment. If they were not within our jurisdiction, his complaint, grounded upon their not having been discussed, would appear exceedingly frivolous. Had any point of real difficulty arisen in the course of the scrutiny *upon which the fate of the election depended*, it would then have been time enough to demand counsel to discuss it. Had we found ourselves in any want of legal light to direct us, the Recorder of London and Mr. Common Sergeant are the proper counsel to advise, and are always ready to assist us with their opinions.

Upon the whole, Gentlemen, we submit it to you, that our conduct was clearly consistent with law; and that Mr. Roberts, far from having any just reason to complain, ought rather to have apologized for the manner in which he attempted to mislead the Sheriffs into an act not warranted by law or usage, and which in the mode of it would have been partial and unjust.

We are, with all due respect,

Gentlemen, your most humble servants,

STEPHEN SAYRE,
WILLIAM LEE.

TO RICHARD HENRY LEE.

LONDON, 17 March, 1774.

My dear Brother:

I must give you a little dissertation on Politics. The American business engages at present the whole attention of every one here, from the K[ing]

to ye shopkeeper. The inclosed paper will give
you a sketch of the bill that is to be brought into
the House of Commons to-morrow, respecting Boston;* but I am told by several members (for none
but members are admitted when American affairs
are on the carpet,) that Lord North said, in the

---

* It was on March 11th that Lord North asked for leave to
bring in a bill removing the customs, courts of justice and all
government offices from Boston to Salem. Gibbon wrote on
the 16th: "Something more is, however, intended, and a committee is appointed to inquire into the general state of America.
But administration keep their secret as well as that of Freema-
sonry, and, as Coxe profanely suggests, for the same reason."
Lord Dartmouth was firm in wanting an alteration of the Council of Massachusetts Bay, but was opposed to bringing offend-
ers to England for trial, wishing them to be tried at Nova
Scotia. Hutchinson was told by John Pownall that the Cabinet
was at one time determined to have the principal "incendiaries"
of Boston sent over for trial, and Franklin suspected such a design was on foot. Mansfield persuaded the Cabinet to give
over this project. The division of party feeling given by Lee
must have been based largely upon rumor, for there was little
or no opposition to ministerial measures, either within or out of
Parliament. "The violent destruction of the tea seems to have
united all parties here against our province, so that the bill now
brought into Parliament for shutting up Boston as a port till
satisfaction is made meets with no opposition." *Franklin to
Cushing*, 22 March, 1774. "I mentioned that the bill brought
into Parliament, for punishing Boston, met with no opposition.
It did, however, meet with a little before it got through, some
few of the members speaking against it in the House of Commons, and more in the House of Lords. It passed, however,
by a very great majority in both, and received the royal assent
on Thursday, the 31st past." *Franklin to Cushing*, 2 April, 1774.

bill, some alteration of the charter of the Massachusetts bay would be introduced, and declared
that the punishment of Boston was intended as an
example to all the other Colonies, who should be
treated in the same manner whenever they dared
to resist the shackles which the K[ing] is determined they shall wear (perhaps the last sentiment
was not conveyed in my words, but the meaning
was truly the same), but that it was necessary and
prudent to punish one colony at a time, and Boston
being the foremost in asserting their rights, it was
proper to begin with it first. This you may be assured is the language of every ministerial scoundrel.
The intention of this act is totally to annihilate the
town of Boston, which will most effectually be
done, if the people there permit it to be carried into
execution. Lord North, Dartmouth, and some
say, Lord Mansfield, have been against these measures; but the K[ing] with his usual obstinacy
and tyr——l disposition, is determined, if it be
possible, to inslave you all; the Bedford Party,
Lord Temple and the remnant of the Grenville
party, Lord Suffolk and Wedderburne, wish the
same as well as to make their court to the K[ing],
so that Lords North and Dartmouth have been
over ruled in the cabinet, where the whole business
is settled, and P[arliamen]t made the instrument
when it is tho't convenient; for the mode of business is quite changed in this country from what it

was formerly. Neither K[ing] nor Minister ever do anything wrong, because P[arliamen]t is very ready to sanctify what the K[ing] or Minister determines to be right.

These violent measures would never have been attempted (for there is not a more certain truth in nature than that Tyrants are always cowards) but upon the following principles or reasons; from the conduct of the Bostonians in admitting the troops in 1768 to land and be quartered in the Town without any resistance, tho' they had an act of Parliament in their favor, and after they had made the world believe by a great deal of blustering, and everybody here firmly expected, they would proceed to extremities, in so much that the stocks here fell upon it, as if war had been actually declared against France or Spain : the K[ing] and his friends, as they are called, think there will be no resistance now. Secondly, they believe that the other Colonies will look on quietly and see Boston destroyed. In both these conjectures I flatter myself they will be mistaken. The people of Boston seem to me to have been preparing for such a stroke for some time: I think they are now provided, and the less they talk the more I expect they will do, especially as they know the European powers are ready at any moment to give them any assistance they want. As to ye second reason, I cannot believe the other Colonies will not interfere, and that very warmly. Everything at present seems to me to be very properly situated in N. York, Pennsylvania and So. Carolina, and if the Virginia Assembly does but stir in the business, I have no doubt there will be a perfect union among all the Colonies, which is indeed more absolutely necessary now than at any time before, as the attack is intended against the whole, and I am of opinion it will check the sanguinary spirit of your enemies here, if they find the Colonies are firm and closely united. Indeed, it is evident you have no alternative, but to resist united and most probably be free, or to submit and be slaves at once. The plan I leave to you. You have many friends here upon principle, as you will perceive from the inclosed printed letter to Lord North, signed E. B., which is supposed to be Edmund Burke's, who is the mouth of the Rockingham Party; which should be reprinted in all ye American papers. Write me often, especially from ye Assembly. Yours.

TO FRANCIS LIGHTFOOT LEE.

LONDON, 16 July, 1774.

My dear Brother:

Capt. Nicks now goes out a passenger in the Bland, Capt. Danby, and, as I cannot help thinking you will in Virginia cordially join the Marylanders in stoping the exportation of Tob^o. after a certain period, Capt. Nicks, if such resolution sh'd take place, has agreed to wait on you immediately, to be advised if you can load a ship for me in Potomack or Rap^{k.} before the exportation is stop^{d.,} and if one is to be got on charter you will please to take her up for that purpose, and put Capt. Nicks into her. 'Tis impossible for me to be farther particular in this business, as the whole must depend on the particular situation of things and circumstances which you on the spot can only judge of; therefore shall trust the transaction entirely to your prudence and discretion, only observing that in all probability, should a nonexportation of Tob^{o.} take place, it cannot continue above one year; because in that time the contest must be settled one way or other, and a ship load coming at so critical a period, will save me from the general devastation and the consigners from the increase of price will get as much from half a crop, as from the whole if there is no interruption in the trade. Should it be requisite to think of the above, in my opinion only our Br. R. H. Lee and the 'Squire* sh^{d.} be consulted before it is put in Practice, and I w^d not have you wait for Capt. Nicks if he does not come to you immediately on his arrival, as no time can be lost if the Scheme is put in Execution at all.   Y^{rs} Sincerely. †

---

* Richard Lee, of Lee Hall.

† From the *Lee Papers* in Harvard University.

TO RICHARD HENRY LEE.

LONDON, 10 September, 1774.

My dear Brother:

I have perused your letter to our Bro. A,* as he is absent on a tour to Italy. I find from a letter of our Bro. F. L. L. † an idea has been entertained in Virginia of paying for the East India Co's tea destroyed at Boston; I cannot think such a measure will be adopted at the Congress. In my judgment it is totally wrong, and cannot be supported on any principle of Policy or Justice; my reasons for this opinion are too numerous to be set down here, especially as they can be of little use, since the measure must be fully canvassed before this gets to hand; however, as it appears to me, that whatever may be determined at the Congress, or at your meeting at Williamsburg the 1st of August last, that the difference between this country and America cannot be settled until a new parliament meets. I will give some hints of what in my opinion ought to be your conduct.

A settled plan is laid to subvert the liberties and constitution of this country, as well as that of America. You are personally obnoxious to the King and his Junto, as having shown more spirit in support of your rights, than the people of this country, who are immersed in riches, luxury and

---

* Arthur Lee.   † Francis Lightfoot Lee.

dissipation. Therefore, every nerve will be exerted to subdue your spirit, and make you first bow your necks to the yoke, which will prove a useful example to the people at home.* The plan is deeply laid by the King, Lords Bute, Mansfield, and Wedderburne; for which purpose they employ the most useful tools in the kingdom: Lord North, a tyrant from principle, cunning, treacherous and persevering, a perfect adept; and his Brother in Law, Lord Dartmouth, who will whine, preach and cry, while he is preparing privately a dagger to stab you to the heart.† Under this direction, the several acts against Boston, the Massachusetts Bay, and Quebec act, have passed the last sessions; to enforce them soldiers and ships of war have already been sent to Boston, and many more will follow on the

---

* In 1772 Burke had said: "There is no proposal, how destructive soever to the liberties of the kingdom, which the ministry can make, but what the people would readily comply with."— *Parliamentary History*, XVII, 836.

†Lord North married for his third wife, Katherine, daughter of Sir Robert Furnese, and widow of the Earl of Rockingham. The marriage occurred in the summer of 1751. Some one said it was very hot weather to marry so fat a bride, when George Selwyn responded, "Oh! she was kept in ice for three days before." She died in 1776.

Lord Dartmouth's piety was noticed by his contemporaries. Richardson said he would have been the living Sir Charles Grandison, had he not been a Methodist: and Cowper celebrated the peer "not too proud to pray." Horace Walpole once described him as in "the odour of devotion."

least occasion. General Carleton, the ablest officer
in the British service, is sent to his Government of
Quebec, to embody 30,000 Roman Catholics there.
The Ministers have offered to General Amherst the
command in chief of America, and to Gen. Sir
William Draper, the government of New York.
General Amherst has not yet agreed to accept, but
has it now in consideration. Amherst, Gage, Carleton, and Draper, are to be employed against you.
From these facts it is evident that open war is intended against you, provided the people here sit
still, and the question is, how are you to oppose it.
In my opinion every method is lawfully warrantable. As the first blow is struck by the Ministry,
and every tie of allegiance is broken by the Quebec
act, which is absolutely a dissolution of this Government, the compact between the King and the people is totally done away with. The people of New
England have been prudently providing for the
worst event by lately having two entire vessels,
privately loaded with arms and ammunition from
Scotland, with twice as many small arms, and
double the amount of Powder, that was usual,
shipt from hence.* I wish every colony had been
as provident, but I do not find that they have.
However, let us consider what peaceable steps

* Hutchinson speaks of the shipment of some arms, but they
were for government. 1 *Diary*, 218.

should be first pursued, that your last efforts may be warrantable in the eyes of God and Man.

The first object should be to form a Federal Union with all the Colonies, as the States General of Holland, or the Amphyctions of Greece. If it is practicable, get Quebec into the union. Delegates or Representatives of the Colonies should certainly meet in Congress once at least in every year. In every Colony incessant pains should be used to engage the yeomanry or people at large in the same spirit of opposition with the principal men, and by degrees lead them on to the last point, if it should be necessary. In this progress you will no doubt find many obstructions from the slavish principles of some, and the prospects of rewards and preferments, which are liberally held out from hence, to some principal people in all the colonies, and particularly in New York; but with perseverance I think those obstacles may be easily surmounted. By no means trust anything to the merchants, for, in general, gain is their God; but force them to co-operate with the wishes of the people. For this purpose you will have abundant time, as I am convinced the business will not be speedily ended, unless a thorough change of ministers and favorites should take place here. As I take it for granted, the Americans will be firm, and persevere to the utmost extremity. It is the part of the leaders to engage the Body of the people,

step by step, till they have advanced too far to retract. To accomplish these points in America, it
will require infinite perseverance, address and assiduity. The leaders in Boston have the most fore-
sight, and those of Philadelphia much sagacity, but
not as determined as the former; with these you
should co-operate in every measure, as they really
have the best and earliest intelligence of everything
that passes here, and are better prepared for resistance. This arises from their situation and nature
of their trade. Next you are to endeavor to raise
up a formidable opposition here, which is to be accomplished by only two methods that I know of:
a total suspension of all commerce whatsoever with
this country by stopping all exports and imports to
and from G. B.; one without the other will be of
no service, but rather injurious, as it can militate
only against yourselves: and by making a prodigious cry against the Quebec establishment. I take
to myself no small share of merit, from sounding
the first alarm, and raising up the opposition to it
in the H. of Commons and the City, by keeping a
continual fire in the papers. The principles of this
act are abominable beyond expression; but what
hurts me most is the ministerial plan openly
avowed, to make use of the Canadians to enslave
all America, which may be possibly be accomplished in a few years, if the act is not repealed, as you will be hemmed up between two

fires, the Canadians on your back from Hudson's Bay to the Mississippi, and ships of war on your coast.

The people here, however, will not make any opposition to the act on this ground. They are, nevertheless, very greatly alarmed at the threatened establishment of Popery by law, and raising a formidable Roman Catholic army; and if these apprehensions are aided and increased by proper representations from the Colonies, I shall not be surprised if the Quebec act proves as fatal to Lord North as the excise scheme was to Sir R. Walpole.* 'Tis not uncommon to hear, pretty openly expressed, that a Revolution is become necessary, and many cast their eyes on the hereditary Prince of Brunswick, tho' it is too evident to doubt that the design of Lord Bute and Mansfield is to restore the abdicated family of Steuart. Had Lord Rockingham one spark of the spirit of Pym or Hampden, great changes would ensue; but both he and Sir G. Saville, the two great leaders of the old Whig interest, have too much of the milk of human kindness in them, to entertain one bold or daring idea. The body of the people is still incorrupt,

---

* "It would have been far better to have given civil rights to the Roman Catholics before making them soldiers; they would now, no doubt, willingly employ the arms in their hands to destroy the privileges of which they were not suffered to partake."
—*Shelburne, Parliamentary History*, XVIII., 724.

but leaders are wanting, or else things would not have gone on as they have done. Lord Chatham seems to me the most decided friend America has here among the great men, but he is very infirm and has little influence since his acceptance of a Peerage, tho' united now with his brother-in-law, Lord Temple, whom he has nearly made a full convert of respecting American rights. I have had the honor of many conferences with his Lordship on the subject; like B. G. Grenville, he will not entirely give up the Parliamentary right of taxation, but he acknowledges the putting the right in execution was a most unhappy attempt, and that the present taxes should not only be repealed, but that the like attempt should never be made again; but when money is wanting from America, it should be obtained, as formerly, by requisition. Lord Chatham, like himself, speaks out and says: "The Parliament has no right under Heaven to tax America." These noblemen, however, most ardently hope that on your part, a firm and invincible opposition will be made, as they are free to declare, that from the complexion of the times, they have no prospect of saving the liberties of this country but from the exertions of America; and it might prove of some use, were you to let me have a proper political letter for the inspection of these noble Lords, with both of whom I have the honor of a correspondence, now they are out of town.

Lord Chatham's band in the House of Lords is himself, Temple, Camden and Shelbourne; in the House of Commons their band is small in number, but able in capacity: Barré, Dunning, Captain Phips, and one or two young Grenvilles, with some others. Could a sincere union be brought about between the Rockinghams and the Chathams, the present set of infamous ministers would soon decamp; but I fear such a measure could not be accomplished, and yet I am convinced unless it is, a new parliament will not make any alterations in the ministry. Lord Shelbourne I always thought as wicked a man in Politics as any in the nation (Lord Mansfield not excepted,) and now I am perfectly convinced of it, as we know for a certainty we owe the Boston Port bill meeting with no opposition in the H. of Commons to his concurrence with Lord North in the measure, for which he was to be paid with the Lieutenancy for Ireland, and Barré was to be his Secretary. I am rejoiced that North has cheated him, for after the dirty work was done, they would not give him the bribe. He is a complete Jesuit, * and thereby has ever deceived our Bro. Templar † whom I cannot convince that he is a villain, though he cheated us in a bare-faced manner about our first petition to the House of

---

* The King spoke of Shelburne as "Malagrida" and the "Jesuit of Berkeley Square."

† Arthur Lee.

Lords, against the Boston Port Bill. He undertook to deliver and support it, and promised he
would have a division on the bill in the House of
Lords, if no other Lord but himself was against it.
By this means he prevented us from getting into
better hands, and served his friend North's purpose most effectually. He delivered our petition,
but said not one word in its support,* nor did he
make any division against the bill. I suspect this
Jesuit is now on some dirty work. From the complexion of things lately in Europe, and particularly
in France since the new king's accession, there is
reason to apprehend a general war soon; therefore
Shelbourne and Mansfield, tho' 75 years old and
very infirm, are gone to Paris, as it is supposed to
buy a continuance of peace at any price with
France, that all the power of this country may be
employed to subdue and enslave America.

From great rogues, let us come to small ones.
The American merchants are very quiet, and consequently the manufacturers for the merchants,
particularly in the tobacco trade, will not entertain
an idea that it is possible for you to determine on

---

* This statement is not entirely correct, as Lord Shelburne
did speak against the measure. "The House allowed me very
patiently, though very late at night, to state the tranquil and
the loyal state in which I left the colonies, with some other very
home facts; and I cannot say I met with that weight of prejudice I apprehended."—*Shelburne to Chatham*, 4 April, 1774.

a non-exportation of tobacco. In this they have
been encouraged by letters from [Edmund] Pen-
dleton and Mr. [Robert Carter] Nicholas to Mr.
Norton, and hearing that Mr. C. C.* of Corotoman,
T. Nelson, and Col. Carrington, were against it at
the meeting of 26 members in Williamsburg, I confess I have some doubt of the measure being adopted,
from the above circumstances, and seeing the resolves of Prince George, Col. R$^{d.}$ Bland's County,
which for unmeaning insignificancy, excel anything that has ever appeared in print. I therefore
now am very impatient to know the resolutions of
the General meeting the 1st of August at Williamsburg. The merchants are almost universally your
enemies, therefore, instead of doing you any good,
their whole influence will be against you, unless
you force them thro' interest to take an active part
in your favor, and this can only be done by stopping both exports and imports to G. B. A non-
importation will affect all the merchants from Pha.
to the northward, and a non-exportation, all to the
southward of Pha. Therefore the two schemes
will unite the whole body of N. American merchants in your favor, among whom I do not know
that you have one friend at present, but Mr. Tri-
cothick,† who is rendered incapable of business by

---

* Charles Carter.

† Alderman Barlow Trecothick. In 1766, when serving as
sheriff, he attracted attention by giving away an appointment

an unlucky stroke of the palsy, 9 or 10 months ago; Mr. Bromfield, * a native of Boston, in the New England trade, Mr. Johnson, † a native of Maryland in that trade, and myself. From this real state, does it not occur to you as a measure absolutely among other things requisite to be adopted in America, to agree in supporting those merchants, effectually and only, who have openly and avowedly espoused your cause with infinite danger to themselves, while so many have been busy in traducing you, and forwarding the late iniquitous measures with all their force?

If something like this is not done, I will venture to foretell that you will never hereafter find one

---

that was usually sold for £1500. He had been a prominent adherent of Wilkes, and was chairman of the committee of the American merchants in 1767, urging upon Townshend the repeal of the acts against America. In 1770 he proposed in Parliament the repeal of the duty on tea. In November 1774, he resigned his gown as Alderman, because of ill health.

* Thomas Bromfield. Governor Hutchinson called on a Mr. Brousfield, at Islington. The poor editing of his *Diary* may have metamorphosed the name. I., 234.

† Gadsden & Johnson were a firm of American merchants in London, and John and William Johnson were signers of the City petition of 1774. It may possibly be Joshua Johnson, born in Maryland 25 June, 1742, went early in life to London, where he married Catharine ——. On the outbreak of the Revolution he went to Nantes, and after the war, returning to London, was the first American consul at that port. His daughter married (1797) John Quincy Adams.

merchant who will dare to open his lips in your behalf; for indeed by threats and a thousand other dark devices, they have already frightened all those I have mentioned into silence, except myself. You will easily conceive under these circumstances what little mercy I shall find here if the exports are stopped and my debtors will not remit, should it be known here that I have advised the measure. But does it not strike you as a folly of the first magnitude to put power and importance in the hands of your enemies, thereby enabling them to do you the most essential injury? I have just received a letter from Dr. Franklin, which concluded thus: "The magnanimity of the Virginians will amaze this ministry, which has no idea that any such thing exists anywhere as public virtue." You have not done the Americans justice who petitioned against the Boston Port and other Bills, by not publishing their names as well as those few who would not sign, that these names may be handed down with contempt to the later generations. You had the list per Gibson, and copies since. 'Tis necessary not only to encourage the virtuous in these days of profligacy, that they go on in the right way, but to hold up the wicked to contempt, that they may reap the fruits of their villainy, and thereby be prevented from a repetition of it. I have been endeavoring to get the American merchants to begin a subscription for relief of the poor sufferers in

Boston, but cannot get any one to begin it, tho'
they know I have orders from two first-rate gentlemen to subscribe £200 for them, whenever the
subscription is begun. Does not this show their
dispositions plainly? Indeed Champion,* one of
the most considerable and oldest Boston merchants,
when appealed to, declared that he would subscribe
largely to induce the Bostonians to submit and
comply with the requisitions of the Boston Port
Bill, but he would not give one shilling to support
them in their present state of rebellion—or words
to the same effect. I will, notwithstanding, endeavor to bring this measure to bear. Every body
here waits with impatience to know the result of
the Congress; till then all things will be at a stand.
We know that orders have long since been sent to
General Gage, and the other governors, to prevent
the Congress if possible; but we do not learn the
mode that has been pointed out to accomplish this
end. I am told, but cannot vouch it, that the
ministry have in contemplation a bill to defeat
your schemes of non-importation and non-exportation, if they can venture to bring it forward. I
wish they may, as it will be the most effectual plan
that can be devised to rouse the people here. 'Tis
no less than to make a monopoly of the whole
American trade, to confine exports and imports to-

---

*Probably Richard Champion, of Bristol. See Burkes' Cor-
res., II., I.

tally to G. Britain, and this commerce only to be in the hands of such merchants as are licensed by government. This plan you may think too daring and foolish for even the present weak and wicked ministers to think of; but in my opinion, 'tis the strongest reason imaginable for giving credit to the report.

I have been thus prolix in order to give you as full an idea of the state of things here, as I do not know of any opportunity I shall have of writing again before Xmas, and shall refer you for further information to the papers, etc., that go with this.*

---

* "I hope you will kindly assist Captain Brown as much as you can in leading the adventure, which will certainly be for your interest, as the price here must be very high next year, and you will always find me attentive to your benefit. The gloomy appearance of affairs between this country and America makes the mercantile body very apprehensive of the consequences, and for my own part must confess, I wait the issue with fear and trembling." *William Lee to Moore Fauntleroy,* 22 December, 1774. "Your manly associations prevent any goods from being shipped . . . . It will depend entirely on the manœuvres of Parliament this session; should our wicked ministry continue hostile to America, all mercantile business must be at an end. What tobacco next year you ship may be disposed of as you please, and it will certainly be to your advantage to ship all you can, as the price must be very high here. The merchants are in motion, and we are to have a meeting the 4th of next month in order to consider what steps we should take. In my opinion the Americans have acted wisely in not applying to anybody here but the king. By all means adhere firmly to every tittle demanded by the Congress; do not accept

TO FRANCIS LIGHTFOOT LEE.

LONDON, 24 December, 1774.

* * * I was sincerely anxious to accomplish the design I long since mentioned of visiting Virginia the next spring, but viewing with calmness the precarious state of public affairs, and considering every circumstance in its proper light, it is not

---

a *part* without the *whole*. You must succeed if you persevere. I have reason to suspect, from the manner in which some very wretched tools busy themselves (of whom, no doubt, you will hear many brags by and by) that the ministry (who are really frightened out of their wits) have a design to comply with *part only* of your demands, hoping thereby to dissolve the American unaminity. I wish you to be guarded against this wicked ministerial trick. You have every advantage now in the contest, and one year's firmness and perseverance must infallibly procure you full redress of your grievances; therefore, for God's sake, and everything else that is dear to you, do not shift your ground, but stand firm where you are." *William Lee to Landon Carter*, 22 December, 1774.

"I know your sagacity will point it out so strongly to be your interest, since the price of tobacco will be immensely high here on your stopping the exportation. When this event happens, it is to be hoped the poor tobacco merchants will find a little harmony, if they come amongst you. I see you want to come to poor *old England* again *freight free*. The Revd. Thomas Smith, chairman of a (as Lord Bute calls them) set of Traytors, etc., etc. How will you answer this when at the bar of the Old Bailey? 'Tis pity the American sheriffs are out of office, as their countrymen are likely to fill Newgate, which is now rebuilding much enlarged for their reception. After all, you may quiet your fears; for, if you adhere firmly to the plan already adopted by the Congress, you will unquestionably at least get

to be accomplished with any degree of prudence, therefore have adopted the mode which you will well know by the accompanyments with this, as ye most eligible at present in every point of view, and entirely in conformity with our Brother A's opinion and other real friends to me. No other argument is wanting to convince me that my presence in Virginia would be of infinite utility to my own affairs than your opinion, but it cannot be accomplished this season. However, the summer after, if American rights are not then settled on a firm and solid basis, let the consequence to me be what it will, I am determined to pay you a visit and perhaps a serious one; for the present difference between G. Britain and the state of America appear to me in a much more important light than

---

all your grievances fully redressed; tho' not without reluctance on the part of the K—, and our ministers, who will try a great many shifts and tricks in order to try at a division of the colonies, before they comply with the whole. But they must yield at mercy in the end, if you persevere." *William Lee to Rev. Thomas Smith*, 22 December, 1774. "However unsatisfactory the London prices may have hitherto been to you, this season will probably make amends for many losses if you ship largely, for the price of tobacco must be higher in this market than anywhere in G. Britain when ye exportation stops, which I suppose will certainly be the case, as I do not believe your grievances will be fully redressed before another session of Parliament; and without compleat redress, as the game is now in your own hands, you must be madmen, to give up for part only." *William Lee to Thomas Bartrand Griffen*, 22 December, 1774.

it does to most people here. I trust that America is sound; and I know them here to be so rotten that I cannot really think the contests can be finished in less than two years at least, and without an explicit compliance with the terms insisted on by the Congress, I, as an American, will never cease my opposition, and I hope no other American ever will. * * * Our brother Arthur has undertaken to write you fully on politics,* so have nothing to say on that head but earnestly to advise that every measure may be taken to confirm the Americans in their present spirit, and to take every possible prudent measure to defeat the most hellish and diabolical schemes that are planning against you. Trust not to any specious appearances or flattering words; depend upon it, I am not deceived in assuring you that the K., Lords B[ute] and M[ansfield] are your inveterate enemies, and that nothing but necessity will induce them to change the present iniquitous system. In less than 12 months after the American trade is compleatly stopped, the merchants and manufacturers will feel that your cause is their own and will consequently fight your battles. At present the trading interest is quite easy, owing to your exports continuing a year longer than your imports.† * * *

---

* See *Arthur Lee to Ralph Izard*, 27 December, 1774, in *Correspondence of Ralph Izard*, I., 35.

† "American affairs still wear a dismal prospect; next Wednes-

TO RICHARD HENRY LEE.

LONDON, 1 January, 1775.

My dear Brother:

* * * As to Politics, I refer you to the Magazines and Papers: our ministers seem to have totally forgot the connections of Great Britain with Europe, and their whole attention is fixed on subduing America. Indeed, you ought to stand firm and united, and then, it will not be in the Power of this, or any other Country, to hurt you.

Every real Patriot in this Country admires the Spirit that has already appeared among you, and the last Resolves of the Virginia assembly * have struck a greater Panic into the Ministers than any thing that has passed since the Stamp Act: and from some late advices, it is expected, that the northern Colonies will send Home Articles of Impeachment against Lord Hillsborough, and also against Lord Dartmouth, for signing the Letter respecting the Rhode Islanders. You see, by this,

---

day the merchants and traders in London meet to consider what can be done in the melancholy occasion. They will no doubt apply to Parliament for redress, and we hope for yᵉ assistance of all yᵉ merchants, traders, and manufacturers in the kingdom." *William Lee to William Hicks*, 31 December, 1774.

* This could hardly have reference to the proceedings of the Assembly proper. In August a meeting of delegates from the counties assembled at Williamsburg, and again in November, but the proceedings were not fully reported. It was to this last convention, probably, that Lee referred.

what an idea is entertained of your Spirit. * * *
Farewell.

TO JOHN LIDDERDALE.

LONDON, 2 January, 1775.

Sir:

Mr. Browne* received a letter from you which I
am to answer in part, as he was too busy in putting
things to rights before his departure for Virginia
where he is ñow gone (in a ship of mine) to return
in September. The plan was fixed only a few days
before it was put in execution. The very gloomy
prospect of American affairs rendered this step absolutely necessary in order to get as much property
home as possible, before the dreadful storm bursts,
which is now inevitable; for I have the best information that administration are fixed in the resolution of pursuing the same measures as they have
done lately, and I am also as well informed that all
America will persevere in the plan pointed out by
the Congress.† In this situation you can judge as
well as any man what must be the certain event to
every merchant, trader and manufacturer in the
whole Kingdom, that is concerned in American
commerce or that have any property there. Noth-

---

*Edward Browne, a business partner of Lee.

† The Association articles of the Continental Congress were
known in London, November 10th.

ing can be more clear than that the first blow struck cancels every debt due to Great Britain. For these considerations I am sure you will commend my prudence in sending Mr. Browne away as expeditiously as possible, before what I know, is also publickly known, which at present is not the case, as in general it is believed some accommodating plan will be adopted. * * * The merchants of London are to meet the 4th inst., to consider of some measures to be taken respecting American affairs; in my opinion they will have little weight with Parliament, unless they are joined by all the trading and manufacturing interests in the Kingdom. * * *

TO ANTHONY STEWART.*

LONDON, 4 January, 1775.

My dear Sir :

* * * I find by the public papers you have been as active in making bonfires in Annapolis as you were in protesting. The captain was not to blame as you must know ; but the tea was deservedly burnt, tho' the vessel should have been saved. However, I am well pleased at the whole transaction, as I understand you are to be paid for the

---

*Of the firm of Dick & Stewart, of Annapolis. He was prominent in the troubles of 1768, over the non-importation agreements in Maryland.

vessel, and with the public here who do not know this, it has had more effect in making them look on the American business as too serious to let the ministers trifle any longer, than almost anything that has happened.* The merchants are to meet this day to consider what they shall do; but for my own part I am well assured no accommodation will take place this session of Parliament. You may rely on what I say respecting the disposition of things here, and if you have any reasons to believe that the Americans will persevere in the plan adopted by the Congress (which, by the bye, is thought by every one here, wise, temperate, and much more modest than was expected), and will stop the exports in September, or sooner, I would by all means advise you to purchase immediately 1000 or 1500 hhds. of your very best tobacco, and ship it off in ships of about 350 or 400 hhds., by which you may make a fortune. You will say perhaps, where is the money to do this? I will tell

---

* In October, 1774, the brig *Peggy Stewart*, owned by Anthony Stewart, arrived in Annapolis with a cargo of general goods, including some tea—then a contraband article. Stewart, although he did not own the tea, paid the duties on it, and was waited upon by his indignant townspeople, so harassed that he publicly apologized in the most humble terms for his offence,—"a most daring insult, and act of the most pernicious tendency to the liberties of America"—was tried in a meeting of delegates, and sought a return of confidence by firing his vessel with his own hand. Scharf, *History of Maryland*, II., 159-161.

you—draw on me at 60 or 90 days sight, when the ship sails, order insurance, and consign the tobacco to me. In this case the bills will be paid. You will find Molleson's agents purchasing all they can lay their hands on. The price should not be the least obstacle; give what others do without hesitation, provided you are clear of the firmness, &c., of the Americans, on which head your judgment may be directed by observing what quantity of tobacco is planted. * * **

---

* "Besides, we acted on patriotic principles. Had you all stopped your exports and imports last fall, you might have expected redress this session of Parliament; as it is, you must wait another season, but in the meantime I trust your spirit and unanimity will increase instead of diminishing. By all means be prepared for the worst, and resolve to browse with the goats on the mountain shrubs, or meet death with intrepidity, rather than voluntarily to submit to be the veryest slaves this earth beholds. You have no friends at Court, but what is much better, you have it in your power to be friends to yourselves and have the means of redress in your own hands; and if you do not use them, no one will pity you. Persevere strictly in the plan adopted by the deputies of the American States, provide for war, and depend upon it all will be well. G. B. had better contend when united cordially with you against all the power of Europe for 7 years, than with you alone for 2 years; for the latter must be infallibly ruined. Everybody is pleased with the proceedings of the Congress." *William Lee to Dr. William Shippen, Junr.*, 4 January, 1775.

TO FRANCIS LIGHTFOOT LEE.

LONDON, 13 January, 1775.

My dear Brother :

Having never rec^d a line from you since Aug^t , dated at Urbanna, I sh^d have been a good deal alarmed on Acc^t of your health, had not our mutual friend, Mr. Giberne, frequently mentioned you in his let^rs. I have wrote you pretty fully on business by the Adventure Ca[ptain   ]on, who has been unfortunately detained a great [

] the downs by contrary winds. I have not much to add [   ] Mr. Fauntleroy's bill to Mr. Page, jun., is paid. The sum is above £100; therefore with propriety you may urge him to ship largely. I have not rec^d one shilling from Fauntleroy at Greenspring, nor a letter, except 3 or 4 lines in Jan. '74 since he went on the estate. The tobacco is this year in much worse condition than ever it was, and will not sell for as much as it would have done by ½^d p. lb., if it had been put up neatly and free from sand and dirt, as it used to be. It would have been some satisfaction had I known what plan has *been thot of to* support the Negroes in *clothing* this and next year, and how I am to get anything from it for my own support. We have a report from Glasgow that Ld Dunmore is dead; should he not, I hope the Assembly when it meets will roast him well for his many vile and infamous governmental Acts. The Merchants and

Traders in London have agreed on a Petition to Parliament for redress of American Commerce. I was one of the Com̅ᵉ for drawing it up and one for presenting it and managing it—therefore have had full opportunity of knowing. There is nothing very serious in this business, therefore do not expect any great good from it, for really nothing can rouse the good people here till they *feel*, which is not the case at present, but will be woefully so in 12 months. You must persevere in the plan adopted by the Congress and leave it to work here. My political sentiments are fully conveyed to R. H. L. by this opportunity which you will know. * * **

---

*From the *Arthur Lee Papers* in Harvard University.

"We have also this day heard that . . . . the tea in yᵉ Virginia, Captain Easten, is burnt, and the ship ordered home in ballast. This, with intelligence this day by 4 ships from N. England, that all America is firm in supporting the resolutions of Congress, has amazingly staggered all our pitiful time serving merchants, and to morrow I expect at the meeting to be unanimous." *William Lee to Edward Browne*, 3 January, 1775.

"The merchants and traders in London are drawing up a petition to the H. of C. for redress of American grievances. In this they will be followed by many towns in the kingdom, but believe me, there is some cheat in this business, as the most ministerial merchants, &c., are busyest about it. You must know how much censured I was last year by almost every merchant here for endeavoring to get them to petition against the Boston port bill. I still bore my testimony against it, and the other Boston and Quebec Bills by petitioning both houses of Parliament and the king against them. You must not ex-

TO RICHARD HENRY LEE.

LONDON, 17 January, 1775.

In confirmation of what has been wrote to you by this opportunity, I am now to inform you from

---

pect full redress this session of P—t, as the people here do not yet feel enough to make them *serious* in applications in your favor. Adhere strictly to what the Congress has already agreed on, and depend upon it by next Winter, you will have many, many thousands at Westminster to fight for you. I cannot too much urge you to pay no attention to the proceedings of the merchants. I am one of a Committee for drawing their petition, and can assure you it is only a blind to recover their lost reputation in America. They will not go any farther than the ministers choose, for there is a good understanding between them; but this time next year they will feel so much that they will speak for themselves without ministerial orders; therefore, do you attend to your manufactures, which will certainly save America." *William Lee to Richard Lee,* 9 January, 1775.

"It is now determined by administration most assuredly not to relax in their measures against America; the merchants have consequently become luke-warm and timid; but there is a fire kindling among the people that will blaze most furious in about a year." *William Lee to Edward Browne,* 17 January, 1775.

"F—n is stirring up a meeting of the merchants in London, who profess not to trouble themselves about the political dispute, and only pray in general for the care of their interest in America: and they chose what was called a good Committee, except the late Sheriff Lee, and one other person, who it is supposed will draw the rest farther than they intended." *Hutchinson to Green,* 10 January, 1775.

"If the merchants had thought fit to interfere last winter, the distresses of this might certainly have been prevented; conciliatory measures would have taken place; and they would have come with more dignity, and with far better effect, before

unquestioned authority, that last night a full
Council was held on American measures, at which
Lord Bute assisted, when it was determined to per-
severe in every measure oppressive to America.   I

the trial of our strength than after. But a confidence in ministers, and a dread of the imputation of giving countenance to
what those ministers called faction, rendered them all passive,
and some worse than passive, in the plans then adopted. By
means of this reserve, the authority of the mercantile interest,
which ought to have supported with efficacy and power the opposition to the fatal cause of all this mischief, was pleaded
against us, and we were obliged to stoop under the accumulated
weight of all the interests in this kingdom. I never remember
the opposition so totally abandoned as on that occasion. Now,
as it was foreseen, they begin to stir, because they begin to feel.
But still the same influence which hindered them from taking
any previous measures to prevent their disaster, will, I fear,
hinder them from taking any effectual measures to redress it.
The meeting in London was large, and the sense of their situation as lively as possible; but as far as I could find, they had
nothing like the sentiments of honest, free, and constitutional
resentment, which Englishmen used formerly to feel against
the authors of any public mischief; and they seemed to entertain full as great apprehensions of taking any steps displeasing
to the authors of their grievances, as they showed desire of re-
dressing them." *Edmund Burke to Richard Champion*, 10
January, 1775.

"The petition as it was first prepared by the merchants, was
to the last degree cold and jejune. Not a word purporting the
least dislike to the last Parliament. Not a syllable that indicated a preference of one system of American government over
another. But Baker [William Baker, of Bradford-bury], with
great address and perseverance, carried some distant reflection
on the American laws, and some compliment on the beneficial

do not know, certainly, all their Plans, but in
general I am told that some of them are foolish to
an extreme. Time will show what they are.*

The ministerial runners have been busy in the

---

effects of the repeal of the stamp-act. This petition is far, and
far enough, even now, from what in common sense it ought to
be ; for by putting the whole of the sufferings of trade from the
resistance of America, it sets the nation in a very humble, and,
in truth, an abject state, in case of a concession. Had indeed
the ministry been disposed, or any *prevalent* party in parliament been disposed, to overturn the obnoxious acts, as being
fundamentally unjust and impolitic, the merchants might come
with great weight and propriety to speak of their effect upon
trade. At present we have no reason assigned by those who
have any strength, either within or without doors, for giving
way, but the opposition our acts have met with." *Burke to
the Marquis of Rockingham*, 12 January, 1775.

This plan of petitioning the king was attributed by the Marquis of Rockingham to William Lee's endeavors, but it was not
acceptable to many of the merchants. Baker and David Barclay were opposed to it ; the West India planters and merchants
refused to join in it.

* Bancroft (VII., 193) mentions a Cabinet meeting that was
held on January 12th. "The current of its opinions drifted the
minister into the war, which he wished to avoid. His colleagues refused to find in the proceedings of Congress any honorable basis for conciliation. It was therefore resolved to inter-
dict all commerce with the Americans; to protect the loyal,
and to declare all others traitors and rebels. The vote was designed only to create division in the Colonies, but it involved a
civil war." Parliament re-assembled on January 19th, when,
by his Majesty's command, the papers relating to the disturbances in North America were laid before it. On the 20th, the
same matters were laid before the Lords by Lord Dartmouth.

city to-day, and the merchants who appeared fore-most in petitioning, which they were *permitted* to do, from the ministry having taken no decided part, and wishing for somebody to point out a path for them to get out of the scrape they were in, are now much puzzled how to act, so as to support their credit in America, and yet please their masters here. Rely not on such wretched creatures, but persevere in your own measures; confirm and enlarge the Plan of the last Congress, and depend on it, 12 months must produce a Revolution here.

Be not surprised if Resolutions in Parliament should pass, that the People of Massachusetts Bay are in a state of actual Rebellion.* They must be supported at every Point, or you are ruined. Again, I conjure you, to be provided to resist Force by Force. Such a contest must terminate in your advantage. Farewell.

Read, seal and forward as soon as possible the enclosed to Mrs. Rind.†

TO RICHARD HENRY LEE.

LONDON, 20 Jan., 1775, 9 o'c. at night.

This minute from the House of Lords.

This day the Lords met according to adjourn-

---

* It was not until February 2ⁿᵈ that North proposed an address to the king to declare that a rebellion existed in Massachusetts.

† Printer of the *Virginia Gazette.*

ment, from the Xmas holidays at 3 o'c. The
American papers were laid before the House, without any message from the King.

Amongst them is the Congress petition to the
King, the Resolutions and proceedings of Congress, with sundry other Papers. The titles being
read, Lord Chatham got up, and speaking for an
hour in an astonishing manner to me,* who never
had the happiness of hearing him in public before,
he moved that an address should be presented to
the King, to remove the troops from Massachusetts
Bay, as an earnest to America, that some conciliating Plan was about to be adopted here;† (remem-

---

* "He [Dr. Franklin] has seen in the course of life, sometimes eloquence without wisdom, and often wisdom without
eloquence; in the present instance he sees both united, and
both, he thinks, in the highest degree possible." *Franklin to
Earl Stanhope*, 23 January, 1775. "I was quite charmed with
Lord Chatham's speech in support of his motion. He impressed me with the highest idea of him, as a great and most
able statesman." Franklin, *Negotiations for effecting a Reconciliation between Great Britain and the American Colonies.*

† For some reason Chatham wished there should be no little
mystery attending his motion. On the 18th, Lady Chatham
wrote of the "infinite pains taken to circulate an authoritative
report, that you are *determined* to give yourself *no trouble* upon
American affairs, and that, for certain, you do not mean to
come to town"—a rumor that her husband characterized as
"the impudent and ridiculous lie of the hour." On the next
day he wrote to Lord Stanhope, "Be so good as not to communicate what my intended motion is to any one whatever;
but the more it is known and propagated that I am to make a

ber I speak from memory, after 6 hours standing in an immense crowd, without any refreshment but that of the mind); however, it appears of infinite importance that you should have some idea of the debate, as soon as possible, and the ship sails to-morrow morning.

He said, if the House adopted his motion, he had a Plan to propose, which he was sure would secure the dignity and supremacy of their country, and at the same time, be perfectly satisfactory to us. His plan, in short, is to disavow the right of taxation explicitly on the part of Great Britain; and, on the part of America, to acknowledge the supremacy of Parliament respecting navigation.

In the course of his speech he said: "My Lords,

---

motion relative to America the better." To Shelburne, he was somewhat more communicative. "It is an address to send im-mediate orders for removing the forces from Boston, as soon as the season may render the same practicable. This is only en-tering on the threshold of American business, and knocking at the door of a sleeping or confounded ministry. . . . Having had no communication of purposes from others, I have made none to any." He also informed Franklin of his intended step, and secured his presence. It is certain that his motion was a disagreeable surprise to some of the Rockingham Whigs, though it is not probable that a previous communication with them would have resulted in any agreement or united action, so divided was the party in opinion. As to Chatham's plan, see Franklin, *Works* (Bigelow's edition), V., 492. The motion was rejected by a vote of 68 to 18—"a very handsome majority" the king wrote to North.

I have read Thucydides, and am somewhat acquainted with the history of the Roman and Grecian States, and I will be bold to say, that in their most brilliant Periods, they will lose by a comparison with the strength of argument, temper, elegance of composition, and deliberate firmness in the cause of liberty in the proceedings of the Congress at Philadelphia."*

---

* "Soon after I had the pleasure of seeing you, I received the extracts from the votes and proceedings of the American Congress. I have not words to express my satisfaction that the Congress has conducted this most arduous and delicate business with such manly wisdom and calm resolution as do the highest honor to their deliberations. Very few are the things contained in their resolves that I could wish had been otherwise. Upon the whole, I think it must be evident to every unprejudiced man in England who feels for the rights of mankind, that America, under all her oppressions and provocations, holds forth to us the most fair and just opening for restoring harmony and affectionate intercourse as heretofore." *Lord Chatham to Stephen Sayre*, 24 December, 1774. "The Congress is in high esteem here among all the friends of liberty, and their papers much admired; perhaps nothing of the kind has been more thoroughly published, or more universally read. Lord Camden spoke highly of the Americans in general, and of the Congress particularly, in the House of Lords. Lord Chatham said that, taking the whole together, and considering the members of the Congress as the unsolicited, unbeseeched choice of a great, free, and enlightened people, their unanimity, their moderation, and their wisdom, he thought it the most honorable assembly of men that had ever been known; that the histories of Greece and Rome gave us nothing equal to it. Lord Shelburne would not admit that the Parliament of Britain could be comparable

He more than once, in his inimitable manner, declared that America ought not to submit to the iniquitous and tyrannic laws for its government; which, if carried into execution, must introduce *Despotism* there, and finally into this country. He also said, America had been greatly *traduced and vilified*, by the wicked artifices of a *puerile, sleeping,* and *abandoned administration.**

Said he, "If there is any of the King's ministers, who shall advise a continuance in these iniquitous measures, what shall I say? I must not say that the King is betrayed, but I will say that this country is undone." On the whole, he did not * * *

He observed that "there were 3,000,000 of men in America, who would not submit to despotic government, and must be joined by every *Whig* in this Kingdom, (the million he would not mention,) and by *every* man in Ireland. With a French and Spanish war hanging over our heads, what must

---

with it, a Parliament obeying the dictates of a ministry who, in nine cases out of ten, were governed by the under-secretaries." *Franklin to Charles Thomson,* 5 February, 1775.

*The words really used were "sleeping and confounded ministry." "Ministers may satisfy themselves, and delude the public, with the report of what they call commercial bodies in America. They are *not* commercial; they are your packers and factors : they live upon nothing—for I call commission nothing. I mean the ministerial *authority* for this American intelligence; the runners for government, who are paid for their intelligence." *Boyd.*

be the fate of this devoted kingdom, if the present
arbitrary American System be persevered in, he
left every Lord to judge."*

This motion and speech drew from Lord Suffolk
a pretty explicit declaration (Lord Suffolk is one of
the Secretarys of State,) that ministry had formed
a Plan, which in due time would be opened by the
Noble Lord in whose department it was; but he
would go so far as to say, that it was not to recede,
but to persevere, and carry into execution by force,
all the late acts of Parliament; and he founded his
hopes of success on the several Colonies being
already disgusted by the Proceedings of the late
Congress, and would not adhere to them.

He gave the House to understand, that part of
the Plan was to increase the military in Boston, to
destroy that town by bombardment, and to send

---

* "This glorious spirit of Whiggism animates three millions
in America, who prefer poverty with liberty to gilded chains
and sordid affluence; and who will die in defence of their
rights as men, as freemen.   What shall oppose this spirit, aided
by the congenial flame glowing in the breasts of every Whig in
England, to the amount, I hope, of double the American numbers? Ireland they have to a man. . . . On the other hand,
every danger and hazard impend, to deter you from perseverance in your present ruinous measures—foreign war hanging
over your head by a slight and brittle thread: France and
Spain watching your conduct, and waiting for the maturity of
your errors;—with a vigilant eye to America, and the temper of
your colonies, more than to their own concerns, be they what
they may." *Boyd.*

troops to every Colony to support the friends of government, as they are fashionably called, who conspire to destroy the Liberties of their country, viz: the Hutchinsons, Ingersolls, De Lanceys, etc.*

Lord Littleton spoke next; abused America in dirty terms, well befitting such a Demon as he is: applauded administration, but * * *   †

---

* In a conversation with Hutchinson on the 22d, Lord Suffolk owned " he looked upon an attempt to enforce internal taxation desperate: asked what effect an explicit declaration of Parliament would have, setting forth the reasonableness of the Americans contributing to the support of Government, and declaring that upon such contribution by the respective Assemblies, it was the determination the acts, except such as regulated trade, should be repealed; and that the monies raised by such Acts as remained in force, should be applied to the support of the Government where it was raised? But he started objections; and particularly that of the Colonies taking advantage of such a declaration as a concession; and insisting more vigorously on the rest of their claims."

† The rest of this letter is missing. Burke outlined the debate in his letter to a *Committee of Bristol*, 20 January, 1775.

"The London merchants have presented two petitions to the House of Commons, of which you have the copies; the papers will show our conduct on our second petition being ordered to lye on the table. We are to persevere with a third petition to ye House of Commons, or one to the House of Lords, perhaps more than one to both Houses; besides application to the throne. Glasgow has petitioned in plainer language than any other place — Whitehaven, Manchester, Liverpool, Dudley, Staffordshire, Birmingham, one in favor of America, and another under the patronage of Bolton, who has rivall'd Pinchback as the K—g's Toyman, insists on enforcing the acts of

TO WILLIAM HICKS.

LONDON, 27 January, 1775.

* * * I have not seen any petition from Whitehaven, and do suppose there is some mistake in
the business, as Mr. James Lowther sent to me on
Tuesday last, desiring I would let him see the
Whitehaven petition, which he understood I had
received from you. The most spirited petition yet
presented is come from Glasgow; it is evident from
the temper and conduct of the King's servants that
moderation and gentle words will not answer with
them. The people must at length, for self-preser-
vation, speak with that dignity and freedom which
is their birthright, or else they, viz! the ministers,
will certainly involve us in a civil war, from which
evil I hope the Almighty will deliver us. You
have herewith a copy of our first petition, which

Parliament; Norwich, two strong ones from Bristol, and many
others expected, are the petitions in favor of a reconciliation
with America; besides a strong petition from the whole body
of W. India merchants and planters united. Notwithstanding
all this, the ministers under the direction of G.— must persevere, and a civil war in my opinion is unavoidable. The minister's Majority in the House of Commons is still near 3 to 1,
which will encourage them to go on.

"Since the foregoing I am informed that one part of the minister's plan is to procure an act of Parliament to shut up every
American port." *William Lee to Edward Browne*, 30 January, 1775. The debate on the Merchants' petition is summarized in I. Hutchinson, *Dairy and Letters of Thomas Hutchinson*, 360.

by a ministerial trick was put into such a train as
to have no effect; therefore, yesterday, we presented another petition praying that the house
would not come to any determination on American
affairs, until we had been fully heard in support of
the allegations in our first petition. This was
ordered to lye on the table. This day we were
called on to come to the bar, which we waived,
telling the House very explicitly, that we would
not go into the examination until the prayer of our
petition delivered yesterday was agreed to. The
ministers must comply at last, if the merchants,
etc., thro' the Island do but persevere in a manly
way. *

---

* "Yesterday being the day appointed for reading the papers
in the H. of Commons, a second Petition was presented from
the Merchts of much the same tenor as the former, which was
rejected by 250 to 89; and then another from Bollan, Franklin
and Lee, praying that the petition from the Congress to the
King might be then read; and this was rejected by 218 against
67. These two petitions took till ten o'clock, so that the papers
are not yet read." *Hutchinson to Gage*, 27 January, 1775.

"I find that the merchants trading to North America and
the West Indies, are petitioning Parliament. Their applications are ill-timed, and will prove ineffectual. Had they joined
us in our petition, we had assurances that the corporation of
London would immediately have followed the example. This
would have put all the manufacturing towns in motion, and
some good might have been done. The truth is, they are, in
general, puffed up with pride and unmindful of the interest of
their employers.

"The tea, which has occasioned so much trouble, would never

TO RICHARD HENRY LEE.

LONDON, 10 February, 1775.

My dear Brother:

* * * Since the 4th of January, I have, as a
Committee man, been every day engaged with the
Merchants' Petitions to the Houses of Parliament
for Redress of American Grievances; insomuch
that I have never got to bed 'till one o'clock in the
morning, and frequently not sooner than 3 or 4
o'clock. * * *

Tho' the merchants have been unsuccessful in
their application to the Lords and Commons, we
are now preparing a Petition to the Throne; if that
has no effect, we shall at last appeal to the People
at large, who, we do not doubt, will pay some attention to us.

You have the Magazine and Papers, which will
show you our Political Madness, and the wickedness of our ministers, &c.; to them I refer you, as
well as to those sent p\[r] the Jett, Capt\[n] Gibson,
which you had better send for, as soon as she

---

have been sent to America, had not many of these gentlemen
offered themselves as security for it. The India company, by
requiring security, showed that they knew how obnoxious a
measure it was; but the merchants, who ought to be the
natural guardians of the interests of America, submitted to the
infamy of becoming parties in the attempt against us." *Ralph
Izard to Thomas Lynch*, 14 February, 1775.

arrives at Leeds Town, if they are not come to hand before you receive this.* * * *

---

* "Being one of the merchants' committee, and having every day since the 4th January been employed in the business of our several petitions to the two houses of Parliament, and the General Meeting having last night determined on a petition to the Throne, since those to the two houses have been ineffectual." *W. Lee to Edward Browne*, 9 February, 1775. "Tomorrow the corporation of London intends also to petition the Throne for redress of American grievances. In a little time I expect a full appeal will be made to the people at large in your behalf. That is the only body now that has any virtue in it. . . . Your own judgment will tell you what line is proper for you to pursue in politics—submit to be slaves, or persevere to be freemen. Col. G. Corbin will, I believe, succeed Jn°. Page, Esqr, as Councillor, for no reasonable man in such times as these would wish his friend in such a post." *W. Lee to Richard Lee*, 9 February, 1775. "The prospect is most unhappy, for the two houses have, by an address to the Throne, in fact declared war against America. Gen'ls Burgoyne, Clinton and Howe are going with 6000 troops to Boston, with a number of ships and vessels of war to stop all the American ports. In one year I expect this country will be in arms. You may easily judge from this that you have but one line of conduct to pursue. Unanimity and perseverance will do wonders." *W. Lee to Col. John Tayloe*, 10 February, 1775. "The American Merchants in London have been acting a part meerly to please their correspondents; the Petition to the Commons, the Lords, and then the King, being a meer piece of form, and I have been told that one of the three merchants who carried up the latter, after he had delivered it, said to the other, 'I am glad I am clear of it,' so loud that the Queen heard what he said."—*Hutchinson to his brother*, April, 1775.

TO FRANCIS LIGHTFOOT LEE.

LONDON, 25 February, 1775.

My dear Brother:

Capt Dobbie has just told me that he goes tomorrow, so I cannot say much; for Politics refer to the inclosures. I am so convinced, and from the best information, that there is no real change intended here in the political plans formed against America, that I shall make none in my mercantile plans, which have been already communicated to you. Capt Outram goes in 8 or 10 daies, but I have not been able to get a charter in him, therefore shall, as soon as possible, send a ship out to be loaded, in James, York or Rappahannock as you may advise. I think my account sales this year will give me the preference on Rap.^k —therefore am much concerned that my continued engagement, ever since the beginning of Jany in the Public concerns respecting America prevents me from sending them now. My correspondents will, I hope, excuse me; it seems to me that 3 or 4 hhds. might be got consigned on York River, and as many on Rap.^k, besides what the Adventure brings, therefore shall provide ships accordingly, if they can be had on reasonable Terms, which is not the case at present; but you may be assured of my sending one at least, by the middle of next month, from hence, of 4 or 5 hhds., which I am sure may be easily loaded, and wish you to be prepared for.

Dan! Tibbs of Westmoreland drew a bill on me
for £10, which, when due, was not bro't for payment; whether it is lost, or gone back I cannot
tell, tho' it has been due ever since the 10th of
Jan.Y. Should this bill be sent back, 'tis not my
fault, as I should certainly have paid it, if I had
seen it, when it became due. All this you will be so
good as to inform M.Ɍ Tibbs of as soon as an opportunity offers, tho' he cannot complain as he never
wrote me any letter about the bill or his tobacco.
I shall write you often, therefore shall conclude,
with Mine, M.Ɍˢ Lee's and the little Patriot's Love
to all at Menoken, and sending you some Rhubarb
seed, to be sowed, as soon as you get it, in good
soil, where, well cultivated and secured from the
extreme severity of the Winter weather, it will in
3 years produce a fine root, better than any you can
import. This grew in England. Some silkworms'
Eggs, for M.Ɍˢ Lee's amusement, which our B.Ɍ
Templar bro't from Italy; and some most excellent
Rock Cantalupe Musk Melon seed, which you are
to divide with our Bro. Thos. Ludwell and Rich.ᵈ
Henry.   Farewell—*

TO RICHARD HENRY LEE.

LONDON, 25 February, 1775.

Tho' much political intelligence is sent to Phila-

---

* From the *Arthur Lee Papers* in Harvard University.

delphia to meet you on the Congress, I must with
only a moment's time inclose you an attested copy
of your Governor's letter to Lord Dartmouth.*
Another attested copy shall be sent to the Speaker
and Treasurer; you will judge whether it may not
be proper to publish it, which may easily be done
in Pennsylvania or Maryland, if the Virginia
printers refuse. The malignancy of it and the
wickedness in urging your enemies to persevere in
their plans of despotism against America should
certainly be exposed, that the minds of men may
be disposed in time to seize his person, when the
first blow is struck in America, and keep it in safe
custody to answer for the life of any American—
life for life. This conduct should be pursued in
every Colony, and also to seize on every K—g's
Officer. Jay, one of the Delegates from New York
to the last Congress, has by letter betrayed its
secrets to administration here:† this can't be absolutely proved, because his letters cannot be come
at, but the ministers have asserted it, therefore

---

*Lord Dunmore's letter, dated 24 December, 1774, is printed
in Force, *American Archives, Fourth Series*, I., 1061.

† This charge against Jay was current in London at this time.
"Permit me to hint to you that it is whispered here by ministerial people that yourself and Mr. Jay, of New York, are
friends to their measures, and give them private intelligence of
the views of the popular or country part in America. I do not
believe this; but I thought it a duty of friendship to acquaint
you with the report." *Franklin to Galloway*, 25 February, 1775.

should he again be appointed, it may be necessary to administer an oath of secresy to each member. Gov.ʳ Colden, Watts, DeLancy, White * one of the Council, M.ᶜ Evers,† and Lott‡ the Treasurer of New York, have written that they will support the ministerial and forming schemes to create a division among the Colonies, and plans against America; on receiving these advices from N. Y. and Virg.ᵃ, together with opposition here gaining ground every day, L.ᵈ North bro't forward his motion, the 20ᵗʰ instant in the H. of Commons which you have herewith; in order that he might easily get the bill passed for starving the 4 New England governments and quiet the minds of people here, 'till his plans were carried into execution, and at the same time divide America as the N. York Traitors had advised. Tho' the motion is so palpably delusive and means—nothing good; for it is not binding even if it had been expressed in explicit terms, yet by finesse inserting in all the papers at first that it was fully giving up to America the right of taxation, and that everything was to be amicably settled, it run like wild-

---

* Henry White, a prominent merchant of New-York: a sketch of him may be found in Sabine, *Loyalists of the American Revolution.*

† A merchant named James McEvers was stamp agent of the Colony in 1765.

‡ Abraham Lott. Died in 1794.

fire in the minds of men that it was so; and when the true motion came out, the original impression was so fixed that people still conceived it to mean what in their own minds, they at first believed; this delusion is however wearing off and from the genius of the people I do expect they will soon be more violent than ever against the ministry. This plan you may be assured was devised by L^{ds} North, Bute and Jenkinson only.—However to prevent your being deceived by false appearances, depend on the following to be the plan adopted and that will for a time at least be pursued ag^t America. The Ministers, alarmed at the conduct of Virg^a and encouraged by the Traitors already mentioned in New York, have determined to send the troops now embarking under Gen^{ls} Howe, Clinton, and Burgoyne to New York, which is to be a place of Arms, to secure that Colony with the assistance of DeLancy, Colden, Watts,* etc, and to prevent any communication or assistance from Virg^a , or any of the other Colonies getting to New England. The Bill inclosed is to pass into a Law and Ld North declared in the House of Commons that the same restrictions were soon to be extended to the other Colonies. But I am as well convinced as I am of my existence that if New York joins cordially with the other Colonies, and you all continue firmly

---

* John Watts and Oliver DeLancy. *See Sabine.*

united and prepared for the last event, the Ministers will instantly retract, for they will never dare
to advance or even to continue the present system,
if all America is united. 'Tis worth all your attention to secure N. York; but should that Colony
fail the common cause, still all the rest should persevere and cut off all intercourse with the town of
N. Y., which in twelve months would bring the
gentry there to their senses, as their trade would
by such a step be almost totally destroyed. In
every Colony as soon as the Assemblies meet they
should pass an Act, to bind every County to keep
at its expence a magazine of Arms and Ammunition in the body of each County, besides what each
militia man is obliged to keep in his own possession. The County Courts to be authorized to give
premiums for encouraging Woolen and Linen Manufactures.

Think of my plan for emancipating the Negroes
and abolishing every kind of Slavery in America.
The inclosed letter you will make such prudent use
of as you may think expedient. Among the mer-
chants here you have some incorrigible enemies—
viz.: all the New England Merchants except M^r
Bromfield; John Blackburn of Pigon & Booth, New
York & Phil^a Merchants; Lanc^l Girt & Thos. &
Rowland Hunt, Virg^a Merch^{ts}; Jno Nutt & Chris^n
Rolleston of the house of Neuffville & Rolleston,
So. Carolina Merch^{ts}. These men sh^d be stigma-

tized in America; particularly M.̲ Lanc.̲ Girt who
being one of the Merchants Com.ᵉ at this time,
never attends, but when it is to carry some ministerial point, and then shows the most rancorous
malignity against America and the people there,
that you can possibly conceive. This ought to be
fully known in Virginia, tho' not that it comes
from me. While the ministers reward their partisans amply, you will contend on very unequal
ground, if you reward the same infamous tools by
placing your property and confidence in their
hands. I shall be always ready, if called upon
properly to state openly some part of his Conduct;
one in particular respecting the Merchants' last
petition to the H. of C. which you have inclosed.
You may assert with confidence that he has in
every instance, when present, opposed any sentiment or expression being introduced into our petitions that should convey to the world an idea of
our taking any part with America, or hinting that
we tho't them oppressed or injured—that he has
always endeavored to get the most servile ideas
introduced to flatter administration and implore
their gracious protection. In the last petition particularly he wished us to assent *indirectly* to the
wicked and bloody address of the two houses, to the
declaration that Massachusetts Bay was in rebellion, and that the other Colonies were aiding and
abetting them. For the truth of this refer enquir-

ers to M Bromfield, M Wooldridge,* M Lee or
M Molleson, all members of the Committee.†

FRANKLIN'S PROPOSITION.

Early in December, 1774, Franklin had drawn up his "Hints,"
embodying what he considered should constitute a reconciliation between the mother country and her colonies, and a plan
for their future relations. In this paper he suggested that "in
consideration of the Americans maintaining their own peace
establishment, and the monopoly Britain is to have of their
commerce, no requisition to be made from them in time of
peace." So cogent were Franklin's reasons for demanding
such a measure, that Barclay and Fothergill agreed to it with
little objection. These Hints reached the ministers, as was intended they should, and were by some of their followers thought
"too hard." Some time later Franklin was made acquainted
with Lord Howe, and at his request drew up a second paper,
for a like purpose of exposing what the colonies desired or
might accede to, in the belief that the ministers were sincerely
desirous of reaching some accommodation. Howe, either of
his own accord, or at the instigation of the ministers, was posing as a peace maker, and had already conceived the scheme of
Commissioners to America, a scheme that long amused the
English, and accomplished nothing in America. He had been
made acquainted with the "Hints" of Franklin and expressed
his opinion very decidedly that there was no likelihood of their
admission. The petition of the Congress citing their grievances
had been received in England, and little could be added to
that; but Franklin drew up another paper, and on the aids

---

* In July, 1777, Thomas Wooldridge was gazetted as a bankrupt. He was described as "of the Crescent, London, Merchant
(Partner with Abraham Lott, of the City of New York, in North
America, Merchant, surviving partner of William Kelly, late of
the Crescent aforesaid, Merchant, deceased)."

† From the *Arthur Lee Papers* in Harvard University.

said: "Then let requisition be made to the Congress of such points as government wishes to obtain for its future security, for aids, for the advantage of general commerce, for reparation to the India Company," etc., etc.

"A generous confidence thus placed in the colonies will give ground to the friends of government there, in their endeavors to procure from America every reasonable concession, or engagement, and every substantial aid, that can fairly be desired."

This Franklin thought covered the project of aids designed in his former paper, and not until the opening of Parliament was he told by Lord Howe that his propositions "were not such as probably could be accepted." Howe doubtless at once communicated them to the ministers, but he was not very deep in their confidence, for they had given him nothing but general phrases, and left him in the dark as to their real sentiments. To Dr. Fothergill, Lord Dartmouth had said that some of the Hints appeared reasonable, but others were inadmissible or impracticable. So that when Parliament assembled, there had not been framed by the ministers so definite a plan, either of reconciliation or aggression, as could be communicated to their adherents, and the bare submission of the American papers was deemed as far as they would go for the present.

Nor was the opposition any the better prepared with a policy. Hutchinson, a partisan of the administration and a very good exponent of what was going on in the government circles, recorded in his letters (10 January) that the plan of the opposition was "to propose nothing themselves, but to inflame the minds of the people against everything proposed by administration." Lord Chatham made his motion to withdraw the troops from Boston without consultation with any of his party or of his followers; and as late as the 29th had not received from or made to others any communication of purposes. Apart from Chatham there was no person in opposition willing to bring forward a plan, and there was much reason for the taunts thrown out by the ministerialists at them for criticising when they had nothing to propose.

That Franklin's propositions had exerted no little influence in the Cabinet is proved by the existence of a minute found among Lord Dartmouth's papers; curious aud interesting as evidencing a very early intention of the ministers to offer a measure of reconciliation.

A minute of a Cabinet meeting, held January 21st, at the house of the Earl of Sandwich, notes as present the Lord Chancellor, the Lord President, the Earls of Sandwich, Dartmouth, Suffolk, Rochford, and Lord North. It was agreed "that an address be proposed to the two Houses of Parliament to declare that if the Colonies shall make sufficient and permanent provision for the support of the civil government and administration of justice, and for the defence and protection of the said Colonies, and in time of war contribute extraordinary supplies in a reasonable proportion to what is raised by Great Britain, we will in that case desist from the exercise of the power of taxation, except for commercial purposes only, and that whenever a proposition of this kind shall be made by any of the Colonies we will enter into the consideration of proper laws for that purpose, and in the meanwhile to entreat his Majesty to take the most effectual methods to enforce due obedience to the laws and authority of the supreme legislature of Great Britain."

In the debates on his motion, Chatham had said that he had thought long and closely upon the subject of reconciliation, and would soon lay before the Lords his plan. This plan was shown to Lord Camden before Franklin saw it on the 27th; and on the 29th it had been thrown into the form of a bill, as Chatham wished to present it at an early day, naming February 1. This was done, and at the suggestion of Dartmouth, who very properly regarded the subject as of too great importance to be decided by an immediate vote, the bill was laid on the table for consideration—a decision that was soon reversed, and the bill rejected as involving too great a concession. This result was somewhat remarkable, in the face of the Cabinet minute. Chatham's bill emphasized the power of Parliament to make laws binding on Colonies where the imperial crown was concerned; it asserted the right of Parliament to regulate trade and navigation ; and it stipulated for a free grant of a certain perpetual revenue to be subject to the disposition of the British Parliament. This was going further than the Cabinet scheme, and apart from the provision for a Colonial Congress, was more in alignment with the wishes of the extremists of the administration's followers. With a little amendment, it could have been made of a scope that the Cabinet minute intended, and, indeed, so far as a measure of concession, it was quite as well calculated not to quiet the disturbances in America. It may be doubted if any act of Parliament would have been accepted as an honest and sincere, as well as final, settlement of the controversy.

Some days afterward (February 4th) Franklin was told that his "Hints" had been considered by administration, and several of them thought reasonable, and others might be admitted with small amendments. The sections covering the granting of aids were approved, but the news from America was turning the administration more to thoughts of war than conciliation. It was not until February 20th that the decision of the Cabinet was made known to Parliament, and Lord North introduced it as a motion of reconciliation :

"That it is the opinion of this committee, that when the Governor, Council, and Assembly, or the General Court of his Majesty's provinces or colonies shall propose to make provision according to their respective conditions, circumstances, and situations, for contributing their proportion to the common defence, such proportion to be raised under the authority of the General Court or General Assembly of such province or colony, and disposable by Parliament, and shall engage to make provision also for the support of the civil government and the administration of justice in such province or colony, it will be proper, if such proposal shall be approved by his Majesty in Parliament, and for so long as such provision shall be made accordingly, to forbear, in respect of such province or colony, to levy any duties, tax, or assessment, or to impose any further duty, tax, or assessment, except only such duties as it may be expedient to impose for the regulation of commerce; the net produce of the duties last mentioned to be carried to the account of such province, colony, or plantation, exclusively."

Franklin was quite correct in his belief that the motion was not submitted as originally framed, for the first form was the Cabinet decision, so strangely overlooked by Bancroft. On January 22d Lord Suffolk—who was at the Cabinet meeting of the 21st—asked Hutchinson some leading questions based upon the decision of the Cabinet (note, page 120, *ante.*), and suggested the abandonment of an attempt to impose internal duties—an idea of Franklin. But Hutchinson also was told by Mauduit on February 17th, that "Lord D[artmouth] had drawn a different way from all the rest [of the Ministers]; and they have so far conceded to him, as that Parliamt in some way or other should signify that if the Assemblies will agree to comply with such requisitions as shall be judged fit, that then Parliament will dispense with its rights of taxation." Three days later the motion was made by North, who had the approbation of the King, but had taken his following by surprise. In the debate there were times when it was thought the Minister must suffer defeat, so strong was the opposition ranged against him. The friends of government opposed it because it was a concession; Burke, because it was no concession. Lord Dartmouth thought it should be expressed in terms more precise; and Hutchinson deemed it "a very poor performance, and dishonors administration." The motion was carried by a majority of 166. Franklin's criticism may be seen in his *Writing's, Bigelow's edition,* V., 524.

"Since Lord North's motion on Monday last, the 20th inst., of which you will have a full account from Wm. Dawson, things have been at a stand, and the buyers of tobacco hang their heads, thinking the price must fall. I know better, therefore proceed on the plan formerly settled, for be assured the ministerial plan of enslaving America will be pursued without one moment's relaxation; this motion was a trick to keep things quiet awhile here, which were just rising into a flame, and to deceive and divide the Americans. I am as certain as that I exist, that the plan of war against America is at this moment positively determined at Buckingham House." *W. Lee to Edward Browne,* 25 February, 1775.

TO FRANCIS LIGHTFOOT LEE.

LONDON, 1 March, 1775.

This goes to the Dow [*ns to*] catch Capt Dobbie. Mr Pross's letter please to forward as soon as possible. The inclosed paper will give you a true Idea of Lord North's motion, that is, what he meant by it. Last night we were heard and produced evidence at the Bar of the House of Commons against the Fish Bill as 'tis called, of which you have a copy. Our evidence has embarrassed the Minister, but still I think the Bill will pass which will embarrass him still more in this Country. Ld North's resolution was reported to ye House from the Committee last Monday, and passed after long debates.* Its fallacy is now well

---

* The bill for restraining the trade of the New England colonies was brought into the House on February 17th, and ordered to be printed. It was read a second time on the 25th, and passed to be engrossed on March 6th, by a vote of 215 to 61.

"In the morning called upon Mr. Ellis, who informed me the Resolve upon Lord North's motion passed the night before without a division : that Burke, Dunning, and some others were absent : that Lord North was explicit that if the Colonies, upon this offer, would not pass any acts for raising money, he would continue the tax acts." *Hutchinson's Diary,* 28 February, 1775.

understood here, and instead of serving his purpose, has made him weaker, as I always expected it wou'd. The War preparations are still carrying on against America. The troops are designed to embark from Ireland in all this month but they will hardly get to Boston or New York before the Middle or the latter end of May. You must take care of yourselves. By all means preserve union among the Colonies and you will be safe. The Packet which arrived yesterday has destroyed in great measure the ministers' hopes of seducing New York, for tho' the Assembly would not confirm the proceedings of the Congress, the Committee unanimously resolved to adhere to the association. You must exert yourself for me this year as we shall have nothing to do the next. Farewell.*

TO RALPH IZARD.

LONDON, 4 March, 1775.

Dear Sir:

I received your favor from Naples and forwarded your letter to Philadelphia.

You are quite mistaken in supposing anything conciliatory towards America is intended. The ministers, with their leader, are violently blowing the coals into a flame, that will lay waste the whole British Empire. From the destruction of so vast a

* From the *Arthur Lee Papers* in Harvard University.

body, new empires and new systems of government must arise. In short a civil war is inevitable.

Large numbers of troops and ships of war, are preparing to go to Boston and New York; a bill will finally pass the House of Commons on Monday to stop all the New England fisheries, to prevent those four governments from having a commercial intercourse with the other provinces and colonies, or any part of the world, but Great Britain, Ireland and the British West Indies.

In a few days another bill is to be brought into the House of Commons, extending the same restrictions to all the other colonies.

America seems firm in preparing for the last event. The assembly of Jamaica has petitioned the King in stronger and plainer terms than the Continental Congress.*

Best compliments to yourself and Mrs. Izard.

TO ROBERT CARTER NICHOLAS.

LONDON, 6 March, 1775.

Dear Sir:

I thank you for the pamphlet you sent me, which Lord Chatham says (to whom I sent it) is extremely well written and in the argument *unanswerable.*†

---

*Printed in Force, *American Archives, Fourth Series*, I., 1072.

† *Considerations on the Present State of Virginia examined.*

Your favor of Sept. 27 did not come to hand till January. It gives me much concern that you cannot give "any *useful* attention to my estate," but as your own immediate concerns employ so much of your time, I must submit with patience. You have enclosed a copy of Lord Dunmore's letter to Lord Dartmouth as lay'd before Parliament. A copy authenticated by a member of the H. of C., is sent to ye speaker by my brother Arthur, that the Assembly may take notice of it, if upon deliberation it is thought proper. The direct charge of *dishonesty* against the whole Colony, and particularly against the Gentlemen, has done much injury to the American cause, and left very unfavorable impressions of Virginian virtues in most men's minds. I shall make no farther comment, but leave it to your better understanding and the feelings of your own breast. The prospect of American affairs is more dreadful than ever; you are *all* by implication declared to be in a state of rebellion; ships of war and soldiers are preparing to go from hence to Boston and N. York. A bill passes the House of Commons this day to prohibit the 4 New England governments from catching even a single fish to eat after the first day of July next, from having any commercial connection from the other colonies, and from any trade whatsoever with any part of the world except Great Britain, Ireland, and the British West Indies. The merchants are doing with faint-

ness and languor what they ought to have done
with spirit last year, and which I believe their
feelings and necessities will compel them to do
with firmness and manly fortitude next year.
Your sincere friends have not been idle, and the
opposition in Parliament, as well as out of it, would
have been much more tremendous to the ministry,
had not an idea been artfully insinuated into the
minds of men, that the Americans want both spirit
to fight and virtue to persevere even in their commercial opposition.* I trust they will in both prove
themselves worthy descendants of their memorable
progenitors. I inclose you a paper which contains
a motion of Lord North's and the truest accounts

---

* "I will sport a line or two on public affairs. I call it sport-
ing because you must be very sensible of the inability of our
profligate and abandoned ministers to carry their schemes into
execution, of enslaving America, provided you have but common fortitude to support your liberties. The ministers are determined to try your metal and the *ultima ratio Regum* is to
settle the dispute. You have been called cowards by a Colo.
Grant, that commanded and was taken prisoner at Fort du
Quesne, in the House of Commons, and by Lord Sandwich in
the House of Lords; you have been declared guilty of high
treason by the two Houses of Parliament in their address to the
King, and by his Majesty indirectly accused of rebellion.
Under these circumstances common sense points out the only
reasonable line of conduct. Force, of course, should meet with
force. The Spaniards will surely be upon us very soon. But,
at all events, you must not yield your liberties, even till the last
gasp. If you do, I will no longer be a Virginian or your dutiful godson." *William Lee to Landon Carter,* 19 May, 1775.

published of what he said on the occasion, as well as others. You will see the only motive was to divide the Americans themselves and their friends here, so as to carry the diabolical ministerial designs of despotism into execution with the greater ease. Nothing shows more fully the extreme unwillingness that 9 men out of 10 have to persevere in this horrible dispute with America, which all men see, if continued, must terminate in the independence of America and the destruction of England, than the avidity with which the motion was at first swallowed out of doors, as thinking the ministry really meant an accommodation; but now the cloven foot appears to every one, which was at first only discovered by a few, and wonderful disquietude again prevails. Your own judgment on the spot can best direct what is proper to be done, but for my own part, I would persevere even to the loss of life and everything else, rather than submit to the most horrible of all slavery, which is intended for you. Should you yield, the lowest cow-herds in Scotland will be your taskmasters in every department, and for them you will be worse than "hewers of wood and drawers of water."* Mrs. Lee joins me in every good wish for yourself and Mrs. Nicholas, trusting you will

* In another letter he expresses the hope that the Americans will not become "hewers of wood and drawers of water" for "every Scotch shoeblack."

find virtue enough in America to preserve the inestimable blessing of Liberty to her sons.

Besides the part of Lord Dunmore's letter of
which you have a copy, and which is all that ministry tho't proper to communicate to Parliament, I
am informed by unquestionable authority, that he,
Lord Dunmore, has wrote to the ministry that the
negroes have a notion the King intends to make
them all free, and that the Associations, Congress
and Conventions are all contrivances of their masters to prevent the King's good intentions towards
them and keep them still slaves; that from this
circumstance, it is probable they will rise and give
their masters employment enough to keep them
from opposing the ministerial measures. These
may not be his precise words, but the meaning is
the same. The folly of this plan is only to be
equalled by its wickedness, since a proper execution of the patrol law will entirely defeat it, and I
have no doubt you will take care that this law
shall be properly executed through the colony.
It is not agreeable to have one's name mentioned
as an authority in such points, but if the public
good, in your opinion and that of the other friends
of Liberty, should *absolutely* require it, I shall have
no objection to being mentioned, as in my opinion
the public weal ought ever to be superior to every
private consideration. I do not know Capt. Foy,*

---

* Foy was the private secretary of Dunmore, and vastly unpopular in Virginia.

nor have I ever seen him, but some here who knew him well have told me it is their opinion the above is a plan of his, and that it is very probable he is now with the Governor's assistance laying the foundation of carrying it into execution. This, however, is only conjecture, but very proper for you to keep an attentive eye on. Perhaps the best method of defeating so dreadful a scheme as is planning against you, would be to emancipate all the negroes yourself by act of Assembly, and instead of their being slaves, make them your tenants. This I acknowledge is a bold idea, but still I am convinced the more you think of it [the better you will like it]. I have a large stake in this business, yet would freely give my consent.

TO JOHN BALLENDINE & COMPANY.

LONDON, 6 March, 1775.

Gentlemen:

I have to apologize for not answering sooner your very obliging favor of the 9th ulto., covering Mr. Cale & Co. draft on Howitt & Co., which should have been done had not every moment of my time been employed in our public affairs. In answer to your question about Virginia and Maryland, however disposed they might have been to renew their commerce with us, and to pay their debts, they will now be absolutely prevented from both, and driven to the wall with the New England governments, by a bill that is in a few days to be brought into the House of Commons restricting their trade and commerce, as that of New England is by the Fishing Bill passed the House of Commons this day: so that there cannot be a doubt of *all American Commerce for ever ceasing* until the present ministerial system is entirely reversed. Your town has a great stake in this business, every shilling of which will be inevitably lost and sacrificed in the contest for a feather, unless a change very shortly takes place here; therefore it is high time the American merchants should bestir themselves *seriously*.

Little has been done here in the tobacco way for some time past, but we are informed the French have wisely taken advantage of the calm produced by Lord North's insidious motion, and bo't 6000 hhd. of tobacco in Glasgow at 3d. The next time they come to market 3½ must be the price, which in my opinion is not too low considering the unhappy situation of things, and if you stand out they must give 3¾ or 4, for they cannot be supplied here. We have here 3000 Maryland hhds., and not 1500 Virginia. No old tobacco can come, as there was none left in the country, so that you have the whole game in your own hands. The country price will, I expect, be universally 25/, and on James River 30/ pr. ct., therefore purchasing will be at much risk, unless we cou'd insure an adequate price here, which I doubt much of, as a great deal will undoubtedly be grown in Europe the next summer.

TO WILLIAM SHIPPEN, JR.

LONDON, 9 March, 1775.

* * * The resolutions and proceedings of your Pennsylvania convention in January last* (which, by the by, we have only seen thro' the ministerial channel, as no copy has yet been sent to any friend of liberty here) please me exceedingly, as replete with wisdom, prudence, and firmness. A bill has now passed the House of Commons, and is now before the House of Lords, totally prohibiting the four New England governments from fishing, having any communication with the other Colonies, from trade or communication by sea with any part of the world except Great Britain, Ireland, and the British West Indies. The inhabitants of the Island of Nantucket are permitted to carry on the Whale Fishery only (but not to get provisions even from the continent of New England) with such vessels as they may be possessed of before the 25th of this present month, March. This day a bill to restrain the trade and commerce of New Jersey, Pensylva-

---

* Printed in Force, *American Archives, Fourth Series,* I., 1169.

nia, Maryland, Virginia and South Carolina, to
Great Britain, Ireland, and the British West Indies
in every article. This bill will complete the firmest
union among all America, and must in my idea
make them entirely independent of this kingdom.
Notwithstanding all this bluster of administration,
I see clearly this country cannot hold out two
years if America perseveres unanimously in with-
holding all concerns with us, but must submit to
the most humiliating terms you may please to demand, even to beheading and hanging the contriv-
ers of all this wickedness. Therefore, like men,
continue steadfast in so great a contest, and prove
yourselves worthy descendants of good Old England. Be firm, temperate, and submit implicitly
to the determination of the Congress of your States
in May, which from their conduct in September
and October last, one must suppose will be governed by manly firmness and admirable wisdom.
* * *

TO LANDON CARTER.

LONDON, 10 March, 1775.

* * * Our political madness is still in its zenith,
and we are consequently taking the most effectual
measures that the wit or folly of man can devise to render America totally independent of this
Country. A bill is passed the House of Commons,

and now before the House of Lords prohibiting the four New England governments from fishing, even from catching a fish on their shores to eat; from any commercial connection with the other Colonies and confining their trade to Great Britain, Ireland and the British West Indies solely. Yesterday another bill was bro't into the House of Commons by Lord North to confine the trade of New Jersey, Pennsylvania, Maryland, Virginia and South Carolina to Great Britain and Ireland only. You have heard of the proceedings of the merchants in London, in which very little serious was intended for the benefit of America, except by myself and one or two others, and our application has accordingly been treated with contempt. The merchants of Glasgow sent up a very spirited petition, but, as we are informed here, they gave Lord North to understand by their member, Lord Frederick Campbell, that they did not mean any opposition by it, but only to get credit in America. Such is the report here. I am every day more convinced of the soundness of my first opinion in this American business, and the ministers are now also convinced that if America continues firmly united and perseveres one twelvemonth in the non-exportation and non-importation, without striking a blow, the distress will be so great in this country, overwhelmed with debt, profligacy, debauchery and luxury, which nothing can support but the most

extensive flourishing commerce, that they must
yield to the most humiliating terms that you can
ask. Therefore, with actual money bribes, places,
pensions, and contracts, they are trying every art
to divide you in the different Colonies, particularly
in New York, and by every irritating and provoking measure they are contriving to force you to
blows, in hopes of rousing the resentment of the
nation against you, which at present is directed
against the ministers, and in twelve months will
be so strong as to bring them to the fate they have
so long deserved, if by their acts they cannot direct
it against you. To defeat all these diabolical
schemes, suffer everything that human nature can
inflict before a blow is struck, attend to manufactures of every kind, especially the necessaries for
clothing. Stop all commerce and intercourse with
this country, and as common prudence directs, be
well prepared to resent any forcible injury that
may be offered when you find it expedient and
prudent so to do. These are my sentiments; if
you approve, and think they will be of use, I do
not care how universally they are known. Your
governor,* I am told, besides his letters which
have been published, has wrote to his masters for
5000 troops, or else he cannot stir in Virginia.
These they cannot supply him with, for they will

* Lord Dunmore.

not be able to find the 10000 which General Gage
has wrote them are necessary for New England
only. Excuse me for saying so much, for my
heart and mind is too full to be silent. Heaven
will give you the means, if you have but the courage to use them, for the preservation of your Liberties, which I sincerely pray may prove the case.
Farewell. *

---

* "I do not claim any merit for having endeavored to do my
duty here to my country in a political line, but surely some
difference is to be made between those who do what they ought,
and those who are violently inimical to you. Was America in
general to make this distinction, she would find many more
friends among the merchants than she has." *William Lee to
John Tayloe*, 20 March, 1775.

"Virginia tobacco has been quite at a stand for some time ;
on the address of both Houses to the King, the stocks fell 2 pr
cent, the buyers of tobacco were all in a bustle. On Lord
North's nugatory and delusive motion, everybody without
thought took all for peace, the stocks got up, and nothing has
been material in the tobacco way since. I know the minister's
thirst after blood is as violent as ever, and if the Americans are
firm, the business will not be settled this year, and that every
one will see before two months expire. . . . If America is firm
and unanimous, she must triumph ; this the ministry know
well. Therefore, every art is tried to divide before the sword is
sheathed in the bowels of the Americans." *W. Lee to Edward
Browne*, 21 March, 1775.

TO THE SPEAKER OF THE PENNSYLVANIA HOUSE OF REPRESENTATIVES.

LONDON, 22 March, 1775.

Sir,

My brother Arthur Lee, not knowing of this opportunity, I take the liberty for him to enclose an attested copy of a letter from Germany, which may be of some importance to your province. The Fishing Act, as it is called, passed the House of Lords yesterday with an Amendment, which is, to restrain New Jersey, Pennsylvania, Maryland and Virginia from the right of fishing, as well as the four New England governments.* The blanks in the bill restraining the trade of New Jersey, Pennsylvania, &c., are filled up. It is to take place the 20th of July next. Therefore all your products for foreign markets will no doubt be

---

* "The Bill for preventing the 4 New England Governments from fishing and confining their trade in every Article whatsoever to G. Britain, Ireland and the Brittish W. Indias, is now before the Lords having passed the H. of C—last night. I prepared a pretty strong petition against it to the Lords, which the London Merchants here will get presented on the 14th inst on its second reading; still the bill will pass. Another Bill is this day bro't into the H. of C. by L.d North to confine the trade in every Article, from and to New Jersey, Pennsylvania, Maryland, Virginia and So. Carolina to G. Britain, Ireland, and the Brittish W. Indias only. Surely these bills will strengthen the union and perseverance of all the Colonies or nothing can do it." *William Lee to Francis Lightfoot Lee*, 11 March, 1775. From the *Arthur Lee Papers* in Harvard University.

ship'd off before that time. You will be so good as to communicate the contents to the Honble Matthew Tilghman, Speaker of the House of Delegates in Maryland, who will probably be in Philadelphia when this comes to your hands.

The above intelligence may perhaps be of service if communicated to the public.

TO RICHARD HENRY LEE.

LONDON, 3 April, 1775.

My dear Brother,

You have, herewith, a pamphlet written by your brother in support of the Congress petition to the King,* the London Merchants', and the House of Assembly of Jamaica's Petition to the King; the Journals of the House of Commons, containing Mr. Burke's motion respecting America, which were made as the creed of the Rockingham Party; and the Lords' protest against the Fishing Bill.

The Livery of London meet in Common Hall, the 5th inst., and I inclose you the draft of a petition which we have prepared for them, and which,

---

* "An appeal to the Justice and Interests of the People of Great Britain, in the Present Disputes with America. By an old member of Parliament." This pamphlet was first published in London in 1774, and by the end of 1775 had run through three editions. A fourth edition, "corrected," was printed in London in 1776, and in New York in 1775, the American edition alone bearing the writer's name.

I don't doubt, will be adopted. These documents, together with the copy of Lord Chatham's Bill, which you have had by various opportunities, show explicitly the sense of all parties here, respecting the American measures—except the ministerialists and the Jacobites, who express their sense fully by the fleet and army, now going to Boston and New York.

You have, also, a copy of the New Jersey, Pennsylvania, etc., restraining Bill, with the Blanks filled up.

The Proclamation of the States of Holland, prohibiting the exportation of arms, etc., shows our wicked ministers are trying every method to keep you defenseless, but it does not appear that they have yet been able to prevail on the Spaniards not to supply America with arms, etc.

Having thus the whole ministerial system, and the sense of Parties here, clearly before you, the mode of resistance, for resist you will to the last Breath, I take for granted, which is most likely to ensure success, you can better judge of than any body on this side of the Atlantic.

In my opinion, you have fully the means of success in your own power; and, we hope you will use them properly: but do not rely on any material assistance as yet from this country—depend upon your own exertions, and act like men, for the contest must now come to a final decision, and in my opinion, it will end in an absolute Independence of the colonies on this country. Perhaps there may continue a favorable commercial League with Great Britain, which is as much as I expect you will grant us in a year or two more.

Whether you come to blows or not, still, for every reason you should persevere in the commercial opposition planned by the last Congress. You will find, more and more, every year, how easily you can live within yourselves, without the assistance of this country, and when remittances are wholly stopped, the Merchants will seriously exert themselves, to put a stop to the ministerial measures; for, indeed, it was shameful to see what shuffling there was about the last Petitions. Perhaps I may hereafter give you a minute detail of the whole Proceedings; at present, I will only say you are not a jot obliged to above 3 in the whole committee, for what was done. The whole was a true piece of Quaker and Scottish Policy to deceive the Americans, and thereby come in this year for the best share of what remittances were made; and, I don't doubt, they will succeed in some Colonies, particularly in Virginia and Maryland.

You must religiously refrain from all connection and intercourse whatsoever, with any Colony that does not adopt the Congressional Resolutions. Here, the Restraining Bills will assist you.

You cannot too much guard against the ministerial arts to divide you; under their auspices, large quantities of goods are now shipping in the Transports hired by Government for *Boston* itself. This will, no doubt, be used by those who wish to break thro' the non-importation agreement, as the argument for it, and the Bostonians will be charged with fraud and treachery, tho' it is universally known, here, to be a ministerial trick.

That there are Rogues of merchants in Boston, as well as London, I suppose nobody will deny; therefore, the landed interest in America has acted most wisely in taking the management of this business into their own hands, and *making* the merchants comply with what is thought best for the general interest of the Community in which they reside, and by which they live. I shall write in 10 days to Philadelphia; so farewell.

P. S. A large parcel of prints are sent by this conveyance, from the most worthy Dr. S. T. Janson, Chamberlain of London, who is, incessantly, at work to serve the American cause, to the Chairman of the Congress, to distribute in every part of America, where they can be of use.

TO RODHAM KENNER.

LONDON, 15 May, 1775.

* * * You must know by this time that our wicked ministers are gone quite mad. Is it possi-

ble that the Americans can bear with patience
such repeated and wanton insults and oppressions?
Every complaint instead of being redressed, produces a fresh grievance and injury. The magazines, etc., will show you the petitions, etc., of the
merchants, etc., and the London remonstrance on
American grievances. The K— and his ministers
have publicly proclaimed you rebels. Everybody
knows what rebels have alone to trust to. The
Lord Mayor very justly observed that a *successful*
rebellion was always called a *revolution*, and from
his confidence in the virtue and fortitude of y^e
Americans, he was not at a loss to determine what
that would be hereafter called, which the ministers
were now pleased to term rebellion. I cannot suppose that any dangers will deter you from persevering to the last extremity in defence of your liberty, and with unanimity you must succeed. The
ministers have sent such violent orders to General
Gage that we every day expect advice of a general
engagement in Massachusetts Bay. The Scotch
gentlemen have got advice of the proceedings of
your last Congress at Richmond.* One of your
flattering resolutions to his Excellency is very different from what we had been taught to expect, as
the ministerial runners in the city had about ten
days ago reported that Government had received

---

* *Force, American Archives, Fourth Series*, II., 165.

advice of a plan deliberately settled in Virginia to sieze the Governor's person, and all the K—'s officers, and keep them as hostages for the safety of such Americans as Gen'l Gage has certainly received orders to take up and send over for tryal. The eyes of all Europe are upon America, and the ministers attend much to the motions in Virginia, for they think *you will fight;* which they have been taught to believe the New England people will not do. Indeed the conduct of Virginia and New England will decide this business, but success will be more easy and certain if all the colonies are united. Wonderful preparations are making in France and Spain; with the latter, we shall certainly come to an open rupture very soon after a blow is struck in America. * * *

TO RICHARD HENRY LEE.

LONDON, 24 May, 1775.

My dear Brother:

I have no doubt of your being pleased with the information contained in the inclosed paper, of my being yesterday elected Alderman of one of the most respectable wards in the City of London. This post is for life, very honorable, and attended with little, or no extra expense; however, it cannot be a disadvantage to appear with more dignity than I have hitherto done, or indeed than my present finances will properly admit of; but this must depend on further contingencies, for I am resolved never to embarrass myself, so as to be under the control of great, rich or wicked men; but if my mercantile business should increase, which I should suppose very probable, I shall act accordingly, both for my own and the honor of Virginia. I wrote you fully on business the other day, by this op^ty, and sent a multitude of papers, etc. You must in America have taken a decided line of conduct by this time, as the Ministerial Plan for your destruction will be fully before the Continental Congress.

I have confidence in your virtue, and being fully satisfied of your ability to succeed in the contest for the support of your liberties, my mind is tolerably at ease, especially too, as I am sure your friends are very numerous and firm: tho', at present, a little lethargic.

The first blow will rouse them, as well as the French and Spaniards. Heaven bless you all! Farewell.

TO FRANCIS LIGHTFOOT LEE.

LONDON, 24 May, 1775.

My dear B^r

Yesterday I had the Honor of being chosen Alderman for one of the most respectable Wards in the City of London. This Post is for Life, Honourable, and attended with very little expence. The Paper will show you the rest. The Scotch we understand are buying up all the Tobacco in the Country; surely no one will trust them without the Cash, for their bills are dangerous. Let them get your property into their hands and then see what will be the end. Let Mr Browne know all the above. Urge and assist as much as you can to procure payments and remittances. Those who won't pay, get from them Bonds and Security if you can. God Bless you all and believe me most affectionately and sincerely yours for ever.

I trust America will be steady and unanimous in support of her Liberty, let the consequence be what it will. A little suffering and endurance for a year or two must be expected, but with fortitude and perseverance the issue will certainly be successful to you. Even loss of Life is, in my mind, a less evil than loss of Liberty. Do you know one John Hipkins(?) I fancy he must be a notorious Sharper. He is getting all the Planters in Excess to draw bills on me at sight. This Puppy's plan is no doubt to injure me if he can, therefore it would be proper to stop him in his Career. A Bill this day appeared on me at sight payable to himself, supposed to be drawn by James Bray. It is protested for want of Advice, and because I do not believe the signature to be the hand writing of James Bray. It appears to me that the Bill is both written and signed by John Hipkins himself. What a noble pair Samuel and John are.*

TO WILLIAM HICKS.

LONDON, 12 JUNE, 1775.

* * * The ministry have last Saturday published their accounts of the unhappy transaction of the 19th April last in Massachusetts Bay,† which is rather more to the disadvantage of the regulars than the accounts we had before. They say that the militia fired first, tho' the contrary is proved by a number of authentic depositions, some of them sworn to by the regulars themselves. If the people of England do not interfere a little more seriously than they have done to stop the wanton effusion of the blood of our American brethren, and put a speedy stop to this most unnatural war, I am sure the consequences must be most fatal to the whole British empire.

P. S. Since writing the above have received your esteemed favor of the 8 inst., for which am much obliged. The New York May packet is arrived that brings home the post officers from that city. The people there have taken possession of the post office, custom house, and castle. They

---

* From the *Arthur Lee Papers* in Harvard University.

† Captain Derby reached London with the news 29th May, 1775.

are in arms, and determined no troops shall land there. Upwards of 2000 men are sent off to the relief of the New Englanders, who to a man are determined to *dye* or be *free*. As far as we can learn all Americans [are] in arms, and that upwards of 50,000 men are embodied. Will the English never again stir in defence of liberty? I trust they will, and that shortly.

TO RICHARD HENRY LEE.

LONDON, 13 July, 1775.

My dear Brother:

Capt. Falconer delivered me safely your favor of May the 10 from Phil.ᵃ The insurances you ordered are made. The uncertainty of this reaching you at Philadelphia, or indeed at all, will prevent me from being so full as I should otherwise be. Our Br. A[rthur] has wrote I believe pretty largely. Notwithstanding the base and wicked attempts of our ministry and Genl. Gage to disguise the truth, 9-tenths of the People here are fully convinced that the civil war was commenced by Genl. Gage. I can with truth and pleasure assure you that the repeated success of the Provincials since the 19th of April gives almost universal pleasure here, but still you are not to expect any really spirited exertions on the part of the people, until they feel, which they do not at present, because large remittances have been made to the merchants in general, and unfortunately chiefly to the most ministerial ones;* who besides, it is said, have privately negotiated with the minister to prevail on the Bank to lend them £300,000—part of which a tobacco merchant is to share, who has made a great parade to his correspondents of his services last winter. Indeed, if things are ever settled, a reform must be made respecting the American merchants, for half the present mischief has arisen from their villainy and treachery to you.

The Governor of Virginia's conduct in robbing you of your powder, and the proclamation against Henry, with the Council's contemptible and stupid address to the people,† makes a fair opening for a reform in your constitution and government, which is founded on as arbitrary and tyrannical a system as can well be contrived; the mode of summoning

---

* "I agree with you in opinion, that the good people of England will not much care whether America is lost or not, till they feel the effects in their purses or in their bellies. While they can go on as usual, they speculate but little as to futurity; or at least their thoughts lead them only to grumble and growl; they must feel and be pinched, and in some tender part too, before they will put themselves to any inconveniency to prevent the impending mischief; that this moment of pinching will come, is certain; but it probably will be felt too late for remedy!" *Duke of Richmond to Burke,* 16 June, 1775.

† The papers on these matters are printed in Force, *American Archives, Fourth Series,* II., 371, 465, 516, 1185.

Juries is open to ten thousand objections, and in process of time will be a dreadful engine of oppression in the hands of a tyrant.

The late Constitution of Massachusetts, or the present of Connecticut and Rhode Island, seem the most eligible.

Now is the time to form a proper mode of internal government which may last for many centuries, and if it is lost or disregarded, the opportunity may never occur again.

We have various reports of what the Congress is about, but nothing shall I believe that is not authenticated with the name of Charles Thomson. Capt. Falconer has all the papers, there are no publications worth sending which you have not already had. The Corporation of London has at last agreed to petition the King in your behalf, a copy of which I enclose. It is to be delivered on Friday, and perhaps you will get the answer with this.* The ministers have however sent orders to Gen'l Gage to persevere and to go out of Boston to dispossess the Provincials of their strong places. Gen'l Carleton is ordered to send down on the back Country the 3000 Canadians which he has

---

* The address is printed in *Annual Register*, XVIII., 255. The king, while expressing his willingness to listen to dutiful petitions of his subjects and to comply with their reasonable requests, asserted his intention of asserting and maintaining the constitutional authority of the kingdom.

wrote he can spare for Gage's assistance (blessed fruit of the Quebec Act), and a highland regiment is to be compleated to 1000 with highlanders, under a Lord John Murray, to be sent as soon as compleated to America.* From Quebec they expect to be able to get fresh provisions sufficient for the army and fleet at Boston. If they get men at all, it must be from Scotland, or among the Irish Roman Catholics, for the American war is really so odious and disgusting to the common people in England, that no soldiers or sailors will inlist, for without pressing they cannot in two months man two twenty-gun ships, nor have they for 3 months past inlisted 20 soldiers in all England, tho' recruiting parties are all over the country.† Added to this, the ship-wrights at Plymouth,

---

*Gage had written that he saw no opportunity for continuing actively the campaign, and desired leave to return to England. Howe was to command in Gage's absence, and Carleton was to be employed in Canada.

†Scotland was, almost to a man, on the side of government, but the prospects of securing a reasonable force from thence were very poor. The king wished to send beating orders to Ireland early in the summer of 1775, but he was overruled by his Cabinet. According to Gibbon, a great effort was to be made in the spring—"Scotch Highlanders, Irish Papists, Canadians, Indians, &c., will all in various shapes be employed." *To Holroyd*, 1 August, 1775. Walpole notes in his *Last Journals* (I., 500) that "the Government [in August] could not get above 400 recruits; and failed in their attempt to raise a regiment of Irish Catholics." In September, the King thought

Portsmouth, Gosport, Chatham, and Sheerness, to amount of 3000, have all left off work, on account of their ill usage, when they have not 3 ships in all the yards fit to put to sea. These men called on me yesterday with their petition, which they are to present to the K——g to-morrow. 'Tis spirited and bold. To compleat the affair two daies

---

that by March, four thousand Germans might be had, in addition to the two battalions of Royal Americans. In October Gibbon informed Holroyd that the "new levies go on very slowly in Ireland," and the refusal of the Empress Catharine to supply mercenary troops induced the King to direct the detachment of regiments from Ireland, replacing them by some from England, depending upon the militia, should an occasion call for defence. At the opening of Parliament the King put on a bold front and asserted that only a small force was sent to America, and offers of reconciliation went with it. The German contracts were made and Parliament voted to increase the army, but the difficulties in the way of securing men increased. "In January, 1776, Lord Barrington warned the King that Scotland had never yet been so bare of troops, and that those of England were too few for the security of the country. . . . New bounties were offered. Recruiting agents traversed the Highlands of Scotland, and the most remote districts of Ireland, and the poor Catholics of Munster and Connaught, who had been so long excluded from the English army, were gladly welcomed. Recruits, however, came in very slowly. There was no enthusiasm for a war with English settlers. The pressgang met with an unusual resistance. No measure short of a conscription could raise at once the necessary army in England, and to propose a conscription would be fatal to any Government." Lecky, *History of England in the Eighteenth Century*, III., 457.

ago an express arrived from Gibralter, by a man of war's cutter. The Captain's brother I have seen, who says, they expected the same wind which bro't him to England would bring the Spanish fleet and army from Carthagena to Gibralter, that the works on the sea side were quite in ruins, and that he does not doubt the place surrendering, if attacked. Europe has not seen such an armament since the famous Armada in Queen Elizabeth's time; 60 sail of the line, besides smaller vessels and transports, with 30,000 land forces, all collected within a day's sail of Gibralter.

Under these difficulties, with every thing in confusion in the East Indias, our Mule and his Drivers B[u]te and M[a]nsf[iel]d are determined to ruin America, if they can. Things look very well. You have nothing to do but to persevere, as we are told you are proceeding. Prepare for a vigorous defence, at the same time hold out your plan of accommodation in the form of an American Bill of Rights, in which you should not forget to new model the several arbitrary Colonial constitutions, such as Virginia, New York, &c. The people should choose all their own officers annually (unless the appointment of the commander in chief remaining in the crown as in the New England provinces). Canada should be reduced to its antient boundaries, where all religions should be tolerated, as in Pennsylvania, but none established. Assemblies should of right be held every year, and a General Congress annually, or once in two years at least, to consider and settle the common interests of all the Colonies. 'Tis reported the General Congress are about publishing a Manifesto to all the World, and to open your ports to all nations; should this prove true, the maritime powers of Europe must fight in your cause for the benefit or your commerce. Should Spain attack Gibralter, you may immediately settle your own terms; if they do not, the Ministers are determined to try the issue of this campaign. If they are unsuccessful, they must yield the contest; if successful, they will go on; but even then, I am satisfied they will not be able to add 2000 men more next year to the present force they have in America. You know whether that will be sufficient to subdue you. The public prints you will see, if in Phila.: if you are not, they will be too bulky to forward with this.

We are all well—Vale.

[No Signature.]

TO GEORGE MASON.

LONDON, 29 July, 1775.

* * * It is clear to me that the American trade to Great Britain can never be restored to its former channel. I have more at stake in this business than most people; however, the love I have for my country, as well as an ardent affection for universal liberty, makes me submit with patience to the decrees of Providence, which I am convinced overrules in this unhappy contest between Great Britain and the Colonies. Therefore am sure, as *justice* is the most amiable attribute of an Almighty direction, that you must in the end be successful. We have only the ministerial account of the bloody engagement on the 17 June at Charles Town, near Boston, which from thence appears greatly to the disadvantage of the regulars. The ministers still have no thought of relenting and fresh supplies of arms and ammunition are preparing to be sent to Boston. All I can say is, "Quem Deus vult perdere, prius dementat." America must now be a great empire, or sink for slaves * * *

TO RALPH IZARD.

LONDON, 14 August, 1775.

* * * Madness in the extreme has taken possession of our ruling powers, and inexplicable folly with unaccountable supineness has seized the friends of liberty in this country, so that a downfall of the British empire seems inevitable. General Amherst, it is said with confidence, has agreed to take the command in America in the Spring. Gage is certainly recalled, and it is said that New York, by advice of some of her sons, is to be the seat of

war next summer. Rich'd Penn, Esqr, is arrived from Philadelphia, and the report this day in the city is that he has bro't a petition from the Congress to the King, the contents of which of course every coffee house politician is acquainted with, and it is already declared that the Ministry have rejected the proposals, tho' hardly three ministers are in town. For my own part, I do not believe any propositions, however advantageous to this country, will be accepted, and that nothing but the fate of war or a convulsion in this country, can put an end to this dreadful civil war.

TO SAMUEL BRAILSFORD.

LONDON, 19 August, 1775.

Dear Sir:

I received your very kind favor of the 10th. inst. which [I] should have answered sooner, had I not waited in expectation of hearing again from you, as several ships have arrived lately at Bristol from Philadelphia, that, as we have been informed, bro't very interesting news from the Congress. Mr. Penn is not yet come to town, and as far as I can learn, keeps his public papers to deliver himself.*

---

* Congress entrusted the petition, the draft of which had been written by John Dickinson, to Richard Penn, who was to present it in company with the Colonial agents in England. Burke declined, as he held his appointment from the General

The Butean and Bedford faction have already pre-
determined not to listen to any terms whatsoever
of accommodation. Therefore, until the people at
large exert their natural rights in this country,
there is little hopes of an end being put to this
unnatural and ruinous civil war. It seems pretty
certain that the Hanoverians are to go to Gibraltar,
to garrison that fortress, from whence the present
garrison is to be transported when recruited to
America, to cut the throats of our fellow subjects
and brethren, and as loyal men as any in the whole
British Empire. The Georgians in full Provincial

Assembly of New York, which had declined to send deputies to
Congress. To present the petition would be to act not only
without, but contrary to the authority of his constituents. Paul
Wentworth (New Hampshire) had declined to present the first
petition, not only pleading the want of instructions, but charging that the paper was an assertion of all their claims in a very
high tone and with very offensive expressions. Thomas Life
[   ] had also pleaded his want of authority. When the
second petition arrived, there was great doubt as to who of the
agents would accept the responsibility imposed upon them.
Charles Garth, member for the Divizes, and agent of South
Carolina, and William Bollan, one of the agents of Massachusetts and Virginia (Arthur Lee being the other), were dependents of the ministry. Penn and Lee alone remained to act,
and they gave a copy of it to the Secretary of State; but on
pressing for an answer, they were told that as the king did not
receive it on the throne, no answer would be given. Two days
later, (August 23d) was issued the proclamation for suppressing
rebellion and sedition.

Congress have adopted the whole of the Continental resolves, and manfully spurned the bait thrown out to bribe them, by their being left out of the restraining acts passed last session.* . . .

TO RICHARD HENRY LEE.

22 September, 1775.

I am afraid the most wicked machinations of Governor Dunmore have by this time involved you in the horrors of war. What the Ministry intend against you and the rest of America, cannot be exactly ascertained before the meeting of the Parliament.† Probably they have not yet determined upon the exact mode of executing their vengeance. You will do wisely, however, in preparing for the utmost extremity that the most unprincipled and deepest revenge can suggest. It is said, and I believe with truth, that the war is to be carried into Virginia, as well as in the northern Provinces, next spring. This winter will be employ'd in providing every means that can shield you from the destruction to which your merciless enemies have destined you. Some precautions will be taken, relative to your Negroes. Some fortifications, in

---

* "The skirmish at Lexington became known in Savannah on the 10th of May, and added Georgia to the Union." *Bancroft.*

† Parliament convened on October 26th.

the places by nature most inaccessible, for Magazines and Refuge will be made. Cannot the Capes, by the co-operation of the two Colonies, be rendered impassable? Should not alarm Houses be erected there as well as the mouths of the Rivers? No precautions can be too great against the dangers that threaten you, especially as no one can tell what foreign foes, taking the advantage of the present state of things, may invade you.

The utmost industry of the Ministry is employd to inflame men's minds here, especially by publishing General Gage's accusations of savageness and barbarity in carrying on the war on the part of the Provincials. These accusations, like those of Bernard and Hutchinson, are made in such general terms, as admit not of a specific refutation, and in a general denial, his word is more likely to gain credit than that of those he accuses.

Whatever may be the real sentiments of People here in this question, it is not easy to conceive more quietism than prevails in general. The interested on each side declare themselves, but the bulk of the Nation is perfectly silent. We therefore see the Jacobites and Nonjurors addressing for coercive measures, the Merchants and Manufacturers petitioning for conciliation, while the Counties and large Cities in general (London excepted), remain unmovd. The increase of taxes, which another year's continuance of violent measures must

produce, will excite much clamour, which will not
be diminished by the interruption of Commerce.*

---

* Burke commented strongly upon the general apathy of the
people, the high spirits of the king, and the ease of the ministers. "No man commends the measures which have been pursued, or expects any good from those which are in preparation;
but it is a cold, languid opinion, like what men discover in affairs that do not concern them. . . . We look to the merchants
in vain—they are gone from us, and from themselves. They
consider America as lost, and they look to administration for
an indemnity. Hopes are accordingly held out to them, that
some equivalent for their debts will be provided. In the meantime, the leading men among them are kept full fed with contracts and remittances, and jobs of all descriptions; and they
are indefatigable in their endeavors to keep the others quiet,
with the prospect of their share in those emoluments, of which
they see their advisers already so amply in possession. They
all, or the greatest number of them, begin to snuff the cadaver-
ous *haut gout* of lucrative war. War, indeed, is become a sort
of substitute for commerce. The freighting business never was
so lively, on account of the prodigious taking up for transport
service. Great orders for provisions and stores of all kinds,
new clothing for the troops, and the intended six thousand
Canadians, puts life into the woollen manufacture; and a number of men of war, ordered to be equipped, has given a pretence
for such a quantity of nails and other iron work, as to keep the
midland parts tolerably quiet. All this, with incredible increase of the northern market since the peace between Russia
and the Porte, keeps up the spirits of the mercantile world, and
induces them to consider the American War, not so much their
calamity, as their resource in an inevitable distress. This is the
state of *most*, not of *all* the merchants." *To the Marquis of
Rockingham*, 23 August, 1775. See also his letter to the Marquis, 14 September, 1775.

Our good friends at Glasgow, are by their Agents here endeavoring to procure a proposition from the Merchants, in conjunction with them, to supply Administration with Money for carrying on the war, provided the forfeited lands in America are secured to them. This money is what the Virginians chiefly have supplied them with, in contemplation of the approaching troubles, by treble Remittances. This is Scotch gratitude.*

Thirty thousand men, is said to be the Estimate of the whole force intended against America, next year; and indeed it is difficult to conceive, where troops and taxes will be found for such an Army. Wherever the storm falls it will be heavy. But that such a force can shake one Province, much less the whole Continent, is to me incredible. I am afraid a total disconnexion between the two Countries will be the consequence of these hostile measures. Common danger, however, if it should occur, would unite them again. The ensuing Session of Parliament, will decide whether we are to have actual War or not. For should opposition be stronger and in earnest, I cannot but think the

---

* "When you write to the Congress, it would be well, I think, to mention that, as all the evils have been produced by Scotch counsel, and those people prosecute the business with more rancor and enmity, a distinction ought to be made between the treatment of them and other people when made prisoners." *Arthur Lee to C. W. F. Dumas*, 13 August, 1776.

calamities we dread will yet be prevented. However this is more to be hoped than trusted to. Parliament is to meet on the 26th of next month. If anything could make us doubt a providence it would be that the lust of Tyrants is suffered perpetually to blot the face of the earth with blood and misery. It seems that Liberty is never to be procured, or maintained, but by the Sword. Be vigilant in providing for your safety against the probable attempts of next Spring; and let not the Philistines come upon you unprepar'd. The union of America once secur'd, her vigilance must render all attempts upon her Liberties abortive.

God bless and preserve You and Yours; and send us a happy issue out of these distresses and dangers.

[The following is written on the wrapper:]

You have another packet of Newspapers by this conveyance. D.ʳ Renaudet deliver'd y.ʳ dispatches from Philad.ᵃ safely. *

TO ROBERT CARTER NICHOLAS.

24 September, 1775.

Dear Sir:

I enclose you a Paper containing a Letter, which has given infinite anxiety and alarm to every

---

* An intercepted letter, now in the Public Records office, London.

friend of America, and especially of Virginia here. If it be in truth the Letter of the person whose name is affixed to it, I hope the same name will never more disgrace the list of the continental Congress. The principles of it are as dangerous, as they are detestable. The speaking so lightly and irreverently of men and things, which ought to be considered with reverence; the indecent reflections upon the Congress itself and upon individuals, intended, as it is made public, to disgrace that august Body in the eyes of the world, and if it had only reached the hand for which it was destind, the effect of it must have been, to impress a dangerous disgust and suspicion on the mind of the Commander in chief. It was from such seeds as these, and by the instrumentality of such unprincipled fools, that the usurpation of Cromwell, and the still more pernicious restoration by Monk took its origin and succeeded.

What a picture that Letter gives of a Representative for the first Colony, of the united Provinces of America. Instead of the wise and grave reflections, becoming such a character, and so awful an occasion, we have the ridiculous amours of Falstaff, and the common place manoeuvres of a Broker for places. Indeed Sir such men and such Letters, will do more dishonour and injury to a cause like ours, which stands upon the perilous edge of opinion, than the long labours of the wise and good can repair.

The opinion taken up here, from this Letter chiefly, that there are secret disagreements and jealousies among the Members of the general Congress. These they hope will in time be exasperated into fixed enmities, and open dissentions. And indeed they reckon upon the natural progress of human depravity, in such little and unprincipled minds. The consequence of this will certainly be, that they will endeavor to give efficacy to their arms, by insidious propositions, and applications to such men as thus shew themselves to be uninfluenced by the great and noble motives, which ought alone to inspire those who are trusted at this important moment. The People ought to be exemplary in withdrawing their trust at this all-important moment, from those who abuse it, or by their conduct shew themselves unworthy of it. Happy must a Commander in chief be in a cause, of as great consequence and difficulty as ever a man undertook, with such a Monitor, and the Secretary he would recommend. Happy the Colony must be, that has no better man, in whose wisdom and virtue she may repose the vast concerns of this solemn appeal. *

* The letter referred to was one from Benjamin Harrison to General Washington, dated Philadelphia, 21 July, 1775. It was, with other letters, entrusted to the care of one Hichborn, and was intercepted at Rhode Island by Captain Ayscough. On August 5th Washington, then at Cambridge, learned of the

The Answer of Your Assembly to Ld North's proposition, is esteemed here a master-peice. I never read anything with more pleasure. The proceedings of the Assembly were not sent to me. They were however lent to me the other day, and finding the Report of the Committee touching the Governor's conduct, and the state of the Colony of much importance, I have sent it to the Press. War is the word, with our just and humane Ministers; but the manner of conducting it next Spring, is not I believe determind.

May the God of Battles guard you, and preserve the Liberties of our persecuted Country.

---

capture, and of the exultation of the captors over the contents of the letters, understood to be of some consequence. "It is exceedingly unfortunate," he wrote to Congress, "that gentlemen should chuse to travel the only road on which there is danger. Let the event of this be what it will, I hope it will serve as a general caution against trusting any letter that way in future." And the biographer of Adams notes that Hichborn in his explanation of the capture, saved his honesty only at the expense of his character for presence of mind. The capture was of importance, for it included two letters of John Adams to his wife, that were written in such frankness that their publication gave him much trouble; and the letter of Harrison's, that attracted great notice from the low tone of morality, public and private, that pervaded it. With this letter before it, why did Congress in September choose Harrison a member of the committee to go to camp? The letter, in part, may be found in *Force, American Archives, Fourth Series*, II., 1697. The omissions of Force are printed in my *Washington-Duché* Letters, 15, note.

[The following is written on the wrapper.]

Administration will certainly be puzled to get 26,000 Men to send to Am.ᵃ in the spring to compleat the Troops now there to 30,000. Englishmen will not inlist—and recruiting and inlisting Roman Catholics in Ireland and the highlands of Scotland goes on very heavily, notwithstanding the great Bounties given. The Ministers sensible of this are endeavouring to negotiate with Russia for 20,000 Russians and with several German Princes for Germans; but it is much doubted whether they will be able to succeed either in Russia or Germany, because foreigners will not venture to America until a Cartel for the exchange of Prisoners is settled, which for that very reason sh.ᵈ not by any means be done for a year or two; for the moment it is, you may be assured the Ministry will attempt to over run you, with Russians, Germans, or Swiss. *

---

*An intercepted letter in the Public Records office, London. The employment of German mercenaries in the British service in America is too well known to require comment. It is doubtful if serious proposals for Swiss troops were made until October 1777, but the Dutch refused to give up a Scotch brigade that they had retained in their pay for some years.

The ministry had been informed by Mr. Gunning, the British ambassador at St. Petersburg, of the concern of the Empress about the troubles in America and of some hints of her readiness to lend some of her troops for the English service. Gunning was instructed to sound whether ten or fifteen thousand

TO BARBEU DUBOURG.

27 August, 1776.

I only arrived home last night. To-day I receive a letter from you from D[uma]s under care to E. B., without date and without name. It contains nothing essential.

I learn that many ships, for different parts of America, chiefly for Philadelphia and the colonies

---

Russians could be had, and the answer was considered so favorable, that the King wrote under his own hand to "Sister Kitty," asking for a force to serve "not as auxiliaries but as mercenaries," the Russian general to be absolutely under the command of the British. This application was known in France in September, and in November King George received a reply to his letter, not at all to his liking. "The letter of the Empress is a clear refusal, and not in so genteel a manner as I should have thought might be expected from her. She has not had the civility to answer in her own hand, and has thrown out some expressions that may be civil to a Russian ear, but certainly not to more civilized ones." *The King to Lord North,* 3 November, 1775.

On September 16th the king ordered a letter to be written to the Lord-Lieutenant of Ireland (Harcourt), directing certain regiments to be taken from Ireland for the American service, offering to replace them by continental auxiliaries. The Irish parliament reluctantly consented to the taking of the troops, but did not accept the substitute, affirming at the same time its abhorrence and indignation over the disturbances in America. This demand for troops, and the subsequent measures, led to a motion to censure Harcourt, and it was admitted by the ministers to have been a very bad bargain, but a majority carried them through. Donne, *Correspondence of George III. with Lord North,* I., 302.

of New England, are shortly to sail from Bordeaux,
Nantes and St. Malo, and a French ship from Dunkirk for P———a; but it would not be prudent to
trust Gammon. He was, I perceive, the agent of
M. Turgot at Dunkirk.

A merchant of Philadelphia, newly arrived from
France, says that several French officers applied to
him to go to America in case he were authorized
to promise them employment. Saturday's Gazette
gives the official account with regard to the check
of General Clinton and Mr. Parker at Charlestown.
It appears that the English loss is much more considerable than the Gazette announces, and persons
from that voyage say that the Bristol and the Resolution, each of 50 guns, are become unserviceable,
and consequently will fall into the hands of the
Americans. General Lee by a forced march arrived in time with two battalions of foot from Carolina and one from Virginia, to perform this service.
What must foreigners think of our government,
which, it seems, last week sent two officers into
France there to spread false reports, that New
York is taken and the Americans totally defeated?

General Wooster arrived in Canada just in time
to conduct the retreat from Montreal, and at
present commands there against Carleton, &c.
Washington and Putnam command at New York,
where they make light of the enterprizes of General Howe. Thirty of the authors of the conspir-

acy are in prison. The Declaration of Independence is generally approved in America, and the utmost unanimity prevails there. Lords S[helbur]ne and Townshend have gone to Paris to remain there until the reassembling of Parliament on the 24th October. The first, by what I am told of his conversations at P., is no friend of the latter, or of the matter which you have so much at heart. Therefore be very reserved with him. Do not forget the tobacco scheme. Great discretion is necessary for its success; for I know there are many people in France who have their attention turned towards that subject. You can write to me quite safely to the address of *Mr. John Banks, Merchant, No. 33 Barking Alley, Great Tower Street, London.* *

TO C. W. F. DUMAS.

LONDON, 10 September, 1776.

Sir:

The 27th ultimo and the 7th instant, in the absence of my brother, Arthur Lee, your two letters for him came safe to my hands. My brother is now on the continent, and perhaps may write to

---

* Re-translated from a French version of an intercepted letter, in the *Archives des Affaires étrangères Etat Unis*, and reproduced in *Stevens' Fac-similes,* No. 581.

you from where he is.* The Declaration of Independence on the part of America, has totally changed the nature of the contest between that country and Great Britain. It is now on the part of Great Britian a scheme of conquest, which few imagine can succeed. Independence is universally adopted by every individual in the Thirteen United States, and it has altered the face of things here. The Tories, and particularly the Scotch, hang their heads and keep a profound silence on the subject; the Whigs do not say much, but rather seem to think the step a wise one on the part of America, and what was an inevitable consequence of the measures taken by the British Ministry. In short, every one wants to form his judgment by the event of the present campaign, as something decisive is expected to happen from the arrangements under General and Lord Howe, and General Carleton, before the meeting of Parliament, which will be the 24th of October.

In the meantime every effort is made to prevent France from taking any open or even private part with America, for which purpose Mr. Stanley, Mr. Jenkinson, one of the Lords of the Treasury, and confidential friend of Lord Bute, and one of the Solicitor-General, Mr. Wedderburne, have been at Paris some time to aid the negociations of the

---

* Arthur Lee was in Paris.

British Minister, Lord Stormont. As far as money will answer for their purpose it will not be spared. The French are generally acute enough in observing what is for their interest, but most people here are at a loss to conceive what plan they have in view, as they have not hitherto, as we know of, taken any part with America.

The public papers will tell you all the material news we have from America, but in general it is supposed the Americans will stand greatly in want of arms, ammunition, and artillery, to oppose such a force as is sent against them, and it is evident they have not experienced officers sufficient to manage such extensive operations as they have in hand. Should you have occasion to write to me, you may address, under cover, as you do my brother.

TO RICHARD HENRY LEE.

DIEPPE, 15 October, 1776.

We have just heard of the proceedings on Long Island, the latter end of August; which is indeed unfortunate, as it will in all probability lead to other events still more unfortunate, because they will inevitably tend, nay, indeed will certainly occasion a continuance of the war.

Nothing, now, in my opinion can possibly prevent it, but the interference of Foreign Powers, who have a strong inclination to it, but still there are some material obstacles in the way: however this winter or next spring will probably produce some great events. Respecting this you must receive from a quarter that you have a right to expect it, much better information than I can give.

The American question seems, at this moment, to be entirely forgot by all parties in England; for neither in conversation, or in the public papers, is the Declaration of Independence mentioned as a matter of the least importance; indeed, it has not been so much talked of, as the capture of one West India ship.

The attention of every one is fixed on the operations of the army; on its success the Ministry build their hopes for continuance in office, and on its discomfiture the Opposition rely for getting into Power. In truth the Interest of England seems to be totally out of the question, on both sides; and the people at large, who are ever easy while affairs are successful, will be perfectly quiet, until a series of ill fortune rouses their resentment: added to this two successive crops, the most abundant that have been known for 20 years, make bread and most provisions cheaper than they have been, while Manufactures increase in price, and Trade flourishes amazingly; for the American war creates an amazing Fund for Commerce. Think what 7 or 8 millions will effect, laid out in the various manufactures and implements for the Army, with the necessary provisions, and transports, etc. This immense sum, too, all passing thro' the hands of Government, keeps the principal agents, and thro' them every intermediate person, down to the lowest, quite easy. You will readily perceive that this system is all a fiction, because in the first instance there is no solidity, viz. money, for these millions are all Navy and Victualling Bills, etc, and have not one shilling fixed by Parliament for the redemption of them.

While the Bubble lasts, it will, however, carry with it all the weight of a Reality; but when it bursts, the crush will be dreadful indeed, and like a powerful torrent will overwhelm the nation with irreparable ruin.

This event it is in the power of France to produce in one day:—A stroke from her would do the business almost instantaneously, and she is sufficiently prepared to give it, if she pleases.

It has been said that the Congress has Representatives at several of the different courts in Europe; but others again say, that they have only one regular Representative in France, and even he has not had any advice from his Constituents since June. It is certainly presumptuous for any individual to attempt to censure the proceedings of so wise a Body, that have hitherto conducted themselves with such admirable judgment; and, indeed, to the utter astonishment of every person: yet one cannot help thinking, it would have been prudent to have had the Declaration of Independence authoritatively proclaimed to every Court in Europe, long before this.

The terms in which it is couched, as we have seen it, might not answer for every climate, but it would have been easy to convey the essence of the thing, in words not altogether inadmissible, so as to answer the purpose. *

I see clearly, that you must have mercantile, as well as other agents, in various places, and as the prospect of starving is by no means agreeable, can't you fix upon some employment for a certain friend of yours,† that is equal to his station in Life, and his capacity, such as it is. You know both, perfectly well, as also his disposition, therefore can judge what is fit for him as well as he can for himself. Shew this to Loudoun, consult with him upon it, as I am sure he will cordially assist if any

---

* "I presented the Declaration of Independence to this Court, after, indeed, it had become an old story in every part of Europe. It was well received ; but as you say you have articles of alliance under consideration, any resolution must be deferred until we know what they are. The want of intelligence has more than once well nigh ruined my affairs. Pray be more attentive to this important subject, or drop at once all thoughts of a foreign connection." *Silas Deane to John Jay*, 3 December, 1776.

† William Lee.

thing can be done. Remember that all countries are alike to a traveller, if he has but health and independence.*

It is ever prudent to try all powders as well as arms before they are relied on for use:—a great quantity of both these have been in the last 12 months, exported from Great Britain by permission to France and other places; such as is carried to the coast of Africa, and is totally unfit for any other purpose, than to scare an African with.

Such as these, I am told is chiefly what has been carried from France to America; try, therefore, before you trust.†

---

*The suggestion contained in Lee's letters was apparently acted upon by Congress, for in February Deane received a letter from the secret Committee, appointing William Lee joint agent with Mr. Thomas Morris, and in March notified Lee of his appointment. It required some time for Mr. Lee to close his mercantile concerns in England, and he arrived in Paris on June 11th, to find the Commissioners in deep embarrassment over the condition of affairs at Nantes, a confusion produced by the incapacity and general misconduct of Thomas Morris.

† "I now advise you to attend carefully to the articles sent you. I could not examine them here. I was promised they should be good, and at the lowest prices, and that from persons in such stations, that had I hesitated, it might have ruined my affairs. But as in so large a contract there is room for imposition, my advice is, that you send back to me samples of the articles sent you. Cannon, powder, mortars, &c., are articles known ; but send clothes, the fusils, &c., by which any imposition may be detected." *Silas Deane to John Jay*, 3 December,

Since the last advice from Long Island, I have
not seen a military man or one acquainted with the
situation of the country; but it appears to me that
the loss was chiefly owing to the want of proper officers, artillery, and perhaps ammunition; tho' indeed, it does not seem by the account, as if the
men fought at all, or else there must have been a
greater loss on the side of the victors. Should a
sound footing once be had, and the command got
of Hudson's River, is there not some reason to

1776. See *William Lee to Robert Carter Nicholas*, 9 August,
1777, post.

"Since my last note I have made a further enquiry about
the Brig Sally, and find from very good authority, that she was
bought from a Mr. Wilcocks, cheesemonger, somewhere near
the old change; that she stood, and I believe does now stand
in the Custom house books of Register, as the property of Alderman Lee, which seems to confirm my former suspicions, and
hope I shall be able to fix the stigma on so *bad* a man as *he* is."
George Robertson to Rev. John Vardill, 18 March, 1777. *Stevens' Fac-similes*, No. 55.

Sometime in 1777 Mrs. Bancroft went to France, taking some
letters from English correspondents of the Doctor, Franklin
and others. A Mr. Hake, under encouragement of the ministry, joined her, obtained possession of the letters, opened
them, and after taking memoranda, resealed them. Among
them was a letter from William Lee to Franklin, in which he
said, "I shall in the course of a few days be able to accomplish
what I hinted to you on the 10th instant relative to P—r and
A—n. Nothing I hope will transpire." It was suspected that
the Alderman was engaged with Mayze and two Wistars in an
extensive shipment of powder and ammunition to the Colonies.

suppose, that the army will be kept recruited to its present number, if not increased by Tories, besides being supplied with provisions?

The fate of things hangs on a critical balance, and I do not know how it may turn, but from the bottom of my heart, I wish there was a happy end of the warfare.

Providence will no doubt protect you, as your cause is just.

Farewell, and believe me ever Yours &c.

Pray let me hear from you when you have an opportunity.

TO C. W. F. DUMAS.

London, March 21st, 1777.

Sir:

Government here has received within these ten days past several expresses from General Howe, at New York, in North America, as late as the 19th of last February, which are, in every respect, very disagreeable indeed. He writes in severe terms against General Heister, whom he calls *an old woman* in the field, and a stupid and incorrigible blockhead in the cabinet; he also says that the Hessians and other Germans are the worst troops under his command, and are not fit to be trusted in any business; he has, therefore, desired several particular English officers to be sent to command

them; some of them that he has pointed out
have refused to go on such a forlorn hope;* but
General Burgoyne, much against his will, is, it
seems, obliged to go,† and one Colonel Charles
Gray, who was only a Lieutenant Colonel upon
half-pay, has agreed to go, being appointed to a
regiment, with the rank of a Major-General, in
America.

General Howe has, with some difficulty and considerable loss, got his troops back to New York,
that had attempted to make good their situation at
Brunswick, in the Jerseys. He has recalled the
greater part of these troops that had been sent to

---

* "In the last war they [the Hessians] were esteemed not
unequal to any troops in Prince Ferdinand's army, and I should
do them much injustice were I not to say they were in very
high order in America." Howe's Narrative, p. 8. But it was
generally believed in America that great dissentions and disputes had arisen between the British troops and the Hessians.
Bowdoin to the Commissioners, 27 February, 1777. And in
England there were hints of treachery on the part of the Hessians, although these mercenaries had twice been thanked in
orders for their good behavior. *London Chronicle*, March, 1777.

† On February 20th the King notified North that Germaine
would on the next day propose Clinton for Canada, and Burgoyne to join Howe. Burgoyne submitted a plan for conducting the war from Canada, and at a Cabinet Council in March,
was chosen to command such an expedition. There is no indication of any unwillingness on his part to accept the appointment, though it practically involved an affront to his superior—
Sir Guy Carleton.

Rhode Island. At New York they were in the greatest distress for all kinds of fresh provisions and vegetables; at the same time, a fever, similar to the plague, prevailed there, that, in all probability, before the spring will carry off to the Elysian shades at least one-half of the troops that remain there, and prepare an immediate grave for the Germans and all the other troops that are about to be sent to that infected place. At the same time we learn that the American army under General Washington increases in numbers every day, and, being accustomed to the climate, have kept the field in all the severe weather. Notwithstanding this melancholy prospect of affairs, our papers talk of a foreign war, but in my opinion we are in no condition to engage in one, for you may be assured that we have not in the kingdom sailors enough to man fifteen ships-of-the-line, though you may see thirty or forty ships put in commission, as the public prints will tell you. And as to soldiers, the draft for America has been so great that we have not ten thousand in the whole Island, yet our Ministers have lately attempted to bully the States of Holland by a high-flying memorial relative to the conduct of some of their Governors in the West Indies.* It might, however, be attended with very

*The governor of Eustatia had returned from his fort the salute of an American vessel, with an equal number of guns. The British minister demanded the recall of the governor, and

serious consequences, if the Hollanders were to take their money out of the English funds.

P. S. If you please, insert the foregoing in the Dutch, Brussels, Frankfort, and Hamburg papers.

INSTRUCTIONS FROM CONGRESS.*

PHILADELPHIA, 1 July, 1777.

Sir:

Herewith you will receive commissioners from the Congress of the United States of North America,

---

a more rigid restraint on the trade than was known to exist between that island and the rebellious colonies—demands that were not conceded.

* On December 24th, 1776, Congress named a committee of five—Gerry, Witherspoon, Richard Henry Lee, Clarke and Samuel Adams— to report a plan for obtaining foreign assistance. This plan was completed on December 30th, and provided for the appointment of commissioners to the courts of Vienna, Spain, Prussia, and the grand duke of Tuscany. Franklin was named for Spain, 1 January, 1777; but before this appointment reached him, the commissioners at Paris had determined to separate—Mr. Lee to go to Spain, and either Franklin or Deane to the Hague—believing that something might be accomplished in those countries. Lee had set out before the commission reached Franklin, who wrote: "The committee in their letters mention the intention of Congress to send ministers to the courts of Vienna, Tuscany, Holland and Prussia. They also send us a fresh commission, containing your name instead of Mr. Jefferson's, with this additional clause: 'And also to enter into and agree upon a treaty with his most Christian Majesty, or such other person or persons as shall be by him authorized for that purpose, for assistance in carrying on the

authorising and appointing you to represent the said
Congress as their Commissioner at the Courts of
Vienna and Berlin. You will proceed with all convenient expedition to those Courts; visiting that first
which, on consultation with the Commissioners at the
Court of France, shall be judged most proper. You
will lose no time in announcing in form to those Courts

present war between Great Britain and these United States.'
The same clause is in a particular commission they have sent
me, to treat with the court of Spain, similar to our common
commission to the court of France, and I am accordingly
directed to go to Spain; but, as I know that choice was made
merely on the supposition of my being a little known there to
the great personage for whom you have my letter (a circumstance of little importance), and I am really unable through
age to bear the fatigue and inconveniences of such a journey,
I must excuse myself to Congress, and join with Mr. Deane in
requesting you to proceed on the former footing till you can
receive a particular commission from Congress, which will no
doubt be sent as soon as the circumstances are known." *To
Arthur Lee*, 21 March, 1777. A new commission, naming Arthur
Lee for Spain, was ordered 1 May, 1777, and then Congress proceeded to fill the other places: Ralph Izard was sent to Tuscany
(7 May, 1777); and William Lee was named commissioner for
the courts at Vienna and Berlin. The draft of the commission
and instructions for Lee was laid before Congress 27 June, 1777,
recommitted on the 28th, and a new form adopted on the first of
July. "We enclose to you commissions and instructions for
Ralph Izard and William Lee; the first, appointed Commissioner to the Court of Tuscany, and the latter to the Courts of
Vienna and Berlin. Their instructions are so intimately connected with your own, that we have thought proper to send
them open to your confidential care, that you may give information to the gentlemen, and take every due step to forward

the Declaration of Independence made in Congress on the fourth day of July, 1776. The reasons of this act of Independence are so strongly adduced in the Declaration itself, that further argument is unnecessary. As it is of the greatest importance to these States that Great Britain be effectually obstructed in the plan of sending German and Russian troops to North America,

---

the execution of the intention of Congress." *Committee of Foreign Affairs to the Commissioners*, 2 July, 1777. John Adams admitted that the missions to Prussia, Austria and Tuscany had been advised by persons, "who knew no better," and in these measures "there was less attention to the political interests and views of princes, than to the ties of blood and family connections."

Lee wrote that the Spanish mission was of all the most disagreeable to his disposition, and was "so very inferior in point of political importance, that I should certainly be of much less utility there than here [Paris]." He wished Franklin to be sent to Vienna, "as the first, most respectable, and quiet;" Deane to Holland, William Lee to Berlin, "as the commercial department;" Izard to Tuscany, and Edward Jenings to Madrid. "France remains the centre of political activity, and here therefore I should choose to be employed." *Arthur Lee to Richard Henry Lee*, 4 October, 1777.

The Committee of Secret Correspondence had no connection with the commercial agencies, a separation that produced no little complication, when in Europe the Diplomatic agents were called upon to interfere in the disputes of Lee and Morris. "As all affairs relative to the conduct of commerce and remittance pass through another department, we beg leave to refer you to the Secret Committee, and Mr. Thomas Morris, their agent in France, for every information on those subjects." *Committee of Secret Correspondence to Commissioners at Paris*, 21 December, 1776.

you will exert all possible address and vigor to cultivate the friendship, and procure the interference of the
Emperor and of Prussia. To this end you will propose
treaties of friendship and commerce with these Powers,
upon the same commercial principles as were the basis
of the first treaties of friendship and commerce proposed to the Courts of France and Spain by our Commissioners, and which were approved in Congress the
seventeenth day of September, 1776, and not interfering
with any treaties which may have been proposed to, or
concluded with the Courts above-mentioned. For your
better instruction herein, the Commissioners at the
Court of Versailles will be desired to furnish you, from
Paris, with a copy of the treaty originally proposed to
Congress, to be entered into with France, together with
the subsequent alterations that have been proposed on
either side.

You are to propose no treaty of commerce to be of
longer duration than the term of twelve years from the
date of its ratification by the Congress of the United
States. And it must never be forgotten, in these commercial treaties, that reciprocal and equal advantages
to the people of both countries be firmly and plainly
secured.

There being reasons to suppose that his Prussian
Majesty makes commerce an object, you will not fail to
place before him in the clearest light the great advantages that may result from a free trade between the
Prussian dominions and North America.

You will seize the first favorable moment to solicit,
with decent firmness and respect, an acknowledgment

of the independence of these States, and the public reception of their Commissioner as the representative of sovereign States. The measures you may take in the premises, and the occurrences of your negociation, you will communicate to Congress by every opportunity.

It may not be improper to observe that these instructions, and all others which you may receive from time to time, should be kept as secret as circumstances will admit.   JOHN HANCOCK,
President of Congress.

SILAS DEANE TO JONATHAN WILLIAMS.

PARIS, 4 July, 1777.

Dear Sir:

Yours of the 30th ulto. and 1st instant are before us. Mr. Morris, were he present, has not the least right to any direction of Captain Wickes or his prizes, and less so to Johnson or Nicholson; they are Continental property, and are immediately under our direction, by the express orders of Congress, and under no other persons.

Inclosed you have a letter to Captain Wickes, and to Captains Johnson and Nicholson on this subject. Mr. Lee's arrival would make no odds in this business,* as

---

* Lee's new position was well known in London. "Dr. Lee's brother, the Alderman of London, is arrived here; he hath accepted of the employment of Commercial agent to Congress. The Alderman is so much of a Courtier that he places all virtue in economy." *Public Ledger*, 22 July, 1777. "What doth the Court of Aldermen say to Lee's departure? He lives in the

it is distinct from anything contained in either of their appointments, and your appointment from us is the only one at present that can be of any force; we therefore direct you not to give way to any pretensions of any one, but consulting with Mr. Ross and Captain Wickes, proceed to dispose of the prizes, and to settle their affairs in the best and most expeditious manner possible. Mr. Deane has wrote to Captain Wickes to address to the house you mention.

SILAS DEANE.

Rue Jacob, in as sparing a manner as American frugality will permit, and yet I am told his allowance from the Congress as their Commercial agent is considerable." *Public Ledger*, September, 1777.

"No doubt but you have missed Alderman Lee before this; he is here [Paris], but don't understand on any business. He proposes returning shortly no doubt, but will carry many letters. There is a great misunderstanding between him and Dr. Bancroft." *Lupton to Eden*, 18 June, 1777.

"Alderman Lee is gone to Havre. I should have accompany'd him, but found 'twould be of more use my staying here. He [is] not liked by any person, in short they will not let him and Bancroft come together." *George Lupton to William Eden*, 9 July, 1777. *Stevens' Fac-similes*, No. 179.

"Alderman Lee is returned from Havre, and so much out of favor at Mr. Deane's that he frequently comes to me to know what's the news." *Lupton to William Eden*, 17 July, 1777.

"Alderman is not liked by the Gentlmⁿ here no more than his brother Arthur, and everything, before his brother's arrival, was kept a profound secret from him." *Lupton to Eden*, 20 August, 1777.

COMMISSIONERS TO CAPT. WICKES.

PARIS, 4 July, 1777.

Sir:

We have appointed Mr. Williams to take the direction of such affairs at Nantes as are more particularly within our department, and, accordingly, advise you to address yourself to him for any assistance you stand in want of, in the disposition of your prizes, or your other concerns; you will give directions to Captains Johnson and Nicholson, which render it unnecessary for us to write each separately.

We are yours, etc.,   B. FRANKLIN.
                                                 S. DEANE.

JOHN ROSS* TO SILAS DEANE.

NANTES, 19 July, 1777.

Dear Sir:

By last post I acknowledged receipt of yours, and then flattered myself that I should to-day be able to communicate Mr. Morris' sentiments to you, regarding

---

*Although a Scotchman by birth, John Ross was a shipping merchant in Philadelphia at the beginning of the troubles between Great Britain and her colonies, and espoused the American cause. He signed the non-importation agreement, received an appointment in the Continental navy (1775–'76) but resigning, was employed by the Congress to purchase supplies for the army. It was when thus employed—naturally under Robert Morris's directions—that he came to France, and was selected by the commissioners to undertake the arrangement of the agency business at Nantes. Ross died in 1800.

what you have recommended. However, for some days could not get a sight of him; how he has been employed is best known to himself. Before your letter came to my hand, I proposed to him to resign the sole management of public and private business, from a conviction of his inattention and neglect in superintending matters of less importance to his own reputation, and to those of his distant connections. To this he replied, he had determined in his own mind not to relinquish the management of either, until he heard further from his brother, whose apprehensions had been ill-grounded, as he could convince him and all his friends, the business had hitherto been conducted with regularity, and that nothing had suffered in what was committed to his care. I took the liberty to contradict his assertions from my own particular knowledge of the contrary, and informed him what such resolutions might hazard, if he persisted, when possessed of his brother's letter, and particularly acquainted with the instructions I had received therewith. At the same time I insisted, if determined to abide by so absurd a contempt of his brother's orders, on his writing me a letter stating his reasons for refusing a surrender of what I knew him incapable of conducting, without risking further sacrifice of the interest of his employers, and an additional loss of reputation to himself, and to those of his connections thereby.

This letter he promised to furnish me, and might serve to justify my attention to the trust reposed by our friend in me, but have not received it as yet. I have, therefore, reason to conclude it will not be possi ble, without positive new powers, for me to command a surrender of the private concerns of his house, and that I shall have the disagreeable task of corresponding with the friends of W[illing], M[orris] & Co., forbidding their future attention to his orders or correspondence.

It is impossible for me or any other person to find out what abuse the house have sustained in point of interest, nothing being entered to afford me the least insight thereto; but I know them to suffer through his folly and extravagance more than he can ever retrieve, respecting their credit and character.

Permit me now to give it as opinion to you and *advice*, that the commissioners interpose immediately, exercise their powers, and place the execution and management of all future concerns of the public in some secure hand. Our friend, Mr. Robert Morris, has placed the utmost confidence in both you and me; we should be wanting, and indeed to blame, did anything escape us under present circumstances in any degree prejudicial to his interest and reputation. *It happened extremely unfortunate at present that Mr. Lee should be deprived from acting, for want of proper instructions respecting his appointment as joint agent.* Your powers, I trust, may nevertheless prove sufficient to supply the want of a former commission until it reach him. Accordingly, if so, and that he does act, it is incumbent on you and me in particular to consult the interest of Mr. Robert Morris in his absence, until we hear further from him, and have his own opinion on the subject. I would beg leave, therefore, to propose a continuation of his *name* in the management of the public business, joined with Mr. Lee, or such other as the commissioners may see fit to appoint on the present occasion, and that everything incumbent on our friend, Mr. Morris, may be complied with on his part as joint agent. I approve that you and I should look out and engage a careful, capable man in character of clerk, to attend the business and to be paid at his expense, until matters can be better arranged more suitable and satisfactory to the parties concerned. You'll believe I am persuaded the opinion urged by me on this subject, cannot proceed from any views of interest to myself. I have in truth no such motives; on the contrary, I may venture to assure such agent as may be appointed here, if Mr. Morris' name is discontinued the business must be greatly lessened by such a loss of connection.

By a letter received from you last evening by Mr. Williams, I perceive you press him to a pursuit of getting possession of the prizes lately arrived. Some are sold, and I fear they may turn out so trifling on the settlement of the whole, I would take the liberty to advise your permitting Mr. Morris to close the sales, and the net proceeds to be carried to the credit of the United States, he being more in advance than will balance such part as can come to their share. Your letter to Capt. Wickes, (which he received from Mr. Williams,) sufficiently guards against any more coming to our friends' hands in the same line, Captain Wickes having already directed the Commanders of the continental ships of force to conform to your instructions in the consignation of all future prizes.*

This, I foresee, will prevent noise, such as ought in our situation to be avoided. I shall be glad to know your determination in course; assuring you of every possible endeavor on my part to facilitate your resolutions, if my services can be rendered useful on the present or any other future occasion, that matters may be conducted in *future* with more regularity and prudence; I trust, more to the satisfaction of all parties. My respects to Mr. Franklin. I sincerely remain etc.†

---

* On the 4th the Commissioners had written to Captain Lambert Wickes to send all prizes to Mr. Williams at Nantes. It was in Wickes' vessel, the *Reprisal*, that Franklin had come to France. As the captains drew on the Commissioners for all expenses incurred in fitting out their vessels, while the commercial agents and others disposed of the prizes, and rendered no accounts, Franklin and Deane issued the orders that prizes should be turned over to Williams.

"Permit me now to inform you, Mr. Morris is possessed of the instructions to Mr. Lee from Committee of Congress on his being appointed Commercial agent here. Since your last letter came to my hand, I suspected this to be the case, from some circumstances, and by accident last evening learnt it to be so. These instructions are contained in a letter addressed to Mr. Lee and Mr. Morris as joint agents, which is similar and of equal force with the separate powers on which Mr. Morris has acted hitherto. I therefore take the liberty to recommend Mr. Lee's repairing hither immediately, to assume the management, being certain Mr. Morris will possess him of this letter, so soon as they meet, though kept so long back, probably from inattention." *John Ross to Silas Deane*, 22 July, 1777.

† From the Laurens Correspondence, 35.

TO ARTHUR LEE.

NANTES, 6 August, [1777].

My dear Brother:

On Monday evening I arrived here, a good deal fatigued, in some measure owing to accidents on the road. The carriage I cou'd have have sent by a F. man to-day, but I apprehend those people w'd not be quite so careful as they ought to be of it; indeed I must say in my judgment, it will be wrong to take the trip to Normandy. My advice would be to keep close where you are and lie upon your oars quite inoffensively until a favorable crisis occurs of gradually coming forward with honor to yourself and advantage to the concerned; for I think the ground is ticklish which requires that every step should be taken with caution and circumspection. If I should blunder, it will not be surprising, since from a certain mysterious concealment of what should be fully communicated, every step is to be taken in the dark. However, I am determined to persevere without complaints. I hope nothing farther has passed about the account. When that business is cleared up, which will be among the first, what is wrong shall be put right: but by chance I have already seen that the produce of what Wickes bro't was expressly ordered for Mess. F[ranklin] and D[eane]. All my attempts have as yet been in vain to get a sight of Mr. M[orris], since Saturday. It is said, no body knew

where he was. This morning he was understood
to be at home, but so firmly barricaded up, that no
creature cou'd gain admittance tho' above twenty
attempts have been made by myself and others.
Be so good as to make my compliments to your associates, and let them know I shall write as soon as
ever it is in my power to say anything satisfactory.
Direct for me chez M.ʳ Schweighauser, and pray
tell how I shall direct for you, so as to avoid double
postage. I long to hear the success of your plan
with G. G,* but from comparing dates and circum-

---

* "By G. G., whom I did not see, I hear that there is great
misunderstandings; I had heard of them before. Let me entreat you to do everything in your power to restore the ancient
necessary harmony. Your trade will suffer without a mutual
confidence; your disposition and capacity to promote the general interest I can answer for. Talk freely to G. G. You will
find him manly, and a hearty well wisher. Do for God's sake
return to one another. Your general interests certainly require
it. I am miserable on the subject; let me hear a pleasing account of your affairs." *Edmund Jenings to Arthur Lee*, 24
September, 1777. G. G. may refer to Carmichael. "You will
I trust forgive the liberty I took in earnestly recommending to
your esteem my friend Mr. Carmichael. I do so again with
more warmth, since I have heard of some misunderstanding between you. I know you both, and am confident that both wish
equally well to their country. You were old collegians together.
I was the means of the renewal of your former intimacy, and
the services of both are necessary for the common good. Do,
my dear Sir, take him cordially by the hand; keep him in
Europe if you can, and I am sure you will have a friendship for
him." *Jenings to Arthur Lee*, October, 1777. See also let-

stances, I am inclined to think he was not the author. It comes from another mint, which you may

ters printed in *Life of Arthur Lee*, II., 100, 101. In the Harvard University MSS. is a letter from Carmichael dated 26
September, 1777, asking Arthur Lee to appoint an interview,
and Lee's reply, naming the day. "I received a card from
Wm. L. with your letters: of course I waited on him to thank
him for the trouble I had given him. The misfortune of these
people is to believe that everybody is plotting against them,
they therefore plot against everybody. They think me leagued
with Mr. D. and Dr. F., at the very time that I really feel hurt
at their public conduct, and the private behavior of one to myself. I hope on my arrival in America to give such a representation of our affairs, as will induce the Congress to change their
European system in a great measure." *Bolton* [*Carmichael*]
to Jean Tourville [*Edmund Jenings?*], 1 November, 1777.

"Carmichael is a very reasonable young fellow, and it's a pity
he could not be brought over to your way of thinking. He informs me that neither Franklin nor Deane are capable of doing
the business for which they are designed. Deane has not the
least politeness whatever, and Franklin is too reserved. Of
course they will never do for this Court—and if I am not mistaken they are falling off very much, which the Congress perceive—notwithstanding the many reports to the contrary."
Lupton to Eden, 15 October, 1777.

October 4th Arthur wrote to Richard Henry, warning him
against Carmichael; and the same warning was made to Francis
Lightfoot, October 7th. "I have mentioned to you a cabal being formed here, under the auspices of Mr. Deane, which has
given me much disquiet, and been very busy to defame me in
my absence. I sent you a copy of a newspaper production
of this cast. Among other things they have circulated a
report both here and in England, which will probably reach
America, of dissentions subsisting among the Commissioners.
I have taken great care to prevent any such from arising, and

conjecture as well as me. A certain Dr. [Frank-
lin?] thinks himself a none such at fine writing.

---

none certainly have yet existed, notwithstanding all their diligence in provoking them. Of these gentlemen, I would wish
to guard you particularly against Mr. Carmichael, of whose art
and enmity I have had sufficient proofs to make me distrust
him for the future." *Arthur Lee to Francis Lightfoot Lee*,
7 October, 1777.

Carmichael had been introduced to Deane in the fall of 1776,
by Nicholas Rogers, of Maryland, and served him in various
ways by copying letters and holding conversations. He was
already known to Arthur Lee, and when he left England for
France in the spring of 1776, he received from him a small
pocket dictionary to serve as a cypher for their correspondence.
Between the blank leaves and the cover were pasted two small
pieces of paper which was represented as containing some intelligence for the secret committee. As Deane was the channel
through which such intelligence was to be sent, the book was
handed over to him, the papers taken out, and found to contain
suspicions against Reed and Langdon. "If you should have
an opportunity of writing to —— [Virginia] before I see you,
caution them against Sir James Jay, Dennis Deberdt, Mr. Langdon, formerly delegate from New Hampshire, Paul Wentworth,
and Mr. William Molleson, a Maryland merchant, with whom
Mr. Tilghman, a delegate for Maryland, corresponds without
knowing that his intelligence goes directly to administration.
Col. Mercer too, who is always with ministerial people, should
not be trusted. I have good reason to fear that Joseph Read in
Philadelphia is a dangerous man." *Arthur Lee to Silas Deane*,
28 July, 1776. The papers were not sent on to Congress at the
time, and Lee was apparently satisfied with this step, making
no complaint until nearly two years after, when he charged
Carmichael with having opened and intercepted them. His
real fault was that he had no confidence in the Lees, and was
thought to be intriguing for the Prussian mission.

I will endeavor to find it out, and you should do the same, but caution is requisite, nor should anything be said until the fact is known.* What a horrible place this is. I tremble at the thoughts of what a friend of ours will feel in being here.

No English papers are to be seen. After you have done with them, can't you contrive to send them once a week by some stage or diligence, when private opportunities do not occur, for the postage is too extravagant. Petrie & Gruel take some in, and amongst you there are a great many others. Another ship is arrived from Charlestown, but she does not bring anything new, as she sailed with the one that arrived 14 daies ago. When you have anything worth communicating pray do not fail to write. The eldest Miss S——r is lately married to a Mr. Dobrée from Guernsey. I am dear Brother, most affectionately.

Addressed "To The Honorable Arthur Lee, Hotel de Angleterre, Rue Richelieu, Paris."

---

* This probably refers to a letter published in the (London) *Public Ledger*, dated Paris, 12 July, 1777 : "Dr. Lee is certainly joined in the Commission, but he understands the business of courts so ill, that not one of the ministers will negotiate with him. He is the straight-laced image of awkward formality. To the preciseness of a Presbyterian he endeavors to add the Jesuitism of a Quaker. The one renders him ridiculous, the other suspected. When he thinks he is imposing on mankind, they are laughing at him."

TO ROBERT CARTER NICHOLAS.

NANTES, 9 August, 1777.

Being here to transact public business which
will fix me in this place, I with pleasure embrace
yᵉ earliest opportunity of renewing our correspondence, which has been unhappily interrupted for
some time. Our country will necessarily have occasion for many [   ] Europe, in procuring
of which, my services [   ] commanded and
I am yᵉ more induced to [   ] them on this
occasion because I have reason to apprehend that
some adventurers, who have neither property, reputation, or good character, either here or in any
other part of Europe, are likely to obtain yᵉ confidence and trust of yᵉ State. I must take the
liberty of advising, if any proposition should be
made, or contracts offered by persons who are not
extremely well known, that yᵉ precaution may be
taken of stipulating that yᵉ effects may first be delivered to you in your country at a certain fixed
price, and be paid for in produces, also at a certain
fixed price, as soon as yᵉ goods are delivered and
found to be right with respect to quality and quantity. It will subject you to yᵉ impositions that it
is well known here have been already practiced, if
a contract is made to pay a certain commission on
yᵉ invoice price, for great advances have been put
on yᵉ real prices, yᵉ quantity deficient and yᵉ quality

insufferable. For instance, powder has been sent
that was hardly sufficient to burst an elder gun,
and guns not fit to shoot snow birds; cannons
made also of a factious metal, composed of improper iron, with small quantities of lead and some
pewter mixed, which have been tried in Europe,
and found to be useless. Such being thrown on
ye hands of ye scheming inventor, have been bo't
up for a trifle and sent to America. You may be
assured that ye above are facts; therefore I pray
you to prove always before you trust. Should it
unfortunately happen that you are retired from
public business, I trust you will lose no time in
communicating what preceeds to those in power,
whom it most immediately concerns; and should
you or any other of my friends write to me here,
there cannot be too strict instructions given to
ye bearer to deliver them into my own hands, for
there has been some very shameful practices in use
of opening and searching letters. This place lays
almost in ye centre between ye following seaports,
viz: Bordeaux, Rochfort, Rochelle, Port l' Orient,
Brest, and St. Marlos, so that with little difficulty
I could transact any material business at any of
these ports. . . . As to public affairs, I am almost
at a loss what to say since all Europe hangs in
suspense on ye issue of the present campaign in
America. However, in my judgment, it may be
fully depended upon, that G. Britain will agree to

acknowledge ye Independence of America next winter upon some advantageous terms in point of commerce, and possibly for some stipulated aid whenever G. Britain is at war with any European State, provided Gen'l Burgoyne is foiled in his attempt on Ticonderoga, and Gen'l Howe does not gain some capital advantage in his operations. My advice would be to close instantly with G. B. on any terms whatever that she can ask, provided that Independence is first admitted, without which it would be madness in the extreme for America to treat at all while she has one hundred men that are able and willing to fight for every thing that is dear in this world. The Americans should never forget the memorable sentiment of ye famous Prince of Parma, "Qu'il se devoit souvenir, que qui met l' epée à la main contre son Prince, endoit à l' instant jetter le furreau." That is, when a subject draws his sword against his Prince, he should not forget that it is absolutely necessary the same instant to throw away the scabbard. Liberty or Death, must be the American motto. As to an European war, 'tis impossible for me to say whether there will be one this fall or next spring; but it is certain that a sufficient train is laid, and no one can say how soon ye torch may be put to it that will set it all on fire. . . .

TO ARTHUR LEE.

NANTES, 12 August, 1777.

My dear Brother:

½ past 12 o'clo. This moment Mr. M[orris]
has sent me two letters addressed to him and myself jointly. They are of little consequence, but
he promises to send me any others he has. Pray
mention this to your associates.

I wrote you last night by M.ʳ Lister Jett, a
Frenchman who expected to see you on Thursday
morning. The letter was directed to the Hotel de
Angleterre, and acknowledged the receipt of your
favor of the 7th, which shou'd have come a day or
two sooner than it did. The business of the prizes
must rest yet a while, as it now stands, for I cannot get a sight of any letters or papers whatever
from Mr. M[orris]. I forced into his room yesterday, after my other effort had been tryed in vain
to get at him, and past 12 o'clo: he was in bed in
a dreadful situation.

I think it is utterly impossible to make any
thing of this strange unhappy man. 750 barrels
of rice arrived here from Carolina on the publick
account, which Mr. M. says is solely consigned to
him, and he has put it into the old hands, which I
cannot prevent, having neither letters, papers, or
any shadow of authority to demand it of the captain. I will, however, try this week out, and if

nothing can be done I will state the facts to the commissioners, and let them do as they please. It has been whispered that Mr. D[eane] thinks of applying for the aid of government to stop the proceedings of Mr. M., and the others, and put the whole into my hands. On this idea I say nothing only that no part of it shall come from me, nor should *you* be *active* in it. Let others do as they please, but it would be highly improper in either of us, as things are circumstanced, to have any part in such a business.

You will see by the copy of mine to Mr. D[eane] that I am disappointed in my design of sending Mr. R[oss]'s letters; it is on the other side.

It is reported at the Court at Westminster that your private letters and papers stolen at Berlin are in the hands of the British ministry.* Some pub-

---

*This curious affair was for more than a century clouded in mystery, when a fortunate recovery of some papers by Mr. Oscar Browning revealed the inside facts. Lee and Stephen Sayre (the latter of whom is described by the Earl of Suffolk, as a "man of desperate fortune, but with a disposition rather than the talents to be mischievous") arrived at Berlin on June 4th, with a purpose of negotiating a treaty of commerce with Prussia, acting under encouragements held out by Schulenberg, as Lee interpreted them. Hugh Elliot, the representative of Great Britain at the Prussian court, was fully aware of these movements of the "rebels' agents" and hearing that Lee kept a journal, determined to obtain a copy. He had false keys made to the door of Lee's room and to the bureau in which the journal was kept, and on the 26th of June, learning that Lee

lication such as I mentioned would certainly be
proper, and it might easily be sent to Bridgen*

and Sayre were to visit M. de Launay in the country, where
they generally staid until late at night, he obtained the coveted
papers. Four gentlemen who were dining with him at once
began the task of copying the papers, while Elliot himself went
to pay visits and show himself until eight in the evening, when
he went to the inn, and finding the Americans returned, joined
them and amused them with conversation for two hours without making himself known. About ten o'clock Lee went to his
room, soon discovered the theft, and raised the alarm. Elliot
drove home, and finding the most important of the papers
copied, in disguise left the originals late at night at Lee's inn.
The complaint to the court was followed by the arrest and examination of all the servants at the inn, and it was learned that
a servant of the English ambassador had tampered with them ;
but Elliot had already sent his servant out of the country, and
waiting upon the Prussian minister, declared that the act was
due to his own imprudence in having shown too great inquisi-
tiveness concerning the Americans, and was due to the excessive
zeal of his servant, who knew of his desires. He gave assurances that his court was in nowise responsible, and to prove his
sincerity he was ready to ask for his recall. The English court,
while glad to be put in possession of the papers, rebuked its
agent, but the letter in which the rebuke is conveyed is a model
of diplomatic language. One thousand guineas were allowed
to Elliot, although his expenses in the matter were only five
hundred. As the Earl of Suffolk wrote, the enterprise could
never have been justified but by the completest success. "Un
Mystère diplomatique : Hugh Elliot à Berlin, 1777." *Revue
d' Historie diplomatique*, No. 2, 1888. A letter from Vergennes
to Marquis de Pons on the subject, is printed in *Doniol*, II.,
710, *note.*

* Perhaps the London merchant who married the daughter of
the novelist Richardson.

thro' the channel he desired. Pray do not act or meddle in the affair of Sollier;* keep silence and let others speak; on all occasions be reserved and backward even to speak, but particularly in writing or acting, for indeed we are both most critically situated, and it is impossible to be too much guarded where certain characters are on the stage. Let me know how the plan succeeded with G. G. and send us some English papers when you can after you are done with them, for not one is to be seen here. Some good opportunities will very soon happen for Virginia and South Carolina, from whence the post goes regularly to Philadelphia. Adieu, and believe me most affectionately yours.

[Copy.]

NANTES, 12 August, 1777.

S. D., Esq.:

I am sorry that I did not have the honor of seeing you before I left Paris, tho' I wrote to you the day before I set out, and sent the letter to your house, desiring your despatches might be with me that evening, as I should leave P. the next morning, from whence we did not depart 'till eleven o'clock. It would give me a great deal of pain if I thought that any part of my conduct could give room for supposing that I cou'd ever make an unwarrantable use of private confidential letters put into my hands. I have no reason in the world to believe that Mr. Ross would not at any time

---

*A banker in Paris, with whom Thomas Morris had dealings. Also noted as *Soulier*.

justify what he had written, but as far as I can recollect the contents of his letters, there is nothing in them that will ever stand in need of justification. However, I am not the less chagrined that I have not yet been able to find them among my books or papers, nor indeed ye copys that I know were taken by your consent. I well remember to have put into my brother's hands some papers which were intended to be ye original letters for you, and it is very possible that in my hurry, I gave him both originals and copies. Be pleas'd therefore, to ask him for ye papers I left with him for you, and if he has not ye originals I will again and again search over all ye books and papers I have here to find them for you, when they shall be immediately transmitted.

I will write you on business as soon as those that have hitherto been concerned here will permit me to enter on any, which has not been the case as yet, nor indeed have I been able to procure a sight of any letters, instructions, or papers whatsoever relative to ye business. On Sunday ye Hancock and Adams, Cap. Smith, arriv'd here from Charles Town, with 750 barrels of rice on the public account. I shall probably have something farther to say about this cargoe per next post. I am &c.

P. S. I have never mentioned to Mr. Ross, or any one else here, that I ever saw any of his letters, nor shall I *do it*.

TO ARTHUR LEE.

NANTES, 14 August, [1777.]

My dear Brother:

Mr. M[orris] has at length put into my hands our instructions. I shall now proceed to get a settlement of accounts, but it is easy to perceive that

the business must not be hurried, or there may be
danger of not getting it done at all. We shall
write on the subject of the prizes, and I will endeavor to get the balance paid to the Commissioners that is due to them as fast as possible, tho'
I am given to understand the Public is indebted to
all its correspondents: we must apply to you for
aid or there will be danger of things standing still.
I beg you will be particularly careful *never* to be
alone with Mr. C[armichae]l. As much and as
well as you think you know him, I can make you
wonder when we meet. If you want your chaise,
say so, for there are opportunities of sending it;
but if you are not in haste, I will keep it a little
longer, for at present it is not clear to me that it
will not be necessary for me to make a trip to
Paris soon. I should be glad to have a copy of
the Commissioners' contract for tobacco with the
F[armers] G[eneral].* We have no American

---

* About the middle of January, 1777, Franklin, Deane and
Lee informed Congress of their intention to contract to supply
the Farmers' General with twenty thousand hogsheads of tobacco. "The desire of getting money immediately to command the preparations for the ensuing campaign, and of interesting so powerful a body as the Farmers General, who in fact
make the most efficient part of government here, and the absolute part in all commercial or moneyed concerns, induced us to
concede to these terms, which may possibly, in the estimate of
the price of tobacco, be low, but which upon the whole we
judged necessary, and we hope will be advantageous." The
proposals to the Farmers of a private company in which Thomas

news, only private letters from London mention
that Cornwallis escaped by burning Brunswick,
and that Ticonderoga was invested. Can't you
contrive to forward the English papers here, after
you have done with them, for not one have we.
Pray send to the Hotel de Grand Villars & Hoch-
ereaus every post to see if there are any letters for
me. I ought to have had a material one by Tues-

Morris was active, to import tobacco, suspended for a time the
signing of the contract, and during this interval, the Commissioners were informed of a grant to them from the King of
2,000,000 livres. "Such was the King's generosity, he exacted
no conditions or promise of repayment." But political considerations were still strong for the contract. "We have at length
finished a contract with the Farmers General for five thousand
hogshead of tobacco. . . . We found it a measure of Government to furnish us by that means with large advances, as well
as to obtain the ground of some of their own taxes ; and finding
the Ministers anxious to have such a treaty concluded, we complied with the terms, though we apprehended them not to be
otherwise very advantageous. We have expectations, however,
that in case it appears that the tobacco cannot be afforded so
cheap, through captures, &c., Government will not suffer us to
be losers." The contract was signed at Paris, 24 March, 1777,
by Franklin and Deane—Lee being on his Spanish mission.
But Lee knew of the proposed contract, and approved of it.
"Our object was to interest government here, through them
[the Farmers General], in our commerce, so much as to secure
their utmost protection of it. . . To compass these objects we
were induced to offer them such tempting terms." *To the
Committee of Secret Correspondence*, 14 February, 1777. As he
later said, "tobacco was the most weighty political engine we
could employ with the French Court."

day [?] sennight's post. Remember, the directions are either Waters, Williams or Thomson. Those to Mr. Grand will probably be directed to Pierre Noé Grand. This I shall send with the song from Miss S——r. The family are well, and seem to be most worthy people. Mr. Hartley * whom you know, the linen draper in Covent Garden, carrys it. He does not intend to go to Passi, as he returns immediately to England; therefore, thinks it will be imprudent. He lodges at the Hotel de Louis Seize, Rue Royale pres le Rue Petits Champs, vis a vis l' Hotel de Mon^s Necker. Sam'l Petrie will be a good hand to plan about sending the papers. Mr. Baylor presents his compliments and begs you will send to the Hotel d' York, Rue Jacob, and inquire if any letters have come there for him, and get them forwarded here to the care of Mr. Schweighauser.

Farewell. Be cautious and guarded in all things. Yours most sincerely.

TO FRANKLIN, DEANE AND LEE.

NANTES, 20 August, 1777.

Gentlemen:

Yesterday arrived here the brig Liberty, Captain Herbert, with 108 hhds. of tobacco on account of the State of Virginia, consigned to J. Gruel & Co.

---

* David Hartley, who carried on such a peaceable correspondence with Franklin through the war.

She left Virginia, July 10, running thro' the fire of 5 men of war that guard the mouth of the Bay of Chesapeake. The captain is a true tar, has not bro't any papers or letters, but what relates to his vessel and cargoe. However, he in great measure confirms the news received some time since from Bordeaux of Lord Cornwallis being defeated in the Jersies. He says he heard about the beginning of July a letter in Williamsburg from Gen. Washington mentioning the defeat of Lord Cornwallis, who lost in killed and wounded and prisoners about 1300 men, that Gen'l Scott and another whose name he forgets, commanded the Americans. He does not recollect the date of the letter, or the day on which the action is said to have happened, but he speaks of the fact in general as universally believed, and being the subject of conversation in all companies; also that *all* the B— troops were driven out of the Jersies. This day two privateers arrived here with two valuable West Indiamen prizes. The privateers are the brig Fanny, John Kendrick, 14—4 pounders, 104 men, belonging to Adam Babcock and Archibald Blair, left Bedford, N. E., July 10th; and the Gen'l Mercer, James Baron, 14—4 pounders, 87 men, belonging to Winthrop, Sergeant & Co., of Cape Anne, sailed July 1st.*

---

*Deane, in his *Narrative*, says these privateers were the *Boston* and *Hancock*. Also the Commissioners in their letter to Congress, 28 February, 1778.

Of the Jamaica fleet consisting of 160 sail, they took two small prizes of no great value near New-foundland, which they sent to Boston; the two they have bro't in were taken the 8th instant in the mouth of the Channel tho' the fleet was convoyed by two 28 gun frigates. Their names, the Hanover Planter, Captain Luny, from Jamaica to London, with 360 hhds of Muscovado sugar, 87 punchions of rum, some logwood, 8—6 and 2—4 pounders; and the Clarendon, Capt. Cowell, from Jamaica to London, with 386 hhds Muscovado sugar, 106 punchions of rum, and 6—3 pounders. The captive people say 11 of the fleet were missing when they were taken. Capt. Kendrick has one paper which is on board at Pembeuf;* he left Bedford July 10th, and confirms the defeat of Cornwallis in the Jersies, but says the last accounts made his loss about 600 men only. His account is that the whole British army some time in June (the date he also forgets) was put in motion in 3 divisions to go against Philadelphia, when the first division was attacked and defeated, on which the others retreated with great precipitation, and imbarked at Amboy as fast as possible, from whence it was expected they would go up the North river. They say there was upwards of 6000 men at Ticonderoga where they think Sullivan commanded, and Gates

---

* Paimbœuf.

was stationed at Albany to take care of that quarter. This is all the news, and you will judge best how much is proper to be given to the public—I mean with respect to the privateers and their prizes, since we have an ugly report here of which we should be glad to know the truth, that an American agent was the other day put into the Bastile on account of some transactions with or for Cunningham.*

---

* The "American agent" was William Hodge, of Philadelphia. Congress had approved Deane's suggestion of armed vessels being fitted out at Continental expense, provided the French Court did not disapprove of the scheme (*Secret Journals*, 23 December, 1776). "Private ships of war, or privateers, cannot be admitted where you are, because the securities, necessary in such cases to prevent irregular practices cannot be given by the owners and commanders of such privateers" (*Committee of Secret Correspondence*, 21 December, 1776). Blank commissions were sent out by William Hodge, who arrived at Paris early in February. "He had a long passage, and was near being starved. We are about to employ him in a service pointed out by you, at Dunkirk or Flushing. He has delivered us three sets of the papers we wanted ; but we shall want more, and *beg you will not fail* to send them by several opportunities" (*Commissioners in France*, 6 February, 1777).

The French court had issued strict orders that American prizes should not be sold in French ports—an order made to appease the rising suspicions of Great Britain. In the winter of 1776–'77, Captain Lambert Wickes had made a cruise, brought five prizes into Nantes, which gave "some uneasiness and trouble to the Court, and must not be too frequently practised." For these prizes Thomas Morris was to account. Wickes was ordered on another cruise, in company with an armed cutter

TO ROBERT MORRIS.

NANTES, 21 August, 1777.

I wrote to the Secret Committee on the 11th inst. via Boston, and the 13th via N. C., advising my being here, and of the arrival of the Hancock and

---

[the *Lexington*] commanded by Captain Samuel Nicholson. "Accordingly they sailed, nearly as I remember, some time in April, 1777, with the design of intercepting the Irish linen ships. They cruised some time in the Channel and Irish sea, and missing the great object in view, they took, burnt and sunk near twenty sail of vessels of small value, and sailing round Ireland returned into St. Maloes and Morlaix in France with a part of their prizes." *Deane's Narrative*, 39. These prizes were disposed of at a prodigious loss. While refitting, orders came from the Court to detain Wickes and Nicholson until further orders, and they were so situated late in August, 1777.

Meanwhile the Commissioners had purchased a lugger at Dover, and sending it to Dunkirk, Hodge gave the command to one Gustavus Conyngham, stripped the vessel of all arms, giving out that a cargo of merchandise was to be taken to one of the ports of Norway. As this declaration was suspected, a pretended sale of the vessel was made to a British subject, Richard Allen, security was given by Hodge, and the vessel was allowed to sail. Once outside the harbor, Conyngham received arms, sailors and munitions, and soon after captured the English packet boat —the *Prince of Orange*—returning to Dunkirk. This was too flagrant a violation of the treaty to remain unnoticed by England. Hodge was imprisoned in the Bastile for six weeks, Conyngham and his crew were placed under arrest, the packet boat was restored to her owners without process, and the lugger (the *Surprise*) seized. The King thought these acts "so strong a proof that the Court of Versailles mean to keep appearances," as to deserve mention in the speech.

Adams with 750 bbls. of rice on the public account from Charles Town, So. Carolina. I shall not write at present to the Committee because I shall for some time longer endeavor to get your brother, Mr. T. Morris, to make some settlement of his former transactions, for as yet I have not been able to procure from him a sight of any books or accounts whatever, nor indeed of the invoice or letters he received per the Hancock and Adams, whose cargoe, expressly contrary to my desire, he has put into the same hands that have transacted all business for him hitherto at this place. The fact is, that Mr. Gruel is the only man here who receives and disposes of everything that comes here and pays or ships goods as is agreeable to himself, and yet the following firms appear at different times in America, viz: Thos. Morris; Thos. Morris, Pliarne, Penet & Co.; Pliarne, Penet & Co., and Jas. Gruel & Co.—which last firm is not known here.* Your

---

* "We also think it advisable that you should be so far on your guard, with respect to Mons. Penet, as not to deviate from the original contract made with him, as we cannot learn that he is known to be a person of substance; at the same time, it is but justice to say that he appears to be active, industrious, and attentive to your interests. He is indeed connected with a very good house in Nantes, M. Gruel, but we know not the terms of that connection, or how far Mr. Gruel is answerable. It seems to us that those houses which are connected in Great Britain are to be avoided." *Commissioners at Paris to the Committee of Secret Correspondence,* 17 January, 1777. Arthur Lee, in

accurate knowledge of business will readily show
you how much confusion will necessarily follow
from this juggle of firms. I will endeavor to have
this remedied in future, but am much afraid your
brother will not leave his present way of life, and
consequently will not give me much assistance.
For further particulars I refer you to Mr. John Ross,
who has been here for some months trying in vain
to bring about some settlement of your brother's
affairs. For the future, I hope particular orders
will be given that all despatches shall be delivered into my hands, and from time to time accounts will be sent me of the cargoes sent from
America to the different ports in Europe, and the
returns ordered from every person, that the same
things may not be ordered here from others. That
I may be enabled to form a proper settlement with
your several correspondents in the different European ports, it would be proper to furnish me with
a state of all the remittances you have made to
them and the returns you have received prior to
this time. I approve much of the plan pointed out

February, 1777, wrote that "the credit and character of Mr.
Gruel are exceedingly well established."

M. Penet was born in Alsace, the son of an artillery store-
keeper who, having many children, could give them but a
mediocre education. This one went to seek his fortune in
America, and, at his departure, did a stroke of business not indeed of a dishonest man, but of a not very scrupulous adventurer.

by the Committee for the conduct of their superintendant commercial agent in Europe in their letter of instructions to Mr. T. Morris, and I shall conform to it until they think proper to make an alteration. You have received many things by the Amphitrite and other vessels, for which I am told you have been written to either by Mr. Beaumarchais or Monthieu, or their immediate agent, Mr. Herries, to remit for the value in tobacco, but as I understand the transaction those goods have already been paid for, and nothing is expected in return; tho' surely the Committee will set this matter in a clear light.* Mr. T. M——s has unfortunately made an unlucky contract with the F——rs G——l for all the tobacco he receives on account of Congress at 70 livres per 100 lbs. French, deducting 26 per cent. for tare, tratt and damage. The price is now from 110 to 120 livres per hundred lbs., with much less deductions, and 130 livres are now asked for what little is to sell. Unless a considerable quantity is shipped off the ensuing Fall and Winter, the price cannot fall. The injury of this contract may be avoided by shipping the tobacco to my address solely, tho' it will be directed in all respects as your other remittances. The Commissioners, viz. Messrs. F.

---

* See *Deane to the Committee of Foreign Affairs*, 3 September, 1777, for the true state of the case. Also *Arthur Lee to the Committee of Secret Correspondence*, 14 February, 1777.

and D., have also made a contract with the F——
G——, for 5000 hhds. of the best York and James
River tobacco, at 8 sous per lb., which is much
lower than Mr. Morris's, and will hardly pay the
present freight and insurance. If what I have
heard relative to this contract be true, which I
have no reason to doubt, the F. G. will have no
just right to complain if the money they have advanced on account of this contract be repaid, and
they do not get any tobacco.* I trust you will
take every thing said here in good part, and that
you will believe, if I can render you or your house
any services on this side of the Atlantic, it will
give me the greatest pleasure to do it, and in the
meantime with &c. &c.

TO ARTHUR LEE.

NANTES, 21 August, 1777.

My dear Brother :

Pray forward the enclosed per post immediately,
unless a private safe and quick conveyance should
first offer.

A large packet was sent from London for me the
7th thro' Bridgen. Pray enquire at my Hotel and
the book sellers for it. When got, forward it by
the first proper conveyance. Your [torn] own

------

* This contract is printed in *Diplomatic Correspondence of
the Revolution*, I., 206.

Hammy, &c., are truly grateful to me, for I must confess my sufferings already on their account cannot easily be compensated for by any good fortune yet to come.

I hope the Commissioners will not delay an answer to Mr. M. and my joint letter by Capt Thompson. Be so good as to inform Mr. Deane that I have advised Penet, and he has promised complyance, to pay Mr. D. the proceeds of 86 hhds. of tobacco, received in March last, and I think it will not be difficult to settle the business with Sollier, provided Mr. Deane will let me know how much he has received on the different funds, viz—on account of the £10,000 salary; on account of £20,000 sterling, ordered to be paid him solely, and whether anything on account of the tobacco. Mr. Gruel & Penet have promised to settle everything fully and fairly. Mr. M. does the same, but I have not yet been able to get a sight of his accounts or papers; tho' in a fortnight, I hope to get things in some order, or at least in a way to it. I find a great deal of management is requisite, and am determined to persevere.

The two prizes last bro't in being private property, by my consent the captains* put into mine and Mr. Williams hands. He does all the business un-

*Captains Babson and Kendrick. Babson in 1780 commanded the *Phœnix*, a brig of fourteen guns, belonging to the Tracys of Newburyport.

der my direction.   Keep this to yourself; let the
knowledge come from other quarters.   The privateers I have ordered to sea immediately, for fear of
accidents, but the captains do not seem to be in a
hurry to go.   However, I shall hasten them away.*
Best respects to Mr. Izard and family.†

---

* "Since writing the above, the two Jamaica prizes are, by
order of court, arrested, and it remains doubtful whether they
will not be restored to the original proprietors.   The captain of
one of the privateers on his passage took on board a lady, who
was prisoner on board an American privateer, bound for Boston.
This he did from motives of humanity.   On his arrival at Paim-
beuf, she wrote to her brother, a merchant at Nantes, who came
down, and hoping to get the consignment of the prizes, offi-
ciously advised the captain to report them as ships laden at St.
Eustatia, which they did, and on their arrival at Nantes, consigned the prizes to Messrs. Lee and Williams, who immediately
made a private sale of them.   Meantime the owners being acquainted with the proceeding, and knowing that the ships and
cargoes, by being regularly entered, were in the hands of the
custom house, lodged claims showing that they had been
falsely entered, and were English property captured by American privateers, and consequently by treaty could not be sold in
France.   This obliged the government to arrest the prizes, or
openly violate the treaty.   Mr. Williams came up a few days
since, and presented a memorial on the subject, but I fear he
will receive an unfavorable answer."   *Silas Deane to Robert
Morris*, 23 August, 1777.   Full satisfaction was afterwards obtained for the captors of the prizes.   "A fresh proof of the good
will and generosity of this court, and their determination to
cultivate the friendship of America."   *The Commissioners to
the Committee of Foreign Affairs*, 28 February, 1778.   See
Deane's Narrative, 41.

† Addressed to Monsr. Lotsom.

TO ARTHUR LEE.

My dear Brother:

This day I received the 26th, and am obliged by the intelligence. The copy shall be preserved. The paper of the 22d. was received before I left Paris, and you took it. Another might be got for writing for. Let me advise you not to be too forward in any business; 'tis the policy of some people by impudent and imprudent conduct to create difficulties and distress, and then leave the burthen of getting out of them upon others. The Bastile business* should rest as it is for me, but in all cases I would only move when the *old* General led the way and was first engaged beyond retreating. This morning the two prizes and their cargoes were seized by order of Government. Mr. Williams talks of setting off to-night for Paris; if he does not, shall write more fully to-morrow, at present have only to say the two captains of the privateers have in every instance acted directly contrary to my advice. Neither prayers, entreaties, threats or orders would make them act otherwise than they have done. The persuasive eloquence of the Rum overbalanced everything else.

They are still in port, but positive orders have been sent down this day to them in writing to go away immediately; but this, I expect, they will

---

* Imprisonment of Hodge.

disobey, as they have done everything else. I do
not blame the government, for I think they cou'd
not have acted otherwise. All that has happen'd
there are a number of witnesses to testify I foretold
wou'd happen unless there was an alteration of
conduct here.* 3 rich Carolina men are taken
with pilots on board in the mouth of Bourdeaux
River. Will this be allowed?

    Adieu.   [No Signature.]†

TO THE SECRET COMMITTEE.

        NANTES, 1 September, 1777.

Gentlemen :

I wrote you 11th ultimo, via Boston, and the
13th, via No. Carolina, advising my being here to

---

* Vergennes informed the Commissioners, 16 July, 1777, on
the return of Wickes from his second cruize, that orders had
been sent to the ports at which American privateers had entered to detain them until sufficient security could be obtained
that they would return directly to America, and for the departure of their prizes. Franklin and Deane replied on the
17th that before the receipt of Vergennes' letter corresponding
orders had been given to Wickes, Nicholson and Johnson,
which these captains were preparing to obey. To the Commissioners the court "privately professes a real friendship, wishes
success to our cause, winks at the supplies we obtain here as
much as it can without giving open grounds of complaint to
England, privately affords us very essential aids, and goes on
preparing for war." 8 September, 1777.

† Addressed to "Mr. Lotsom, chez Mon⁵ Grand, Banquier,
Paris."

take on myself the department you have been pleased to honor me with the appointment, viz., of superintending the commercial concerns of America in Europe in conjunction with Mr. Thos. Morris. As your appointment was made in January last, it is not improper for me to mention the [*instructions ?*] did not get here sooner than the beginning of last month. The latter end of April I received by ye penny post in London, a letter from ye Honb^{le} Silas Deane, dated in Paris the 30th of March, informing me that the Secret Committee had appointed me to superintend their commercial business in Europe, and desiring my answer immediately whether I would accept of ye appointment, that he might advise ye committee thereof. I answered him in a few days saying I would come over as soon as I could venture to stir, having respect to my personal liberty, which at that time was in some danger, being continually watched in consequence of a wicked information being given ye Secretary of State by one Digname,* of which you may have seen some account in ye public papers. Being advised by other letters that ye public

---

* In the London Chronicle, 13 March, 1777, is recorded the evidence against David Brown Dignam for forging an appointment to an office in the Dublin custom house, which he disposed of for £1000 to an enthusiastic place hunter. Mr. Brown also testified that he had purchased from Dignam for a like sum an appointment as writer of the London Gazette.

service required my immediate attendance on this side ye water, I left London ye 7th of June for Paris, leaving behind me all my family, property to ye amount of upwards of ten thousand pounds sterling in ye hands of persons from whom it was utterly impossible to withdraw it in so short a time, a great deal of which, tho' in specialties, I am informed has since been refused to be paid, in consequence of my coming away, and there is no method of compulsion as things are unhappily situated between G. B. and America. As soon as I arrived in Paris I applied to ye commissioners, Dr. Franklin and Mr. Deane, Mr. Lee being then at Berlin, to know if they had received any letters or instructions from ye Committee for me authorizing me to act for them. They answered they had not, and advised me jointly not to come down here until ye former transactions of Mr. Morris were settled, as a gentleman had been here some time on that business, which they undersood was a good deal derang'd. I waited accordingly till the latter end of July, when ye Commissioners informed me that they were advised from hence that Mr. Morris was in possession of my appointment, and had been so for some months, tho' I have never received any letter from him on that or any other subject, and as ye gentlemen had not been [able to bring] about any settlement, they thought it advisable for me to proceed on ye business without delay.

I came here the 4 ulto., since which I have used
every exertion to bring the parties to some settlement, who have been hitherto intrusted with your
property and concerns at this place, but as yet, all
my efforts have been in vain. It appears that all
your remittances to this place lately, have been
by Morris put into the hands of Mr. Penet, who is
in partnership with Mr. Pliarne, and by Mr. Penet
into the hands of Mr. James Gruel, who seems to
have transacted all yᵉ buiness that has been done
tho' not in his own name. Mr. Gruel's accounts
seem so perplexed and complicated, that from what
I am told by the different parties, having not been
able to procure a sight of any books, accounts sale,
or invoices of goods shipped, it will be as difficult
for him as any body else to make a fair statement
of them. *Sometimes the transactions are in yᵉ
name of yᵉ Congress, sometimes in Mr. Penet's,
sometimes in Mr. Morris's name, without any regularity or written orders for so doing, by which
means the Congress will often stand debtor for the
things to Mr. Morris, Mr. Gruel, and Messrs.
Pliarne & Penet in their different accounts.* However, it seems to me at present that Mr. Gruel has
received all your remittances and furnished such
returns and payments as have been made, after he
was in cash, for I do not find that he is disposed to
advance a shilling, tho' he talks of being very
largely in advance; but then he forgets the value

of several cargoes that he has sold, and not yet brought to account, which if done would, I believe, bring ye balance against him. Particularly ye cargoe of 774 whole, and 143 half barrels of rice bro't here since I arrived in ye Hancock & Adams, which by Mr. Dorsius* in Charlestown, was consigned solely to Mr. Thos. Morris, who *contrary to my request*, put it into ye hands of Mr. Penet and he as usual put it into ye hands of Mr. Gruel. I will persevere in endeavoring to get these transactions settled, but in the meantime would take ye liberty of advising that no more remittances or payments be made either to Mr. Gruel or Messrs. Pliarne & Penet, until a full and explicit account be rendered of all former transactions; and least ye difficulties already experienced should be continued, it may be well for you to write to both of them, or at least to Messrs. Pliarne & Penet, with whom you have only corresponded hitherto, desiring they will come to an immediate settlement with me. The Honb^{le} Silas Deane writes me thus ye 27th ulto.:

" Of the £20,000 ordered me by Congress I have not received one shilling, which Mr. Morris very well knows, and that I have repeatedly urged him on ye subject, as a very important commission remains unexecuted for want of it, and myself exposed to blame un-

---

* Of the firm of Livinius, Clarkson & Dorsius.

til it shall be known that I had not the means of executing y.ᵉ order of Congress. As to y.ᵉ £10,000, we have, I judge, received about 70,000 livres. Orders were indeed given for our receiving 120,000 livres in y.ᵉ whole, but these orders, for reasons unknown to us, have been countermanded, and we at this moment are not only without one shilling of that sum ordered us, but in advance for our expenses. This is y.ᵉ general situation of this affair.''

As soon as any value comes into my hands, y.ᵉ first object will be to close y.ᵉ sum ordered to ye commissioners, and afterwards to enable others that you have ordered goods from to comply with those orders, always having regard to those things that appear most essentially necessary for y.ᵉ public service. As I find you have agents in y.ᵉ different States to ship such goods as you intend for Europe, who sometimes order returns to be made in y.ᵉ vessels to y.ᵉ particular state from whence they came, should be glad you would say whether such orders are to be comply'd with, when the situation of affairs here will admit thereof. The 25th ulto., the Abigail, Capt. Jerow, arrived here from Charlestown, with 300 whole and 30 half barrels of rice on your account. Mr. Dorsius has ordered y.ᵉ Abigail to be freighted with salt on your account, to any part of y.ᵉ continent, which shall be done without delay. In my opinion it will be always prudent to give every Captain who sails for you, written in-

structions to make the first friendly port in Europe
that he can, as care will be taken to fix on a proper
correspondent in every port to do ye needful in case
of any of your vessels' arrival there; and if they
should happen to get into any little bye port, where
no such correspondent is settled, it will be easy
for ye captains to send an express or write to me
here, where I think of establishing my general headquarters, as being the most central and convenient
to all ye different ports in France and Spain. The
Captains should be also informed not to speak with
any ship whatever at sea, and generally to make
for a different port from that which he clears out,
which may prevent the bad effects that too often
have arisen already from ye information of spies, or
those who fall into ye enemy's hands. Would it
not be well to have a clause in all charter parties,
that ye insurance and charter shall be void if y^e
owner's captain does not strictly conform to such
written orders as you or your agents may give him?
As the most shameful of all piratical acts., viz.,
running away with your ships and valuable cargoes, has not only been authorized but encouraged
in England by highly rewarding the pirates, as in
ye cases of ye Dickenson,* Aurora,† Mercer, etc.,

---

* The story is told in Force, *American Archives, Fourth
Series*, IV., 658, 659.

† "The Aurora, John Hutchinson master, late the Oxford, of
Glasgow, taken by the rebels, with a party of the 71st regiment

would it not be proper to put in every ship that has a valuable cargo on board, soldiers to do duty as mariners, which will answer the double purpose of securing your property and gradually increasing your number of seamen, which you want sufficiently already and will want much more by and bye, as it is most likely that when the British troops are driven from ye continent the war will be continued for a time by depredations on your sea coasts, until your marine is sufficient to drive

---

on board, and carried into Virginia, is brought into Liverpool, laden with 412 hogsheads of tobacco, on account of the Congress, and bound to Nantz or Bordeaux. She was navigated by 15 men, and had a Mr. Hall on board in the capacity of a supercargo; eight of the crew were Englishmen, and had all been prisoners in America. About the longitude of 16 W. and lat. 47, William Turner, boatswain of a ship, and who had previously sounded the inclinations of the English sailors and found them willing to assist in seizing the vessel and carrying her to England, secured the captain and supercargo in the cabbin, while his companions secured the American sailors upon deck; and they were all soon overpowered, and Turner, who took the command, shaped his course for Liverpool, where he arrived the 29th instant. All the American papers were secured, and the cargo, at the present price of tobacco, is of great value."— *London Chronicle*, 1 February, 1777. "Five of the American sailors assisted in the seizure: Jesse Jenkinson, Jesse Topping, Gilbert Welch, Joseph Walker, and Hugh Johnson. Each of them was awarded £914 as their share in the prize, and each Englishman received £1828." *Do.*, 9 July, 1777. Of the *Mercer* the only reference to be found is a sale of the cargo of tobacco for £31,205. The vessel was carried into Whitehaven by its crew.

yᵉ invaders from your seas. Especially too as no cartel is settled for sailors, and while you are discharging all that you take, those taken on board your ships of war are confined as pirates, and those taken on board your merchantmen are forced on board yᵉ British ships of war to aid in killing or enslaving their countrymen. Some kind of retaliation seems necessary. I trust that my attention and diligence will justify yᵉ confidence you have reposed in me, as I am, etc.

P. S. Please to put your letters for me under cover to Mr. J. D. Schweighauser, at this place.*

TO RICHARD HENRY LEE.

NANTES, 1st September, 1777.

My dear Sir:

Inclosed you have a letter, which, after carefully perusing, you will please to seal and deliver, provided you think it proper. If you do not, you are at liberty to destroy it.† The facts are all strictly

---

* "Mr. Schweighauser was a very solid merchant, highly esteemed by everybody, and highly approved by the Court." John Adams, *Diary*, III., 129. Arthur Lee thought that the intention of the Committee of Secret Correspondence was to place the established credit and character of Schweighauser as a check on Penet, "who had not such recommendations as they [the committee] could wish." Schweighauser was also thought to have an influence with the government.

† Letter to the Secret Committee of the same date.

true, but still circumstances may be such with you as to render it imprudent to mention the names of those who have acted so outragiously ill in your service. Mr. M[orris] in particular exceeds any painting I can draw, as he is actually in a continual state of madness from inebriety and intemperance. This you will keep to yourself, unless the publick service should absolutely require your disclosing it. Mr. Gruel and Penet are, if anything, treated too gently. Nothing farther must go through their hands, at least until they come to a full and fair settlement and refund the public money which they now withhold. They throw all the blame on Mr. M., but he, culpable as he may be, is not more blameable than them.

You will probably hear some complaint from Col. Mason about not paying his bills. If you do, pray request of him to suspend his judgment 'till he hears from me, and he will then be satisfied that his money is safe, and perhaps much safer than in the hands he meant to put it.

Sometime this month I will endeavor to get my family over here, for having once entered on the public business there is no retreating. I find a multitude of perplexities will be to encounter, however, I do not fear surmounting them if there is the same steadiness and perseverance in others as in myself; and as I take it for granted that you have had some share in my appointment, it shall

be my study to do you credit as well as myself. I
think the affairs of Virginia would be somewhat
better managed in my hands than where they are
at present; in this you will move or not, just as
you find the leading gentlemen disposed, especially
those to the southward, for I would not wish to be
employed unless it is with the general approbation.
Communicate this to Loudoun, if you please.
When once a regular system is settled, and things
get into a proper train, which there is reason to
believe will be the case in two or three months,
there will be full leisure on my hands to manage
any publick or private business that can come
here from Virginia—I mean to Europe—during the
continuance of the war.

Your son L[udwell] you have been advised is at
his studies in Paris. Thom is here and seems not
averse to the mercantile line, therefore will probably remain with me. These boys behave well
and I hope will prove a comfort to you and pro-
tectors of their infant relations. This is a dear
place to live in, and to those accustomed to the
English manners, not very agreeable. However, I
shall not repine, if the publick is benefited by my
services. So far removed as this place is from the
center of motion both in France and England, it
will be very seldom that any fresh intelligence can
be communicated from hence; but in general my
idea of European politics is, that King George

would rather risk the loss of his three kingdoms than give up the favorite plan of subduing America, so that nothing but necessity will make him decline persevering in the mad scheme, and I believe *that necessity* will happen next winter if the British armies should be unsuccessful this campaign, which is more than probable, if the accounts we have from thence are to be depended on. France in pursuit of her own interest will feed both parties to keep up the contest; England with promises and professions, and America with more substantial aid when she appears to want it, tho' all under the rose, to prevent an open rupture with England. This conduct though at present it increases the difficulties of America will finally prove advantageous, as she will close the war without any European fetters or engagements. If unanimity and perseverance in America does but continue, she must infallibly succeed in vindicating her liberties and independence, and from what precedes, it is plain she must not too much rely on France or any other power in Europe, but depend on herself. 'Tis no small comfort to reflect that she seems fully able to support her own rights. I have often tho't that Virginia, Maryland and North Carolina might be effectually guarded from invasion by a strong fort on Cape Henry to prevent the entrance of a fleet into Chesapeake Bay. This is certainly worthy of examination by your most skilful engineers.

September 10th. Before this was finished Mr.
King delivered me here your favor from Williamsburg in June. Fauntleroy* has turned out as I
always expected, but there is no helping it now;
but I hope Ellis will do well, as the specimen of
the accounts he has [sent show an atte]ntion to
things that have not been regarded before. I am
fully sensible from my own experience how much
your private interest must have suffered by your
application to public concerns, therefore, instead
of complaining, have to thank you heartily for what
you have done for me. The letters you mention
having wrote from Philadelphia have not come to
hand, nor have I received any from London; I
almost dread to hear what it has to say about my
mercantile concerns. Bad enough they are, I dare
say. Your boys will be taken care of as long as I
am able to do it. L——'s expenses are moderate,
but I fear Thom's has been otherwise at this place,
tho' I have not yet asked for Mr. Schweighauser's
account yet, not being quite convenient to discharge it. Your admonitions to *industry* and frugality may not be of disservice. Their expences in
England were as reasonable as you could wish. I
have repeatedly sent accounts sale and accounts
current to my correspondents, which suppose have
all miscarried, shall therefore send duplicates by

---

* Manager at Green Spring.

Mr. King, who I hope will arrive safe some time in the winter. If Congress should alter my department as you mention, my poor abilities shall be at their service, as I think their generosity will never suffer a man to be ruined who dedicated his time to them. As to the connections you mention with French merchants, it will not only be difficult to accomplish any such thing on account of their strangeness in business, but disagreeable and perhaps ruinous on account of the government, which either forms the merchants, or they form the government, so that without an alteration this can never be a country of very great commerce, tho' it has advantages superior to almost any country in Europe. The merchants here, as far as I have hitherto experienced, either cannot, or will not, advance a shilling to America, either to the public, or to individuals, so that I must begin the world, and go on as well as [I can, in takin]g such commissions as may fall in my way, which may be enough for me, if my countrymen have any confidence in me. I will, however, endeavor to get a ship sent to Virginia this winter if things should look better than they do at present; for we have Burgoyne's account of what passed at or near Ticonderoga to the 8th of July. We are told that Howe is gone to Boston, which some say he will take easily. This I cannot believe. I wrote to Loudoun since I came here, and shall write a short letter now. You forgot to enclose me his account of what was passing in the Jersies. I hope to see America yet, one of the most flourishing empires or states in the world.

My earnest love to all! yours and to Dr. and Mrs. S[hippen] and their little ones. I am most truly and affectionately yours.

P. S. Should Congress resume the idea of sending me to Vienna or Prussia, which at present I presume they have dropt, they should send a commission for each, that both may be tryed, for if nothing further can be done, I am inclined to think that either with one or the other some very beneficial commercial engagements may be made, as most of the capital articles you want, especially for the army, are to be had better and cheaper in Germany than anywhere else in Europe, if funds can be only established for paying for them. Both these powers want much to become commercial.

TO PATRICK HENRY.

NANTES, 3 September, 1777.

Your goodness will, I hope, excuse me for y�: liberty I have taken in putting under cover to your care some letters for my friends. The frequent miscarriages of letters that I have experienced for some years past induces me now to take that method of conveyance which seems most likely to be attended with success. Being settled here in ye public service, it would greatly add to my satisfaction if I can be of any use to my native country, as she will always have a right, and may certainly command at all times my services. Far removed from ye busy scenes of politics, it is not in my power to give you any late intelligence, but in general I think America must depend on her own efforts for working out her salvation from slavery, and not rely too much on any European power. Those States that are not at present ye scenes of war may be very usefully employed in weeding ye bad or suspected plants from ye wholesome corn. This work will be best effected whilst ye din of war is far off. A substantial and explicit oath of allegiance to ye State should be universally administered, and I think it will be found that those who bogle at such an oath while ye British forces are at a distance will to a man aid them when near, either by arms or otherwise, in destroying the liberties of their country. A plain act for describing and punishing of treason against ye State, properly enforced, may do much good and prevent a great deal of mischief.

If this campaign should, contrary to expectation, prove very favorable to ye British forces, it may be expected that next summer they will make some attempt on Virginia, in which they may be effectually disappointed by employing this winter in con-structing a strong fort on Cape Henry, so as to prevent a fleet entering Chesapeak Bay. I am not absolutely certain that a fort there would answer this purpose, but by ye best information I can get from seafaring men it appears to me very feasible, and I have seen some old reports to ye government in England by skilfull engineers who had been on ye spot about fifty years ago, where this very place is pointed out as necessary and proper to be done for ye security of Virginia from invasion. In this work, no doubt, Maryland and North Carolina would cheerfully assist, as they would receive nearly as much benefit from it as Virginia in the security of their property and ye protection of their commerce . . .

TO ARTHUR LEE.

NANTES, 5 September, 1777.

My dear Sir:

I received yours yesterday of the 30th ulto. Have only a moment to say two small vessels are just arrived from Virginia. Their intelligence from Ticonderoga is a fortnight later than Burgoyne's letter; they say about 16 or 17 July, the British were attacked and defeated with the loss of 1000 men killed wounded and prisoners, and 600 of their Battoes burnt. You have from Congress despatches, left two daies ago, bound to Bordeaux, but not so late as this Intelligence, which is given by a sensible gentleman passenger, who read it in a Baltimore paper of July 29, which is in a vessel expected here every moment. I shall write fully, first post. This goes in a moment. Yrs, &c.

You have a line from R. H. L. The news from Ticonderoga seems credibly told. The B. troops advanced to Ft. Edward, Gen¹. St. Clair got behind, attacked the rear; the front attack'd at same time bro't on a general defeat. The British retired to a mountain, leaving their Battoes to be destroyed. I have a great number of papers, the most material you shall have to forward to London per next post, for I have not had time to read one, for my room has been full since 7 o'clo. in the morning. The news gladdens many hearts that were quite sunk last night. Mr. Dobrée* has a letter for you from R. H. L. I know 'tis dated in June, and being large I advise it not to be sent per post for fear of accidents. A private hand will carry it in two daies from this.†

* Peter Frederick Dobrée, in partnership with Jean Daniel Schweighauser.

† "I can hardly tell what to say on politics, for the F— court seems so wavering that one can't know one day how the wind will blow the next. One hour 'tis all war; the next 'tis all peace. We have heard of ye advances Burgoyne has made at Ticonderoga to the 8th of July, as you may see in the Gazette Capt. S. [Skinner] carrys to his Excellency, the Governor. A

TO RICHARD HENRY LEE.

NANTES, 18 September, 1777.

The above is a copy of an original that went to Capt. Skinner under cover to the Governor of Virginia. You have enclosed a copy of the French minister's letter which will show you very plainly the policy of this court. The copy is authentic you may be assured; and it is left to you to determine whether in political prudence it ought to be made public; but at the same time, I think it will be wise to preserve and even to record the letter, as it may hereafter be of use to answer claims that you may be sure will be made, whenever interest prevails, to acknowledge your independency. I shall forbear making any strictures on this letter, being convinced that your penetrating eye will see through the whole in a minute, and also that you will be satisfied the salvation of America must depend on her own virtue and exertions. Depend not on any solid assistance from hence; the policy is to keep up the war as long as possible to weaken

---

little more success on the part of the British troops will be sufficient to encourage G. B. to go on with another campaign, for which America should certainly provide in time ; for if she does not, the war may linger on for some years. But I am firmly persuaded that if America will but continue firm and unanimous, and her sons do not aid in cutting each other's throats, that she must be finally victorious and triumphant, which God grant, I say." *W. Lee to William Aylett*, 10 September, 1777.

both parties, so that F. may be arbiter of each; at
the same time they demand the whole benefit of
the American commerce. I know not what engagements the Commissioners may have come into,
nor can I enter into the spirit of those who would
spill the blood of thousands, and ruin a whole innocent people to pacify private resentments; but
with absolute certainty I can say, if France was to
give America one million sterling per year, she
would be overpaid in the advantages she at present
receives in the monopoly of the American commerce, which they shackle in a most shameful
manner. On this subject you shall have my tho'ts
more at large soon, and also the reasons for my
fixed opinion that Congress should immediately
repeal the resolution prohibiting the importation
of British or Irish manufacturers. My advice
would be to annul the resolution in as few words
as possible without giving any reason for so doing.
Let the wiseacres on this side conjecture what they
please. The prohibition was wise and well intended when first resolved on; but at present my*
opinion is that a continuation will nearly, if not
quite, ruin America. Your conduct must entirely
be regulated by your own particular situation,
which you can judge of better than any person at
this distance, and not from any regard whatever to
promises or professions from a people to whom the
term Punica fides may be applyed with infinite pro-

priety. You can't be too much on your guard against strange adventurers whether in the military or mercantile line, however well they may come recommended, for you may safely take it for granted that 19 out of 20 are no more than the ragamuffins of Europe. Your knowledge of the world will inform you, that letters of recommendation are too often designed to serve the giver as well as the receiver. I hear that the appointment to Vienna has been made, and that the commission and Instructions were sent in the Independence, Capt. Young, which vessel is not arrived, and from the length of time since she sailed, there is every reason to believe she is either taken or lost.* I understand by chance information that the Commissioners have sent the Reprisal, Capt. Wickes, off, with despatches in answer to those they received by a vessel from Baltimore that arrived some time ago at Bordeaux, tho' she sailed some time after Captain Young. How the Commissioners at Paris approve of the new arrangements made by Congress I know not, but from the knowledge I have of a particular character, of whom something has been hinted before, I should not be surprised to hear that insinuations have been made of the inability or something to that purpose. Let others act as they please. I

---

* Captain Young arrived at Passy September 29th, with despatches from Congress, and among them William Lee's commission and instructions.

flatter myself that your friend's conduct will always bear the strictest scrutiny, and that his assiduous attention to whatever is intrusted to his care will obtain success. I wait with extream impatience and anxiety for the issue of the present campaign, for on it a great deal depends. Let it end as it will, no attention should be spared for a body of cavalry similar to the English light horse, and to provide in time every necessary for another campaign, and that earlier than any one yet.

The appointment to Naples of I—d* is proper, for he is a man of fortune and consideration in his country, and it should always be a rule to be cautious of employing people on this side the water who have neither character or property to lose; some such, who have by their wickedness, their debaucheries, their follies and their vices, done a great deal of mischief already, have by intrigue obtained recommendations, as I understand, both to Congress and some members thereof individually. Take care of such characters. I am sure you will take all the care that is possible of my property, and you may rely on my attention to your boys here. Best love and affection attend you all, and with the sincerest regard I am, &c.

P. S. The renewal of the order from Mr. de Sartines was occasioned by two West India mer-

---

* Izard.

chant prizes, bro't in here by Captains Babson and
Kendrick, commanders of the privateers belonging
to Messrs. Babcock & Blair in Boston, and Winthrop, Sergeant & Co. at Cape Anne. These
prizes and their cargoes have been seized, and are
now detained by government here, after the greatest part was sold. The Captains were offered
£16,000 sterling for the two, and the buyers to
take all risks. This they refused, saying they
would rather burn them than take that price.
Afterwards they put them under the care of myself and Mr. Jonathan Williams, a Bostonian, and
nephew of Dr. Franklin, to sell; but their own
conduct was such that it occasioned their seizure,
which I not only foresaw, but foretold to many
here, therefore avoided receiving any part of y^e
goods or money, to steer as clear as possible of
blame. The whole negotiation was left to Mr. W.,
the captains' countryman, I only advising; every
part of which the captains thought fit to disregard,
and now they blame everybody but themselves.
However, it is a happiness that many here can
witness to the probity of my conduct, particularly
Mr. Wm. Blake, a gentleman of one of the first
fortunes and families in South Carolina.

TO RICHARD HENRY LEE.

Paris, 7 October, 1777.

My dear Brother:

Just arrived from Nantes, where I wrote to you, and London, by Capt.ⁿ Rob.ᵗ Barron of Virginia.*
* * *

Just this moment is put into my Hands the Instructions and appointment to Vienna and Berlin. The business is of great magnitude and requires much consideration; therefore cannot do more, by this conveyance than acknowledge the receipt of them, which I have done by a letter to the President of Congress, to whom I can only address myself, having received no letter from any Committee, but the letter of Instructions, which is signed by the Hon.ᵇˡᵉ John Hancock, as President of Congress.

I hope a great deal is not expected, very speedily, from the issues of my Negotiations; for I am sure if anything material is accomplished, it must be by a long, laborious and tedious operation. I shall write you very fully in twelve days; shall only add now, that your sons are well, and that I shall take care of them as long as I can.†

---

* He set out from Nantes, 2 October, 1777.

† "Your goodness, I trust, will excuse me for requesting the favor of you to inform the honorable Congress of the United States of America that this moment (on my arrival here from Nantes, where I have been discharging the public trust reposed

THE MORRIS INCIDENT, OCTOBER, 1777.*

Of what occurred at Passy between William Lee
and the commissioners on October 13th, we have a

---

in me by the Secret Committee of Congress), were put into my
hands the instructions and appointment of me as Commissioner at the Courts of Vienna and Berlin; but not having had
an opportunity of a conference on the subject with the Commissioners here, it is not in my power at present to enlarge on
the business, more especially as I am told that this express is to
be immediately despatched. I understand another will be sent
in ten or twelve days, by which opportunity I shall write fully.
I have only further to entreat that you will assure the honorable Congress of my steady attachment to that respectable
body, and to the rights of America, which I shall invariably and
on all occasions endeavor to support and maintain." *William
Lee to the President of Congress*, 5 October, 1777.

"Dec. 11th. Mr. [Arthur] L[ee] answered a letter he had
received from the Prussian Minister of State, informing him
that a commissioner could not yet be received in a public character at Berlin, and that he did not conceive that any additional light could be given to a plan of commerce at present."

* "Thomas Morris, who I informed before, was an agent for
the Congress at Nantes, and the person appointed by them to do
all their shipping business, &c., has led such a dissipated life for
some months past that Doctor Franklin and Mr. Deane thought
it prudent to appoint another person in his place (say Jonathan
Williams, a nephew of Doctr Franklin). In consequence of
Morris's behaviour, Deane and Franklin wrote to the Congress
(and not to his brother, who put him under their protection),
complaining of the same, and desiring that he might be removed, as he was a detriment to their cause and a disgrace to
America in general. As soon as this news got to America his
brother, Robert Morris, apply'd to the Congress and told them
he would be happy to know if the business transacted by his

record by those present. Izard wrote as follows to Franklin, 17 June, 1778:

"I received a letter in October last from Mr. William Lee, one of the joint commercial agents for conducting the affairs of the Congress in this kingdom, desiring my attendance at your house in Passy, and informing me that he had something of importance to lay before the Commissioners. I accordingly attended, and heard an account of some very extraordinary abuses and embarrassments in the commercial depart-

---

brother here did not merit their approbation. They replied in the affirmative, and voted that the said Morris should be continued in his office, and further, they do not censure the conduct of Deane and Franklin a little; they say he stands too much on trifles. Morris gives out that Deane is to be recalled, which he asserts he has on black and white. The letter from his brother to Deane and Franklin I have seen. Morris, of Phila, therein informs them that they might have wrote to him, and not to the Congress, complaining of his brother's behaviour, and concludes, after many severe reprimands, 'that 'tis not all the Commissioners in France that are able to remove his brother from his present office, in spite of all the nephews or relations they may have or wish to provide for.' . . . Before this news arrived, Carmichael informed me that he imagined Deane would be removed from his present employment and appointed to one of less consequence." *Lupton to Eden*, 23 September, 1777. "The affair between Morris and Deane makes no small noise here, as Morris has pasted up a copy of his letter at Nantes, in order that every American may see the same.

"The affair between Morris and the Commissioners here has not a little humbled their pride. They have promised never to mention anything to the Congress concerning him in future." *Lupton to Eden*, 15 October, 1777.

ment, owing to the misconduct of Mr. Thomas Morris,
late of the joint commercial agents, and to the claim
which certain persons made to the management of the
Congress at Nantes. Mr. Lee complained of great obstructions, which he had met with from these circumstances, that so far from receiving any assistance from
the Commissioners, they seemed to have encouraged
the persons who opposed him in the discharge of his
duty, and that he had repeatedly written to the Commissioners for their support, without ever having been
able to obtain the favor of an answer. He expressed
his desire of returning to Nantes, and using his endeavors to prevent the repetition of such abuses as had
been stated, and did not doubt but with the support of
the Commissioners he should be able to render this
material service to the public. The support which he
required was a letter from the Commissioners, addressed to all such captains of ships as were in the service of the United States, informing them that he was
an agent properly authorized by Congress to manage
their commercial concerns in this country, and that it
would be proper for them to follow his instructions.
This request, which appeared to me extremely reasonable, was to my astonishment rejected both by you and
Mr. Deane.

"This appeared the more extraordinary to me, as
you both acknowledged that you were perfectly convinced of the truth of what Mr. Lee had stated to you,
and said you had laid these abuses before Congress,
and complained in the strongest terms against Mr.
Thomas Morris, whose misconduct had occasioned

some of them; that Congress had given you a tacit reproof, by taking no notice of the complaints you had made, and that Mr. Robert Morris, a member of the Committee for Foreign Affairs, had given you *a rap over the knuckles* for having made them. I begged you to consider that the silence of Congress, which you had construed into a reproof, might have been occasioned by the multiplicity of business they had to transact; or they might have attended to it, and their letter on the subject have miscarried. This you said could not have been the case, as the complaints to Congress against Mr. Morris made but part of your letter; there were several other matters contained in it which were all answered, and as the complaint against Mr. Morris was the only part unnoticed, you considered it as a reproof to you for having written to Congress about it. You had attempted once to correct the abuses which every body knew were practising at Nantes, to a very scandalous degree. Mr. Robert Morris had misrepresented your good intentions, and had insinuated in his letter to Mr. Deane, of June 29th, that your complaints against his brother were made from interested motives, and that you wished him removed to make room for your nephew. As your conduct had in one instance, relative to the abuses at Nantes, been thus misrepresented, you were determined it should in no other, by adhering to your resolution of not meddling with them.

"Your reasons did not appear at all satisfactory to me, and I took the liberty of telling you so, which gave you very great offence. I was extremely sorry for it, but did not at that time, nor have I upon the most mature deliberation since, been able to conceive how it could have been avoided, consistent with my duty. I requested you to consider how unreasonable it was to allow your resentment against the Committee for a supposed tacit reproof, and against Mr. Robert Morris for what you called *a rap over the knuckles*, to operate to the prejudice, perhaps to the destruction, of the commercial concerns of the country. Your answer was direct and positive: 'If these consequences should happen, Mr. Robert Morris and the Committee must be answerable for them, but you are determined not to meddle with the matter.' In this determination Mr. Deane coöperated, and we parted without Mr. Lee's having been able to obtain any satisfaction on the subjects of his complaints, except a promise on your part to countermand an order you had given relative to the sale of one of the prizes at Nantes. The promise, however, I understand was not fulfilled. I most solemnly protest, that I believe this interview to have been the cause of your excluding me from all communications.''

After his arrival in America, Deane saw a copy of this letter, which had been sent to Congress by Izard, and recorded his recollections of the interview, in a communication dated 12 October, 1778:

"I recollect perfectly well the interview at Passy with Mr. William Lee, at which Mr. Izard was present, but I do not remember that any such letter as he describes was either desired or refused. I rather think that Mr. Izard misunderstood Dr. Franklin at the time, or that his memory has deceived him. The facts are these: The late Mr. Thomas Morris had a commission to act as commercial agent; his commission was entirely distinct from, and independent of the Commissioners; he, at least, construed it so himself from the beginning. We were very early informed of his irregularities, and admonished him, and advertised Congress of them. As we could get no account of the disposition of the prizes brought into France, and the expense of repairing and equipping the vessels of war fell on the Commissioners, Dr. Franklin and myself (Mr. A. Lee being then at Berlin) deputed Mr. Williams to take the care of the prizes into his own hands, and ordered the captains to account with him. On Mr. William Lee's arrival at Nantes, he joined with Mr. Morris in writing a severe letter to the Commissioners on what they had done, in which they complained that the office or department of commercial agent was broken in upon, and that we had no power over it. Dr. Franklin, at the desire of Mr. A. Lee and myself, prepared an answer,* in which the reason of our orders was given, and Mr. Morris's conduct urged as our principal motive, but that as he, Mr. William Lee, was there, we would recall our commission from Mr. Williams. Mr. Arthur Lee would not agree to the form of the letter, and, after much dispute upon it, a second was written, when Mr. Arthur Lee observed that his brother was coming to Paris soon to receive his commission for Vienna and Berlin, and as there were then no prizes in port, or expected, the matter might rest. This is the

---

* Printed in the introduction, p. 53 *ante.*

reason why Mr. W. Lee's letters were not answered.
He came to Paris soon after, and represented the con-
fused state in which affairs were at Nantes, and urged
the interposition of the Commissioners to put the whole
agency into his hands. The situation of Mr. William
Lee at that time was precisely this: he had never received any commission, either from Congress or their
committee for the commercial agency, whilst Mr.
Thomas Morris was, and had been, in the possession of
a commission, and in the exercise of the agency.

"Congress had made Mr. William Lee their commissioner to the Courts of Vienna and Berlin, each of
which places is at least a thousand miles from the
scenes of our commerce, without saying anything about
his former appointment, from which it was natural to
suppose his former appointment had been considered
as superseded by the new. We had received intelligence that the information we had given of Mr. Morris'
conduct had been received and read in Congress, and
that Congress notwithstanding chose to continue him
in this situation.* We thought it very extraordinary
that we should be applied to to interfere where Congress, knowing the facts, had declined to interfere, and
still more so, that we should be requested to put (what
indeed was not in our power) the commercial agency
into the hands of a gentleman who must execute it by
deputies; himself at a distance too great either to see
or to correct the abuses that might be practised. The

---

* How this information was conveyed to the Commissioners
is told in the *Deane Papers*, 120, 121.

letter referred to by Mr. Izard was a letter to this purpose, and I remember well (for I avoided bearing any considerable part in the conversation) Dr. Franklin's reply, which was to this purpose, that Congress, by disregarding the information we had given, and continuing Mr. Morris, had impliedly censured our conduct. That Mr. Morris had treated us ill personally, for what we had done, and that Mr. William Lee ought to remember that he had himself, jointly with Mr. Morris, complained of our interfering, as he thought, in that department; and, therefore, he did not incline to subject himself to any further censures, or, as he expressed it, 'raps over the knuckles,' for meddling in the affair. We were, indeed, as much surprised as Mr. Izard appears to have been on the occasion, but our surprise arose from another cause; it was to find Mr. William Lee desirous of holding such a plurality of appointments, in their own nature incompatible with each other, and impossible to have been executed by the same person. But as one of the places was supposed to be a lucrative one, the subject was too delicate to be touched on by us.''

William Lee ''stated that in consequence of the powers given to Mr. Williams, a quarrel had been produced, which made it impossible to conduct the public business with effect till these were recalled and the Commissioners gave their support openly to the agents appointed by the Committee. He said, people in general could not determine who was Commercial Agent, and others took advantage of their mutual pretensions and endeavored to play one against the other. There was a prize, or prizes, lying stripped, plundered, and rotting; no one choosing to become purchaser, under an uncertainty of who had the true authority to sell. He therefore begged to know whether they would recall this order from Mr. Williams, and support him in the execution of his office.. The two eldest Commissioners professéd a willingness to recall the order, but positively refused to give them any support. Thus the meeting ended ineffectually." *Arthur Lee's Narrative.*

On October 7th the Commissioners had written to the Committee of Foreign Affairs: "We are sorry to find all the world acquainted here, that the Commissioners from Congress have not so much of your regard as to obtain the change of a single agent who disgraces us all. We say no more of this at present, contenting ourselves with the consciousness that we recommended that change from the purest motives, and that the necessity of it, and our uprightness in proposing it, will soon fully appear."

TO FRANCIS LIGHTFOOT LEE.

NANTES, 11 November, 1777.

* * * You have also a minute of some things that have been forwarded for the public use. It may be well to enquire about them. Nothing is expected in return except one million of livres that were borrowed on a very injudicious and losing contract for tobacco, which was made without the

least knowledge of the nature of the affair; nor do I know that the contractors had any authority for doing what they did. However, as luckily the time limited will expire before they can possibly comply with their engagement, in my thinking the money borrowed with interest should only be returned to the lenders. I wish you may find that this and the other money has been more judiciously expended than it has been borrowed.

With respect to myself, I know not by what means my line of business has been changed; most certainly the honor is increased, but the profit is greatly lessened, with the difficulty, labor, and hazard greatly enlarged. In the first line I could, and assuredly should, have been of great use to the public, as well as myself, especially if ye Secret Committee would support their own authority and show an insolent meddler* here that they would properly notice his presumption, in taking on himself in many instances to contravene their appointment and orders. In the present line I doubt my abilities, for however anxious and zealous, it must require both much time and more capacity than is common for a man not versed in the crooked paths of court to get into the mysteries of the most subtle cabinet of Europe, and besides, above 40 years old, it is somewhat awkward to go to school to learn

---

*Silas Deane.

languages. All this however must be essayed, and as soon as I find it will be agreeable to the concerned, I shall set out on my mission. I hope, however, it will be considered that having a family, it will be both inconvenient and expensive to move when once fixed. My plan is to move to the northward as soon as I find my presence will be acceptable, leaving Mrs. L. and her two little ones here for the winter. By the spring, I may be able to judge whether it is best to fix at Vienna or Berlin, when she and the children must follow. If nothing very material can be effected in Austria or Prussia, ought not a commissioner to be stationed in Holland; for tho' the Dutch would not receive one openly, yet 'tis possible that under the rose a loan of money might be negotiated much better than by the commissioners here.

Whether your affairs on this side have been as well conducted as they might have been, you perhaps can judge as well as me; but I may venture to assert, they will not be better until there is a clear line drawn and settled, and the commissioners are strictly restrained to ye political part, leaving mercantile business to the commercial agent as long as it is tho't proper to keep one. I have before mentioned a Mr. Carmichael to you, who is here. He is a native of Maryland, tho' of Scotch pedigree, and I believe a distant relation, some how or other, of Col. Lloyd's, at least he gives it out so.

I have had occasion to see and know a great deal of mankind; of all men I ever knew, I have the worst opinion of this man, and I beg you will strenuously oppose any thing that may be proposed, which may occasion any intercourse whatever between me and him, for I cannot trust him in the most distant manner, nor shall any consideration induce me to hold any correspondence or connection with him.*

I wish it was in my power to say anything decisive relative to the general disposition of affairs in your favor. I know not what they are writing about, whose particular duty it is to inform you truly of the disposition of Europe. In my opinion you ought principally to depend on yourselves, and at all events make every possible preparation for another campaign. We have heard of Burgoyne's drubbing Arnold to ye 20th of September, but should B. and his whole army to a man be cut off, and Howe be able to get into Philadelphia, it will be sufficient for a mad king and a wicked ministry to try another campaign. Make all the friends you can in Europe, but trust none of them more than needs must; for all that has, or will be done, will proceed more from enmity to Great Britain than love for you or ye glorious cause in which you are contending.

---

*See Adams' *Diary* III, 142.

There was an affair that happened at Nantes that has given me a great deal of uneasiness. I will state it fully, that you may be master of ye business, since I apprehend it will, or ought to be, ye subject of public consideration, and request you will not lose a moment in communicating to R. H. L. exactly what I say, as my time will not permit me to enlarge so much on it to him. On the 20th of August two New England privateers, commanded by Captains Babson and Kendrick, brought into Nantes two British West India ships with valuable cargoes as prizes.* Before I saw them they had got with an Irish tory at Nantes, to whom they communicated everything they had done, and fully informed him of their whole situation. They had besides in many other respects conducted themselves very imprudently. As soon as I got sight of them I gave them the best advice I was capable of giving. Afterwards they put ye sale of the prizes into the hands of Mr. Penet, a partner of Mr. Pliarne, whom you have seen, Jonathan Williams, a nephew of Dr. Franklin, and myself. As I had seen enough of the conduct of these people to make me doubtful of their prudence or discretion, I took no part of the conduct of ye business on myself farther than to advise Mr. Williams, who being a countryman of the two New England captains, I tho't would please

---

* William Lee to the Commissioners, 20 August, 1777, *ante.*

them best. However, unfortunately, no part of my advice was carried into execution, for ye business was carried on in so open a manner, and ye captains with their people acted so imprudently that before the vessels and cargoes were sold ye English ministry knew every circumstance relative to them, and on making application to ye French court the whole was seized, and has since, by order of the French ministry, been returned to ye former British owners.

It must not be forgot that just at the time of these prizes coming in, we heard at Nantes of a Mr. Hodge of Philadelphia being put into ye Bastile, on account of some irregular conduct in fitting out a privateer at Dunkirk, commanded by Capt. Conyngham, on private account, tho' it is hinted now that ye expence of ye outfit is to be placed to ye public account, for the scheme has not proved a profitable one. This intelligence made me apprehensive, and I instantly wrote a particular account of ye privateers and their prizes to the Commissioners at Paris, desiring their advice how we ought to proceed. From the date of my letter to ye time of ye prizes being seized, 10 daies elapsed, without their giving any answer or taking ye least notice of my letter, nor do I think since that they have made the least application on ye subject to ye French ministry, tho' Mr. Williams came up from Nantes on purpose to engage them

to do so. Indeed a *private* French gentleman*
undertook ye business for Mr. Williams, but as yet
with very little effect. This procedure will appear
very extraordinary when contrasted with the following circumstance mentioned to me in a letter from
Spain, received this day, where neither Dr. F. or
Mr. D. have acted as commissioners. Extract of
a letter:

"A prize sent into St. Sebastians, ye governor tho't
fitting to stop and prohibit the sale of ye cargo. The
ship and cargo was sold to a French merchant, who
immediately applied to ye Spanish ministry, orders
came by the return courier to ye governor to take off
the arrest, with orders not to intermeddle in future in
those matters. The ship and cargo was immediately
delivered up to ye purchaser."†

Thus you have a full and fair account of this
business which has given me infinite vexation in
every stage of it, because I am greatly apprehensive it may be productive of much mischief to y^e
general interest of America. From the unsettled
state of things with you, I can easily conceive that
many irregularities would easily arise, but I live
in hopes of seeing order grow from confusion, and

---

* Deane speaks of Chaumont as active in this affair.

† This affair was not settled so easily, for in January, 1778,
Arthur Lee was informed of the imprisonment at St. Sebastians
of the sailors "who carried in a prize made by an American privateer, and the seizure of the prize."

that in a little time every man will be kept to his proper business and be made to account regularly for every part of his conduct. With respect to my conduct relative to the prizes, I will refer at any time to ye testimony of Wm. Blake, Esqr, a gentleman of one of ye first fortunes and families in South Carolina, who was at Nantes the whole time and acquainted with the whole transactions. I still think, however, that the French court will indemnify the American captors in meal or in malt, for the loss of these prizes.* Things are not yet ripe for their plans, and a little temporizing to hoodwink the already blinded English, might be political and wise. You have a copy of a letter from Mons. de Sartines, which I before sent to R. H. L. By that you will see they begin to open their plans. I know you are not over fond of much business, but still it is incumbent on you to get some more active person to call immediately for an expenditure of y^e *several millions of livres,* which ye commissioners (at least ye acting one of them in these affairs,) have received in this country for ye public use. Such an account in my opinion it is absolutely necessary should be immediately furnished to you, otherwise you may when it is too late repent the delay. Should there be an

---

* The captors received the sum of four hundred thousand livres. *Deane.*

idea of continuing ye appointment of a commercial superintending agent, you will render ye public an essential service in my opinion in forwarding ye appointment of Mr. John Lloyd, of South Carolina, who is now settled at Nantes. He is an experienced, intelligent merchant, and of fair character. Mr. Lawrence,* of South Carolina, knows him well. Care should be taken this winter to fortify Charlestown against any attack in that quarter, for you will see by the king of G. B.'s speech, inclosed to R. H. L., that another campaign is determined on. . . . †

TO RICHARD HENRY LEE.

PARIS, 24 November, 1777.

My dear Brother:

I have received the appointment of Congress for me to go to Vienna and Prussia as their commis-

---

* Laurens.

† "The Courier de l'Europe some time since dispersed Lord Stormont's tale of Howe's victories over Washington, but ye last posts from England discountenanced ye report. Ye fact is, that no *real* accounts whatever have been received from the quarter of Philadelphia, since the packet that bro't despatches from Howe, which were published some time since in the London Gazette. Whether Washington has beaten Howe, or Howe defeated Washington, no one in Europe knew when the last post left England." *William Lee to John Bondfield,* 17 November, 1777.

sioner, and by this opportunity have wrote to Congress addressed to ye Secretary, Charles Thomson, Esqr. As no particular mode of correspondence is pointed out in my instructions, that letter will no doubt be communicated to Congress, to which therefore be pleased to refer, but I will add to you that the clerk who wrote the commissions has in both made some capital mistakes. In one, the state of Virginia is twice mentioned in ye title, and in the other the State of Maryland is twice mentioned. I should suppose and humbly submit that ye style and title in such commissions should run thus: "The Delegates of the Independent and United States of &c., &c., &c., in North America, assembled in Congress" have determined so and so. I presume 'tis the intention of Congress to put all their Commissioners on the same footing as those at Paris, see their votes of Sept. 28, 1776, especially when 'tis considered that Vienna is as gay and expensive a court as any in Europe; but by some accident they have omitted to make any provision for Mr. Izard or myself. This I hope you will contrive to have regulated soon, which I should suppose may be done without seeming to be too personally busy in it yourself. The line that Congress has tho't proper to place me in, on reflection I rather doubt my abilities to succeed in, agreeable to their wishes or those of my particular friends, but on mature consideration, I am resolved to enter on the service, because I do not know whom they could get here that is unemployed, to execute those necessary functions, better than myself, and because I find from experience that it is not in my power to render the public any essential services in the mercantile line, since Mr. Deane has *in fact* taken on himself the authority of suspending the Secret Committee's appointment of Mr. Thos. Morris and myself, as mercantile agents, by appointing Mr. Jonathan Williams, a young man of about 22 years old, nephew to Dr. Franklin, as agent for the public business at Nantes, and ordered him to take charge of selling all prizes made by Continental armed vessels, giving orders at the same time to the captains to put their prizes into Mr. Williams' hands, tho' he knows perfectly well that the sale of prizes was expressly committed to Mr. Morris and myself by the Secret Committee, see their letter of Octr. 25, 1776, to Mr. T. M. In this last business Mr. D. says he acted with the approbation and consent of Dr. Franklin, but the letters on the subject, I am well informed, both to Mr. Williams and the captains, are signed by Mr. Deane alone. His view in appointing Mr. Williams must be so evident to you and every one else that I have no occasion to mention it.* I could not therefore continue to act for the public without

---

* See *Deane to Robert Morris*, 23 September, 1777.

coming to an open rupture with Mr. Deane, which at this critical moment might be attended with bad consequences to *our public*, because it would lessen us in the eyes of Europe, and give our enemies at least some exultation, if not an opportunity of operating something greatly to the disadvantage of America.* I therefore wait with patience, not doubting that the Committee will vindicate their own appointment; for if Mr. Deane has any charge [against] Mr. Morris, I fancy he will not presume to make any against me. If he does, I am perfectly ready to meet him on that ground. In fact, the public business in this country has been, and is likely to continue in strange disorder; nor is it likely to mend until the Secret Committee confine all this mercantile business to their mercantile agent, and keep the Commissioners to their political duty, which *may* be neglected from too much attention to private schemes of commerce on public funds and contemptible private jobs. I am now out of the question, therefore cannot be charged with partiality in my advice: but if it is tho't proper to

---

* "On my arrival here in October. I applied personally to those gentlemen on the subject, when Dr. Franklin and Mr. Deane promised that they would immediately recall their orders to Mr. Williams, which I do not find has been done yet. So far from it, a very few daies afterwards these gentlemen wrote to L'Orient, giving directions about the sale of the prizes bro't in there by Capts. Thompson and Hyndman." *William Lee to Thomas Morris*, 27 November, 1777.

continue the appointment of a mercantile superintendent, I do not know any one that will serve the
public better than Mr. John Lloyd, of South Carolina, who is now settled at Nantes. He is a merchant of very fair character, much experience and
ability. You will have from another hand a state
of what supplies have been furnished for public use
by our friends here and in Spain. I have now sent
a copy to our F. L. Lee. The manufactured articles should be enquired for, as we do not hear of
any miscarrying that have been shipped, except a
part of those sent by the Seine. Mr. Francis Lewis
of New York, is a sensible, intelligent merchant; I
have therefore sent him a copy of these supplies,
that he may act in the business as he finds necessary. I have often heard that short accounts make
long friends; therefore as the Commissioners have
already received in money *three millions one hundred and eighty-seven thousand five hundred livres*
for your use,* is it not incumbent on you to call
immediately for an account of the expenditure of
this money? Certainly you ought, without a day's
delay. I understand there is a negotiation on foot
for borrowing a considerable sum of money, which
I dare say will easily succeed, if Gen'l Howe does
not get possession of Philadelphia. Should this
money be borrowed, it should by all means be kept

* Two millions from the Court, and one million advance from
the Farmers General.

as a sacred deposit, not by any means to be touched
without the express orders of Congress.*   'Tis absolutely certain that all the articles you can want
for the army from Europe can be purchased very
considerably cheaper and infinitely better in quality
in Germany and Sweden and the northern countries, than they can in France or anywhere south—
such as brass and iron ordnance of all kinds, fusils,
powder, sulphur, copper, steel, bombs, shot, cloth,
linen for shirts, stockings, sail cloth, anchors,
cables and all kinds of cordage. 'Twill be perfectly
easy to get any of these things shipped from some
of the northern ports, provided there is proper prudence and secrecy used, sometimes directly to
America round Scotland, sometimes to the ports of
Spain and France to be reshipped from thence.
Two or three ships covered under foreign names
might be very beneficially employed in this business.   A cargoe now and then of tobacco, rice and
indigo or furs sent round Scotland by Embden in
the Prussian dominions, would turn to good account and would be gladly received there, but these
cargoes should be trusted with careful and diligent
captains, with faithful officers, and some soldiers
on board to act as mariners, or else there will be
danger of the sailors running away with vessel and
cargoe, as they have often done already.   This

---

* This scheme for a loan came to no issue.

plan will answer the double purpose of saving your property and breeding seamen.

I am just informed that at first Mr. Williams was sent to Nantes by all the commissioners to superintend the shipping and buying some arms, &c., for them in the early part of last Spring, as they did not choose to trust that business with Mr. Thos. Morris; but since that, Mr. Deane, long after I came to France, took from Mr. M. and myself the sale of the prizes as before mentioned, and now seems to think his appointment of Mr. Williams ought in all cases to be superior to the Committee's appointment of Mr. Morris and me. If the Committee submits to this, or do not explicitly stigmatize such presumptious conduct, I am perfectly confident that their business here will grow more and more disordered than it is already, and it is bad enough at present in all conscience. Your greatest enemies could not wish your affairs to be more deranged than they are on this side, and they are likely to continue so, until order and regularity is established on your side, where the power rests. I have just discharged what I think my duty in thus giving you a true state of your affairs here, and shall from henceforth take my leave of this department, keeping my attention entirely to the charge which is committed to my care.

The general system of politics in Europe the Commissioners will no doubt give you. In my private opinion there will not be any war soon on this side the Atlantic. France and Spain wish you success because they think whatever takes from the strength of Great Britain adds to their own; whatever *covert aid* therefore that they can give, you may be sure of receiving; but the disorderly conduct of some of your privateers and their crews, has given a great deal of embarrassment because they are in no preparation to go to open war with England; at the same time wish to harrass her as much as they can. Too much care cannot be taken in regulating your privateers. Any irregular conduct or breach of the laws of nations with respect to neutral powers should be severely punished, or else whenever ye war ends the whole sea for a long time will be infested with pirates. The present system and connections between the different powers of Europe have been formed on a supposition of a certain strength in G. B., and until it appears that you are able to support with certainty your Independence, that system cannot easily be changed. Otherwise we should have been at war before this day. The first rupture on this side will most probably spread war and devastation over every country in Europe. In my last to the Secret Committee of this date, I have mentioned y^e plans proposed by me to Messrs. Montaudouin Fréres, of Nantes, and Mr. And$^{w.}$ Limozin, of Havre de Grace, for undertaking the public business, and now enclose you y^e papers that you may be fully master of y^e subject. But Mr. Limozin's letter to me, dated 5 October, 1777, I beg you will carefully preserve, as it may be of use hereafter. So strangely is business managed here, that [it] is now above a fortnight since I have been waiting for a copy of the treaty to propose to Vienna and Berlin, and have not yet got it from the Commissioners, tho' there are three or four hangers on, that are maintained at ye public expense, and for some of whom there will probably by and bye be a charge made as Secretary to the Commissioners. I have thus discharged my duty and my conscience in giving you a full state of some proceedings here, of which I have no doubt you will make a prudent and discreet use.

TO RICHARD HENRY LEE.

PARIS, 30 November, 1777.

* * * The Commissioners will no doubt write fully on politics, but there is one point I think I may venture to assure you of with great confidence, which is, that France and Spain are sincerely friendly to you, and will do every thing to assist you that can be done without bringing on an immediate rupture with Great Britain, for which they are not yet quite prepared. Some transactions will I dare say be insinuated to you as proof of ye contrary by those who have been extremely culpable, and may endeavor to throw ye blame off themselves on the French court. I mean the imprisoning Mr. Hodge for forfeiting his bond to ye Admiralty on sending out Conyngham in a privateer from Dunkirk and restoring the two British West Indiamen bro't into Nantes. In ye Dunkirk business Mr. Deane, in my opinion, was wrong because it was expressly contrary to the promise of the Commissioners made to the French ministry, and directly contrary to the ministers' injunctions that any privateer should be fitted out in Dunkirk. They were so anxious to prevent any noise on this affair, that the ministry sent orders to Dunkirk to pay every expense attending Conyngham's outfit, and to take the vessel themselves, but she was pushed out of port before such orders could be executed.* All this I have from such authority that I not only believe it, but fancy, if any inquiry was necessary to be made, it would prove to be true. The seizure of the West Indiamen at Nantes was regular according to the French maritime laws. I know the whole of that business, and do not think the French court in the least to blame. In general, with respect to Mr. D—'s conduct, I think the public interest has not much to thank him for, and his conduct to our brother has been reprehensible

---

* See *Deane to Robert Morris*, 23 August, 1777. Deane, *Narrative*, 39–40.

in the highest degree, of which he will, or surely ought, to give you a full account.

TO CHARLES THOMSON, SECRETARY OF CONGRESS.

PARIS, November 24, 1777.

Sir:

Be so good as to inform the honorable Congress of the United States of America that I have received the commissions, whereby they have done me the honor of appointing me their Commissioner and Representative to the Courts of Vienna and Berlin. In consequence of their instructions, I have applied to their Commissioners at the Court of Versailles for a copy of the treaty originally proposed by Congress, to be entered into with France, together with the subsequent alterations that have been proposed on either side, which I presume they will furnish me with, and in the mean time I have been taking, and shall continue to take, measures to get the best possible information, which of these Courts it will be most for the interest of the United States that I should visit first, in order to accomplish the most urgent object of Congress, that of preventing Great Britain from obtaining more German troops to send to America. For this object, my views shall be extended to Russia, as far as the situation of affairs in Europe will admit.

Colonel Faucitt, the British Agent, has been most of the year in Germany, and about two months ago, General Haldimand, who was appointed and embarked to go and succeed General Carleton as Governor of Quebec, was recalled and sent to Germany as it is supposed, to aid Colonel Faucitt in obtaining more German troops. What success they will meet with, I cannot at present speak of with certainty, but you may rely on every exertion in my power to obstruct their operations, and I have some hopes of succeeding so far as to prevent their obtaining more than to make up the number that the States of Hesse, Brunswick, and Anspach, have formerly contracted to keep in the pay and service of Great Britain in America. It would certainly add to their difficulty and embarrass the British Ministry, if there were only an appearance of beating up for men for the United States, in some of the free towns in Germany, where all the world by custom is permitted to recruit and enlist men. Something of this sort might be attempted, sufficient to give a great alarm and create a diversion in your favor at a very little expense, if prudently managed.

I shall pay strict attention to my instructions, and embrace the first favorable opportunity of prevailing upon the Courts of Vienna and Berlin to receive the Commissioner of Congress as the Representative of a sovereign State, which will necessarily carry along with it an acknowledgment of the independence of the thirteen United States of America; though in this business I apprehend the other Powers of Europe will wait for France and Spain to take the lead, as they are known every where to be friendly to the American States, and to have received hitherto greater advantages from the American commerce than any other kingdoms, and still have not determined as yet to receive the American Commissioners as the representatives of a sovereign State. I hope I shall be excused for observing, that neither my commission nor instructions authorise me to conclude any treaty with the Courts of Vienna and Berlin, even if I should find those Courts at any time disposed for such a measure. Congress will determine whether it may be prudent to enlarge those powers, when they consider the distance between the two countries, and the time it will take to write to Congress, receive their answer, return to them the treaty, and then again receive their ratification.

It occurs to me that it will be extremely proper for me to have a cypher to carry on my correspondence with Congress, more especially if any supplies of cordage, arms, cannon, or ammunition are purchased in the northern countries, where, it is beyond a doubt, they may be had infinitely better in quality, and very considerably cheaper, than what have been sent already, or may be sent from

France or Spain, particularly iron and brass ordnance, ball, shot, fusils, woollen and linen cloth for soldiers' clothing, and tents, sail cloth, and cordage. Ways and means may be contrived to ship any of these things from the northern ports as easily as from the southern ones. If this idea is approved by Congress, any cypher you send me shall be used when necessary. As there is no particular mode pointed out in my instructions how I am to correspond with Congress, I have adopted the method of addressing myself to you as their Secretary, it being the usual practice in similar cases in Europe ; but if I am wrong, I shall hope to be better informed by the next dispatches I receive.

TO THOMAS ROGERS, LONDON.

PARIS, 8 December, 1777.

Dear Sir:

As things seem to be from strong appearances in all quarters in a very unsettled state, there is a probability, if not a certainty, that by taking ye opportunity by the forelock, a great stroke may be made and very considerable advantages gained by your stocks, and as it may fall in my way to see how things will turn as soon as most people, with your aid in London, ye business might be successfully accomplished, and having a high opinion of

your judgment, honor, integrity, secrecy and caution, would willingly engage with you in a scheme
of that kind, you to be one third interested, and
ye other two thirds here, for which two thirds I
must stand answerable or to be the receiver. This
I must enjoin you never to mention to any person
breathing, either directly or indirectly, unless it is
your partner, Mr. W.,* for whom I have a very
high regard and esteem, and to him only under the
strongest injunctions of secrecy. If you decline
the proposal, I request this may be immediately
committed to the flames. If you approve, let me
know it directly, giving your letter to Mr. B.,†
who will deliver this, that he may return it by y^e
same messenger who carrys this, as he may not
stay in L. longer than a day or two.‡ Mr. B.
knows nothing of the contents. Should you approve, it will be left with you to determine what
fund to make ye essay in. I should suppose, from
my idea at present, that India will tumble most
when the cloud breaks, but on this I may hereafter
perhaps be able to give you a proper hint when the
period arrives. All that you will have to do will
be to send a *trusty* person to Boulogne, near Calais
and opposite to Dover, to stay there, if it is for a
month or more, till he hears from me, that he may

---

* Welch.
† Browne.
‡ Ed. Capes.

be with you as speedily as possible. He should be
ordered to write to me per post, directed to me
"chez Monsr Holleville, Maitre Tailleur, vis a vis
la Samaritane, a coté de la Café de Parnasse," telling me particularly the house, the name of the
landlord, and the name of the street in Boulogne,
in which he lodges. He should be ordered also
never to be many hours at a time out of the town,
because the loss of an hour may lose a great deal.
The sending this person need not be done untill
you receive a short line from me saying only
"Send to Boulogne." Such a short epistle may
go by post, for if opened, no one but yourself will
understand it, and I will take care to give you notice of this, that he may be there in time; for it
will be better that he should be there a month before hand, than half an hour too late. For fear of
accidents I shall only say "buy so many pounds
of hops for me," nor should the person you send
know anything of the *real business* he comes
about. As in a business of this sort, there must be
confidence on both sides, your answer need not be
long, whether tis in ye affirmative or negative,
and it had better be directed to me as if in London. . . *

---

*Stock jobbing appears to have been very general among
those having a somewhat immediate interest in the war. Ed-
wards, Dr. Bancroft and Paul Wentworth—British spies—were
suspected of having transactions in the Alley, and Major Thornton, Arthur Lee's secretary, was implicated.

TO JOHN BONDFIELD.

CHAILLOT, rue Bataille No. 5,
près Paris, 13 December, 1777.

Sir :

I had the pleasure of writing to you the 6th. current, since which received yours of the 5th, and this moment yours of the 8th. current. By the last I perceive your modesty has a *second* time got the better of your judgment. I wish you had taken up both Capt. Walker and the prize, and if in future any one addressed to me at your port should apply to you, if it is not inconsistent with your other plans or engagements, I could wish you would do their business for them, as I have no doubt of your capability, and think what you have suffered in the American cause, entitles you to a preference. I tho't one of my former letters would have conveyed this idea sufficiently to you. There can be little doubt of the prize being disposed of before this gets to hand, but could wish you would endeavor to learn the price and let me know it, also whether well sold or not.

By letters from England it appears the nation is more enraged at the American minister, Lord George Germaine, on account of Burgoyne's fate than from any circumstance that has happened. *

---

* Austin had arrived in Paris on December 4th, bringing intelligence of Burgoyne's surrender, and of the battle of Germantown.

What will be the issue, time must discover, but this discontent will be increased when 'tis generally known that besides the commander, Col. Donop, near 700 men were lost in yᵉ *unsuccessful* attempt on the fort at Billing's point,* which loss is concealed in the last extraordinary Gazette. They say also that General Vaughan and 2000 have been made prisoners up the North River, which circumstance is likewise unnoticed by the Gazette. Letters from Rochefort mention the arrival of a French vessel there from America, which brings advice of Howe and his army surrendering to Washington the 9 November—the Hessians refusing to fight. This wants confirmation. . .

TO SILAS DEANE.

CHAILLOT, 17 December, 1777.

Sir:

Your long card to my brother, dated Saturday 2 o'clock, which has been just communicated to me, it is in some respects incumbent on me to answer, because it would be extreme folly in me to let it go forth uncontradicted to the world, that any *misstating* or *misunderstanding* of my actions or words should be construed into any approbation [of], or in any manner countenancing *your* superceding

---

* Billings Port.

the Secret Committee's appointment of their commercial agents. I must call it *your superseding* the Committee's appointment, because I am well informed that the letter to Mr. Williams for that purpose was signed by you alone. I am also informed that the correspondence since on the subject has been in your single name, tho' the style of *we* has been used in the letters, and I believe I shall not be contradicted in saying that Mr. Williams's letters in reply have generally been under cover directed to you solely. You say in your card to my brother: "Mr. Lee will recollect that he was present when his brother resolved on delegating his power as commercial agent to Mr. Montaudouin without any consultation with Mr. Morris." So strange and fictitious an assertion I am at a loss to account for, and it would be still more strange if my brother should recollect what *never* happened, and which I assert was never in my contemplation. 'Tis true that I applied to all the three Commissioners when present, not to any one singly in a corner, stating the propositions I had made to Messrs. Montaudouin of Nantes, to undertake the public commercial business of America, on terms which I knew were more advantageous to America than any that had been proposed by any other person, or had been accepted by any other house; at the same time observing, that I had no power to compleat this engagement without the concurrence of Mr. Morris, who I was apprehensive, from his attachment to another house, would not agree with me in opinion, and desiring in that case the advice of the Commissioners how I should act. *You* immediately proposed that the Commissioners should interpose and suspend Mr. Morris, for without that, in your opinion, Messrs. Montaudouin could not undertake the business in any shape; another of the Commissioners observed that the question was not about suspending Mr. Morris, but whether Mr. Lee should not appoint a proper person to act in his stead. To this I made no reply, and there the conversation ended. In consequence, I afterwards informed Mr. Montaudouin personally that I was not vested with sufficient authority in my own person to conclude such an engagement, but that I would represent his obliging willingness to serve America to the Secret Committee, who I did not doubt would be happy in such respectable correspondents.

With respect to Mr. Moylan,* I did not send him to L'Orient. I thought Mr. Moylan a capable and deserving man, and therefore promised him all the

---

*John or James Moylan. The commissioners promised to give him what public business they had at L'Orient, provided he could connect himself with some merchant there able and willing to advance for the public as occasion should require. He formed a partnership with one Gourlade, who had assisted Captain Wickes in 1777.

aid and support that I could personally give him, and at the same time advised him to endeavor to obtain Mr. Morris's approbation also, that we might cordially intrust to his care the management of any public business that was under our joint control. I also wrote Mr. Williams, in answer to a letter from him on the same subject, that if he and Mr. Moylan could agree between themselves, any aid I could give to forward the business successfully should not be wanting. This shows that tho' Mr. Williams had been made the instrument of a personal injustice to me, I bear him no ill-will on that account.

Had the joint letter of Mr. Morris and myself, early in August, or my own letter to you of the 28th of August (which in course of post would reach you the 31st of August), been favored with any answer, the length of this might have been perhaps unnecessary. I had always understood that every gentleman had a right to expect an answer from another to a civil letter, but my late experience teaches me I am not always to expect that civility. However, I must take the liberty of recapitulating some facts relative to your superceding the Committee's appointment of commercial agents. You know that I was appointed by the Secret Committee, in conjunction with Mr. Thomas Morris, commercial agent for the affairs of America in France. You know that I left England to take upon me that office, and arrived in Paris early in June, where I remained several weeks under your advice, being then a total stranger to the powers and authority vested in me by the Committee, having never had any information on the subject by letter or otherwise. In July, without saying one word to me, you wrote to Mr. Jonathan Williams to take upon himself the sale of prizes made by Continental ships of war, to give orders accordingly to ye commanders of Continental armed vessels, and also to superintend the management of such armed vessels ;* in consequence of which, Mr. Williams, with the aid of a Frenchman, got possession of one or two prizes, which I believe at this moment have not been accounted for to the public, or other proprietors—at least, I am sure they were not when I left Nantes in October last. Mr. Morris, as was his duty, remonstrated against this order, and sent you an extract of the Secret Committee's orders on the subject. Still there was no alteration on your part, and I was permitted to go to Nantes the beginning of August without one syllable being mentioned to me about the business. In August Mr. Morris and myself wrote a joint letter from Nantes, requesting this order might be withdrawn, at the same time sending a copy of the Secret Committee's instructions to us on the sub-

---

* See page 197, *ante.*

ject. This letter has to this moment remained un-
answered. Early in October, when I came to
Paris from Nantes, I personally applyed to *all* the
Commissioners present, to recall that order to Mr.
Williams, stating the mischiefs that had already
arisen from it to the public interest, and fairly saying that I could not intermeddle with the commercial affairs of America until that was done. A
promise was made that the order and appointment of Mr. Williams to supersede Mr. Morris and
myself, should be immediately withdrawn, as the
Commissioners had no authority whatsoever to
control the Secret Committee's appointment of
commercial agents; yet so far from this promise
being complied with, Mr. Williams writes thus
from Nantes the 6 December, 1777, and addressed
"The Honble Commissioners of the United States:"
"You have never recalled your order to me relative to the management of the ships of war, prizes,
etc." Here is an unequivocal proof that the
promise solemnly made of recalling these orders
two months before had not been complied with.
Who Mr. Williams supposes to be the Honble Commissioners of the United States I do not know, but
it is evident he cannot mean Mr. Lee to be one,
because he never received such orders from him.
On the contrary, Mr. Lee has ever disavowed such
orders, and the authority of the Commissioners to
interfere in such matters. This, when fully con-

sidered, is really a very curious business. A vessel comes from the United States of America expressly addressed to William Lee and Thos. Morris, as their agents; when Mr. Jonathan Williams, as agent of Mr. Deane, expresses his dilemma whether he ought not under Mr. Deane's appointment take the management of this vessel out of the hands of Mr. Lee and Mr. Morris.

On the same principle, sir, I should suppose that whenever you think it convenient, you have as good a right to order your servant to take my coat off my back and put it on his own. These are facts that I can hardly suppose will be controverted, and it is these facts that have determined me not to interfere any further with the commercial affairs of the Committee till their pleasure is known; and I should think myself very deficient in my duty were I not to state the case very fully to the Committee, and leave it with them to determine as they please on the occasion; for the motives of my conduct being public good, much more than private emolument, where I can't do real service, I will do no injury, which might possibly be the case were I in this country at this critical juncture publickly to assert the rights that are vested in me; and that is the reason why I pass over in silence with Christian forebearance the personal injustice and injury that has been done to me. It is a matter of perfect indifference whether this letter meets with the same fate of silence and disregard that my others have, but I must desire it may be kept, as I mean it to be a formal and written protest against any one of the Commissioners, or the whole together, undertaking to supercede the Secret Committee's appointment of their Commercial Agents. I beg it may be remembered that the merits or demerits of Mr. Williams are totally out of the question; 'tis undue exercise of a power with the shadow of authority in superceding the Secret Committee's appointment of their Commercial Agents, and without assigning any reason for such procedure, that I complain of. I should suppose that in candor, when you mention that one of the Agents has left the business, you should mention also the reasons which induced him to do so, which it is not probable you were unacquainted with before. However, you now have them from under his hand. I have endeavored to express myself clearly and fully, and I hope with decency; therefore have only to add that I an your obed't humble servant. *

TO T. ADAMS [EDWARD BROWNE].

PARIS, 18 December, 1777.

Dear Sir:

The 9th Mr. Capes was wrote to by a private

---

* See Introduction, p. 58. Deane to the President of Congress, 12 October, 1778.

hand, since which Mr. J—nes's* letter of the same date came to hand, and clears up ye bill business, only subsequent postage to the first account seems to be omitted, and the pro. on F—w was not sent; let it come per first post if not sent before. Pray tell him this, as also what follows. If 'tis not done already, there is no anxiety for finishing ye bond, if ye money can be of use to Mr. J.—But I would advise caution, for tho' the times look well for speculation in almost anything, yet they also seem big with universal bankruptcy, both public and private. Perhaps it may be well to see first how the Xmas settlements are likely to pass over, and forever make it a rule in speculations to buy at the very beginning of a rise and sell at the very beginning also of a fall. The particulars of Hunt's bills are requested, their different sums and times of payments. He is a comical genius. What was directed with No. 39,152 was no more than was invariably ye practice when distant persons were interested. Be so good as to deliver ye inclosed to the person to whose favor, at your request, it is granted;‡ the sum shall be enlarged whenever you require it, and when it is found that this will be of any avail, which perhaps may be better received, and more

---

* Jones, also intended for Browne.

‡ A letter to Welch, Rogers & Co., asking them to advance £500 to Browne.

effectually answer the purpose than if it was larger: but double the amount shall be sent when required, if you find this is received well, and properly attended to. Please to desire S. T. to call on the Leadenhall Street Alderman, and to insist on being informed whether he knows anything of ye extract of ye letter in ye Gazette of December 1st. If he does, there is no doubt of his denying it; but ye truth will appear by a strict attention to ye countenance, and humming and hawing. His correspondent S. P. of T.* house yard was possibly the writer, from the folly and nonsense of the style. The travelers are all well and request to be remembered with cordial regard. Our old acquaintance [W. L.] thinks soon of taking a long jaunt, but he will write himself before he sets out.

No appearance of peace I think yet, and sincerely wish ye good folks at W[estminste]r would grow a little more temperate and wise; for if they go on with the horrible business of man killing, I fear they will not only depopulate poor O. E., but ruin every inhabitant with the expence. Those who have tobacco lodged in Dunkirk have written over if 200 livres per 100 lbs. can't be got for it, to send it to England. That price will not be got there, consequently it will not be shipped. Judge then what effect that will have on ye London market.

---

* Samuel Petrie, of Trinity.

Some people may judge it prudent to speculate in insuring against a French and Spanish war for 12 or 6 months. There is a risk always in those things, but this might not be a bad one at present, as our rulers seem to be running quite mad. * * *

TO CHARLES THOMSON.

PARIS, December 18th, 1777.

Sir:

Enclosed is a copy of what I did myself the honor of writing to you by the Independence, Captain Young. Be pleased to inform the honorable Congress that, upon application being made to his Prussian Majesty, he has prevented the Hesse and Hanau recruits, for reinforcing the British army in America, from passing through his territories on the Rhine, which has kept those troops still in Germany, who otherwise would, by this time, have been on their voyage to America; and it is now doubtful whether they will ever be permitted to go. Our friends at Court here are of opinion that it will be better for me to visit the Court of Vienna first, as it may be of use to strengthen and unite all the branches of the family compact in the measures they have determined to take here in our favor; therefore, as soon as the ceremony (which is a pretty essential one) of *signing* and *sealing* has taken place, I shall set out for Vienna, as it is

thought most advisable to wait till something decisive is absolutely concluded with the Court of Versailles, because on *that* must be grounded my operations at Vienna and Berlin.

With respect to the latter, trade must be the
principal object, though the friendship of the King
of Prussia will be of use to keep Russia quiet,
and to prevent Great Britain from getting any material aid from that quarter in case of an European
war, while she is mad enough to continue the war
with America. Nothing material relative to commerce can be effected in the north till late in the
spring, because their ports are all frozen up during
the winter. His Prussian Majesty seems well disposed to our cause, and I trust will give us every
encouragement in time that we can wish; but in a
country where there is very little foreign commerce, it must be raised gradually and by experi-
mental conviction of its benefits. To me it seems
evident that the commerce between America and
the Prussian dominions must be considerable, because the natural productions of the former will
come to as good a market in the latter as almost
any part of Europe; those from the latter are what
we have been heretofore obliged to get from England. I shall omit no safe opportunity of informing Congress of my proceedings; and with due consideration and regard, I am, sir, etc.

TO THOMAS ROGERS.

PARIS, 18 December, 1777.

Dear Sir :

Circumstances are such that I can't wait as I intended to do; therefore, send this by express to desire you will sell for me stock to the amount of two hundred thousand pounds, and as much more as you please for yourself, against the next settling day after the Xmas settling day is past. I mean that our settlement is to be fixed for that which is to come next after the Xmas settlement. The choice of the fund or funds (for I should think it will be better not to deal all in one) I leave to your judgment. For it is certain that tho' low now, they must grow lower; however, I willingly venture, and should there be a loss, you may depend on being immediately reimbursed by me, for whatever loss may fall to my share, tho' of that I think there is hardly a possibility.   *   *   *   *

ROBERT MORRIS TO HENRY LAURENS.

MANHEIM, 26 DECEMBER, 1777.

Sir :

On the 17th inst., I received at this place two letters from my friend Mr. John Ross, dated in Nantes, the 2d of August and 20th of September, which came via Virginia, in a sloop called the Congress, lately arrived there. These letters were written for the purpose of making me acquainted with the unworthy conduct of my brother, Mr. Thomas Morris, in Nantes, and their contents shocked me to the very soul; I perceived instantly how grossly I had long been imposed on, and deemed it my duty to have him immediately discharged from the agency in which he was employed for the public. Accordingly, I wrote that very day to the Hon. William Smith, Esq., a member of the commercial committee, an account of this intelligence, and enclosing a letter for Mr. Thomas Morris, one for Messrs. Pliarne, Penet & Co., and another for Mr. J. Gruel, requesting they might be signed, if approved by the committee, and despatched in order that Mr. Morris might be dismissed, and the business that had passed under his direction be brought to a settlement soon as possible. All these letters I wished to have laid before the Congress for their approbation, and in order to prove *that I had not a wish* to retain my brother in the public service one moment after I knew him to be unworthy of the employ. I then thought these letters would be all that was necessary on the occasion, and that my brother's dismission would have wiped away the discredit his conduct had brought on our commercial department, and the final settlement of the accounts have ended the disgrace he has brought on me, leaving only himself the victim of his folly. But on the 23d instand, I received several letters from Mr. Deane, by the eastern post, wrote in consequence of one that I had unfortunately written to him the 29th June last, whilst under the influence of an unjust and erroneous opinion that the commissioners had used my brother very cruelly in their manner of mentioning him to Congress. In this letter I censured them freely, believing that I had sufficient reason for doing so. These censures of [and] the very unwarrantable use Mr. Thomas Morris made of the letter, have excited the keenest resentment of the commissioners against me, and, I confess, as things are really circumstanced, I am not surprised at it. This resentment has impelled them to put the harshest interpretation on some passages in my letter, and to represent my conduct, in respect to my brother, in colors it does not deserve.

The receipt of these letters distressed me exceedingly, because I had been convinced by Mr. Ross that I was in the wrong with respect to the commissioners, and had determined to acknowledge it fully and freely to them; but on finding that, although my letter to Mr. Deane was a private one, and his to me the same, yet he desired I should lay his before Congress, it was compelling me to open before that august body a dispute that I thought they ought not to be troubled with; yet, as his letters insinuated many charges against me, I concluded to comply with his request and vindicate myself against insinuations and reflections not founded in justice or reality. I find, however, by a letter received yesterday, that copies of these letters from Mr. Deane to me have already been read in Congress, consequently that it is unnecessary for me to bring the original; and my design in giving you, sir, the trouble of reading and Congress of hearing this letter, is not to recriminate on Mr. Deane, but to justify myself; and this I propose to do by a plain narrative of the facts that have led me into the present embarrassments, and I must ask a patient and candid hearing from you and them.

Mr. Thomas Morris and myself are descended from a father, whose virtue and whose memory I have ever revered with the most filial piety. Our mothers were not the same, and this youth was born after our father's decease, without any sufficient provision made for his maintenance. The tender regard I bore to the parent, I determined when very young to extend to his offspring; and no sooner had I fixed myself in the world than I took charge of this brother. I gave him the best education that could be obtained in Philadelphia, and took as much care of his morals as my time and capacity enabled. When he was arrived at a proper age, I took him into my counting-house to instruct him in the profession from which he was to draw his future support. In this situation he remained about three years, during which time he discovered on all occasions a good understanding, sound judgment, and clear head, with remarkable facility in despatching business. His behavior was then modest and innocent, his heart pure, and he possessed a mind strongly actuated by principles of honor; at least these were the opinions I had formed, and such was the character he bore amongst his own acquaintance; from hence I formed the most pleasing expectation, and saw but one source from whence any reverse could spring. This was a fondness he early discovered of being the head of his company, a disposition more dangerous to youth than any other, and which in fact has been his ruin.

This it was that first led him to seek improper company, who, readily granting him the pre-eminence he delighted in, soon carried him into the practice of their follies and vices. When I discovered this to be the case, and found that advice had not its proper weight, and thinking frequent exercise of authority might be dangerous, I fell on the expedient of sending him to Spain (in order to break off his connections with worthless companions), and there placed him in an eminent counting-house, where he gained much knowledge and experience, and where he acquired the French and Spanish languages so as to write and speak both with great fluency. At a proper season I recalled him to America, and took him as a partner in our house, promising myself assistance and relief from his abilities, and *expected* assiduity, and for some time had great satisfaction in him; but unfortunately his former associates found him out and again led him astray. At this period the commercial business of America was interrupted by certain resolutions of Congress, and, fearing that idle time and these associates would bring him to ruin, I determined on sending him to Europe well recommended, with money in his pocket, in hopes to open his mind, extend his ideas, and give him a habit of keeping and seeking good company. He travelled through Spain, Italy, and into France, with reputation kept by means of introductions. I procured for him the best company in every place he went to, and I had the pleasure to receive many letters from my friends as well as from himself in the most satisfactory style. These letters, his assurances, and those from some friends on his behalf, regained my confidence. I judged he had now arrived at the period of proper reflection; for such usually happens to young people who have been too volatile in the first stages of manhood. At this period it happened that a commercial agent became necessary to have a general superintendency of the public business in Europe. My brother was then in France (as I thought) possessed of my good opinion; and, reflecting that he was qualified for that agency by his education in two counting-houses, where he had seen and executed much business; by his perfect knowledge of the languages, and by his being connected with some of the best mercantile houses in Europe, and known to many more, I was prompted to offer his services to the committee, firmly believing he would be extremely useful, and do honor to himself and me. Here I must observe that no part of his conduct had ever given me the least cause to suspect any want of integrity or breach of honor. Therefore, the only doubts I did or could entertain were, whether he would bestow that attention that he ought to his business; and for this I depended on the assurances he had given in his letters of a faithful execution of any commands I might lay on him. The committee, of which Dr. Franklin was then a member, was pleased to accept the offer, and on the Doctor's going to France, he promised me to become a friend and adviser of my brother if he found it necessary. Mr. Deane had promised this before his departure, and to make me acquainted with his conduct. I reposed myself in confidence that he could not do any harm, (as I should hear how he managed, and could act accordingly,) that he might do much good. At the same time that I recommended him to the agency, I entrusted him to collect the debts due to our house in Europe, and pay the balance we might owe there; and since then have continued to employ him in the management of our business. This must convince every person that I had full confidence in him, as I would not have intrusted my own property and affairs in what I could think doubtful hands.

I have given this long detail to show the foundation on which I recommended my brother to his employment, and I think any other person in my situation would have done the same thing. However, if I am any ways culpable in having done so, it is the event and not the intention that makes me so; for could I have had the least idea of what has happened, I would sooner have perished than he should have been trusted.

The next thing I am blamed for is granting greater faith to my brother's representations than to the commissioners' letters. This was only the case in part, for I had other evidence than his letters; however, I must also account for my conduct in this respect by a detail of circumstances.

It happened very unfortunately that, about the time Mr. Thomas Morris was appointed in America to this agency, he had gone from France to London, where, totally unable to withstand the tempting scenes of pleasure *that sink of iniquity affords*, he gave in to the pursuit with an eagerness (as I am now informed) that debauched his mind and laid the foundation for all

that has since happened. He was in London at the
time his letters of appointment arrived at Paris. Mr.
Deane sent for him. He came and promised a faithful
attention to business; he repaired to Nantes, and finding Mr. Penet had been intrusted with a contract for
public business, part of which had been executed, he
readily fell into the proposals made by that house and
became a party to it, but on what terms I do not know;
consequently he put the public business into their
hands (which was not inconsistent with the instructions under which he acted). Whilst these things
were in this train in France, I received a letter from
the gentleman in Cadiz with whom my brother had
lived, a worthy man, who had great regard for him and
wished to promote his welfare. He gave me reason to
suppose his conduct in London had been out of character, and this gave the first alarm to my fears.

In consequence of which I wrote letters on the 31st
January last to Mr. Deane, to Mr. Ross, and to Mr.
Thomas Morris, informing them of this intelligence,
and pressing their immediate care of and attention to
the public business, should he neglect it. I requested
my friend Ross to visit France on purpose to watch
and inform me truly what was his conduct, and insisted
to my brother that if he had been guilty of any neglect
of duty or misconduct in discharge of his public trust,
that he should resign it into the hands of Mr. Deane
or Mr. Ross, empowering them *regularly* to act for him
until new arrangements were made. This done, I
awaited impatiently for the event. In the meantime,
some disputes and mutual complaints had arisen be-

tween Mr. Deane and my brother, and, on the arrival
of the above letters, the latter went to Paris, where
they so far settled matters that he returned to Nantes
with Mr. Deane's sanction, (Mr. Ross, being at Hamburg, did not arrive until long after.) Some ships arrived from Philadelphia at Nantes about this time with
cargoes on public account, consigned to the order of
Thomas Morris; particularly the Success, Captain An-
derson, and Elizabeth and Mary, Captain Young. By
the return of one or both of these (I think) came letters from the commissioners, saying, to the best of my
remembrance, "that Mr. Thomas Morris must be immediately displaced from his agency," and another,
quoting the paragraph of Dr. Lee's letter from Bordeaux. Having no private letter *then* from Mr. Deane
on this subject, I was astonished at the style of these
to Congress; for, supposing my brother guilty of some
inattention, which was the most I did suppose, I could
not think it right to blast entirely a young man's reputation that was just setting out in the world, merely
because he was fond of pleasure; and as the letters he
had written respecting the business under his care were
full and clear, they were produced to Congress in his
justification, and to prevent any hasty measures. I
then related to Congress the substance of what I have
now written, but not so fully; and many members, as
well as myself, were surprised at the affair as it then
stood. In consequence of what the commissioners had
wrote, I referred myself to Mr. Thomas Morris' private
letters more particularly. I found there was no good
understanding between Mr. Deane and him, (but of

Dr. Franklin he wrote respectfully,) and he intimated that Mr. Deane was privately his enemy. Not trusting, however, to his letters, I applied to several persons that came from Nantes, who assured me there was nothing amiss in his conduct that they knew or heard of; but more particularly one person who had transacted business with him. This gentleman assured me over and over that he lived two months in the same house with my brother; that he saw him assiduous, attentive, and industrious; that if it had not been for him the business of those ships would not have been done in any reasonable time, and that I might depend my brother would give entire satisfaction; at least he was fully persuaded of this. He said he knew well there were persons in France that envied his appointment, and would leave nothing undone to have him displaced, and particularly mentioned Mr. Williams, who he heard was nephew to me and concerned in trade with another of the commissioners, as the person intended to supply his place. The relator of this account is now in America; a man of character, sensible, and capable for his sphere of life; and when Mr. Deane arrives he shall have the satisfaction of seeing and examining him; till then I think it best to keep his name for my own sake.

This relation and others less full, my brother's and other letters, and Mr. Deane's silence, led me to give some credit to the story; and although I was ever willing to displace my brother on the least just cause appearing, yet I confess I did not like that he should be sacrificed to make room for another person; and when Mr. Deane's first letters on the subject of my brother did arrive, they did not remove the impressions I had received. Still I had not full confidence that some cause for what was written had not been given on his part, and I supposed his neglect or misconduct to have been magnified in the account given thereof to the commissioners, who could not have been eye witnesses. In this situation, I wrote the letter of the 29th June, that has so irritated them; telling very fully what I had heard, and censuring fully what I thought wrong. Before I sent this letter I showed it to some members of Congress, relating truly, as I have now done, the circumstances that induced me to write it; and they thought me right as things then appeared. When Mr. Ross arrived at Nantes, he advised me of it, and promised immediately to enter into an examination of my brother's conduct, and give me a faithful account of it; but he was above ten weeks there before he wrote that account, and I do suppose was trying what he could do by exhortation, etc. At last the shocking account came on the 17th inst., and that day I requested my brother might be dismissed from his employment, giving notice to Congress of his malconduct.

Here, Sir, have I given a candid account of my reasons for introducing this unhappy man into public employ, and for not sooner soliciting his dismission. I did the first in hopes of his being servicable to the public, at the same time that he would enjoy an honorable and beneficial employment. I have done the latter as soon as I was convinced it ought to be done.

Until now I had no conception that it was possible for him to act the part he has done, and nothing carries stronger conviction of his being irretrievably lost than his behaviour with my letter of the 29th June. Congress will observe that Mr. Deane complains of my having urged him to resent the injuries I believed they had done him. The paragraph of my said letter to Mr. Deane on that subject is as follows: "I think those public letters were cruel to my brother and extremely unfriendly to myself. I shall inform him of them, and if he has spirit to resent them, I hope he will also have judgment to do it properly."

This letter was enclosed to my brother with the following paragraph: "I now wait with impatience to learn the result of your journey with Captain Bell to Paris, for on that and your future conduct depends your commission as commercial agent to the United States of America, and I find there are those that envy you that appointment and wish it out of your hands, as you may see by the enclosed letter for Silas Deane, Esq., which I send open for your perusal; and if you can determine to merit the continuance of that commission by good behavior, I think I can maintain it for you in spite of all endeavors to the contrary. But if you will not deserve it, I shall be the first to take it from you, and in that case it would hardly be worth while sending the letter to Mr. Deane, only there are some commercial matters in it. Therefore you must *seal and send it to him.* As to what I have said about your resenting their letters, I think you had best not think of any thing of that kind, lest your past behavior will not support you in doing it; and the best satisfaction you can have will be by holding your post under such good conduct as will deter them from attacking you again."

Thus, Sir, you will observe I only hinted resentment in the letter to Mr. Deane, and in fact retracted the idea in this to Thomas Morris, and I solemnly declare these are the only lines I ever wrote in that style. Here it also appears that my design was to have the letter delivered immediately without any person seeing it but Mr. Deane and himself. Had that been done, you would not have been troubled on the occasion, but it would have remained a private affair.

The other charges and insinuations are chiefly founded on the ill use Mr. Thomas Morris made of this letter on conjecture and on misinformation. If Mr. Deane had seen the whole of that long private letter he speaks of, he would have seen how false and groundless the several stories told him of it were. Indeed, the contents of that letter, except the paragraph above quoted, would ill suit Thomas Morris to show any one; for, knowing his own conduct, they must have stung him to the very soul every time he read them, unless his soul was grown too callous to have a feeling left.

Mr. Deane seems to remark on my private letters. requesting him to displace Thomas Morris from his employment if found unworthy of it, as if I meant thereby to exercise an undue authority as member of Congress. But this is a strained construction; the only authority I must or could mean to exercise was that of an elder brother over a younger, dependent on him for his support and accountable to him for his conduct; and, under this idea, I insisted he should empower Mr. Deane or Mr. Ross to act in his stead and under his authority if they thought it necessary, which shows I had no design of exercising any other authority than the influence I expected my letters, as an individual, would have had on my brother; and I still think if these had been insisted on at that time, he would have yielded to them. As to the expressions I used, of "supporting him in his appointment if his conduct would justify it, and that all the commissioners together should not remove him if he did his duty," etc., they may have been too strong; but I was writing these under the influence of a (groundless) belief that they had done him an injustice, and I knew Congress would not displace him or any of their servants that did their duty.

Upon the whole, this was a private letter that has produced these animadversions on my conduct, and therefore not wrote with any particular guard or caution; but it adds very much to the distress and unhappiness this unworthy young man has involved me in, to think I should have passed censures on Doctor Franklin and Mr. Deane, (Doctor Lee was not mentioned,) which they did not deserve. I did it under a deception that most men of feeling would have fallen into, and I shall as freely own it to them as I do to you, holding it more honorable to acknowledge an error and atone for any injuries produced by it, than with a vindicative spirit to persist, because you happen to have committed it. The account given both by Mr. Ross and Mr. Deane of Mr. Thomas Morris' conduct so far surpasses anything that I could have an idea of, that I do not pretend to animadvert on any part of it. My distress is more than I can describe; to think that in the midst of the most ardent exertions I was capable of making to promote the interest and welfare of my country, I should be the means of introducing a worthless wretch to disgrace and discredit it, is too much to bear. I hope, however, that no pecuniary loss will happen to the public, and that the disgrace and discredit will be wiped away by his dismission. From this hour I renounce all connection with him, although I cannot help lamenting the loss of what he was capable of being. I shall enclose Mr. Deane a copy of this letter for his satisfaction, and make what I think suitable acknowledgments to both Dr. Franklin and him.

Should Congress think there is anything more on my part to be done, I am ready to obey their orders, and with the greatest respect I remain,

Sir, your most obedient servant,

ROBERT MORRIS.

TO RICHARD HENRY LEE.

PARIS, 2 January, 1778.

My dear Brother:

* * * I before mentioned that Congress had omitted to mention any appointment for supporting my mission to ye Courts of Vienna and Berlin. The commissioners appointed for Versailles have hitherto been and are likely to continue in possession of all your funds on this side the Atlantic. As yet they decline furnishing either Mr. Izard or

myself with any money for our support, because
they say they have no orders so to do. If Congress
should determine to supply me for my expenses
thro' the Commissioners here, I hope ye orders will
be positive and ye sum mentioned, leaving nothing
to be solicited as favor here; and I could also wish
that whenever dispatches are sent to Europe, I may
be informed by letter addressed to myself of what
has happened, and also the public papers might be
sent to me particularly; or else, being so far removed, I shall be totally uninformed of the true
situation of things, which will make me appear
very ridiculous and insignificant in the Courts
where I am. For I am convinced from ye mode
of carrying on business here, that I shall not be
informed of anything from hence until it has been
in half the Gazettes of Europe.* For the three
months that my brother was in Germany, not a
single letter was ever written to him from hence,
tho' he wrote at least a dozen to ye gentlemen here.
I should be glad to be informed by you whether it
is not the design of Congress to put all their Commissioners on ye same footing—see their resolves of
September 28, 1776.†

---

* The Lees and Izard all complained that Franklin and Deane
did not communicate freely with them.

† Some determination in this matter was reached by the
Commissioners, for they feared lest the public interests
might suffer by delay. They asked William Lee what sum

The papers sent herewith will show you the number of troops voted by Parliament for next campaign, and also ye measures that ministry are taking to prevail upon the people at large to support their measures. They are also still busy in endeavoring to procure more additional troops from Germany; tho' every measure is taking to obstruct their negotiations in Germany, which will probably prevent any great success from that quarter, and I do not think with all their efforts, they will be able to get more than four or 5000 men at ye utmost from Great Britain and Ireland. Yet in common prudence you ought to take every measure to defeat them, supposing that all their plans should succeed. There are a number of reasons [which] might be urged in support of this advice, but a principal one in my opinion is, that the King of Great Britain is so inveterate against ye United States, that he

would be necessary; he replied that he could not ascertain the exact expenses of his mission in advance, but suggested that a credit of two thousand louis be given him at the bankers, he to draw from time to time what was absolutely necessary. This was done, and a similar credit given to Izard. To the surprise of Franklin and Deane, these credits were at once drawn to the full amounts, and the money so placed that only Lee and Izard could draw it. As this occurred at a time when the demands on the Commissioners were pressing, and money was needed to pay for what Congress had ordered and were expecting, the trick greatly embarrassed Deane and Franklin. In about ten months' time both Lee and Izard were pressing for further advances.

would rather sacrifice everything that is now left him, than not wreak his vengeance on them. Therefore, I conjecture that tho' France and other powers acknowledge your Independence, it will not occasion an European war; consequently, all the force that may be willingly put into the hands of the King and his ministry by the people of Great Britain, to prepare for an European war, will be employed to crush you.

This you will observe is my single conjecture, principally founded on my knowledge of ye ruling passions of ye King of Great Britain, and his secret advisers. Be therefore prepared to meet their utmost efforts, and if they are foiled next year, you may absolutely depend on ye war being at an end, unless you choose to continue it till Canada, Nova Scotia, Newfoundland, and the Floridas are united to you.

You must be sensible of ye advantage it would be to you to have the Portuguese ports open to you. The politics of that country are entirely changed since the death of ye late King and ye disgrace of his favorite minister, the Marquis of Pombal. Therefore, in a little time I expect Portugal will be as friendly to the United States as either France or Spain, unless some injury done them on the high seas should prevent it. For this and other more cogent reasons, you can't be too strict in ye instructions given to American privateers, or too rigid in punishing any transgressions of them. This principally relates to the New England States, from whence most of the privateers are fitted out. Their delegates should therefore attend to it, and immediately.

My letter to Congress will show the present disposition of the King of Prussia. You may now be assured of his ports being open to American merchantmen. Therefore, if captains can be found that understand ye navigation round the north of Scotland, Embden, near Hamborough, will be an excellent port for a cargoe of tobacco, rice and good indigo, that which is most like ye St. Domingo indigo. The returns from thence will be greatly beneficial to America. Be so good as to send me a list of the Congress, the members of the several committees, and such resolutions as it may import me to know.

Our brother Loudoun has wrote me that my houses in Williamsburg have been made barracks of, and greatly injured. He supposes ye public will make a recompence for it. Would it not be well to make ye application the first meeting of Assembly, before too many things of the same sort come on the carpet, and I should think it wise while paper money is plenty to lay taxes for support of ye war, because people pay chearfully when they have abundance of the commodity in their hands which is to be paid—at least I wish this method may be early adopted in Virginia. As soon as a treaty is concluded here (which we have reason to expect will take place in a few daies) I shall set off for Vienna, and shall carry on my negotiations with Prussia. I have waited here some time, that my motions may be regulated by what is *absolutely concluded* with France and Spain; because, I know many things have fallen out between the Cup and the Lip, therefore am not greatly inclined to rely too much on promises only. * * *

What has become of your Dear Brother and Sister Shippen, and their young tribe? I have just looked over your last 3 letters of Ap¹ 17, June 7, from Philadelphia, and of June from Virginia, by M⁷ King.* With respect to myself, I do not see after maturely weighing every circumstance, any more than you did, how it was in my power to take any other line than I have done, however disagreeable, laborious and unprofitable it may be. Your wise caution will be attended to, and let the issue be what it will, I shall endeavor to be content; tho' you must acknowledge it will not be over and above comfortable to be tossed about continually, from one post to another, with a family to carry along with me. I am determined, however, not to complain, for if my Country is benefited, and our

---

* John King, a merchant of Hampton.

glorious Cause is successful, my greatest object will be accomplished.

With respect to my Estate and affairs in Virginia, I cannot give any particular directions; they must be left to the friendly care and guidance of yourself and our brother F. L. L., only remembering, that if the course of events should hereafter call us to reside in Virginia, we would wish to find something comfortable to set down with at the close of life.

If my continuance in the North should be of any duration, as soon as our boy Thom: is sufficiently qualified to serve his Country and himself, my present plan is to send for him there, where there must be employment enough for him, and which he may make advantageous to his Country, honorable and beneficial to himself.

My whole house, Mrs L., her son and daughter are well. We join in most sincere and affectionate love to our dear Sister and all the children, being most truly, my dearest brother's sincere and lasting friend.

TO CHARLES THOMSON.

PARIS, 2d January 1778.

Sir:

I had the honor of writing to you by the Independence, Captain [John] Young, a copy of which went since.

It is with infinite pleasure that I congratulate Congress and America on the favorable change in our affairs in Europe, since advice was received of the noble and spirited exertion of the northern army and militia, in making General Burgoyne and his army prisoners. The purport of the last and present despatches from the Commissioners at the Court of Versailles, will show how pleasing and encouraging the prospect before us is in this country at the present moment.

I must beg you to lay before Congress, that though we had received repeated assurances from the King of Prussia of his good wishes for our success, and indeed had experienced his operations in our favor, by his forbidding his officers to permit the Hesse and Hanau recruits for the British army in America to pass down the Rhine, yet, since the late advices, his Prime Minister writes more decidedly than before, for he says: "I can assure you, sir, his Majesty will not be the last Power to acknowledge the independence of the Americans, but you must be sensible it is not natural for him to begin it; and that at least France, whose political and commercial interests are more immediately connected with yours, should set the example."

From this I conclude that as soon as France has entered into a treaty with you, the King of Prussia will not hesitate to do the same. This shows that my former opinion was well founded when I observed to you that it was probable most if not all the European Powers would follow the example of France and Spain, in acknowledging the independence of America. I have so far been able to prevail with the Emperor, by negotiations with his Minister, as to get his Imperial Highness to discountenance the practice of the German princes hiring their troops to Great Britain for the purposes of the American war. I have been waiting some time for the conclusion of certain affairs here, on which I presume the Commissioners at this Court will write fully. When they are clearly decided, signed, and sealed, I shall then immediately set out for Vienna, where it is thought my first visit will be most proper and beneficial, and then I shall proceed to Prussia, where I can venture to assure Congress that American merchant ships will be now freely admitted for commerce.

Embden is a convenient port where many American articles will come to a fine market, such as tobacco, furs, rice, and indigo, of that quality which is most like St. Domingo kind. The returns in woolens, linens, naval stores, arms, and ammunition, will be greatly beneficial to America. I shall, by all safe opportunities, regularly inform Congress of my proceedings, continuing to address my letters to you until I have other directions, not having received any instructions on that head as yet. It will certainly be of great use to keep me regularly advised, and as early as possible, of all the material occurrences in America. I cannot omit to mention it as my opinion that, let the events in Europe be what they will, you ought to prepare for another vigorous campaign, in which, if Great Britain is foiled, you may assuredly compute on the war being at an end.

I have the pleasure to inform Congress that from the best intelligence, I learn that Great Britain has hitherto been very unsuccessful in her attempts to hire fresh German troops for the American war, but the diligence of the Ministry is greatly increased in endeavoring, by every artifice and allurement, to raise men in England, Scotland, and among the Roman Catholics in Ireland. I am inclined to think that even there they will find themselves a good deal disappointed ; but a few weeks will show their chance of success with certainty. ' At all events, the troops they raise will be raw men, and not able to encounter your veterans, aided by a well disciplined and spirited militia. The plan of the next campaign is, I believe, as yet to be settled ; the earliest information I can get on that head, which is to be depended on, shall be immediately transmitted to Congress.

I am, with all due regard, &c.

TO JOHN BONDFIELD.

CHAILLOT, RUE BATTAILE NO. 5, PRÈS PARIS,
2 January, 1778.

Sir:

I have before me your esteemed favor of the 19th and 24th ult., and thank you for the information given me relative to the disagreeable situation of Capt. Walker; but I trust that with exertions of Messrs. Delaps and the laws of the country Mr. B——* will be severely handled for his extraordinary and unwarrantable conduct. If such proceedings are not strictly censured, the trade between France and America will labor under very heavy inconveniences. As Capt. W. is in confinement I have addressed a letter to him by this post, chez. Messrs. Delaps, and I shall be obliged to you for letting him know that if there is anything in which I can serve him, I will do it with the greatest chearfulness.

Conformable to what I hinted to you the 6th. ulto., I am to leave this in ten or twelve daies for a far country, from whence the period of my return is very uncertain. This puts a stop to the ideas I had entertained (at least for this winter) of being concerned in adventures for this country. Otherwise the plan you have last mentioned would be extremely agreeable to me. If there should be war soon, insurance in my opinion will fall, because in

---

* Beaumarchais?

such an event the British cruisers will have enough
to do in protecting their own trade, without attending much to interrupting that of America. War is
as much talked of here as with you, but I do not
see any symptoms of such an event happening
speedily, unless it should be true what we hear from
Portsmouth, and what has been let drop from Lord
Stormont's confidants, that six English ships of the
line and two frigates that sailed from Portsmouth
about six weeks ago, were ordered to seize the
Spanish flota that is expected home in a month or
six weeks; or to take all the French West Indiamen
they can meet with. I shall write you again before
I set out, advising how to direct to me, as I have
desired my friends in America to address letters for
me via Bordeaux to your care.

TO FRANCIS LIGHTFOOT LEE.

PARIS, 4 January, 1778.

My dear Loudoun:

If accidents, which are not uncommon in these
times, do not interfere, you will receive from me
many and some pretty long letters, that I have
written to you within the last six months; and I
will again thank you for your two letters of 22
April and 8 July last from Phil^a. If you should
meet with Mr Wm Stevenson who carries this, I
must entreat your kindness and friendly offices to

him. A letter to Col. Lloyd and also to some leading person in or about Washington [?] may be of much service to him. Mͬ S. is a native of Maryland somewhere about Chester River, a Nephew of our relation Edmͩ Jenings, Esqͬ, of London, and has been some years settled as a Merchant in Bristol, where from the unhappy times and his steady attachment to the cause of America he has suffered very greatly. He now goes out with the hopes of getting in something to support his wife and 6 or 7 children. He has something due on James River which occasions him to want a good introduction in that quarter. * * * I am this moment informed that Mͬ Stevenson has not met with very genteel treatment here. After being given to understand that he was to be the Bearer of the dispatches to Congress from the Commissioners at this Court, two of them joining have determined that Mͬ S. shall only carry them to Nantes and there deliver them to Mͬ C[armichae]l, of whom I have repeatedly wrote you to beware, who is to carry them to Congress. Mͬ S. has therefore, in my opinion, with very great propriety declined taking charge at all of their letters, but he carrys our Brother's, Mͬ Izard's and mine. I trust therefore you and all your friends will be more particular in your attentions to Mͬ S.* The

* Franklin explained that a Bordeaux house had sent him word that they intended to send a packet every month to

wonderful alteration that has happened in our favor
in Europe and particularly in this country since
the Account was received of the Captivity of Burgoyne and his Army, shows to demonstration that
our salvation from British Tyranny and savage
cruelty depends entirely on our own exertions.

America on their own account, and offered to take charge of the
Commissioner's despatches. Not knowing what degree of confidence could be reposed in the captains, Franklin did not
make use of that offer. "These are the packets I mentioned to
the gentleman as likely to afford him the convenience of a passage, and he understood more than I said to him, when he imagined there was a packet to sail soon with our despatches. I
knew of no such thing proposed ; and certainly, if it had been
proposed by me, or with my knowledge, I should have acquainted you with it." *Franklin to Arthur Lee*, 17 March,
1778. See *Deane's Narrative*, 54; *Life of Arthur Lee*, I, 373,
374.

Stevenson had been introduced to Arthur Lee by Jennings.
"His conduct at Bristol has made him obnoxious to the worst
men there, who have injured him." 22 December, 1777. A
William Stevenson, of Bristol, merchant, was gazetted as a
bankrupt in February, 1777.

"Mr Stevenson returns his Compliments to Messrs Franklin
& Deane & as he is well assur'd Mr Arthur Lee has already
done them ye justice to acknowledge that he told Mr Stevenson, He had propos'd His taking charge of & delivering the
Commissioners Despatches to the Congress, which had been
agreed to ; Mr Stevenson flatters Himself Messrs Franklin &
Deane will do Him equal justice, in acquitting Him of ye
charge, that it was any Supposition of His, that they had
changed their intention. From what passed at Mr Deane's
Lodgings when Mr S. call'd with Capt Jones on Thursday

Before that, the Ministry lowered, most people were shy, and, indeed, Mr Hodge of Philadelphia, one of Mr Deane's Agents, had been confined six Weeks in the Bastile at the instance of Lord Stormont, the B. Ambassador here; but since B[urgoy]ne's fate was known, every thing wears a

---

Morning, Mr S. had no reason to imagine that it was meant He should carry ye Despatches to Nantes—only on ye contrary when Mr Lee told him a few hours after that ye Commissioners had agreed to his carrying their Dispatches to Congress, He reply'd that He had just understood ye same from Mr Deane.

Mr S. concluded it was so determin'd by ye Commissioners : Mr Stevenson readily acknowledges that nothing pass'd on ye subject between Doc.^r Franklin & Him, but He is persuaded Messrs Franklin & Deane will now be convinc'd that Mr S.^s refusal to carry ye Despatches to Nantes, did not arise merely from a *supposition* of His being ungenteelly treated & if there was any misapprehension about ye matter, it did not originate with Him : Mr Stevenson will venture to say that no Person wou'd be more happy to serve His Country on every occasion, without any view of Self Interest & He has only to regret that His ability to render it essential services, is not equal to His wishes. Had any pre-engagement been hinted on ye first mention of this Mr S. wou'd certainly have given neither ye Commissioners *or* Himself any trouble ye occasion. Mr Stevenson will only add that He is extreamly sorry He shou'd become ye subject of an altercation on this occasion, as it is His constant wish to avoid everything of that kind, but He thought it highly necessary in vindication of His conduct, to endeavor fully to explain ye matter & He trusts that Messrs Franklin & Deane will candidly acquit him of having acted merely on supposition, as His expectation must appear to be well founded.

Paris Hotel Vauban Sunday Night 4 Jany 1778.

different face—we are Smiled on and Caressed
everywhere; what temper the Ministrv and the
King here are in you will fully learn by the dispatches of the several Commissioners to Congress.
The British Ministers are exerting every nerve to
get supplies of Men from E[ngland], S[cotland],
and Ireland, to carry on the next Campaign, as
they have been much disappointed in Germany,
but I shall be much mistaken if they are not nearly
as much disappointed in their plans in G. B.
They may make a figure in subscriptions of Money,
because their Agents know the Treasury is to pay
the roast, but they will find great difficulties in
procuring the Men. However you should be prepared at all events to baffle their utmost efforts, in
which case, you may rely on this year finishing
the War.

The plan of the Campaign is not yet settled you
may be assured, nor do I believe they have yet
agreed on the outlines or even the Commanders.
They talk of recalling Howe, in which case 'tis
probable Murray will succeed, this will be our
benefit, for he is a more hot headed, imperious,
rash fool than Burgoyne. You should prepare for
6 or 7000 men, including recruits, fresh men, and
everything they can send from Europe for this
year, which I suppose may be about the mark,
unless Burgoyne's Army should be permitted to
come away, in which case you may assuredly rely

on an equal number, (if not the very same men in Corps under different names,) being sent from Ireland or Gibralter, where B[urgoy]ne's men will be sent in their room. In order to weaken your Unanimity, in which your Strength consists, L.ᵈ North and his Masters, Bute and Mansfield, are contriving some fallacious propositions to be proposed to you thro' Parliament. Such pitiful snares I apprehend will not operate much on your Side but they may help to blind some well meaning people in England, whereby the plotters will gain something. You see I talk as if nothing was to happen in Europe. Indeed I do not think, with all the flattering appearances, you ought to rely on an European War; I will not, till a serious Blow is struck. You must depend principally on yourselves, and with Unanimity and a proper Exertion, this Winter and next Summer, you may assuredly chase away all your Invaders.* * * *

TO THOMAS MORRIS.

CHAILLOT, 4 January, 1778.

Sir:

Captain Jones delivered me your esteemed favor of yᵉ 28th ulto. I presume when you wrote you

---

* From the original in the Lee Papers of Harvard University. I am indebted to the courtesy of Mr. Justin Winsor for copies of these papers,—one of the many obligations I am under to him.

had not received mine of ye 23^d ulto, which would
have informed that I entirely agree with you in
opinion that we should not interfere with ye political part of ye American business, and I only
wish that others would cease to interfere with the
commercial business, which by ye committee had
been entrusted to us. I am informed you have
delegated all your power as commercial agent at
Nantes to Mr. Williams. The commissioners
being in possession of all ye public funds and
credit of Congress, and having hitherto given all
orders relative to continental ships of war, not to
you or me, I presume they will continue to do
ye same in ye present instance. Therefore, until
ye committee see proper to arrange affairs differently, I do not think I can with any propriety or
to any good purpose interfere with Captain Jones
or his ship, as I do not find he has any orders to
apply to us relative to ye disposal of himself or
ship. If the committee choose to let things go
on as they have done, I shall cheerfully submit
with this consolation, that I have endeavored to do
as much good as was in my power.

TO THOMAS MORRIS.

CHAILLOT, 8 January, 1778.

Sir :

I had ye pleasure of writing to you the 4th instant by Mr. Stevenson, a countryman of yours, and a gentleman that I trust you will find very deserving of your civilities, and who I think you may safely trust any to, as he carries several despatches to Congress, which he is to deliver himself, and consequently will go in Captain Nicholson. I understand that Captains Thompson and Hyndman refused to let you have anything to do with the prizes they bro't into l'Orient; that they have accounted, or say they will account, with the gentlemen at Passi * for the Congress share of the prizes, and that to them only have they applied and been directed since they came to L'Orient. Judge then what must be my surprise to have ye other day presented for payment bills to the amount of near seventy thousand livres, drawn by these captains on you and me. I saw these captains twice while they were up here, but they never communicated to me one syllable of their affairs, and I only know from common report that they are in the continental service. There is something very odd in this transaction, and I could wish you would find out by whose orders they drew so largely on us at the

---

* "Captains Thomson and Hinman arrived in the month of November, 1777, in two of the Continental frigates at Port L'Orient with two prizes, which they sold without difficulty, but at a low rate. Their equipments exceeded the continental share to a large amount." *Deane's Narrative*, 41. The instructions under which the captains cruised are printed in the *Works of Franklin*, VI. 112.

moment they were about to sail. As you are much
in the way, and will frequently have opportunities
of recommending consignments from this country
to your brother's house in America, you will excuse
me for hinting that I should think you ought not
to neglect any opportunity of that sort. I hear
that Mr. Deane's brother, Mr. Simeon Deane, is
just sent out to America to settle a house in Virginia as Messrs. Simeon Deane & Co., and that he
is promised more of the consignments from this
country and Holland.* Who compose ye company
you know as well as I do, for I have not heard that.
Mr. Williams will not, I suppose, hesitate to tell
you who signed the letter to him directing him to
undertake the sale of prizes made by Continental
armed vessels. This letter I have repeatedly endeavored to get recalled, and was solemnly promised it should be done, but I am informed it never
[has been recalled].†

---

*Simeon Deane had been forced to put back, the frigate meet-
ing with an accident, and reaching France soon after the signing
of the treaty, a copy was sent by him to Congress in another
vessel, *Le Sensible*. A letter from him to his brother was intercepted by the British, and printed in *Lloyd's Morning Post*, 26
August, 1778.

† It was not until the 25 May, 1778, that the powers of Williams
were formally revoked. "It is not from any prejudice to you,
for whom we have a great respect and esteem, but merely from
a desire to save the public money, and prevent the clashing of
claims and interests, and to avoid confusion and delays, that we

TO RICHARD HENRY LEE.

PARIS, 9 January, 1778.

My dear Brother:

This I hope will be delivered to you by Mr. Stevenson, by whom I wrote already very largely to you, Loudoun, Congress, directed to ye Secretary, C. Thomson, Esqr , and several other friends. If my writing to Congress, addressed to the Secretary is not approved, let me be directed otherwise, and apologise for me, as it is ye usual mode practised in Europe. Mr. Stevenson has thought himself very ungenteely treated by some of the Commissioners here; he will state ye case to you himself. To me it seems a continuation of the *little* intrigue, which has been constantly practised here between Mr. D[eane] and Mr. C[armichael] to ye infinite disgrace of ye American cause, in so much that if ye success of ye northern army against Burgoyne had not been so great, I am convinced that ye Americans would have been by this time *driven* with disgrace from ye French ports, and it was very likely at one time that if G. B. had desired it, ye Bastile would have been a lodging place for him who by his folly, to say no worse, was the means of getting poor Hodge, a Philadelphian, there for six weeks last summer. With respect to

have taken this step." *Commissioners to Jonathan Williams,* 25 May, 1778. See letter of Williams, 22 July, 1778, in *Papers in relation to the Case of Silas Deane,* 130.

Mr. Deane's conduct, you will hear enough of that from various hands, I don't doubt; but I should think myself very culpable both to my country and to you, were I not to caution you in ye strongest manner against the wiles and intrigues of Mr. Carmichael. As to his public principles, you will soon have reason to think of them in ye same manner that I do; and as to his private principles, I never knew a man in my whole life that I would not sooner trust. I have for some time been obliged to avoid being *ever alone* with him, and for fear of some plot, I have avoided trusting him with my hand writing, even for the superscription of a letter. Weigh with caution, but trust not any thing that comes from him, whether it is on paper, or verbal, or by insinuations, or little hints, or private anecdotes. A fertile brain is never at a loss for *invention*, when schemes, too dark to bear ye face of day, are in agitation. I could such tales relate, which, as Shakespeare says, would harrow up your soul. I know Mr. C. has a strong recommendation to Congress from Dr. F. and Mr. D. The secret of all this would be too long for this letter, but I am much mistaken if the givers of that recommendation will not be quite satisfied if it is lay'd by as waste paper. The *giving* has paid the debt between him and Mr. Deane, who knows him too well, and is also too much in his power, to let him go away discontented. Besides I remember an *old cunning man* used to say : that smooth words, or letters of recommendation, where others were to pay the roast, cost a man very little, and therefore a *sagacious* man should never refuse them.* I beg your patronage and that of our friends to Mr. S., for I fear ye intrigues of C. may hurt him, especially if he knows what letters Mr. S. has in his possession, which will throw some light on ye real character of Mr. C.

I suppose Mr. R. Morris will not think himself much obliged to Mr. D. for ye treatment his brother, Mr. Thos. Morris, has received here. I have done everything I could to support Mr. T. Morris, but the Commissioners being in possession of all ye money obtained here for your use, the point is completely gained against Mr. Morris, and Mr. Williams seems now ye only agent at Nantes. He has already received about £500,000† of the public money, and now asks for £200,000 more, without any account returned how the five hundred thousand livres have been expended. I must again give it as my opinion that in duty you are called upon immediately to require a full, clear, particular and explicit account, with proper vouchers, of

---

* See *Franklin to a friend*, date unknown, in his *Works*, VI, 99.

† The French *livre* is intended. Why this credit was given is explained by *Franklin to Arthur Lee*, 6 April, 1778, *Works*, VI, 162.

ye expenditures of ye very large sums, that have and will be received for your use, on this side of the Atlantic. Remember how Virginia suffered for want of this precaution in ye case of ye late treasurer R[obinso]n.* Will it not be wise in Virginia while paper money is plenty, to begin directly in laying taxes to pay off our proportion of ye heavy sums that will be expended in ye course of the war.

I understand Mr. Simeon Deane, who carried lately from the commissioners some dispatches to Congress, is sent by his brother here to settle in Virginia as a merchant, under the firm of Simeon Deane & Co. Who is to form the Co., you can guess as well as me. However, I hear much industry is used and great pains are taking to throw all the consignments from this country into that house, which may very easily be effected, if the

---

* John Robinson—the defaulting treasurer of Virginia. He was a man of large estate, and for nearly twenty-five years had been Speaker of the House of Burgesses. When Treasurer, he had loaned the public money to his personal and political friends, to curry favor in the House, an example taken from English methods, and in his private ventures. Finding himself on the verge of ruin, he concocted a device for a public loan office, from which money would be loaned to individuals on landed security, hoping in this way to cover his deficit by transferring his liabilities to the Colony. The scheme was defeated by Patrick Henry or Richard Henry Lee—or both—and four years later the death of Robinson exposed his frauds.

disbursement of the public money on this side continues as at present. The house of W. and Morris seems to be forgot entirely in this plan. I need not mention how our public affairs go on here, because I know they are fully stated by your brother, who writes this day. With respect to the charges against Mr. D. and Mr. C., I think you should weigh the matter with Loudoun very cautiously and only move when you see the way very clear.* In the arrangement that has been mentioned about commissioners at the different courts, I have been, it seems, left out of the question. However, I shall say nothing on that head, because ye arrangement seems to me a little visionary at present, and that at any rate some years must pass before it could be brought to bear with you, and every month may produce events that

---

* Arthur Lee, though he forwarded a formal charge against Deane to his brother, Richard Henry, was disinclined to appear as the accuser. "Perhaps it would be wiser for me to support than commence an accusation, for every day will furnish new matter of complaint, and some one will speak at last" (26 January, 1778). "If the conduct of these two Commissioners [Franklin and Deane], which has been neglectful, and I am much mistaken if it has not been dishonest too, towards the Public, and affrontive to Individuals, who were not their creatures, is not yet sufficiently known and censured with you, and if Mr. Morris does not mean to pursue his point against them, the time is not come for me to hazard myself." (16 January 1778.)

might render the arrangement improper. Strange
as it may appear, that a man without education,
without family, without fortune, and without
character, in short without a single requisite but a
talent for low intrigue, should think of being
placed in high and responsible situation, yet I
have good reason to believe that Mr. C. has had
vanity enough to suppose he can manage the
Congress, so as to get appointed commissioner to
Prussia. However, I shall think it more strange
than any thing that has happened yet, if he suc-
ceeds in that, or indeed in any other of his plans.
If my appointment is ever changed, I should prefer for myself England first, and Holland next, for
I am now satisfied that in less than three years
America will have a commissioner publickly received in both those places. But I apprehend my
station will be continued in Prussia (between
which country and America there must be a great
trade,) even if Dr. F. should be sent to Vienna,
for which court he is certainly the fittest person, as
Holland would suit Mr. D—'s abilities. You will
also want a commissioner in Portugal. If a respectable man will not come over from your own
body, there is a Mr. Thos. Digges in England, a
son of Wm. Digges in Maryland, opposite to Gen'l
Washington's, who is sensible, spirited, and has
been invariably and usefully employed in his
country's services ever since the commencement

of the dispute with G. B.* There are also here
two respectable gentlemen of South Carolina,
Dan'l and Wm. Blake, brothers, either of whom
would do, and I dare say would accept such an
appointment. Col. Laurens knows them well.

Our affairs are come to such a point here, that
my departure from hence will take place very

---

* A more unfortunate nomination could hardly have been
made. Digges was a Maryland merchant residing in London,
and representing himself as a zealous advocate of America, undertook the task of relieving the sufferings of American prisoners in English prisons. From time to time he drew for his
expenses on Franklin, until he had received £495 sterling,
when Franklin learned that he had pocketed all the money
save about £30, failed, and absconded. " I received your re-
spected favor of the 20th past, and am shocked exceedingly at
the account you give me of Digges. He that robs the rich even
of a single guinea is a villain; but what is he who can break his
sacred trust, by robbing a poor man and a prisoner of eighteen
pence given in charity for his relief, and repeat that crime as
often as there are weeks in a winter, and multiply it by robbing
as many poor men every week as make up the number of near
six hundred? We have no name in our language for such
atrocious wickedness. If such a fellow is not damned, it is not
worth while to keep a devil." *Franklin to William Hodgson*,
1 April, 1781. He afterwards had a conversation with John
Adams in Holland, and doubtless was employed by the British
Ministry. Adams' *Writings*, I. 355.

" It has also fallen very practically within my knowledge
that Mr. Thomas Digges, of Maryland, has exerted himself with
great assiduity and address in gaining intelligence and doing
other services in England." *Arthur Lee to the Committee of
Foreign Affairs*, 19 December, 1777.

shortly, and after France has acknowledged our independency, you may reckon on most of ye Powers of Europe immediately doing ye same, except ye Emperor of Germany, and his mother, ye Empress, who still keeps possession of all ye Austrian dominions, and rules without letting her son, ye Emperor, having anything to do with ye government. He is only at present commander-in-chief of her army. I shall therefore have a difficult task to manage in that court where there is a double cabinet, one of ye reigning sovereign, and ye other of ye heir apparent. I shall, however, do every thing in my power to accomplish the desires of Congress, and ye wishes of my country. A vessel from Virginia with 180 hhds of tobacco, I don't know whose property, was taken last month on this coast by an English man of war and carried to England.

TO T. ADAMS [EDWARD BROWNE].

12 January, 1778.

Dear Sir:

Be so good as to let our friend E. B. know he was written to ye 9th via L——t C—t* about insurance, but as delay or miscarriage may happen, communicate to him that 'twas to the following effect. I hope something, if not ye whole of the

---

* Lambert Court.

sale of *Hops*, has been done that T. R. was written to about. The annual policy being really out, on a war between France or Spain and Great Britain, be so good as to get insured for me against that event taking place in four months from this time, as far as to take £1500 sterling in premium, provided it can be done at 15 per cent. prem? or under. But if the prem? should be higher than 15 per cent., go as far as 20 per cent., and in that case only insure as far as to take up £1000 sterling in premiums. I have no doubt that my request will be complied with in ye best manner and on the cheapest terms. Care should be taken that the underwriters be good, and the best way to get ye business expeditiously done is to give orders to different brokers, B—d and L—, Let—r* and others that are known to be clever in that way. Be so good as to advise what is done. Sums and dates should be mentioned, and when a safe opportunity offers, sums and names as they may stand on ye policy. When it is known what is done ye premio shall be supplied. We have not any news here that is to be depended on; every one looks to the English papers, but accounts are so various in them that one hardly knows what to believe. Best wishes and esteem from every one here attend Mr. J—nes ye Traveller, and respects

---

* Bird, Lewis and Letillier.

are desired to Serjeants and Senoakes. How is y^e
alderman business settled? Kindest regards to the
Haberdasher.

TO THE BARON DE SCHULENBERG

PARIS, 16 January, 1778.

Sir:

My brother, the Honorable A. Lee, Esq., has
communicated to me the contents of the letter
which you honored him with of the 23d ultimo,
and I shall with pleasure and expedition obey the
summons when you are pleased to inform me of
his Royal Majesty's opinion that my arrival at
Berlin may be of mutual benefit to his Majesty
and the United States of America. Being well
acquainted with the nature and extent of the commerce between America and Europe, I flatter myself it will be in my power to point out such plans
as may in the present situation of things be carried
into execution, and will be productive of great
advantages to his majesty's dominions, as well as
to America; and I have strong hopes that the period
is not far distant when several of the European
powers will acknowledge the independence of the
United States, since it is now evident that they are
fully able to maintain their rights, against the
utmost efforts of Great Britain. The very high
respect they bear for his Prussian Majesty makes

them extremely anxious to rank him among their first and best friends. At this moment it would be the most signal mark of his Majesty's friendship for the United States if he would use his influence in obstructing Great Britain from engaging any more German troops to serve in America.

We have not received any late dispatches from Congress. When we have any thing authentic, I shall lose no time in communicating the same to your Excellency. By Gen'l Howe's last dispatches to England, of November 29, you will see that the American Forts on Mud Island and Red Bank, on the river Delaware, had been evacuated. The greatest advantage that General Howe will receive from this will be that his escape from Philadelphia is rendered less difficult than it was, provided he leaves it before the ice obstructs the navigation of the river. General Washington's main army was posted only ten English miles from Philadelphia, without any river between him and General Howe, and a strong American corps of observation was posted in the Jerseys, about twelve miles from Philadelphia, so that General Howe is under the necessity of forcing a general engagement, or of leaving his present station. We are assured from England, that he has positively demanded to be recalled, which is a decisive proof that he does not like his situation; and the very great decline of the English funds proves that the basis of the

British strength, which was their credit, is done away.

PARIS, 22 January, 1778.

Sir :

Be so good as to inform Congress that I have communicated to them by several letters addressed to Charles Thomson, their Secretary, my proceedings hitherto, in consequence of their appointing me their Commissioner at the Courts of Vienna and Berlin. I am now to add that having lately had a conference with the Imperial Ambassador at this Court, he observed immediately an imperfection in my commission, as it only authorizes me to treat with the Emperor of Germany, and not with his mother, who is the reigning and sovereign prince over all the Austrian dominions, as well in Germany and Flanders as elsewhere.

She is extremely jealous of her power and authority, not permitting her son to interfere in any manner in the government of her dominions. Her title is, ''The Most Serene and Most Potent Princess Maria Theresa, Queen of Hungary and Bohemia, Arch Duchess of Austria,'' &c., &c. The Emperor her son, though heir to her dominions, is, at present, only Commander-in-Chief of his mother's army, and as Emperor is the head of the German Empire. I therefore beg leave to submit to Congress whether it may not be proper to send another commission to treat with the Queen of Hungary, &c., since, in fact, there are two Courts to negotiate with, though they both reside in the same city, viz: with the Emperor, so far as relates to the German Empire, such as obstructing Great Britain from procuring German troops to send to America; and with his mother, for the purposes of commerce with the Austrian dominions, &c., &c.

There is every reason to believe that our affairs will be finally settled here, and the compact signed and sealed in a few days; after which I shall immediately set off for Vienna, since from that quarter we have most to apprehend, as there has been always a particular intimacy between that Court and the Court of London, at least for the present century, which had not been interrupted but during the last war with France.

Notwithstanding the promising appearance of things at present, I cannot forbear giving it as my opinion that every possible exertion should be made to prepare for a vigorous campaign next summer.

I am, with sincere esteem, &c.

TO RICHARD HENRY LEE.

PARIS, 24 January, 1778.

My dear Brother :

In course of ye last two months, as well as ye present, I have wrote you a variety of letters, all

which are on board ye Independence, Captain
Young, and ye Lyon, Captain Nicholson, two Continental vessels, that from ye most outrageous ill-
management of your directors here, are I believe
at this moment in ye river Loire, on which Nantes
is situated, with ye cloathing for your army, which
ought to have been in America three months ago,
and which most certainly in other hands would
have been so, ye danger of the enemy excepted.
Things cannot go otherwise while public interest
is sacrificed to private jobs. There is only one
remedy that I know of for such crying evils, which
is to call immediately for a fair, explicit and particular account of ye expenditure of ye very large
sums that have already been, and will hereafter be
received for ye use of ye United States, on this side
the Atlantic; with regular vouchers, at least for
large sums; not remaining contented with an account that so much was paid to such one's draft,
or to Mr. C[armichael], or to Mr. R[oss], or to Jno.
W[illiams], or Mr. any body else, for the public
use, without a particular account is also rendered
from these individuals, how the money furnished
them has been expended, whereby you will be able
to judge whether justice has been done or not.
Added to this, strict injunctions should be sent to
your commissioners or deputies not to meddle in
any manner with contracts, trade, or sale of prizes.
Leave all that to your mercantile agent, as well as

furnishing all supplies you want, which ye Commissioners should be advised of your ordering from ye Agent, and at the same time directed to furnish, out of ye money they receive here for you, ye agent with the necessary funds for payment, when your remittances in ye way of trade are not sufficient. By this means there will be some cheque on ye expenditures, which there is not at present, and I will venture my reputation on it, that your supplies will be more regularly forwarded than they have hitherto been; especially, if a proper person, (such as Mr. John Lloyd of South Carolina, tho' now at Nantes, whom I mentioned to you before) is appointed ye commercial agent. It would be as painful for you to read, as to me to give an account of the various malconduct here; but if a day of reckoning comes, as I trust it will, I shall not hesitate to state what I know to be true.

Mr. Thos. Morris, I apprehend, has pretty effectually thrown himself out of the agency line by devolving his authority on Mr. Williams, Dr. Franklin's nephew, of Nantes, whom ye Dr. and Mr. D., has set up there in opposition to Mr. M. As Mr. Deane's brother, Simeon, is sent out to establish a house in Virginia under ye firm of S. Deane & Co., that will have all possible interest made here to get ye chief of ye consignments from this country, which probably will take a great deal from ye house of W[illing], Morris & Co., if things continue here as they are at present. You very well know how much credit and influence the power of disposing of large sums of money always gives.

By the agreement to be made with this country, it is stipulated that consuls are to be admitted in the French ports to watch over the interests of American commerce. Marseilles, Bayonne, L'Orient and Dunkirk are to be free ports for the admission of all American commodities; therefore, I presume at each of these ports an American consul will be appointed. This arrangement may not immediately take place, but when it does, I could wish that Mr. Edward Browne, my former partner, may be appointed the consul at L'Orient, because I know his capability for such an appointment, and his uniform attachment to the cause of America. If Mr. B. is so appointed, I will endeavor to establish him as a mercantile house there, and put my nephew T[hom] L[ee] in partnership with him, which appears to me at present as eligible a plan as can be devised for Thom., and in which, by a few years' industry and attention to business, he may make himself entirely independent. * * *

It is understood that most of the powers of Europe are now disposed to acknowledge the independence of America, and unluckily when ye commission from Congress appointing a commissioner to the Court of Vienna was shown to the imperial ambassador here, he immediately discovered what I had remarked before to you, that the commissioner [was] only empowered to treat with the Emperor of Germany, and not with the Empress Queen, who, it is to be observed, is ye actual reigning sovereign over all the Austrian dominions, both in Germany, Flanders and elsewhere, the Emperor being only a nominal title as head of the German empire or Germanic body and King of the Romans. He is also commander in chief of his mother's army, and heir to her dominions. Her title is the most serene and most potent Maria Theresa, Empress, Queen of Hungary and Bohemia, Archduchess of Austria, &c., &c., &c., &c. She is extremely delicate with respect to her rights and powers, and will not suffer ye Emperor to interfere in the most distant manner in ye government of her dominions. You will therefore see the necessity of expediting a new commission to me, authorizing me to treat with her, leaving that already sent relative to the Emperor uncancelled, because tho' mother and son are residing together, they must be treated as two separate and distinct powers.

The Commissioners here, tho' possessed of great funds belonging to Congress, which are disbursed most plenteously and without account to dependents, favorites, relations and for private purposes, have declined supplying anything to ye Commissioners to the Grand Duke of Tuscany, Vienna and

Berlin, to bear their expenses in their mission. You will see from this how necessary it is for Congress to give positive orders on this head and to inform the several commissioners interested with what is ordered. That you may not be imposed on by ye assuming arrogance of some people, give me leave to assure you (as I have been an attentive observer and eye witness of all the turns and changes here) that ye alterations of late in our favor on this side the Atlantic, have been totally and entirely owing to ye success of the American arms last year, and particularly in ye captivity of Burgoyne and his army.

I must again caution you against C[armichae]l, who goes in Capt. Nicholson. In order to know your plans and worm himself into your confidence that he may betray you, he will in the grossest manner abuse those he thinks you dislike—particular Mr. D. and Dr. F., tho' I am greatly mistaken if Mr. D. has not particularly recommended him to Mr. H—n of V—a,* to make a party against you. Watch him well, and then judge for yourself. Our country has been generally the scene of plunder and imposition for vagabond strangers that have credit enough to buy a fine suit of cloaths. There is more occasion now than ever to guard against them, both in a public and

---

* Benjamin Harrison, of Virginia.

private view. A Mr. Holker is gone over with
Mr. Deane, and I apprehend with recommendations from some here.* It may be well to attend
with circumspection to his motions. The inclosed letter is entirely on the omission in the
commission to Vienna; the subject of funds has
never yet been mentioned by me to C.; that I leave
to the care of particular friends, and as I do the
care of my private fortune, to you and Loudoun,
to whom you'll be pleased to communicate this.

---

* Holker was associated with Chaumont, but was charged by
the French ministry with verbal instructions to report upon the
circumstances of America, the disposition of Congress, the resources at command, and especially to induce the Congress not
to listen to advances for peace from Great Britain which did not
at the same time guarantee peace to their allies. "There has
arrived here a Mr. Holker, from France, who has presented a
paper to Congress, declaring that he comes with a verbal message to Congress from the Minister of France, touching our
treating with Great Britain, and some other particulars, which,
for want of his paper, we cannot at present enumerate. The
style of his paper is as if from the representative of the Court,
but he has no authentic voucher of his mission for the delivery
of his verbal message. We desire of you, gentlemen, to give
us the most exact information in your power concerning the
authenticity of Mr. Holker's mission for this purpose." *Committee of Foreign Affairs to the Commissioners*, 21 June, 1778.
Vergennes, upon being questioned, denied that Holker had any
verbal commission from the ministry; but being informed that
Holker was going to America, Vergennes had desired him to
write, from time to time, the state of things and the temper of
the people. Doniol regards Holker as the agent of Maurepas.

LETTERS

OF

WILLIAM LEE,

SHERIFF AND ALDERMAN OF LONDON; COMMERCIAL AGENT
OF THE CONTINENTAL CONGRESS IN FRANCE; AND MIN-
ISTER TO THE COURTS OF VIENNA AND BERLIN.

———

1766=1783.

COLLECTED AND EDITED BY

WORTHINGTON CHAUNCEY FORD.

VOL. II.

BROOKLYN, N. Y.:
HISTORICAL PRINTING CLUB.
1891.

CONTENTS OF VOL. II.

(iii)

1779.

TO RICHARD HENRY LEE.

4 February, 1778.

My dear Brother:

Mr. Thos. Morris died at Nantes the 31st ulto. The inclosed letter will tell that I am waiting for an order from Court to put me in possession of his papers, which are sealed up by the king's officer agreeable to ye laws of this country in case of the death of a stranger:* I shall before I leave this appoint proper persons in ye different parts to receive and dispose of any cargoes or property that may arrive in any port on account of the public.

---

* "Feb. 2d. The Commissioners received an account from Mr. Ross, at Nantes, that Mr. T. Morris was at the point of death, and if that happened his papers would be seized by the officers of the crown. Mr. Lee went with his brother to Versailles, to get an order for the delivery of the papers which concerned the public business, to the other commercial agent. M. Gérard said this would be done with all possible expedition, if the commissioners would present a small memorial for it to the minister."

"3d. Mr. L. drew up a *mémoire*, desiring an order for the delivery of Mr. Morris's papers to Mr. W. Lee, the other commercial agent, which the other commissioners signed. On the 4th, Mr. W. L. waited upon Mr. Gérard with the *mémoire*, and he promised to expedite it with all possible despatch." *Arthur Lee's Diary.*

This arrangement when made, I shall give the committee a particular account of, that they may confirm or alter as they think proper; but if they should think of appointing any other commercial agent before they hear from me again, you can't, I think at present, do better than endeavor to get Mr. John Lloyd of South Carolina appointed, who is now at Nantes. I fancy a *Scotch* gentleman, a Mr. John Ross, who is here from Philadelphia, will endeavor to get the appointment thro' Mr. R[obert] M[orris]. I have for my own part many solid objections to such an appointment, which I have not time to mention now, but I hope 't will not take place. Our business is not yet finally settled yet at this court, but so near it that I hope nothing will prevent the conclusion, as everything is written fairly and agreed, only remains to sign and seal. Everything is settled in G[erman]y, where there will not be any war. The King of Prussia's minister has written that his M[ajest]y will acknowledge the Independence of the United States as soon as France has done so. In England the king has determined to pursue his utter ruin, and every exertion is made by y[e] M[inisteriali]sts, Jac[obins], Tor[ies] and Scot[chme]n to procure men for another campaign, which you ought to provide for with your utmost vigor, and with this confidence that it will assuredly be the last unless your armies should everywhere be cut to pieces, and totally dispersed, which I think is too improbable to be even supposed.*

The uneasinesses and bickerings that have been on this side begin to subside, and I believe will soon totally vanish, as the principal fomenter, Mr. C[armichael] is now on his way to America. It is inconceivable the mischief this man has been the cause of by telling untruths from one to another, whispering and insinuating what never happened or was said, and a thousand other little artifices, for no end that I conceive but a natural delight in mischief. If he will give from under his hand plain and specific charges against any one, it may perhaps be worth attention; but otherways what is said in dubious terms or whispered, should be totally disregarded. This would be my advice even if he was to attempt a charge against a man I have the worst opinion of. I can't omit advising you never to be in his company alone.

TO RICHARD HENRY LEE.

NANTES, 13 February, 1778.

My dear Sir:

I have been two daies with the King's order to get possession of Mr. Thos. Morris's Papers, that I may be able to make some settlement of the public

---

* Lord Dunmore had proposed to the king to raise four regiments of Scotch and to be appointed Colonel himself. The ministry talked of sending 26,000 men to America.

affairs that have been in his hands before I go to Vienna, for which place I should have set out by this time, had not the death of Mr. Morris obliged me to come down here to put the public concerns under some regulations first.*

As soon as everything is regulated I shall give the Secret Committee a full account of the whole; but in the meantime I must advise you, that there is here a Scotchman, named John Ross, who has taken upon himself to forbid Mr. Penet, (that with Mr. James Gruel, has managed here all the public business, which was addressed to Mr. Morris,) to give me any public accounts, or to come to any settlement with me.

This is the more unwarrantable in him, as he knows how difficult it will be, without any interruption, to get those accounts settled with Mr. Gruel and Penet; and the more insufferable, as he has no kind of authority whatsoever for such conduct, the whole of which shall be fully stated to the Committee. He gives it out here that he expects to be appointed Commercial Agent, probably

---

* On Morris' death, it was represented to the Commissioners that Penet, on the plea of some partnership with Morris, might claim his papers. It was, therefore, thought best for William Lee to go to Nantes, armed with an order from the King, to receive the papers, and to deliver to Ross such of them as might relate to the operations of Willing and Morris. Lee quarreled with Ross and brought the whole trunk of papers to Paris.

thro' the interest of Mr. Robt Morris, whom he calls his friend; but I shall think it passing strange indeed if America was to choose a person, for such a very confidential and important trust, from that country whose natives have been assuredly the cause of all her most grievous miseries and sufferings.* * * *

You will probably hear before this gets to hand of the full Alliance made between you and this Country, on which I congratulate you, as our Independence is now firmly established, and probably the Internal war with you at an end; but I count it as an absolute certainty that, at the utmost, it can't last this year out, because a war between this Country with Spain against G. Britain is inevitable. Peace, here, cannot continue above two months, perhaps, not as many weeks.

Capt Young of the Independence, is still here tho' his dispatches were sent from Paris, the 1st Decr. What has detained him so long, I cannot learn from any one, but I shall not be surprised, if he and Mr. T. M[orris] in his letters should lay the blame on me, tho' I was away from hence the whole time. When he arrived I was here, and put the repairs and outfit of his vessel under the care of Mr Schweighauser, who had funds in his hands sufficient for the purpose, if they had been properly conducted. Mr Morris and Capt.ⁿ Young were then both absent, and when I went to Paris in consequence of my appointment, every thing was going on very well. On their return they threw everything into confusion, and Captain Young wrote to me repeatedly, that he would not follow my orders, nor would he have anything to do with Mr Schweighauser. He also told the same to Mr Lee, who was acting in Mr Schweighauser's Counting House.* If you should not now be of the Committee, I hope you will take care to possess fully some proper member with these facts.

There is one part of the Treaty of Commerce which I do not by any means approve; but I would not say a word on the subject that in any manner might create contention, as on the whole we may esteem ourselves well off, were I not convinced that the ministry will alter it, if the Congress, tho' confirming what is done, should order the Commissioners to represent that they think that part not equal. It is, I think, the 12th article where 'tis engaged, that no duties shall be laid on anything exported *from* the United States to the West Indies, in consideration of no duties being laid on Molasses

---

*"Mr. Lee's Nephew, a son of the honorable Richard Henry Lee, is in the house of Mons. Schweighauser, at Nantes, as a clerk or as a partner—I am informed the latter. Commercial affairs and the disposition of prizes are put into the care of this house, while a near connection of Mr. Schweighauser, at Guernsey, or Jersey, is employing himself in sending out cruisers on our commerce." *Deane to the President of Congress,* 12 October, 1778.

only exported *to* the United States. This latter
part was directed by Congress to be asked, but in
their Instructions they desire it to be given up,
rather than that it should impede the Treaty.
When 'twas asked, the ministry, at first, said it
was a thing they never intended to do, as they
could not lay any impediment in the way of ex-
porting Molasses, without altering the whole system they had established for regulating the commerce of their Islands; but afterwards, they proposed as an equivalent that no duties should be
imposed on Tobacco exported to France. Some
of the Commissioners then proposed the equivalent
as it now stands; this the three were not unanimous in, when one* proposed that the opinion of
M.ʳ Izard and myself should be asked on this point,
as we were both in Paris; this the other two would
not agree to—when the dissentient conformed to
the majority rather than create a difference or any
disturbance, at so critical a monent.†

---

* Arthur Lee.

† This is not a true statement of this incident. The thirteenth
article of the treaty proposed by Congress, exempting from all
duties molasses purchased by Americans in the French islands,
was considered by Gérard an unequal stipulation; and to remedy
this defect the XIth and XIIth articles were framed. The first
conceded the exemption of molasses from duties, and the XIIth
stipulated that no duties should be imposed on merchandise exported from the States for the use of the French islands. The
Commissioners unanimously agreed to accept these articles, but

My late letters from London say, "the raising of men goes on very slowly in Great Britain; we shall not send many to America this year; but we shall block up their Ports, and carry on the war by sea, for we cannot give up our Sovereignty."

If this was the case before they knew what has been done here, you may easily judge how things will go, when they come to be informed of this decisive blow against them.

The paper sent will shew how the minority has

---

almost immediately after, Arthur Lee conceived some doubt of their expediency, and wrote to Franklin and Deane to prevent their being embodied in the completed treaty. Though not recognizing the mischievous consequences that Lee attributed to the 12th article, Franklin and Deane gave Lee a letter to Gérard, requesting the omission of the two articles, a letter which was delivered by Lee in person. "Mr. Lee discoursed on the subject with M. Gérard, who satisfied him, as he thought at the time, and as we all then thought, of the impropriety of making any alteration in the treaty after it had been so maturely considered ; had been fully agreed upon by us all ; had been approved of in form by his Majesty, and ordered to be transcribed and signed. Neither Mr. William Lee nor Mr. Izard ever spoke one word to me on the subject ; and I did not think myself authorized or at liberty to consult them or any other person on the subject but my colleagues." *Silas Deane to the President of Congress*, 12 October, 1778. See *Diplomatic Correspondence of the Revolution*, I, 470–473. *Life of Arthur Lee*, I., 383 *et seq.* Lee forwarded his objections to Congress, and it was from thence that Franklin first learned of their having been sent. *Franklin's Works*, VI., 200, 201.

increased of late,—it never voted on any question for 4 years past above 105, and on American questions before, not so high as 90, and now you see, they amount to 165.*

You know best what remittances the Committee has put into the hands of Mr. John Ross. I know he received from the Commissioners here, at least

---

* "The foundations of the North Ministry were sapped by the unfortunate turn of the American war. Their majorities in both Houses indeed continued large; but the country party began to hesitate in their support of this ruinous contest, to look with some dismay on increasing taxation, and to distrust the abilities or the honesty of the present rulers." *Donne*, II, 127. On February 2, Fox introduced a motion on the "State of the Nation," and in a speech of two hours and forty minutes described the misconduct of the war. "I went over the whole of the American business, and I really thought the House went a good deal with me in the most of it . . . . We had several Tories with us, and I really think it was a great day for us. The ministry, not by concert, but, I believe, by accident, did not say one word, which scandalised even their own friends a good deal, as I had opened the affairs so very fully. They now pretend to say that Ellis and Wedderburne were up (I did not see them), and, while they were complimenting one another, the question was put. The fact is, that it is such a cause as no man can defend well, and therefore nobody likes to attempt it." *Correspondence of Charles James Fox*, I, 168. The division stood 169 to 259—a surprise to the minority. "I trust," wrote the King to North, "that when next the Committee on the State of the Nation is resumed, gentlemen will be more ready to speak." North was eager to resign, and only remained to gratify the urgency of the King. On February 17th, North introduced his measures for conciliating the Colonies.

£20,000 sterling above 8 months ago, to purchase goods for the Congress. You ought to know whether he has sent those goods or not.

I wish the Secret Committee would attend more to business as a Body; for the Congress never could intend that any *one* should do the whole, or they would not have appointed a Committee, but have left it to one.

The Commissioners here, about 7 days ago, have given Mr. Izard and myself, each 2,000 Louis d'ors to support our Embassies, of which I shall inform the Secret Committee, to whom I had before wrote, that I should keep what money I had in my hands, belonging to them, to bear my expenses in Germany. Still it would be well for Mr. Izard and myself to have some authority in future to call on the Commissioners here for the funds to support our expenses, at least.

There are 50,000 land forces ordered into Normandy and Brittany on the coast opposite to England; most of them are already there, and while they continue, you need not fear that any more men will be sent to America. Thom. and Ludwell, and all your connections here, are well. Best love and wishes attend you and yours, and Loudoun and his.   Adieu.

TO RICHARD HENRY LEE.

NANTES, 15 February, 1778.

My dear Sir:

I before informed you by Mr. Stevenson, that it was agreed here to make Dunkirk, L'Orient, Bayonne, and Marseilles free ports for the admission of American vessels and produce of all kinds, duty free; and as France is to be allowed to appoint Consuls in the different American ports, to take care of the rights of the French Commerce, and America is to be allowed the same privilege here, I presume Congress will appoint Consuls at all the above free ports; in which case I wish much you could get Mr. Edward Browne, my former partner, appointed the Consul at L'Orient, or Dunkirk, (the former, viz.: L'Orient, I should prefer,) because I certainly know his capability for such an office, and his sincere attachment to our general Cause. If he is appointed, I will exert myself to get him established as a respectable house there and put Tom: in partnership with him, which, in my opinion, will be as happy and independent a situation for Tom: as can be wished.

With respect to the affairs at Green Spring, in general they must be left with you to act as you see best.

I wish particular attention may be paid to rearing young Negroes, and taking care of those grown up, that the number may be increased as much as possible; also putting several of the most promising and ingenious lads apprentices to different trades; such as carpenters, coopers, wheelwrights, sawyers, shipwrights, bricklayers, plasterers, shoemakers and blacksmiths; some women also should be taught to weave.

The planting of white mulberry trees should not by any means be neglected; the corners of the pannels of the fences, round all the fields, will be proper places.

If ever I return, the culture of silk will be my principal object; which I am morally certain will succeed even to the most sanguine expectations. No doubt care will be taken to receive the interest regularly of such money as may be placed in the Continental Loan office, and by adding it to the Principal increase the Capital fund. If the estate of the late Honble P. L. L.* is in a condition to pay off the legacy, which now amounts to upwards of £2,500 st^g, that may be placed in the Continental Loan office.

Every good attend you, I sincerely pray, and remain most affectionately

Yours &c.,

---

*Philip Ludwell Lee.

TO JOHN LLOYD.

CHAILLOT, 25 February, 1778.

Sir:

I had the good fortune to bring the trunk* with me here, sealed as you left it. The officers had more civility than a Scotchman [Ross], for they took my word for the contents, and let it pass untouched; if therefore, you and Mr. Blake have no objection, I shall be obliged to you for transmitting me a certificate stating on such a day at my request, you went with me to the public office of Monsieur Delicpore, avocat au Parlement et Greffier en chef de le Présidial de Nantes, where a trunk containing the papers of the late Mr. Thos. Morris was opened, and upon being examined by Mons.ʳ Delicpore and compared with the record he had before made of them, he found they were the same as when delivered to me; after which, they were all put again in the same trunk, which was locked and sealed by you and left in my possession. If Mr. R—d† was willing, he could not with propriety sign this, because he was not present at the last sealing, nor is his name on yᵉ paper attached to yᵉ trunk. I must beg your answer as soon as possible, because my stay here will not be long.

Nothing is yet settled about the appointment,

---

* Of Thomas Morris' papers.

† Perhaps a misreading for *Ross*.

though I have mentioned my plan, which you know, to the several commissioners, to which no reply has been made; some arrangement, however, shall be made in a few daies. Dr. F., indeed, I tho't did not seem displeased at the plan; but he replyed, that he tho't it was business in which I had the sole authority to act as I tho't proper, and that the Commissioners had nothing to do with it. I knew that as well as him, but at the same time would wish to act so as to meet the approbation of all parties.*

There seems to be nothing but confusion in England. The King and his ministers are as distracted as it is possible to conceive. Their rage for revenge and the utter incapability of gratifying it cannot be so well expressed in words, as Cibber has done it in the excellent representation of a raving madman over the gate of Bethlam Hospitals. The issue must shortly be, either a general war, or universal peace; but it is curious to observe as the tone of war increases on the other side, things be-

---

* This refers to the appointment of agents in the various ports of France. "Mr. Williams wrote me that although he had hitherto done the business at a moderate rate, with the view of serving his country, he could by no means accept of Mr. W. Lee's offer of dividing the commissions with him, but would sooner resign the business entirely." *Deane's Narrative*, 49. On the other hand Lee produced sworn affidavits by John Bondfield and J. D. Schweighauser that no demand for any commission, gratuity or reward was made for the appointments.

come calmer here; and when peace is the theme there, we are on all sides here—blustering for war. I hope you will commend me in your warmest manner to your excellent rib.

TO BENJAMIN FRANKLIN.

CHAILLOT, 25 February, 1778.

Mr. Lee presents his respectful compliments to Dr. Franklin, and begs leave to inform him that in consequence of his appointment yesterday to come here this day at 11 o'clock to examine yᵉ public papers that were to be taken out of yᵉ trunk bro't from Nantes, containing yᵉ papers of the late Mr. Thos. Morris, he got the favor of Mr. Izard to attend, as he knows the seal and hand writing of the Gentleman in whose presence the trunk was sealed at Nantes. However, as something has prevented Doctor Franklin from attending this day, and Mr. Lee is very desirous of getting away to Germany as soon as possible, he begs Dr. F. will be so good as to attend to-morrow at 11 o'clock precisely, or mention any other day and hour that will be more agreeable to him to finish that business. Mr. L. wishes for an answer per the bearer, as he has also wrote to Mr. Deane on the subject, and hopes he will attend whenever it is agreeable to Dr. F.*

---

*Lee desired that "to prevent reflections or suspicions, it

TO EDWARD BROWNE.

Dear Sir:

A letter to Mr. G[ran]d of the 20th, came safe and mentions one of the 6th which from his being absent on a journey has some how or other been mislaid *here* (it is verily believed) so that the contents are unknown where they were intended. For two packets came by L——t C——t, but in neither was anything from F——y street, nor is it conjectured what the strange news can be. Senoakes indeed hints about some one having lost country house and all, and obliged to appear to his creditors; who it is we can't guess, unless M—-l—-n.*

---

might be opened and the papers divided in our presence. We consented to this; and I went to his house for that purpose, where Mr. Izard attended to verify the seals of the two gentlemen that were on the trunk. But, Mr. Deane being hindered from attending by accident, the business was postponed; and, as I soon after understood by your letters, that Mr. Lee had had the papers under his particular examination several days before that formal sealing, of which I therefore did not see the use, and apprehending some danger of being involved in your quarrel, I refused on consideration to have any thing to do with the opening and sorting of the papers." *Franklin to John Ross*, 26 April, 1778. Lee, on going to Germany, left the trunk in Franklin's hands, taking his receipt for it, witnessed by Deane and his brother, and Izard and Pringle. Lee retained the key of the trunk.

* Molleson?

"A great Virginia house of the name of Moll—n is said to have stopped last Saturday; it is supposed that instead of carry-

If so, give a hint so that it may be understood. I
admire that there is not a word whether anything
has been done in y.e *Hop* or *Insurance* way. If
that of the 6th. contained anything material to be
known, it should be repeated. Pray look close
after the Jew and C—lb—g's affairs. Henrisod
should be tho't of when any insurance is to be
done, because whatever the premio is, will be so
much gained. The Adelphi should not be spared,
for he has proved himself as bad as most people before supposed him. Therefore lose not a moment
in inforcing the law in the most effectual manner.
Compliments to Mr. W., and tell him this, requesting his aid and advice. Relative to the H—ts,
they can't complain if the parchment is given
them, for it is only restoring things as they were,
and if this won't content them, they must be left
to their own meditations. Should the boasting
crescent get on again, take advantage of the first
moment of opening, and get as much as possible
if not the whole. A certain lady is extremely
anxious for her new tea urn, if good luck should
offer any opportunity so that it might get to the
bankers here in 11 or 12 daies, from this time. A
snuff box was carried by Mr. T——n,* who must

---

ing on his mercantile business, he had commenced politician,
and ruined thereby the fairest prospects." *Jenings to Arthur
Lee*, n. d.

* Thornton?

have delivered it by this time. All the travellers are well, and join in sincere good wishes for their old fellow-traveller. 'Tis certainly better to be born fortunate than rich. I——n and R—dl—ly * sent a little vessel, that when they bo't her was called the Mary Carrol, to Lisbon. She loaded with salt, when vessel and cargo was not worth £600 sterling. She went to Maryland, sold her salt at £10 currency a bushel, which bro't £25,000 currency. She has returned with tobacco, that will nett £7000 sterling, and left above £20,000 currency in the country. Astonishing as this is, it is certainly true. You'll observe that she was British property, which proves that some people had better steal a horse than look over the hedge. Think of the noise that was made in 1775 by some people about a book and a piece or two of linen.

TO RICHARD HENRY LEE.

PARIS, 28 February, 1778.

The unexpected and unlucky return of Mr. Deane gives me a moment to send you the inclosed copies of some former letters and also copies of the correspondence between Mr. Ross and me relative to Mr. Morris's papers, which will give you the facts so far, to form your judgment on†. Tho' I

---

* Mathew Ridley?

† "For my part, Sir, I shall ever maintain and declare openly

wish to avoid all comment on these extraordinary
productions, yet it is impossible to forbear observing how this insignificant Scotch pedlar talks as if
America was all his own, and Congress his instruments only. Strange indeed it would be if a North
Briton should accomplish by assurance what his
countrymen have not been able to do by force of
arms. He knows best what he means by insinuating that *treasonable correspondence* was to be found
amongst Mr. Morris's papers; at all events I can't
conceive that Mr. R. Morris or any other connection of the deceased ought to be much obliged to
him. It was much against my own wishes that I
went to Nantes, but all the commissioners here thot

my sentiments on the subject, nor shall I relinquish my opinion
until you convince me of an essential service rendered to *our
Country*, by your sagacity and assiduity to get possession of
treasonable correspondence by this strain and exertion of your
powers, under the cover of your *pretensions* to the measure."
John Ross to William Lee, Nantes, 13 February, 1778.
"In the next place permit me to observe that I do not consider you on this occasion, in any degree *concerned* or interested
from your appointment as Joint Agent, to *assume* or *interfere* in
the inspection of the public or private affairs of the late Mr.
Morris, or those of his connections under present circumstances. Because you have no authority from the *Brother*
[Robert Morris] nor from the house of W. M. & Co., [Willing,
Morris & Co.] neither have you ever *join'd* or superintended
any part of the public business with Mr. Morris as agent or
otherwise, consequently not responsible to the public for what
came under his management." *John Ross to William Lee*,
Nantes, 13 February, 1778.

it was a duty I owed the public, and accordingly they made a joint written application to the minister for an order to have the papers delivered to me. When I went down, the commencement of Mr. Ross's conduct you will learn from his first letter to me and my answer. To his last letter I made no reply, but in order to disappoint the breath of malignity, I had the trunk (without even opening it myself) carried to the public office, where the Greffier, examining them in the presence of Wm. Blake, Esq., of South Carolina, and Mr. John Lloyd, merchant in Nantes, found they were the same as when delivered to me; after which they were again put into the trunk and sealed by Messrs. Blake and Lloyd, and so I bro't them all here, where they wait for the attendance of the Commissioners to take out the public papers, when those of a private nature will be again sealed up and left with the commissioners for the legal claimant. I should not have given you so much trouble about this business, but that I am informed that Mr. Ross has laid a plot to make it a subject of public conversation in America, not only by writing to Mr. Morris (whose letter inclosed you will please to seal and deliver after perusal), but by impressing the minds of two passengers in his ship, the Brune, Capt. Green—a Mr. Brown, of South Carolina, and Mr. Verplank, of New York—with a false state of the transaction. Neither of them

know one single fact relative to the business themselves; only as they have been informed by Mr.
Ross, or others that he has told his tale to. He
depends on his influence with Mr. R. Morris, and
on that gentleman's influence in Congress; but I
have some reason to think he may find that he
reckons without his host. However, you will act
as the occasion requires. The letters inclosed to
the Secret Committee, will show what authority
he has assumed to himself in their affairs, and you
may communicate the first or the whole of his letters to me, as you think proper. My letter to Loudoun is chiefly political. You will please to open
it in case of his absence from Congress. It seems
to me at present that in order to keep peace here,
I shall be obliged to appoint Mr. John Lloyd and
Mr. Jonathan Williams, Dr. Franklin's nephew,
commercial agents at Nantes, until the pleasure or
the Committee is known; but I beg that such appointment may not be considered as a recommendation of either from me, and for very good reasons I must in particular beg to withdraw anything
I have before said in favor of Mr. Lloyd.* We
have all been dupes long enough to serve the private
views of others. As soon as ever the Commis-

---

*As late as 22 August, 1778, Arthur Lee wrote to Richard
Henry in very high terms of praise for Mr. J. Lloyd. *Life of
Arthur Lee*, II., 143.

sioners will finish the business of Mr. Morris's papers, I shall immediately set out for Vienna, from whence I hope to send you some agreeable intelligence in my next. Your son Thom seems happily fixed with Mr. Schweighauser, who appears a very worthy and respectable merchant, very fit and proper to be your agent at Nantes.

TO FRANCIS LIGHTFOOT LEE.

PARIS, 28th Feby 1778.

My dear Sir:

Since the original above copied, I wrote you from Nantes by a vessel of Messrs Pliarne and Penet's to South Carolina, giving some accounts of the extraordinary conduct there of Mr. John Ross, relative to Mr Thos Morris's papers; and also from thence sent two Pamphlets and a paper, by a Mr Brown of South Carolina. I have now wrote fully to R. H. L. on that subject, desiring him to communicate the contents to you, or in case of his absence that you will open his Packet, and do the needful, to prevent the effects of the calumny of Mr Ross, which I have understood since, is to be aided by the oral report of some passengers in his ship, the La Brune, Cap: Green, to whom he has strangely misrepresented facts, and they have not heard one word from me, nor do they know one

single fact themselves; the whole of their knowledge being founded on M.̲ Ross's acc.̲ of things to
themselves or others.

The Political Part you shall have to communicate to our brother. The unexpected and unlucky
return of M.̲ Simeon Deane occasions this dispatch
to be sent off in such a hurry, that we shall hardly
be able, (at Chaillot) to write so fully as we could
wish.

My last advices from England, which are as late
as the 20.th ins.̲, say Gen.̲ Howe is universally condemned. He sent a message by Lord Cornwallis,
that if Lord Geo. Germaine continued in office, he
must desire to come home. Lord Geo. G——ne, on
being told this, with a greatness of mind peculiar
to himself, immediately begged leave to resign, but
his Majesty, with a judgment and goodness natural
to him, refused his request.

Howe, it was thought at first might be quieted as
other Commanders have been; but considering the
whole matter it has at length been determined to
recall him, with intimation that his Majesty expected he would have done more; and Gen.̲ Clinton
was to succeed to the chief Command; but unluckily Gen.̲ Clinton being now returning to Europe with leave, another express has been sent off
after the first to stop Gen.̲ Howe, if Gen.̲ Clinton
has sailed. In short, there have been four ex-

presses on this subject; which will be to effect no
one here can guess at present.*

Lord North has opened his plan of conciliation,
which is both a silly and knavish piece of work.
A vile attempt has been made here to induce Par-

---

* Howe had asked to be recalled, and the King was convinced
that it would be as difficult to induce him to remain as it would
to get Lord George Germaine "to act towards him in such a
way as will make the efforts of others not prove abortive."
The King to Lord North, 13 January, 1778. On February 2d,
the recall of General Howe was a settled measure. Germaine
at this time did not think the repeal of the Boston act would
lead the Colonies back to their allegiance to the crown; the
declaratory act was what galled them. He therefore wished to
repeal all legislation subsequent to 1763, but hesitated on the
policy of such a measure, doubtful whether it would hurry
France into a treaty with the rebels, or would lead the colonies
to break with France. Lord George supported the pacific
propositions of Lord North. Germaine was directed to write a
"suitable letter to Sir W. Howe that may encourage him to act
with spirit until the arrival of his successor," but he prepared
a letter so "cold" in tone that the King objected to sending it.
His favoritism to Sir Henry Clinton had disgusted Howe, while
his profuse promises of reinforcements and supplies, and scant
performance, had rendered abortive the plans of the American
commander. In less than a month after Germaine wrote to
Howe of his recall, he had himself resigned because of a fancied
slight upon him by the King's rewarding Sir Guy Carleton with
a sinecure.

Franklin was at this time writing to Hartley:—"America has
been *forced* and *driven* into the arms of France . . . They can
never persuade her return and submission to so barbarous an
enemy" as Great Britain.

liament in a Treaty of Peace to declare that the currency of America shall not be admitted as legal tender.

The attempt is ridiculous and malicious. You know well one of the Signers, (viz.: M—l—n*); it is necessary, however, that he should appear soon to his creditors, so far my letter says.

Tho' you will have the two Bills, by this conveyance sent to Congress, I will mention that the first *enacts* the right of imposing *even Internal Taxes* upon you; which is going farther than the Declaratory Act, as that only in general terms, *implies* the right of Taxation. Tho' this right by the Act is to be suspended, yet another Parliament, even another day, the same Parliament, may, for good reasons, resume that right. The Act of Parliament is still more impudent; I can't call it illusory, for it is too explicit to be misconceived. The Commissioners are to be vested with full powers to do all imaginable mischief and villainy, without the shadow of authority to do any good, until it is confirmed by Parliament, viz.: they may proclaim a cessation of the *Land* war, and break it at pleasure, so that if the American Army disbands, on the faith of their Proclamation, the war may be commenced at any moment they please, when they are most sure of doing the greatest mischief.

---

* Molleson.

No truce should be admitted or Treaty commenced within 3 or 4 months after every British soldier has been embarked from the Continent; or rather until their arrival in Europe, with Bag and Baggage, is authenticated.

Again the commissioners may suspend the Prohibitory Act, and enforce it at pleasure; so that if American vessels venture to sea, on the faith of the Proclamation, they may at any time be taken in the trap, by the law being enforced. Besides it should be remembered, that even if the Act was entirely repealed, you can't get military stores from Great Britain nor manufactures, because these last are prohibited by your own resolutions.

'Tis not possible to conceive that the British ministry, idiots and wicked as they are, can be such perfect fools, as to expect any benefit from these Acts; the Truth is what they publicly boast, that their greatest reliance is on Bribery, if they are but once admitted to have free access to the Members of the Congress; for it is in every one's mouth, that near half a million of guineas are sent over.*

---

*Franklin gave a calmer estimate of North's propositions, but not less unfavorable to their sincerity. "What reliance can we have on an act expressing itself to be only a declaration of the *intention* of Parliament concerning the *exercise* of the right of imposing taxes in America, where, in the bill itself, as well as in the title, a right is supposed and claimed which never existed; and a *present intention* only is declared not to use it, which may be changed by another act next session, with a pre-

The actual situation of things here, and the number of land forces on the coast, will certainly prevent any more troops being sent over this spring to America, even if Great Britain had them, but in fact they neither have or can get any more to send. A gentleman writes from England that it is possible Manchester may afford a small regiment of Weavers in 1779 for America, but it is now quite certain they cannot do it in 1778.

The clouds seem to gather, and threaten a war in Germany, tho' everything seemed settled a few weeks ago. The Emperor, and Elector Palatine, had agreed between themselves about the division

---

amble that, this *intention* being found inexpedient, it is thought proper to repeal this act and resume the exercise of *the right* in its full extent. If any solid benefit was intended by this, why is it confined to the colonies of North America and not extended to the loyal ones in the sugar islands? But it is now useless to criticise, as all acts that suppose your future government of the colonies can be no longer sufficient.

"In the act for appointing Commissioners, instead of full powers to agree upon terms of peace and friendship, with a promise of ratifying such treaty as they shall make in pursuance of those powers, it is declared that their agreements shall have no force nor effect, nor be carried into execution, till approved of by Parliament; so that everything of importance will be uncertain. But they are allowed to proclaim a cessation of arms, and revoke their proclamation, as soon as, in consequence of it, our militia have been allowed to go home; they may suspend the operation of acts prohibiting trade, and take off that supervision when our merchants, in consequence of it, have been induced to send their ships to sea; in short, they may

of the Estate of the late Elector of Bavaria, but the
King of Prussia says, he must have his share of the
plunder, or some equivalent, to increase his strength
in proportion to that of the house of Austria; otherwise he will try what is to be got by war; which
disposition England will no doubt endeavor to support, in order to embarrass France, that will probably take part with the Emperor.

I hope however things will be settled by negotiation, as there is a probability at present; otherwise
I shall be much embarrassed in my negotiations in
that quarter, *being only detained for the Commissioners to finish the necessary proceedings relative to
Mr. Morris's papers; which being done I shall set*

---

do everything that can have a tendency to divide and distract
us, but nothing that can afford us security. Indeed, sir, your
ministers do not know us. We may not be quite so cunning as
they, but we have really more sense, as well as more courage,
than they have ever been willing to give us credit for ; and I am
persuaded these acts will rather obstruct peace than promote it,
and that they will not answer in America the mischievous and
malevolent ends for which they were intended. In England
they may indeed amuse the public creditors, give hopes and expectations that shall be of some present use, and continue the
mismanagers a little longer in their places. *Voilà tout.*" *Franklin to Hartley*, 26 February, 1778.

The King thought he was making "generous offers" to the
Colonies, and doubtless he and North were sincere in their
wishes to conciliate. Even Franklin said the propositions
"would probably have been accepted, if they had been made
two years ago." *Franklin to Gérard*, 1 April, 1778. See Lecky,
History of England in the Eighteenth Century, IV, 76.

out immediately for Vienna. According to the usual mode of doing business here, that which ought not to take up more than 2 or 3 hours, will I expect keep here me Ten or Twelve days.

'Tis extremely irksome, even to think, much more so to write on the horrid management of your business in this quarter. Cap.ᵗ Young of the Independance is still in the river Loire, tho' his dispatches were sent from hence the 1.ˢᵗ Dec.ʳ So are all the supplies for your army, that ought to have been in America three months ago, when they would have gone much safer than now.

I know the excuse will be contrary winds, and the fear of the British cruisers, but be assured that there is not a syllable of truth in either. Letters from Nantes yesterday (one of which I enclose) say the ships are not yet all loaded.

The whole arises from mal-conduct at Headquarters, and the persons he employs follow his own example of being more intent on private gain than public good.

The remedy must come from your side, and speedily, or the mischief will be irremediable.

The secret committee, as well as the other committees, should attend more to business as a body, and not leave the whole to the management of any one member; *and here the political and mercantile characters should be entirely distinct and separate, and both of them executed by persons of your express appointment. If this regulation does not take place soon an infinite deal of mischief will, inevitably, ensue.*

Congress will, no doubt, be pressed for remittances, and to comply with an unwise, injudicious and unauthorized Contract made here with the Farmers General for 5,000 Hds. of Tobacco; altho' more money comes in here from voluntary contributions than will furnish all the supplies you want, and pay the interest of all the money you have borrowed in America; for the expenditure of which no account is rendered, nor can any be procured.*

The contract for tobacco should be let to sleep; return the money when you are able with the interest.

Congress can't too soon positively forbid the money to be borrowed in Europe, which they ordered in Dec.ʳ 1776.

Mʳ Beaumarchais makes a considerable or rather an enormous demand against you, which is thought utterly unjust. Congress is desired to let it be settled here. Endeavor if possible to prevent this request from being complied with; order the whole to be stated to Congress, when the demand will be entirely relinquished, or, if persisted in, will discover such a connection and proceedings as will certainly produce very great public utility.†

* This was an entirely gratuitous supposition and statement.

† "We have, to avoid disputes at a particular time, delivered

I pray you to send me by several opportunities a list of Congress, and several Committees; the Constitution and Laws of Virginia, as now settled; and how long you and R. H. L. can be permitted to remain in Congress; and the names of such in case of your absence, that you think it will be safe and prudent in me to correspond freely with.

It seems as if the minister of this country, and one or two others, wish to keep at peace with Great Britain, but the King and everybody else is strong for war; and things are in such a state, that it hardly seems possible to maintain peace for 2 months.

This country and Spain have not been during this century so well prepared for war as at present.

Two of the Commissioners, at present talked of in England to be sent to you, are Wm Henry Littleton, Lord Westcoate, late Governor of South Carolina, a Lord of the Treasury, and Hans Stanley, Cofferer of his Majesty's household, and Governor of the Isle of Wight,* both members of Parliament.

---

up the cargo brought by the Amphitrite to Mr. Beaumarchais. We hear he has sent over a person to demand a great sum of you on account of arms, ammunition, &c. We think it will be best for you to leave the demand to be settled by us here, as there is a mixture in it of public and private concern which you cannot so well develop." *Commissioners to the Committee of Foreign Affairs*, 16 February, 1778.

* Hans Stanley, a grandson of Sir Hans Sloane, was negotiating a treaty at Paris in 1761 and 1762. Early in 1780 he com-

These men are thought deep, overreaching gentry, and to be as faithless as any of the British ministry. The last (H. S.) is an old stager, and as much experienced in the art of bribery and corruption, as any man in England.

Take care how you let them come among you, or even into the country.

TO THE PRESIDENT OF CONGRESS.

PARIS, February 28th, 1778.

Sir:

The unexpected return of Mr. Simeon Deane gives me the opportunity of enclosing you a copy of my last, which went by an express from Spain, to which be pleased to refer. I should before this have set off for Vienna, but the Commissioners at this Court have not yet found time to examine the papers relative to the commercial concerns of Congress, taken from the private papers of the late Mr. Thomas Morris, as Mr. Deane's card of this date (a

---

mitted suicide in a fit of momentary frenzy—as his father had done before him.

William Henry Littleton was a brother of George, Lord Littleton. On his way to South Carolina in 1755 he was taken by a French vessel and carried a prisoner to Nantes. "He is a very worthy young man, but so stiffened with Sir George's old fustian, that I am persuaded he is at this minute in the citadel of Nantes comparing himself to Regulus." *Horace Walpole's Letters.*

copy of which is enclosed) will show. As soon as
that business is finished, I shall immediately set
out to execute your commands in Germany, where,
I am sorry to inform you, there are now appearances of an approaching rupture between the Emperor and King of Prussia, relative to the possession of the late Elector of Bavaria's estates. The
Elector Palatine, who is the rightful heir, has
agreed by treaty, signed the 12th ultimo between
him and the Emperor on the division of the Bavarian estates; but the King of Prussia is not satisfied
because he has not a share. He has, therefore,
commenced a negociation with Great Britain and
the Princes in Germany to support his pretensions
to some parts of Germany, founded on claims of
right that go several generations back. Great
Britain, you may be sure, will instigate him to go
on, because, if war ensues, France will probably
take part with the Emperor, which will render
their meditated attack on her more likely to succeed; but I still hope peace will be maintained by
negociation in that quarter.

The British Ministry are now fairly pushed to the
wall; after exerting every effort to procure men for
the ensuing campaign, both at home and abroad,
and finding it impracticable any where, so odious
are they and their measures, they have recourse to
acts of Parliament, which are so presumptuous and
treacherous that it is hardly possible to say in

which they excel. You will have the two bills by this conveyance, which are too plain to be misunderstood by any one who knows the framers; therefore, I shall only observe that by the first the *right* of taxing you is explicitly enacted, though suspended for the present, which is going something further than the declaratory act, for by that the right of taxation was only implied. By the second bill, the Commissioners are vested with full powers to do all possible mischief to you, and no possible good until it is confirmed by Parliament. Under these circumstances I do not well see how any treaty can be commenced, nor perhaps will it be prudent, in the moment of their weakness and distress, to agree to a cessation of hostilities by land unless your enemies will remove all their troops to Europe.

The situation of Spain, her millions being yet on the sea, and the circumstances in Germany beforementioned, I believe induce this Court still to continue the injunctions of secrecy relative to the treaties; but if war is not declared before, I do not see how it can be avoided as soon as you publish them, which I suppose will be done as soon as they come to hand, or at least such parts as will announce the fact to the world in such a manner that it cannot be doubted.

The number of French troops that are now on the coast in Brittany and Normandy, with the powerful naval preparations both in this country and Spain, would effectually prevent Great Britain from sending any more troops to America this year even if she could get them.

I have the honor to be, &c.,

Mr. DEANE presents his compliments to Mr. Lee: As to-morrow is fixed by the Minister for sending off the despatches, it will be impossible for him to attend the examination of Mr. Morris's papers before his brother sets off. As Mr. Deane had the honor of mentioning before, it shall be his first business after the despatches are gone.

Saturday Morning.

TO JONATHAN WILLIAMS.

CHAILLOT, RUE BATAILLE,
près PARIS, 5 March, 1778.

Dear Sir:

I have before me your favors of the 24th and 28th ults., and agree with you that it is not worth contending the commission on the captain's venture of vice with Mr. Peltier,* tho' it is not right, because expressly contrary to verbal agreement. But it is lamentable to think that some people are not to be bound by anything that you have not in writing; however, I can't help again saying that this should caution you in your transactions with Mr. P.——.

---

* Peltier du Doyer.

The best way will be to settle immediately with Mr. Peltier, and receive the balance, taking on yourself to answer, so far as you receive, for any allowance that may be judged right to make Messrs. Berthault and Landlazuge. But as I understand the case at present, they have no just claim at all, tho' there seems so general an opinion in a certain country that every individual has a right to plunder the Americans, and particularly the Congress, that I am afraid if the claim is persisted in they will gain their point. You will, however, do the best you can, and advise with Mr. Lloyd and Mr. Schweighauser whether it is most proper to refer it to the merchants on change, or to your merchants' court.* You formerly hinted your surprise at my silence relative to your question about being answerable for a proportion of the advances for Babson and Kendrick. You could not be more

---

* "I send an order this day to suspend the action against Mr. Peltier. But surely he acted very irregularly to sell a cargo consigned to us, without our orders, and give the produce to another. We ourselves never had any dealings with M. Beau marchais, and he has never produced any account to us, but says the States owe him a great deal of money. Upon his word only we gave him up the cargo of the *Amphitrite;* he promised then to give us an account, but has never done it; and now by means of M. Peltier he has seized another cargo. I imagine there is no doubt but M. Peltier would be obliged to pay us the money if the action were continued. And methinks every man who makes a demand ought to deliver an account." *Franklin to Williams,* 19 March, 1779.

surprised than *I was* at the *request*, as the thing
appeared to me at the time. Just before the receipt
of that letter from you, I had been told that your
bill for £50,000 on their account had been accepted,
and would be paid when due. You had not mentioned a syllable of it to me, which occasioned
my surprise, and therefore I chose to wait in silence
till this seeming mystery should be cleared up by
time. The other day, by accident, I learned that the
50,000 livres were not paid, but certainly would be
soon, and probably the whole value of the prizes.
You mentioned also my refusal to lend my name
in the business; but you will recollect that was
only to a letter to the Captains ordering them to
sea, which I refused for two reasons: because I did
not chuse to trust these strange kind of men with
my name, and because, from the general course of
their behavior, it appeared to me the most likely
way to prevent them from going. But you can't
forget that I signed the contract for the sugar, and
in consequence had the honor of becoming acquainted with the nature of a process verbal. I
have entered into these points because I apprehend
you must have talked of them, since I find a *malignant spirit* * has charged them to me as crimes,
leaving them to you now to put them right, if he
is capable of it. I presume Mr. Lloyd has men-

---

*A reference to Ross.

tioned to you the scheme proposed of appointing you and him joint commercial agents at Nantes. The business was yesterday fully talked over with the Commissioners. None of them had any objection, but they did not seem to think they ought to interfere in the appointment. Dr. F——n declared for himself that he could not in consequence of his connection with you, least he might bring censure on himself, but tho't I must do as I pleased. I see not at present anything to prevent its taking place, and 'till the business is finished I have only to add that I am, etc.

TO BARON SCUHLENBERG.

PARIS, 6 March, 1778.

Sir:

I have to acknowledge your obliging favor of the 3d ulto., which from my being at a distance from home at the time of its coming here, did not come to my hands as soon as it otherways would have done. The assurance of the continuation of his Majesty's good disposition towards the United States of America is particularly pleasing at this time, because there are letters from London that say "we have detached the King of Prussia from the American cause by paying his demands." This, I trust, is only a finesse on the part of the British Ministry to impose on us a distrust of our best friends, among whom we shall ever be happy to rank his Prussian Majesty.

The exhausted state of Great Britain and the utter incapability of her ministers to prosecute their weak and mad contest with America by arms, is so fully apparent from the bill carried thro' the House of Commons, and their other public proceedings, that I shall not detain you with any strictures on that head, because I am sure your penetration will see their pitiable situation in as clear a light as I do. We have advices from America as late as January 22d. General Washington was then encamped within a few miles of Philadelphia, where General Howe was so closely beset that he could not venture out to forage but with his whole army; and notwithstanding the aid from the ships of war, the Americans had taken in the river Delaware several transports laden with clothing, arms, etc., so that the American army was clothed and supplied with ammunition in great measure by the British ministry. Gen'l Gates had taken Fort Independence, which prepares the passage to New York, that will probably return that city into the hands of the Americans, if the winter, as usual, is severe enough to render the ships of war useless. General Burgoyne was then at Boston, with such of his troops as had not deserted.

On the whole, I think it more than probable that in 12 months from this day, G. B. will not be in possession of one foot of land in all North America.

TO JOHN LLOYD.

CHAILLOT, RUE BATTAILLES,
près PARIS, 7 March, 1778.

Sir:

I should not have been so long in acknowledging the receipt of your obliging favor of the 28th ulto., (the contents of which were quite as desired,) but that I was in hopes of making one letter do for the whole. However, as according to the usual mode of doing business here, every little thing is to be trained out into a tedious negotiation, so that I am at last compelled to write, tho' the agency business is as unsettled as it was ten days ago. Mr. Izard has already informed you of the proposal I made to the commissioners, which Dr. F——n positively declared he would not interfere in, in any manner whatever. Mr. D. made no positive objection, but I could not learn he approved. Therefore to reduce things to a certainty, I have written to them, mentioning my plan, and desiring their sentiments on it; to which they have not given an answer as yet. If it comes to me in time, a copy shall be sent with this, and that you may judge fully, I will mention the plan I proposed, viz.: to appoint you and Mr. Williams jointly for Nantes and all the parts in Brittany; A. Limozin for Havre, S. & S. H. Delap for Bordeaux, and Mr. Bondfield for Rochelle, Rochfort and Bayonne. Mr. Izard observed that he imagined this plan did not come up to your ideas, as he tho't that you expected to be placed in exactly the same situation as Mr. Morris and myself. I told him this part had not been explicitly entered into between us, and that I was sure the material part of the business would arise in Nantes, and the ports of Brittany. However, if that was any objection with you to engaging in the business, it should be removed in a moment, because I would make the appointment to you and Mr. Williams *general*, recommending Mr. Bondfield to be employed, if anything should occur to be done in the ports I had allotted to him, and Mr. S——r at Nantes, if it was necessary at times to employ a French house. But we are totally at a loss what to do, because in your letter to him you say: "if a perfect confidential and satisfactory assent can be obtained from the Hon. Commissioners to an appointment for me as public agent, but without it, I would not by any means accept the office." From what Mr. I[zar]d and myself have told you, you'll see how little prospect there is of obtaining *such* assent. I shall however wait for your own determination, which I beg may be sent by y.ᵉ return of post, so that I may have it by Saturday or Sunday (15) at farthest. It seems to me that the appointment in the manner you wish from the above words will not be in my power or that of your particular friends to get accomplished. In that case all that remains for me to say is that I shall be very ready to authorize you, if you remain here, to take up any vessel or transact any mercantile business that comes to France addressed to me individually or jointly with Mr. Morris as commercial agents for America. The rest will remain with the Secret Committee to make such arrangement hereafter as they may judge proper. Mr. Ross is certainly not quite right in his mind, for in a letter to ye Commissioners he seems to bear as hard on Mr. R. Morris as in one of his to me; I may surely be content to bear the misfortune of laying under his censure since he deals so freely with the person he calls his friend. But perhaps he wants to be as conspicuous as his namesake and countryman (probably relation) Captain Ross, who acted so extraordinarily in London about that Yankee privateer, and for which an English Jury made him pay soundly.* Mr. Ross has at last declared that the cargoes of the Henrietta and Le Brune are public property, also the latter vessel; but it is a pity he had not attended more to their despatch than attempting to breed riots, whereby

---

* See introduction, page 40, *note.*

"Yesterday came on before Lord Mansfield and a special jury, in the Court of King's-bench, at Guildhall, London, the trial of an indictment, removed into that Court by certiorari, against Captain R——, for an assault committed by him on the Royal Exchange, upon Mr. Alderman Lee. The Jury withdrew for an hour and a half, and brought in a verdict finding the defendant guilty." *London Chronicle,* 1 March, 1777.

possibly they might have got away with convoy, and the Henrietta escaped seizure, which may be yet attended with disagreeable circumstances.

TO BENJAMIN FRANKLIN.

CHAILLOT, 12 March, 1778.

Sir:

In your favor dated the 6th instant, which you did me the honor of delivering in person last night, you are pleased to tell me that my proposition about appointing agents in the ports shall be laid before the Commissioners when they meet. 'Tis now five days since I wrote to the Commissioners on that subject, and am sorry they have not in that time found ten leisure minutes to answer my letter on business in which I conceive the public to be much interested. You add that in looking over mine of the 2d instant, you observe an expression which you do not like, which is this: "I am always willing to submit my judgment to yours, therefore will deliver the trunk." You continue: "This implys that I had advised the delivery of the trunk to me, which you comply'd with contrary to your own judgment." My conduct afterwards proves so clearly my meaning that implication is unnecessary to show that I understood the proposition in that light, as I acted accordingly. I went to Nantes to take possession of Mr. Thos. Morris's papers, as being his late colleague in the commercial agency, not only under the sanction and approbation of the Commissioners, but by their advice with very great inconvenience to myself. When I got there, Mr. Jno. Ross tho't proper (tho' I am sure totally unauthorized) verbally and by letter, which you have read, to prohibit my executing the public business which had been entrusted to my care. Judging from what I had before experienced (and the issue has proved that my judgment was right,) how much countenance Mr. Ross would receive here, I tho't it advisable to have the papers sealed up as delivered to me, and to bring them to Paris, that, in the presence of the Commissioners as ye representatives of America in France, those relative to the public concerns might be taken out and those of a private nature left in their hands, until some person properly authorized should appear to demand them. On my arrival here, I gave the Commissioners an account of my proceedings, and also of the unjustifiable behavior of Mr. Ross ; proposing at the same time that they should see the public papers taken out as before mentioned. This was not only agreed to, but yourself, Mr. Lee and Mr. Izard attended for that purpose, when the business was postponed by Mr. Deane's being prevented from attending by an unforeseen accident, which occasioned a delay of some days. I had returned about 8 days, and never heard any ob-

jection made to this mode, until a letter to the
Commissioners from Mr. Jno. Ross was received,
which tho' in my opinion highly deserving of very
severe censure, was not only indirectly approved
of by you, but that censure transferred to my conduct. You then tho't proper to refuse absolutely
to proceed in the manner before agreed on, and
pointed out another, which I complyed with,
anxiously wishing to avoid disputes of every kind,
and the imputation of censure from every individual. I have now done my public duty in our
one department, as far as I was permitted by a
conduct that appears to me utterly unaccountable,
and am about to proceed on another; but I can't
take my leave without observing that instead of
receiving that aid and assistance which I had a
right to expect, I have met with every embarrassment that could be possibly thrown in my way.

TO BENJAMIN FRANKLIN.

13 March, 1778.

Sir:

Before I quitted this place, it was my wish to
put the public commercial business, as far as I was
empowered, into such a train that it might be conducted with harmony and effect. I had experienced in myself that the partiality you and Mr.
Deane manifested for Mr. Williams, and the powers

with which you thought proper to invest him, had greatly impeded me in conducting the public business. Much more reason was there for apprehending the same impediment to a person of my appointment. I had a good opinion of Mr. W's intentions, but did not think his experience equal to the discharge of the business, if he was alone.

In these circumstances, I proposed to unite Mr. Williams with Mr. Lloyd, a gentleman of approved knowledge and experience, and desired your concurrence. You chose to refuse it. Mr. Lloyd, viewing the matter in the same light, and being apprised of your refusal, does not choose to undertake the business, nor can I press it.

This new embarrassment thrown in my way delays my departure upon my other public business to arrange this anew. I add this new complaint to those I have already made of the embarrassments thrown upon the execution of my duty by those of the Commissioners who have taken the management of the business to themselves. The delicacy you are pleased to mention with regard to your relation, Mr. Williams, as a reason for not concurring in a plan so well intended and so unexceptionable, is the less satisfactory, as it is known to me, and is indeed notorious to all the world, that you have not only concurred in appointing him to a similar office, but have put near a million of the public money into his hands.

TO SILAS DEANE.

CHAILLOT, Monday, 16 March, 1778.

Sir:

In your letter received late last Saturday night you express your surprise at my asking for a literal and attested copy of such parts of Mr. Ross's late letters as relate to me, meaning that the copy could be attested by you or any one else who read the original. I cannot help thinking such surprise would never have existed had you attended to your former letter, where in a very material part you give me your explanation only of what Mr. Ross writes, and not his own words ; and I still think as Mr. Ross's letters are looked upon by you as charges against me, that you cannot in justice refuse to give me a literal copy of his own expressions.

Upon a revisal of your own conduct on former occasions, you will find that your sentiments were not always the same relative to private correspondence as expressed in your letter.

You have much misconceived what I said to you the other day relative to the sale of prizes being taken out of the hands of Mr. Morris and myself as commercial agents, and put into the hands of Mr. Williams, contrary to the appointment of the Secret Committee. I only meant to inform you that I was mistaken, not "grossly deceived," in attributing that act *to you solely*, because I was then satisfied that Dr. Franklin had taken his share in the transaction. But it is not an exculpation of the action, that you were only a copartner in it. I always tho't the act wrong, and shall continue to think so, until you show me good authority for doing it, and good reason for throwing such a slur on my character, thereby in great measure incapacitating me to render that service to my country which I wished to do, when, on the appointment of the Secret Committee, I gave up a very respectable station which was for life, and sacrificed no inconsiderable part of my private fortune to enter upon their business. You had Mr. Morris's sentiments and mine on the subject, in our joint letter to you and Dr. F—n; and mine farther, in my particular letters to you. The transaction appears to me a reflection on the Committee, and an injury to Mr. Morris and myself, totally uninvited I am sure on my part; and that injury aggravated by repeatedly promising many months ago to recall Mr. Williams' appointment, which has never that I know of been complyed with. As such, I have ever mentioned it, and, you know, have wrote about it, tho' not so fully as to yourself.

Insinuations or opinions I shall decline taking notice of, especially when coming from Mr. Ross ; but if you have any explicit charge against me, either from written or viva voce evidence, you will always find me ready to give an explicit and satisfactory answer.

TO JOHN LLOYD.

CHAILLOT, 21 March, 1778.

Sir:

I duly received your obliging favor of the 12th current, which should have been answered sooner, had we not been so much taken up with a variety of pressing and important affairs. The plans conceived relative to the agency are all reversed, since you decline it and Dr. F. has declared he does wish Mr. Williams to be concerned.

With respect to the continental dollars, I fear it will not be practicable to invest them here, for on enquiry I am told there are a great many in Paris that have been sent from England to try if they could not be changed with the Commissioners or the Americans. Howe took the State chest at Wilmington, with £30,000 in it, which were advertised for sale in London; besides, an immense number have been forged, on Lord Dunmore's and the Scotch plan, which have been endeavored to be contrived into circulation in order to injure the American credit. Tho' it may be difficult to exchange them, yet I should think any merchant would take them as a collateral security for what he might advance.

Last Tuesday in the Houses of Lords and Commons, it was decided for war by a great majority, and it was accordingly declared in London against France on Wednesday last. We have had here two expresses from London that have been only 40 hours each on the way.*

Yesterday in form the American Commissioners were introduced to the King at Versailles, and to-morrow they are to be introduced to the Queen. War will probably be declared here in a day or two. You have probably heard before what is public here, that Mr. Deane is recalled, and Mr. John Adams appointed in his place, who is expected every day. Mr. R. Morris has retired for two months, but will then return to Congress again, being chosen a delegate for Pennsylvania this year.

TO FRANCIS LIGHTFOOT LEE.

PARIS, 23 March, 1778.

My dear Brother:

When this will get to your hands I know not, but request you to attend to the inclosed, which will clear up, so far as I am concerned, the business of the two West Indiamen prizes last summer at Nantes, which I am just informed our good

---

* On March 17th North laid before Parliament a message from the throne, containing information of the treaty between France and the United States, the recall from Paris of the British ambassador, and his intention of repelling the insult and maintaining the reputation of the country. In the Commons the government obtained a majority of 150, and in the Lords, one of 43.

friends here (Mr. C[armichae]l at their head) have assiduously circulated in England (possibly in America) was entirely owing to my refusing to take an ample price for the whole. I mean thus to put you in possession of ample proof to silence such assertions, should they be made, or even whispered with you. I have with this sent a large pacquet to R. H. Lee, which you will please open and do what you think is necessary and proper in the business, provided he is not at Congress.

I leave this to-morrow, heartily fatigued by the extraordinary conduct of your servants here, for my destination in Germany, where the utmost address and management will be necessary to accomplish in any degree the wishes of Congress.*

At all events it must take a great deal of time, perseverance and patience, for the last post informs us that _war_ is actually commenced between Austria and Prussia, in which France has positively declared she will not take any part, having enough to do to fulfill and secure her engagements to you. In this situation neither Austria or Prussia can be expected to declare hastily in your favor, altho' the King of Prussia's minister three months ago wrote positively that his Majesty would acknowledge the Independence of America as soon as France had done it. This you will

---

* Lee was thus not in Paris when Deane left the city, on the night of March 30th.

know France has done openly, not only by avowing her treaty with you to the British Court, but by receiving publickly your Commissioners at Versailles the 20th inst., where and when they were in form introduced to the King by the Secretary of State, Count Vergennes, with Mr. Izard and myself, as commissioners to other courts. 'Tis said here that war was declared in London against France on Friday last, but this wants confirmation. The only reason we have to believe it is, the inconceivable folly of the British ministry. If war is declared, you may fully count France, Spain, Portugal and America against Great Britain and Ireland. Holland will be neuter, and stick to the plunder on all sides. Russia is on the eve of a war with the Turks, and all Germany will be fully employed between Austria and Prussia. Thus you will have little else to do but to take to yourselves the Floridas, Canada, Nova Scotia, Newfoundland, excluding Great Britain from a share in the cod fishery, while France takes the East Indies and she with Spain divide the West India islands. So that you see there will be sufficient work for all your forces for one year at least. But if the British ministry have a single grain of common sense, they will let France alone, acknowledge your independence, keeping Nova Scotia, Canada and a right to the fishery jointly with you and France, making peace immediately, passing an act of oblivion, for Great Britain as well as for those that may be in Canada,* &c., granting a mutual right of citizenship and paying for towns burnt and other damages. If Great Britain can obtain peace on these terms, it will be very fortunate for her indeed. I pray you to send me by different opportunities a list of Congress, and the different committees, specifying when each member was chosen and for how long a time he can continue; also copies of the Constitutions of every State and the General Confederacy. It seems to me that the British Constitution, if cleared from its impurities, is as well adapted to maintain the general liberty of the subject as any that has ever yet been devised; therefore, in my opinion, those States that lay that down as a model to improve on, will keep their liberty the longest of any. Let me hear from you by all opportunities under care to Mr. Schweighauser, merchant at Nantes, or Mr. John Bondfield, merchant at Academie, Bordeaux. . . .

P. S. You have often had my opinion of Mr. Carmichael, who is going out in Captain Nicholson. Should by his artifices any employment be

---

* "I will never consent that in any treaty that may be concluded a single word be mentioned concerning Canada, Nova Scotia, or the Floridas, which are colonies belonging to this country; and the more they are kept unlike the other colonies the better, for it is by them we are able to keep a certain awe over the abandoned colonies, where good garrisons must be continually kept." *The King to Lord North*, 26 March, 1778.

proposed for him, wherein he is to have any kind of connection with me, I beg of you explicitly and publickly to declare my dissent; for being most perfectly and thoroughly acquainted with his *principles* and abilities, I am determined that no consideration whatever shall induce me, either to hold any correspondence, or have any kind of intercourse with him.

My services to America want not my own blazoning, nor any false coloring to heighten their merit. Mr. Car—l indeed may stand in need of such aid, and I will only say with Iago "he that steals my money steals trash—'twas mine, 'tis his, and may be anybodies. But he that *filches* from me my good name, steals that which not inriching him, makes me *poor indeed.*" Read the character of Iago in Othello, and the character that the ghost and Hamlet give the King, Hamlet's uncle.

TO RICHARD HENRY LEE.

PARIS, 23 March, 1778.

My dear Brother:

I refer you to the inclosed copy of mine per Mr. Simeon Deane of the 28th ulto, who carried also several other letters from my brother and me, for which a receipt was given to my brother, a copy of which he will no doubt send you, for really there has been such conduct here, that there is no knowing whom to trust.

I now send you the whole correspondence relative to the papers of the late Mr. Thos. Morris, to enable you to set the business in its proper light to all the world, and particularly to Mr. R. Morris, on whom Mr. Ross solely depends for gratifying his resentment on being disappointed in his favorite wish of having the whole American commerce in his unhallowed North British hands.

I think you will be at no loss to determine from various letters of Mr. Ross, that he has been very long planning to get the American agency out of the hands first of Mr. Thos. Morris, and then out of his and mine too—all upon a private letter from Mr. R. Morris only (a copy of which is inclosed), whom he seems to think is King of America, as having unlimited power in Congress ; at least he flatters him as such, in the same line of conduct for which his countrymen are famous. That Mr. Ross should be countenanced here by Mr. D. is not surprising, because he hopes through the aid of Mr. M. to escape the censure with you which he has so much reason to apprehend. I can only add, that if the secret committee do not fully and explicitly reprimand Mr. Ross, and in future attend to their business *as a committee*, without permitting any *single* member to exercise the power of the whole body, they will never find an honest or independent man that will act for them. In consequence of the strange conduct of the commissioners here, I have been left alone to act for the committee in appointing agents in the best manner I could, and accordingly have appointed Mr. Andrew Limozin at Havre de Grasse, Mr. Schweighauser at Nantes, and Mr. John Bondfield at Bordeaux and its neighborhood, who are in my opinion the best men in the different places; and if the committee continues a mercantile body (which as far as I can judge now will be totally wrong and highly injurious to America,) they ought to be employed, until by positive misconduct they should chance to forget the trust reposed in them. I know the house of S. and J. H. Delap at Bordeaux is greatly in the favor of Mr. M., so is Mr. Ross; therefore should not be surprized if he endeavored to throw the whole American business into their hands. He may trust his own where he pleases, but I should be very sorry indeed to find any part of the public interest put into their hands; having unanswerable objections to both, which would be too long to enumerate here. I have not sent to the committee any part of Dr. F—n's correspondence, or any others, since the trunk with Mr. Morris's papers was put into his hands; but I can't enter into the reason of his *expressed* scruples about Mr. Williams, when he is the very man that Dr. F—n and Mr. D. tho't proper to appoint to sell the prizes in direct contradiction to the Committee's instructions to their agent, and to whom they have in the course of the last 8 months, intrusted the expenditure of near a million of livres of the public money.

I come now to Mr. Carmichael, who is gone over in Capt. Nicholson. This character I have often mentioned to you and Loudoun, and I must again repeat that from the most perfect knowledge of his abilities, and particularly of his *principles*, I am irrevocably determined that no consideration in this world shall ever induce me to hold any kind of correspondence, or have any kind of intercourse with him. 'Tis said here that Mr. M. has wrote to Mr. Ross (which letter is lately come to hand) that C——l is appointed secretary to the embassy at this court, and I am just informed that he went over on a plan concerted between him, Mr. D. and a Dr. Bancroft that is here, to get appointed deputy to Prussia, on the pretext that Vienna and Prussia was too much for one person to execute; which being obtained, the field would be left open for Dr. B., his rival, to get the secretaryship at this court. The scheme, I am told, is deeply plan'd, therefore attention to the measures of C—— may be necessary. I trust you will endeavor to prevent Congress from being precipitate in any measure relative to Vienna or Prussia, because from the present appearance of things, there is the greatest probability of my being publicly received at Berlin and being rejected at Vienna, in which case, if the appointment to Berlin is changed, I shall be let down into a very shabby situation indeed, after having had all the trouble and accomplished the greatest, at least most important to us, part of my mission. I shall set off certainly for Germany the day after tomorrow, and shall immediately give Congress a true account of the real situation of affairs there, when they may be able to form an accurate judgment of what may be necessary and proper for them to do. Every day a war is expected between Austria and Prussia, and until things have taken a decided turn there is no man breathing that can say it will be prudent or advisable for you to take any new measures for that quarter. The wisest thing you can do is to remain quiet a little while, more especially as France has now taken an open and decided part, which establishes our independence beyond a possibility of doubt, and a speedy end of our troubles, on which I most heartily and sincerely congratulate you and my country. We must, however, not rest without the whole continent to the Mississippi, excluding the British from the Newfoundland fishery.

Should Mr. R. Morris take up Mr. Ross to vindicate his conduct, ask him for authority for such vindication, and the only reply necessary to anything Mr. R. may have written or propagated against me, is to desire proof of his assertions. Mr. John Lloyd, of South Carolina, was a witness of all that passed at Nantes. He is going over soon to Congress, and I have no doubt will speak the truth if called upon.

TO THE PRESIDENT OF CONGRESS.

PARIS, March 23d, 1778.

Sir:

To the enclosed copy of my last* be pleased to refer. I have the pleasing satisfaction of congratulating you and my country on the independency of the thirteen United States of America being now openly acknowledged by the Court of France, which must soon put a glorious end to all our troubles. About fourteen days ago the French Minister in London formally avowed to the British Ministry the treaty which His Most Christian Majesty had made with you, and on the 20th instant your Commissioners were, in form, introduced to the King and his Ministers at Versailles, as the representatives of a sovereign State, and on Sun-

---

* "I am not in much spirit to write, for the prospect of things is far from being agreeable. The public news is that the French ambassador has left London ; that Lord Stormont leaves Paris to-morrow morning without taking leave, and that to-morrow the American Commissioners are to be publicly presented to the K. at Versailles. A blind man may almost see the issue of of all these things." *William Lee to Edward Browne*, 19 March, 1778. The Marquis de Noailles left London on the 20th, "not without some slight expression of ill humor from John Bull." Lord Stormont arrived a few days later, and had an audience with the King on the 27th.

day last they were introduced to the Queen and all the royal family.

The British Ministry, as usual, have blustered a good deal, but have not ventured to declare war, that we know of. If they do, our business may the sooner and better be finished. I set off to-morrow for Germany, where the prospect of a war between Austria and Prussia seems to thicken, although this Court uses all its influence to prevent one, and has explicitly declared to both parties that she will not in any manner aid or assist either side, as she is determined to exert all her force in supporting her new alliance with the States of America. I have already claimed the King of Prussia's promise to acknowledge our independence as soon as France has done so; his answer I shall meet in Germany, and, as far as one can judge at present, there is a greater probability of my being sooner openly received at Berlin than at Vienna; but on this head, and at this critical moment, it is impossible for any man in the world to form a decisive opinion, because the issue will depend on events that are yet in the womb of time; therefore, all that is in prudence for me to do is, on the spot, to seize the first opening that is made on either side in our favor; and I shall take care to give you the earliest intelligence of every thing material that occurs in my department.

I have the honor to remain, &c.

TO SAMUEL THORPE. [?]

My dear Sir:

'Tis a long while since I had ye pleasure of hearing from you, nor can I well account for the loss of one letter from you that I was informed about six weeks ago should have come by the French ambassador's courier. Several others, particularly one from L. S., that were put in ye same channel never came to my hands. I cannot well conceive any other motive for this conduct but the French minister's suspicion that I was at heart too much attached to ye good old country and people, and wished if it was possible to bring about an accommodation with Am———a before they had compleated their schemes, and therefore they were desirous to know what kind of correspondence I had. The independence of America is now established beyond revocation; but her trade and affection for Great Britain may yet in a great measure be retained, if the British ministry have but common honesty and common sense enough to take advantage of the passing moment, by adopting instantly the sage advice in all its parts as given by ye Duke of Richmond lately in the House of Lords, adding to it an act of general oblivion for what has passed everywhere, and giving every subject of ye United States a right of citizenship in Great Britain, and every other part of the British

Dominions; at the same time giving up all hostile designs against France. America, thus left to her own feelings, I am convinced would do as much as any honest Englishman could wish. At least for myself, I can truly say that I would instantly forego every other object and pursuit to labor at accomplishing a happy issue to the unnatural quarrel, provided I saw the proper basis lay'd by act of Parliament, and a cabinet established in which one might reasonably expect to meet with fair and upright dealing; but I must say that in my opinion Lords Temple and Shelburne are as little to be trusted as Lords Mansfield and North. If the above plan is not adopted, and instantly too, I do not think it within the chapter of possibilities that Great Britain can be saved from utter perdition. If war at this time takes place against France, common sense tells us that America must of necessity join the latter, in which case Great Britain *alone* will have to contend against France, Spain and America, when she is already more exhausted than she ever was by any former wars; and France and Spain more vigorous than at any period for near 100 years past. Things so situated, what possible chance can there be of Great Britain retaining one single possession without the island, if she goes to war with France, all this being so plain that it is impossible for the meanest comprehension to have a doubt about it. There-

fore I cannot help hoping that the plan of peace
will be speedily and seriously adopted, which will
bring happiness. I still retain the hopes of embracing all my friends with you, 'till which happy
period I beg them to accept my warmest and most
grateful wishes. However, if at any time, you and
those who have the best right to speak desire that
to be returned which they gave, I shall ever think
myself bound to obey their commands. I
presume M—y's motion about the C—y seal arose
from a concerted plan to assert the right to control the H—l proceedings and estates. By refusing to let the seal be applyed, taking care to choose
as proper an occasion as possible, you may bring
the point to a decision, and it will always be better
to be on the defensive than the offensive. I wonder that W—ge being on yᵉ spot, or his man W—h,
does not think of a mandamus to compel the
wicked and infamous bookseller to show cause, if
he or his adherents have any, for such extraordinary conduct. These miscreants have nearly run
their race, but I fear they will not get to the end
until they have totally ruined their country. All
the European world seem to be on the eve of falling together by the ears, but still there is some
hopes of peace, tho' indeed they are very small.
. . . .

TO EDMUND JENINGS.

FRANKFORT SUR LE MAINE, 11 April, [1778].

. . . We hear of nothing here but war, which will be a great interruption to commerce. Had it not been for this, trade with ye spring would have borne a most lively appearance; but now, one hardly knows where to turn for fear of being involved in some difficulty on one side or other, since the two champions of Christendom are on the point of measuring swords with no little personal animosity against each other. This country is in a most dreadful situation, being on the eve of a war which seems almost inevitable, and if once commenced promises to be the most bloody and desolating that Europe has known for this century past. Each of the combatants have now in the field above 200,000 of ye finest troops, well appointed, and commanded by the ablest generals now in Europe. It is pleasant to observe the pompous account in the London papers of the reception of the rebel agents at Versailles, and the tete-a-tete conversation between the French king and Dr. F——. These things must make you and I laugh. However, a gentleman of credit, who was present out of curiosity, tells me that he was at ye king's side when they were introduced, and that he said to Dr. F. "he might assure the Congress of his friendship;" to which the arch Rebel replied, "that his Majesty might rely on their

faithful adherence to their engagements.'' After
which he retired into another room. The French
say their King is as steady in adhering to his word,
as our most gracious sovereign is firm in adhering
to his purposes. This indeed he gives some proof
of, by an unshaken attachment to the minister of
his choice, which all the intrigues of the most intriguing court in Europe cannot shake. Notwithstanding the perilous situation of Great Britain, is
it not astonishing to see the lethargy that possesses
every individual, even when particular ruin stares
them all in the face? Lord S—— has now proved
himself in ye face of ye world, what you and I
always tho't him. . . . *

---

* In letters from this time, William Lee employed no less
than four different cyphers. Two, which were based upon a
transposition of the alphabet, I have succeeded in decyphering.
A third, in which a system of numbers were used to denote persons, places and certain transactions, I have only partially completed, as the material at hand has not proved sufficiently full
to give me the whole. The fourth system has baffled all my
efforts to solve it. It was probably based upon some dictionary,
or similar book, and so each word has a separate and distinct
symbol. For example: 110 a xxviii. would represent a word,
the letter between the figures being a or b, and the Roman
figures never going above xxxviii. These circumstances led me
to conjecture that the book on which the cypher was based was
a dictionary printed in double columns. The first numeral referred to the page (which might be any where before or after
the real one on which the word intended was to be found); the
letter told whether it was in the first or second column: and
the Roman showed the position from the top or bottom of the

TO ARTHUR LEE.

FRANKFORT, 23 April [1778].

My dear Sir:

Many thanks for the communications of the 14th and 16th, which came together yesterday; that mentioned containing the substance of the letters to me is not yet arrived, and I suspect it is still in the Post-office at Paris, for want of franking.

I could wish all from *America** to be forwarded here except that from the Committee, of which a literal copy may be sent. The original may at present be more useful with you; but I would have a copy sent to Mr. Bondfield, who may probably be as much plagued with Deane's emissaries, Delap and the little pert Scotchman, McC[reer]y,† as Mr. S[chweighauser] is likely to be with Mr. W[illiams], for no doubt R[oss] will be as busy there, as he has been at Nantes. I always told you that W[illiams]

---

column. No work that has been placed under my notice will supply the key, and the little "red book," mentioned in one of the letters, is too indefinite a term to point to any one work. From the fact that Entick's *New Spelling Dictionary* was used by the Secret Committee of Correspondence for its cypher, I thought that Lee used the same; but I have been unable to discover a copy of an edition prior to 1783, and that one will not fit the symbols. I print such words as were written in cypher in the original, italicized.

* Italicized words were written in cypher.

† William McCreery had insinuated to John Adams that "the Lees were selfish, and that this was a family misfortune."

had neither sense or judgment, tho' he has a tolerable share of low cunning and a kind of seeming good-natured plausibility; which is fully proved by his suffering himself to be made a cat's paw of by R[oss].*

I think it would be quite proper on the letter from the Committee to apply to the old fox [Franklin] for the certificate before requested, which being signed by all three, and sent to S[chweighauser], would completely crush all the dirty Scotch pedler's intrigues.

The old buck would be puzzled to find out an excuse for refusing to sign such a certificate, especially if it is asked in the presence of *Adams*, and it is ready prepared for signing to prevent being put off for want of time, &c. If he does, the plot in favor of the nephew will be made manifest.

As to proving the plots of *Deane*, I should think great caution ought to be used, as 'tis most probable the exculpation, and indeed applause, may be over before the charges can be got to the scene of action; tho' if any thing decisive can be got at, no time should be lost in conveying it.† In my mind

---

* For a sharp letter to Ross from the Commissioners see *John Adams*, III., 152.

† Arthur Lee placed himself in an awkward position by a letter to Grand, the banker, directing him to accept no bills or pay out any money to the credit of the commissioners without

there is no doubt of the criminality of *Franklin*. He will therefore use every wile to ensnare your circumspection; therefore it is requisite to lull as much as possible the suspicion natural to a cunning and guilty mind, unless a solid and effectual blow can be made; and I am sure it will be wise not to hurry *Adams* too much; to lead his ideas as softly as possible may be well, but if I am not mistaken in his character, he will not be driven, and has too high a sense of himself, to take up hastily the opinions of others. Carmichael is so complete a wretch that there is no depending on what he may do; but I apprehend that *Deane* will reap no inconsiderable benefit from a strict union with M[orri]s, being characters pretty similar; and there can be little doubt of the latter intriguing to get R[oss] appointed. In this he might be disappointed if Ll[o]yd would go over immediately, and could get to *Congress* before M[orri]s' leave of absence expires, which will not be till the last of June, especially if a recommendation for him could be got from *Adams*. Consult with *Izard* immediately on this, as no time is to be lost, and if 'tis not approved I don't know a fitter person to set on this business than J[ohnso]n of M[arylan]d, who

---

a joint order; and to deliver all letters addressed to Deane, to the Commissioners. Franklin did not fall into the trap, and his reply may be found in his *Works*, VI., 176.

came to Paris with S. D.* the 15th of March. It
was a capital stroke in *Deane* & *Franklin* to get
61† to go ; the measure surprises much every one
in this quarter. The stealing the letters I am inclined to impute to the two you mention, and not
to Hynson.‡ I do not recollect any of mine but a

---

* Simeon Deane.

† This seems to refer to Beaumarchais, or one of his agents,
perhaps Holker.

‡ Hynson "received Deane's letter of the 7th of October
(being then fitting out a ship) at Havre de Grace, with the
Congress dispatches which were directed to Folger and *him*,
and Folger being ready and willing to sail away with them immediately, he Hynson took an opportunity of sending Folger
out upon some business in the Docks while he slipping off the
string, which was intended to secure the end of the packet, he
got possession of the dispatches, that I have had (I hope to be
right in saying) the happyness of delivering to you, and then
making up paper, equal in length and thickness to what he
had taken out, he dexterously filling up the vacancy, shut
up the end of the bundle, passed back again the same string,
and upon Folger's returning with a Mr. Moyland, he had
the bundle well cover'd, put in a bag, seal'd and delivered
it to Folger, in presence of Moyland, never to be given again
out of Folger's hands (unless to be thrown overboard in case
of meeting with one of our ships, or in the hands of those
they are directed for). Hynson then set off next morning for
Dieppe, got over last night to London." *Lt. Col. Edward
Smith to William Eden*, 20 October, 1777. Deane soon discovered Hynson's treason, for a letter of his to Hynson dated
Paris, October 26, was intercepted in the mails. He said "I do
not write you to reproach you for the ungrateful and treacherous part you have acted ; I leave this to your own reflections.

short one to the President of Congress, of no importance, and perhaps a short one to R. H. Lee; from the last letter of *Deane* to me, I am convinced that all our letters sent to P[ass]y have been open'd at least, if not detained; therefore I would advise copies of all that are material to be sent, and a copy of Simeon Deane's receipt for such as he had to carry; for there is too much reason to believe that they were all opened, if not entirely secreted.

But as you have had the assurance to write to me, and to propose the betraying your new patrons, in the manner you have wickedly but in vain attempted to betray your former, and with them your country, I must tell you that no letter from you will hereafter be received by   DEANE."

"No doubt but you have seen or heard from Hynson, as I met him going into London, as I was coming out. Happy for him that he left Paris the time he did, as there was an order issued for apprehending him on suspicion that he was a spy from your court on the court of France." *Lupton to Eden*, 31 December, 1777.

"You will see the facts attending my enquiry into the robbery of the despatches, which should have been carried by Folger. Comparing and connecting all things together, it is my private judgment that this Mr. Chaumont was employed by the 243 a xvii to take the public despatches; and that he availed himself of the opportunity to take my letters for Mr. Deane and Dr. Bancroft, with whom he was in close connection." *Arthur Lee to James Lovell*, 3 June, 1778.

On January 11, 1778, Captain John Folger arrived at York, bringing packets for Congress from the Commissioners at Paris, which on being opened, were found to contain "only an enclosure of clean paper, with some familiar letters, none of which contained any political intelligence."

You know that Penet has already settled his accounts with me, and since his leaving Gruel and
joining with D'Acosta, the business of the house
seems to be carried on with regularity and in a
merchant-like manner.

The resolution, with respect to Burgoyne should
be published in England ; but those relative to Independence I think for the present, had better be
withheld.—Pray send me here the most correct list
you can get, of the present members of Congress,
and the several Committees ; also a copy of the last
Articles of Confederation drawn up by Congress.

[The minister] of *Prussia* has been here and by
desire *W. Lee* waits till [an answer] can come from
Berlin, so that there will not be any motion from
hence, till the next month begins.

Will it not be a good political stroke to give out
among the Commercial powers, that the United
States will not trade with those who do not immediately acknowledge their Independency ?

France may at once decide either *Vienna*, or
Berlin, by speaking a little plainly, but while nothing is said to either, both will be afraid of *Great
Britain.* For my own part I think in policy on
every account France should decide for 18,* but in
this perhaps it will not be well to stir, until you
hear from me again.

---

* Berlin? The usual symbol was 8, but the sense points to
Berlin.

War is not yet commenced in this country, that we know of. The armies are assembled not very far from each other; and the Generals on each side with them; so that we may expect every day some important news from the North. Desire F. to show you my letter to him, if you have not seen it already.—All here desire their best love to you and L[udwel]l whose good fame had reached this before we came. Remember us to Radswill and his host.

Adieu, and believe me always most sincerely

Yrs

Ri.^P Lindsay,

Give the earliest notice when there is a design of going to *Spain*, and say is there any alteration of *A. Lee's* powers in *France.**

---

* "I hope as my countrymen have now got rid of that nest of vermin the North Britons (who not only sucked the heart's-blood out of our particular country, but have unquestionably been the occasion of all the heavy mischiefs that have fallen on America), will pay more attention to trade than they formerly did, and keep it in their own hands, for they should consider that the occupation of a merchant in a commercial country, is as honorable as any other in ye society. A North Briton is something like the stinking and troublesome weed we call in Virginia wild onion. Wherever *one* is permitted to fix, the number soon increases so fast, that it is extremely difficult to eradicate them, and they poison the ground so, that no wholesome plant can thrive." *William Lee to Raleigh Colston*, 30 April, 1778.

TO ARTHUR LEE.

FRANKFORT SUR LE MAIN, 30 April [1778].

My dear Sir :

To-morrow I expect to hear from you at least to receive a letter that layed some time in the Paris postoffice for want of being franked.

On reflecting about the dispatches that have been stolen, I have not a doubt of its being done by *Deane* and that *Carmichael* knows it at least, but most likely was as much concerned in the act as the other. Tho' *Dr. Franklin* may know the whole, no eclaircissement is to be expected from him; on the contrary every finesse will be used to conceal the Truth unless he finds *Adams* determined to find out the whole. It will be proper to know from Lim[ozi]n the precise day that Hynson went off ; if he went away before they got to H. he can't be even suspected. I tho't it extremely odd at the time, but I remember perfectly well that the countenance of *Carmichael* expressed great and secret pleasure when the news first came to P[ari]s of Hynson's being gone off, instead of resentment or anger. Again it will be proper to trace every hand through which the packets went until they came to Folger,† and if not too late, they should on the other side carefully compare the blank paper that was put in the covers instead of the letters, with the paper on which the letters

* Captain John Folger.

of *Deane* and *Franklin* were written, or enclosed.
Also the same thing should be done with respect
to the letters of *Carmichael* and 11 ; for if on examination the blank paper is the same with either of
the others, the mistery will then be very plain.
For as there is a very material difference in paper
which is easily discernible by a skillful or attentive
observer, 'twill not be very probable that exactly
the same kind, in texture, thickness, largeness,
color and marks should be found in places so distant. There is a considerable difference even in
the shades of white paper, when compared together.

Are the despatches gone that I left with you, and
by whom ? When do you send any more|? If *W.
Lee* should not be properly received at *Vienna*, in
case the course should be bent that way, do you
think he ought to remain there, to wait the course
of events ? Perhaps it may not be improper to stay
and the point of indignity may be got over from
the mistake in the *commission*. No decided resolution can be taken yet for some days in consequence of what was communicated the 23ᵈ , but as
far as any judgment can be formed at present,
Vienna will be the course at last. However, advice
will be given as soon as any determination is made.
I observe since *Adams came*, the *puffs* of *Franklin*
and *Deane* in the 50* *papers* have ceased. This

---

* English ?

proceeds from the *cunning* of *Franklin*, who is afraid of giving offence until his *nett* is *wove*.

Stockings, shoes and coarse cloths can be got much cheaper here, when delivered in *Holland* than with you ; blankets also much better and something cheaper. Is such ample provision made else where as to render the sending any from hence unnecessary. I have but a very small fund in my power to lay out ; but I am sure 100,000 livres might be employed here to great advantage, which would fully compleat from head to foot with a blanket for each, 2,000 m. Give me an answer to this per first post, directed here. I see nothing is yet particularized about the Free Ports ; as was desired, I frequently mention'd them to R. H. L. He will think strange of me when he comes to read 30. You should touch on the business, tho' there is no necessity for hinting about what I have said about a particular being *consul.* We have all little coughs, but hope they will pass over ; tho' we have a memento of eternity every day, for almost daily, one, sometimes 2 or 3, go by our window to the church yard.

Our last post from London missed; so that we have nothing new from that quarter. The Heroes in the north have been each some weeks at the head of their respective armies, which are assembled within a day's march of each other, and no blow struck that we hear of. Indeed the strongest rumor is peace; and that the King of P[russia] is to have Dantzig and something else to indemnify him; I should not be surprised if Bremen and Verden were added, on which perhaps he has as just a claim as the El[ecto]r of H[anove]r.

Respects to all with you, and receive our best wishes. Adieu.   I. McCULLOCH.

P. S. It will be well to get as much in writing as possible, relative to Mr. W[illiam]s' proceedings at Nantes, because one day or other it may tend to illustrate some other proceedings.

Pray do not let my letters lay open or be exposed to every inquisitive eye. I may sometimes write to you from the Book. *

---

* "'Tis strange how secrets get out. The secret mission of Th[oronto]n and his commission is all blown here, tho' kept so secret at Ch[aillo]t. We have the particulars of Pultney's negotiation at P[ass]y. The particulars of Destaing's fleet, its sailing and the passengers, were known at Westminster the 19th April—quick work indeed. About 2000 men, recruits and all, have gone this year from Germany to America. The last division, about 800 are probably just sailing now from Portsmouth." *William Lee to Arthur Lee* (?), May, 1778. Major Thornton had been sent to England by Franklin to transact some business relating to American prisoners in British gaols· Pultney had come to Paris late in March to lay certain propositions of reconcilation with America before Franklin, who at once communicated them to the French ministry. Gérard took with him to America a copy of these propositions, which Franklin said "would probably have been accepted, if they had been made two years ago."

TO THE AMERICAN COMMISSIONERS AT THE COURT OF FRANCE.

FRANKFORT ON THE MAINE, 8 May, 1778.

Gentlemen :

I have been detained here longer than was intended by a personal application from one of the King of Prussia's ministers. I have now received an answer from Berlin, which informs me that his Majesty chooses for the present to decline acknowledging the Independency of the United States, or to enter into a commercial treaty; consequently my route is fixed for Vienna, where, if I am not wrong inform'd, an application from the French ministry will easily induce that Court to comply with the wishes of Congress; especially if the application is made while the affairs in Germany continue in their present state of suspence.

It will be of essential service in the direction of my movements for me to know what measures the French ministry intend to take in this business, for which I must rely upon you to inform me. The safest way will be to send your letter under cover to Messrs. Bathman Frere, Banquiers in this Town, from whence it will be forwarded to me, and perhaps be less liable to meet with any interruption than if sent by the post direct from Paris to Vienna. As the negotiations between the Emperor and King of Prussia still continue, many are of the opinion that at last an accommodation will take place, instead of war. I have the honor to be with great esteem, gentlemen, your most obedient and very humble servant.

TO RALPH IZARD.

F[RANKFOR]T, 10 May, 1778.

I wrote to you the 19th and 30th ulto, which I presume you received. A decisive determination is come from 18, [Berlin?] where nothing can be done at present, nor do I think much ever will unless 'tis dearly paid for. I am well informed that the *King of Prussia* is to [form] *a confederacy of all the northern powers against* [   ] 47*; in which England *is to be included.* This object will hardly be completed, but still *France* should look well to it. You may depend upon the fact relative to the plan. To-morrow I intend to set out for *Vienna*, where everything depends on the *French court.* One line from 113 will make everything go on smoothly, but without it, very little can be expected in the present situation of things. You will, therefore, I am sure, do all in your power to forward the necessary measures from that quarter. I have wrote to the *ministers.* What they will do, I can't tell, not knowing the trim since *John Adams* was added, and *Deane* subtracted; but un-

---

* Russia ?

less *Franklin* is counteracted, I am not to expect anything, unless he has some private end to answer.

The Duke de Choiseul can do much in my station, knowing the trim of everything there, a letter from him, if it could be got, would be of much use. . . . What hopes have you from the Dr. and Temple's mission? Has there really been any contentions in South Carolina as mentioned in the English papers? . . . Be cautious in mentioning what is said above about the *King of Prussia*, lest it should injure our affairs; tho' the *court of France* should know it.

THE COMMITTEE ON FOREIGN AFFAIRS TO
WILLIAM LEE.

YORK, May 14th, 1778.

Sir:

Your favors of November 24th and December 18th, reached us only the 2d of this month, with the letters of our other friends at Paris, from whom we had not received a regular packet for eleven months. You will readily conceive how much we have wished to hear from you, and how very agreeable your information would have been at an earlier period. It is evident that you were yourself in a degree of doubt as to the conduct of France, even after the conference of our Commissioners in December; you will, therefore, be naturally led to give us due credit for the resolute manner in which we proceeded upon the two draughts of bills which the British Ministry had hurried over to America. Be assured we were acquainted with the spirit of the French Court. The decisive part it has taken was really unexpected, judging from the accounts we had collected from travellers. The dates of the papers herewith sent will enable you to put this matter in a clear point of view.

The turn of affairs in Europe will make it needless for us to attempt the finesse of recruiting in Germany, which you hint at, and which would have a good effect in case of necessity. Mr. Arthur Lee's letters make it quite probable that your commission will prove successful at Berlin, and there appears the best agreement between the King of Prussia and the Emperor.

The enclosed resolve of Congress, of the 7th instant, will show their intentions with regard to your support, which was not properly attended to when your commission was made out.*

---

* "*May* 7th, 1778. *Resolved*, That the Commissioners appointed for the Courts of Spain, Tuscany, Vienna, and Berlin, should live in such style and manner at their respective Courts as they may find suitable and necessary to support the dignity of their public character ; keeping an account of their expenses, which shall be reimbursed by the Congress of the United States of America ;

"That besides the actual expenses of the Commissioners, a handsome allowance be made to each of them as a compensation for their services ;

"That the Commissioners of the other Courts in Europe be empowered to draw bills of exchange from time to time, for the amount of their expenses upon the Commissioners at the Court of France."

Other papers herewith sent will give you a general
idea of our situation. You may be assured that independence is firmly adopted by the States, and the
unanimity of Congress is truly emblematic of all
America. Nova Scotia has long ago expressed its
wishes to be adopted by us, and now afresh solicits.
Canada will be greatly affected by the news of our
alliance with its former parent State. In short, sir,
every thing which could be added to our own determination of being free and independent, is ensured by
this eclaircissement of the Court of Versailles. Our
army is growing daily, so that if we are to negociate
with Britain, we shall do it in a proper posture. There
are some reports of her drawing away her troops that
she may with a better grace enter into parley. But
this must be done without disguise, or no treaty can
be held; surely no one can suppose that we shall now
give up a point which we had made a preliminary before we knew what powerful friendship was secured to
us in Europe.

The powers which had been given to our Commissioners in France, and our great anxiety to keep perfect faith in treaties, induced a caution with regard to
the powers given in after appointments, which is now
become unnecessary. Perfect equality being the basis
of our present treaties, without any exclusive privileges
to France, there can be no chance of discontent from
the conclusion of similar treaties with other Powers of
Europe; therefore, we shall doubtless soon forward to
you more full powers than were sent with your commission. As you seem to think it may be advantage-

ous to have a cypher for a correspondence, we would propose the same which has been mentioned to Dr Franklin formerly, by Mr. Lovell, and this is the rather chosen because it may serve between the Doctor and you, or any number of your friends, taking a different key-word for each.

We are, with great regard, &c.,

R. H. LEE,
JAMES LOVELL,
ROBERT MORRIS.

P. S. You are to have a plenipotentiary commission with instructions, *not* limiting the term of the proposed treaties of amity and commerce.

JOHN ADAMS.

The arrival of John Adams in April, introduced a new element into the commission, that promised at first to increase the differences existing among the members. While at Bordeaux he was informed by William McCreery, of "a dryness" that subsisted among Franklin, Deane and Lee, and was exceedingly disquieted by accounts of the rancorous animosity shown, that had divided the ministers and all connected with them into parties. Franklin also, at a very early moment, spoke to him of the "coolness" between the American ministers, and described Lee's anxious, uneasy temper, Izard's violent and ungoverned passions, and the disputes they had caused,— embarrassments to which William Lee had contributed not a little. After being presented at court, Adams determined to accomplish something towards introducing system into the conduct of the commercial agencies. On the 13th of April, four letters were sent out by the commissioners. Ross was informed that he could not have any further advances, and must account for the money already sent him. Williams was directed to incur no further expenses, and to close his accounts for the present with as little expense as possible. Mercklé, a Dutchman, was somewhat brusquely told to expect nothing more at the hands of the minis- of the ministers, and a merely formal letter of thanks was sent to Bondfield. (*John Adams' Works*, III., 128, 129.) Of William Lee, Adams wrote that he "had been a merchant in London, and I believe an alderman, had been appointed by Congress their commercial agent and a general superintendent of all their commercial affairs. Congress was our sovereign lawgiver, prince, and judge, and, therefore, whatever, was done by their express authority, we, as I believed, ought to respect and obey. Mr. William Lee had appointed Mr. Schweighauser commercial agent for the United States, under him, and Mr. Schweighauser was a very solid merchant, highly esteemed by every body, and highly approved by the court. Mr. Jonathan Williams, a relation of Dr. Franklin, whom I had known in Boston, as well as his father, uncle, and cousin, who was a clerk in my office, I had the best disposition to favor, as far the public service and my own sense of propriety would permit. Dr. Franklin and Mr. Deane had employed him in transactions which appeared to me to be commercial, and, in this, had differed with Mr. Arthur Lee, and interfered with the province of Mr. William Lee. I therefore, united with Mr. Lee in this and many subsequent proceedings, requiring the settlement of Mr. Williams's accounts. Dr. Franklin, finding that two of us were agreed in opinion, subscribed the letter with us."

But Adams soon discovered that his attempts at reform, however well-meant, were not crowned with the success he anticipated. "Whatever was done or said by Dr. Franklin, or by me when I agreed with him in opinion, was censured and often misrepresented by one party; and whatever was done or said by Mr. Lee or Mr. Izard, and by me, when I thought they were in the right, was at least equally censured and misrepresented by the other. I was so thoroughly disgusted with the service, and so fully convinced that our whole system was wrong, and that ruin to our affairs abroad, and great danger and confusion to those at home, must be the consequence of it, that I thought it my indispensable duty to represent my ideas in America." He therefore wrote to Samuel Adams, 21 May, 1778, representing that one minister at Paris would be sufficient, he should have no connection with the commercial affairs of Congress, and his salary should be determined, and not left an uncertainty. (*Diplomatic Correspondence of the Revolution*, II, 540). A few days after Arthur Lee added the weight of his advice: "I am of opinion, with my colleague, Mr. Adams, that it would be better for the public that the appointment of your public ministers were fixed, instead of being left at large, and their expences indefinite. From experience,

I find the expense of living in that character cannot well be less than three thousand pounds sterling a year, which I believe is as little as is allowed to any public minister beyond the rank of consul" *To the President of Congress*, 1 June, 1778. And Franklin also wrote 22 July, 1778. These letters doubtless contributed much to the changes in the foreign commissions made by Congress in September, 1778; but the salary of the ministers was not fixed till 4 October, 1779, when a minister was allowed £2500 sterling a year, and his secretary £1000.

In the meanwhile the powers given to Williams were revoked (25 May, 1778), Schweighauser recognized as agent under William Lee, a rap administered to John Paul Jones, and Ross and Bondfield ordered to render accounts. The letters were written by Adams, and signed by Franklin "composedly;" and the report was that Adams had gone over to the Lee faction.

". . . Does the appearance of *Adams* make any alteration in the powers of *A. Lee* in *France?* Is every thing right in *Spain*, and is there any prospect of going there soon? It will be of essential service in directing the judgment and conduct of *W. Lee* with respect to himself, if he could but know particularly the present situation and influence of *Robert Morris* in *Congress* and *America*, and whether R. H. L. and Loudoun are likely to continue as before. Also what 142 [Ross?] is doing at N[antes]." *William Lee to Arthur Lee*, 3 June, 1778.

John Adams was not a bitter opponent of Deane. He questioned the wisdom of some of Deane's acts,

and believed that America had not received a full
equivalent for the "immense sum of money" that was
gone or owing. "If I had been strongly against Mr.
Deane, I should certainly avow it and make no secret
of it at all. I have never been used to disguise my
sentiments of men whom I have been against in public
life, and I certainly should not begin with Mr. Deane,
who is not and never was a man of importance enough
to make me deviate from a rule that I have observed
all my life, viz., when obliged to be a man's enemy,
to be openly and generously so." *Adams to William
McCreery*, 25 September, 1778. He admitted that
Deane was "active, diligent, subtle, and successful,
having accomplished the great purpose of his mission
to advantage."

TO CONGRESS. *

[VIENNA, 30 May, 1778.]

* * * The undecided and critical situation of
affairs [at] this moment between the King of Prussia and the House of Austria, he knew would prevent this Court from taking any open part with us
in a hurry, for fear of throwing the weight of G. B.
into the scale of Prussia; therefore he was of
opinion, that I should not hastily take upon myself
in publick the character with which I am vested;
but remain for a time as an American Traveller;

---

* From a much mutilated letter book. I presume the letter
was written to Congress or to one of its committees.

in short to act as your commissioners did for above
a year at the Court of France. Accordingly he has
introduced me as a traveller to the Minister, all the
great officers of State, ladies of the Court, and all
the foreign ambassadors and ministers, except from
G. B., and Hanover, and I have reason to believe
that some progress will be made, in getting the
better of the strong penchant that has prevailed for
many years in this court for G. B., with which
there has been the strongest alliances for near a
century against the House of Bourbon, except in
the last war.

My first object shall be to obstruct as much as
possible the operations of G. B. in hiring more
German troops; in which I flatter myself with having already had some success with the Princes of
H. D. and of B. D., at whose courts I have been for
that purpose. The British agents are however at
this moment busily employed among all the petty
princes in this country to get more subsidiary men
and recruits for their army in America; which,
with sending Governor Johnstone, the secret, tho'
devoted, agent of Lords Bute and Mansfield, as one
of the Commissioners to treat with you, show in-
contestably what little sincerity there is in the
B[ritish] M[inistry], and how little they are to be
trusted.

The Emperor and King of Prussia are now, and
have been for some weeks, on the confines of their

dominions in Silesia, each of them with upwards of 100,000 men, and the largest quantity of artillery that has ever before been brought together. They are within a few hours march of each other, and tho' their troops are in cantonments, they are so disposed, that they can be encamped in two days time. This great object close at home, engages the attention of all the politicians in this country, and until the contest between these two mighty Monarchs about the Bavarian succession is settled in a solid peace, or bursts out in flaming war, our business must necessarily move slowly. I shall, however, watch every favorable opportunity of accomplishing the wishes of Congress. I have the honor &c.

TO RICHARD HENRY LEE.

V[IENNA], 30 May, [1778.]

The last date I have received from you was that of June last from Williamsburg and G[reen] S[pring]. 'Tis probable your letters to me have met with the same fate that mine have to you and C——ss. The nest of wretches that were guilty of that and other dirty work are now somewhat dispersed, but still the oldest is left, who can breed mischief enough for twenty worlds. I have so often mentioned two of the characters, that you can hardly be at a loss to know who I mean.

I shall be much mistaken if Congress gets any satisfaction from the inquiry they have ordered to be made relative to the loss of the letters that ought to have been carried by Capt. Folger in October last. You should have received by that conveyance one from me, and Congress another. I have no doubt in my own mind of the parties that intercepted and stopped them, but as it will be difficult for me to bring the proof home, I shall say no more.

I have wrote fully to Congress of this date, but as I have not received any letters from America for a long time, I cannot judge whether you will be at Congress when mine gets there. Therefore, will give you some account of the state of affairs in this country. On the Duke of B—a's death in December last, the Elector Palatine as heir, ought to have succeeded to all his dominions. But the male line of B—a was extinct, the house of Au—a [claimed] part as fiefs in reversion to that house, and in January a [treaty] was signed between the Emperor and Elector Palatine, settling a partition, when we thought that everything would pass w[ithout] noise.* But the Duke de Deux Ponts, who is heir

* Maximilian Joseph represented the younger line of the house of Wittelsbach, and by his death that line became extinct. The next heir was Charles Theodore, the Elector Palatine, and representative of the elder line of Wittelsbach. The claim of Austria was desisted from on her obtaining from Bavaria the frontier district which bears the name of Sunviertel, or the quarter of the sun.

with [   ], who is old and without children, would
not agree to this partition. [Where]upon the Kings
of F—ce, Pru—a, Sweden, Denmark, and [other]
powers, that were guarantees of the treaty of Westphalia [   ] of P has taken up the affair. F & S,
as yet, decline interfering [   ] mediators. The E.
and K. of P. have collected their armies, each above
100,000 men, and the largest quantity of artillery
that was ever bro't together, on the confines of their
dominions in Silesia, within a few miles distance
of each other. They have been thus situated for
above six weeks, and, as no blow has been struck,
the world suppose the time has been spent in negotiation, and what will be the issue nobody can tell.
The emperor has already raised 40,000 recruits to
complete his army, and within these few days,
orders have been issued for raising 30,000 more,
which has not a very peaceable aspect. In this
situation you may be assured that both parties are
trying their utmost skill to engage G. B. on their
side, which will of course for a time prevent either
from acknowledging our Independence. But I
have reason to think that as soon as this great object is resolved into a solid peace or dreadful war,
one, if not both these powers, will openly avow their
attachment to us. In the meantime I must wait
with patience, and do what is possible to obstruct
the negotiations of G. B. for more German troops
to send to America, in which her agents are very

busy at this moment; which shows how little good they expect from their Commissioners that they have sent out to negotiate a peace with America. Before this unlucky event here, the K. of P. professed much friendship for us, and had promised to acknowledge our Independence as soon as France had done so. But now he declines it for the present, as the affairs of Germany require all his attention, and he has no marine to support such an acknowledgment. Mankind is a strange animal. The country, people and all, for which this mighty contest is likely to be waged by the E. and K. of P., if put up to sale to morrow, would not sell for half the money that has already been spent.

Mr. Adams has been arrived two months, and I have not yet received the last Articles of Confederation. Be so good as to have sent me by every express that is dispatched, such proceedings of Congress for the last and present year, as are permitted to be known; with a list of that body, and the several committees, marking in the margin the time that each member can serve according to your Constitution.

Governor Henry, I understand, has sent over a person to France with orders for me to buy arms and ammunition for the State of Virginia to the value of one million of livres, about £44,000 sterling, but I do not hear that he has sent any regular authority from the State to borrow the money;

without which, you know, the goods cannot be bo't, and indeed it will be a difficult task at present to borrow so large a sum, even if the authority from the State was distinct and regular. But I hope our credit will increase every day, and in the meantime we must try what our good friends, the French ministry, will do for us. The State of Georgia, tho' so much younger in business than Virginia, sent over a person last winter on the same business, with powers very clear and regular. If, contrary to all appearances, the British troops should this campaign meet with any signal success, we may have another year of war; but according to every reasonable judgment, this will prove the last. * * *

TO ARTHUR LEE.

V[IENNA], 10 June, 1778.

Dear Sir:

Thanks for yours of the 29th ulto. Three letters before this have been written to you from hence. The weather in this quarter has not changed for the better; it lowers a good deal. We shall, however, wait a little to see what course it will take. The American war seems to engage conversation much more than the differences in this country. Like the climates, one is free for all the world, and the other is a sacred arcana, that none but the priesthood are permitted to know or even to talk about. However, there is no war yet here, tho' the immense preparations on both sides are continued with equal activity and vigor. I have noted the admirals. We are all impatient to hear what is become of 158. 57 [Count D'Estaing?]. The earliest intelligence will be acceptable. Not a word of Nicholson, Green, &c., &c. . . . I am glad to hear that *John Adams* goes on well. He must be let to lead, or at least to think he does so. Remember the maxims of De Retz and Clarendon's character of Hambden. From hints dropped here, I fancy *Franklin* has planned to be fixed alone where he is, which is to be accomplished by *Beanmarchais* and *Deane*. Penet should first send the goods for the State of Virginia that he engaged to do last September, which was not done, or even thought of when I left N[antes] last. Some people unhappily are too ready to engage without ever afterwards thinking of the execution. Our best chance will be with the *Court of France*. Apply there by all means, and if successful I will execute the . . .

TO ARTHUR LEE.

VIENNA, 20 June, 1778.

Dear Sir,

This moment was received a letter of the 4th or 6th (I can't tell which) that ought in regular course to have been here 4 days ago,—thanks for the intelligence, tho' the situation of A—d is greatly to be lamented.

I predict that nothing material will occur this year, in America, as a resolution of Congress I have seen will certainly prevent Washington's army from being complete. I suppose Capt Le M.* will soon return from St[rasbur]g; he has written and sent me the prices of some things, which show that we cannot have anything to do there. I have answered his letter and told him so.†

In a few days I shall write you fully, by a safe conveyance, relative to that business, as I have some hopes given me here that *court of France* will do the most material part that we want. In the meantime I leave it with your prudence to determine on the propriety of letting 164 [Vergennes?] know that the Empress has taken a decided part with England against America. You will hear more particularly from W. Lee when the opportunity is proper; in the meantime he is not idle,

---

*Le Maire, commissioned by the State of Virginia to purchase some war supplies in Europe.

†"Poor Lemaire was sent about Germany to find goods and credit, which consumed a great deal of time to little purpose. Several of the manufacturers wrote to me that they would furnish him on my promise of payment. I referred them to Mr. Lee." *Franklin to Patrick Henry,* 26 February, 1779. See *William Lee to Governor Jefferson,* 24 September, 1779, *post.*

and has other prospects in view, the issue of which time must decide. You will address for him, always as before, to F—t, which is found to be the most proper, and oftentimes most expeditious. If no steps have yet been taken with *French court* relative to Le M[aire]'s business, 'twill be best to wait till I write by the conveyance mentioned above.

We see they are in a wonderful bustle in England—for what reason I don't know, tho' I conjecture, the scheme has been judicious to occasion it.

Lord Shelburne's coming in will occasion a continuance, certainly, of the war against America; experience will prove the wisdom of taking the thorn out of the feet of others, and putting it in his own. Here there is no war yet, and in my opinion there will be none, tho' probably the bustle may not subside, and things be quite settled for some time; however the general cry is strongly war, and the public movements tend that way.

The Austrian troops are almost all drawn from Moravia to the borders of Bohemia, where the Emperor is, and the report is, that orders are given for raising 80,000 recruits, which make an addition of 50,000 to what was before mentioned; but this last report I don't credit. What a fine expedition Thompson and Hynson have made—indeed little better could be expected from them, when the manner of their first setting out is well considered.

Such conduct should have been severely reprimanded in the beginning, instead of being applauded; for if the strictest regimen is not observed with such people, great inconvenience and mischief will inevitably follow.

TO ARTHUR LEE.

[VIENNA], 24 June [1778].

I hope my several letters from hence will reach you safely. His excellency the Baron de Breteuil having kindly promised to mention the arms, etc., that are wanted by the State of Virginia to Count Vergennes, I hope he will assist us in the business, for which reason it will be well for you to wait on him as soon as you receive this, which goes by the ambassador's courier. I have given the ambassador a list of the articles wanted, which he will probably enclose, or send a copy of to Count Vergennes. If the ministry should determine to let us have the articles out of the public stores, still one or two hundred thousand livres will be wanted to pay incidental charges of Insurance, and to make advances in part of freight to the vessels that must be ch[artered] to transport the goods. But as it will be an [   ] task to charter vessels, they must be taken where they [are] found, in France, Holland, Denmark, or Sweden; [and] small vessels, so as to divide the risk and make [the con] veyance more sure, because small vessels ca[n go] into several little creeks on the coast, where [large] vessels cannot enter. I should prefer Danmark for the ch[arter] of vessels for this business, because if taken, it m[ay at] least have the effect of inclining that Power, partly from resentment against England, to join France, and as this will be a naval war principally between F[rance] and G[reat] B[ritain], it seems to me that Sweden and Danmark will be much more useful allies, than either Austria or Prussia; because the two former have not only ships of war, but a great number of excellent sailors; while the two latter Powers have neither ships nor sailors.

On these considerations, as well also, as that with money, the articles may be bo't and shipped, with infinitely more secresy and safety, than if taken from out of the King's stores. I would prefer your requesting the Count Vergennes to lend on account of the State of Virginia, one million of livres, which it is computed will be the least that the goods and charges necessarily to be paid with money will come to; this sum to be repaid by the State as soon as ever their trade is sufficiently open to allow them to export their commodities. The money in fact will not be wanted these six months, because, after a credit is fixed for the sum with a banker in Paris, it will take at least two months to prepare the goods and vessels to ship hem in; and I have no doubt, but that they may be bo't with bills at four months, which together will make six months before there will be occasion for the money to be actually paid.

If the ministry are disposed to assist the State in this business, [but] should not approve of lending the money, but rather choose to furnish the articles in their kind, we must request that they will order them to be supplied out of the arsenals in, or nearest to the ports where vessels may be found to charter. The importance of this supply to the general cause you know as well as me, and can state at large to Count Vergennes, who may possibly think that the application ought to be made to him by the Commissioners of Congress. But he should be informed that it is a particular commission in which neither Congress or their Commissioners have any immediate concern, tho' it is, notwithstanding, of most material consequence to the general welfare; because by the Constitution, every particular state is bound to furnish the soldiers they supply for the Continental army, with arms, &c., besides what are necessary for the troops that each [State] must keep on foot to protect and defend their own country. The [necessi]ty of this supply is now become greater since Nicho[lson was] taken, and I hope on this occasion the French Cabinet will [recall] a maxim of the Great Sully—when speaking of the [French] affairs, that were then,

something as ours are now, he [said it] is a maxim
that he who gives plentifully at once, gives [some-
thing] to which he will add; that he who gives by
halves gives nothing.

If you should have applied already to Count Vergennes in consequence of what I before wrote, still
I think it by all means advisable that you should
do so again, because it is probable that the ambassador's representation may have its due weight.
The sooner you advise me of the issue of this business the better, for if the funds can be obtained,
there is no time to be lost, that the vessels may be
despatched in good season.

There is no alteration in our affairs at this court
since I wrote last, but these uninformed politicians
begin to look wise. For I am told on hearing the
fate of the Conciliatory Bills in America, they have
not yet got out of their dream about the invincible
power and inexhaustible resources of G[reat] B[rit-
ain]. I have, indeed, met with two or three pretty
deep political [   ], but believe me they are
not of German heads ; for as far as I have seen,
there is more in the K[ing of] Prussia's head, than
in all the other Germans put together. * * *

TO THE REV. JAMES MADISON.

V[IENNA], 24 June, [1778].

* * * The heaviest and most dreadful [   ]

of the contest is, thank God, now over. The Independence of the 13 United States is fixed, and in my opinion will be acknowledged by all Europe, even by G. B., before the end of 1779. Let us then look a little forward for a moment to the period of peace, and in time provide the most essential means for the happiness and prosperity of our country. For this great end, I know not of any method more essential than taking care of the education of our youth, for tho' in old countries, perhaps, 'tis the laws and constitution that form the morals, manners and genius of the people ; in new nations, as ours now are, this system must be reversed, and the morals, manners and genius of the first and second ages will have to establish laws and customs that must influence the well being of many generations to come. On this view it gives me much comfort to observe from whence you date your letter. From your abilities and good dispositions, our country may expect a pletiful crop of PATRIOT SONS to supply the void that has been made by a destructive war. The seminary, as far as I am acquainted with it, is well calculated for instruction ; the rest must ever depend on the professors, and as far your department extends, I rely on every benefit to the community.

The turn that things have taken in Europe within the last six or seven months has given G. B. something else to contemplate on than the conquest of America. Tho' no war is declared, they are at this moment in the most alarming confusion from the apprehension of a French invasion. The reinforcements sent to America this year do not exceed 2000 men, many of which can't be arrived at this time, and the whole destined for Canada, Nova Scotia and Newfoundland, to secure, if possible, the remnant of the British Empire in N. A. from the power of the United States; so that if G. Washington has his army tolerably compleat, Phila. and New York must be evacuated, as Boston was, by the B. troops, or they must be taken Prisoners.

Every moment we expect a most dreadful war in this country between the Emperor and King of Prussia, which, if once commenced, will be bloody indeed. They have each armies, well appointed, of above 200,000 men, and have been for some months in the neighborhood of each other, on the confines of Bohemia and Silesia. France and G. B. are also on the point of measuring swords, or rather trying their naval forces; one with a strong fleet of 21 large ships at Portsmouth, and 12 or 14 at Plymouth ready for action; and the other with 30 odd large ships at Brest, ready for sea at a moment's warning, and much better provided than the English, besides several more ships at the different ports, above 60,000 troops commanded by their ablest general, Mareschal Broglio, on the coast opposite England. ,The English militia, with the few regulars they have, altogether to the amount of about 35 or 40,000 men, are on the different parts of the English coasts. So that the eyes of all Europe are gazing to see where the mighty storm will burst.   *   *   *

Poor Mr. Norton now sleeps with his fathers. Young man [   ] of a consumption in great distress, and young John Lewis ended his [   ] in France, and James Wormeley is in the British army, and I believe [   ].

TO EDMUND JENINGS.

V[IENNA], 24 June, [1778].

Many thanks for yours of the 9th, received yesterday, and for the intelligence it contained. While the cabinet continues as it has been and is, the Tory Quaker will always have intelligence quicker than those who ought to be first informed of what relates to *America*. I have reason to think the *British Court* have *a copy of* 1. You may conjecture as well as me thro' what channel. I wonder you did not know of Nicholson's being taken, which we had here from London two days ago. You will no doubt believe that Posterity will not be puzzled to decide between Sr W. T. and *W. Lee*, when you know that he intends to leave this place in about eight days. His return here will depend upon circumstances, on which it is not in his power to decide. The conduct of the *Emperor's Court* has not been the most pleasing, and as appears to me infinitely more insulting to *France* than *America*, because the thick heads look on the business as a matter entirely between *England* and *France*, leaving the other totally out of the question. Some of distinction, however, are warm for the part of America, and in the beginning spoke freely to the great mortification of 50–2;* but since the *Emperor* and *King* have taken their high line, mouths are in some measure shut. 'Tis possible that 47 [Russia?] may alter things, but whether he does or not, 'tis some comfort that the first object of *Congress* will be accomplished as well as the nature of things will admit, without being under any obligation to either the *Emperor*, *King*, or 47. [Russia?] * * *

We have no war here yet ; but some that pretend to be in the secret say in about a fortnight it will be [   ] for Peace or War, tho' between ourselves I don't think that any of them know any more about the matter than you.

From what has appeared of the proceedings in [America] I am inclined to think the operations of this year will [be very ex]pensive and nothing decisive; for I am very clear the [mili]tia, at least

---

* British ambassador?

in any material numbers will not join [   ]
W[ashington]. Certainly F[rance] will soon begin
to make reprisals on B[ritish] merchantmen, otherwise she will be presently in the same situation she
was at the declaration of last war, with one-fourth
of her seamen prisoners.   *   *   *

TO JOHN PAGE.

VIENNA, 24 June, [1778].

The letter you did me the Honor of writing the
12 March has reached me here. I have been some
months in this country on the public service, and
may possibly continue some months longer, after
which, in all likelihood, I shall return to France,
and pursue my old occupation in serving my
friends. I am happy to find you had in prospect
to finish the war this campaign, before you could
possibly know the turn our affairs had taken in
Europe, which I trust will not have the effect of
making you less vigorous in your measures. Were
you not so fully masters of your own business, and
so fully sensible of the weakness, wickedness and
treachery of the British ministers, as you really
are, it would be still unnecessary to caution you
against them, because every step they take leaves a
visible mark of the cloven foot. Congress have
wisely determined that an explicit acknowledgement of your Independence, and withdrawing the

British fleets and armies from the territories of the United States, must be the preliminary articles to any kind of treaty.

If these ministers were not perfect Idiots, how could they expect any good from sending out as a commissioner, a Scotchman, who is well known to be the devoted tool of Lords Bute and Mansfield, and that they have kept him as a spy among the opposition for many years, to be masters of their secrets.* If the British army at Philadelphia is bro't to share the same fate this campaign, that Burgoyne's army did the last, this may be the [last] of the war; but if that is not the case, you should look forward to another. For I trust there is not a man in America who does not feel the justness of the great Prince of Parma's observation, that when the sword is drawn in certain [   ], one should never forget to throw away the scabbard ; and [while] we have every reason to be content with our new allies, the French, yet it is always more secure to take care of ourselves, than to trust to our friends for protection.

But if in the din of war, one moment can be spared to look forward to time of peace, let me request your attention to the mode of levying taxes for supporting the heavy expences of this war, and to the college for the education of our youth. The

* Gov. Geo. Johnstone.

immense importance of both these objects to the
future prosperity and happiness of our country, is
so obvious, that it is unnecessary for me to press it
on you; therefore will only mention that, after having well considered the various subjects of taxation
that our country is capable of, except a few articles
of luxury at present of no great importance, a poll
tax seems to me the best, as being easiest collected,
with the least expence, and as equal, if not more so,
than any other. A tax on lands must be always
very unequal, and taxes on articles of commerce,
either export or import, generally take a pound
from the community for every shilling they bring
into the public coffer.

For months past we have every moment been
expecting the commencement of a most tremendous
war between the King of Prussia and the Emperor
of Germany, and between France and England.
Still there is no declaration on either side yet.
The English men-of-war and privateers in most
parts of the world, even on the coasts of France,
continue to take the French merchant vessels,
which we cannot, in common sense, suppose
France will suffer much longer without making
reprisals, especially as she has now a powerful fleet
ready, and is better prepared for war, than she has
been any time in this century. They never were
more alarmed in England than they are at this
time, every moment expecting an invasion from

France, which gives so much employment that they have little time to think of conquering America. * * *

TO MR. ELLIS.*

VIENNA, 24 June, 1778.

I am glad to hear that my estate under your management is bro't into some order, and I hope in a little time you will be able to make me amends for not having received anything from it for three years past. It is not in my power at this distance to be very particular, but in general I wish you to get as much of the swampy lands as possible made into timothy meadow, and instead of selling any hay or fodder, I think they will be more beneficially employed in increasing and supporting well a large stock of cattle and sheep to manure your lands, and the rams should always be kept from the Ewes till the fall, so that no lambs may be dropped till the middle or latter end of April. I wish to have a large quantity of white mulberry trees raised; they should be planted by the sides of the fences round all the fields. Take care of the fruit trees and gardens, and put some promising young lads apprentices to all the useful trades, such as carpenters, house joiners, wheelwrights, sawyers, blacksmiths, brick layers, and ship carpenters. The

---

* Manager at Green Spring.

tobacco that is made at present may as well be sold in the country, and what money is raised from the estate may be put into the public loan office till there is an opportunity of sending me some remittances. I can't too much recommend to you (tho' I hope there is no occasion for it,) to take all possible care of the people. The women with child should never be hard worked or oppressed in any manner, and the children should always be plentifully fed and have necessary clothing. I wish them all to be treated as human beings whom Heaven has placed under my care not only to minister to my luxury, but to contribute to their happiness. In return for which I have a right to expect their faithful, honest and diligent service. I shall be glad to hear from you. The Rev. Mr. Madison at William and Mary College will tell you how to direct to me, and I dare say will take the trouble to forward your letters. I wish you health, &c.

TO ARTHUR LEE.

V[IENNA], 27 June, [1778].

* * * I only mean now to beg you will suspend making any contract or engagement with P[ene]t & Co. I am satisfied the business will not be properly done by them. I presume it is with P[ene]t himself that the negotiation is going on, but whether 'tis or no, I can't think in any manner

that it will be right. I have many invincible
reasons too long to recite now.

You have above some parts of the bargain proposed at S[trasburg] to Captain Le M[aire], which
exclusive of the prices, show that nothing can be
done there. Indeed at first sight, a place so remote
from any sea port, must appear improper, not only
on account of the charge of transport, but the
length of time to get to a port, which will be much
longer than the voyage. I trust the whole of the
first order will be furnished by the *Court of France*
—if not, we must essay other methods. I know
not the orders given at Ch[aillo]t to Capt. Le M.,
therefore shall only say to him in general, that I
do not think we can do any thing at S. He will
then of course, pursue his orders . . .

MEMORANDUM.*

Although the Emperor of G., when crown'd,
takes an oath, that he will, as much as possible,
prevent emigrations, yet all the Princes and sovereign powers, claim the privilege of making treaties
with, and selling their subjects to any foreign
powers, provided such engagements are not contrary to the peace, liberty and interests of the Germanic body. This privilege has been fixed and
ascertained by the treaty of Westphalia in 1648,

---

* From William Lee's letter book.

which is guaranteed by France, Sweden, Danemark, &c., &c. France, in consequence of this
treaty, as well as other neighboring powers, have
ever since been in the exercise of hiring German
troops from the several powers; and at the death of
the late Elector of Bavaria,* in December, 1777,
actually had a treaty with him for that purpose.
This prior to [   ] extremely anxious of maintaining [   ] it cannot be expected of her, to
move in the design of obtaining a resolution of the
General Diet against emigrations, unless it is on
the principle, that being sent over the sea, they
must be forever lost to their country, and in case
of danger to the Germanic body, their distance will
certainly prevent their being returned in due time.

TO ARTHUR LEE.

FRANKFORT, 16 July, [1778].

My dear Brother :

I wrote you the 14th in answer to one received
that day without any date, and yesterday I received
yours of the 9th covering one from R. H. L. Please
to forward the rest that came with it, by the first
post, and I beg you will remember that if you ever
forward to me a letter without the original cover,
that you will preserve the cover for me, marking
on it when the letter it inclosed was received, from

---

* Maximilian Joseph, son of Charles Albert.

whom, the place and date, when it was forwarded
to me and by what conveyance. This particularity
I know will appear trifling to you, but I have my
own private reasons for desiring it to be done. You
remember that on Mr. S[imeon] Deane's return,
many other letters were written and delivered to
him. You must remember also some particulari-
ties that happened at that time. R. H. L. acknowledges receiving by him my letter in December, but
not that in February. This business should be
fully investigated. I wrote by Mr. S[imeo]n Deane
to R. H. Lee dated February 28, 1778, covering
copys of mine from Nantes of the 13 and 15 of February. Also to F. L. Lee, Robert Morris, the Secret Committee and President of Congress, all of
date February 27. These I think were put under
cover addressed to the P—t of C—ss. I likewise
wrote to Genl. Arnold and sent him an engraving.
You have Mr. D's receit for these letters, a copy of
which you ought to send R. H. L. immediately,
and inform him of the above particulars.

Pray send me the explanation about your present manner of using the red book, for I do not
understand how you have fixed it with R. H. L.
Let me know if there is any opportunity to America. *W. Lee* says he would by all means avoid
any kind of *difference with Adams*, or even a *cooll-
ness*. Let the appointment go as it will, *A. Lee*
should not meddle at all, which will embarrass

Franklin more than any other conduct; but it will be certainly right in you to inform the present Deputys, where the power is now lodged that they may pursue such measures with respect to themselves as they think proper. The Baron De Breteuil has interested himself in favor of a Mr. Comyn at Marseilles, to be appointed in that port. He has written to Mr. Grand to apply to the Commissioners for him, and I must request you will do Mr. Comyn all the service you can, in return for the obligations we are under to the Baron de Breteuil, who has given all countenance to our affairs. He is esteem'd a sage and deep politician, and I think bids fair to be one day at the head of affairs in his own country.

With respect to the business of Virginia, I have so often desired that no contract or engagement for goods may be enter'd into with Messrs. Pliarne, Penet, D'Acosta & Co. on account of the State, that I have only to confirm now what I have before written on that subject. So far as we can get funds to be sure of the payment, I can buy the goods, particularly the fusils, at least 20 per cent. cheaper than they supply them at. This is paying too extravagantly for their credit, besides which they will expect the returns to be consigned to them, the profits whereof, you may in some measure conjecture. I must request you will explicitly and fully inform me of what measures you have taken and are about to take in this business, for it is impossible to judge from hints or general expressions, how to conduct myself.

I have nothing else at this time to attend to, but laying in these goods, for our general affairs here must stand still as they are now, 'till the close of this campaign, which letters from Saxony and Vienna say was commenced the 5th of this month, by the King of P. entering into Bohemia. Saxony gives a considerable advantage to the Prussians, and Vienna of course to the Austrians. The real truth I cannot as yet find out; but this seems certain, that the war is began. All I want of you is to negotiate the loan, on which subject I wrote you you fully from Ratisbonne, but I am convinced and can prove it that we had better give 8 or even ten p.r c.t interest for the money, than enter into the contract proposed to get the goods on credit.

If you can contrive safely a line to E. J[enin]gs in London, pray tell him I have wrote 2 or 3 letters since I went to V[ienn]a, and not receiving any answer, I fear they have been intercepted in England; but if 'tis so, he need not be under any apprehensions on that account. With respect to Franklin, W. Lee desires Arthur Lee to remember what Homer says of Nauplius, King of Eubœa, who being irritated against the Greecian chiefs, for having condemned to death unjustly his son Palamedes, thro' the *artifices* of Ulysses, placed false fires on

Mount Capharea to lead the Greecian fleet to their destruction against the rocks; but the cunning Ulysses, conscious of what he deserved from Nauplius, went another course, and escaped the destruction intended for him. We are all well, and send our best love. Adieu. Yours sincerely and truly.

TO EDMUND JENINGS.

F[RANKFOR]T, 19 July, [1778].

* * * The English papers tell us that the [   ] to acknowledge the independence of America and make peace. 'Tis certain they now have the fairest opportunity that they can wish for, to make such a [   ] relished by almost the whole nation, by means of Gen'l Howe, [if they] do not wait too long, but assemble the Parliament immediately to give them full powers and authority. I will then proceed to give you what I think they ought to do in order to succeed. By all means avoid a war with F[rance]; restore the two frigates and other captures, which may be done with honor, as they have certainly been taken contrary to ye laws of nations, and 'tis always more consistent with the dignity of a great nation to repair the errors of her servants, than obstinately to persist in supporting them. Withdraw all the B[ritis]h troops and ships to Halifax at least, if not to G. B. Acknowledge the independence of the 13 United

States, fix their boundaries as contended for by G.
B. against F. in 1754. Each party to have free
liberty of fishing on the Banks of Newfoundland.
G. B. to pay for towns burnt and private property
destroyed on land by her troops during the war; a
mutual right of citizenship in all respects, to the
subjects of each party in either country, and a free
right of entry and commerce of the ships and merchandize of either party into the ports or territories
of the other. British and American property that
has been or may be confiscated in America, to be
made good, and a general act of oblivion passed on
both sides. I do not think any propositions less
than these will answer, nor will these be accepted
unless they are made neatly, plainly and fully at
once, and by some person like yourself, whose
honor, integrity and justice cannot doubt; for you
may be assured there is a party in America and in
Congress, tho' not the majority at present, [   ] or
fully sensible of their strength, wish not for [   ]
G. B. has any share of the Newfoundland fishery,
or is in possession of C., N. S., and B., or the
Floridas. This party has much address in negotiation, and will prevail in their schemes unless the
B. M. adopt the open, candid and plain part above
mentioned. Mr. Fitzh[ug]h may assert what he
pleases, but he must excuse me for not giving the
least credit to what he advanced. I am convinced
that America will treat as readily at least, with the

present ministry as the opposition, if they will but go plainly to work, and by such men, [of] whose honor and honesty the Americans have an opinion. I am sure that not one of the three commissioners* last sent out will be trusted by a single man in Congress. With these sentiments of the agents, you may easily judge what will be the issue of their negotiation.

TO ARTHUR LEE.

F——T, 30 July, [1778].

My dear Brother:

I received here yours of the 21st June, sent to N—, and yesterday another of no date, with several accompanyments, Nos. 1, 2, 3, 4 and 5. You seem to have adopted Mr. Burke's principle, that the representative when once appointed is no longer amenable to the controul of his constituent. You will remember that the contract with P[enet] & Co., was from the beginning objected to, and with the power a positive injunction against it was sent, both which were received before the contract was finish'd. However, as that and the one at Klingenthal are compleated, I shall decline farther observations. I wish to have as soon as possible, full copys of the last Invoice, power to borrow the money, and the letter accompanying them. At

---

*The Earl of Carlisle, William Eden, and George Johnstone.

the same time say if with respect to the loan you
have applyed to *French court*, G[ra]nd, the F[arm-
ers] G[eneral] and M—de, or to any of them. From
this answer a judgment may be formed whether a
trip to P[aris] is likely to produce any good effect.
I am convinced that *Deane* and the tribe have corrupted *Franklin*.

I wish to know also, whether any thing about
the State business is known *at Passy*. Tell our
friend at Radswil, before he complains of want of
intelligence, he should answer my last letter from
V[ienna]. The bringing an English Frigate into
Brest, taking most of the Guernsey and Jersey
privateers, the order for the Brest fleet to sail, the
arrival of the Spanish flota, and lastly, the order
for reprisal on the British Marine dated the 10th
inst., which I only heard of two daies ago, are
surely too trifling objects of intelligence to be
mentioned from your quarter. I expect it will be
the same when news is received at P. of the arrival
and operations of D'Estaing's squadron and Byron's 3 sixty-four-gun ships; and 3 or 4 frigates
despatched immediately will be exactly in time to
secure all the Newfoundland Fishery, which would
be almost as heavy a blow as destroying Keppel's
fleet. If you think so, you know where to mention it, but no time is to be lost. I hope you have
particularly mentioned my letters sent by D[eane]
that have not been delivered. You see by the

Committee's letter that my two to Congress in February have not been received. I think if you have been precise this matter may be fixed, which will explain, tho' not legally prove the stealer of the other letters.

The northern post last Monday the 27th, bro't advice that a truce for 6 weeks between the Emperor and King of Prussia had taken place; that commissioners on each side were appointed to meet at Glatz to settle the peace; that in consequence the King had retir'd from Bohemia into Silesia and Prince Henry had also retired from B—a to Saxony. This news is denyed here by the Austrian party, but to-day's post will confirm or contradict. If I hear anything in time you shall know it at bottom. The whole is not very likely, tho' it is probable the armies have retir'd from Bohemia for want of provisions, as the Austrians themselves have laid waste the countries and the inhabitants have some time retired by command of the Emperor to the interior parts. Probably too, the King, grown old, is not so venturesome as formerly, and does not choose lightly to risk his great reputation so dearly earned, therefore he has not attacked the Austrian lines.

Kniphausen and many other officers from N. Y. are arrived in England. The dragoons and guards are on their way back. Lord North keeps in, and I believe will to the end of the chapter. What a wretched lot the whole opposition is? Can they expect to be ever in any degree respectable, while they continue to receive with open arms every scoundrel that the ministry choose to discard, such as Bur[goy]ne. I presume the commissioners will inform Congress of the conduct of 142 [Ross?]. I would not wish you to be hasty in mentioning Mr. Comyn, least it may be a reason for another to object. Nor do I understand that you have authority to appoint any consuls, but only mercantile agents, which appointment for the present might satisfy Mr. C. All here are as usual, except the little Rose Bud, who has suffer'd and is now suffering as much with the chicken pox as she could with the small pox.

I hope you will in one instance prove like the priests—practice differently from what you preach; that farther you will pay due attention to my several complaints and let me have the earliest intelligence of every material occurrence. I do not press for secrets, but only that I may not be expos'd to ridicule in asking others and learning from public Gazettes, what I ought to be informed of first . . . . Adieu.

TO M. NEUFVILLE.*

F[RANKFORT], 27 August, [1778].

* * * In 6 or 7 days I shall set out for Paris, where my stay will not be above three weeks, or to the latter end of September at furthest. On my return here I could contrive to meet you at some place on the road, or by going somewhat out of my way, provided you are assured by Mons. le. P.† that our meeting will be of any essential service in accomplishing the business we have been agitating. On this you can give me your opinion in ten days or a fortnight by a line addressed to myself, and put under care to Mons. Grand, Banquier in Paris, writing on my letter that it is not to be delivered into any hands but my own, when I can in answer fix the time and place of our meeting. You may be

---

*Jean de Neufville was then at Aix la Chapelle, and writing to Lee before the latter's departure for Paris, arranged for a meeting at Aix. Lee left Frankfort on the evening of the 31st, and the meeting seems to have occurred.

It is uncertain what incident first led Lee to propose a treaty. Some letters from England for him had been sent through the Pensionary in March or April of this year, and in April Franklin had sent to the Pensionary a copy of the treaty entered into by France. How Neufville, who figured a year later in a remarkable proposition to Franklin (*Works*, vi, 334), became connected with the negotiation, I have not been able to discover. From the beginning, Lee appears to have acted upon his own responsibility, without consulting any one but his brothers and Izard.

† The Pensionary.

assured of the good disposition of my principals, towards the good people and States of Holland, and if the same inclinations prevail in your quarter, I do not fear concluding something that will be equally satisfactory to both parties. It will be advisable for you if we meet, to bring with you a letter from Mr. the P., to lay the foundation of our future proceedings. I hope you will not find any difficulty in the business of the loan, which will be the best corner-stone to lay for the foundation of the building we propose to raise, and if you find it can be accomplished, the sooner we come to the terms the better. * * *

TO THE COMMITTEE OF FOREIGN AFFAIRS.

PARIS, September 12th, 1778.

Gentlemen :

I have just arrived here from Germany, and finding the bearer of this about to set off in a few hours, I cannot omit saying a word or two, though it will be impossible to be so full as I could wish. I wrote to the President of Congress from Vienna, the 30th of May last, which was forwarded from hence, to which be pleased to refer; since then I have received your first and only letter, dated from Yorktown the 14th of May last, wherein you acknowledge the receipt of mine of the 24th of November and the 18th of December; but I am surprised at your not receiving also two other letters from me, dated the 28th of February and 23d of March last, which were sent by Mr. Simeon Deane, and addressed to the President of Congress.

Since my last of the 30th of May, when the war broke out between the Emperor and the King of Prussia, on consultation with the French Ambassador at Vienna, it was agreed to be most advisable for me to retire to Frankfort, and wait there until the several Powers in Germany and the rest of Europe had taken a decided line in this war, when we might be able to direct our operations to the most advantage for America, since it was evident that neither the Court of Vienna nor that of Berlin could, in their critical situation, take an open part with us, for fear of throwing Hanover, with a body of thirty thousand men, into the scale of the adversary, especially, too, as France had declared a neutrality, on the urgent application of the House of Austria for aid, under the treaties subsisting between them and France; to which, however, France replies with truth, that the case does not exist as specified in the treaty, which obliges them to aid the House of Austria. The two mighty Powers have been in the field opposed to each other ever since the beginning of July, when the King of Prussia entered Bohemia with his army; but no battle has yet been given, or anything material passed on either side. There have been perpetual skirmishes between the foraging parties and advanced posts, which on the whole seem rather in favor of the Prussians. In the course of the winter or spring, we hope things will take such a turn as to enable me to operate to advantage with one or the other of the parties ; but at present I think you may be assured that such measures have been taken as will effectually prevent our enemies from obtaining any further aid from any part of Europe, if they should continue the war against us another year, which I can hardly expect they will do, for I am informed, and have reason to believe my information true, that orders have been already sent to their Commissioners in America to acknowledge our independence, if nothing else will answer, in order to commence a treaty and make a peace.

After my arrival at Frankfort, finding an opportunity offered to me of negociating a treaty of commerce with the United States of Holland and West Friesland, I embraced it, and have proceeded so far as to agree on the draught of a treaty, with the regular representative of the Pensionary and Burgomasters of the city of Amsterdam, of which I have not time to send you a copy by this conveyance, but I am sure you would approve of it, as it contains all the substantially advantageous articles of the commercial treaty with France, and some beneficial and agreeable additions.

So far, the business has been conducted on both sides with great secrecy, which is absolutely necessary in order to procure final success with the united States here; for though the city of Amsterdam and the States of Holland pay, it is supposed, about five-sixths of the whole taxes for the support of the Government, which consequently gives them very powerful weight and influence, yet they have no power, by their constitution, of entering into such a treaty, without the concurrence of the other united States, in some of which the Prince of Orange has an over-due influence, and all the world know his blood connexions with the King of England, as well as that he has the same designs against his country that have been attempted to be carried into execution against us, and which he hopes to succeed in by the aid of his cousin of England, with whom he is in the strictest intimacy. This renders secrecy of the last importance, until the patriots in Holland have secured success, before the business is agitated in the General Assembly of the States, where it must come, to have full authority.

Here I find myself embarrassed because I have no power to sign such a treaty, and I know not how to determine as yet about communicating it, in the present situation of things, to those who have a power to sign it in your name, because it is well known that some of the most important negociations and proceedings here, relative to your affairs, have some time past been very speedily communicated in England, and I have not yet been able to learn that the old channel is stopped. I shall, however, proceed in the manner that shall, on the maturest reflection, appear the best to forward the wishes of Congress, and advance the prosperity of our country.

In a week or ten days I shall return to my station in Germany,* and watch with careful attention over my charge there, and when any thing material occurs you shall be duly advised.

I have the honor to be, &c.

TO RICHARD HENRY LEE.

PARIS, 12 September, 1778.

My dear Brother:

I am just arrived here from Germany and find the bearer, M.ʳ Gilby, just setting out with dispatches for Congress, and have only a few minutes to write to you.

I wrote you from Vienna 30.ᵗʰ May, and have since received Loudoun's of May 16.ᵗʰ last, for which thank him, and give our love, as I can't write now having no time. I have received from you 25.ᵗʰ Jan. last from Green Spring, and 13.ᵗʰ May

---

* "In eight days at farthest I shall return to my old station at Frankfort." *William Lee to E. Browne*, 15 September, 1778.

from York town; in the last you mention receiving by Mr Simeon Deane and Capt Young mine of Nov: 24 and 30, and 3, 6, and 18 Dec^r; but you say nothing of one dated 28th Feb:, covering copies of what I wrote you from Nantes, about a fortnight before; which was enclosed to the President of Congress, with one to Congress, another to the Secret Committee, and another to F. L. Lee Esqr, all of the same date with your's, and this packet delivered to Mr Simeon Deane, for which he gave a receipt, but I do not yet learn that any of them have been delivered.

Mr Silas Deane went from hence as far as Versailles with his brother Simeon, when he set out with the dispatches the beginning of March, and they staid there together all night. I hope you will inquire about these letters, and if they have not been received, that the transaction may be sifted to the bottom.

There was a letter from me also to Mr Robt Morris in the same packet, and of the same date, viz: 28 Feb: 1778.

You will see by my letter to Congress of this date how far I have gone in negotiating a treaty of Commerce with their High Mightinesses, the United States of Holland, etc; but it is really a lamentable circumstance that I forsee the business will be obstructed, and I am afraid fatally because I have not power to sign it, and if communicated here,

where the only power of signing is at present
vested, it is most probable, that intelligence of it
will speedily get to England; as has for a long time
been the case with all the most important and critical transactions relative to America.

This channel which was fixed long before Mᴿ
Adams came, I am afraid is not yet obstructed.   I
think you must have reason to fix at least on some
of the agents, and tho' the great patrons and pro-
tectors are removed, yet one at least of the instruments remains, and is enabled as much as ever to
carry on the old game.

I see a thousand difficulties on every side, but
my whole object will be to accomplish the wishes
of Congress, and effectually serve my country.

I know perfectly those that are on the watch to
catch, at every step that they can torture, to serve
their *selfish* purposes, but I know too, that when a
man exceeds his authority, success will varnish
over every irregularity, and sometimes blots out the
remembrance of the most horrid iniquities—when a
failure draws along with it, not only censure for the
simple act, but a load of reproach, which is often
unmerited.

'Tis most certain that if this negotiation is
known in England, or even to the Prince of Orange's party in Holland, before its success is secured, that it will be effectually prevented.

I must return to Germany in about 10 daies, to

watch over my charge there, which for the present is at a stand, as you will see by mine to Congress; and yet it will be some time before any one can possibly judge what turn affairs will take in that quarter; it seems to me most probable that the war will continue some years, and that peace will not arrive until many bloody and terrible battles are fought; however you may be assured that Great Britain will not get any more aid from Europe to prosecute her ridiculous war with America, which in fact I look upon as good as ended. However after 'tis finished Congress will nearly have an Augean stable to cleanse in correcting the disorders that must have crept in, and in punishing the corruptions and peculations that no doubt have been practised. * * I have sent from Holland 2,000 Dutch blankets and 3,000 p^r woolen stockings, on acc^t ofthe Secret Committee.

My best love and wishes attend you always.

Adieu.

COMMISSIONERS TO WILLIAM LEE.

PASSY, September 26th, 1778.

Sir:

We have considered with some attention, the papers which you have laid before us, containing a project of a treaty to be made between the Republic of the United Provinces and that of the United States of America.

As Congress have entrusted to us the authority of

treating with all the States of Europe, excepting such as have a particular commission designed by Congress to treat with them; and as no particular Commissioner has been appointed to treat with their High Mightinesses, we have already taken such measures as appeared to us suitable to accomplish so desirable a purpose, as a friendship between nations so circumstanced as to have it in their power to be extremely beneficial to each other in promoting their mutual prosperity. And we propose to continue our endeavors in every way consistent with the honor and interest of both.

But we do not think it prudent, for many reasons, to express, at present, any decided opinion concerning the project of a treaty which you have done us the honor to communicate to us.

We cannot, however, conclude without expressing our real disposition to treat upon an object, which, besides laying the foundation of an extensive commerce between the two countries, would have a very forcible tendency to stop the effusion of human blood, and prevent the further progress of the flames of war.

We have the honor to be, with the utmost respect, sir, your most obedient humble servants,

B. FRANKLIN,
ARTHUR LEE,
JOHN ADAMS.

TO ARTHUR LEE.

FRANKFORT, 8 Oct.ʳ 1778.

Dear brother:

I wrote to you the 4th and yesterday I received yours of the 1st. I forgot to mention that directions were given to Mʳ Sauvage, orfévre à l'ainean blanc, quai des orfévres, pont neuf, to make his estimate for a small portable vice; as well as the the Seal for the State of Virginia; but on reflection I think the vice will be unnecessary, because they must have had something of this sort to use their former seal with; therefore all that is now wanted will be the two silver pieces properly engraved to make the proper impression on each side of the wax.

This can't cost near what you talked of, nor can it be difficult to execute. Let me know if you can have it done in Paris, if not I will have it done in Holland.

Design of a Great seal for a State. On one side of the seal the impression should be Virtue, the Genius of the state, dressed as an Amazon, resting on a spear with her left hand, and holding a drawn sword in her right hand, with Tyranny under her feet, a crown falling from his head, holding a broken chain in his left hand and a sceptre in his right hand.

In the exergue the word " Virginia " over the head of Virtue, and below the words

"Sic Semper Tyrannis."

On the opposite side of the seal should be Liberty
holding a spear in her right hand, with a cap at the
end of the spear.   On one side of Liberty should be the
goddess Ceres, with her horn of plenty in her left hand
and an olive branch in her right hand.   On the other
side of Liberty should be Eternity with a globe in her
left hand and a phœnix in her right.

In the exergue the words

" *Deus Nobis, Hœc otia Fecit.*"*

TO S. THORPE.

F[RANKFORT], 14 October, [1778.]

* * * The election of a new Mayor seems to
show that instead of mending things are growing
worse and worse, therefore I shall not be surprised
if N—m, (whose political principles I think you
had always a much better opinion of than they
deserve,) should succeed the little petulant, silly,
proud creole.   Our enemies, I am informed, are in
their hearts, well pleased at the resignation not being made, because it makes them more strong in
the Court; at the same time, with their usual
effrontery, they are on all occasions abusing me

---

*Indorsed on the original design of the great seal, the fol-
lowing names.

Leonard, graveur a la monie on Au Galarie du Louvre.
Lorthior, rue de la Monie.
Gammot, vis-a-vis Sainte Chapelle, Cour du Palais.
Sauvage, orfévre, Quai des orfévres.

personally. 'Tis not in my power to express the painful sensations I have experienced since we parted, on viewing at a distance the course of public affairs. For the downfall of poor old E[nglan]d seems to be decided in the registers above. The utter blindness, folly, madness, and distraction, that prevail thro' all orders and degrees, appear to be totally incurable. For private and particular reasons, I am much pleased that the inland trade last spring has been so brisk and profitable, but I fear it will prove in the body politic as in the human frame, that the cheeks glow, the spirits are most lively, and the blood circulates quicker than usual, when the poor creature is at death's door in the last stage of a consumption. * * * Manufactures are declining in price, tho' the number of manufactures are greatly diminished by many circumstances, but particularly by the number of people in arms. A manufactory in one of the most curious and principal branches in which England excelled, is established in this country (viz. Germany), where I have been. There are now above 400 men employed. The principal and by far the greater part of the manufacturers are Englishmen. These are bad symptoms, but they might be cured, if there was any soundness in the body. The French prizes, tho' they benefit individuals, will most certainly injure the Community, because like the lotteries, every one will expect the great prize, and on that presumption will neglect his fair trade, and live on his imaginary gain, till the Gazette awakes him from his reverie. With respect to America, her Independence is irrevocably fixed. The conduct of opposition has, with respect to that, been as foolish and inconsistent as on almost all other occasions; but the ministry know from repeated experience how little their feeble efforts can interrupt any measures they wish to carry into execution. Therefore any excuse on that head is really trifling with common sense. I should suppose that peace may be made, and a treaty of amity and commerce entered into with America, without saying one word about Independence. There is a great probability that before this reaches you, some intelligence will be received from thence, which will show the necessity of such a measure's being speedily adopted, even to the most blind and obstinate. * * * All which she probably may preserve by a peace this winter. The East and West Indies, she holds only by the mercy of France and Spain. In this lamentable situation of things, you cannot blame my resolution fixing on this quiet and retired place for my winter quarters; but it has, and does give me pain, to reflect on my keeping that place which might be properly filled by another, and whilst it is impossible for me in the present circumstances to execute the duty thereof. When my constituents are desirous of it, I shall at any moment be ready to put it in their power to choose another; for, in truth, I should have done this long ago, had I not apprehended that they were not provided with a successor that they approve of.

As to myself, I am no stranger to the many aspersions that have been cast upon me; but I bear them with patience, in confidence that those who really know me, will be satisfied my conduct has been entirely directed by the wish of giving as much satisfaction to my constituents, as my situation would admit of, without a single view to myself. I am not insensible of the favors they have done me, and shall be always happy in the opportunity of testifying my gratitude whenever I can do it with propriety. It is said "Interest on the one hand, and necessity on the other, may for a time unite France and America; but their union cannot be lasting—the resentment of the latter will in time subside, and they will again look to G. B. as the land of their forefathers." All this might prove very true, provided things are not carried too far. * * * Old women and children, with the savage butchery now practicing by a refugee from Newgate, now ycleped Col. Butler, with the Indian allies and faithful auxiliaries of the B. M., on the babes and sucklings on the frontiers of Virginia and Pennsylvania,* will naturally produce very different

* The massacre at Wyoming had occured on the 3d of July. Col. John Butler being the British commander.

feelings from those of affection or esteem. It remains entirely with your ministers to decide (but this decision they will not long have in their power to make), whether or not America shall be forever firmly united, as well by affection, as by gratitude and interest, with France. Let them then look well to this, and before 'tis too late, or they may rue the consequences. . . . *

TO RICHARD HENRY LEE.

FRANKFORT ON THE RIVER MAIN IN GERMANY, }
15 October, 1778. }

My dear Brother:

I wrote to you the 21st Ult? from Paris, when I sent to Congress a Copy of a Plan of a Treaty between the seven United Provinces of the Netherlands and the United States of America, which had been digested by me and an eminent Dutch Merchant of Amsterdam, who represented the Pensionary of that City. I sent also from Paris a duplicate copy of this plan to Congress, and a copy of my Letter to you. By this Conveyance I send a copy of this Plan, and have wrote pretty fully, to which be pleased [to refer]. How the Commissioners at Paris will proceed with this treaty, can't be positively said; but I conceive 'twill go, as I mention'd in my last, of which you have a copy. In your re-

---

* This letter is much mutilated.

plys to me, pray note the particular dates of such letters as you receive from me, as also whether they are originals or the 1st or the 2^d copies.

You will receive with this a power of attorney relative to the Estate in Virginia and the necessary Letters. The determinations you take in this business and the conduct of it afterwards, you are very sensible, will be of such high and lasting importance to me and mine, that I am sure you will deliberate fully with our Dear Brother F. L. L. before you take any measures in it, or communicate the design to any person whatever; and if the resolution is to sell, I think no time shou'd unnecessarily be lost. All this your wisdom and judgement will direct properly, but I beg you will give me the earliest and repeated information of what you do determine on, and particularly relative to the plan or constitution of the Continental Loan Office. Besides by the Public expresses, which are generally the safest with regard to the Enemy, you may write by the way of Nantes, or to the care of Mr. John Bondfield, merchant in Bordeaux. I have before me ye following letters: 25 Jan., '78 from G. Spring; 13 May, '78 from York, and one Copy of it; and 6 June, 1777 which you sent by the Eastward and only came to hand last month. With respect to the first, the most material part is answer'd by by the power now sent. Ellis sent me his Accounts by which I perceive the number of Negroes are less than when they were divided. Now the Courts are open, 'tis presumable that Fauntleroy may be made to account for what he has received from the Estate. 'Tis now upwards of 3 years since I received one shilling from the Estate, and the last remittance, in 1775, was about 15 hhds. of Tobacco and £40 or £50 Sterling. This consider'd, I can't suppose that it will be expected that I shou'd be able to send any supplies from Europe, until something is sent that will enable me to do so. Those who have claims on me for Ballances in consequence of former mercantile transactions, must be sensible that while such large ballances are detain'd from me in the Country, I cannot pay their bills here; therefore if they draw, their bills will be returned. Besides, if it was ever so much in my power, I can't see the justice or reason for my paying in Europe what I owe, and being obliged to receive in the Country (or not receive it at all) what is owing to me, at a loss of 5 or 600 per cent. On the principle then of equal justice, I hope my Brother F. L. L. will pay off all my creditors without distinction, in the same manner and with the same Currency that he receives from my Debtors.

The crop of tobacco made in 1777, I suppose, will be sold in the country, where I am informed the price has been 65s, 70s and upwards per hundred weight. The crop made in 1778, I would not have you in a hurry about disposing of it, because 'tis probable that, should the war continue another year, France will judge it advisable to afford convoys for the American trade and particularly to Virginia ; in which case my tob? may be sent to Europe always consign'd to myself or orders. I hear a good account of M.ʳ Ellis from various quarters, and if you determine on keeping the Estate, I shall hope he will continue ; but in that case, I wish the removal of the people backwards and forwards from one plantation to another may as much as possible be avoided; because it prevents me from clearly determining about their increase or decrease. I will order the few things M.ʳ Ellis desires to be sent by the first good opportunity from France, with some bark for yourself. The wines of that country are all very improper for your habit, subject to the gout. Besides the medicines sent by M.ʳ King, your son Thos. was order'd to send 2 lbs. of Bark by the Independence, Cap.ᵗ Young, and the same quantity by another opportunity, all which I paid for. I am sure you know me well enough to be certain of my lasting gratitude for the care and attention you have bestow'd on me and my concerns, which I hope you will continue. Ludwell has grown much of late, is likely in his person, fond of reading and has a good genius, so that I think he will do very well, especially as he must early in life learn to provide for himself, which will force his natural talents into full exer-

cise in due season. He is still with his Uncle.
Thom. is still with M.ͬ Schweighauser, and if I
may judge from his Letters, he improves a good
deal ; and besides, I understand M.ͬ S. has begun to
employ him in active business, which from his
great caution and circumspection I think he
would not do, unless Thom. was trustworthy. He
shall continue where he is, until I can find some
better plan for him. Indeed he is still but 20 years
old and another year's apprenticeship will be
perhaps requisite to give him a proper knowledge
of business. I mention'd before (one of which letters by the way I have reason to apprehend has
been intercepted and kept by M.ͬ D.) and I hope
you will not forget it, that whenever the Idea is
taken up of appointing consuls in France, I cou'd
wish you would endeavor to get M.ͬ Edw. Browne
my former Partner appointed Consul at L'Orient,
if it is fix'd on for a free Port; if it is not, for Dunkirk or Holland. I know his worth intimately
well and can answer for his principles. By all
means prevent the power of nominating Consuls
from being delegated to any Persons in Europe, for
really at present a certain person, 169 *b* xxi in.
————* seems to think that Congress is bound to
follow his Mandates, and that it is highly presumptuous to do anything without his orders. I have
always admired the wisdom of Congress, and am

* Benjamin Franklin.

sure if they have determin'd wrong on any occasion, it has been owing to their being misinformed and deceived. Their Wisdom is evident in the express orders they have given relative to the application of the money they have ordered to be borrowed in Europe, and I assure you, it will be necessary to repeat them frequently; for notwithstanding the positive orders you have already given, attempts, I am well inform'd, have been made to divert this money into another channel and employ it in the old way. I have no doubt 115 b xxxviii* will 92 b xxvii—259 b xxxii with 110 a xxviii—which would not have been the case had 426 b xxviii taken care to 177 a xvi, 415 a x timely 39 b ii of his 305 b xxx. 'Tis of infinite importance to have the earliest notice of important resolutions, and some hints how parties stand with you. 'Tis sufficient to mention only the initial letters of people's names, and I must beg you to be particularly cautious in showing my letters to any person whatever except Loudoun; for in times like the present, he that professes himself the greatest Friend to-day may to-morrow prove your bitterest Foe. A Person that I dare say you cou'd not suspect, has, I understand, mention'd on this side the Water by way of reproach to me, the contents of some of my letters to you, which he says you show'd him. In your last letter, (the date of which I have forgot, having put the letter

---

* Deane.

among a number of papers and can't immediately
lay my hands upon it) you advise me to be cautious
in my public proceedings. I thank you for the
hint, at the same time assure you that I have been
in all points as circumspect as it was possible for
me to be, and if by any intrigues, what I have
done with Holland shou'd not be approved by
C[ongress], I shall never expect approbation unless
I turn Rogue like others, and mind my own private Interest more than that of the Public. I know
more than one instance on this side the Water of
persons who two years ago to my certain knowledge were not worth one shilling, without a prospect of ever becoming richer, that under the pretext
of serving the Public are now become men of capital fortune; one in particular 373 a xxxiv, 253 b xxi
of 169 b xxi in*, I am sure in the above time has made
£40,000 sterling without one shilling to begin with
of his own, and I fancy Mʳ. Ross the friend of Mʳ
R. M[orris] has done much more.† I have been

---

* Williams, nephew of Franklin.

† "It is not a little unpleasant to be deprived of that praise
which constant toil and assiduity in the public service have deserved, and submit to be traduced by those who, instead of consulting the public interest, when in office, have made immense
private fortunes for themselves, and their dependents, who are
occupied in two things only—their own gain, and the abuse of
every one who will not sacrifice the public to their views. Mr.
D. is generally understood to have made £60,000 sterling while
he was commissioner; his clerk, from being penniless, keeps

about 18 months in the Public Service, and have not made one shilling for myself, but on the contrary have sacrificed several thousand pounds by leaving England. I have never yet asked for anything from Congress, but when they do send a Commissioner to Holland I profess, as my former line of Life has been changed, I shou'd not dislike that appointment and I think if any change takes place in my present department, there is no person so proper as D.ʳ Franklin to be sent to Vienna. At all events I am determin'd to attend to the appointment of Virginia. My B.ʳ and myself have already done a good deal, and I am now endeavoring to borrow the money to compleat their orders; and if there is occasion, you may assure the State that I will do everything that is possible to comply with all their orders. It would

---

his horse and his carriage. Mr. Williams, Dr. Franklin's nephew, from being a clerk in a sugar bake-house in London, is become a capital merchant here, loading a number of ships on his own account, while the gentlemen of the first fortunes of America, cannot get remittances or credit for their subsistance. These things are notorious; and there are no visible sources of this prosperity but the public money and state secrets to trade upon." *Arthur Lee to Bland*, 13 December, 1778.

"Sir James Jay insinuated that Mr. Deane had been at least as attentive to his own interest, in dabbling in the English funds and in trade, and in fitting out privateers, as to the public; and said he would give Mr. Deane fifty thousand pounds for his fortune, and said that Dr. Bancroft too had made a fortune." *John Adams*, III., 138.

have been very agreeable, and will be so still, to know by whose means and from what motives my Commercial line was changed to a Political one. I am inclin'd to believe the true motive was to get me out of the way of my former mercantile associate T. M. I hope you have been sufficiently upon your guard against the Intrigues of C[armichael], whose real character you must be fully possessed of; but if I am not mistaken he has found very able supporters who only mean to make him the instrument of bringing D[eane] to Justice. You know the common saying, "Set one Rogue to catch another," but still, neither the one or the other should be trusted. Mr D. will no doubt make the most of the credentials and the advocate he carried, or rather, that he went with. Wise men, however, without saying much, will know well how to apprize both justly. *Verbum sapienti sat est.* Take care of yourselves and trust not too much to others. You will excuse my saying one Word with respect to yourself: I know you so well that I am sure you will sacrifice your time and Estate in the Public Service, as you have already done heretofore, without gaining one single shilling for yourself; but do not involve yourself in unnecessary embarrassments that only tend to shield those plunderers who have grown fat on the public spoil. You have been a Member of the Marine and Commercial Committees and Board of War; thro' these

Channels, most of the Public Money must have been spent. I am sure you have not touched any of it, tho' a great deal may have been misapplyed; to save the Public and exculpate yourself you can't be too urgent in insisting on those several bodies making up their accounts and returning them to Congress; and if anything is objected to what has been done, let them answer for it who have had the chief direction and have fingered the Public money. While writing I have received considerable pleasure in learning by accident from the American papers how Congress has treated the 2ᵈ foolish and impertinent letter from the British Commissioners. Indeed, Governor Johnstone should not be permitted to send his silly and ridiculous, tho' wicked and infamous, letters into the Country. I am assured that 3 months [ago orders] were sent to the B. Commissioners to treat with you on your own terms, but since that, the B. Ministry, or rather their Master, growing bold on a few French prizes being taken, and the hopes that Count D'Estaing's fleet will be destroyed, the present determination is to continue the War another year, and Howe is to return to the command. Thus you see their determinations change like the wind, but you may decide positively yourself whether the War will be continued another year or not, when you know the full issue of this Campaign; for Nothing but dire [necessity] will compel the silly Mule, to relinquish his wicked attempts against you, therefore provide accordingly and in time. I trust you will not quit Congress until Peace and regular order afterwards is establish'd, unless you should be call'd home to fill the important place of Governor there.

Heaven bless you. Adieu.

13 December 78. I am obliged to you for the Congress manifesto, which looks well. If they have taken proper measures to get information of what is plan'd at N. Y., they may give timely notice at Chas Town of the expedition, in which it may fail of success, for the chances must be against them unless the people in Carolina are taken by surprize; this expedition and the forces sent to the W. Indies as must weaken Clinton so much that I should hope Washington will return the Compliment to N. Y., which they intend for Chas Town Nothing would have been more easy if Count D'Estaing had gone straight there from Boston; but things in that squadron have gone hitherto in such a train from the beginning that I expect nothing of eclat from the end. I never expected any good from Penet's house as my former Letters will tell, but it seems to me quite necessary that you should give immediate and repeated notice to the State of the conduct of this house; for Penet has gone out there near 4 months ago, and you know how he is calculated to deceive and impose on our

countrymen, fine cloathes a cringing, flattering and lying ges——in whom there cannot be the least confidence placed; that will promise and agree to everything and never perform a single article. Iron *Cannon* can be got at *Leige* of any size, and in any quantity, from 15 to 17 £ the quintal, the transport to a Sea Port about 5 £ the quintal more, which will make 22 £ the quintal ready money; but then they can't be ship'd [erased] and to ship them from Dunkirk [torn out] the risk passing thro' the channel will be fully equal to £ the quintal, so that on the whole if the Cannon at Bourdeaux are deliver'd on board at £ 27 the quintal, if they are sound and good, and the seller will wait for payment till remittances can come by the vessel that carrys them, I think we should not hesitate about taking them, if there is any convoy to send them by, because I take it for granted that sooner or later in their spirit of [devas]tation they will make an attempt on Virginia, against which every provision should be made that is possible. I mean the heavier Cannon, for I suppose you recollect that besides what were order'd by Le Maire and the subsequent Invoice that you had, 20 thirty-six pounders were order'd in May last to erect a fortification at York Town. 50,000 Livres would send as much Iron Cannon as is necessary, with Ball and powder sufficient. Clinton is under great apprehensions for N. Y., and I have no doubt

that the Regiments now on foot in England and
Ireland will be sent to him as soon as possible.
Cannot the F[rench] Ministry be prevailed on to
sent out a force to intercept them on the passage.
I wish you had told me whether my draft on the
Comm'ee for £ 24000, in favor of Mr. Grand
was to be paid or not. This Bill I sent to Mr.
Grand from hence the 9th inst., and at same time
by Letter advised the Comm'ee of it. Be so
good as to let me know by return of post what is
done. [Torn out] I suppose the privy Councillor
C—t in the Garde [erased]; some other rumors will
be consulted before an answer is given to y^r proposition made to the *Ministers.* We wish you
all a happy new year, etc.—Adieu.*

TO THE COMMITTEE OF FOREIGN AFFAIRS.

FRANKFORT, October 15th, 1778.

Gentlemen :

I have the honor of forwarding to you herewith a
third copy of a plan of a treaty of amity and commerce, between the Seven United Provinces of the
Netherlands and the United States of America,
which you will perceive was settled by M. de Neufville, as the representative of Mr. Van Berckel,
Counsellor Pensionary of the city of Amsterdam,
and myself. The Burgomasters of Amsterdam had

---

* From the *Lee Papers* in Harvard University.

authorised Mr. Van Berckel to treat in this business in their name, and the Pensionary regularly authorised M. de Neufville, a capital merchant of Amsterdam, to treat with me. I forwarded two copies of this plan from Paris last month, where I went to communicate what had been done to the Commissioners there, as I did not think myself authorised to proceed any further alone.* They were fully informed by me of the state of politics in Holland, and that a great deal of management and secrecy in the present stage of the business would be requisite to complete it successfully, be-

---

* Dumas had interested the First Pensionary of Amsterdam in the cause of America, before William Lee appeared upon the scene. Lee, acting through M. de Neufville, a merchant of Amsterdam, received from Van Berckel, the Pensionary, a declaration of the good intentions of Amsterdam, given on the supposition that it was being made to one of the Commissioners at Paris. Dumas very naturally complained of this attempt of Lee to undermine him, "when I thought he had enough to do to fulfil his commissions through Germany, and, therefore, was very open and unaware in my letters to him."

The framing of this treaty was a piece of unnecessary activity on the part of Lee, as well as of Van Berckel and de Neufville. Amsterdam repudiated the venture, Congress never approved it, and even the Commissioners at Paris refused to give it any consideration. It is of historical moment only because the paper was taken by the British when Henry Laurens was captured, and was made the occasion for such demands of the Dutch that they were driven into war.

The treaty is printed in full in *Sparks' Diplomatic Correspondence of the Revolution*, I., 608.

cause the English party having the Prince of Orange at its head is very powerful, and might effectually obstruct the progress, if the negotiation comes to their knowledge before the Pensionary and Burgomasters have made sure of carrying the point in the Assembly of the States-General.

The further progress in this business your Commissioners at Paris will no doubt communicate to you. However, it appears to me of no inconsiderable importance that I have obtained from the Pensionary an engagement, that the States-General shall not take any measures that may be injurious to the United States of America, provided America shall not take any measures injurious to Holland. This engagement the Pensionary is alone capable of complying with, because his single negative is sufficient to prevent the States-General from entering into any such measures, and consequently the States will be prevented from giving any aid to Great Britain against our good ally, France.

I have so often given you a full account of the situation of affairs in this quarter of the world, that I have little to add on that subject. Though the King of Prussia was prevented, by the critical situation of politics here, from complying with the promise he had made of acknowledging our independence as soon as France had done so, I thought it proper to write to his Minister to know whether our privateers and armed vessels would be permitted to enter and refit in the Prussian ports; to which he replied, that his Majesty's absence from Berlin, and his continual application to the great object in which he is engaged, prevents him from being able at present to make me a favorable reply, but he hopes that circumstances will soon enable them to make us more advantageous proposals than they have already done.

The campaign has ended for this year, and nothing material has passed. There are some politicians who think the winter negotiations will produce peace, and if they do, I think the King of Prussia will not then hesitate to enter into a treaty with us. As to the Court of Vienna, you know my commission only authorized me to treat with the Emperor, who has been since the beginning of April with his armies in Bohemia ; however, while I was at that Court our affairs could not be advanced there, because both the Emperor and the King of Prussia stand in the same predicament with respect to Hanover, which has now increased its army to near thirty thousand men. The Emperor wishes to keep Hanover neuter, and the King is exerting all his political abilities to have the Hanoverian army active on his side. This winter will, it is generally believed, decide the part that Hanover will take if the war continues in Germany, in which case the opposite party will soon join issue with us; in the meantime, we must have patience,

as at present neither side can in prudence enter into any measures with us, unless France makes a
point of it.

With the advice of the French Ambassador at
Vienna I shall remain here, as being a central place
for Germany, until we can see with more precision
how to direct our future operations. I understood
from his Excellency Count de Vergennes, when I
saw him at Versailles last month, that he thought
our business by and by would go forward at Vienna.
As the Court of Versailles can at any time influence
that of Vienna with respect to us, I presume some
plan of that sort is now in agitation, of which I
expect due information from his Excellency the
Baron de Breteuil at Vienna; but I must remind
you that, under my present commission, I have no
authority to conclude, or even to treat of any thing
with this Court. This I explained fully to you in
my letters last winter, which you must have received.

I am, gentlemen, with the highest esteem and
regard, &c.

TO ARTHUR LEE.

FRANKFORT, 18 October, 1778.

Dear Brother:

I wrote to you the 4th and 8th, which I dare say
you will particularly answer as soon as you can.
I thank you for the intelligence relative to the

operations at Rhode Island. You have with this, some packets for America, which I request your particular care of: let them only be sent by some of the most probably safe conveyances, viz., an express that you can trust, taking a receit for them, to be transmitted to me. Whether it is owing to the measures of the Old Fox I know not, but certain it is, that since my return Old D[uma]s has not answered two letters I wrote to him, tho' before he was always precisely punctual. Perhaps he may be traced out in some of his manœuvers. Don't you think that by watching a favorable movement for the application, we might obtain all the cannon and ammunition we want?

Mons.ʳ Beaumarchais's great ship, the Roderigue, was loaded fully out, and the whole cargo was purchased by the State of Virginia. If it can be done conveniently, I cou'd wish to know what this cargo consisted of, because 'tis more than probable that most of the articles were such as I was before desired to send. Surely this ship bro't letters for me, and I don't suppose it will be offensive to inquire for them.

We have no news in this quarter, as the great armies are returned to winter, the K. of P. in Silesia, and P. H. in Saxony.

I wish I could whisper in Mr. S[arti]ne's ear the necessity of taking care of the French commerce, which would be infinitely better done by strong convoys and keeping the best sailing frigates and men of war cruizing after the Privateers and armed vessels, than by great fleets peeping out of port and returning *re infecta.* The valuable prizes already taken will make the people in En[glan]d mad for a continuance of the game. So that Lord Sandwich will have every man's aid to cover his past iniquities. Every moment I expect Mrs. L. to tumble to pieces. The little Gen! has been unwell for some time, and is now very thin. The young lady is as fresh as a rose, and as frolicksome as a young fawn. Let me have I pray you the earliest advice of what you received from America. Our best love attend you and Ludwell. Adieu.

Notwithstanding the late affectation of throwing aside the title of Doctor, I see your neighbor at P[ass]y is among the list of M. D.'s lately incorporated by his most Christian Majesty for examining and licensing all quack medicines. How does this square with the resolve of Congress relative to those they employ in foreign offices? Is it not something of a piece with the snuff box and picture?

(No Signature)*

---

* Addressed to "His Excellency Arthur Lee, Esq!, Minister Plenipotentiary from the United States of America to His Most Christian Majesty, at Paris."

COMMITTEE OF FOREIGN AFFAIRS TO WILLIAM LEE.

PHILADELPHIA, October 28th, 1778.

Sir:

The enclosed resolve, it is hoped, will be productive of singular advantage, so far as relates to you, who must depend greatly for American intelligence on your connexions in Paris. Congress have been and are exceedingly loaded with business, and of late have met with some singular interruptions in the intended general arrangement of their foreign affairs, so that they have yet only decided in respect to Dr. Franklin, their Minister Plenipotentiary at the Court of France.

Our first and most pressing business is the appreciation of our currency. This point accomplished, our enemies themselves will acknowledge their hopes of conquering us at an end. The British Commissioners, sent on a foolish and wicked errand to America, are returning home completely disappointed; and there is reason, from appearances, to think that the land forces of Britain are gradually withdrawing from these States. It is probable that the Marquis de la Fayette, by whom this letter goes, will obtain in Boston further knowledge than we now have of the destination of a fleet lately departed from New York, amounting to about one hundred and fifty sail.

We shall desire Mr. Adams to give you all possible information on the arrival of this packet, and shall soon despatch other letters from this part.

With hearty prayers for your welfare, we are, sir, your affectionate friends,   R. H. LEE,

JAMES LOVELL.

[From the *Pennsylvania Packet*, 12 December, 1778.]

To the Printer:

Observing that Mr. Deane in his late publication says that it is probable that the Honorable William Lee, Esquire, Commissioner of the United States at the Courts of Vienna and Berlin, and Commercial Agent for the Congress in Europe, still holds the office of Alderman of the city of London, I have consulted on this point the Royal Kalendar, or Annual Register, for the year 1778, and find the following list of Lord Mayor and Aldermen of the city of London for the year 1778 :—

The Right Honorable Sir James Esdaile,
Knight Lord Mayor.

Wards.

Bridge Without,	{ Robert Alsop, Esq., Father of the City.
Farringdon Within,	William Bridger, Esq.
Portsoken,	{ Right Hon. Thomas Harley.
Bread-street,	Brass Crosby.
Bishops Gate,	James Townshend, Esq.
Queenhithe,	Frederick Bull, Esq.
Farringdon Without,	John Wilkes, Esq.
Langham,	John Sawbridge, Esq.
Aldersgate	Sir Thomas Halifax.
Recorder,	John Glynn,
Cripplegate,	Sir James Esdaile.
Castle Baynard,	Samuel Plumbe, Esq.
Cornhill,	Brackley Kennet, Esq.
Cheap,	John Kirkman, Esq.

Billingsgate,	Richard Oliver, Esq.
Lime-street,	Sir Watkin Lewis.
Brassishaw,	William Plomer, Esq.
Walbrook,	Nathaniel Thomas, Esq.
Coleman-street,	Robert Peckham, Esq.
Cordwainer,	George Hayley, Esq.
Vintry,	Nathaniel Newnham, Esq.
Aldgate,	*WILLIAM LEE, Esq.
Broad-street,	Richard Clarke, Esq.
Bridge Within,	Thomas Woolridge, Esq.
Dowgate,	John Hart, Esq.
Candlewick,	Thomas Wright, Esq.
Tower,	Evan Pugh, Esq.

OBSERVATOR.

---

* Cum tot sustineas, et tanta negotia solus,
————————in publica commoda peccem
Si longo sermone morer tua tempora, Cæsar.—*Hor.*

[From the *Pennsylvania Packet*, 16 December, 1778.]

To the Printer of the PENNSYLVANIA PACKET:

Your inserting the following extract from the sixth Article of the Confederation of the United States of America, will, I have no doubt, enable the citizens of America fully to judge of the propriety or impropriety of employing William Lee, Esq., an Alderman of the city of London, as an Ambassador of the United States of America at a foreign Court.

—— "Nor shall any person holding any office of profit or trust under the United States, or any of them, accept of any present, emolument, office or title of any kind whatsoever, from any King, Prince, or foreign State." PLAIN SENSE.

TO RICHARD HENRY LEE.

FRANKFORT IN GERMANY, 20 December, 1778.

You will receive with this, my dear Sir, some papers that will in part inform you of what has passed in Holland, relative to the piratery that has been practised by the British men-of-war, armed vessels, &c., on the Dutch trade.

The British partizans, headed by the Prince of Orange and aided by British guineas, had nearly prevailed to destroy the freedom of the Dutch commerce, and overthrow the rights of the Republic; but the firmness of the Regency and Pensionary of Amsterdam, supported by the Body of the Merchants, at the head of whom was placed Mons[r] Jean de Neufville, has hitherto saved the Republic from the evils it was threatened with, and the patriotic party seems to gather strength ; for on the last question in the General Assembly of the States, two other cities, and three members of the nobility voted with Amsterdam, so that by perseverance it is expected the patriotic measures will finally prevail; all which would be greatly to our advantage.

If Col. F. is at Congress, you will of course communicate this to him; if he is not, please to read this letter and then forward it to him.

This being a very uncertain conveyance I can't be very particular.

I have wrote frequently to Congress, from whom I have not heard of a later date than May; nor do I learn, that the gentlemen at Paris are much better informed than me.

The English papers tell us of a thousand divisions and distractions in America, and even in Congress, not a word of which do I believe, tho' Govr Johnstone insists that a great deal of his money was received, which was laid out to produce these effects.

Tho' there has not been any general battle in this country, yet there has been on the whole a great deal of fighting between the Austrians and Prussians, nor have they ceased until the quantity of snow that has fallen seems to have made them a little quiet. Prince Repuin has arrived at Breslau in Silesia (where the King of Prussia had fixed his winter quarters), as Commissioner from the Court of Russia, to meet a Commissioner from France as mediators to make peace between Austria and Russia; however I do not find that the French Commissioner is yet named, nor any from Austria, for it is understood that the place is not yet agreed upon; France and Austria naming Augsburg or Nuremburg, while Russia and Prussia fix on Breslau. In my private opinion it will be impracticable to bring about peace this winter; the King of Russia has got possession of Austrian Silesia, which he easily will not relinquish; while Austria will make efforts before she cedes that valuable part of her paternal inheritance.

Our affairs of course, in this undecided state of things, must remain at a stand; for unless France makes a point of it on either side, and demands an acknowledgment of American Independence, neither will probably do it, for fear of decidedly throwing Great Britain and Hanover into the opposite scale.

Hitherto France has kept aloof in that respect, probably to avoid being an active party in the German war.

I cannot learn that Great Britain has been able to engage any fresh troops from this quarter for the American war, on the contrary I am assured from all the quarters that she will not be able to procure near the number of recruits necessary to complete the German corps now in America.

You ought to have the earliest intelligence from Paris of what is going on in England; my remote situation prevents me from writing so often as I should otherwise do.

The designs of the British ministry can't be exactly understood, because their plans are changed so frequently; however I think they are determined on essaying another campaign to recover America; and that most of their operations will be of the predatory kind, and ravaging the Back country with the Indians. They may be puzzled by threatening an invasion of Canada and Nova Scotia, being as well as possible prepared for any sudden attempt on the coast of Virginia, and on Charleston, which from resentment Clinton will wish to destroy; and by sending an effectual body against St. Augustine, the nest of Pirates.

Tho' if the French fleet keep on the American coast, many of their schemes must as heretofore prove abortive.

I can't help expecting that during the winter, in the time of Clinton's weakness, some successful attempt will be made on New York; for believe me the best method is to keep the enemy in perpetual alarm by continual attacks.

A court martial is to be held on Admiral Keppel on the complaint of Sir Hugh Paliser, for misconduct in the engagement of the 27 last July with the French fleet; it is supposed Paliser will be tried also. It is supposed as the King and ministry hate Keppel, that he will be sacrificed tho' innocent, and Paliser being a favorite will escape, tho' guilty; which I wish with all my heart may happen as most likely to create a mutiny in the fleet.

At all events a good deal of hot blood will be created, and I hope all the Whigs will be taught how dangerous it is to trust their lives and reputations in the hands of the present ministry.

'Tis my duty to mention and you may be assured of the fact, that Lord North declared publickly in the House of Commons, that if the Congress had assented to treat on the terms proposed by the British commission, he would not have confirmed them; after this, what American in his senses can listen one moment to any terms whatsoever, proposed by the British ministry, unless they are warranted by a plain and positive Act of Parliament? This should be published through all America, and if 'tis necessary you may give me for the author.

Mr Deane it seems has written over that Congress had plans of changing all their appointments in Europe, and that he was coming over in a very lucrative employment.*

I had no doubt that he and his coadjutor Carmichael would carry on intrigue and trick wherever they were; but my opinion of Congress must be greatly changed from what it is, before I can believe it will be deluded by them: however I trust you will give me the earliest information if any changes are made or intended.   *   *   *

Farewell.

---

* There was a plan for appointing Deane to Holland.

COMMISSIONERS TO WILLIAM LEE.

PASSY, 13 January, 1779.

Sir:

The letter which you did us the honor to write us on the 15th of December we have received. As we have heard nothing further of the Congress in Germany, which you inform us was talked of, we presume that no such measure will take place.

However, whether there be a Congress or not, we cannot comply with the terms of the gentleman you mention, nor advise him to take any steps in the business.

We have also the honor of your letter of the 9th of December, informing us of your draft upon us for twenty-four thousand livres, at one month's date, payable to Mr. Grand. The bill of exchange itself has also been presented to us, and accepted.

We have the honor to be, &c.,

B. FRANKLIN,
ARTHUR LEE.
JOHN ADAMS.

TO ARTHUR LEE.

FRANKFORT, 27 January, [1779.]

I wrote the 19 directed to Challiot, and ye 23d under cover to ye Banker. Yesterday received yours of the 20th. The packet was received right. One letter by mistake was not inclosed. The address of Durbrick & Co: is *au soin de Monsr F.*

Bowenes, Nego. *a Ostend*. Loudoun only says 300 and *odd* dollars were lent Maj.ʳ Wrixon; but whether the odd number was *one* or *ninety-nine*, I don't know. Capt. Molesworth, brother to your acquaintance the Major, called at T[owe]r Hill, in September last, and left his address, which he desired might be sent to you and me. You know best if he is wanted by *Congress* or for their own purposes in *Virginia*. The inclosed please to forward. There is no saying here whether the *ship* is *dear* or *cheap*. If any thing is wrong the agent is to blame, because he is perfectly acquainted with these things, and had formerly a good character for honesty.

The very heavy losses the French commerce have sustained must in a great measure put a stop to all the F. trade, and in particular that to America, where the risk is so great, and the expence so high in the proportion of the fund, which must be layed out in the vessel, that the goods ought to sell immensely high, to bring any profit to the adventurer; but my last advices from Virginia and Carolina in October, mention the price of tobacco and other things so enormously high, that no *extraordinary* profit will remain even if the vessel of the adventurer should return safe. The plan of *Holker* & Co., seems to be a pretty sure one on the supposition that *America* is sure of *Independence*, of which there seems to be little doubt. We are beginning to freeze almost entirely; much colder, tho' clear, than in Virginia, which does not much agree with any of us, and will consequently stop William's journey for the present. Give us the news from America as soon as you get it. Accept all our loves. (No signature).*

TO ARTHUR LEE.

F[RANKFOR]T, 7 February, 1779.

I was impatient to hear from you, when Mr. I[zar]d the 30th ulto. inform'd me that you had been ill for a fortnight, but was then better. I hope sincerely that you are now quite well, and that in a day or two a letter from yourself will tell me so, but least it should be otherwise, this is sent inclosed to Mr. I., as I wou'd not wish to have your mind ruffled, if your body is weak. I do not believe you see the *St. James's Chronicle.* If you do not, you should send for that from 26 to 28 January, No. 2789. In it there is a long letter from Silas Deane, which fills up more than 3 columns, dated Philadelphia, November, 1778, and published in Dunlap's *Pennsylvania Packet,* Dec. 5, 1778, addressed to yᵉ free & virtuous citizens

---

* Addressed to "The Honorable Arthur Lee, Esqʳ, Minister Plenipotentiary from the United States of America, No. 5 Rue Battailles, a Chaillot, pres Paris."

of America. This letter is entirely a charge against
yᵉ Lee family. You are the first object and greatest culprit; myself the second, and R. H. L. the
next. It is filled with the most impudent falsehoods I ever saw. With respect to myself, I can
prove them to be so, and what is more I can prove
that he knew some of them to be so at the time he
wrote them. Indeed R. H. L. had documents in his
hands, and the Secret Committee also to prove
some falsehoods. Yet by the New York paper ot
December 22, it appears that R. H. L., in answer,
addresses the public to suspend its judgment until
the charges against his family are inquired into.
To which Deane replies as Congress is now disposed to listen to his plaints, he has no occasion
for the mediation of the people. I can't enter into
this extraordinary performance, which tho' very
illy written, must be fully answer'd; therefore 'tis
quite necessary that you should have the paper.
If you do not get it from England I must send you
the one I have. 'Tis very clear, however, that
Deane not finding Congress disposed to send him
back, has impudently asserted falsehoods, in order
to get one or both of us recall'd to answer them; in
which case his chief object would be answered of
having us displaced like himself.* I shall prepare

---

* The knowledge of Deane's address affected Adams quite as
strongly as it did the Lees, and led to the expression of opinions
so heated as to at once deprive Adams' judgment in the matter

my answer directly; but I wish for your opinion, whether it will be most prudent to forward it immediately, or wait 'till we hear from Congress; and as this is an address to the People, whether an answer also should not be given to the people besides what is sent to Congress. On these two points I

---

of much weight. It was "one of the most wicked and abominable productions that ever sprang from a human heart; that there was no safety in integrity against such a man; that I should wait upon the Count de Vergennes and the other ministers, and see in what light they considered this conduct of Mr. Deane; that if they and their representatives in America were determined to countenance and support by their influence such men and measures in America, it was no matter how soon the alliance was broke; that no evil could be greater, nor any government worse, than the toleration of such conduct." Deane's conduct was an evidence of "such a complication of vile passions, of vanity, arrogance, and presumption, of malice, envy, and revenge, and at the same time of such wickedness, indiscretion, and folly, as ought to unite every honest and wise man against him; that there appeared to me no alternative left but the ruin of Mr. Deane or the ruin of his country; that he appeared to me in the light of a wild boar, that ought to be hunted down for the benefit of mankind; . . . that this measure of his appeared to me to be so decisive against him, that I had given him up to Satan to be buffeted." He was greatly perturbed for days: he foresaw the dissolution of the Constitution; the confidence of the French court would be lost, and the other nations of Europe would be indisposed to treat with America, where now a civil war impended. On the 11th he had already taken the somewhat unusual step of writing to Vergennes a defence of Arthur Lee, and denouncing Deane's paper, a letter that the Count answered diplomatically, disclaiming very properly any concern, as minister, in the matter. On the 12th of February,

beg your answer directly. Tell me also the present disposition of *Spain* with respect to *America.*
We are so-so in health, and impatient to hear of
your recovery. We send you in the meantime our
best wishes.   Farewell.

———

TO RICHARD HENRY LEE.

FRANKFORT ON THE MAIN IN GERMANY.
10 February, 1779.

My dear Brother:

I wrote you the 20 Dec.ʳ ult., which if it ever
gets to hand will go with this ; but the uncertainty and risk will prevent me from writing to
Congress or from saying so much to you as I would
otherwise do; however I can't refrain from informing you, (which information you may with confidence communicate to those it immediately concerns) that in consequence of the engagements
entered into by me with the city of Amsterdam, of
which Congress has been repeatedly advised, and
the measures I have taken since, the States of Holland first and afterwards the United States of the

---

1779, he learned of the choice of Franklin to be sole minister at
the court of France, and with a sigh of relief, he laid aside the
horrid visions he had conjured up, and threw the entire responsibility on to Franklin. March 12th he was at Nantes on his
return to America.

Deane's address, and the replies it called forth, will be printed
in a volume of this series.

Netherlands, have come to a resolution, that if the English ships either visit or interrupt their merchant ships in their commerce, that the United States of the Netherlands will look upon such visitation or interruption, as a declaration of war on the part of England.

This declaration is decisive, not only of the part that Holland will take with France, but also with America.

As to Germany, there has been some time since much talk of peace, but lately the rumor dies away, and in my opinion the chances are much in favor of war.

I am still in continued correspondence with the Courts of Berlin and Vienna, and in my judgment, if peace takes place in Germany, both those courts will immediately acknowledge the Independance of America; and if war continues Prussia, Russia, and Great Britain may be leagued together, when France will join Austria, and the latter enter into a treaty with America.

However I am happy to tell you that Great Britain has been defeated in all her attempts for the last twelve months to get fresh troops from Germany, to prosecute the American war; she cannot even get a sufficient number of recruits to complete the German corps now in America. All the recruits she can get will be a few hundreds; however, I am told that the British ministers mean to

leave Ireland, and even Great Britain, entirely defenceless, in order to send reinforcements sufficient
to maintain the ports of New York and Rhode
Island, and, if your defenceless situation will admit,
to ravage and plunder your sea coasts. You will
therefore do well to be prepared in time.

The enclosed papers will speak for themselves,
but I am decidedly of opinion that the British
agents, the mortal enemies of America, do not wish
for anything better at this moment than appeals
to the people at large, against Congress. I wish
you would not only consult my particular friends,
but even Congress itself, before you publish either
of the enclosed papers. However, I wish you to
communicate them to Congress; and if it is thought
decent and proper that either of them should be
published, I should wish the address to the public
to be published first, and then if Mr. Deane renews
his assertions, publish the affidavit.

A full statement shall be transmitted very soon,
but in the meanwhile let me intreat you as much
as possible to prevent all cabals or parties from obstructing the necessary measures for your security
and defence against the horrid machinations of the
British ministry and their agents.

As to myself having never solicited anything
from Congress, and my present appointments being
at first not only highly disagreeable to myself; but,
I am sure, contrary to the wishes of my real friends,

yet, being now engaged in the political line, as long as I can be of service to my country, I shall have no objection to continuing in it; however, if Congress shall have determined otherwise, I shall submit without repining.

It must, I should think, at first sight have struck every mind that Mr. Deane, exasperated at his disgrace in being recalled, wished to have those he calls his Enemies put on the same footing; therefore he hazards the most audacious falsehoods to get my brother and myself recalled to answer them; in which his chief point would be carried, and he himself when proved guilty of being *a false* accuser could not be more infamous than he already is.

Remember, I pray you, not to let any of his accounts for the expenditure of publick money finally pass without the most authentic vouchers; upon proper inquiry into this business, I can boldly assert that most infamous transactions will be brought to light. From this apprehension arises Mͬ Deane's and Dͬ Franklin's mortal hatred to my brother and myself.

Pray call upon the President, Mͬ Laurens, to inform Congress of what he has received relative to Mͬ Deane from Mͬ Lloyd, his friend, from the information of Mͬ Carmichael, and what Mͬ Izard has wrote relative to Dͬ Franklin. * * *

My stay here will probably not be long, for as

the future political system of Europe will be settled by the spring, when that is fixed, I shall be
called from hence to prosecute the commands of
Congress. I shall conclude therefore with assuring
you of the constancy of my affection & esteem.

TO ARTHUR LEE.

F[RANKFOR]T, 21 February, 1779.

W. Lee desires me to say that he wrote yesterday
acknowledging the receipt of a card of ye 12th
from *A. Lee*, and he says further that, after the
deepest reflection on facts and probabilities, as far
as he knows, he cannot decide on the propriety or
impropriety *of going to Paris.* Many certain inconveniences are foreseen, without knowing any
certain good. Why has such reserve taken place
in a business of such importance? It would appear from the last public accounts that *Deane* has
been foiled in his schemes, but whether he has or
not, 'tis more than probable that interested views
of others may occasion the *recall* of *W.* and *A.
Lee.* This must now be decided, and where then
can be the hurry to go to work in the dark 'till the
decision is known, or at least ascertained. In order
to determine *W. Lee going to Paris*, he wishes immediately to be informed whether R[ichard]
H[enry] L[ee] was at *Congress*, when ye last letters

came away; when the decision was likely to be made; some account of the state of *parties;* will *Izard* give a certificate to *W.* and *A. Lee* of what he personally knows; has he been *attacked by Congress* or *America;* is he likely to *continue* as *at present.* These and other informations *W. Lee* wishes to have immediately, and also that his letters may be at same time forwarded; and if before they arrive he should see good reason for the jaunt and set off, no inconvenience can arise, because they will be in good hands during his absence. Has *A. Lee* any idea of going to *America* in case of the worst?* . . .

---

* "We see in the papers a letter of *A. Lee* relative to *Deane;* hasty measures are often injurious. We learn from the papers that the Marquis de Fayette has been some time arrived at Paris, from whence letters, in the old channel, make Dr. F. not only minister plenipotentiary to Versailles, but to all the other Courts in Europe; this is making him K[ing] or rather E[mperor] of America with a witness. America has therefore struggled to a fine purpose to make a Ben. instead of a Geo. her absolute lord and master. . . . Peace in Germany seems now agreed on all sides, therefore it seems there will be work enough soon for *W. Lee* and probably for *Izard.* . . . Mat. Clarkson, Mr. D[eane]'s advocate in Philadelphia, was a Scotch notary; no doubt he thinks at present with his countryman Mr. R[o]ss, that they have the control and command of America under their patron *Robert Morris.*" *William Lee to Arthur Lee,* 27 February, 1779.

TO THE COMMITTEE OF FOREIGN AFFAIRS.

FRANKFORT, February 25th, 1779.

Gentlemen :

I have the honor of enclosing to you with this a fourth copy of the plan of a treaty, arranged, as you will see, between M. John de Neufville, on the part of the Pensionary and Burgomasters of Amsterdam, and myself on the part of the United States of America. This plan, I presume, will meet with the approbation of Congress; and if it can be carried through in the General Assembly of the Seven United States of the Netherlands, America cannot have any just grounds of complaint. If any further steps are taken by you in this business, it will be necessary to authorize some person to complete it in your name, who must advance it with the States-General as he finds the temper of the times and politics; for it is to be observed, that by their constitution, in all cases of treaties, alliances, peace, or war, the unanimous consent of all the States is requisite; however, it is with pleasure I inform you, that in consequence of the negociation with Amsterdam, and the correspondence I have kept up with the parties, that city (by far the most important member of their union) has with infinite firmness and resolution opposed all the intrigues of Great Britain, countenanced as it is said by the Prince of Orange, to involve the Republic in a war against France, and consequently against America.

The efforts of Amsterdam have at last prevailed on the States-General to come to a resolution lately much in our favor; that is, that they insist upon Great Britain's strictly adhering to the treaty of 1674, whereby the Dutch commerce is allowed to be entirely free; and if Great Britain will not accede to this, they will convoy their trade with ships of war, and repel force with force. They are accordingly making a very respectable addition to their navy, the care of which Amsterdam has taken on herself.

With respect to Germany, our affairs seem to wear a more promising aspect than they have done for some time past. Letters of good authority from Vienna, Berlin, and Breslau, the present residence of the King of Prussia, speak with confidence of the terms of peace being fully settled between the House of Austria and Prussia, under the mediation of France and Russia, that of Great Britain being equally slighted by both parties. There has been about ten thousand men raised in this country, under the title of free corps, for the two contending Powers, all of whom will be dismissed as soon as peace is signed, and will be ready to enter into any service that will pay them. It will require infinite address, industry, and management, to prevent Great Britain from gaining advantage from this circumstance, which will no doubt be attempted by their agent, General Faucet,* who is now in this country, endeavoring to buy more human flesh to sacrifice to the demon of tyranny in America. To this object I shall apply at present my principal attention, at the same time keeping a watchful eye upon the Courts of Vienna and Berlin, to take advantage of the first favorable opening for us that appears at either.

I think it most probable, that one or both of those Courts will begin a negociation with us, in a very little space of time after the peace between them is finally settled; however, for the present the King of Prussia has formally engaged, by a letter from his Minister, who writes in the King's name, the 17th instant, "that the merchants of North America, who should come with their merchant vessels into the ports of his Majesty to trade there, in merchandise that is not prohibited, should have full liberty, and should be received in all respects as the merchants of other countries." This looks to me as if they wished the trade to be commenced between America and the Prussian dominions; but the European merchants, and especially those who are not accustomed to a foreign commerce, which is almost universally the case with the merchants in the Prussian dominions, are cautious, and do

---

* Faucitt.

not care to venture hastily in a trade which they do not understand. A vessel or two from America, arriving in the port of Emden, would convince the Prussian merchants more of the practicability of this commerce than a volume of the most demonstrative reasoning that ever was written. You will judge then of the propriety of encouraging the American merchants to undertake a trial of this commerce.

This will be delivered to you by Samuel W. Stockton, of New Jersey, who has been with me some months, in the capacity of Secretary to the Commission at the Courts of Vienna and Berlin, for which purpose he left London in May last, where he had been some years pursuing the study of the law. He now returns to his country, because we do not see clearly how the expense of a Secretary is to be supported, since the American Commissioners at the Court of Versailles have lately demurred at paying my draft on them for my expenses, conformably to the resolve of Congress: and though they have allowed me some money, I am given to understand that it is the last I am to expect from them; therefore, if you should agree in opinion with most others on the propriety of keeping up the Commissions in Germany, it will be quite necessary to establish some sure funds to support the expense. Mr. Stockton has received from me 3,732 livres for his expenses, and I am obliged to refer him to Congress for such further consideration as they may judge he deserves, not having it in my power to make him that compensation for his services to the public which I think him entitled to. However, justice calls upon me to say, that he merits consideration and esteem for his zeal and readiness to serve his country, whenever it was in his power, and therefore I am sure Congress will render him ample retribution.

To Mr. Stockton I refer you for further information relative to the general state of political affairs in this quarter of the world; and expecting shortly another opportunity, I shall write again, when I hope to be able to give you very pleasing accounts of the progress of my negociations in this country. I have not received any letter or intelligence from you of a later date than May last, therefore I have no reply to make.

I have the honor to be, &c.

TO RICHARD HENRY LEE.

FRANKFORT ON THE MAYNE,
Germany, 25 February, 1779.

My dear Brother:

I have not heard from you, nor of you, but in the English papers, since May last. I have wrote to you repeatedly within that time, some of which letters I hope will reach you, particularly one of the 10th instant, via Holland to Boston, enclosed to

Samuel Adams Esqr, a copy of which was sent to Paris, to be forwarded from thence. Both these covered my affidavit in reply to Mr Deane's charge against me in his letter published Decr 5th in Dunlaps' paper, of receiving a share of the commissions charged by the Commercial Agents in France, and a short address to the public, one, or both, or neither, you will publish as Congress shall judge advisable; for in so critical a time for our Country, I would avoid all public contestation, as far as it can possibly be done with propriety and a due attention to one's character. For, unless that is clear, half a man's powers to serve his country are taken away. You have now with this a copy of the affidavit, confirmed by certificates from one of the Commercial Agents and his clerks. I have drawn up a full state of all my proceedings in the public service from the time I first received notice of my being appointed one of the Commercial Agents, until I left Paris in March last to come to Germany. This state shall be sent by the first safe conveyance that is likely to be quick, in which Mr Deane will be proved to have acted a most reprehensible part, and his *insinuations* to my prejudice will appear as wicked and unjust, as his only positive charge against me will be proved untrue.

I hear by private report that the plot contrived in August or September last by the remnant of the old Junto in Paris and Nantes to injure the reputation of M.̲ Schweighauser and his Son in Law, M.̲ Dobree, has been transfer'd to the Agents of the Junto in America, where of course the principal censure has been thrown on me and has been industriously propagated from Philadelphia to Maryland and Virginia, because M.̲ S. was appointed one of the Commercial Agents by me. I am surprised that so barefaced an attempt to injure me was not immediately quashed, as it cou'd have been done so easily by letting it be known, that I have had nothing to do with that department for many months past, as the Secret or Commercial Committee early in the last year appointed the American Commissioners at Paris, superintending agents of their Commercial affairs. From the experience I have had of the wickedness of our enemies, who I know will not stick at any falsehood or villainy to accomplish their vile purposes, I think it prudent to enclose you a copy of the Baron de Breteuil's letter to me approving of my conduct at Vienna, and also copies of recommendatory letters of M.̲ Stockton, who has been with me as Secretary, which you will keep and make known if you find occasion, for 'tis not impossible that some forg'd aspersions may be circulated against my proceedings in Germany; especially as the negotiation I have had with the city of Amsterdam has given mortal offence to a *certain person* * who wishes to be

---

* Franklin.

esteemed not only the sole legislator for all America, but also the sole and absolute director of all her proceedings. However I pride myself on that measure, and the good effects are visible in the steady and firm opposition of Amsterdam to the designs and intrigues of G. Britain. Congress will certainly pursue that negotiation and leave nothing untried to gain the whole republic of the 7 Provinces, decidedly and openly in our favor. Congress will judge who is the properest person to be employed in that business. It wou'd be at this moment of great advantage to America if she had some active and well informed agent (tho' not in a public character) at the Courts of Petersburg, Copenhagen and Stockholm. This agent shou'd be a Gentleman and by his appointment enabled to keep the better sort of company. If he had any address, he might pave the way for those powers acknowledging our Independency, at least he might prevent G. B—n from getting any assistance or countenance in prosecuting the war against us and France. It will be somewhat unlucky for America if Congress shou'd pay so much attention to the calumny of M.r Deane, as to leave this department vacant at this critical moment; for now hostilities have ceased between the Emperor and the king of Prussia, and peace is certainly settled, there will be work enough for an American deputy in Germany, and it may happen with a good deal

of management, that the king of Prussia may do
more than any other power in negotiating a peace
between us and G. Britain. I shall write again on
this subject, if I find my plans are likely to take
place, which at present wear a favorable appearance.

I have long since commenced some negotiations
with Denmark, from whence before long we may
expect some favorable issue ; at present things are
not so decided as to permit me to speak with certainty, tho' the prospect in general looks so well,
that I think it more than probable that our Independence will in a few months be acknowledged
by several of the powers in Europe. My family is
not very well in health, however we send our best
love.

P. S.—I do not mention anything to Congress
about Mr Deane, as it appears to me that it wou'd
be irregular, as I only have heard of his proceedings thro' the medium of the public papers.*

TO ARTHUR LEE.†

28 February, 1779.

I wrote yesterday to my friend Thomson that I
should prepare to set out for *Paris* about the 8th

* From the *Arthur Lee Papers*, in Harvard University.

† Addressed to "Monsieur Lotsom, No. 5 Rue Bataille, a
Chaillot, pres Paris."

of next month, as soon as answers were received to some letters. This determination will be executed unless sickness, &c., prevents. B[rutu]s still continues ill, and I begin to think his course will not be of long duration. However, in the present state of things 'twill be impossible to leave this place. *William Lee* has received a letter from *the French Court*, from *Passy*, saying no regard or notice will be taken of the *publications* of *Deane*. 'Tis *private* and nothing to *the French Court*.* *W. Lee*, therefore, advises *A. Lee* without delay (especially before there are any *advices* of ——) to get there a letter of *approbation*. Circumstances unknown to *W. Lee* may render such an attempt improper, but as

---

* "Dr. Franklin says in his last letter, that he has no concern or interest in Mr. Deane's accusations." *Arthur Lee's statement.* "I was confined to my bed when Mr. Deane's letter was announced for the next week in the *Courrier de l'Europe*, a paper printed in France, and read through Europe, because it is in the French language. I sent my secretary to Dr. Franklin to desire his concurrence in writing to M. de Vergennes, to request him to forbid the publication of that letter, as it was likely to injure and disgrace the cause of our country. Dr. Franklin not only did not concur, but by not making me an answer he kept me in suspense till my application was too late. Thus this libel upon Congress and their servants was permitted to be circulated through all Europe. Dr. Franklin, like Mr. Deane, appeared totally regardless of the mischief it might do to the public, provided it would defame me." *Memorial of Arthur Lee*, 1 May, 1779.

far as he knows at present, it seems requisite to be
done for more reasons than one.   Farewell.

(No signature.)*

---

*"There has been no time lost, for I am told the defence, &c.,
of *W. Lee* is nearly finished.   The plot formed at *Passy* before
the *departure of Deane* seems to have taken by the *appointment
of Franklin.*   It seems to me likely that the whole will succeed.
The *disgrace* of *W. Lee* and *A. Lee* does not hurt me so much
as the reflection on the unhappy and deplorable situation of
America, which could induce such measures to be taken to be
at the feet of *France.*   We say here that the Peace in Germany
is settled and absolutely fixed." *William Lee to Ralph Izard,*
2 March, 1779.   Franklin received intelligence of his appointment as Minister Plenipotentiary at the French Court on 13th
February, 1779.

"The English have taken St. Lucia from the French.   'Tis
an island of no great consequence, and the French expect
every day to hear that D'Estaing has taken Antigoa and St.
Kitts.   Campbell with troops from New York has landed in
Georgia and defeated a party of militia.   He is to attack South
Carolina, where he will probably meet his match.   The people
all over England have nearly gone mad with joy on Keppel's
acquittal, particularly in London, &c., where the people have
done greater feats than in Wilkes' time.   All ministers' houses
were nearly pulled down.   This spirit of ye people has done
more to bring ye K— and his junto to reason, yn all the opposition in Parliament, where the leaders are playing the same
idle tricks as usual.   The people unhappily want leaders, more
than spirit.   There is certainly to be peace in Germany."
William Lee to E. Browne, 8 March, 1779.

"The uncertainty of the vessels being gone prevents my writing to Virginia, but if there is time for you, I beg you will write
a short line directed to the Honble John Page, Williamsburg,
Virga, and tell him the reason I do not write, but assure him

CONFERENCE WITH FRANKLIN.

PARIS, 15 March, 1779.

Waited this day on the Honble Doctor Benjamin Franklin, minister plenipo: from the U. S. of America at the Court of Versailles; congratulated him on his appointment; gave him an account of the political state of Germany and Holland, of the danger there was of G. B. getting a considerable number of troops in Germany as soon as the peace between the Emperor and King of Prussia should take place, as there would be 20,000 disbanded, and there were a number of B. agents now dispers'd over Germany waiting to engage them. That I wished him to aid me in an application to the French ministry, to get their influence and assistance in the most effectual measures for preventing so heavy a blow on us. The Doctor replyed, that he knew so little about the situation of affairs in the north, he cou'd not meddle in it. I then told

from me that the B. ministry have ordered Virginia to be invaded as soon as the reinforcements reach Gen'l Clinton at New York, which are about this time sailing from Portsmouth. This information may be depended on. I hope therefore they will provide against it as well as possible, and particularly that they will take care of their public records. This resolution, 'tis reported, has been taken in consequence of some letters intercepted in a vessel taken coming from Virginia to Nantes, one of them from Carter Braxton Esqr in Virginia to Mr. Jno. Ross in Nantes. Some of these letters we shall no doubt see in the English papers." *William Lee to Thomas Lee*, Paris, 22 March, 1779.

him that I had strong reasons for believing as soon
as the German peace was settled, the courts of
Vienna and Berlin, or at least one of them, wou'd
acknowledge our independence, provided the Court
of Versailles would assist us in negotiating this
business, which I tho't it probable the French
ministry would do, if he would go with me to
Count Vergennes that we might jointly urge this
measure. The Doctor replyed that it was a matter
to be considered whether it was worth our while to
ask any of the Courts of Europe to acknowledge
our Independence. This, I confess, astonished me
greatly. However, I calmly replyed that I tho't it
of infinite importance for many reasons, but particularly it appeared to me the most probable way
to bring Great Britain to her senses, and to make
the K. and his ministers enter into a peace with us,
for my first object and wish always had been, and
still was, to obtain peace on honorable and independent terms. The Doctor said that I might apply
myself to Count Vergennes about it, but he was so
ill that he cou'd not go to Versailles. I asked him
then if he would write a short letter by me to
Count V. excusing his not going with me in person
on account of his health, but that he had confer'd
with me on the subject of my visit, which he
much wish'd to be adopted. I farther urged that
it was in some measure necessary, as it was the
form in all the Courts of Europe, for the public

ministers of any country, residing at a foreign court, to wait on the ministers of that court, to introduce any subject of his Nation, especially if that subject was in a public capacity. That this mode of proceeding seemed to me more necessary at this particular time as Congress had recommended confidence and harmony to all the representatives to the different Courts, and to show the ministers here that the public business would not be affected by the late extraordinary proceedings of Mr. Deane in America. All that I cou'd urge had no effect, and the Doctor plainly refused either to go with me, or to write by me.

I observ'd to him, that as he had refused to accept or pay the draft I had some time ago drawn on the Commissioners in France for my expences, agreeable to the order of Congress, it seem'd necessary for me to know of him, whether he intended to pursue the same conduct in future, and whether I was to depend on him or not for supplies to support the expences of my commission, that I might inform Congress accordingly. He replyd that he had no money, and therefore would not engage to supply me, for no supplies came from America except tobacco, which was delivered to the Fermiers Generals, under the old contract made by him and Mr. Deane.*

* "Mr. A. Lee has retired from Chaillot to Paris, and his

TO THE PRESIDENT OF CONGRESS.

PARIS, 17 March, 1779.

Sir:

Your Excellency will most particularly oblige me by laying the enclosed papers before The Honorable Congress of the United States of America, as soon as they come to your hands, with my most humble respects and duty, and I trust their goodness will excuse the length of them; for the field that Mr. Deane has open'd is so large, and the matter so abundant, that it was impossible to comprise even a summary state, so as to be clearly understood within a shorter compass.

I have the honor to be, with the highest respect and consideration.

Your Excellencies, &c.*

---

brother has come on a visit from Frankfort. He talks of a Congress to be held in Germany, and seems to want me to advise his attendance there incognito. I know nothing of it, and, therefore can give no advice about it. He talks of 20.000 men at liberty by the German peace to be hired by the English against us, and would be employed in preventing it. What do you think or learn of these circumstances?" *Franklin to Dumas*, 18 March, 1779. The Congress was that held at Teschen.

* Endorsed. "Read August 30." Although the defence is dated the 8th of March, I place it after the letter of transmittal.

TO THE PRESIDENT OF CONGRESS.

8 March, 1779.

Sir:

I had not been a great while in France, before I was convinced, from observing the extraordinary manner in which the public business of America was conducted, that some day or other a public enquiry into those proceedings must take place; therefore, as my duty to my country call'd upon me to do, I observ'd with attention such facts and circumstances as came within my knowledge; tho' it must be confess'd that, almost on every occasion, infinite pains seem'd to be taken by the parties most concern'd in those extraordinary transactions, to keep me as much in the dark as possible; therefore 'tis reasonable to suppose that what I did know and observe, is by no means the whole of what was done against the interest and benefit of America.

I had some time since drawn up a short note of several facts, to be at the public service whenever the day of enquiry should arrive; but a late publication in the London newspapers, said to be taken from Dunlap's Pennsylvania Packet of December the 5th, 1778, signed S. Deane, and addressed "to the free and virtuous Citizens of America," which has just come to my hands, renders it necessary that I shoud enlarge a little; but I will endeavor to avoid prolixity, as far as a strict regard to truth, and a clear exposition of facts will admit; which will oblige me in the course of this narrative, often to mention the name of Dr. Franklin, his nephew, Mr. Jonathan Williams, as well as of other persons.

Mr. Deane, in the letter above mentioned, says: "In February, 1777, I received a notification of the appointment of William Lee, Esqr, to be one of your Commercial Agents in Europe, of which I gave him notice. As your commercial affairs were, at that time, in such a state as to require much attention and care, I press'd this gentleman, then in England, to come over immediately, and execute his office; but heard nothing from him till the month of June, when he arrivd at Paris. At this place he continued till about some time in August, when he went to Nantes. There he was loudly calld to regulate certain affairs, which he prudently declin'd; lest, as he observed, his property in England should be affected. In September or October he return'd to Paris, and there receivd his appointment of Commissioner to the Courts of Vienna and Berlin. He continued nevertheless, inactive at Paris, until the month of December, carefully concealing his appointments, which might indeed have militated against his office of Alderman of the city of London, which he had then, and probably does still retain. When the news of General Burgoyne's defeat and surrender arrivd, it produced a revolution in the minds of many, and among others, inspired your commercial agent and political Commissioner, the Honorable William Lee, Esqr, with some degree of activity in your favor. That I may not be under a necessity of mentioning this Gentleman again, I add here, that he hath since gone to Vienna, having first appointed sundry commercial agents for you at the several ports, and in one instance remov'd the person* who had faithfully done your business for 2 p^r C^t, in favor of another, who is to receive 5 p^r C^t, of which, as well as of the like Commission at other places, Mr. Lee receives a share, for superintending at Vienna the business on your account, a thousand miles from his place of residence.''

I have with design put the whole of Mr. Deane's charge against me here, because the following state of facts will be the compleatest answer that can be given, and will shew at the same time what induc'd Mr. Deane to make it.

Mr. Deane says ''that in February, 1777, I receiv'd a notification of the appointment of William Lee, Esqr, to be one of your Commercial Agents in Europe, of which I gave him notice. As your Commercial affairs were, at that time, in such a state as to require much attention and care, I press'd this Gentleman, then in England, to come over immediately and execute his office; but heard nothing from him till the month of June.''

About the 21st. of April, 1777, I receivd by the Penny Post in London, a letter from the Honorable Silas Deane, Esqr, dated Paris, March the 30th,

---

* Here a note of Mr. Deane's letter mentions Mr. Williams as being the person displaced by me.

1777, directed thus—"To Alderman William Lee, Esqr, London," in Mr Deane's hand-writing and sealed with the initial letters of Mr. Deane's name, vizt. S. D. Mr. Deane's hand-writing being then well known in London, and his name just before, having been often mentioned in almost every company and public Gazette in England, in consequence of the proceedings of John the Painter, I thought at the first moment, that the letter was a snare laid for me by the tools of the ministry; not then conceiving that it was possible for Mr. Deane, who had been entrusted by Congress, to be capable of such indiscretion, or that he had any latent design of injuring me, with whom, at that time, he had no connection, or of injuring my relations, who had never given him any offence that I knew of. The sequel will shew whether I judg'd too favorably of Mr. Deane or not. In this letter, Mr. Deane only informs me, that the Secret Committee of Congress had appointed me joint Commercial Agent with Mr. Thomas Morris, and desiring my immediate *answer*, whether I wou'd accept the appointment or not, as he was to write to America in a few days, and wish'd to communicate my resolution; without saying a single word about the state, nature, or situation of the commercial affairs in France; or in the most distant manner hinting, that my presence was necessary or wishd for : on the contrary, the whole spirit of the letter seemed to say " You need not come."

On the same day that Mr. Deane wrote the above laconic letter of advice to me, he wrote the following letter to Mr. Jonathan Williams, Dr. Franklin's nephew, who had left London, and gone to Paris in about six weeks after Dr. Franklin's arrival in France, and was then at Nantes.

PARIS, 30 March, 1777.

Dear Sir:

I wrote you a few days since that we had purchasd the whole Magazine of Monthieu, and inclosed you his order for the delivery. From all appearances of affairs we shall have many concerns at Nantes for some time, and as I have great confidence in you, desire you woud in return have so much in me as freely to state the terms on which you can undertake our business, as I can by no means feel easy at your being in a state of uncertainty on that subject, and it is on our side proper that we should fix on some certain conditions. It is probable that our affairs may amount to five or six hundred thousand livres at Nantes in the course of this year, and if you determine on fixing at Nantes it may give you a good introduction.

The ordinary post from Paris to Nantes is three days, and three days from Nantes to Paris, so that Mr. Deane might have had Mr. Williams' answer with ease, near a fortnight before I received his letter above mentioned: Every person is left to judge for himself of the probability of this answer being receivd, before the letter to me was sent from Paris.

It is proper to mention here, that notwithstanding Mr. Deane acknowledges he was advisd in February, 1777, that I was appointed one of the Commercial agents; yet Dr. Franklin and himself enterd into a contract in behalf of Congress, with the Farmers General of France on the 24th of March, 1777, to deliver in France in the course of that year five thousand hogsheads, or five million pounds of James and York River tobacco (the best kind that is made in that State) at the rate of forty livres for every hundred French pounds, which make above 107 pounds English, with an allowance of 4 p^r ct. and eight pounds p^r hhd. to be deducted from the weight of the tobacco; 2 p^r ct. discount on the money, and all damaged or rotten tobacco to be cut off; which on some occasions might amount to 40 or 50 p^r c^t more; also all the tobacco that Congress could send to France over and above the 5000 hogsheads, was to be delivered to the Farmers General on the same terms, and at the same price; altho' it was then publickly known that Mr Thomas Morris, as commercial agent, had contracted in the month of January preceding with the same Farmers General for all the tobacco that shoud arrive in any of the ports of France on the public account, during the continuance of the then existing war with Great Britain, either of the growth of any part of Maryland or Virginia, at the rate of seventy livres for every quintal or hundred pounds; the hogshead to be weighed with the tobacco, and from the gross weight 26 p^r c^t was to be deducted for the weight of the cask, trett (?) damage, and every other kind of allowance whatsoever. I shall not make any remarks either on this proceeding of the two honorable commissioners, nor on the difference of advantage to America in the two contracts; the meanest capacity is capable of forming a clear judgment on both; but I must mention, that at this time Dr. Franklin being not only sole minister to the Court of France, but also superintending commercial agent, all the tobacco that arrives now on public account is delivered to the Farmers General under this unequal contract made by Dr. Franklin and Mr. Deane, which hardly pays the first cost, exclusive of the freight, insurance, &c.

But to return to myself. Altho' the manner of Mr. Deane's letter coming to my hands, its unusual direction, and its contents, occasion'd many reflections in my mind ; yet the urgent desire I not only then had, but always had and still have, to serve my country, immediately decided me to accept the appointment. But I cannot suppose there is any man in the world, who will not join with me in opinion, that it would have been folly in the extreme to answer Mr. Deane by the post ; because my letter being intercepted, would have been sufficient ground for my being put in prison, where I

might have remained untryd to this moment:
especially too, as at that time I knew that spys
were set to watch me, when I went out of my
house, in consequence of an information having
been given to a Secretary of State, that I was concerned in a conspiracy with some of the most
respectable persons in England, to take away the
King's life.*

I waited therefore to find a private conveyance,
and on the 30th of the same month of April 1777,
by an American gentleman, who left London that
night to go directly to Paris, I wrote to Mr. Deane
that I had receivd his letter, and would go over to
France to execute the appointment, as soon as I
coud possibly settle my affairs in England.

This letter Mr. Deane acknowledged to me in
Paris that he had receivd. Indeed he could not
quite so well have denyd it; because the gentleman
happened to be there in Town. I also wrote to my
Brother, Arthur Lee, then one of the commissioners in France, on the 2ᵈ of May following, that I
wou'd go to France, as soon as it was possible to
execute the appointment, and requesting him to
communicate this determination to those whom it
concerned. This letter Mr. A. Lee received, and
did communicate my determination to Dr. Franklin and Mr. Deane, before he left Paris to go to

---

* An absurd matter, for which Sayre was arrested and put in
the Tower.

Berlin, which was on the 15th of May, 1777. Mr. A. Lee is now in possession of my letter, and is ready to verify, when called upon, that he did make this communication. I set to work with the greatest diligence to settle my affairs; well knowing that when I left England it must be forever, and probably, too, all the property that I left behind me : but every one in the least conversant in trade will know, that it must require a considerable time for any London Merchant, who has been in a pretty extensive commerce for upwards of seven years, to settle finally and close all his business. However, hearing from general report, that the commercial affairs of America in France were in disorder, and very ill conducted, I determined to sacrifice my private concerns, to the public service of my Country; and for that end, to leave London immediately. As it was impossible in so short a time to settle my own business fully, I was obliged to leave it unfinish'd, and much of my property behind ; by which I can make it appear that my private fortune has sufferd to the amount of several thousand pounds sterling. Added to this, I left Mrs. Lee not recovered from her lying in, with an infant about three weeks old. I quitted London the 7th of June, 1777, and arriv'd in Paris the 11th of June : I wrote to Mr. Deane immediately, informing him of my arrival, and of my being somewhat fatigued with my journey, which prevented

my waiting on him that evening ; but that I wou'd
do myself the pleasure of calling on him the next
morning, if he would be so good as to let me know
what hour woud be most agreeable to him. To
this I receivd in answer the following curious
card :

Mr. Deane has the honor of presenting his compliments to Mr. Lee. Mr. Deane will be at his Hotel to-
morrow morning at 10 o'clock.''

Notwithstanding this reply, I went to Mr. Deane
precisely at 10 o'clock the next morning, vizt.,
June the 12th. I told him that I was come in consequence of the letter he had been pleased to write
to me, informing me of the Secret Committee of
Congress having appointed me their Commercial
Agent, and desired to know if he had the appointment. He replyd he had not. I then askd, if he
or the other Commissioners had any authority,
under which I cou'd act. He answered that he
had not, nor did he believe the other Commissioners had; but he had a private letter from Robert
Morris, Esqr, Chairman of the Secret Committee,
mentioning my appointment, and desiring him to
give me notice of it; but the letter being a long
one, and chiefly on private business, he cou'd not
give it to me. He then entered into a long detail
about the conduct of Mr. Thomas Morris, joint
agent with me, and said that a Mr. Ross (a Scotch
Merchant that had been some time in Philadelphia,

but had left it in 1776, and gone to Hamburgh,
from whence he had come at the request of Robert
Morris, Esq.) was then at Nantes, settling the
former transactions of Mr. Thomas Morris; which
were in a very disordered state, and until Mr. Ross
had finished that business, he thought it wou'd not
be adviseable for me to go to Nantes; however
when Dr. Franklin came, who was expected every
moment, they woud talk over the business together. I replyd that I thought it my duty, and
that I was ready and willing to render the public
every service in my power; however, being entirely
unacquainted with the nature, extent and situation
of the Committee's business, and also of the then
state of politics in France, I shou'd submit my
conduct wholly to the direction of himself and
Dr. Franklin, who, knowing those things at that
time much better than myself, were the best judges
of what was proper to be done for our Country's
benefit. I waited for Dr. Franklin till 2 o'clock,
who not coming when dinner being ready to be
brought on the table, and not being asked to stay
longer, I went away, but was desird by Mr. Deane,
to call again in the evening, as Dr. Franklin woud
certainly be there then. I did call at Mr. Deane's
the same evening, but did not have the pleasure of
meeting Dr. Franklin. I went to Passy the next
morning, when Dr. Franklin was come to town.
I return'd to Mr. Deane's where I found Dr. Frank-

lin. After waiting in an ante-chamber about an hour and a half, I had the honor of a conference with the two gentlemen, Dr. Franklin and Mr. Deane, which was nearly the same as what had passd the day before between Mr. Deane and myself; and the conclusion was, their joint opinion and advice, that I should not go to Nantes, till Mr. Ross had finished the business he was then about; especially too, as it did not appear, that I had any regular authority from the Committee to act. I waited accordingly in Paris 'till the latter end of July (except a little excursion of a few days to Havre de Grace) very frequently calling on Mr. Deane, and often on Dr. Franklin; to both of whom I always express'd my anxiety to enter on the public business, if there was any for me to do. Mr. Deane, who kept up the correspondence at Nantes, and indeed seem'd on all occasions to act the part of the principal mercantile agent, continually replyd, that Mr. Ross had not finishd the business he was upon; but expected to end it very soon. About the latter end of June, while I was thus waiting in Paris, under the directions of Mr. Deane and Dr. Franklin, several prizes were sent into France, that had been taken by the Continental armd vessels; Reprisal, Capt. Wickes; Lexington, Capt. Johnson; and Dolphin, Captain Nicholson. These prizes Mr. Thomas Morris claimd the disposal of, under the Secret Committee's appointment and instructions; but Mr. Deane thought proper to order Mr. Williams to get possession of, and dispose of them; and when Capt. Wickes, who acted as Commodore, returnd into port, he had orders from Mr. Deane to put the prizes made by his little squadron into the hands of Mr. Williams, who was also appointed to superintend the refitting of these armd vessels. These orders and directions of Mr. Deane, he says, were given with the consent and approbation of Dr. Franklin. Be that as it will, Mr. Morris opposd the execution of them, and remonstrated against them by letters to Mr. Deane, to whom he sent a copy of the Committee's instructions relative to prizes sent into France. This made no alteration in Mr. Deane's conduct; and what is still more remarkable, tho' I had been in Paris for some time, and was then waiting there, under the advice of Dr. Franklin and Mr. Deane, always ready at any moment to enter on the public business, for which purpose I had left England, the whole of this transaction about the prizes was kept a profound secret from me. About the latter end of July, when Mr. Morris's opposition had given Mr. Deane's agent, Mr. Williams, a good deal of trouble; and seemd as if Mr. Morris was determin'd to thwart the schemes that had been plan'd to take his business from him (the day my Brother, Arthur Lee, returned to Paris from Berlin), Mr. Deane told me that he understood my letters of appointment, from the Secret Committee of Congress were then, and had been for some time, in the hands of Mr. Morris at Nantes; and as Mr. Ross had not been able to compleat the settlement of Mr. Morris's former transactions, he thought I had better go down to Nantes. I waited on Dr. Franklin at Passy the next morning, and informd him of what Mr. Deane had told me the day before; when Dr. Franklin agreed in opinion with Mr. Deane, that it was adviseable for me to go to Nantes; but neither by the one nor the other was a syllable mention'd to me about the affair of the prizes.

They then wrote me the following letter:

PARIS, 31 July, 1777.

Sir:

The hope of obtaining previously by means of Mr. Ross a clear state of Mr. Morris's proceedings in the commercial affairs of the Congress (which was our inducement to advise your stay here for some time) being vanish'd, we now think it prudent and right for you to proceed to Nantes as soon as possible, and there take such measures as to you shall appear most for the public interest, which we accordingly advise you to do; and are with great esteem, sir, your most obedient hble servants.   B. FRANKLIN,
                                   SILAS DEANE.

WM. LEE, Esq.ʳ

I accordingly left Paris in the morning of the 2nd. of August to proceed to Nantes. I hope to be excused for mentioning here a circumstance, tho' it does not immediately relate to me; because it marks, as strongly as what has preceded, the spirit with which the public business of America was conducted at that time at Paris.

Early in June, 1777, the owner of the ship Richard Penn, mounting 14 guns (a sufficient force then to keep off the British letters of mark, a fine vessel and good sailer, built at Philadelphia) came to Paris and offerd to sell her to the commissioners, to carry stores, &c, to America. She cou'd have been in a very few weeks in any port of France ready to take in her Cargo for America. The owner, I believe, did not wish for a higher price than £2500 sterling or at the most £3000 sterling. This offer, however, was refus'd, because it was plan'd for Mr. Williams to buy a vessel at Nantes, just then put upon the stocks, which did not sail from France 'till the last of February or March, 1778, and cost the public about £15,000 sterling. It was also plan'd, to serve another favorite, to buy an old vessel at Havre de Grace; which, after much expence, and remaining in port several months, was sold, or the property chang'd, at how much loss to the public, I will not pretend to say; and also to serve some other purpose, a large and extraordinary vessel in her construction, was began to be built in Holland, which after costing upwards of 300,000 livres of the public money, was left where she was began to be built, and I believe at this moment has not been fitted to go to sea. From these proceedings, and a multitude of others of a similar, or more glaring nature, it happened that the supplies for the army, which were ordered in September or October, 1776, were not all even despatched from France 'till February and March, 1778; altho' during that period several millions of public money pass'd thro' the Commissioners' hands; or at least were disburs'd under their directions.

Such proceedings certainly merit public enquiry; and no doubt that will take place, when things are more compos'd than they are at the present. It was many days after my arrival at Nantes, before I coud get a sight of Mr. Morris: but at the first interview he inform'd me of the before mention'd transactions relative to the prizes; which 'till that moment had been conceal'd from me; and complain'd as much of Mr. Deane's conduct in general, as Mr. Deane had before complain'd of him. As I was conscious of having been in Paris before the commencement of this transaction; and had been waiting there during the whole time of its negotiation, under the express advice of Dr. Franklin and Mr. Silas Deane, and to their knowledge ready at any moment to enter on the public business; it appear'd wonderfully strange that neither of these gentlemen had said one word to me on the subject:

especially as Mr. Morris inform'd me there had been a considerable correspondence about it. On further enquiry, I found that Mr. Williams, in consequence of his orders, had, with the assistance of some Frenchmen, one of them named Peltier du Doyer, got possession of some of those prizes, which then remain'd unsold, and continued so when I left Nantes in October; tho' one of them was almost new and a well form'd valuable brig: but wishing to avoid as much as possible entering warmly into the resentments on either side, I only agreed with Mr. Morris on writing a civil joint letter to Dr. Franklin and Mr. Deane, stating some of the injuries to the public that had arisen from Mr. Williams being appointed to sell the prizes, in contradiction to the Secret Committee's instructions to us; at the same time sending an extract from their instructions, with which we presum'd they were unacquainted, otherwise the orders wou'd not have been given to Mr. Williams and Captain Wickes as before mention'd; which we requested they wou'd countermand, that the public business might not be any farther interrupted. To this letter no answer was ever given, nor were the orders it complain'd of ever recalled.*

---

* So far from these orders being recalled, Mr. Williams writes thus to Mr. Deane, August 21st, 1777. "I have received your favor of the 18th Instant, and observe that matters relative to ships of war and prizes are to continue as they were." And

The whole of my proceedings while at Nantes have been so often and so fully communicated to the Secret Committee, thât it is unnecessary to repeat them here; but it may not be amiss to mention that the only cargoe on the public account that came under my management at Nantes, was 315 barrels of rice, received by the Abigail, Captain Jenne from Charles Town; which vessel was dispatched back again in three weeks; on which inward cargoe and the returns by Captain Jenne, my commission amounted to 1761 livres, 7 sols, which is the whole that I can properly say I have receiv'd for my public commercial agency at Nantes.

'Tis not my business here to say anything about Mr. Thomas Morris; but Mr. Deane says I "was here loudly call'd to regulate certain affairs, which I prudently declin'd." I can only say it was very prudent in him to decline mentioning what those certain affairs were; because he cou'd then have been brought to conviction, as he will be in every thing he has particularly mentioned as a charge against me.

I shall leave these "certain affairs" then with

Capt. Weeks, in reply to a letter from me desiring he would put the prizes into the hands of Mr. Morris and myself agreeable to the Secret Committee's instructions, writes to me thus the 9th of September, 1777, "As to the prizes, they are at the disposal of the honorable Commissioners at Paris, whose orders I have received on this head, and must act in conformity."

Mr. Deane; being very confident that he cannot easily invent any, in which Congress is concern'd, that I declin'd to regulate when it was in my power. 'Tis too evident to want any proof, that it was my earnest endeavor to regulate the public business in various instances, which has brought on me Mr. Deane's resentment, as well as the ill will of others of the same character as himself. During my residence at Nantes, besides the before mention'd joint letter from Mr. Morris and myself, I wrote several times to the honorable the American Commissioners at Paris: some of the letters on affairs of consequence; to none of which did I receive any answer. Late in September being advisd by a private letter of my being appointed a Commissioner to the Courts of Vienna and Berlin, I left Nantes the 2d. of October, 1777, to go to Paris. On the 6th of October I saw the Commissioners, who deliver'd me my commission; and, an express just then setting off with despatches to Congress, I had only time to write the following short letter:

[Here was inserted his letter of 5 October, 1777, printed, p. 254, note, *ante.*]

This letter with the Commissioners' letter to Congress, and those written particularly by Arthur Lee, Esqr, that shou'd have gone by the same conveyance, were stopp'd, or rather stolen, by some person; and tho' Congress has ordered this black

transaction to be enquir'd into, yet so many obstacles have been thrown in the way, that the culprit has not been discover'd.

A few days after this (viz! on the 13th day of
October, 1777,) I had by appointment, a conference
at Passy, with the three Commissioners of Congress at the Court of Versailles, vizt. the honorable
Benjamin Franklin, Silas Deane, and Arthur Lee,
Esqrs., at which, by my desire, the honorable
Ralph Izard, Esqr, commissioner to the court of
Tuscany, attended also. At this meeting I laid before the Commissioners the several abuses and
mismanagements of the commercial business of
Congress, and the disorder that those affairs were
then in; which I had found impossible to remedy
or rectify; for they arose not so much from the
conduct of my colleague, as from Mr. Williams
being appointed to interfere with us in our business, and take out of our hands the sale of prizes,
which had been entrusted to us by the Secret
Committee: against which appointment Mr. Morris and myself had written a joint letter to Dr.
Franklin and Mr. Deane, which they did not an-
wer. I mention'd also the prizes then remaining
unsold, and wasting every day in value for want of
care: all of which proceeded from the contest about
the right of disposing of them; since in that situation no man in his senses would purchase a thing
to day of one, which another might take from him

to morrow. That the loss in the prizes was not the only injury; for this interference of one, in another's department, had occasioned a spirit of confusion and disorder in every branch of the public business at Nantes, and the neighboring sea ports. At the same time I reminded those gentlemen of my having been at Paris, waiting under their advice, at the very time that this appointment was given to Mr. Williams, which they had conceal'd from me; which surpriz'd me greatly; but that I was still more surpriz'd at the joint letter of Mr. Morris and myself on the subject not having been answer'd. However, as I did not know of any urgent reason for my immediate departure for Vienna and Berlin, and as I was always anxious to do everything in my power for the interest or advantage of my country, I was willing to return to Nantes, and endeavor to reform and regulate for the future the Commercial Business of Congress, before I went to Germany; provided they wou'd immediately recall the orders given to Mr. Williams, which had been complained of; and give me all the assistance which their influence as Commissioners enabled them to do; not only to correct my colleague, but to obtain a settlement of the public accounts from those persons, who had been before entrusted with the public property; and that I was very certain, if they wou'd do this, the public business might be put in a regular and orderly

train; when it wou'd be very easy to obtain credit
for Congress to a very considerable amount.

To this Dr. Franklin principally reply'd. He
said, that for his part he wou'd not interfere in any
manner with respect to my colleague Mr. Morris,
altho' he was fully sensible of his misconduct, for
they had already written to Congress about it ; for
which he had got a *rap over the knuckles* from Mr.
Morris's Brother, Robert Morris, Esqr, Chairman
of the Secret Committee, who had used very disre-
spectful language relative to him, in a letter he
had written to Mr. Deane ; but the orders given to
Mr. Williams about the prizes shou'd be immediately recal'd ; and that an answer had been written
to the joint letter from Mr. Morris and myself, *but
something had intervend which had prevented its
being sent.* This was all the excuse he made for
not answering the joint letter ; nor did he make
any excuse for not answering my own letters. Mr.
Deane propos'd the absolute suspension of Mr.
Morris, which the other two Commissioners did
not think they had any right, or authority to do.
After this Conference, I waited about a fortnight
(which time was employ'd in getting Mrs. Lee and
my family from England) expecting to receive from
Dr. Franklin and Mr. Deane the revocation of the
orders before given to Mr. Williams ; but not receiving it, and understanding by report, that the
subject of the conference had given great offence to

those Gentlemen, I gave over all thoughts of taking any further active part in the Commercial business, and apply'd my attention to that of a Commissioner at the Courts of Vienna and Berlin.

I therefore apply'd in person to Dr. Franklin for a Copy of the Treaty, that had been propos'd by Congress to the Court of Versailles, conformable to the Instructions I had receiv'd with my Commission. This he promis'd I shou'd have in a few days ; but, waiting a considerable time and not receiving it, I thought proper to write the following letter, which was deliver'd to Dr. Franklin, at Passy :

HONORABLE BENJAMIN FRANKLIN, SILAS DEANE AND ARTHUR LEE, ESQ^{RS}, COMMISSIONERS FROM THE UNITED STATES OF AMERICA TO THE COURT OF VERSAILLES.

CHAILLOT, 10 November, 1777.

Gentlemen :

In consequence of the Instructions to me from the Honorable Congress of the United States of America, I am to request that you will be pleas'd to furnish me with a Copy of the Treaty originally propos'd by Congress to be enter'd into with France; together with the subsequent alterations which have been propos'd on either side. As my instructions came inclos'd to you for perusal and delivery, you cannot be strangers to their Contents; therefore shall be particularly oblig'd by your giving me any information that you think will tend to forward the wishes of Congress, in appointing me their Commissioner to the Courts of Vienna and

Berlin; especially, that you wou'd advise which of those Courts it wou'd be most proper for me to visit first. You having told me that Congress has omitted to direct what fund is to supply my expences and appointment, I have only to request on that head, that you will be so good as to take notice of that omission in your next despatches. I am, &c.

To this letter no written answer was ever given: but some days afterwards meeting Dr. Franklin in Company, he told me that I shou'd have a copy of the Treaty as soon as it cou'd be got ready; however, this Copy I did not receive until the 12th of January, 1778. In the meantime I was employ'd in negotiating the public business by Correspondence with the Prussian Minister at Berlin, the substance of which has been communicated to Congress in Letters, which have been receiv'd. It is to be observ'd, that the advice of General Burgoyne's Captivity, with that of his Army, did not arrive at Paris till the 4th of December, 1777 ; so that the preceding letter, and the Conference before mention'd with all the Commissioners in October, &c., is a full answer to Mr. Deane's charge against me of remaining inactive in Paris during the months of October and November. If there was anything criminal in my staying in Paris for those two months, 'tis evident that the Commissioners are culpable, and not me.

I hope to be excused for observing here, that in

August and September we had advice of General Burgoyne's taking of Ticonderoga, and being at Fort Edward; which in the minds of most people look'd ominous against America, and certainly influenc'd the conduct of the French Ministry in putting Mr. Hodge, a Gentleman from Philadelphia, into the Bastile; tho', perhaps, on enquiry into this business, the principal blame will be found to ly on Mr. Deane. Notwithstanding these unfavorable appearances, I left Nantes the beginning of October, in a few days after receiving advice of my appointment as a Commissioner, and was as active, during the months of October and November, as I was permitted to be, by the Commissioners at Paris; altho' during that period, we had from time to time accounts of General Howe's landing at the head of Chesapeak-Bay, the battle of Brandywine, and his getting possession of Philadelphia: all which when fairly consider'd, proves in the clearest light, the injustice and malignity of the insinuation, that my conduct in the service of my Country, was directed by Events and not by principle.

Having received a copy of the Treaty the 12th of January, 1778, I requested a conference with the Commissioners at the Court of Versailles, to settle with them the articles that might be proper for me to propose to the Courts of Vienna and Berlin; this Conference I obtain'd on the 16th of January; and

as the treaties with France were then settled, and
only waited for copying to be sign'd, I thought it
adviseable not to leave Paris before that ceremony
was over; of which I have repeatedly advis'd Congress. It must be observ'd that during the whole
time of my being in Paris, no letters, nor anything
relative to the commercial business of Congress,
was communicated to me by Mr. Deane, (tho' he
continually carry'd on a considerable correspondence on that subject) until the first of February,
1778, while I was waiting only for the signing of
the Treaties with France, in order to depart for
Germany, which Mr. Deane knew perfectly well;
but on his receiving a letter from Nantes, from
Mr. John Ross, advising him of the dangerous
state of Mr. Thomas Morris, he immediately sent
it to Mr. Arthur Lee, desiring him to communicate
it to me; and on the 3d of February, receiving a
letter of advice of Mr. Morris's Death, he sent it to
Dr. Franklin, desiring him to communicate it to
me also; which was done. As Mr. Deane was well
inform'd that I had for some time given over all
thoughts of being further concern'd with the commercial business, and that this resolution had taken
place for the reasons before mention'd, and because
he had assum'd almost entirely to himself the
direction of that department (which I can prove by
letters to him and from him) I was surpriz'd at
this repeated application, and must confess, that

my own Judgment directed me not to meddle with the business in any manner. For knowing the characters that were then acting in the direction and management of the Commercial business of Congress, I foresaw the Consequences that did happen, and that it wou'd be impossible for me in the then situation of persons and things, to render the public any very essential services.

However, submitting my own opinion to the judgment of others, I undertook to postpone my journey to Germany, and go to Nantes in order to try to put the Commercial business under some tolerable arrangement before I left France. The whole of my proceedings on this occasion have been communicated to the Secret Committee, which they, or at least their Chairman, have been in possession of many months; and also of the Copies of the letters, that pass'd between me and Mr. John Ross and others on the occasion: therefore it is unnecessary to repeat them here, as full information may be had by referring to those letters now in possession of the Secret Committee; but I think it will appear evidently, from Mr. Deane's before-mention'd publication, that this latent design, in having communicated to me the death of Mr. Morris, was to treasure up a charge of negligence against me, if I did not undertake the business, and if I did, knowing from Mr. Ross's first letter of advice that he expected to be put into possession of all the papers of Mr. Morris, and intended to take upon himself the management of the public concerns, which I cou'd not agree to; it was more than probable, that a difference wou'd arise between me and Mr. Ross, who being patroniz'd by Robert Morris, Esqr , wou'd find support, and aid Mr. Deane in the Schemes, 'tis now prov'd he had long plan'd and been executing to injure me.

I come now to the last, and most positive charge which Mr. Deane makes against me in his Address to the Public; vizt —that before I departed from Paris, I had appointed sundry Commercial Agents at the several ports, and in one Instance remov'd the person, (vizt Mr. Williams before mention'd) who had faithfully done the public business for 2 per cent., in favor of another, who is to receive 5 per cent., of which, as well as the like Commission at other places, I receive a share.

To this bold and untrue assertion, the following facts will fully answer. It is proper to observe here that the promise which Dr. Franklin and Mr. Deane gave early in October, 1777, as before mention'd, of recalling the orders to Mr. Williams which Mr. Morris and myself had complain'd of, was not comply'd with; at least it was not the 16th of December, 1777, because Mr. Williams expressly says so, in a letter from him of that date, address'd to the Honble American Commissioners at Paris;

and Dr. Franklin, so far from recalling those orders, as he had promis'd, writes thus to Mr. Williams:

PASSY, 22 December, 1777.

Dear Nephew:

You need, however, to be under no concern as to your orders being only from Mr. Deane. As you have always acted uprightly and ably for the public service, you wou'd be justifyd if you had no orders at all. But as he generally consulted with me, and had my approbation in the orders he gave, and I know they were for the best and aim'd the public good, I hereby certify you that I approve and join in those you receiv'd from him, and desire you to proceed in the execution of the same. I am ever your affectionate uncle

(Sign'd)   B. FRANKLIN.

After the business about the late Mr. Morris's papers had been settled, by leaving them all seal'd up in the possession of Dr. Franklin, I wrote the following letter, which was deliver'd to Dr. Franklin at Passy:

CHAILLOT, 6 March, 1778.

Gentlemen:

In conformity to the general instructions of the Secret Committee that you shou'd be consulted and advis'd with in all important cases relative to their Commercial affairs, and Mr. Thomas Morris, joint Commercial Agent with me, being now dead, and as I am just on the point of setting out for Germany; I think it expedient to advise you, that in order to pre-

vent the business of the Secret Committee from getting
into improper hands, I intend to appoint persons in
the different ports of France to take care of any remittances, vessels, or cargoes that may arrive on account
of the Secret Committee, until their farther pleasure
is known. For this purpose I think of appointing
Mess.rs Lloyd and Jonathan Williams for the port of
Nantes, and the other ports of Brittany; Messrs. S. and
J. H. Delap at Bordeaux; Mr. Andrew Limozin at
Havre, the two last Houses being strongly recommended by the Committee; and Mr. John Bondfield
for the ports of Rochelle, Rochefort, and Bayonne.
These three ports I put under the same direction, because it is not probable that many vessels will arrive
at them, and the accidental ones that do arrive there,
will not be more than Mr. Bondfield can easily manage.
I shall be happy to find that this arrangement meets
your approbation: but if it does not, be pleas'd to point
out any alteration you wish to have made; and due
attention shall be paid to it.

I have the honor to be, &c.

Signed,   W. LEE.

*Hon. Benjamin Frankin, Silas Deane and Arthur Lee,
Esq.rs Commissioners from the United States of America in France.*

I thought it a lucky circumstance for the public,
that such a Gentleman as Mr. Lloyd was in France,
to undertake the Committee's business; a merchant of respectable character, who had early in
the present war quitted England with his family,

to settle at Nantes, and carry on a Commerce to his own Country, South Carolina, in which State he holds considerable property. Consequently I propos'd to him to undertake the business, which he positively declin'd; unless it cou'd be done with the full approbation and countenance of the American Commissioners at Paris; in which case he wou'd readily undertake it; and he suppos'd the most likely way to obtain that approbation and countenance wou'd be to join Mr. Jonathan Williams in the appointment with him; who being an active young man, might be of considerable assistance to him: as his uncle, Dr. Franklin, and Mr. Deane, had already employ'd him in laying out a great deal of the public money, he imagin'd their favor and protection wou'd be continued to him; and therefore without his being join'd in the appointment, it was probable the same distractions and divisions wou'd be continued in the public business, which had already prevail'd to the very great detriment of America; and in that case, he cou'd not agree to be in any manner concern'd. I mention'd therefore to Mr. Williams, that I had a design of appointing him in conjunction with Mr. Lloyd, Commercial Agent at Nantes; to which he reply'd that he shou'd be intirely directed by the advice of Doctor Franklin. Things were thus situated when I wrote the foregoing letter to the Commissioners: to which Dr. Franklin deliver'd me his answer himself at Chaillot the 10th of March, 1778, in the afternoon, in a letter dated thus:

PASSY, 6 March, 1778.

Your proposition about appointing agents in the ports shall be laid before the Commissioners when they meet. In the meantime I can only say, that as to my Nephew Mr. Williams, tho' I have, from long knowledge and experience of him, a high opinion of his abilities, activity and integrity, I will have no hand in his appointment, or in approving of it ; not being desirous of his being any way concern'd in that business. And the other gentlemen I know so little of, that I can have no objection to them, but I do not see that I have anything to do with their appointment.*

---

* Franklin complained that Lee's agents and the captains of vessels were continually writing to him on matters of which he was ignorant. "I see clearly that many of the captains are exorbitant in their demands, and in some cases I think those demands are too easily complied with by the agents, perhaps because the commissions are in proportion to the expense. . . . The commissions demanded by the agents seem to me in some cases very high. For instance, Mr. Schweighauser, in a late account, charges five per cent. on the simple delivery of the tobacco to the officer of the farmers-general in the port, and by that means makes the commission on the delivery of the two last cargoes amount to about six hundred and thirty pounds sterling. As there was no sale in the case, he has, in order to calculate the commission, valued the tobacco at ninety livres the hundred weight; whereas it was by our contract with the farmers, to be delivered at about forty livres. I got a friend, who was going upon change, to inquire among the merchants what was the custom in such cases of delivery. . . . In conse-

It is to be observed that Passy is about half a mile distant from Chaillot. I must confess that I never cou'd see the propriety of this refusal of Dr. Franklin to agree to the appointment of his nephew, Mr. Williams, and his *apparent* delicacy on the subject; as I knew he had employ'd, and was then employing him in the commercial business of the public to the amount of above a Million; as will appear by Mr. Williams' accounts, and Dr. Franklin's letter to him before mentioned, of the 22d of December, 1777; and had by one single order given him authority to draw on the public Banker for half a million of money.

Mr. Deane gave me his answer as follows:

PASSY, 11 March, 1778.

Sir :

I can have no objection to the Persons you propose appointing to act under you in the Commercial Agency, nor can I take any active part in that affair.

Thus disappointed in the plan of having Messrs. Lloyd and Williams appointed Commercial Agents at Nantes, with the approbation and countenance of the American Commissioners, I had no other

quence, I refused to pay the commission of five per cent. on this article; and I know not why it was, as was said, agreed with him at the time of his appointment, that he should have five per cent. on his transactions, if the custom is only two per cent., as by my information." *Franklin to the Committee of Foreign Affairs*, 26 May, 1779. The charge was abated to two per cent.

resource than to refer to the recommendation of
the Secret Committee, and that was, to Mr. J. D.
Schweighauser, who (among all the Cabals at
Nantes, and the number of wicked insinuations
and private slander of almost every Person in any
manner concern'd there with American affairs) has
maintain'd a clear and unsullied reputation, and
was highly esteem'd by all the Americans who
were, or had been at Nantes.

I shall proceed then, to give Copies of my Letters of appointment to the several Agents, asserting here what I have already made oath to, that I
did not in any manner whatever, demand of either
of the said Agents to receive a part or share of the
Commissions that they might get, in consequence
of my appointment, and that I have not received,
nor do I expect ever to receive, directly or indirectly, any Commission, gratuity, or reward whatsoever from those Agents on account of that appointment. And I will further assert, that what
Mr. Deane charges (untruely) to me as a crime,
was actually done by Mr. Williams, Dr. Franklin's
nephew, whom he speaks of in the highest terms
of commendation. I can prove by Mr. Williams's
own letter that he agreed with Mr. Thomas Morris
to do the public business and charge 5 per cent.,
which they were to share between them, and Mr.
Williams's accounts since render'd to the American
Commissioners at Paris, will shew that he has

actually charg'd and received 5 per cent. Commission on that business.

TO MR. ANDREW LIMOZIN, AT HAVRE DE GRACE.

PARIS, 21 March, 1778.

Dear Sir:

I duly receiv'd your esteem'd favor of the 13th instant, and note the contents. By the death of Mr. Thomas Morris, the Commercial Agency for the Secret Committee of Congress has fallen on me alone; and I am happy in conformity to their recommendation, in appointing and authorizing you, as I do fully by this letter, to take up and dispose of such vessels and Cargoes as may be lucky enough to arrive at your port, in which the said Secret Committee may be interested, whether address'd to me solely or to Mr. Thomas Morris and myself as joint Commercial Agents; always taking care to advise the Committee of your proceedings, and giving the American Commissioners at Paris notice when any vessels arrive at your port in which the Committee are interested. I sincerely wish that you may have frequent occasions of showing your continued attachment to the interest of America in general and to that of the Secret Committee in particular. I am, &c.

(Signed)   W. LEE.

TO MR. JOHN DANIEL SCWHEIGHAUSER, NANTES.

PARIS, 21 March, 1778.

Sir :

I was duly honor'd with your esteemed favor of the 11th current and note the contents.

As the superintendence of the Commercial Concerns

of the Secret Committee of Congress has devolv'd on me solely by the death of the late Mr. Thomas Morris, I am happy in pursuing their recommendation by appointing you to take up, and dispose of any vessels or Cargoes that may arrive in the port of Nantes or any other port in Brittany, on account of said Committee; requesting you always to govern yourself in this Agency conformable to such Instructions, or advice as you may receive with such vessels or Cargoes; whether they are address'd to me solely, or to Mr. Morris and myself as joint Commercial Agents; and that you may be fully inform'd on that head, you are hereby authorized to open any letters that may come to your hands, directed to me only as Commercial Agent, or to Mr. Morris and myself as joint Agents for America. In order to prevent as much as possible any interference with you, or any interruption in this business, I enclose you a certificate, and a letter from the Chairman of the Committee, dated February the 3^d 1777, to shew my authority, if any one shou'd entertain a doubt about it.

You will please to give the Committee regular advice of your proceedings, and also give the American Commissioners at Paris advice whenever any property arrives in which the Committee is interested. Shou'd any cargoes arrive in the above mention'd ports address'd to me, being private property, you will please to dispose of the same in the best manner you can for the interest of the concern'd, and follow their directions in making returns for the same. Be so good as to forward any letters that may come to your hands, directed for me, to Mr. Grand, Banquier in Paris.

I have no doubt of your conduct in this agency giving entire satisfaction to all parties concern'd, and wishing you success therein,

I have the honor, &c,

(Signed)   W. LEE.

MR. JOHN BONDFIELD, BORDEAUX.

PARIS, 21 March, 1778.

Sir:

As the Commercial Agency for the Secret Committee of Congress has devolved solely on me by the Death of Mr. T^s Morris, and having a good opinion of your abilities, industry and integrity, I am induced to request you will take upon yourself the management of any vessels, and the disposal of such Cargoes, as may arrive in the Ports of Bordeaux, Bayonne, Rochelle and Rochfort, belonging to said Committee, in which they are interested or concern'd; hereby authorizing and impowering you to act in all such Cases as fully as I cou'd do, if personally present; always wishing you to attend closely to such Instructions or advice as you may receive with said vessels or Cargoes, whether address'd to me solely or to Mr. Morris and myself jointly. And that you may be fully inform'd, you are farther authoriz'd to open any letters that come to your hands directed to me solely as Commercial Agent, or to Mr. Morris and myself as joint Agents. The House of Messrs S. & J. H. Delap formerly did business for the Secret Committee, but the enclos'd letter (which you will please to deliver) will shew the reason of the alteration, and to facilitate your operations for the benefit of the concern'd, I have thought it advisable to inclose you a certificate; also a letter from the Chairman of the Secret Committee, Robert Morris, Esq.ʳ, which will fully shew my authority, and consequently that under which you are to act. I wish you to give the Committee the earliest advice of this arrangement, and on all future occasions that you wou'd advise them of your proceedings. It will be proper to inform the American Commissioners at Paris, when any property arrives in which the Secret Committee is interested. I have not the least doubt of your giving entire satisfaction in whatever is committed to your care, and wishing you both ease and success in the management.

I am, &c.,

(Sign'd)   W. LEE.

The Secret Committee were informed by letter from me dated March 23d, 1778 (which they have receiv'd) of these arrangements being made, only until they shou'd give further orders therein; also of the reason why the House of Messrs. S. & J. H. Delap was omitted at Bordeaux; tho' I had acted upon my own judgment alone, there was another much more forcible reason with me for such omission; which being mention'd to Dr. Franklin, on my first coming to France, and he to Mr. Deane, the latter, I understood, had prevail'd on the former, to think that my Information was not well founded; (the private connections between Mr. Deane and that house were too publickly known to require mentioning by me;) therefore I submitted; and that house seem'd to grow afterwards into higher favor with those Gentlemen, than it had been before. I had never the most distant private connection or correspondence with this house, nor the honor of being acquainted with any one of the partners: therefore my conduct cou'd not possibly arise from personal motives. However, to avoid all misconception 'tis proper to add a Copy of my letter to that House, which was enclos'd to Mr. Bondfield.

MESSRS. S. & J. H. DELAP, BORDEAUX.

Gentlemen :

I wrote you from Nantes the 14th ult^o advising you that by the Death of Mr. Thomas Morris the Commercial Agency for the Secret Committee of Congress had fallen on me alone, and desiring you wou'd favor me with your account current against said Committee, with account sales of such goods as you had receiv'd on their account: To this letter you have not been pleas'd to favor me with any answer, therefore conclude you do not chuse to act any farther for said Committee; consequently by virtue of the powers vested in me by said Committee, I have authorized Mr. John Bondfield, who will deliver this, to take up, and dispose of such Cargoes or Vessels as may arrive at Bordeaux on account of said Committee, or that may be address'd to me solely, or to Mr. Morris and myself as joint Commercial agents. This I think it proper to give you due notice of, not doubting that you will act in conformity.

I am, &c.,

(Sign'd) W. LEE.

I have now given a plain and unvarnish'd account of all my conduct in the Public Service, relative to their Commercial Affairs, the Truth of which I am ready to verify on oath; besides being possess'd of the original writings and testimonials, that prove the most material parts: which shall at all times be open to the perusal of proper persons; yet still I think it expedient to mention that Congress did on the 9th of February, 1778, before the date of the above mention'd appointments, resolve, that the Committee of Commerce shou'd write to the Commissioners at the Court of France, desiring them to appoint commercial agents; the Commercial Committee did write to the Commissioners accordingly on the same day, which letter was received in France, some time in May or June; since which time I have not had any concern with that department; if there had been any sufficient ground for altering the appointments I had made, there can be no doubt but that they wou'd have done it long since. In September, 1778, I heard that the same dark agents, who had long been employ'd in traducing every person that had been employ'd in the affairs of America, unless he was of their society, coîmmenc'd an attack on the character of Mr. Schweighauser, and his son-in-law, Mr. Dobrée, which began by dropping anonymous and undirected letters on the tables of the Commissioners, full of charges and insinuations against these

Gentlemen; at length one of these Letter droppers, being discovered, was called upon for the Author, which he refused to give up; however the charges I have understood, have been enquired into, and I suppose the issue of that enquiry has been communicated to Congress by the Commissioners; but I must beg leave to add here extracts of a letter to me from John Lloyd, Esqr, and of a certificate sent to the American Commissioners at Paris on this subject by Daniel Blake and John Lloyd, Esq^rs, of South Carolina; where they both have considerable Estates, and are well known to be gentlemen of the highest Integrity, honor and good sense.

NANTES, 19 September, 1778.

The unjust, base and villainous attack made upon Mr. Dobrée and Mr. Schweighauser must have originated in hearts capable of the blackest crimes; and those who countenance such assassin-like proceedings, are not in my opinion less culpable.

(Signed)   JOHN LLOYD.

NANTES, 19 September, 1778.

Being informed that some malicious person or persons, hath been, and are still endeavoring, by the most infamous means, to deprive Mr. J. D. Schweighauser of his good name, and being apprehensive that the intention is to prejudice him in the estimation of the Honorable Commissioners; we think it an act of justice due to injur'd merit to acquaint you, that we have employ'd, and are now employing that Gentleman to transact for our friends and ourselves to a very large amount. The satisfaction that they and we have received from his assiduity, honor and integrity, will induce us to pursue every means in our power, after our arrival in America, to serve him; being confident that as a merchant he most justly deserves public and private confidence. He has had, and continues to transact, a very considerable part of the business to and from America; and we have always heard the Americans, who have had any connection with him, speak of him in the most respectful terms.

(Signd)   Danl. Blake,
John Lloyd.

These certificates, given six months after my appointment of Mr. Schweighauser as one of the Commercial agents, by gentlemen who were on the spot to see and judge for themselves, are surely a full vindication of my choice, had I not been authorized to make it by the Committee's recommendation, which was strengthened by my own observation and Judgment.

Nowadays it seems to be the mode to circulate dark and wicked insinuations, by whispering in corners, and by anonimous Letters, and when the plot is sufficiently ripe, the insinuations are converted into *stubborn and undeniable facts*, and the anonymous Letters into proof as clear as that of holy writ : But whether these charges and insinuations against Mr. Schweighauser or his son-in-law, be true or false, let the accus'd answer for themselves : but I will observe that the accusations, and even the subject of them, are of a date long after my appointment of Mr. Schweighauser, and long after the Commercial Agency was taken out of my hands by Congress. Indeed I have been informed that the direct attempts to blacken the character of Mr. Schweighauser, who was the only agent appointed by me at Nantes, were soon given up, as it was found to be rather too arduous an undertaking ; but the indirect attempts were continued, thro' the medium of his relations with his son-in-law. These relations being charged by hearsay, with enmity to America, it was infer'd that Mr. Dobrée was guilty, and as surely his father-in-law, Mr. Schweighauser, must be guilty also. 'Tis very certain that there is something very curious in this mode of accusation ; but I wonder these accusers do not recollect the case of Dr. Franklin (whom they and Mr. Deane extol to the skies, and who is absolutely trusted by Congress), and his only son, Governor Franklin, whose former and present conduct is too notorious in America and even in Europe to need mentioning here.

It is now made evident that every positive charge which Mr. Deane has brought against me, is not only unfounded, but directly the reverse of truth ; and it is somewhat curious that the only thing which he mentions as being *doubtful*, happens to be a truth: this is, that I *might* be an alderman of

London at the time he was writing his letter. The fact is, I was then an Alderman of London, and, as far as I know, am one at this moment.

As soon as I got my family from England, I wrote to one of my Common Council, saying that I was ready to resign my Gown, as soon as my constituents were ready to receive it. The answer was, that the majority did not wish me to resign it. I wrote several times to the same purpose, and receiv'd the same answers: when at length I determined to wait no longer, and on the 13th of November I sent my resignation in form, but this not getting to hand until the 22^d or 23^d occasiond the proceedings at the Wardmote, the 21st December (last St. Thomas's day) which having been publish'd in almost all the London papers, it is unnecessary for me to repeat here. Although my constituents have been actually in possession of my resignation ever since December last, they have not yet thought proper to make use of it, because they say, they wish to find a successor to fill my place of sound old whig principles; for which, it is certain, they honor'd me with their Choice. One of the Common Council in last month (vizt Feb. 1779), wrote to me thus: "It is certainly the wish of my brethren and self that the resignation shou'd not be made until we request it, i. e., supposing you are no ways injur'd by this." The injury must be very great indeed, that will induce me to be guilty of ingratitude to men, who have not only honor'd me by their choice, on the noblest principles of liberty, but have even shown themselves warmly attach'd to the Cause of America. I speak of a great majority of my Constituents; for which reason I think it a duty incumbent on me to let them proceed in their own business as they judge right; and in this I am confident, that every honorable and impartial man will accord with me.

I have the honor to be,
with the greatest respect,
your Excellency's most obedient
and very humble serv!

W. LEE.

Frankfort on the Mayn in Germany, March 8th, 1779.

HIS EXCELLENCY PRESIDENT JAY AT CONGRESS.

PARIS, March 16th, 1779.

I have just had communicated to me the copies of two letters from Mr. Silas Deane, address'd to Mr. President Laurens, dated Philadelphia, October 12th 1778, and a separate paper relative to the 11th and 12th articles in the Treaty of Commerce, between his most Christian Majesty and the United States of America; in which letter, so far as respects me personally, he has asserted nearly the same groundless charges as in his letter to the public, which have been already so fully reply'd to, and prov'd to be utterly repugnant to truth. Had Mr. Deane made these very extraordinary assertions only once, he might have had some shadow of excuse, tho' it is a very bad one, by pleading a weak memory; but a deliberate repetition of them, after an interval of time amply sufficient for recollection, shews a heart and designs of such a complection, that all good men shou'd avoid and guard against. Mr. Deane concludes with the following assertions by way of summary of all he had before advanced:

1st That I never had a Commission to the Commercial Agency. What Mr. Deane may stile *a commission*, I do not know; but he knew by a letter to himself from Mr. John Ross in July, 1777, of which he knows I have a copy, that I had as sufficient authority to act in the Commercial Agency as Mr. Thomas Morris, and that I did act in that department accordingly. But if Mr. Deane knew I was not Commercial Agent, how can he palliate so bold and daring an imposition on his most Christian Majesty and his Ministers, as to represent me in that character to them; which he did do in the letter sign'd by him to his Excellency Count de Vergennes, in February, 1778, representing that the late Mr. Thomas Morris's papers might be put in my possession, as then being the sole Commercial Agent of Congress. But indeed we ought not to be surpriz'd at any imposition whatever on the part of Mr. Deane, when he impos'd himself on the

King of France, his ministers, and the whole world as a Commissioner of Congress on the 20ᵗʰ of March, 1778, when he confesses that on the 4ᵗʰ of that month he received a resolution of Congress recalling him to America. I also refer for his conviction to the Letters and proceedings of the Secret Committee.

2dly. Mr. Deane says: "Mr. Lee's caution was such, that he never even answer'd my letters to him in February or March, informing him that Mr. Robert Morris had written to me, that he was appointed; nor did I hear anything from him of his intentions until he arriv'd at Paris the summer following, where also he acted with the greatest caution, while he waited the return of his brother from Berlin." One cannot here omit observing the studied latitude of expression. Mr. Deane talks of his letter in *February* or *March*, and that I came to Paris in the *summer* following. Will Mr. Deane say how many letters he wrote? I never saw or heard of but *one*. Will he please to say whether that one letter was dated the 1ˢᵗ of February or the 31st of March? for the difference of *two* whole months makes a very material alteration in the consequence he means to draw from the assertion. I will answer, that his only letter is dated the 30ᵗʰ of March, tho' he acknowledges his having receiv'd a *notification* from Mr. Robert Morris in February of my appointment; and at the same time was desir'd to give me information *immediately* of it. It has been also prov'd by Mr. Deane's letter to Mr. Williams on the same day, vizt March 30th, that he was plotting a contention and rivalship in this Department long before it was possible for him to know my determination on the subject. Again, will Mr. Deane specify what time in the *summer* I arriv'd at Paris? because here it is left to be understood, either the first day of June or the last day of August; which makes a still greater difference than the former expression. I I will assert, what I can prove, that I arriv'd in Paris the 11th of June; and that besides receiving a letter from me himself in the month of *May*, he was personally told by my Brother, Arthur Lee, by my desire, in the beginning of May, that I wou'd come over as soon as possible to execute my appointment; and so far from waiting in Paris for my Brother's return from Berlin, it has been prov'd already, that I waited by the express advice of Dr. Franklin and Mr. Deane until the 31st. of July, 1777, as their letter to me of that date will shew; which was nine days after my Brother's return from Berlin to Paris.

The manner in which Mr. Deane sent me the letter informing me of my appointment, join'd with what is now manifest, a form'd design in him and Dr. Franklin to make Mr. Williams (nephew of the latter, and who now appears connected with the former in private mercantile business) commercial agent in opposition to the Secret Committee's appointment, renders it evident that he expected either the interception of that letter, or of my answer, wou'd have subjected me to imprisonment and secur'd their plan. It is this disappointment that makes Mr. Deane so outragious against me, for not having committed so great an act of Imprudence, situated as I was, as to be writing to him by the post upon such a subject. That this scheme of Mr. Deane might be more effectual, notice of my appointment was circulated upon the Royal Exchange in London, before I receiv'd Mr. Deane's letter; and not long after, it was publish'd in the newspapers in authentic letters written from Paris. Now, as Mr. Deane acknowledges that *he* receiv'd the letter announcing my appointment, it must have by *him* that others were enabled to write and publish it to all the world; while my *Life*, *Liberty*, and *property*, were at stake. It is hardly in charity to believe, that these were not the intended victims of Mr. Deane's conduct.

3ly. He charges it as a crimes, that I was circumspect in my conduct, on my first coming to France, for fear of prejudicing my interest in London.

Will any man in the world call circumspection a crime, where ostentation wou'd have been not only useless, but highly ridiculous, and when my family, and nearly the whole of my property in Europe, were in the power of the enemy?

I have in the former part of this narrative shewn, that my urgent desire of serving my country, and its glorious cause, had induc'd me to quit England so hastily, as to leave behind me Mrs. Lee not recover'd from her lying in (which event was daily expected when Mr. Deane's letter was receiv'd) my children, House, Furniture, and property to the amount of many thousand pounds sterling; the greater part of which has been with held from me, in consequence of my coming away. It is some what curious to observe that almost in the same breath, Mr. Deane brings a heavy charge against Mr. Arthur Lee for being ostentatious in his proceedings, and as heavy a one against me for conducting mine with caution: but this is among the least of his inconsistencies and contradictions of himself.

4thly. Mr. Deane says: "So far was he (meaning me) from ever executing or publickly attempting to execute that Agency until after the news of General Burgoyne's defeat had arriv'd in France, that he did nothing that ever I heard of, which cou'd have prevented his returning to the exercise of his Aldermanship of London."

If anything could astonish me that comes from Mr. Deane, surely here is abundant matter for astonishment. He had just before, from under his own hand, on the very same paper, acknowledg'd my having attempted to exercise that appointment, in the joint letter from Mr. Thomas Morris, and myself as Commercial agents, to himself and Dr. Franklin in August, 1777, which he calls *severe;* but which I aver, is a very civil one, and that it does not contain a single harsh or offensive expression. He acknowledges also the conference I had with all the Commissioners in France, in October, on the subject of the Commercial business, when Mr. Izard was present. He knew also that I had receiv'd a cargoe publickly at Nantes, belonging to Congress, by the Abigail, Capt Jenne; which vessel was loaded again by me, and despatched back for America in three weeks; while other American vessels of no greater size, or importance, were detain'd at Nantes from two or three months. He knew also, or ought to have known, that I had written a letter address'd to all the commissioners, Dr. Franklin, Mr. Deane, and Mr. Arthur Lee, on the 10th of November, 1777, which was deliver'd to Dr. Franklin as eldest commissioner the same day; wherein I requested a copy of the Treaties that had been proposed to the Courts of France and Spain, agreeable to my Instructions from Congress, that I might not as a Commissioner of Congress, propose any thing repugnant thereto, to the Courts of Vienna and Berlin. After these things, and a continued series of operations in the public service (all of which Mr. Deane was acquainted with) from the time I was permitted to act by himself and Dr. Franklin until the 4th of December, when the news of General Burgoyne's defeat arriv'd at Paris: with what face cou'd Mr. Deane make such an assertion as he has done? Most of these things also, being of public notoriety, and capable of being prov'd by a multitude of witnesses; can any one suppose Mr. Deane so totally ignorant of the Laws of England, as to imagine he cou'd think I might return "to the exercise of my aldermanship of London," without being a madman desirous of hanging himself.

This Gentleman attempts to excuse himself and Dr. Franklin for not answering the joint letter of Mr. Morris and myself, by laying the blame on Mr. Arthur Lee; not a syllable of which was mention'd at the conference I had in October, 1777, at Passy, with all the Commissioners, when Mr. Izard was present; and which Mr. Lee has answer'd himself; but he omits to say why my several letters from Nantes, as Commercial Agent, on public business, to the Commissioners, were not answer'd, and of which I not only complained at the Conference, but since. In order to invalidate what Mr. Izard has written, he totally misstates the purport of the Letter, which Mr. Izard complains of Dr. Franklin and Mr. Deane's refusing to write. This letter, as desir'd by me, was a general one to all Captains and others, informing them that I was a Commercial Agent of the Secret Committee of Congress, and that in consequence they ought to follow my directions and orders, in all matters relating to the Commercial business of the Committee.

So far from my proposing the suspension of Mr. Morris, I never thought the Commissioners had the least shadow of authority to do it. 'Tis certain that Mr. Deane not only propos'd the suspension of Mr. Morris at this Conference, but at several other times. As a confirmation of this assertion I beg leave to give the following extract from Mr. Deane's letter to me, dated

PASSY, 18 December, 1777.

My advice before your appointment (as was well known) was to supercede Mr. Morris, and appoint another, until the pleasure of Congress shou'd be known. I was always of the same opinion after your appointment, that you ought to conduct the business alone; these are well known to have been my uniform sentiments.

With regard to the 11th and 12th Articles of the Treaty of Commerce, 'tis certain that I did not speak to Mr. Deane about them; because his conduct has been such, on almost every occasion, that I had determin'd never to speak to him singly on any public business whatever; but I spoke to Dr. Franklin largely on the subject, and surely Mr.

Deane cannot forget that when a proposition was made to him and Dr. Franklin, by desire of Mr. Izard and myself, that we might have a conference with them on those articles, they rejected the proposition with contempt and with insulting terms.

Mr. Deane labors much to throw an odium on me, as wishing to monopolize to myself the places both of honor and profit. Probably from the weakness of his memory, he forgot that in the Commencement of his address to the public he states that before September, 1776, he "had the honor to be the *Commercial* and *political* agent of America in Europe." He also forgets that the first cause of any difference between us was his usurping the exercise of the Commercial agency, to which Mr. Morris and myself were appointed by the Secret Committee, while he was not only one of the Commissioners to the Court of Versailles particularly, but generally authoriz'd to that with every power in Europe—the influence and patronage of which very extensive commission, he was perpetually endeavoring to retain entirely to himself. He also seems to be ignorant of what, I suppose, is known to most people in Philadelphia, that his "Venerable Friend," as he calls him, Dr. Franklin, is at this moment, not only *sole* Minister Plenipotentiary to the Court of Versailles, but also in fact, *sole* superintending Commercial Agent in all Europe.

I have the honor to be with the greatest Respect and consideration your Excellencies Most Obdient & Most Hble Servt   W. Lee.

*His Excellency Mr. President Jay at Congress.**

TO RICHARD HENRY LEE.

PARIS, 25 March, 1779.

My dear Brother,

The original of my last letter by Mr Stockton, which is copied on the other side, may not perhaps reach you as soon as this.

M^r. Adams had left this place to go to Nantes to be ready to take his passage in the Alliance for America, before I got here, in which I was unlucky, as I much wished to have some conversation with him before his departure.†

With this goes a full vindication of myself against the aspersions of M^r. Silas Deane, under cover to his Excellency President Jay, to be laid before Congress.

I do not make any address to the public, because as far as I am acquainted with the actual situation of things in America, such a step would be highly improper, as tending to draw the attention of the

---

*Endorsed. William Lee's vindication in answer to the publication Dec. 5, 1778, signed Silas Deane. Received October 11, 1779.

†Adams set out from Passy on the 8th, and reached Nantes on the 12th.

people from the reverence and respect of Congress, which is the grand basis of the security of America, and which our enemies have been, and are still trying by bribery, and every insidious to bring about; and because I fear, that if the attention of people is taken off from exerting every effort in providing for their security against our inveterate enemies, they may be taken unawares and suffer irreparable injuries. If you however being on the spot judge it proper that any public reply on my part should be made, 'twill I suppose be amply sufficient to select some of the striking facts, out of what is sent to Congress, and publish them. Such as, that Mʳ. Williams actually agreed to do the public business for Mʳ. Morris, and divide the 5 pr cᵗ. between them, (I have Mʳ. Deane's letter on this engagement, which he approved); and that Mʳ. W. has actually charged and received this 5 pʳ cᵗ..

The certificates of the agents appointed by me, viz: Mss. Limozin, Schweighauser and Bondfield, whose certificate has been already sent to Congress.

That Congress in Feb. 1778 put the commercial agency under the direction of the American commissioners at the court of France, which authority Dʳ Franklin, as minister here, is now exercising alone, and such other facts as you may think prudent and proper to publish.

From my own letters to you, as well as my brother's to you and Mʳ S. Adams, you can shew that so far from my desiring to keep the commercial Agency in my hands, while I was acting as a commissioner, as Mr Deane and his partizans insinuate, we both recommended Mr Lloyd to the commercial agency. And as they charge us with an engrossing disposition, will they show what part of profit any of the family has, or ever had?

Mr Deane's fortune when he came over here must be well known in America. Every body knows he has now much money.

The critical situation of Mr R. Morris, at the beginning of the American War, was not only generally known in London and Holland, but in other places; what is it now?

What has Mr Carter Braxton, Mr Williams, Mr John Ross, and a multitude of other dependants of Mr Deane and Mr Morris? Have they made these immense profits with their own or the public funds? as to myself I shall be perfectly easy if Congress, in the arrangement of their European affairs, should leave me out entirely.

I never did ask for, nor ever wished for my present appointment; however I trust there will be justice enough to reimburse me what I have lost by coming from England, to enter on the public service, that my family may not starve while it is impossible to get any supplies from America; for I know not any part of Europe where we could get 50 guineas to keep us from a jail. I can by a fair account prove that I lost by coming from England above £6,500 Ster.lg, all money out of my pocket.

If on the contrary, I should be continued a minister, 'twill be as necessary for Congress to fix some more decisive mode of supplying the expenses of the commission, than the resolution of last year, that the commissioners at the other courts should draw on those at Paris for their expenses; for in consequence thereof, I drew last Sept.r on the commissioners here for 1.000 Louis d'ors, which D.r Franklin refused to accept: he also refused to accept M.r Izard's draft for 500 Louis d'ors, however the other two commissioners accepted both our drafts.

Now D.r Franklin is sole minister and sole commercial director; he told me the other day, that he would not pay any of my drafts for my expenses;—thus does he presume to contravene the appointments and orders of Congress, and he had even the assurance when I mentioned to him, the resolution about unanimity and cordiality here to reply that Congress should set us the example by their own conduct. *

---

* "In this situation I have been applied to by Mr. William Lee, and lately, through our banker, by Mr. Izard, for more money for their expenses; and, I am told, there is much anger against me for declining to furnish them, and that I am charged with *disobeying an order of Congress*, and with cruelly attempting to distress gentlemen who are in the service of their country. They have, indeed, produced to me a resolve of Congress,

For my own part, I cannot any longer submit to the insolence and tricks of this old creature, who is perpetually surrounded by persons to whom his papers are exposed, that he has been again and again cautioned about, and whom everybody but himself take to be spies for our enemies. But they flatter his vanity, and tell him he is absolute Lord of America. This is with him a most decisive proof of their merit and integrity.

I do not know that it has been yet explicitly, and in regular manner settled between the King of France and the United States, that the guarantee on both sides mentioned in the Treaty of Alliance has now actually taken place. This is a point of so much importance that it can't be too soon or too explicitly settled. If this guarantee has actually taken place, surely Congress did not consider that

---

empowering them to draw on the Commissioners in France for their expenses at foreign courts; and doubtless Congress, when that resolve was made, intended to enable us to pay those drafts; but as that has not been done, and the gentlemen (except Mr. Lee for a few weeks) have not incurred any expense at foreign courts, and, if they had, the five thousand five hundred guineas, received by them in about nine months, secured an ample provision for it, and as both of them might command money from England, I do not conceive that I *disobeyed an order of Congress*, and that if I did, the circumstances will excuse it; and I could have no intention to distress them, because I must know it is out of my power, as their private fortunes and credit will enable them at all times to pay their own expenses."
Franklin to Committee of Foreign Affairs, 26 May, 1779.

peace must be actually made here, when they determined to leave all their political and mercantile interests in this country, in one and the same hand. I know that what is agreed here, must be ratified by Congress, to be binding; but I know as well how difficult it will be to resist even a very bad arrangement of the Pacification that is agreed to here, therefore too much care cannot be taken to prevent such an evil.

It seems to me that immediate instructions and very explicit should be sent to the minister here, not to consent or even undertake to recommend to Congress any plan of pacification without the consent and approbation of all the deputies, that Congress may have in Europe; who can be easily assembled here, on such an important occasion. Communicate this idea to the Aristides of America, S. A.* with my very best respects, and to such others as you know love their country and liberty, better or at least as well as themselves.

I have not followed the example of M.ͬ Izard, and my brother in requesting to resign; because I do not approve what they have done; for the greater the danger, the more I am firm; and at this moment, the danger to one country seems to me more tremendous than ever, from the inveteracy of our enemies and the abandoned profligacy of those who having plundered millions of the public money

---

* Samuel Adams.

wish to realize what they have hold of, by a secret convention with our enemies to be secured, if by private machination they can bring about a subjugation or pacification on dependent principles.

I did not believe Gov.ʳ Johnstone when he boasted to the British cabinet, and his confidential friends of what great things would arise from the effects of his private operations in America; but some late proceedings, particularly the not censuring Silas Deane for his daring publication have had a bad appearance; however I am determined to stick the closer to the operations of the secret and underhand operations of the enemies of our country.

I am assured that what a certain *Great Man** as he is called, has done for Silas Deane and his Junto, is not entirely approved of at Versailles; and he is consequently coming away.

This to yourself.—I have surely great reason to be offended at giving up all T. Morris's papers after what had passed here; which was not very wise; for there is great reason to believe they contained something highly important for Congress to have known, from the letters of M.ʳ John Ross, who was a good deal in the secrets of Silas Deane, and R. Morris with you.

I am inclined to think the former chairman†

---

* Gerard, the French minister in America.
† Robert Morris.

concealed my letters, and documents sent with them, from the secret committee, or Congress, until he obtained the resolve for the papers to be delivered up to his order. Pray tell me how this business was really managed with you.

I burn to write my mind truly to M.ʳ R. Morris, on the subject, but I wish not to be hasty, because my conjecture may be ill-founded. Will not M.ʳ Deane's publication show to Congress the necessity of adopting the mode practised by every power in Europe, of administering an oath of secrecy to all their public ministers or commissioners. Those with you may do it before they come away, and those in Europe, on having the form sent them, should be obliged to take the oath before a proper officer in the country where they are, and to return at least 3 certificates to Congress of his having taken this oath.

The receipt of the following letters written by me and delivered here to M.ʳ Simeon Deane, in Feb: 1778 has never been acknowledged, viz: to yourself dated 28.ᵗʰ Feb: 1778, conveying copies of mine to you on the 13ᵗʰ and 15ᵗʰ of Feb.ʳ 1778 from Nantes, and copies of some of M.ʳ Ross's letters relative to M.ʳ T. Morris's papers; to R. Morris, Esq.ʳ 28ᵗʰ Feb. 1778; F. L. Lee Esq.ʳ same date; Secret Committee of same date; President of Congress, same date, viz. 28ᵗʰ Feb.ʳ 1778. All these were put up in one packet and directed to the

President of Congress; also a letter to Genl. Arnold with an engraving,—the history of the Revolution in Switzerland.

Pray inquire and let me know if all, or any of these letters have been received; for I never supposed it was for much good, that Mr Silas Deane went from hence with his brother Simeon, after he had these dispatches as far as Versailles, where they staid together all night; and from whence Silas brought an impertinent letter from his brother Simeon to our brother Arthur Lee, for demanding a receipt from his brother Simeon for these letters.

It seems that no interest is to be paid in France for any money put into the Continental Loan Office after March 1778. I don't see therefore what benefit will arise to me from putting any of the annual produce of my estate into the office and for what has been put there, I wish you to send me the bill here, at least for the amount of the interest. I have already, I fear, written too much, and yet have a great deal more to say. Our best love and wishes attend you and yours, and I remain, &c.

P. S.—Your sons are well, and I suppose write to you frequently. The linnen you desired is sent in the Govr Livingston, Capt Gale for Virginia, to the care of my steward, Mr Ellis.

TO THE COMMITTEE OF FOREIGN AFFAIRS.

PARIS, March 25, 1779.

Gentlemen :

Be pleased to refer to the foregoing copy of my letter to you of the 25th ultimo by Mr. Stockton, which may not get to hand as soon as this.

On the 10th instant an armistice was published between the Emperor and King of Prussia, and the same day the conferences were opened at Teschin in Austrian Silesia, to consolidate and reduce into form the treaty of peace between the two contending Powers, the important articles of which have been already agreed upon by both parties. The operations of war have consequently ceased, but perhaps the final signature of the peace may not take place for some weeks.

The principal objects of my coming here were to engage this Court to aid and assist me in adopting the most speedy and effacacious measures to prevent our joint enemies from reaping considerable advantage from the peace in Germany, by engaging a vast number of the free corps that have been raised for this war, to the number of fifteen or twenty thousand men, that will all be disbanded as soon as the peace is signed, and to aid me in endeavoring to get the German Powers to acknowledge the independence of America, which would certainly have a decided influence on Great Britain, and induce her King and Ministers to make peace with us on the footing of independence.

As it is the regular and usual mode in Europe for one nation to treat with another on public business through the medium of their public Ministers, I applied to Dr. Franklin on my arrival here, as the American Minister at this Court, to go with me to his Excellency Count de Vergennes, to consult with him on these points. The Doctor declined doing so, saying he was so little acquainted with German affairs that he could not meddle with them. I told him that it was not his knowledge or idea of the German politics that was to be communicated to the Minister, but mine, on which the Minister would form his own judgment with respect to the propriety of my propositions; but unless they were made to him in the regular mode by the Minister of Congress at this Court, it could not be expected that he would pay much attention to what came from me, as an individual unauthorized by Congress to treat with him on great political subjects. The doctor still refused either to go with me, or to write by me on the subject to Count de Vergennes. I shall, however, do every thing that is in my power to accomplish these desirable ends, and from the present appearance of things, it appears to me most probable I shall succeed in one, if not both the objects in view, if I can obtain the aid and concurrence of the Ministry here.

These are certainly objects of high importance, especially with respect to the troops, as the British Ministry have now several officers in pay in Germany waiting to engage them. Our enemies it seems are determined to prosecute the war against us, at least for this year; their plan must be begun before this gets to hand, and therefore opened to you, which renders it unnecessary for me to mention anything on that subject.

With this is a letter to President Jay, covering my reply to the allegations of Mr. Silas Deane against me, in his letter to Congress of the 12th of October, to be laid before Congress, which I flatter myself will, in the mind of every impartial person, be not only a full vindication of my conduct, but also prove how little credit is due to any assertions of Mr. Deane. As to myself personally, I am perfectly at ease with respect to the weak and wicked attempts of Mr. Deane to injure me, for I am shielded with the invincible armor of innocence; but the injury his daring publication has done to the common cause of America in Europe, is not easily to be delineated, and I can assure you, with truth, that our enemies are more elated at it than they would have been with a capital victory. The reason for their exultation is too evident to require mentioning.* Besides, it has created a diffidence

---

* "If we may credit the late accounts from America, a dawn

in the minds of the Europeans, which will embarrass extremely every attempt at public negociations; since few Ministers will treat with a people who permit every thing that passes to be wantonly published to the world with impunity. I trust, however, the wisdom of Congress will not let its attention be drawn off from the great and principal object of providing effectually for defeating the open and secret efforts of our enemies against us, and finally to force them to an honorable peace;

---

of hope has at length broken forth upon the despair of administration. Silas Deane is returned to Philadelphia from the Court of France, deeply incensed at his recall, which he attributed to the influence of the two Mr. Lees, in Congress, who in conjunction with their brothers at the Courts of Versailles and Vienna, have been endeavouring to induce that body to break their faith with the French nation, and sacrifice America to the English Ministry. In fine, the seeds of dissension are at last sown in Congress, and there is no doubt, but that every means will be used on our part, to make them vegetate and expand throughout America." *The London Packet*, 27 January, 1779.

"Great dissensious prevail at this time among the rebel Colonists. Silas Deane is openly arraigning the conduct of Congress, while the Congress condemn him as the author of confusion and distrust in every department in which he has been employed ; and Gen. Arnold has been censured in a long string of allegations, setting forth the tyranny of his behavior, and the several disadvantages suffered by the state through the impropriety of his commands." *London Chronicle*, 17 April, 1779.

"The reports of disputes in the Congress are confirmed. Discontents universally reign out of it." *Letter from New York*, 27 February, in *London Chronicle*, 27 April, 1779.

which I am convinced they will not accede to until they are driven off the continent. I have the honor to be, &c.

TO FRANCIS LIGHTFOOT LEE.

PARIS, 26 March, 1779.

My dear Brother:

The inclosed copy of mine of the 20 Dec.ʳ Ult.º contains almost as much as I can say on my private affairs, except that you may deliver or not, as you think best, the inclosed Letter to Col. G. Mason, if I have time to write one. I now understand that all my property of every kind is taxed 1 ½ pC. in Virg.ª ; so that what money of mine has been put into the Continental Loan Office, which has been sufficiently reduced already, will soon come to nothing at all. If I am to receive paper for money advanced in London, surely the same paper must be legal payment to my Creditors for Sterling debts, and I beg it may be tendered to them. As to the annual produce of my Estate and the interest at least of what has been already put into the Continental Loan Office, I cou'd wish it to be remitted to me in Bills on Paris, if they are to be got, which I suppose is possible, as there have been a great many drawn on the Commissioners here and some purchased at 300 pC. My object in desiring this remittance is to get something for my family to live on, since it seems more than probable that my present public appointment either is already, or will be soon [revoked] and if it is not, unless Congress fall upon some sure mode of supplying the expenses, the Commission must cease of itself, for notwithstanding the resolve of Congress last year, Doc.ͬ Franklin has refused to supply either M.ͬ Izard or myself with any more money. 'Tis true the other two Commissioners did last Jan.ʸ give to my dft 1000 Louis d'ors, but if I should be permitted to go to Vienna or Berlin this year (which at present does not seem to me very improbable) what remains of that sum now will last but a very little while indeed. At Vienna the English and French Ambassadors' House rent alone costs 1000 guineas a year. If no material alteration takes place in my appointment I shall be obliged to you for getting the Committee for Foreign Affairs to write at least to the Minister here insisting on his complying with the former resolution of Congress relative to our Expenses. At the same time you will please to let me know what is done on this point that I may be able to regulate my affairs in time accordingly. I have written so largely to Congress and to R. H. Lee, that I have little to say here, but I agree entirely with the wise Man (you know who) that wrote me 18 months ago, that it was certain if you were ruined, it must be by ourselves. I cannot yet believe that C[ongress] is so lost to itself, or the people of America so blinded, as to be duped or led into acts of folly and dishonor by the impudence and wickedness of S. Deane and his party, but I know him and C[ar]m[ichae]l so well that I am sure they will be perpetually busied in some plot, and I wish that Congress may not spend more time about them than 1000 such —— are worth, and by that means neglect some considerations that are essentially necessary for your security and defence ; for our Enemies seem more elated with what they think a great division in Congress and among the People at large, and the success they have had in Georgia, than they have ever been yet, so that they are determin'd at this moment on their old plan of unconditional submission.   I think the prospect seems to look as if the War wou'd still be long, and surely in common sense America shou'd look forward and be provided as well as she can for such an Event, which will be the most effectual mode of shortening its duration.   But you may lay it down as a maxim that the Obstinacy of the King of G. B. (who is as absolute in G. B. as the K. of Prussia is in Berlin) is such, and his malignity so great, that he will never make peace on Independent or honorable principles for Am.ª while there is the least glimmering hope of success.   Lord Bute and the Scotch are his only favorites, and you know too well what the Scotch are.   We have a great deal to do, against this Brute and his Scotch mirmidons before we can hope for Peace, and I am sure they must be driven from off the Continent before they will be bro't to Reason. Take all the care you can of False *Brethren* among yourselves; Govr Johnstone says there are some working for his Wages and I think they may be discover'd, for surely their first object will be to create dissentions and with the true *Scotch cunning* flattering the People into an Idea of their Security, while fire, sword, chains and tortures are preparing for them. If you are but properly on your guard, and United, I do not fear what our Enemies can do against us; and your best security will be to rely on your own efforts and not to rely too much on any external aid. I wish you may be properly supplyed for this Campaign, for I understand that no part of the contract made with nobody knows who, under the name of Hortalez & Co., will be complyed with; at least, nothing that I can hear of, has been done yet. Your sound judgment needs no caution, but I wish some of our near friends wou'd remember that it is not all gold that glisters, and that all the funds which some people have to traffic on, are fine words, professions and promises, which they never think of afterwards, unless 'tis to laugh at those who think they mean anything by them. Give this hint to those you may think want it. Spain as yet keeps aloof, but her immense preparations for War continue with as much vigor as ever, and she is more formidable at Sea than she has been since the famous Armada. 'Tis supposed she will either force a peace, or commence the War with G. B. before this campaign is over. I cannot pretend to say what is in the womb of time, but it appears to me not within the chances hardly of possibility, that G. B. should subjugate America, if she is but firm, active and unanimous. I came here for reasons you will see mention'd to Congress, but D^r. F—— no doubt from motives of malignity and something worse, refuses to give me any assistance. I shall however do all that is in my power for our Country and shall return in a day or two to Germany. The Doctor and his Junto, it is said, expect S[ilas] D[eane] over here every day, cloath'd in Triumph and cover'd with honors; however his great support with you is recalled, and a much better Man apparently, appointed to succeed him. I left my Family not very well tho' 'tis increased by a Boy that is call'd Brutus, least there sh^d be in his [   ] a Tarquin or a Cæsar in America.*

* * *

TO BENJAMIN FRANKLIN.

PARIS, Hotel D'Espagne,
Rue Guenegeaud, 30 March, 1779.

Sir:

I had the honor of writing the 23 of January last

---

* From the *Arthur Lee Papers*, in Harvard University.

to the Commissioners of Congress at the Court of Versailles, requesting that they would in consequence of the recommendation of Count de Vergennes, apply to the Prince De Mont Barey for certain artillery, arms, and ammunition for the State of Virginia, which I had authority to engage that State to pay for, as soon as it was practicable to send their commodities to Europe for that purpose. To this letter I have not received any answer, nor do I know whether any application on the business has been made to Prince De Mont Barey or not. I am now therefore to request, that you, Sir, will be so good, as Minister Plenipotentiary here from Congress, to do this favor to the State of Virginia, in which case I will do myself the honor of waiting on you any time to-morrow that you shall appoint; with a list of the articles wanted, the particulars of which were annexed to my letter above mentioned. Those things that appear to me most necessary to be immediately despatched are 20,000 stand of fusils, with bayonets compleat; 30 tons best cannon powder ; 20 ton best fusil powder, and the more so, as I apprehend Congress depends on each State for supplying these things for the troops they raise for the general service this campaign. I have the honor, &c.

P. S. The favor of an answer is requested by the bearer.

BENJAMIN FRANKLIN TO WILLIAM LEE.

PASSY, 30 March, 1779.

Sir:

I do not recollect to have seen the letter you mention. When Capt. Lemaire came over last year, and made known here the wants of Virginia, I found three different merchants of ability who offered each of them separately to supply the whole. I do not know why their offers were not accepted, and the business hitherto remains undone. I have heard that cannon and some stores have been obtained of the government by your brother, but know not the particulars. I shall be glad to see you on the subject and to be better informed. I shall dine to-day in the city, and will do myself the honor of calling on you between 5 and 6 o'clock. But if it should be inconvenient to you to be then at home, I will expect you at Passy the morning following. I have the honor &c.   B. FRANKLIN.*

FRANKLIN TO WILLIAM LEE.

PASSY, 2 April, 1779.

Sir:

Before I apply for the arms you desire, I wish to be informed whether your brother did not apply for them at the same time he applied for the cannon he obtained, or since, in consequence of the letter you mentioned to have sent us in January last, and whether they were refused or promised.

---

* See *Franklin to Patrick Henry*, 26 February, 1779.

Since I had the honor of seeing you I have received an application from the government of Maryland for a similar quantity of arms and military stores, which I am requested to obtain in the same manner, and these, with the orders of Congress, will make so vast a quantity, that I apprehend greater difficulties in obtaining them. I should be glad, therefore, if a part could be obtained elsewhere, that the quantity now to be applied for might be diminished. On this occasion permit me to mention that the D'Acostas have presented a memorial to me setting forth that they had provided arms, etc., to a great amount, in consequence of a contract made with you through your brother, and that for no other reason but because they were not finished at the time agreed, there having been a delay of a month, which they say was not their fault, but inevitable, he had refused to take them. Upon this they desire that I should procure justice to be done them, or that I would approve of their sending the goods and endeavor to have the contract complied with on the part of Virginia. I declined having anything to do with the affair, but I wish you to consider whether it would not be prudent to moderate this little difference with those people, and take the advantage of sending those arms, which have been proved good, and I suppose still lie at Nantes ready to be shipped immediately, rather than wait the success of a doubtful application.

I have the honor to be, sir, etc.,

B. FRANKLIN.

TO ARTHUR LEE.

F————T, 17 April, [1779.]

By mistake the original bills of *neave* at D. were
bro't away. They amount to 12,200 livres. He
has sent his whole demand, which is £12,921.3.*
In some things it is rather more than what is right
tho' on the whole not worth a dispute; therefore he
ought to be paid the balance, which is £721.3s;
that is £12,200, the bills which I have, and £721.3
makes £12,921.3, the whole amount of his demand: which please to settle and pay finally. I
have Deane's letter to Beaumarchais—a great part
is in cipher, but I think I can make out abuse
of Congress, the dissatisfaction of *Beaumarchais*,
telling who and who are together, &c. It is dated
December 3d., and has been published at New
York.† He says the debt of America is about 100

---

* Livres.

† An extract from this letter was printed in the London Chronicle of March 27th: "I have now spent near five months in
this city, and though I have wrote ten letters to Congress, have
been unable even to obtain an answer, and shall reap no satisfaction by my voyage hither, but the knowledge of our affairs,
and of the method in which they are conducted, if that can be
called a satisfaction. Flour is now eight pounds per cwt. in this
once plentful city, and about 20 at Boston, and everything in
proportion, from which I leave you to draw your conclusions, as
to our money, and what must be our public debt soon, it being
near one hundred millions of dollars, one-half of which has been
contracted the last campaign."

millions of dollars, the half of which was spent in the last year (viz. 1778); he gives a dreadful account of the situation of things in America. He adds: "Berkenhout has been imprisoned here. Pray get a minute account of that man's correspondence with Mons. Lee at Chaillot, and ask Petrie for a copy of a letter which he received in March last from London, or an extract from it which gave the information of the signing the treaty." This accounts for the opening and stoppage of letters, for we may suppose some letters have got to hand with the same request. You may have a copy, if you want it, or send for y*e* paper, which is the *Morning Chronicle* No. 3074, of March 27, 1779. I think it will be quite necessary for *Izard* and *W. Lee* to put down all that they know which passed relative y*e* 1*s* while they were about; to counteract the combined wickedness of Deane and *Beaumarchais*. I suppose it will be allow'd that the proposition of *W. Lee* was well founded, and ought to have been adopted, of insisting on *Franklin* demanding a categorical answer from *the French Court* relative to the precise present construction of 1. I hardly expect any advices from Congress very speedily, tho' I have now very little doubt about what will be their complexion when they do come.

Besides the recruits and new Scotch corps, now sailing for America to the number of 5000 from

England, there will go or rather have already gone from this country about 3,000 recruits, which will make Clinton's reinforcement at least 8,000, so that with his refugees, he will be much stronger than last year. I wish this may be known in time in America, and that they may also be advised that they must depend entirely on their own efforts, as they will not have the least foreign aid. Is *Arthur Lee* quite sure that 172 is entirely trust-worthy? Folly and self-conceit sometimes does much more harm than even a wicked heart. *W. Lee* says he cannot be quite satisfied with himself, as he is afraid he was lately much too open with 172—notwithstanding he was then, as he is now, convinced that he ought to have been much on the reserve.

I have not heard one word about the box of tea which I left under my bed in the chamber, and wrote from Meaux desiring it to be sent here by the diligence. My love to Ludwell, who I hope mends in his new employment. He forgot to re-mind me of the pen knife which was of course bro't away. Peace is not finally concluded here, but it looks as if it would be so, about the last of the month. When you have anything authentic from America, be it good or bad, let me know it. My compliments to Mr. Ford and all friends. All our best wishes attend you. Farewell.

P. S. This moment was received your billet of

the 11th. It will certainly be proper to demand of Petrie an *explicit* account of those concurrent circumstances, without any prevarication, or any of his northern wit. If you please to demand of him in my name, to whom I wrote giving an account of the signing of the Treaty, the words and date of my letter, and to whom it was addressed, or who it was that authorized him to—but upon recollection I think it more proper to write to him on the subject myself. Therefore, beg you immediately to transmit me a copy of his letter to you, also what Mr. F.* heard B.† say on this subject and the copy of my letter to Dr. F. which was left when I came away.

The children are somewhat better than they have been, and the two Simons are indifferent. Pray do not delay your answer a single post, least I may be so occupied as not to be able to pay proper attention to P[etrie].‡

TO MONS.^R LE BLANC.

19 April, [1779.]

Yours of the 4th instant did not get to hand by some days so soon as it should have done, by which means several principal people had left this place

---

*W. T. Franklin.   † Bancroft.

‡ Addressed "Monsieur Lee, Hotel d'Espagne, Rue Guingeaud, Faubourg St Germain, à Paris."

before I had an opportunity of talking with them on the subject. However, I have spoken to some about the business, but you know the people of this part are naturally slow, and sometimes over cautious about ingaging in new schemes. They seem however to relish the business as I have represented it to them, and some have promised to make a tryal, but they all object to sending any advice whatever to Versailles of their cargoes or destination, for they recollect the conduct of the English last war with respect to the Dutch, and they are apprehensive that by some means or other, the English may get information of their designs and seize their vessels. Therefore, if that point was insisted on, they declare they cannot attempt the trade. I have therefore ventured to say, that they may be assured their vessels will be freely admitted to trade in the French West India Islands without giving ye information to Versailles, as you desired, and I now wish you to tell me whether this is approved, and whether I may be authorized to write to some sea ports on the same plan. The measures I have taken and shall take, I hope will be productive of good effects, but still it will not be prudent to rely too much on their success; for it will not be an easy matter while the British fleet is the strongest in the West Indies to get your Islands properly and fully supplied with provisions. Therefore every method in your

power should be used, and with the greatest diligence, to accomplish so desirable an end. Some-
how or other all your proceedings, especially with
respect to the Marine, do get very quickly to England. Surely some method might be fallen on to
stop this, at least to prevent such communication
from going by the post, and at least to delay it,
when sent by particular persons. For many
months past two of the cleverest and most expert
clerks have been selected out of the Postoffice in
London, and one of them placed at Harwich, and
the other at Dover, in the post offices there, to open
and examine all the letters that come down there
to come to this Continent, by Calais, Ostend or
Holland. For instance, all the letters, or at least
the greater part of them, that come from London
on the Tuesdays, and get to Dover and Harwich
on the Wednesday, are kept for the packet boat
that sails on the Sunday following, in which time
they are examined, and such as the examiner
thinks proper are returned to the ministry in
London, and those letters that are sent from London on the Friday night and get to Harwich and
Dover on the Saturday, are kept for the packet
boat that sails on the Thursday, and so they go on
in rotation, unless by contrary winds the packet
boat is detain'd long enough for the examination to
be finished.* If some plan similar to this is not

* This statement is fully verified by the *Stevens Fac-similes.*

practiced in France, I am sure it should it should be done; for nothing would be more easy, by stationing a proper person at Boulogne or Calais, and at the last post in France on the route to Ostend and Holland, which would be much better than having it done in Paris. What a great stroke it would have been, had measures been taken to intercept the British convoy, the troops and prisoners for New York. Your letters should not have the Versailles postmark on them.

TO BARON D' ARENDT.

GHENT, 20 April, 1779.

I have had the honor of receiving your favor of the 15th inst., and am sorry that I was so unlucky as to leave Frankfort before you arrived there. I had before the pleasure of receiving two or 3 letters from you from Breslau, that came under care to Mr. Artope, which I should have duly answered had you not forbid it. As far as you have been pleased to communicate to me relative to the intentions of the court where you have been, with respect to us they appear to me much less favorably disposed than they were some time ago; for the free entry of American merchant vessels into their ports was always agreed to, even when our affairs were in the most perilous situation. There were promises once to go much farther, and at present I cannot see any reason that should prevent his Majesty from openly acknowledging our Independence, which measure would unquestionably be of infinite benefit to his dominions as well as of very great advantage to his revenue. I am authorized by Congress to treat with his Majesty, but have no power to appoint a substitute for that purpose, nor is there any person in Europe that has such a power; however, if you find it will be of any use or advantage to the cause of America you are authorized to say that I am now impowered to enter into a commercial treaty with his Majesty, on terms which in my opinion are infinitely more advantageous to his Majesty than what will be granted to any power in Europe a few years hence; and finally I conceive that America, like a rich young virgin heiress, just ripe for the joys of matrimony, should wait to be wooed and not go a wooeing, especially where she has so much more to give than she can receive. . . . *

TO JOHN DE NEUFVILLE AND SON.

FRANKFORT, 22 April, 1779.

Gentlemen:

I have before me your esteemed favor of the 16th

---

* "But I have never yet changed the opinion I gave in Congress, that a virgin State should preserve the virgin character, and not go about suitoring for alliances, but wait with decent dignity for the applications of others." *Franklin to Arthur Lee,* 21 March, 1777.

inst^t. , and hope the city of Amsterdam will succeed at last in bringing the whole seven provinces to agree in supporting a respectable neutrality and protecting their commerce to the full extent of their Treaties with G. Britain. The Swedes do not triffle as your States have done, for I find their Men of War have already convoyed into France a large fleet of their merchantmen loaded with naval stores. I shall always be happy in rendering you any services in my power, and I do not doubt that your house will gain credit and influence in every part of America, if any of the intelligence I have sent, relative to what we did at Aix, does but luckily arrive.

I am well convinced that G. Britain wou'd long ago have given up the point and let your commerce be free and not interrupt it, as they find that France alone with America is more than they can well manage; but the British ministry depend on the P. of O., and some other dependents that they have among you, to embarrass your proceedings and prevent the body of the Seven Provinces from exercising their just rights. Pray did you see Dr. Franklin when you were at Paris? The scheme you propose of small vessels to carry on the American Trade seems to be a very good one, and I will try to get you some adventurers in this Country, but you know the people here are slow in determining, therefore we must work with patience.

The provision trade to the French West Indies I see very little risk in, and a Prospect of great Profit. The vessels should go to Ireland and load beef and pork, salted and clear, for St. Eustatia, and send flour from Holland. This vessel might easily slip into a French Island. Be so good as to forward the inclosed letter to Mr. Stockton, if he has left your city.* I am &c.

TO ARTHUR LEE.

FRANKFORT, 4 May, [1779.]

Just as usual. I requested in my last that *three* papers might be sent to me, and only ONE of the three is sent. However, you seem to have been in high spirits the 27 ult°., and I wish you had given us some hint of the cause, that we might have participated; for nothing very exhilarating appears in our horizon.

Be so good as to let your next cover the copy of

---

* Amsterdam.

"M. Neufville's first propositions were so much out of the way that I could not accept them. He required a fifth part of the loan to be sent over to him annually during the first five years in the produce of America for sale, and the money to remain in his hands as a fund for paying off the debt in the last five years. By this means he would have had the use of our money while we were paying interest for it. He dropped this demand on my objecting to it, and undertook to procure a subscription on reasonable terms." *Franklin to Dumas*, 18 March 1779.

my letter to Doctor F—n which I left with you
when I came away last. 'Tis to be hoped that Mr.
F[or]d's sudden decampment is on some really important object, which may be some small consolation for the disappointment it is to me, as I intended him to be the bearer of the inclosed letter
to Saml. Petrie. * As it is, unless some more
proper person happens to be with you, I must request that either yourself or Ludwell will deliver
it into his own hands, first taking a copy of it, and
then sealing it, if 'tis tho't proper it should be so.
The answer must be insisted on to be given in
writing immediately to the person who delivers
my letter. Of this answer I request you or the
person who receives it to take a copy, whether 'tis
seal'd or not, and let it be kept with the copy of
my letter. The answer you will please to enclose
and direct à Mons.ʳ Duncombe, au soin de Mess.ʳˢ
Freres Overman, Negociants, Bruxelles, and put
your letter under a blank cover directed to that
house. Let me intreat you to be particular in conducting this affair in the manner I desire, for it
embarrasses and perplexes me exceedingly when

---

* "As this Mr. Petrie is a stock jobber himself, and united
with those Americans here, who are in the same line, I imagine
that the having imputed the intelligence to my brother will appear, upon inquiry, to have been originally a trick of these
People, such as is very common in the alley; which Mr. Deane
has converted into a criminal accusation against me." *Arthur
Lee to the President of Congress*, 26 April, 1779.

things are put into an entire different train from the arrangement made by myself. If sickness or something as material does not prevent it, I propose to be at Bruxelles the 15th, where I may meet your answer, and if it should be necessary, I shall proceed to Paris; of this you may judge by the tenor of Petrie's answer. At all events I wish to have a line from you at Bruxelles, where 'tis probable I may not stay longer than the 16th Surely you will let me know when Spain speaks out, as it must have a great influence on my conduct and affairs. We have no certainty of the German peace being signed; tho' there does not seem to be the least doubt of every point being settled on all sides, but the terms are not known here exactly, nor is there a certainty of *American Independence* being a part. From some hints to me here, it is probable that *Beaumarchais* is at the bottom and contriver of the Bastile report in the E[nglish] papers and other things in the Leyden Gazette. Can't he be search'd out? Our best compliments to Mr I[zard] and family. His letter of the 27th. ulto. was received. Madame, Mademoiselle, and the Postilion, &c., are in the usual way, neither very well, nor very ill; tho' the weather is disagreeable for the season. The proclamation of the government of Georgia will show pretty clearly to the rest of America, what they might expect under the British government. A few Scotch adventurers, coun-

cillors, judges, attorneys, secretaries, &c., &c., &c.
Our best love attends you all.

TO SAMUEL PETRIE.

FRANKFORT, 4 May, 1779.

I have been long sensible that many unwarrantable calumnies have been propagated with respect
to me, but I was never able to fix precisely on the
author, or propagator of any of them, until this
day, when my brother, Arthur Lee, Esqr, has
favored me with the copy of a letter from you to
him, dated April 9th, 1779, wherein you say:—

"I well remember reading to him (meaning Mr.
Deane) a paragraph out of a letter which I had received from London, stating that intelligence of
the signing of the Treaty with France had been
transmitted there the very night on which it was
signed, expressed in terms which cou'd not have
been misunderstood, and which intelligence from
a concurrence of circumstances appeared to have
been communicated by your brother, the alderman.
When I show'd the letter to Mr Deane, I meant
only jocularly to upbraid his secresy respecting a
transaction, which I understood your brother had
unreservedly communicated several weeks before."

Now, sir, I do not intend at present to make any
observations on this letter, nor do I intend to be
jocular; but to insist seriously, first, on your giving me explicitly your authority for charging me

with having transmitted to London intelligence of the signing of the Treaty with France, the very night on which it was signed, and which, you add, I communicated unreservedly. Secondly, I insist on your naming the persons to whom in London I communicated this intelligence unreservedly, of the signing of the Treaty with France, the very night on which it was signed. 3dly I desire you will precisely mention those terms which could not have been misunderstood.

To these questions I expect precise answers, without any evasion or prevarication; otherwise you must be considered and treated not only as the propagator, but as the author of this calumny.

The gentleman who delivers this will receive your answer, which I insist on your giving to him immediately, that I may know what further steps to take, being determined to make the business very short.

TO FRANCIS LIGHTFOOT LEE.

FRANKFORT IN GERMANY, 10 May, 1779.

My dear Brother:

I wrote to you from Paris ye 26 of last March which I suppose will go in the Alliance, and this hope will reach Paris in time for the Chevalier de La Luzerne, who is appointed to succeed Mr. Gerard. The letter you will forward, or not, as you think proper, agreeable to what I desired with the original. I only wish you to inform me whether you have sent them or not. The Baron de Breteuil's letter is only intended to enable you immediately to put a stop to any misrepresentations (if any should be propagated) relative to my conduct at Vienna. My proceedings since, I am well satisfied, will appear fully to my honor and credit whenever they are fully enquired into, at least as far as obtaining the general acknowledgment of the Independence of America by ye principal powers of Europe shall be tho't praiseworthy. The 3 sheets from pages 1 to 12 inclusive are intended for your information and R. H. L's. The copys of the letters are faithfull, and you may assert them to be such any where and on any occasion. The remarks and observations on the letters are intended to give you some further idea of the Partys and their proceedings, than perhaps you have already. Some late proceedings with you appear extraordinary, but I am not surprized at them, knowing how deeply a certain great man* (as he is called with you) is leagued with Mr. D.† and his partizans on both sides of the water, in private interested schemes. This may account for ye zeal in attempting to get Hortalez & Co. paid over again their enormous demand. I suppose you know who

---

* Gerard. † Silas Deane.

they are that compose this famous company; for with all the industry imaginable, I can't find out who they are; when things look prosperous, and property is to be got hold of, there are enough of Mr. D's old connections ready to seize it; but when anything is to be done, or money demanded, nobody can find out a single person that composes this company. You may be assured that the *Great Man* wrote to his Principals, when Mr. D—'s first publication came out, that he was unanimously approved in Congress. You know whether this is true or not; but it may serve to shew what confidence ought to have been placed in his Testimony in favor of D. with you, and I think shows clearly that D. would not have dared to do and say half that he has done, if he had not been sure of being backed by ye other. These things, however, will cost our dear country all the blood, treasure, devastation and massacres of this campaign, which I am perfectly convinced would never have taken place—without they had happened to encourage our enemies in making one or more attempt to accomplish their diabolical purposes of subjugating and inslaving America.

By a resolve of Congress in Febry. 1778, the commissioners at the Court of Versailles were authorized to appoint Commercial Agents in ye different parts of Europe. This power is exercised now by Dr. F. as the sole minister at that court, and I suppose his caution will prevent him from giving any formal appointment to his nephew, Mr. Williams,* tho' he may be principally employed in ye mercantile business; but it looks at present as if the plan was forming to appoint *nominally* a Frenchman, named *Peltier Du Doyer*, who has acted at Nantes sometimes as Agent or Head Manager for Mr. Williams in his former transactions, sometimes as agent for Mr. Monthieu, sometimes as agent for Mr. Beaumarchais. I am still of the same opinion now, which I frequently communicated to you and others during my stay in France, that Congress should not have anything to do with commerce on ye Public account—for if they have, individuals, and perhaps not the most honest or deserving of ye community, will receive all the advantages, while the publick funds must furnish

---

*"I have no desire to screen Mr. Williams on account of his being my nephew; if he is guilty of what you charge him with, I care not how soon he is deservedly punished and the family purged of him; for I take it that a rogue living in a family is a greater disgrace to it than one *hanged out* of it. If he is innocent, justice requires that his character should be speedily cleared from the heavy charge with which it has been loaded." *Franklin to Arthur Lee*, 27 March, 1779. When Arthur Lee was asked to state his objections to Williams' accounts, he wrote to be excused, "now that it was no longer his indispensable duty, from concerning himself with a business which is in much abler hands. If Congress should call upon me for further reasons than those I have already given, it will then be my duty to act, and I will obey."

the expense and pay all the loss. Such has been
y̆ issue of such conduct in all times and in all
countries. Therefore, we may safely say it will be
so again. But if ye spirit is so strong that there is
no resisting the torrent, you may surely prevail to
have the political and commercial affairs in Europe
placed in different hands, uncontroled by and un-
connected with each other; that is, in y̆ direction
and management of their separate departments,
each agent to be answerable only to Congress for
his conduct, and both the political and mercantile
agents should be nominated by Congress. The
political agent or minister should have nothing
more to do with money or mercantile matters, than
to obtain money or loans from governments, &c.;
and to supply the mercantile agent with what he
wants from time to time, that he may comply with
the orders of Congress. This plan is so plain, not
in y̆ least complicated, and so unobjectionable,
that I think with y̆ least industry you might be
able to get it carried into execution, and I will
pledge myself that in a very little time the good
effects to the Public will be plainly visible. Therefore I beg you to consult R. H. L, and other sound
patriotic members on it, as well as what follows,
which is of the highest importance.

'Tis now evident that the Peace of America must
be settled in Europe, perhaps at Versailles, where
you have now but one Minister, who will in that

case have the fate of America in his hands. I know that before any peace can finally take place, it must have the consent of Congress; but you and every man will easily see how difficult, nay almost impossible, it will be for America to resist an arrangement for peace that is made between France, Spain and England, tho' America may think it a very bad, injurious and dangerous one. Prudence then directs that every precaution should be taken to prevent such a disagreeable occurence, and without delay: for no one can say how soon, or how late, such an arrangement may take place. The only possible preventative that occurs to me at present is, for Congress by a firm, explicit and positive resolution to order y° minister in France not to approve here, or recommend to Congress, any arrangement or plan of Peace without having previously consulted *all* y° public ministers or commissioners of Congress in Europe, and obtained the approbation of at least a majority of them for such plan. On such an occasion, they might all easily be assembled at Paris, to consult together personally on such a very important business.

On these two points I must beg you to let me know, what you think of them, or may do in them. I really am so totally uninformed about the state that my private affairs are in that I cannot say anything about them; and the uncertainty of what may have been the determinations of Congress

relative to their European arrangements prevents
me from saying anything about myself, or my designs for a future livelihood. For indeed, I cannot form or even think of any plan until I know
what has passed with you, so that you may easily
conceive that only breathing from day to day, is
not the most enviable situation in the world; however, I am every moment attentive in rendering
our country every service in my power, some fruits
of which have already appeared, and more important ones I expect will appear very soon; and tho'
the Tory, Mr. C[arter] Braxt[o]n may choose or
wish to disbelieve it, I can with truth assure you
that our affairs have a better prospect in Europe in
general than they have ever had yet, and I hope
neither folly or roguery in America will put them
in a worse state. I hope soon to hear that Prevost
and his army are either prisoners, or at least driven
out of Georgia. Let America look at the list of
names published by Prevost and Campbell for their
Utopean government of Georgia, and then she must
tremble at the idea of what would have been her
fate had she submitted, or was she now to submit
to the tyrant of G. B. and his Scotch mermydons.

    *   *   *   *   *

P. S. I have furnished you with some materials
and information to guard you against any attempts
that may be may be made to injure our country by
interested and designing men ; but I think Har-

mony should be cultivated as much as possible, at least 'till we have peace, and therefore, unless the public safety renders it unavoidable, all contention should be stop'd in the bud.

TO ARTHUR LEE.

FRANKFORT, 10 May, [1779.]

The letter was to Dr. Fra—n of date ye 9th. ulto. which he has never answered. Ludwell's fame has reached this. The letters have been ever used exactly as you mention, except in the first instance to Mr. I[zard], but if the application in one way would not answer, there was only another, in which they cou'd possibly be used.

I wrote the 8th, and shall expect an answer from the commissioners. * * *

The documents you sent are too informal to borrow money on in this quarter, especially from individuals, which I wonder at, since Mr. [John] King was particularly informed what would be necessary. I presume you have kept a copy of the articles wanted; if you have not, and can find the funds, I will return this. Perhaps *the French Court* may do the thing if properly applied to. I mean to set off to-morrow for *Vienna* but still wish letters to be sent here as formerly until you are advised otherwise. Ludwell should remember that tho' I can sometimes make out he means *the* by two scratches and a dot, it is impossible for me to make out strange names of persons and places by hieroglyphic characters. In the Courrier de l' Europe, No. 34, April 28, there are some curious particulars about Capt. Jones; and it is somewhat extraordinary that the single house attack'd in Scotland, belong'd to the Earl of Selkirk, who from first to last has been alone among the Scotch Lords, a friend to America. If you proceed in the scheme of borrowing money, can't £40,000 sterling, or about 1,000,000 of livres be added for the State of Virginia, in which case the goods they order can be bo't at the best market, and I am quite certain that the whole can be got in this quarter at least one fifth part cheaper than in France. Answer me on this subject.

All here are in better health than my self, travelling perhaps may reinstate me. I have been of some service here, in obstructing a British contract for 2000 troops. Our love attends you all. Farewell.

TO MONSIEUR MARBOIS.

FRANKFORT, 16 May, [1779.]

Sir:

It gives me singular pleasure to comply with the request of his Excellency, the Baron de Breteuil, to forward to you letters of introduction to some of my friends in America, which are now inclosed, and I shall be happy if they prove of any utility to you; for the terms in which his Excellency makes mention of you, give me the most flattering hopes of great and good consequences from your going to America; therefore I sincerely wish you a quick and happy passage, and that on your arrival there you may find everything to your satisfaction.

'Tis very clear now to all the world, that our enemies, the King, ministers and people of G. B., place their chief and only hope of getting again any footing in America, on the dissentions that their emissaries will create, not only in Congress, but among the army and people at large, and by circulating awful falsehoods and insinuations, to occasion distrust between America and her good ally, the King of France, and the French nation.

'Tis therefore evidently both prudent and circumspect on those persons who wish to confirm and strengthen the union between France and the United States of America, and to render their present alliance as durable and advantageous as possible to both parties, to exert themselves in putting a stop to all dissensions and differences in America, as soon as possible. There ever was, and always will be, parties in all governments, particularly in popular ones; therefore they must be expected in America; but I shall be concerned to hear that there is any party existing there, that is designated otherwise than by the names of American, or Whig

Party, and the English or Tory Party: to the first
of these every good patriot will unite himself, as
well as every well wisher to France, for 'tis evident
that the true interest of France and America are
now the same; and tho' I fear America has yet many
severe struggles to undergo, before she happily
arrives at Peace, I have no doubt of her being
finally successful and that she will firmly and
gratefully adhere to her engagements and alliance
with France.   I have the honor &c.

TO FRANCIS LIGHTFOOT LEE.

FRANKFORT IN GERMANY, 20 May, 1779.

I wrote you a long letter ye 10 inst., that with
the inclosures made 3 full sheets, which I hope you
will receive.   Since that (tho' I have not received
a letter from you of later date since May last, nor
one from our brother R. H. L., of a later date than
June) I have heard that my letters to you both of
Oct? 15 ult. have been received, and I hope the
power of attorney that went with them, is safely
received also.   I learn with very great concern that
R. H. L. intended to resign his seat in Congress in
April last, which for ye welfare and happiness of
America I hope most cordially he has not done,
unless it is to fill some important office in our own
particular country.   I should suppose he will have

considered this is as critical and dangerous a time for America as she has yet experienced, and therefore the wisest heads and most honest hearts will all be wanted, to save her from great and impending evils. 'Tis true that some late public proceedings would be sufficient to disgust a man of fair and honorable principles in common times, but in the present moment of peril all private feelings should give way to the salus Respublica. Besides, by a resignation ye wicked ones would gain a triumph, and in short there are a thousand strong reasons against it. You can't say that my practice and preaching are different, for besides the loss of upwards of £6000 sterling of my property, I have given up an honorable and respectable office for life in the first city in ye universe, which no American ever had the honor of filling before me, and in fact sacrificed my own and whole family's peace by entering into ye pubic service. For really ye wonted happiness we enjoyed before has been a stranger in my family for two years past. We breath indeed, and that is all. Y^e wandering and unsettled state we are in, makes our living expensive, tho' it is considerably worse and more disagreeable than ever I experienced before, which makes things unpleasant at the moment, and more so on reflexion, as it is at ye public expense. All this I bear with fortitude from the invincible zeal I have for liberty, and from ye love of my country whose cause I am serving, and shall continue to serve to my latest breath in spite all ye D's, the C's, the F's, the B—ns,* &c., on the face of the earth. I wish only to know the resolution and plan of C: with respect to me, for in a state of uncertainty, it is impossible to conduct my affairs with any degree of propriety. Therefore I beg you will write me fully and particularly every thing that relates to myself by several opportunities, for 'tis of little use to me what is written to our brother at Paris. I do not write to R. H. L., from ye uncertainty of his being at C[ongress], but if he is, with you there, pray give my love to him, and show him this, and also let him know that his four pieces of linen have been bo't ever since Xmas, tho' they are but just sailed for V[irgini]a in ye Govr. Livingston, and addressed to the care of Ellis at G[reen] S[pring]. I can't complain of either of you for not writing to me, because I am sure you have been both fully employed in our country's service; but I must beg that one of you at least will drop me a line by every opportunity, putting it under a blank cover addressed to M^r. Grand, Banquier, Paris.

You will have so much intelligence from Great Britain by the Chevalier de La Luzerne, that I shall only give you my clear and decided opinion, that the war will continue another year, unless we

---

* Deane, Carmichael, Franklin, Braxton.

or our allies gain such decided advantages this
campaign as to bring our enemies to their senses,
for they seem to be more and more enveloped in
folly, obstinacy and wickedness every day. The
British Ministry weak as they are, seem to have
got on the blind side of the Spanish Court, for it
seems pretty clear that they will be duped this year
as they were last year, at least so far as not to declare till 'tis too late to do anything this Campaign,
which is the great object of the British Ministry.
For which purpose they flatter in the basest manner and promise a thousand things, not one of
which they mean to perform.* Our friends in
Holland gain ground every day against the English party, tho' the Prince of Orange is at its head.
Sweden and Denmark have fitted out fleets as well
as Holland, to protect their commerce from the
British piracy, and the Empress of Russia, who
was the only power that they boasted of as their
firm ally in Europe (you know they boast publicly

---

*It was Spain that was duping England, and with consum-
mate diplomacy, holding out the expectation of her complete
neutrality. But France was also deceived by promises of assistance, often promised but always deferred when the time for action came, until April, 1779, when a formal agreement between
the two powers was attained. France was to invade Britain,
and assist Spain in recovering Minorca, her stations in Central
America and Florida ; and neither court was to make peace until Gibraltar had been restored. On June 16th the Spanish
ambassador at London declared war.

and even in P[arliamen]t of their savage and barbarous Indian allies in America,) has lately declared to the British Court, that if any of its ships of war or armed vessels should presume to stop, arrest, or even visit or search a vessel under Russian colors, she will take the captains and crews of such British vessels and treat them as pirates. This is a manly and decided declaration. The peace between the Emperor and King of Prussia is just signed, therefore I can't say as yet with certainty what effect that event will have on our affairs in this quarter. But it is probable the King will look at the business a little longer before he strikes, and I shall not be surprised if he waits to see the issue of this campaign. The Emperor cannot do much without his mother, who at present thinks more of the other world than she does of this.

JOHN BONDFIELD TO RICHARD HENRY LEE.

BORDEAUX, 20TH MAY, 1779.

Sir:

* * * * * * *

It is with concern we have seen the effect of M͏ʳ Deane's imprudence ; giving thereby the most convincing proof of his unfitness to discharge the appointment he filled in the European department, and the justness of his recall, as all the calumnies he has published are founded on suppositions, and being groundless, will of course bring on himself the contempt due to his conduct. As part of his charge against Mr William Lee glances obliquely on the appointment I received from Mr Lee, as his deputy at this port, I hold it incumbent in justice to him, as also to myself, to expunge that part of the charge ; in consequence I enclose to you a certificate (duplicate I have transmitted to Mr Lee,) which you will please to lay before the Committee of Congress charged with the examination of this affair.

Monsieur La Motte Picquet sailed from Isle Daix 7 ins.^t . He has with him five ships of the line, five frigates, sixty armed transports, eight thousand troops, also many American private ships. You will undoubtedly have heard of him before the receipt of this.

An expedition from St. Malo went against Jersey. The alarm was given in England ; the fleet destined for North America, under Admiral Arbuthnot was sent to relieve the Island, by which a diversion was given that will retard the departure of the ships from Europe, at least a month, and will thereby give M. La Motte Piquet leisure to execute his mission without interruption.

Peace in Germany [will soon] be established, by which England and France [will be the] only contending powers.

The unfunded debt, which it's said amounts to upwards of twenty millions sterling, will cramp the operations in Great Britain, and force her to accept of terms, which the longer deferred become the more ruinous.

Ireland appears ripe to tread in the path of America. They have entered into a confederation not to consume or import any of the manufactures of England, until their remonstrances are attended to, so that what with open war, private cabals and empty treasury, Great Britain casts a most dismal aspect. How unforeseen events may change the prospect, time only can evince, for probabilities are against her.

We flatter ourselves convoys will be established to protect our trade with you, and thereby enable us to renew our operations your way, which the obstructions of late have totally stagnated.

I have the honor to be, respectfully, sir, your very hum^{ble} servant,

JOHN BONDFIELD.

TO ARTHUR LEE.

LISLE, 26 May, 1779.

My dear Brother:

I received here this day yours of the 22d and 23d. with the inclosures, and thank you much for the measures you have taken about the sorry creature. *
I send another letter inclosed which you will please to deliver and get his answer, if you judge it proper under the present situation of things, to [?] farther until he says himself he is in a condition to do what is right. Mr. Jenings told me what you say he told you, and I shall be very easy if all the World knows, for I am not afraid or asham'd of what I did. In truth I did ever believe the farce

---

* Petrie.

about secrecy relative to signing the treaty was all a little trick of Mr. Deane's and his Junto's contrivance that they might gamble more successfully in the English funds; notwithstanding this, I never hinted the business to any person in Europe that was a stranger to its beginning and progress, except Mr. Jenings after it was finish'd, and then in such a manner that nobody but himself coud guess at what I meant. Mr. Jenings's conduct and character I fancy is too sufficiently known in America to render an apology necessary for such communication to him. I am sorry for R. H. L.'s determination of resigning, and hope it will not take place until there is Peace, which certainly must happen before next year is ended.

You must be mistaken in the dates of my letters he received. You say they were of the 15 and 21st of October, and that my powers about the estate were not received. Now I find that I did not write to him the 21st of October, and the power went enclosed with my letter of the 15th. of October. Pray clear up my doubts in your next, as I wish to be certain about the safety of the power, and send me the copy of the letter to Dr. F. as soon as you have time, for I want to write to him again on the subject. On this you may write to me at F——t as soon as you please, and give me any other American intelligence that you can, such as the members of Congress now, particularly from Virginia. Who is likely to succeed Henry as Governor? Is General Lee again in actual service? Where is Mr. Adams and Mr. Ford? What has induced R. H. L. to think of resigning? Don't send both my answers to Mr. D[eane] by the same ship. The 4 pieces of linnen for Chantilly are gone in the Gov.ʳ Livingston, and it would be well to send 6 lb. of bark and a few capital medicines, salt. of tart. emet, Rhub., some common purges, opiates, tinct. antimon., &c., for R. H. L. and F. L. L. by the Chevalier de la L[uzerne] or Monsʳ M[arboi]s. Nothing particular has lately happened in my quarter worth communicating to America, unless it is that our friends gain ground in Holland, and have, you know, lately obtained a final resolution of the States General for unlimited convoys, and the declaration of the Empress of Russia to the British ministry that her ships of war shall seize any British armed ship that shall presume to visit or arrest any vessel under Russian colors, and that the master and crew shall be treated as pirates. This is a plain and manly declaration. My return home being somewhat uncertain, I would not have you send anything relative to Petrie from you before the 10ᵗʰ or 12ᵗʰ of next month, that every possible accident may be guarded against, for all letters are open'd that come in my absence. Remember me to all friends particularly to all at the Hotel de Tholouse. Adieu

TO BARON DE BRETEUIL.

FRANKFORT, 6 June, 1779.

Sir:

* * * I have the pleasure to inform your Excellency of the arrival of an American vessel that left Virginia the 1st of May; the captain of which reports that just before he sailed they had advice of a general engagement in Georgia, between the American and British forces, wherein the British army was defeated with the loss of 200 men killed and wounded, all their artillery, which they left on the field of battle, their baggage and tents. That what remained of our enemies were driven back to Savannah, from whence by means of their ships they may possibly escape to Florida. I understand that some supplies for America have sailed with Mon.^r De la Motte Picquet, taking the advantage of his convoy as far as they go together.

Since the pacification of Germany, to which your Excellency's able negotiations have so greatly contributed, has not produced any advantage to America, we have only to guard against any injury that may arise to us from it. Therefore I hope your Excellency will excuse me for again mentioning my apprehensions with respect to Russia attempting to interfere. She cannot indeed hurt America directly, but she may be of some injury to the marine of France, and thereby be the means of incouraging our enemies to continue the war.

I am induced to mention this, because I have just received information which appears to me authentic, that Prince Panin in particular, and his court in general, are inimical to the cause of America.

As the events of this campaign are uncertain, in prudence we ought to look forward in time and prepare for another. France has hitherto gone on with her Peace Establishment, while the expense of our enemies has been enormous, and their credit exhausted; but then we should not forget that by the means of their East India Company, they will next year raise their supplies easier than they did last year: however, a few vigorous efforts on our part will soon end the contest. My idea is that a vigorous and spirited war, tho' more expensive in the beginning, is always the most economical in the end. I remain, &c.

TO HENRY LEE.*

FRANKFORT IN GERMANY, 7 June, 1779.

Dear Sir :

Unfortunate as I have been in not receiving letters from my friends in Virginia for near four years past, yet their *Letters of Exchange* find their

---

* Henry Lee was a cousin of William. He married, 1 December, 1753, Lucy, daughter of Charles Grymes, and sometime known as the "Lowland Beauty" of Washington's early romance. He was the father of "Light Horse Harry."

way, tho' not one farthing appears for the debts
due to me. Among the rest I find one drawn by
you, which surprises me a good deal, because I
must suppose you sufficiently informed to know
that it could not be paid. You are a Legislator and
a Magistrate to render justice to others; therefore
you cannot forget the Golden Law, do to your
neighbor as you wou'd have done unto you. You
have made laws and ordinances (the justice or propriety of which I do not mean to call in question)
whereby all those who owe sterling debts, are authorized to pay off those debts with paper. In that
manner I am obliged to receive many thousand
pounds sterling for money advanced in London upwards of seven years ago, under an express and
positive stipulation that the same should be repaid
in sterling money in London without any deduc-
tion or charge whatever. Now, my dear Sir, I
conceive that regulations and laws made by yourselves, must be equally binding on you as on me:
on the other side, if my debtors are compelled to
pay me in sterling money in London, I shall then
be fully enabled to pay with ease every farthing of
sterling money that I owe, as in that case the balance would be many thousand pounds in my favor.
Therefore all I shall add on this head is, that with
the same commodity, whatever it is, which I am
compelled by your laws to receive for my debts, I
must and can only pay what is due from me. So
far on the justice and equity of your demand.

But it is proper to say a word or two on the impossibility of paying your draft. 'Tis now exactly two years since I left England to enter into ye service of my country, and being suddenly called away it was impracticable to settle my affairs or to collect what money was due me there, almost the whole of which has been detained from me in consequence of my being in the service of Congress. Since 1775, I have not received one farthing of remittances for ye larger debts due to me in America, nor for the produce of the Estate at Green Spring. 'Tis true, that for the greater part of the time since I left England the expence of my living has been paid, but that living has been infinitely worse than I had known for near thirty years before; and the fatigue and vexation beyond comparison greater than I ever experienced in my whole life. My employment 'tis true is honorable, but the reverse of being profitable; therefore, you may now easily determine that it is by no means in my power to pay any debts here that were formerly contracted, even if there was the fullest justice in the demand, and my inclination ever so urgent to comply with your request. The same answer I have given to Col. Mason, and the same I must give to every other person. On cool and calm consideration I have no doubt but that great share of justice and good sense which you both possess, will make you perfectly satisfied with my conduct. The post I

am in I look upon only as placing me as a mark
for envy and detraction, for there are in the world
unhappily too many Mr. Deanes, and C. Braxtons;
but I am much mistaken if either of them would
take my place, especially the latter, who from a
ruined fortune is now amassing an immense Estate
from ye distresses of his country. I have sent to
Congress a full answer to Mr. Deane, which I conceive every unprejudiced and impartial man will
allow to be completely satisfactory, and I hope
they will permit so much to be published as may
be necessary to refute his groundless aspersions.

I must say a word or two about ourselves, tho'
I have not yet had the pleasure of receiving the
letter which I understand you sent by Capt. Robinson. The shining merit of your two sons Henry
and Charles I hear of from various quarters with
infinite satisfaction, especially as your niece has
selected Henry as a godfather to our sweet little
Portia, now two years old, who is lovely as the
rosy morn, and mild in temper as the heavenly
cherubims. Pray let him know this. Our eldest
son, William Ludwell, has all the fire and vivacity
of his grandfather, with too great a portion of his
feeble constitution. Our young son, Brutus,* now
8 months old, has been constantly ill from his birth,
arising in great measure from the uneasy state of

---

* Brutus died June 12, 1779.

mind his mother was in during her whole pregnancy. My dear Rib is better in health than myself, for I am nearly worn down. However we always think of you with the greatest affection, and beg that you and our dear aunt will accept of dutiful remembrance. I beg also to be remembered in the kindest manner to the Squire of Lee Hall, who by the bye can easily satisfy your debt, as he owes me four times as much sterling money as I owe you. As to public affairs, I can only say in general, that ours in particular wear a more promising aspect every day; but this truth you should never lose sight of, that the best security of America will be her relyance on herself alone.

TO ARTHUR LEE.

FRANKFORT, 10 June, 1779.

Dear Brother:

I received yesterday yours of the 3ᵈ and shall be very happy to forward the Commodore's plan, if he will tell me how, or in what manner I can do it. I do not know any of the Marine Society or Hassenclever's address.* He is you know a

---

* Commodore Gillon had a scheme for the relief of Carolina, which appears to have been laid before the American Commissioners. He proposed to use the *Alliance*, then devoted to a special purpose and really not subject to Franklin's orders, and to raise a sum of 1,800,000 livres by subscription throughout France, to be advanced to the State on interest. "I cannot

Schemer and without money, but he talks a great deal and with much confidence, but I much question his being able to bring them into the scheme of the Frigates; however, there is no harm in making yᵉ essay. The Marine Society, I understand, is composed of private merchants. I do not know how you got into correspondence with 155. We have most assuredly been wrong from yᵉ beginning, as he has no more to do with what concerns us than a captain in the army. He continued his correspondence with *Carmichael*, who showed his letters to every one in *America*, that would read them. Perhaps this correspondence is kept up now. Pray give my compliments to the Commodore, and tell him he may command any services in my power.

This moment I received a billet of the 5ᵗʰ with an extract from a letter of Loudoun's, the date of which is not mentioned. If the determination about *Deane* is not made before 61 * leaves *America*, the issue may be different from what is expected;

---

out observe," replied Franklin, "that the agents from our different States running all over Europe begging to borrow money at high interest, has given such an idea of our poverty and distress as has exceedingly hurt the general credit, and made the loan for the United States almost impracticable." *Franklin to Gillon*, 5 July, 1779. Peter Hassenclever appears to have been a merchant in Prussia, perhaps of Embden. See *William Lee to Hassenclever*, 2 October, 1779, *post*.

* An agent of Beaumarchais.

however, such proceedings have generally taken place on similar occasions; but at present I think the same principles that induced to resist one kind of oppression and one set of villains, should operate to persevere opposing another set of perhaps more abandoned villains. Let the determinations of *Congress* be what they may, the wickedness and plots of the Junto should be fully exposed. I hear that in *Virginia* the Cabal prevails as strong as in 122. The reason is plain. Next year the *governor* is to be *changed* and R. H. is to be put out of the question. If the letter of *Deane*, first published in *New York* Gazette, and your brother's in Gazette, do not open men's eyes, they must be determined to continue blind. As to *W. Lee*, he thinks at present, as he tells me, of giving up all concerns with public life as soon as the affair is decided in *Congress*, whatever complexion that decision may be of, as it does not appear to him that he can be of that service which he wishes. * * *

TO SAMUEL W. STOCKTON.

FRANKFORT, 13 June, 1779.

* * * You must have seen many American papers and got a good deal of particular Intelligence from the 4 captains, all which I hope you will communicate fully to me, as you know that an American paper hardly ever gets here, and that the in

telligence from Paris is generally very imperfect
and unsatisfactory. 'Tis a happy thing that Prevost has got a drubing in time, for now it appears
that the plan of our enemies was to keep on the
defensive during the Summer, while Butler & their
savage Allies were ravaging the frontiers, and in
the winter Prevost was again to commence his
offensive operations. By a hint in an old English
paper it seems as if the Enemy had received a considerable repulse by Moultrie at Beaufort, wch I
never heard anything of before. In England they
say positively in Parliament, that Spain has decidedly joined France, but I do not hear with certainty as yet of any movement that proves this, or
that has committed Spain ; a few weeks, however,
must surely clear up all doubt. * * * The new
French Minister, the Chevalier de La Luzerne, left
Paris on the 3^{d} ins^{t}., but from what port, or in
what vessel he sails I do not learn, nor can I learn
what is become of Mr. Adams or Mr. Ford. Dr.
F——'s appointment as sole minister took place in
September ; thus Mr. Adams has been left ever
since unnoticed, which appears unaccountable and
very surprising.* It seems the Prince of Orange is

---

* "The alderman is recalled, or rather dismissed. One resolution of Congress was to recall him and Mr. Izard, and this was
followed by another that they need not return; so that they are
properly dismissed, and their commissions totally vacated.
Prince Arthur will be left unrecalled and unemployed, so that

determined that the Dutch trade shall not have unlimited convoys. This business must come to something serious at last. Pray enquire and let me know what writer in French gives the best account of the French negotiations with Holland, and their Wars from the treaty of Westphalia in 1648, to the treaty of Ryswick in 1697, particularly during the period of the famous Pensionary John De Witt : for I do not know any English book that treats fully of the points. You never yet told me who first put into the hand of 100 the copy of what was done at Aix.* I should like to know what additions or alterations are made.

TO ARTHUR LEE.

F——T, 14 June [1779].

The vessel is gone, for *Saint Eustatia*. £150 sterling is *incurred*. 170 has *paid* more than his *share*. He wants £200 *Sterling*. Prepare for this on which you will hear farther in a little time.

Mr. Stockton now at the Hague intends to cross

---

the family compact will be totally broken. If Roger could be disposed of in a similar way, with one or two more, all might yet go tolerably well. But of late a minority, and that a small one, has been able to oppose successfully any vote, and often to carry it in Congress against a large majority of the members. This is certainly a solecism in the political world." *Silas Deane to his brother*, 16 June, 1779.

* The treaty of Lee with Neufville.

the sea soon, and wishes much to be charged with
your dispatches if you have any to send—Indeed,
he would wait some time for them. His address is
Chez Madame la Veuve Loder, à la Haye, and if
Mr. Pringle has left you, you can send Mr. S. a
letter or two of introduction by the post, as I mentioned to Mr. Izard the 5th. instant. You will
oblige me by sending a letter or two of introduction
to Mr. Stockton, if you have no public dispatches
to send.

Mr. Sayre is at Amsterdam which is all I hear
of him, except that he had the command at Copenhagen of as much money as he chose. How he
obtained this I know not.* The 7th. instant
another vessel arriv'd from Virginia at Amsterdam,
but she sail'd before the one that bro't the account
of the Victory gain'd in Georgia. There is now 4
or 5 American vessels at Amsterdam, some of which
stand a good chance to get safe. Pray tell me the
date of Loudoun's last letter, and also particularly
the date of my letters that R. H. L. acknowledges
to have received, for what you wrote me before
must be a mistake. As the business with P[etrie]†

---

*Sayre had written to Franklin for employment, but the
Dr. replied that it was not in his power to give him "any employ worth your accepting." *Franklin to Sayre*, 31 March, 1779.

† "As this Mr. Petrie is a stock jobber himself, and united
with those Americans here who are in the same line, I imagine,
that the having imputed the intelligence to my Brother, will

must be decided somewhere in this country, there can be no after claps, nor subsequent testimony necessary. Therefore what *A. Lee* mentions about that does not hold ; however, if he sees any impropriety in his being present, he had better not attend. Mr. Pringle* would surely be a very proper person, if he is in the way, as I suppose 172 was shy and declared off. The 3 following things I must beg you to get immediately :

1st. 172's state of what he says is the fact, in writing and signed by him.

2d. to ascertain whether S. P[etrie] had not the same disorder on the 10th of May that he has since complain'd of.

3d. A copy of what Sam. Wharton gave to Mr. Izard denying what had been imputed to him relative to stock jobbing.

172 should state how the letter was signed and to whom it was directed.

The whole of the business when fully and fairly

---

appear upon enquiry to have been originally a trick of these people, such as is very common in the Alley, which Mr. Deane has converted into a criminal accusation against me." *Arthur Lee to the President of Congress*, 26 April, 1779. Petrie refused to reply to William Lee's demand, and was promptly challenged. The challenge was accepted, and a place near Valenciennes named for the meeting. Lee, accompanied by Mr. Pollard and Dr. Bush, was there on the day, but Petrie did not appear.

* John Julius Pringle.

stated, so far from being criminal, is in my opinion at least innocent, if not commendable, but the wretched junto by mentioning a little, omitting the most material parts, adding a good deal of untruth, and insinuating a great deal more, endeavor by such vile tricks to support their horrid plots. I pray you to tell me if the Baron De Breteuil from Vienna, is come to Paris. Mr. Grand, being his banker, can tell you. Is Mr. Adams and Mr. Ford gone, and in what ships?

Our dear little patriot Brutus now rests in Peace. His time here was very unpleasant, but I trust he has amends now. His mother feels his loss. Best compliments to Mr. I——d and family, and love to Ludwell. Farewell.

TO HENRY LEE.

FRANKFORT IN GERMANY, 14 June, 1779.

Dear Sir:

I had the pleasure of writing to you pretty fully the 7th inst., relative to your bill on me in favor of Capt. Robinson, since which, I received your favor of the 27th of last February, wherein you state the injury you would sustain by receiving your debt in Virginia in paper @ 33½ difference of exchange. How much greater injury then shall I sustain by being obliged to receive several thousand pounds of sterling debts at the same rate. As for instance your brother, yᵉ Squire, owes me £200 sterling for money advanced long before my debt to you commenced. I owe you fifty odd pounds sterling. Now supposing I am to receive my debt in paper, and pay you in Europe, it will take the Squire's £200 sterling debt and about £30 sterling more to pay you your fifty odd pounds sterling in Europe. So much for yᵉ Justice of my paying what I owe with cash in Europe, while by laws made by yourselves, I am obliged to receive paper for what is due to me. One word only on the impossibility of paying in Europe, which has been fully explained in my letter of the 7th, to which I will only add, that the commissions I have hitherto received for doing the public business for two years past does not amount to seventy pounds sterling. * * *

You can hardly want any reply from me to Mr. Silas Deane's libel, since I see a very sufficient one in yᵉ Virginia Gazette of March 5, under the signature of Detector, which it would appear Mr. Purdie has inserted with some reluctance. What Detector says relative to me is perfectly true, but he might have gone much further, and said that Congress in February, 1778, put the superintendence of their commercial affairs in Europe under the care of the Commissioners in France, and that Dr. Franklin, as *sole* minister Plenipotentiary in France, is now exercising that authority alone. Indeed the only thing like a charge of criminality that Mr. Deane mentions against me, viz., of my bargaining with the commercial agents appointed by me to receive a share of the commissions they charged for doing the public business, is proved to be totally false and groundless by certificates from those agents, already sent to Congress; and I have also proved that Mr. Williams, whom Mr. Deane praises so much, made the very bargain with Mr. Thos. Morris, relative to the public business, that Mr. Deane charges me with, which bargain between Mr. Morris and Mr. Williams was approved by Mr. Deane. Congress has my answer in full, but I can't help observing that this very insignificant character could never have occasioned any ferment, if unhappily there had not been too much combustible matter ready to take fire from the least spark. Whether the guineas of the enemy have worked this effect, time will show; as to myself, I am perfectly easy, being conscious of having served my country and its cause with strict fidelity and disinterested zeal; and before the enemies of our name have a right to clamor, let them show what profit or gain any of us have made at the public expences. The fact is, that the Tories ever have and always will hate the Whigs, and those Whigs that have been most active and constant in their country's cause, will be the first objects of Tory Vengeance. My fervent wish is, to see all private animosity give way to Love of our Country, and that every heart and hand may be united in defence of its liberties and independence, which our enemies are working as hard to destroy now as they ever did. * * *

TO CAPTAIN JOSIAH ROBINSON.

FRANKFORT IN GERMANY, 14 June, 1779.

* * * It would be a sensible satisfaction to me if I could give you the least useful information relative to the prize money of Capt. Lambert Wickes. 'Tis true I did endeavor to get some account of his prizes, but to little purpose; the first prizes Capt. Wickes made, were all in the hands of Mr. Thos. Morris, and his agents, but I never could find any regular or the least intelligible accounts kept by Mr. Morris relative to these prizes, or any thing else. The second prizes Capt. Wickes made were in company with Capts. Nicholson and Johnson; as there were many of them, and it was supposed they were valuable, Mr. Deane tho't proper to appoint Mr. Jonathan Williams to take the sale of these prizes out of the hands of Mr. T. Morris. This, as might naturally be expected, created great confusion in the business, Mr. Morris getting possession of several of the prizes, and Mr. Williams of others, one of which was a very valuable, well found, and almost new brig. Each of these gentlemen, I suppose, sold what they got

possession of, but I could never get the least
account of their proceedings from either of them.
Mr. Jonathan Williams, I believe, is still at Nantes,
and also Mr. John Ross, who as attorney for Mr.
R. Morris, of Philadelphia, has possession of all
the books and papers of the late Mr. Thos. Morris.
To these gentlemen, then, you can apply for the
accounts you wish. * * *

_____

TO _____

17 June, 1779.

Dear Sir:

The cruel and unmerited treatment that you
have received not only from those who you have
uniformly endeavored to serve, renders an apology
unnecessary for the proposition I am now going to
make you; but I will premise that it gives me a
solid pleasure in reflecting that I have in some degree the power of showing you the gratitude I feel
for your unwearied services in the cause of Liberty,
and the general rights of mankind. That the success of the horrid and savage war, which Lord
Bute, his pupil, and his minions are carrying on
against America must inevitably put an end to the
remaining liberties of Englishmen, is a truth now
so clear to the commonest capacity, that it is impossible to suppose your penetrating mind has
not viewed it in this light long ago; and tho' that

kind of antipathy between a Frenchman and Englishman which was commenced and has for a long series of time been cultivated with so much art, that it has now almost become a natural passion in ordinary men, your liberal mind and good sense must despise such weak prepossessions, and induce you to look on all mankind as that are occupied in a commendable and glorious cause, as your friends, and worthy of every aid in your power to give them; at least, while they are so employed. For this reason I presume you can have no objection to undertake to give me regularly the information I want, if it is in your power to procure it. I wish, Sir, to have the earliest advice of all the determinations and designs of the British Secret Cabinet, of every plan of operation against America and her allies, as soon as it is concerted, or even proposed, with an exact account of all the measures and force that is planned to carry the operations into execution. An exact and immediate account of every expedition or attack that is designed against America or her allies, with the force proposed to execute them. The secret instructions given to the Commanders by sea and land, as well as to Ministers and Governors abroad. Every secret negotiation that may be proposed, or attempted to be carried on with foreign powers. The *real* contents of the despatches received from their foreign ministers, from their commanders by sea

and land and governors abroad. In short I wish
to have immediate and accurate intelligence of
every movement in the British Secret Cabinet, and
of all secret intelligence that may be conveyed
there from every quarter. In the prosecution of
this plan, particular attention will be necessary to
the Admiralty and Secretaries of State's offices,
tho' perhaps if a key cou'd be found to the Secret
Cabinet itself, it will be the shortest way of going
to work, as well as the surest. The vague reports
in the public papers, and even what is going on in
the ports and dock yards, are not of such moment
as to require great attention, unless in particular
cases, where there may be a collateral proof of the
soundness of the secret information.

In order to enable you to execute this plan, I will
engage to furnish you with £200 sterling every
quarter of a year, and besides, when the importance of the intelligence requires it, you may send
an express to some part of the continent, as shall
be hereafter pointed out, the expence of which express shall be repaid to you, exclusive of the £200
p. quarter, the time of which will commence from
the date of your answer saying that you will undertake this business, and the first £200 shall be remitted as soon as possible after the receipt of the
first secret intelligence you shall communicate. If
you undertake this business, your answer need
only say, "I have received a letter of date —, the

contents of which are agreeable and shall be complyed with." Direct this to "Mr. Thos. Tomlin,"
put this under a cover directed thus "A Mons.ʳ
Richards, chez Mess. Frederic Miller et fils, Negociants, Frankfort sur Maine," and send it by the
common post via Ostende. I believe it will be
necessary to frank this letter in London.

I have taken proper measures that this letter
shall get safe to your hands without being opened,
which may occasion its being longer than the usual
time per post on the passage, and when I write
hereafter by the post, it will be in such a manner
that if opened no danger or inconvenience whatever shall happen to you. On your part you will
take such precautions as prudence shall require,
but I think it may not be amiss to give you an
alphabet, with the use of which you may write by
the post, without danger of discovery

a b c d e f g h i j k l m n o p q r s t u v w x y z
i j k l m n o p q r s t u v w x y z a b c d e f g h

In this alphabet use the letters (when writing) of
the second line to mean the letters of the first line,
and when reading, suppose the letters of the second
line are always used for the letters directly above
them in the first line. As for instance, King of
France may be written thus sgvownnzivkm, and
sometimes to render the decyphering almost impracticable & and ᶮ may occasionally be introduced
between the letters in the same word, and are to

have no meaning. Knowing the conveyance to be safe, I have written freely and fully; nothing remaining to be added but directions how to address your letters of information by the Post, and where to send the express when one is necessary, all which I can do by the ordinary post, as soon as I know your determination, in such terms that nobody but yourself shall understand, even if it should be opened, of which at present there is no great danger. * * *

I think the orthodox creed of every true Englishman should now be, success to the Enemy, until our liberties are secured, our Constitution reform'd, and Scotch tyrants brought to condign Punishment. The immortal Hampden, &c., aided the Scotch, then called the natural enemies of England, to begin the War against the tyrant Charles the 1st., and the godlike Russell and Sydney leagued with France to save their country from the attempts of the abandoned Charles 2, and infamous James 2, to destroy it.

TO SAMUEL W. STOCKTON.

FRANKFORT, 17 June, 1779.

Dear Sir:

I am much obliged to you for your favor of the 11th, and the intelligence it contains. You had from me long ago the outlines of 100's schemes and wishes; it is most probable that he will be disappointed, for ye reasons you mention, and I shall be greatly deceived in ye men if he is not left in the Lurch by those who have held up to him the flattering prospect. The intelligence about Ireland appears to me a visionary romance, not worthy of the smallest credit; if it was true, he that could divulge it in ye present state of the business as supposed, or even c^d give ye most distant hint about it, must be either a Fool, or a knave, perhaps both; but being as I conceive altogether a Fiction, it appears to me an edged Tool, that is more likely to do mischief to him that plays with it, than any body else; however, it may be adviseable for you to get the precise words of the Letter, its date, by whom written and to whom addressed, all these I should wish to know. I could wish also to have it clearly ascertained y^t the K. of Prussia has agreed to furnish IN *the French seaports* wood for building ships, when it was made, and how long it is to continue. If 'tis certain, perhaps our business may bear pressing home in the north. Letters in this town from good hands speak that Spain would make her declaration to ye British ministry on the 11th or 12 Ins^t of openly joining France, and consequently America. If this has been done, you must know it with certainty by the time this reaches you, but, from the profound and universal Lethargy that has seized the King, M[inistr]y, and

People of England, I don't think this will awaken
them.—The cannon must rattle in their ears at St.
James, to bring them to their senses. We are not
in luck, or else by one stroke the war might have
been ended—Arbuthnot and Darby with 15 sail of
the Line, the N. Y., Quebec and Newfoundland
Fleet, about 400 sail, went out of the channel the
30th of May, and D'Orvilliers with 28 sail of the
Line, besides Frigates, sailed from Brest the 3d. of
this month. Had he sailed the same day that Arbuthnot did from Torbay, they might easily have
met, when the business must have ended the war.

Deane's libel has occasion'd much heat in America. No dispatches from C—, but it is said ye late
President Laurens, and Mr. Penn, members of
C— for N. Carolina, and one of Mr. R. M[orri]s
partizans, have had a duel about their political disputes. This is much to be lamented; however, I
still hope they will not neglect the main business
and prepare a proper reception for Master Clinton
when he attempts to steal out of his hive. You
may see in ye London Even^g [Post?] the beginning of this month, an insolent Letter to Govr Liv-
ngston from C—^{r} Common Sense has given Mr.
Deane several repeated chastisements which you
may see in the Remembrancers, if you can get
them. * * *

TO ARTHUR LEE.

[FRANKFORT ON THE MAINE],
20 June, [1779.]

Lord Granville, the wisest man and ablest minister of his time used to say, that he did not think any intelligence worth attention that was not accompanied with dates. Neither the date of Philalethe's letter or the date of its publication are given. I wish you had mentioned T. Digges' direction, for I have written months ago two letters directed as he desir'd, neither of which he has answer'd ; therefore, I suppose he has not receiv'd them.*

I do not see of what great use the certified copies will be to meet this vague charge. As the name of no particular person is mentioned, and the word *Friends* is used, so that these wretches may say their denial only goes to Mr. T.†—Nor does this agent of Mr. Williams mention by whom or where in France this *creditable report* was made ; therefore it must come to a simple denial on my part, until they are more explicit and come to particulars, when they may be convicted of falsehood and defamation. That such a report may have been in the circle of the Junto at Nantes is possible enough, but the truth of that report I most posi

---

* Digges was then in England.

† Major Thornton.

tively deny. Indeed, the whole of the letter consider'd and Cutler's confession of his agency, is sufficient for any impartial man to see the falsehood and intent of the charge. This plot is what I expected in consequence of the mortal offence the Treaty with H[olland] gave at P[ass]y, and you see how soon the enemies were set to work, to prevent C[ongress] from authorizing me to conclude that business. If C. will be duped by such flimsy artifices, there is no human prudence or rectitude of conduct on my part that can prevent it. This credible report smells too strong of Mess. Williams, Johnson, and Ridley and Ross, to doubt of the manufactory. Mr. Jenings came about the same time from London as Mr. Ridley. Does he know anything of this business? I can't help thinking the determination on Deane's affairs will be different from what F. L. L. apprehends, for I greatly fear the Cabal have deeper designs, viz., of selling our country as the Scotch did their king for English gold, and a flagrant injustice for D. would ruin their main design, as it might open the eyes of the world before things were ripe for execution.

We have London papers to the 12th, in which there is nothing new that is material. Poor Conyngham of the Revenge is at last taken and carryed to New York. Will Mess. R[oss?] and H[olker?] claim the property now?

I observe what is said about M. M—t, on which

you will hear farther another time. We expect
every post will now bring something interesting
from your quarter. We send you our love and
best wishes. Adieu. (No signature.)

P. S. By the time you receive this old D[umas]
will be in *Paris* or at P[ass]y with a *treaty* with
Holland; in which it is said some trivial alterations are made in what was done before, but with
no further confirmation or authority.

TO SAMUEL W. STOCKTON.

FRANKFORT, 20 June, 1779.

Dear Sir:

An anonymous writer, under ye Signature of
Philalethes has published in the Pennsylvania
paper, the following Letter:

BOSTON, 21 November, 1778.

To the Hon. Silas Deane, Esqr :

Sir, Agreeable to Mr. Williams's request I have to
inform you that I arrived from France with his accounts to lay before Congress, with a letter and other
papers to them, and two letters for you, which I am
to deliver to you; that honor I shall have as soon as
the weather will permit. At the time I left France
(the 28th Sept.), it was credibly reported that Wm.
Lee, Esq., then alderman of London, had wrote his
friends there, that he should not resign his gown, as
he intended to return and take it again, and convince
the world that he had while in the service of America

been acting for the good of England as well as of the United States.

I am with respect, &c.,

SAMUEL CUTLER.

You will no doubt agree with me that so vague a charge, and coming professedly from an Agent of Mr. Deane's party and so foolishly brought in neck and shoulders as to show clearly that it was coin'd to answer ye momentary occasion, cannot have the least weight on candid and impartial minds; but when people are heated, the most absurd and ridiculous fictions are sometimes by design, sometimes from blindness, taken for clear and decided truths. This Mr. Cutler I never before heard of, but he tells us himself that he is Mr. Williams's agent sent over by him to America to settle his Accounts with Congress—those accounts which my brother, A. Lee, would not settle in France, thinking them unjust and unwarrantable. Hence one cause of Enmity against me. Another cause you know, and may remember that I told you when we were together in Paris in September last about the T[reat]y with Holland, that I expected some attempt would be made to injure me in consequence of having succeeded in that business and you see I was not mistaken, for the plot was lay'd before the month ended. Tis not easy to bring direct proof in contradiction to the false charge meant to be insinuated by this letter of Mr.

Cutler's, or to convict him of being a false reporter; for he does not mention the name of any one in France, who made this *credible report*, nor does he give the name of any *one of my friends* in London to whom I wrote ; therefore such an insinuation can only be met by a declaration from those who being most with me, are the best judges of the probability of the truth of it. If you have no objection I think something like the following by way of Letter to a person in America, would answer the purpose :

Sir:

The following letter having been published in the Philadelphia papers by a writer under the signature of Philalethes, viz: (here should follow yᵉ letter). Altho' I am no partizan, nor ever will be a party man, yet justice and truth call upon me to say that yᵉ charge meant to be convey'd against Mʳ W. Lee by the above letter, is totally in my opinion void of foundation. I lived with Mʳ Lee in Germany from June, 1778, to March, 1779, during which time his whole conduct and conversation was directly contrary to such an idea as returning to the exercise of the office of Alderman of London, which I know he could not do, after what he had done for America, unless like a suicide, he had chose to hang himself. As a convincing proof that the charge against Mr. Lee is unjust, I can assure you that to my personal knowledge he sent to London in November last a formal resignation of his Aldermanship.

This you are at liberty to make as public as you please. I am, etc.

Such a letter sent to Dr. Witherspoon, and enclosed open to Dr. Wm. Shippen, Junr., of Philadelphia, to deliver, by two at least of the American vessels now at Amsterdam, may answer the purpose of defeating this calumny. I have only to add that if you have any kind of repugnance to this measure, I do not by any means wish you to take it, nor would I have you on any account say one word relative to me, that you do not most sincerely believe to be just and true.   *   *

TO RALPH IZARD.

FRANKFORT, 20 June, 1779.

Dear Sir:

I wrote to you the 5th, which you ought to have received when you favored me with yours of 11th, for which I hold myself much indebted, and must again say that your letters are so explicit and satisfactory that they give me more solid information than any correspondence I have. I have the highest opinion of F. L. Lee's clear and penetrating judgment of men and things, yet I can't help thinking with you about the strength of Mr. D's party, unless they have at bottom the design of selling our Country to our Enemies, and they may fear that a hasty determination in favor of Mr. D.

may open the eyes of the people before their plans are ripe for execution. Whatever is the real fact, the consequences I am afraid will be fatally injurious to America, unless M. de La Luzerne gets over in time to prevent it. It gives me much pleasure to find that your judgment of that gentleman corresponds with y⁹ character I have of him from various quarters where he is known, and I hope you and my brother have both given him and Mr. De Marbois particular letters of recommendation.

We have London papers to the 12ᵗʰ, but not one word of the Spanish declaration, nor even a rumor that it was expected. Had Monsᵣ D'Orvilliers sailed from Brest the same day, and with the same wind that carried Arbuthnot and Hardy from Torbay, they might easily have met, when at one stroke the war would have been ended, without the assistance of Spain. There was timely notice of Arbuthnot's situation and design, but I think we have not hitherto been in luck with our naval operations. Don't you think that everything relative to America had better be sent in the first instance to Millar, for the London Evening, than to Almon? This man, besides that he is not in my opinion friendly to our cause, plays so many tricks as a publisher, that the intelligence is seldom so public as it ought to be. You say our letter about Folger's despatches is perfectly satisfactory, but how? is the iniquity cleared up, or the thief discovered and held up, as he ought to be, to public infamy? You have no doubt seen Phila letters (the date of which, or that part of the Philadelphia Paper it is in I do not know) with Mr. Sam! Cutler's letter to Mr. D. Who this Mr. Cutler is, I know not; unless he is a clerk of Mr. Williams's, nor where he picked up what he calls his *credible report*, unless it was among the Junto at Nantes. I foresaw that the deadly offence which the negotiation with H[ollan]d gave at P[ass]y, would make me a marked and odious man; I said when at Paris on that business in September last, that some plot against me would certainly be contrived, and you see it was so before the month expired; and one obvious design of this report was to prevent C. from intrusting me with the conclusion of the business with Holland. But Mr. Cutler's letter is sufficient of itself to convince any impartial man of Common Sense of its falsehood and folly. In the first place I must have been a perfect idiot to have wrote that I intended to do that which all the world, as well as myself knows I cannot do; secondly, if I had wrote what Mr. Cutler so obligingly imputes to me, to several persons, for he says friends, his *credible reporters* might easily have mention'd the name at least of one of those Friends, when it would be very easy to have convicted them of falsehood and defamation; however, it is some comfort that I have a copy of my resignation dated the 13th of Nov.,

1778, and Mr. Stockton copied my letter to the Ward on that occasion, of both which you have a copy inclosed, and of which you will please to make mention in your first letter to America. For my own part, I am of opinion 'tis not an improper use of time to be employed in clearing up the infinity of aspersions that flow from the fertile Junto; every moment should be employed in searching out their villainy, and guarding against their machinations to ruin our country. As to my post, poor Devils, they are heartily welcome to it, but with all their creative faculties I am much mistaken if they do not find it a barren and unproductive occupation. * * *

P. S. Pray send me a copy of what you had from Sam. Wharton relative to the stock jobbing business.

RALPH IZARD AND ARTHUR LEE TO WILLIAM LEE.

PARIS, June 22d, 1779.

Sir:

We had the honor of receiving your favor of the —, in which you ask our advice relative to an application to the King of Prussia to comply with his promise, made through his Minister, Baron de Schulenburg, "that he would acknowledge the independence of the United States as soon as France had done so," and whether it would be proper to change the channel of application from Baron de Schulenburg to the Minister of Foreign Affairs.

It is with great pleasure that we contribute whatever is in our power to assist your judgment in what so materially concerns the public good.

We are of opinion that in the present state of expectancy from Spain, it will be prudent to wait till her example also, has given encouragement to the Court of Berlin, and contributed to counteract the motives from Russia, which withhold that Court from pursuing its interest and inclination in openly espousing our cause. That when it may be proper to move the question, the promises should be touched with delicacy, by stating that the good will towards us, which the King had formerly declared, having been suspended in its operation by the war in Germany, you hope that their objection being now removed, he will not delay to give the world a decided proof of his sentiments, in the acknowledgment of the independency of the United States of America, which cannot fail, by the weight of such an example, to stop the further wanton effusion of blood.

As the King of Prussia is in fact his own Minister, we should imagine that it might have a bad effect to change from Baron de Schulenburg, whom he seems to have appointed to transact this particular business. But in this, a knowledge of the actual situation of that Court must decide, and of that we are not informed.

We wish you every success in this important negociation, and are with the greatest esteem, dear sir, yours, &c.,

RALPH IZARD,
ARTHUR LEE.

TO RICHARD HENRY LEE.

FRANKFORT IN GERMANY, 24 June, 1778.

My dear Brother:

'Tis a long while indeed since I have received any letter from you, tho' I hear that our brother at Paris has received a letter from you dated in February, and another from our brother F. L. L. dated ye 22 April last. I know little of their contents, except that you both had a design of quitting C.—Whatever you do in this respect I cannot find fault with, because I am so well satisfied of ye good sense, solidity of judgment, and fixed attachment to ye cause of Liberty and our Country, which you both possess, that I am sure you would not take such a step unless you found it impracticable to do ye good you wish, and that it was necessary to do so for your own honor; but I must lament from the bottom of my soul that such a necessity should exist. The imprudence, the folly, the barefaced contradictions and falsehoods, so conspicuous in the publications of Mr. Deane and his partizans, would not in temperate and well regulated times, have afforded conversation for a day: and his daring abuse and insult to Congress would have met with the censure and punishment that it so obviously deserves. From what causes the present temper arises, you on ye spot can determine better than me at a distance; for I am not willing to credit Govr Johnstone's assertion that his pecuniary and *prom-*

issory operations last year have produced their effect; but let y.ᵉ cause be what it will, our dear Country will feel at least y.ᵉ bad effect from it of this campaign, which I sincerely hope will not turn out as our Enemies expect. You and our dear brother have certainly reflected, that in all cases that ever happened in the world, in y.ᵉ least similar to the present case of America, plotting and wicked genius's have started up who, by cunning, treachery and villainy, have too frequently deprived their Country of that blessing which everything has been risqued to preserve. The first step always was to traduce the first leaders, and endeavor by every possible means to get them out of the service of their Country, that their wicked game may be played without obstruction; for these considerations I shall still hope that you and our brother, who stood foremost in the risque of life and property, to save our country from the cruelties of the British Tyrant, will still persevere in endeavoring to rescue her from the infamous designs of her present more insidious and not less dangerous internal enemies.

With respect to myself, I am perfectly indifferent about what may be the determination of C., for I know that my *real Honor* cannot be tainted but by a bad action, committed by myself. If I am relieved from my present employment, I shall have more leisure, and perhaps more opportunity of searching out and exposing to public view the parricidal designs of some people against their country. If I should be continued, unless I receive the thanks of Congress for the negociations with Holland, I shall certainly resign, altho' my cares and solicitude for y.ᵉ general welfare of my Country will not be in y.ᵉ least abated. I have sent by two conveyances a full answer to Mr. Deane's letter published the 5th. December, and a memorial he gave in to Congress the 12 Nov.ᵗ so far as they relate to me; at the same time have exposed to view some of his plots and those of Dr. F. It would seem by some American papers that what they make the most noise about respecting me, is relative to the Aldermanship. The Common people in America may possibly not know it, but it is hardly credible that D. and his Junto should be so dreadfully ignorant, as not to know, that after having been publicly in y.ᵉ service of C., it is not in my power (whatever might have been my inclination) to return to ye exercise of y.ᵉ Aldermanship of London. These brawlers will be hushed, when it is publicly known, that above two years ago I quitted the Aldermanship of London, to enter into the service of my country, and finding that they would not proceed to choose another alderman in my room, I wrote to the Lord Mayor and Court of Aldermen in November last, desiring that they would proceed to have another Alderman elected. This will prove

what credit is due to Mr. Deane's agents, as well
as the folly and wickedness of Mr. Williams' clerk,
Mr. Cutler.

The commission of 5 per cent. charged by y^e
agents appointed by me and Mr. Williams charging only 2 per cent., seems to be dropped by y^e
Junto; I suppose, because they see from Mr. Williams's accounts that he has charged 5 per cent.,
which he did in consequence of an agreement he
made with Mr. T. Morris, which agreement Mr.
Deane knew of and approved before he went from
France. What wretches then are these people?*

You may see in Mr. Deane's letter of the 5th
of December, he insinuated that our brother, A.
L., gave information of the signing the Treaty
with France the very night it was signed, and then
gives the copy of a letter which he says a *gentleman of character* told him, his correspondent in
England had seen. By an intercepted letter of
Mr. Deane's since publish'd in the New York
Gazette, it appears that this *gentleman of character*
was a Mr. Sam! Petrie, the son of a Scotch merchant in London, and also a great intimate with

---

* "Your testimony with regard to Mr. Wm. Lee is fully sufficient to remove the suspicion of his sharing in your commission. I mentioned it not as a charge against him, but as an
excuse for you; five per cent. being, as I understood, more
than double of what is usual." *Franklin to Schweighauser*,
17 September, 1779.

Fordyce the Banker, that made so much noise in
London by his Bankruptcy in 1772.* This Mr. S.
P., after making his father a bankrupt, and ruin-
ing the whole family by his extravagance, &c., for
which reason to this moment he has not been able
to obtain his certificate, came to Paris in 1777,
where he has lived ever since in a pretty expensive
stile; by what means the world in general does not
know. He soon became a retainer to Mr. Deane
and his party, from mutual motives of Interest,
which were pretty evident to those who knew their
objects. Mr. S. P., on being questioned by our
brother in Paris relative to this business, has
deny'd it positively so far as it relates to him, but
as I am absent, he has changed his ground and

* The London *Chronicle* of 11 June, 1772, announced that
"Mr. F———, the banker, who disappeared early yesterday
morning, with an immense sum of money, we are informed,
has not been heard of." He was said to have remained with
his clerks all the preceding night examining his accounts, became convinced of his bankruptcy, borrowed largely upon the
credit of the house, composed of Henry Neale, William James,
Alexander Fordyce and Richard Down, of Threadneedle Street
Bank, and left the kingdom. His flight was followed by a run
upon other private bankers, and many failures resulted. The
deficiency was stated to be some £34,000, and his wife sacrificed
her property to make it good, but the firm was gazetted as
bankrupt, June 20, 1772, and Fordyce's real debts amounted to
upwards of £200,000. He was receiver-general of the land-tax
for Scotland, and the government claimed his estate at Roe
hampton.

says now that he understood the letter was written by me ; therefore to stop the operations of ye Junto on this head, I will state the fact so far as I am concerned, which you may make public whenever you see occasion.

When I left England in June, 1777, Edmund Jenings, Esq., of Maryland, stayed there. This gentleman's attachment and services to his country and its cause, are too well known to you, as well as to many gentlemen in Maryland, particularly to Mr. Carroll, who was in Congress, and Mr. Carmichael, now in Congress, for me to mention them here. Mr. Jenings and myself kept up a correspondence together, the whole object of which was the service of America. Some time after the Peace was signed I wrote to Mr. Jenings, letting him know that our business was finished, in such terms (not those which Mr. Deane has mentioned) that no person breathing but Mr. Jenings, or with his interpretation, could understand what was meant; and besides, the letter was signed by a fictitious name and addressed to a fictitious person. This letter was sent by the common post, and, as a proof that it was not sent the same night that the Treaty was signed, the 6th of February, 1778, was Friday, and the post from Paris to London only goes twice in the week, on Mondays and Thursdays, at 10 o'clock in the morning. This is the plain matter of fact, which is essentially different from one of Mr. Deane's household writing over to London, *before* the Treaty was signed, and mentioning ye precise day on which the Treaty was to be signed; desiring his correspondent to make his speculations accordingly. Of this truth Congress must before now be in possession of proof. This fact proves the true motive for Mr. Deane's talking to those who were not of his cabinet, about keeping ye business of ye Treaty a secret; it served also another end, being made use of by him and Dr. Franklin as a pretext why Mr. Izard and myself should not be communicated with on the subject, and why we should not be furnished with copys of the treatys, agreeable to the order of Congress. I always tho't, and still think, that if Mr. Gerard did mention anything about secrecy in ye latter stage of this business, the thing was suggested to him by Mr. D. or Dr. F., for the reasons above mentioned. However, 'tis a notorious fact, that ye Treaty, its commencement, progress, and conclusion, was a subject of general conversation in Paris, nor was it possible to be otherwise when the proceedings were so extraordinary and open to numbers.

About 10 or 14 days ago, Monsr Le Chevalier de la Luzerne sailed from France for Boston, to replace Monsr Gerard; by him you will know that Spain has at last determined to take an active part with us, and that a really formidable fleet sailed from Brest y⁰ 4th Inst., to join y⁰ Spanish fleet that is still more formidable, from Cadiz and Ferrol. The first object of their operations is still a secret. The British grand fleet is not, that we know of here, yet gone from Portsmouth. Adm! Arbuthnot sailed out of y⁰ channel the 30th of May, with 5 ships of the Line, the Experiment of 50 guns, some frigates, and about 300 transports and merchantmen—The latter for Quebec and New York, the transports with near 8000 troops, and provisions, for New York. Sir James Wallace in the Experiment, with 4 or 5 frigates, are to cruize all the summer from the capes of Delaware to Georgia, to intercept the commerce, while Clinton is to pursue his operations by land with the aid of his savage allies under Butler. All these attempts I hope you will be prepared to meet, for, now Spain has declared, it does not seem within the chapter of possibilities, that our Enemies can be able to carry on another campaign in America, since they have not one ally in Europe, but on the contrary, have by their uncommon insolence and general piracy on all nations without distinction, made those who were formerly their most zealous friends, at this time their decided foes. Ireland is also on ᵗᵉ eve of a general revolution.

The Chevalier de la Luzerne and his secretary Mons. De Marbois, have so high a character wherever they are known, that I am sure you will find them with sentiments and conduct such as you would wish them to be. This change proves the sincerity of the Court of Versailles, and it is much to be lamented that such a character had not been the first representative of his most Xtian majesty in America.

We have hardly got settled in this country from the late tremendous clamor of war, but in a few daies I expect to hear something decisive from Berlin relative to our affairs, which prevents my writing to C. by this uncertain conveyance; but I must say that in my opinion the King of Prussia, as well as ye H. of Austria, Holland, &c., will wait ye issue of ye present campaign, before they take a decided part with us. This you may be assured of, that ye more evidently America appears able to support herself, the sooner she will find friends in Europe, and I am of ye same opinion now as at the beginning of the contest, that our best security was, and is, in our own efforts, constancy and unanimity. With respect to Mr. D. and his partizans, I think the best way will be to expose their wicked plots and designs, without spending too much time in replying to the infinite number of falsehoods that they propagate, for every hou they coin something new in their fertile manu factory. . . . *

* "Your city, since it has been honored with the residence o Mr. Deane, seems to have been the seat of confusion and dis

TO RALPH IZARD.

FRANKFORT, 25 June, 1779.

* * * The French captain's tale about yᵉ situation of affairs in South Carolina, does not seem very credible; they have in England letters and papers from New York to May 6th, and later, from whence it does not appear that they have yᵉ least idea of Prevost's being able to advance into South Carolina; on yᵉ contrary he must be distressed, as Hopkins with a squadron of frigates, had taken two transport ships laden with stores, provisions and

cord, which I am not surprised at, for I believe if it were possible that he, or one or two more of his party, could get into Heaven itself, they would breed dissension and discord even there; however it is for the sake of humanity, for the sake of our country, much to be lamented that things have been in such a ferment, and yᵉ minds of men so heated by such an insignificant object as Mr. D., because from that source will flow all the miseries and calamities of the present campaign in America, which it is very certain our Enemies would never have undertaken, had they not been encouraged by what has passed among you last winter. That Providence which has hitherto so remarkably protected America from yᵉ attempts of her external enemies, will I hope still lend her benign influence to protect the heavenly cause of Liberty and America from the parricidal attempts of those, who now are aiming their secret and mortal stabs against yᵉ existence of both. The Whigs must all firmly unite, to save their country from yᵉ secretly united efforts of the public enemy without and yᵉ private enemy within." *William Lee to Dr. William Shippen,* 24 June, 1779.

"I can't help expressing my indignation to see how much

presents to ye Indians, 3 brigs, and 2 schooners, with goods and provisions from New York to Georgia. Their greatest hopes seem to rest on their copper colorer'd allies, the Indians, who indeed may do a great deal of mischief. If they continue this horrid war, I think retaliation will be justifiable, and I am sure it is in yᵉ power of America. St Johns in Newfoundland can burn, and yᵉ. Negroes in yᵉ West Indies can cut a Scotchman's throat as well as an Indian savage can knock out yᵉ brains of a helpless American infant.

---

relyance our enemies have on yᵉ effects of yᵉ dissention their agents and emissaries have created in Congress. On a motion of Sir W. Meredith's, yᵉ 11th inst. in the H. of C. leading to Peace with America, which was overruled, G. Johnstone said, he saw great hopes of yᵉ Colonies returning *separately* to their dependence on G. B. The people were for it in general; and it was only yᵉ Congress, who from ambition and selfish views were against it. Lord G. Germaine was in high spirits and bold, declared his aversion to treat with Congress, but his hearty desire to treat with the Provinces separately or any body of Americans; that yᵉ King by the Prohibitory Act had authority to *grant Pardons*, &c., therefore there was no occasion for any farther Parliamentary authority. He knew from yᵉ *best authority*, that the Congress were divided into parties; and at this hour, if it was not for the fear they stood in of Washington's army, a *part* of that Congress would offer terms to G. B. Thus you see, the old maxim, divide et impera, is still their sheet anchor, but God forbid that the Liberty and Independence of America should depend on yᵉ Tyrant of G. B., or on the pleasure of W's army, or any army in the world." *William Lee to S. W. Stockton*, 24 June, 1779.

English papers to ye 15th, say nothing decisive about Spain, whose conduct to me has been, and is utterly inexplicable.   I already set it down that all ye bluster will end in smoke, and nothing any way decisive be done.   Poor America will alone feel the most dreadful horrors of war.   *   *   *

END OF VOL. II.

LETTERS

OF

WILLIAM LEE,

SHERIFF AND ALDERMAN OF LONDON; COMMERCIAL AGENT
OF THE CONTINENTAL CONGRESS IN FRANCE; AND MIN-
ISTER TO THE COURTS OF VIENNA AND BERLIN.

———

1766=1783.

COLLECTED AND EDITED BY

WORTHINGTON CHAUNCEY FORD.

VOL. III.

BROOKLYN, N. Y.:
HISTORICAL PRINTING CLUB.
1891.

CONTENTS OF VOL. III.

1779.

TO SAMUEL W. STOCKTON.

I wrote to you the 24th with some letters for America, all under cover to M^r. D. N.,* and last post, the 25th, bro't me your favor of the 21st., which informs me of your design of going in ye Virginia pilot boat being changed. You would surely have found a welcome reception in America, had you been the bearer of the news of the declaration of Spain, which as I told you before, would not rouse our enemies from their lethargy and from their thirst of gorging themselves with American blood. The opposition in England seems as much besotted as the King and his ministers. Indeed the wickedness, ye villainy, and profligacy of these People seem to surpass those of Sodom and Gomorrah; however, it will certainly be of use to carry as quickly as possible to America ye Parliamentary debates, and the Revolutions of Sweden, by Sheridan, should now be read with attention by every man who has anything to do with public affairs in our country. I am not at all surprised that the captains in the service of a certain house in Philadelphia,† should be impregnated with ye heat that has been created in America by Mr. Deane and his

---

* De Neufville.   † Robert Morris.

partisans, for in fact ye business has totally changed from its original appearance. The issue is not now, whether Mr. Deane shall glut his personal vengeance against whom he looked on as ye principal causes of his not returning with charte-blanche as minister Plenipotentiary to Holland, and General Commercial agent and Director over all Europe; but whether those who have fingered more than half ye amazing number of millions (Mr. Deane says about one hundred) that America now stands indebted, shall escape scot free, and without rendering any account—Mr. Deane, for many millions received in France, and his chief patron in Philadelphia for ten times as many millions received by him in America. Of course this enormous sum of money must have procured ye Principals many advocates and defendants: however, I can't help having many apprehensions, that these unhappy circumstances will be attended with most fatal consequences this year to our Country, for you do not say one word about measures taken to provide against this campaign, and against the horrid Indian war. The Spanish declaration having come so late, all ye force that our enemies have, will for this campaign at least, be employed against us alone. I have seen in ye Virginia Gazette, in March, a very full reply to Mr. Deane's charges against my brother and me, under the signature of Detector, the writer I know not, and am told that there have been many satisfactory replies in y. Pennsylvania Papers which I have not seen. * * *

TO BENJAMIN FRANKLIN.

FRANKFORT, 27 June, 1779.

Sir:

By the letter you did me the honor to write to me y. 17th inst, I perceive you are still under a mistake relative to the contract made with D'Acosta & Co. There never was to my knowledge any contract made with that house for the same things that I requested you to apply for to the French Ministry on account of the State of Virginia. D'Acosta & Co contracted to send some thousand fusils and other trifling articles for the State of Virginia, which they expressly stipulated to ship from France before the end of last September; otherwise the contract was to be entirely void. This house failed to comply with their contract, and even without making any apology or giving any reason for so doing, which I have since tho't a most fortunate circumstance, not only for the State of Virginia, but indeed for America, having authentic information that within the course of 12 months past many thousand fusils have been sent out from Leige to a clerk of that house, many of them of so base a quality as to cost only seven livres, the fusil and bayonet. In my judgment it is an unpardonable cruelty to put such implements into the hands of brave men, who are not only fighting for their own lives, but in the defence of the liberties of their country. The most important part of the supplies that the French ministry are requested to furnish for the State of Virginia are the cannon, howitzers, powder, mortars, ball and shells, none of which have ever been contracted for with any one, and if they should be sent to Boston or Charlestown for Congress, they cannot be of any more use to Virginia while the War continues and the enemy have the superiority in the American seas, than if they were in France, and as the principal military operations this year will most likely be in the southern States, there is much reason to apprehend that the want of good fusils will be severely felt in that quarter. I therefore hope you will endeavor to get the supplies requested sent to Virginia as soon as possible, since they may even now be got there before the campaign is ended. In doing this you will certainly render an essentia service to the common cause, and highly oblige him who has the honor to be with very great re spect, Sir, &c.*

---

* When the application of Virginia was first made, William Lee being absent, Franklin found three merchants of standing each of whom was willing to fill the entire order. But tw withdrew their offers when they learned that Arthur Lee wa concerned, and the third was not given the contract. Lemair

TO ARTHUR LEE.

F——T, 29 June, 1779.

You have enclosed Gov. Henry's letters of 1 & 22 Dec.ʳ '77, & 3 Mar. 1778, all by Capt. Le Maire. W. L. to Dr. F. of 30 Mar., and 27 June '79. Dr. F. to W. L. 30 Mar. & 2 April, '79. There can be no doubt of a stab being intended, and that both are yᵉ objects. The same thrust is to kill us both, and I have had so little share in the business, that I do not know what defence to prepare; therefore, shall wait till I see farther what is done. 'Tis probable Le M. will be the conveyer as well as the administrator of the poison. I have mentioned to you often what I tho't extremely reprehensible in his conduct about the contract at Strasburg, which is all I know about him. I have no papers or letters of any kind relative to C——t, nor ever had, except copys of the two notes for £20,000 and £30,-000. A gentleman here told me that Ch[aumon]t abused Beau——s to him in the grossest terms; if these two fall out, 'tis better to let them alone in exposing each other. No notice having been hitherto taken of a joint letter to *Izard* and *A. Lee*, I shall

---

was sent over Germany to look for credit and goods, quarrelled with Lee, who finally agreed with Penet and D'Acosta for the articles, and fell again into disputes with these merchants. *Franklin to Governor Henry*, 26 February, 1779, and *to William Lee*, 2 April, 1779. In the *Virginia State Papers* will be found much relating to Lemaire's mission.

mention it this day to *Izard*. Mr. Jno. Temple is expected every day in an armed Brig from Boston. He had been at Congress, therefore 'tis probable he brings despatches. The Spanish declaration so far as words go is rather against than for the United States of America, since they are still called the K. of G. B—n's colonies. We send you our love.

P. S. This moment received yours of 23. Your inclosures answer the most material parts. The charges in *America* seem now to be more against *W. Lee* than *A. Lee*, of whom *Adams* does not seem to have said anything. However I am glad you have found in time that my judgment about his conduct and designs was not wrong. What 172 has said appears to me sufficient; for my own part I shall never be ashamed or afraid of the real truth being publickly known; but there is no occasion to gratify the vile Junto, by telling them the fact. I am almost exhausted by drafts from Virginia for payment of old scores, while sterling debts due to me are pay'd off in paper, the exchange being now 10 for one. If I go on I shall not have one shilling left here. Necessity will therefore compel me to stop my hand; however, I could wish you would in conversation mention this to *Izard*, and ask him if he does not think I shall be fully excuseable, both in justice as well as law, to send the Virginia bills back as they come. Most of the debts due to me were by contract to be repay'd in sterling money in

London, clear of all charges or deductions whatsoever. . . .

TO ARTHUR LEE.

7 July, [1779.]

My dear Brother:

I wait with impatience to receive the bills I wrote for in mine of the 25th ulto., as the money is now wanted. I pray you therefore not to delay sending it to me.

You may remember I told you in Paris in March, that the Invasion of Virginia was intended, which a friend of ours would not believe, because I was not at liberty to tell from whence I had the information; but what is surprising, a letter I put into the Po: office there, giving advice of this to go to Virginia by the way of Nantes, was never forwarded. The declaration of *Spain* is strangely worded at this stage of the business; tho' the present shyness may be accounted for, as *America* is bound by the separate articles, while *Spain* is totally at liberty. There may be also other motives which time must clear up, but I think you should try every means to get an authentic copy of the ultimatum that was rejected by *Great Britain*, which will prove the true design of *Spain*.

Mathew's expedition was surely intended to favor the operations of Prevost. The mischief to individuals is considerable, but I am inclined to think it will ultimately be of service to the general cause.

Mr. Temple must surely have given you a full account of the state of every thing in America, and I shall be happy to hear that they have not forgot to take proper measures for this year's operations. It is very possible that all the supplies will fall into the enemies hands, for the Capt. is among the unlucky ones; but had they been in the country, they might have shared the fate of those at Portsmouth, where it does not appear they had anybody to take care of them.

Sir G. Collier may be a good seaman, but his letter does not show him to be much of an officer, or to be overburthend with sense or judgment.

The alarm in England is great, and thro' all their blustering you may see a great deal of fear, if the combin'd fleets do not trifle their time away, but quickly advance and destroy Portsmouth and Plymouth docks with ease. *Carmichael* is I suppose coming to fill his snug post of S[ecretar]y, while Du[ma]s and 11, are both eyeing a residency in *Holland*. Our best compliments attend Mr. Iz[ar]d and his good family, and our love is with you. Adieu

(No signature.)*

---

* Addressed to "Honble Arthur Lee, Esqr &c., &c., Hotel d'Espagne, Rue Guinegaud, à Paris."

TO SAMUEL W. STOCKTON.

FRANKFORT, 8 JULY, 1779.

Dear Sir:

I have now before me your favor of the 30th ulto. My last of July 1st. will show you that I do not take amiss an open and candid letter. The English proverb is a good one, "that nobody can tell better where the shoe pinches but he that wears it." The trials I have had for two years past are rather too much for a temper naturally quick, and for one that feels for liberty and his country as I do. The intrigues and practices that I found at Paris, and which instead of decreasing have since spread wider, 'till at last they seem to threaten the existence of our country as a free and independant nation, have left me few peaceable or calm and temperate moments. But enough of self. "Speak of me as I am; nothing extenuate, nor set down aught in malice. I have done the state some service; and they know it." Mr. Temple must surely have brought some later intelligence from C[ongress] than you mention about Mr. D[eane]; for that you know I mentioned to you above a month ago. The fatal effects of the dissensions now begin to appear. As you know I mentioned to you in the beginning, I do not hear of any preparations for this campaign, while the Enemy, tho' considerably weaker than they have been for 3 years past, are almost unopposed, making ravages over the continent. Nothing yet from *Berlin*. It cannot be expected that the powers in Europe will be in a hurry to form connections with us, while they see the consequences of Mr. D's publication and some subsequent affairs, in the great advancement of the enemies forces. You no doubt have seen the London Gazette with the accounts of the invasion of Virginia. What the enemy have done is of little consequence, only that it is a good station as long as they can keep it for obstructing the whole trade of Virginia and Maryland. The French and Spanish fleets are joined, but what will be their operations we do not know. A little fleet of 7 sail under American colors, commanded by Commodore Jones, about 200 guns and near 1500 men in the whole, were seen the 20th. ulto, in the Bay of Biscay, opposite the mouth of the Garonne, which leads to Bordeaux. We shall soon, I suppose, hear something of its operations, which I wish may be in the flames of Glasgow. America should act like Rome who, leaving Annibal and his victorious army in Italy, sent Scipio to fight their enemies at the gates of Carthage. I am clearly for an invasion of G. B., and leaving Clinton and his savage allies to do what they can in the meantime in America. The thing is certainly practicable if men would but accustom themselves to look at it calmly; therefore, I hope you will make it a subject of general conversation when you get over. If you learn anything comfortable from the gentlemen lately arrived from America relative to the general capacity and preparations for defence and offence this campaign, I beg you to let me know it. Clinton cannot now have at N. Y. more than 5000 effective men; what an opportunity then is there for general Washington to make an attempt on that nest of Pirates. Mr. Carmichael is, it seems, expected in France every day, as he was to sail some time in May. What post he comes to fill we do not hear.

TO M. BARTHELEMY.

FRANKFORT, 12 July, 1779.

I have had the pleasure, my dear sir, of receiving the letter you did me the honor of writing to me the 1st. of this month, and congratulate his Excellency that he did not suffer very materially by the explosion of the powder magazine near him, which I see by the Gazettes did a great deal of mischief. How much better would it have been, had the contents of this magazine been safely lodged in the possession of our friends in America.

I rejoice heartily with you at the decision of Spain, which gives us a right to expect a successful end of our dispute with Great Britain; but as I never like to flatter myself too much with the prospect of advantages for fear of being disappointed, my opinion is, that the most decided and united efforts of France, Spain and America should be exerted to reason. By the American war their funds have been pretty well exhausted, but they have this advantage, that their troops and navy are in full practice, while France and Spain come into the field after a long idle peace, which always makes both soldiers and sailors a little rusty: therefore if our joint enemy should unexpectedly gain some advantages in the beginning, it will not discourage me in the least; notwithstanding the phrenzy for privateering among our enemies which trains a number of seamen for their navy, yet I know the resources both for men and money in France and Spain are infinitely greater than in Great Britain.

Reflecting on that period of history when Louis the 14th invaded Holland by the intrigues of the Stadtholder, almost all Europe was combined in a league against France, as if her king was attempting at universal Monarchy; I am astonished to see that now when G. Britain insolently and loudly claims the universal monarchy of the sea, all the maritime States of Europe sit still and leave France and Spain to contend for a freedom of navigating the open seas, in which all those powers are as much interested as France or Spain Can you tell me to what causes such extraordinary apathy and unconcern in the maritime states of

Europe are to be ascribed? 'Tis but the other day an Austrian merchant vessel bound to Ostend, was boarded by the crew of an English privateer, who robbed the Austrian vessel of sundry articles and beat the Flemings because they had not more good things on board their vessel. This is a fact that can be easily proved at Ostend.

You are pleased to say that you have nothing to tell me from the country where you are;* I did suppose that after the declaration of Spain, the disposition of the good people where you are would have become more favorable to America. However, we must wait with patience, for I cannot suppose they will continue much longer blind to their own interest. By this moment some great blow may be struck, if 'tis against the fleet of Sir Charles Hardy. I cannot help flattering myself that it will prove a coup de grace to the naval power of our enemies—in the pleasing contemplation of so fortunate a circumstance, I have the pleasure to assure you of my most perfect esteem and friendship.

---

* Barthelemy was at Vienna.

TO RALPH IZARD.

FRANKFORT, 12 July, 1779.

Dear Sir:

I have had the pleasure of receiving your obliging letter of the 2d., and thank you for the copy of
Mr. Wharton's letter, tho' until that gentleman
mentioned the subject to me I never knew that
fertile geniuses among their other inventions had
dubbed me with the title of stock jobber. However great a secret the fitting out and destination
of Commodore Jones' squadron may have been to
you, I see by a letter from Edinburg, the 15th of
June, that the whole was no secret there. One 64
gun ship with the squadron, would certainly enable it, if so designed, to settle the business easily
in Georgia, Carolina, and Virginia. What General Lincoln is about I can't tell, but this seems
clear to me, that if he does not attack Prevost,
Prevost will attack him, and he that begins the
attack, almost always gains the advantage. The
refusal of a passage to Mr. F[or]d* is of a piece
with sending an express from 16 to 12 in the beginning of *March* just before *W. Lee* got to *Paris*
with advice of 61 being *recalled* &c without letting
Izard or *A. Lee* know anything of it. This
arrived at 12 in a short time. These and similar

---

* Rev. Hezekiah Ford, who had served as Arthur Lee's secretary. Serious charges were made against his loyalty from
Virginia.

facts should be well noted, as they may be of use at one time or another. I told you before that the conduct of *Spain* was inexplicable to me; it may be found out in the recesses of *Passy*. I wish most heartily that *America* was out of the scrape. Mr. Stockton will escape Sir George Collier, as he goes in an armed brig to Boston. I wish Mr. Ford stood as good a chance, tho' in a small vessel he may escape if he gets into the capes at night. Pray tell me if my first defence went by him on the Chevalier de Luzerne. I wish the same game may not be continued in 28 *Congress*. I wrote to M. de M[ar]b[oi]s inclosing some letters of introduction, to which he never gave any answer.

By this time, I suppose, you must have had from Mr. Temple a full account of the situation of affairs in America, tho' my letters from Holland do not mention whether he is bound to Paris or London; he is said to have been much on the reserve, and to speak very little on public affairs, which of course you know will make warm spirits conjecture a great deal, tho' I rather conclude that there was not a great deal material to say. The New York papers mention a great deal of mischief done by the Indians, whom they call their good allies, and that Clinton has taken the field, which I do not believe, as he can't have more than 5000 effective men, and leaving N. Y. &c. nearly defenceless. We are all impatience to hear of the movements of the combined fleets, tho' few people will believe that an invasion is really intended, notwithstanding all the noise and talk about it. You will see by the papers what general terror there is in England, where nobody seems to have acted a consistent part but the city of London. You must allow that the Duke of Richmond has improved in *brass*, if nothing else, from the lectures of his tutor, Gov. Johnstone. He says that after their money is all gone, they may learn from America what can be done with paper. Can his head be so thick as not to know that they have been supported by paper these 50 years past, and that at this moment their specie does not bear so high a proportion to their circulation as one to a hundred? How much farther they will be able to stretch this string before 'tis snap'd, will be proved in a year or two more.

When you have any important news, we hope to hear from you, as 'tis hardly possible that this summer can pass away without some important events taking place, and of this, I think, we may be most certain, that unless the British possessions are attacked with vigor this summer, in the winter and spring they will attempt some bold desperate stroke against the possessions of France or Spain. for as L'd Chatham by a trope conquered Canada in Germany, so his grace of Richmond must trope also and *conquer* America in France and Spain.

I fancy *Carmichael* is coming to enjoy his snug

post of secretary at *Passy*, but I shall be much mistaken if he stirs from where he is until *Deane's* affairs are determined, which I wish was done, let the issue be what it will. For the time already wasted on such a worthless subject will cost *America* many, many millions of money, and many, many innocent lives. Your next will tell me, I expect, of the proper advances having been made by *Spain;* if there are not, don't you think that *A. Lee* should write there? but if he does, I am of opinion he ought first to consult *Vergennes* and act by his advice. Such a step with 164 will please him better if done verbally than by letter. . . .

TO ARTHUR LEE.

FRANKFORT, 14 July, 1779.

The packet boats from Dover to Calais were stopped last month, and two French mails then due if sent over to Dover, are to be return'd back to Calais (that is, I suppose after the letters have been examined); by the way of Ostend your letters and newspapers from London will be a day later than before. The English ministry and people seem to be terribly frightened, and know not well what to do. Wedderburne says peace must be won by conquests abroad, and hints that America must still be the prime object, where the plan of Clinton seems to be to amuse Washington by preparations and attempts 'till he gets his reinforcements, than to attempt at securing the whole North river from N. Y. to Albany. Prevost and Mathews are to be employed in making diversions as well as they are able, to prevent any aid being given to Washington from the southern states. Two British regiments are sent from New York as a reinforcement to Mathews. If the North river can be secured, the latter end of this campaign and the next, the great force is to be turned against the four eastern states. This is the plan against America. Orders are already sent to attack the Manilas. The opposition in Parliament have outrun the Ministry in delivering up everything unconditionally to the Crown, and a bill of Lord North's for doubling the Militia, thrown out as to that point by the Lords; among whom were the opposition and most of the Bedford party. So that Lord North seems to totter and the opposition seems to be in hopes of catching a crumb or two. Rutland, Derby and Ancaster have offered to raise regiments. They were insulted at the first offer, but they seem to be in a way to accomplish their point. The Common Council of London seem to be the only consistent body in the Kingdom. They agreed to address the King, which was little more, when drawn up, than telling him in plain terms what a wretch he was, and how wicked his ministers were, and that they ought to be immediately dismissed. Afterwards they agreed not to address, and not to open a subscription in the chamber to give bounties to seamen and soldiers.

Sir Charles Hardy's fleet is to be augmented with ten ships of the line, which from appearance will join him before there is any movement from Corunna; his fleet has already taken some prizes off Brest and Belle Isle, among them a Virginia boat of 60 tons, Capt. Luner commander, with goods from Nantes, bound to Virginia. I hope this is not Mr. Ford's vessel. The fleet from the Streights and Portugal of 30 vessels are all arrived safe, and the 10 East-Indiamen, expected now every day, I suppose will do the same. A very large fleet from the West Indies are expected from the 1st to the 20 August. The N. Y. Gazette has made hearsay of Lincoln's being totally defeated and driven from Parisburg; but this with other absurdities seems to me to be coin'd in England to keep up their spirits. I expected by this time to have heard from you what Mr. Temple brought from America, for surely he must have wrote to you or Dr F—n. A passenger in the same vessel says that people's eyes in America began to be opened with respect to the conduct of Mr. Deane.

If you have not yet, I presume you soon will hear something from *Spain*. If the great line is not pursued and Jamaica not attacked, surely from the Havannah an expedition to St. Augustine and

Georgia should take place. The paper will tell you that Sir J. Yorke has made a demand of the States General for the succors stipulated by treaty. I have no doubt of their being refused. British cruizers are prohibited from staying more than six days with the prizes they take in the Portuguese ports; they should not be permitted to enter at all. I wish the French ministry would be made sensible of the mischiefs that arise from their privateers ransoming almost all the prizes they take, by which our enemies have almost double the number of sailors prisoners that France has, and if the privateer is taken, the ransomers being on board, the whole profit of the cruize is lost. Some French privateers have been taken with 10 or 12 ransomers on board. The American privateers are also extremely wrong in discharging their prisoners gratis, while their countrymen are dying in the English jails for want of being exchanged.

TO RALPH IZARD.

FRANKFORT, 17 July, 1779.

I wrote to you the 12th; since then I find that two other vessels from Boston have arrived at Amsterdam. They sailed the latter end of May, for they bring papers of the 27th of that month, in which there is nothing materially new, except accounts of some horrid ravages by the Indians on the frontiers of Pennsylvania and New York. Mr. T[em]ple is gone to Spa. The passengers that came with him think he has not any regular commission, but that he expects to meet at Spa with some person of consequence from England to confer on American affairs. If this conjecture is well founded, it will in my opinion be highly injurious to America; for our enemies are so thoroughly faithless and perfectly wicked, that they never should be treated with but in open conference. These private and underhand conferences only give them opportunities of learning how they may more effectually pursue their infernal plan of seduction and propagating fatal divisions.

This is the state these gentlemen give of Mr. D——ne's party in Congress. The Delegates of the 4 Eastern States (who know him best) in general against him; Pennsylvania divided; Maryland for D.; Virginia divided; N. Carolina for D; S⁰ Carolina divided; Georgia, for D. My first short reply to Mr. D. sent from hence via H⁴ in February, is arrived in B[osto]n.

The packet from Dover to Calais being stopped, you perhaps have not yet got into the method of having the English papers by the way of Ostend. An express sloop is arrived at Portsmouth that left Byron at St. Lucia May 14th. Government has had published everything, but it seems fair to conjecture that D'Estaing has had some advantage, for the captain of the sloop says that after the two fleets had cannonaded each other for some time without any material damage on either side, the two fleets returned to their respective ports, Byron to St Lucia, and D'Estaing to Port Royal.

A 14-gun sloop, the St. Helene, politely set out of Brest the latter end of last month, found her way into Sir Charles Hardy's fleet and carried with her some of the French signals and advice of the Spanish force that had joined Count D'Orvilliers at Ferrol; on which Sir Charles returned to Torbay for reinforcements, where it is supposed by this time ten other ships of the line have joined him; so that his force may be now 40 ships of the line. If he remains there, it is a fine place for such a genius as De Ruyter or Heemskirk, commanding the united fleets, to give a finishing blow to the naval power of Great Britain. Letters from Holland say that the States are determined to maintain strict neutrality, notwithstanding the demands of our enemies for succor, and the urgent endeavors of the Prince of Orange and his party to engage them in war. Amsterdam continues as firm as a rock with us.* . . .

---

* "I hear that our haughty and imperious enemies, the British nation, have demanded assistance from your States, to enable them to continue the War that they have began against France, Spain and America. This demand I have no doubt will be refused, as it is quite clear to all the world that they

RECALL OF LEE'S COMMISSION.

Congress had appointed a committee composed of a member from each state, to take into consideration the foreign affairs of the United States, and the conduct of the late commissioners. The members were Whipple, Gerry, Ellery, Ellsworth, Duane, Fell, Searle, McKean, Paca, M. Smith, Burke and Laurens. Their report, as presented on the 15th of April, gave the following conclusions :—

1. That the commissions of Franklin, Arthur and William Lee and Izard were in force.

2. that ministers plenipotentiary should be sent only to Versailles and Madrid.

3. that complaints had been made against the commissioners, and of Deane's political and commercial conduct.

4. that suspicions and animosities had arisen among the commissioners, which may be highly prejudical to the honor and interests of these United States.

5. that the appointments existing be vacated, and new appointments made.

6. that only one plenipotentiary minister or commissioner be at a foreign court.

---

have wantonly made the attack on France and Spain, therefore they can't have any right from the treaties to ask for aid; and besides, if they had a right, they have very lately told you about your ships, that they would not regard any treaties they made with you but such as they found were for their interest or convenience. The English ministry should now have the same answer returned to them." *William Lee to J. de Neufville & Son*, 18 July, 1779.

7th. that no such representative exercise any other public office while serving.

8. that the appointed officer shall be a citizen of the United States, and have a fixed and permanent interest therein.

9. that proper persons be appointed to settle accounts in Europe of American officials, and

10. that a certain salary be appointed for each representative.

The first and second paragraphs were adopted with little question. When the fourth was reached, Meriwether Smith, seconded by Carmichael, wished to strike out the words "which may be." Five days later a vote was taken on this motion, and the words were struck out, only two members (Ellery and Spencer) voting against it, and no state. The paragraph was then taken up in part, and, on the motion of Duane, seconded by Gerry, the words "late and present" were substituted for the word "said," making it read "that suspicions and animosities have arisen among the late and present commissioners." Gerry, supported by Muhlenberg, wished to make a further alteration, so as to read "*some of* the late and present commissioners," but the States were equally divided in the vote. To secure delay, R. H. Lee moved to postpone the 4th article until the 5th had been passed upon; but the States again were equally divided. Duane, with Morris, then wished the names of the commissioners to be inserted, the sense of the house being upon each name, and this suggestion met with favor. Franklin's name was inserted without question, but in every other instance the yea and nay votes were recorded, on demand of Meriwether Smith. The votes were almost unanimous for inserting the names of Deane, Arthur and William Lee, and Ralph Izard, only two or three negatives being given—and Ellery and Searle voting *no* steadily. A proposition to insert the name of John Adams was rejected, New Hampshire, Maryland and Virginia giving their votes in its favor, while Massachusetts and Rhode Island being lost by division. The first clause reading "that suspicions and animosities have arisen among the late and present commissioners, namely, Dr. Benjamin Franklin, Mr. Silas Deane, Mr. Arthur Lee, Mr. Ralph Izard and Mr. William Lee" was adopted—only the votes of Whipple and Armstrong (Pa). being thrown against it. The second clause—"highly prejudicial to the honor and interest of these United States"—did not fare so well, for New Hampshire and Pennsylvania were against it, and the influence of South Carolina was lost by division. In no case do the votes give any indication of the division of party in Congress.

On the fifth clause the question of recalling each minister was put, and here the feeling aroused was strong and of some definiteness. Franklin's name was first on the list. Virginia and North Carolina voted to recall ; Connecticut and New Jersey lost their votes. Gerry (Mass.) G. Morris (N. Y.) Paca (Md.), Smith, Griffin, and Nelson (Va.) and Penn and Burke (No. Ca.) voted for his recall. This was a trial vote, but it was plain that the unanimity was only apparent, for Congress was torn by faction, and the foreign affairs were a center of activity, as was the Arnold. The vote on Franklin was taken April 22d. On the 30th Paca laid before the house a paper, signed by himself and by W. H. Drayton, containing intelligence respecting Arthur Lee. This was done after the question of recalling Lee had been stated, and contained a very sharp arraignment of Lee on the ground that he was not trusted by the Court of France, and it would therefore be highly improper to continue him as one of the commissioners to negotiate a general peace. On the following Monday (May 3d) Carmichael rose, and presented to the house in writing his statement of the situation in Europe, after which the question of recalling Lee was put, and the States equally divided. New Hampshire, Massachusetts, Connecticut and New Jersey, voted against a recall; New York, Maryland, Virginia and North Carolina in its favor; and Rhode Island, Pennsylvania, Delaware, and South Carolina were lost by divisions. As the vote for recall may be regarded as a fair indication of what members were hostile to Lee, their names may be given: Gerry (Mass); Collins (R. I), Jay, Duane, G. Morris and Floyd (N. Y); Fell, (N. J); Atlee, Muhlenberg and Wynkoop (Pa); Dickinson (Del); Paca, Carmichael and Henry (Md); M. Smith, Griffin and Fleming (Va); Penn, Burke and Sharpe (No. Ca.); and Drayton, (S. Ca). Fifteen members voted against a recall, and twenty one in favor—a majority being against Lee.

Izard's name was not taken up until the 20th May and a vote was not reached until June 8th, when his recall was determined. New Hampshire, Massachu-

tts, Pennsylvania and South Carolina voted no, and
1e other States (New Jersey excepted), voted ay.
hirteen delegates voted against a recall, and twenty
1ree in its favor. The one affirmative vote of the
hode Island delegate counted as much in determining
1e question as the four negatives in the Pennsylvania
-The individual votes were not very different from
10se cast in the Arthur Lee ballot. Ellery (R. I),
herman and Spencer (Conn), Lewis (N. Y.), Plater
1d Jenifer (Md), joined the hostiles, while Drayton
5o Ca) and Henry (Md), voted against a recall.
uane, seconded by Armstrong, moved that "Mr.
zard be informed that it is the sense of Congress that
e need not repair to America until it suits his con-
enience." Sherman, seconded by Lovell, wished to
rike out the words "until it suits his convenience,"
hich was agreed to, thus leaving Izard removed from
ffice but not recalled.

William Lee, on the same day, and by nearly the
ame vote, was removed from office, and was not re-
uired to return to America. The vote on recall was
s follows:

Jew Hampshire,	Mr. Whipple,	no	} no
Iassachusetts,	Mr. S. Adams	no	
	Gerry	ay	} no
	Lovell	no	
	Holten	no	
Rhode Island	Mr. Ellery	ay	} ay
	Collins	ay	

Connecticut	Mr. Sherman	ay	
	Huntington	ay	} ay
	Spencer	ay	
New York	Mr. Jay	ay	
	Duane	ay	
	Morris	ay	} ay
	Floyd	ay	
	Lewis	ay	
New Jersey	Mr. Scudder	no	} div.
	Fell	ay	
Pennsylvania	Mr. Armstrong	no	
	Shippen	no	
	Searle	no	
	Muhlenberg	ay	} no
	M'Clure	no	
	Wynkoop	ay	
Delaware	Mr. Dickinson	ay	} ay
Maryland	Mr. Plater	ay	
	Paca	ay	
	Carmichael	ay	} ay
	Henry	no	
	Jenifer	ay	
Virginia	Mr. Smith	ay	
	Griffin	ay	} ay
	Fleming	ay	
N. Carolina	Mr. Penn	ay	
	Burke	ay	} ay
	Sharpe	ay	
S. Carolina	Mr. Laurens	no	} no
	Drayton	no	

For recall, 25; against, 12.

JAMES LOVELL TO WILLIAM LEE.*

PHILADELPHIA, July 17th, 1779.

Sir:

The Committee of Congress for Foreign Affairs are officially instructed to inform you that on the 8th of June last past it was resolved to recall you from the Courts of Vienna and Berlin, to which you had been appointed. But you are also to be informed that it is the sense of Congress that you need not repair to America.

You may see the proceedings, at length, respecting this business in their Journals, printed authoritatively by David C. Claypole, and being in the hands of Dr. Franklin or Mr. Arthur Lee, at Paris.

We are, sir, with sincere regard, &c.,

JAMES LOVELL,
For the Committee of Foreign Affairs.

TO LEBLANC.

20 July, 1779.

About 4 weeks ago 4 Englishmen passed through this town, having come from London in 5 days. They only dined here and went on their journey. They appeared as common passengers and talked at the hotel as if they were going to Vienna. I have just heard that they were only 7 days in going from hence to Venice, where a vessel was hired ready for them, in which they immediately em-

---

* See letter to Richard Henry Lee, 14 October, 1779.

barked and set sail for Alexandria. They are said to have carried orders to the E. Indies to attack the settlement of our Allies at the Manillas. I am informed that our enemies have planned, as soon as the campaign is over in N. America, where they expect great success, to send a large body of the troops they now have there to attack some of the French or Spanish settlements in the W. Indias. This plan might be easily disconcerted by orders being immediately sent for some of the Spanish ships now at the Havannah to go and destroy our Enemies' naval force in Georgia and Chesapeak Bay in Virginia. Now 'tis in our power, we must attack our enemies in all quarters and not wait for them to attack us. I hope an attack on Jamaica and Barbadoes is already planned. October, November and December are the months for effectual operations in the West Indias. The French privateers, as well as the Americans, too often make a practice of ransoming the prizes they take. Is not this tho't an impolitic conduct, for by this means our enemies have always their sailors ready for their ships of war and their privateers, while all the French sailors that are taken are confined in jails to dye with diseases. Sir Charles Hardy, on taking the King's sloop, the St. Helene that went out of Brest, learnt from her that the Spanish ships at Ferrol had join'd Count D'Orvilliers; on which he returned to Torbay for reinforcements; and be fore this his fleet is augmented to 41 ships of the line. If the West India fleet that is expected in 10 or 14 days arrives safe, they will get sailors enough to man Sir Charles Hardy's fleet fully, and two or three ships more. This W. I. fleet might be easily intercepted, which would be a very heavy blow to our enemies. It is talked in England that the packet boats from Dover to Ostend will soon be stopped, and they expect at Ostend that the fishing boats will be stopped there from going to England, as the English take by force all the men and put them on board their ships of war. I mention this, that in time a plan may be adopted for getting intelligence from thence. I will only add one word *of opinion*. I know our enemies so well, as to be sure they never will consent to any peace that we can accept, until they are heartily beaten and loose some of their important possessions; therefore every proposition that comes from them should be considered as it is intended and meant by them, only as a finesse to impede and delay our operations.*

* "The papers say 97 (A. Lee) is minister to 148 (Spain); 90 (Izard) and 96 (W. Lee) being layed by on the shelf, they must look for some retired corner to breath in. If 'tis in his power 97 (A. Lee) should take care of himself, that he may not want when the stroke comes upon him." *William Lee to Arthur Lee*, 24 July, 1779.

TO ARTHUR LEE.

17 August, 1779.

Dear Brother:

I got home the night before last and found your two favors of the 23d. ulto. and 7 inst. You will surely have justice enough to take to yourself all the consequences of 170 transactions being known, which now seems to me inevitable, from the bill not being sent as desired, on which the loss would have been less than will be on the money. What N[eufville] & Son know is of no importance of itself, but may tend to clear up other points for which I believe a person was sent to O[stend]. I am of opinion with you, that no notice should at present be taken of a certain set of wretches, but it may hereafter be of much use to the Public that their wicked operations should be generally known; therefore if you can contrive to get certain information of the author of what is in the Whitehall Evening Post, from 26 to 28 July, I beg you will do it. I will write to T. D[igges] about it, but do not know by what name to direct to him, having written twice long ago, and never received any answer. Mr. Jackson, manager of the Ledger, writes to me thus:

"Your brother should have had that, and a great deal more information from me, had I not been informed that when he invited me to dine with him at Paris, he desired Carmichael to be present to push

about the bottle, and to pump from me what I knew.
Carmichael had all I knew, and I trust he made use
of it for the service of America.''

This informant is pretty evident, tho' not mentioned by name; however, I have written and requested he would name him; and if he does, you
shall have a certificate of the whole. That the
party intended *Carmichael* for *Spain*, I think there
is little doubt, but the completion of this scheme
will much depend on the tenor of the despatches
that were sent from *Passy* to 61, the beginning of
March. You have no doubt seen the Courier de
l' Europe of 16 July. Whether the proceedings of
C[ongress] on the 16 of April were omitted by
design or not, I can't say. However the report of
the Committee is pretty explicit. Article 3d and
4th involves indiscriminately Messrs. A[dams],
I[zard], you and myself in the charges; art 5 is
judgment and condemnation of M^r I[zard] and both
of us; art 7. is intended to incapacitate me, and
art. 8., to incapacitate you from being re-elected.
It remains to know whether these reports are confirmed. The determination, however, with respect
to me seems so clear that I think myself warrantable in declining any farther operations in the
public line, and shall accordingly write to Congress as soon as I can; for which purpose I beg you
to let me know whenever there is a good opportunity. I shall without waiting for farther advice

look out for some quiet place to fix my family in before the winter sets in, on which subject I am not a little perplexed, for there are clouds gathering in this quarter that may burst out in a dreadful storm, in which case Flanders will again become the seat of war.

I saw at Bruges the captain of the Congress frigate, now at l'Orient or Brest.* He told me that he left Paris the 1st. of this month, and that D^r B[ancroft] told him Charles Town was taken by Prevost, and that Lincoln was wounded in an engagement near it. He said also that a French gentleman in Paris told him that he had just come from Spain and had travelled part of the way from Madrid to Cadiz with a Spanish Marquis, who was going as Minister to Congress. I also met on my route with a gentleman from Holland who assured me he had the day before seen an American on his route from Paris to Holland, who assured him that he came from Congress with despatches to Dr. Franklin, amongst which were advices of Prevost

---

* "I wish you could discover what was the *real business* for which Capt. Barnett, commander of the Congress frigate, was sent to Bruges and Ostend. He said his Business was to get American sailors at Ostend for his frigate. This is too improbable to be believed, for he might as well have gone to Vienna for that purpose. He is a Bostonian and impressed with the highest idea of 54 (Franklin), 40 (Deane), & the whole —— at P[assy], N[antes] and B[ordeau]x." *William Lee to Arthur Lee*, 22 August, 1779.

and his army being totally defeated. These reports it may be of use to you to know. . . .

TO RALPH IZARD.

FRANKFORT, 31 August, 1779.

* * * By this time I suppose you are convinced with me that Prevost has met with a Burgoynade at Charles Town, and if Clinton or his successor, Cornwallis should pursue the plan laid down for them, to penetrate into New England after getting possession of the North river to Albany, they will probably meet the same fate. I think after considering the proceedings of 28 (Congress) in the paper you gave me, the determination is too plain to be mistaken; therefore in my opinion neither 90 (Izard), 96 (W. Lee) nor 97 (A. Lee), can with propriety act any longer in their former capacity as 38^s (ministers). Give me if you please your opinion on this. The Exposé des Motifs of France and the Cedula published in Spain, should be well considered, that a strong remonstrance may be immediately drawn up and immediately transmitted to 3 (America) against any longer trusting the whole interests of 3 (America) in the hands of 54 (Franklin). After the offer to guarantee to Great Britain, Rhode Island, New York, Long Island, Staten Island, Portsmouth in Virginia, Beaufort in South Carolina, and every inch of

Georgia, I should not be surprised if the next offer was to give up the whole to G. B.

There are great movements in this quarter. Russia is working hard, for it seems agreed on all hands that she has offered her mediation to G. B. and P. Panin is gone to Sweden from whence he goes to Denmark, as is believed, to form a combination with R. to take an open part in the war, if her mediation is not submitted to. The same intrigues have been tryed at Vienna and Berlin, at both which places, things are now in a great deal of fermentation. Prussia recruits with as much activity as in the last year, and measures are assuredly taken to be ready at a moment to enter into the field. I cannot get any sure information of the real design of the cabinet at Berlin, but at this moment all our proceedings are at a stand there. He is wise however, and I hope is our friend. 'Tis said with confidence that propositions between France and Great Britain have been already exchanged thro' Russia. Powerful mediators are always dangerous especially when they are not so impartial as they ought to be; for 'tis very certain that in the present instance the secret design of R. is to make matters up between G. B., F. and S., and leave America entirely out of the question. Thanks to the contrariety of interests however, between the 3 great powers in this quarter, which, if properly managed, may save us from the threatened mischief. 'Tis astonishing to see how we have sunk in the estimation of the Powers in this quarter since they have known the late proceedings on the other side, and they now give up the idea of America maintaining independency. The last address to the people demanding 60 millions of dollars to be raised this year, has completely satisfied all politicians of the north that our case is too desperate to be supportable. 'Tis strange that nobody but Dr. F. had letters by the last express from C[ongress] arrived at Brest from Boston. . . .

TO BARON D' ARENDT.

FRANKFORT, 23 August, 1779.

Sir:

I had the honor of writing to you the 11th inst., in answer to your favor of the 22 of July, which was the only letter I received from you since you left this place; and this moment is come to hand yours of the 12th inst., which appears to have been 11 daies on the road, which I cannot account for. The security in Europe which is required will I apprehend be as difficult to obtain as the money; indeed, it is in fact the very thing we want to find in your country, as at present our affairs in every quarter wear a favorable appearance. I should hope the merchants in Prussia will readily see that there is very little risk indeed in giving credit to the state of Virginia. 'Tis now certain that General Prevost and the British army have been defeated in South Carolina, the remnant driven on board their ships and escaped to Georgia. The expedition to Virginia has ended in a pillage, burning all the houses they dared to venture to, and massacring in cold blood, *a la savage*, all the unarmed men, helpless women and children they could lay their hands on. They made an attempt on the little town of Hampton in Virginia, but were repulsed with considerable loss. I conclude that General Clinton does not find himself in a condition to do so much at New York, since about a fortnight ago two of his best generals, viz. Sir Wm. Erskine and Genl. Jones, have returned to England. The public gazettes will tell you the state of our allies in the British channel. We trust much to the friendship and good intentions of his majesty toward us, and I hope to hear soon something satisfactory and pleasing from your quarter. You remember my having mentioned the circumstance of a proposition being made at the last Congress at Teschen, for all the contracting parties to acknowledge the Independence of America. Can you contrive to get an accurate account of that proceeding and let me know all the particulars? . . .

TO ARTHUR LEE.

F——T, 1 September, 1779.

Dear Brother:

I think you fix the 20th of October for the period when a draft on M—t will be paid for the bal.—— On that I shall form my plan, as perhaps it will be more advisable to have the money somewhere else than at *Paris*. You will, however, have notice of what is to be done, but if you should think of changing your residence to *Spain*, you should give me as early advice as you can that everything may be settled before you go. The fixing my residence is a very serious and perplexing business at present, especially with the prospect of an increasing family, and no part in *France* will do for me as things are at this time. At B[russels] a house must be taken for 3 years, and then to be furnish'd, which looks like fixing for life almost. 'Tis very certain that when things are settled, there will be a great deal of business done at both Cadiz and Lisbon, therefore I should like much a correspondence with Mr. Dohrman, but at this moment it would be better for Mr. D. to write to me, stating his plan and desiring a connection, provided he chooses it. 'Tis probable that with a proper credit on Paris or Amsterdam I may be able to get the vessels he wants on much better terms than he can, and many articles that are absolutely necessary for his purposes must come from this quarter, which may be sent in the vessels to Lisbon, to have salt, &c., added to her cargoe. The fair is commenced here, and if orders were received here in 15 or 18 days from this time, good purchases might be made of linens and woollens. If you have no employment for T. Lee, perhaps Mr. D. might take him to Lisbon and send him Super Cargo, with his first adventure; after which, if he managed well, Mr. D. might establish him there as his agent. Will you please see, if the Mr. Hall that is come from V. is not the same, that was carried into Liverpool in 1776 by the crew who run away with a ship loaded in Virginia with tobacco on account of C[ongress]. What he says about D—'s acquittal is I suppose the construction that the world puts on the report of the Committee that we see published in the Cur. de l'Europe. That report, if confirm'd, is indeed a full acquittal of D., and a full condemnation of those he accuses.

No answer yet from I—n, and I fear he will not give any, if he does you will know it. The paragraph in the Whitehall Evening Post from 26 to 28 July is "A private letter from Paris informs us, that a certain Alderman of this city was beheaded privately in the Bastile for various frauds and forgeries, notwithstanding Dr. Franklin's endeavors to save him." Is there not a mistake in the brass cannon and mortars being charged at 180 livres the quintal, which is 36 sols the pound, though they were old, when Helenius's prices for new brass cannon was 124 livres, and Monthieu's, 136 livres he quintal? The difference in value between old and new brass cannon generally is very great, as commonly the first is only at the price of old stuff to be refounded. By the English papers it appears hat some time last month a privateer in the Bay of Biscay took an American packet boat with dispatches from Congress, which were saved and sent to the British Ministry. Every day we expect to hear of a battle between C^t D'Orvilliers and Hardy. f gained by the former, the British Empire on the ea must be at an end. You say nothing about peace, but I think you may be assured that propositions on that head have lately been made and I fancy exchanged. If you see L'd Mountstewart at Paris you may reckon on the principal points being agreed. This letter is only for your own perusal. We expect all the important news from your quarter.

My tribe, with myself, send you our love; little [orti]a would win your heart were you here. She is so good, and begins to lisp her words so sweetly.

TO FRANCIS LIGHTFOOT LEE.

2 September, 1779.

The perusal of the inclosed papers and considering what G. B. possessed at the *time* the propo-

sitions were made (viz. early in May, 1779) wil
show what sort of a peace the Dictator [Franklin
which Congress has appointed for America i
Europe was willing to make for you. Your ow
sense and judgment will render any comment o
the whole business unnecessary, as you will readil
see that it is the *Good Genius* of America alor
that has saved her in this instance, as in man
others, from utter perdition. You must now k
convinced of what has been often said to you, tha
America had never greater need of the services (
her wisest and most honest sons than at this preser
period; but we shall leave politics to the *most ab*
and incorruptible Messrs. W. H. D[ra]yt[o]
C[arte]r B[raxto]n, and C[ar]m[ichae]l, &c.

The French and Spanish fleets have at last g
into the B. Channel. We have not yet heard
any engagement, but 'tis probable there will k
one, which may be as undecisive as the one la
year. However, 'tis thought the season is too f
advanced to admit of any farther material oper
tions even if the B. fleet should be entirely defeate

Negotiations for peace are again renewed; t?
terms are not fully known, but as 'tis public, ar
has been for some time, that the B. army has be
totally defeated before Charles Town, and th
Clinton cannot do anything at New York, 'tis to
hoped that the terms for America will be somewh
better than those proposed before. I do not he

that any despatches from C[ongress] dated within
the present year have been received. We have
seen some proceedings in April last, first published
in France, and from thence copied into most of the
French gazettes in Europe, relative to D—e's
affairs. By a private person I hear that both you
and R. H. have refused to go again to C., which
for the sake of America and the noble cause of Liberty, gives me great concern, but I hope you will
both still continue to watch over the affairs of your
particular country.   *   *   *

TO ARTHUR LEE.

FRANKFORT, 4 September, 1779.

'Tis certain that negotiations for peace have been
for some time and are still on the carpet. The
terms proposed on either side I do not know, but
the issue will probably depend on what has happened within these 14 days past, or may happen
within this month in the Channel. Before this a sea
battle must have taken place, but an invasion will
not you may be assured; perhaps we may have a
second edition of the Jersey business. Captain
B[arnet] assured me he came from Boston in the
Congress frigate of 22 guns, but that she would
carry 28, which he intended to put on her; that he
arrived at L'Orient some time in June, and had
made some prizes; that he knew *W. Lee* the

moment he saw him, from his likeness to *A. Lee*
whom he knew at *Paris*, and had in a strange
place, where not a creature knew *A. Lee*, addressed
him by name, &c. This Captain, I have reason to
believe, was returned to Paris on or before the 16th
of August. A gentleman also told me he had seen
his commission from Congress. The Captain told
me that W[illiams] was agent for the sale of prizes
at N[antes], and Moylan and Nesbitt, his partners,
were agents at L'Orient. These things you may
inquire into, as well as to have it fully ascertained
that Jones's squadron is on private account, for the
loss on that business must be immense. Therefore
it is to be apprehended that by some legerdemain
America will be brought in to pay it. *W. Lee* tells
me he does not think there is the most distant
probabilty of obtaining the *agency* in *Virginia*. It
is certainly a desirable thing, but the success must
be certain, and the advantage very considerable, to
induce *W. Lee* to go to *Paris*, which at present he
thinks of never doing again, unless he has substantial reason to alter his opinion of the *Passy Court*.
If *A. Lee* can obtain it for *W. Lee* he will of course
have a full share of the advantages, tho' there is no
objection to its being to the two jointly if it can be
accomplished; but it seems most likely to succeed
if *A. Lee* is proposed, as he has been in that way.
It should be remembered that on such occasions
Comis are often of more *weight* than *principals;* and

in this case *Saint Marc* the *treasurer* is of as *much consequence* as *Pauly*. Say what you think can be done, but try cautiously that the old Spider [Franklin] may not know anything of it . . . *

TO ARTHUR LEE.

12 September, 1779.

* * * Captain Robins† being taken is very unfortunate, but I hope he had not much value on account of the state on board; I always understood that the whole belonging to the state was shipped in the Gov. Livingston. Unless convoys are given to the trade with America, none but madmen can think of venturing, nor will any venture; therefore I am sure that America will be more distressed for goods, this winter and next summer, than she has ever been yet.

This moment I received yours of the 6th and thank you much for the Intelligence, which is important and may produce a peace; for which I am

---

* "I see in the papers a good deal about a Capt Hutchins and two others being taken up for treasonable correspondence, which seems to be a most ridiculous business; for if one may judge from what has appeared, this Triumvirate will turn out to be of the Honble Order of Swindlers. Are they so hard run, as to be obliged to such shifts to amuse the public attention?" *William Lee to Richard Weld*, 15 September, 1779.

† Of the *Hunter*, on board of which were some of the supplies ordered by Virginia.

quite sure negotiations have been already commenced. The Gentlemen at P. have forgot that Hall says the brothers of *W. Lee* refused to serve any longer in *Congress*, which you know to be true as they both long ago determined to resign, and I fancy their resignation has startled the Junto and made them afraid to push their plans till they see the effect of their resignation, which may account for not hearing of their determination. I think from considering all circumstances, it is probable that the appointments of *Izard* and *W. Lee* are annulled, and no new one made; that *A Lee* continues as yet in his place.

So Hardy is safe in Plymouth and D'Orvilliers in Brest, and the embarkment forgot. Sic transit gloria mundi! You can't forget the song we used to sing when boys, of somebody with 40,000 men, going up a Hill, and then coming down again.*

---

* On August 31st a wind drove the combined fleet from the Channel, and Hardy with great skill brought in his ships, anchoring at Spithead the following morning. The King sent positive directions to Lord Sandwich to acquaint the admiral that he expected the "enemy is not to be permitted to quit the channel without feeling that chastizement which so base a conduct deserves." *The King to Lord North*, 4 September, 1779 The combined fleet, however, suffered from another source too heavily to permit it to await an attack. For a terrible disease broke out among the men, and the signal for retiring to Brest was given. For months the pestilence raged, and nearly 6,000 men perished.

The *agency* is surely desirable, if attainable. I wrote about it the 4th but I think whatever is done should be done with great caution, and as much secrecy as possible that neither *Franklin* or any of the *junto* may know anything of it even after it is settled. The whole negotiation must rest with *A. Lee*, as *W. Lee* will not turn towards *Paris* unless success is certain; in that case *A. Lee* will advise *W. Lee*, who will be ready at any time to do what depends on him. * * *

TO THE COMMITTEE OF FOREIGN AFFAIRS.

FRANKFORT, 28 September, 1779.

Gentlemen:

I have not had the honor of receiving any answer to the various letters I have written to you since my coming to this country, nor any letter from you since May, 1778, except a short one of the 28th of October last, which, added to my never receiving intelligence, information, or assistance of any kind, from your Minister at the Court of Versailles, has rendered my situation extremely embarrassing; and therefore, if my success has not been so complete as could have been wished, I shall hope for the indulgence of Congress, especially when it is considered that the general system of affairs in Europe, for eighteen months past, has been so very critical as to puzzle the deepest and most refined politicians.

Not being able to prevail on your Minister at the Court of Versailles (as I mentioned to you in March last) to aid me in getting the French Ministry to exert themselves in endeavoring to obtain a declaration of American independence by all the northern Powers of Europe that were interested in the Congress held at Teschin, in Silesia, last spring, I was consequently disappointed in the full hopes I entertained of obtaining so desirable a point, which there was the greatest prospect of succeeding in, if the Court of Versailles had made a point of it; at least, I am assured that the King of Prussia would not have had any objection, and from the very great influence he has in the Cabinet of Petersburgh, there is little doubt but that he could easily have prevailed with the Empress of Russia to have given her consent. Had this point been gained, our enemies would have been deprived of every ray of hope of obtaining any assistance to continue the war against us, for the great object of European politics has been, and is still, to draw the Empress of Russia into their quarrel.

We had not in this country got sufficiently quieted, after the signing of the peace of Teschin, on the 10th of May last, to make it prudent for me to take any public steps under the commissions I have from Congress, before the negotiations for peace under the mediation of Spain were drawn to a conclusion; but as the rescript delivered in June by the Spanish Ambassador to Lord Weymouth, in London, said not one word in our favor, but rather seemed to look on the Thirteen United States of America as being still colonies, or provinces, belonging to Great Britain, it became absolutely necessary for me to wait until this enigma could be cleared up, and till I could get sure information of the real designs of Spain, and the measures she intended to pursue.

As soon as I had got this information, I made a formal requisition to the Prussian Minister, hoping that, as the late war in Germany had prevented his Majesty's former declarations in our favor from being carried into effect, and as that obstruction was now removed, his Majesty would not delay to acknowledge the independence of the Thirteen United States of America, which might be the means of putting a stop to the further wanton effusion of human blood. To this requisition I received the following answer from the Minister:

"With respect to the declaration, which you again desire of the King in favor of the independence of the Americans, I have frequently explained, that his Majesty having, by the position of his dominions and those of his neighbors, very different interests from those Powers that are properly called maritime ones, he had no right to expect a direct influence in maritime affairs, and that he could not in wise policy take any measures in those affairs, because they would always be unfruitful, as they could not be supported by a war like marine. The support of the maritime Powers wi make the balance incline in your favor more effectuall than all the declarations in the world, and Spain, b joining with France to make war on England, rende you the most essential services, without havin acknowledged your independence. The King, i making the declaration now which you desire, wou only embroil himself with England, without renderin the smallest service to your country. These are th reasons which induce the King to confine himself present to the facilities which his Majesty has offer at different times with respect to commerce, in assuri you, which I do again, that merchant vessels of Ame ica, that choose to enter into the ports of the King, sell their goods and to buy ours, shall be received in friendly manner, and treated on an equality with t merchants of any other country.''

It has long been one object of my policy to e gage the King of Prussia to act in our favor as mediator for peace, whereby, if his mediation w agreed to, he might render us much more effectu service than by sending an army of fifty thousa men into Hanover, which step he could not ta. without arming the Emperor and the whole Ge man empire against him. I have good reason believe that the King is much disposed to act the quality of a mediator, but he is too wise to of his services without being previously assured th they would be accepted by both sides; howev

ve may expect very essential benefits from his influence with the Court of St. Petersburgh, who, it
is said with confidence, has offered its mediation,
and that it is accepted by the parties. I am informed that the first proposition to be made to
England by the mediating Powers, as the commencement of the negociation is, that America
shall be treated as independent. There is a strong
inclination in Prussia to enter into the American
commerce, and there is now a scheme in agitation
under the direction of the Minister to make the
trial, which, if the commencement is successful,
will be carried on upon a very large scale, and will
more effectually engage the King in our interests
than any thing else. For this purpose, I think it
would be of most essential service if two or three
American vessels were to enter into the port of
Emden, which is a good harbor, lying between
Hamburg and Amsterdam, and as easily got into
as any of the ports of Holland.

I have continued my correspondence at Vienna,
but having no powers to treat with the Empress
Queen, who is still sole sovereign over all the
dominions of the House of Austria, and the Emperor being much disgusted with some proceedings
during the late war, and more so with its conclusion, is become, of course, much more disposed in
favor of our enemies than he was, and consequently
less inclined to serve us; therefore, little advantage

can be expected from that quarter at present. Our friends in Holland increase every day, and I am still in regular correspondence with those who regulated with me the form of the treaty of commerce, copies of which have been sent you by various conveyances; and even now if the Stadtholder were to refuse to receive an American deputy, I have no doubt of his meeting a cordial reception from the city of Amsterdam, whose weight and decisive influence in their association you must be fully informed of.

Letters of good authority from England say that the British Ministry would willingly agree to give up the independence of America to obtain peace; but it is feared that the obstinacy and folly of their master will prevent them from executing their plan; however, I am still firmly of opinion, that the best security and success of America will depend on her own efforts—her wise, steady, and uniform conduct. As the obtaining a fresh supply of troops from this country has been a favorite point with our enemies, I have paid continual attention to that object, and have the pleasure to inform you that, at present, there is not any prospect of their obtaining fresh troops from this part of the world, as they have hitherto been defeated in all their various negociations for that purpose; but as this campaign has passed away without any blow being struck in Europe, all the English fleets from the different parts of the world arrived safe, without the least molestation; and the King's hands are so much strengthened by the exertions of all parties in England to repel the invasion which they have been threatened with all the year, that I think it is most probable the war will continue another year at least, for which, I suppose, proper provision will be made in America.

I have the honor to be, &c.,

TO GOVERNOR THOMAS JEFFERSON.

FRANKFORT, 28 September, 1779.

Sir:

His Excellency Gov.ʳ Henry was pleased in 1777, with the advice of the Council, to appoint me agent in France for the State of Virginia, and in 1788, by the same authority he sent me a power under the State seal, to obtain arms, artillery, ammunition, &c., of his most Xtian Majesties ministers, or any other persons, to the amount of 2,000,000 livres, or to borrow money to that amount to purchase those articles with; invoices for which were sent, for the artillery, arms and ammunition by the Governor; for linens, woolens and other merchandize, by Mr. Smith, the State agent in Virginia; and for paper and printing materials by Mr. Webb, the Treasurer. These documents came to me last year when I was at Vienna, in the public service, where I was fortunate enough to prevail with the French Ambassador at that Court to solicit the Court of Versailles to grant us the artillery, arms, and ammunition, and I also sent a power to my brother, Mr. Arthur Lee, who was then at Paris, to solicit this business for me at the Court of Versailles, and to try what could be done in France towards procuring the other articles. In consequence of these measures, there was obtained from the French ministry cannon, mortars, ball, bombs, &c. to the value of £219,489.7.4. and my brother advanced the money for the purchase of swords, pickaxes, hatchets, &c., which with Capt. Le Maire's and other expences amounted to about the sum of £45,000.

My brother chartered vessels to carry these articles to Virginia, and I believe they were all shipped in the Governor Livingston, Capt. Galer, and the Hunter, Capt. Robins: He also made a contract with Messrs Penet, D'Acosta Frères & Co, of Nantes, for several thousand stand of arms, and some other articles which they contracted to ship from France by the last of September, 1778, on the same terms which Mr. John King had agreed to in October 1777, with these gentlemen under the firm of Jas. Gruel & Co, for sundrie articles for the State. No part of the contract made with Mr. King was ever complyed with, nor was any part of the contract made with my brother complyed with, which

I now think a fortunate circumstance, having lately had authentic information, that several thousand muskets were in the course of last year sent from Liege to Nantes, addressed to a clerk of that house, which were of such a base quality as to cost no more than £5 a piece. I hope none of these guns will ever reach Virginia. Truth obliges me to say, that I have always found this house extremely ready to engage, but never so to execute.

My brother has given Governor Henry advice from time to time of his proceedings, and now he writes me that he has no more money to advance, and the owners of the ships in which the goods were shipped are in extreme want of the money for the freight, which amounts to about 27000 livres. Having no money myself to pay this freight with, we shall be greatly distressed, unless you are good enough to hasten some remittances either in bills or American produce, which I must earnestly request of your Excellency to have done. 'Tis necessary that I should inform you of what my brother has before advised Govr. Henry, viz., that the French ministry did last Spring demand payment for the cannon, &c, furnished by them, but on its being represented to them that we were utterly unable to make this payment, and that the State had not had time to make the necessary remittances, they agreed to wait some time longer.

I have not received any letters from Congress for

a long time, but there are some private letters in Europe, as I am inform'd, which say that Congress has dispensed with my services. Therefore my stay in this country will not be long, and when you are pleased to write to me, be so good as to put your letter under cover directed to À Monsieur, Grand, Banquier à Paris, if the conveyance is to any part of Spain, Portugal or France; and if the conveyance is by Holland, put your letter under cover directed À Messieurs, Mess. Jean de Neufville & fils, Negociants, Amsterdam. If you remit any produce, the Captain should be directed to make the first port in Europe that he can get to, and let him address his cargoe as follows, giving me notice of his arrival under cover to M.ʳ Grand. At Cadiz to Messrs. Rey & Brandebourg; at Lisbon, to M.ʳ John Henry Dohrman; at Bilboa, to Mess. Gardoqui & fils; at Bordeaux to M.ʳ John Bondfield; at Nantes, to Mess.ʳˢ Schweighauser & Dobrée; at Amsterdam, to Messrs. Jean de Neufville & fils.

As the enemies cruizers and privateers have the ports of Portugal to run into, they very greatly infest all the Bay of Biscay from Gibraltar to the English Channel, so that it is very difficult indeed to escape them. Therefore, I think the risk of being taken would be much less to come round the north of Scotland to Holland or Embden in the Prussian dominions, where they would be well received, and find a better market for tobacco than in France or Spain, and could get woollen and linnen goods better in quality and much cheaper. The want of money has prevented the articles ordered by Mr. [Thomas] Smith, State Agent, from being purchased, as well as the paper and printing materials ordered by M͏ͬ Webb, the Treasurer, which can only be got in London, for the types by orders cannot be purchased anywhere else in Europe. The first cost of M͏ͬ Webb's order will amount to about £1500 sterling.

I was last year flattered with the hopes of obtaining a loan in France for the 2,000,000 livres, but the large sums borrowed by their own government, from which the lender draws about 9 per cent interest, disappointed my expectations, tho' if this had not been the case, it could not have been accomplished under my power, which only expresses the Governor's authority, by advice of the Privy Council, without any act of that Council to show its consent; and besides they conceived that the State could not be bound without some formal act or Resolution of the whole Legislature. I applyed also in Holland where money abounds, and the terms were all agreed upon; but when the power was sent, the same objections were made to it that had been made in France and farther: 1st, As it specified that the money was to purchase arms and ammunition, such a loan could not be negociated without engaging their government in a dispute with G. Britain; therefore the power should only have expressed that it was to borrow so much money generally, without naming to whom application was to be made for the loan; and after the borrowers had got the money they would be at liberty to lay it out as they tho't proper. 2^{ly} They desired some clear and certain information by some public act, how far any particular state was authorized by the terms and articles of the General Association or Union of the 13 United States, to borrow money on its own single security. But they rather wished to have the guarantee of Congress added to that of the particular State for which the money was borrowed, as one State might be conquered by, or make some accommodation with G. Britain, and the rest remain independent. They think themselves justified in this reflection by the history of their own country, where their first association or union against Spain consisted of 17 Provinces; but 10 of them being conquered or seduced by bribes and solemn contracts and promises, which were never kept, submitted to the tyranny of their old masters, and are Slaves to this moment, while the other 7 Provinces, that were steady and true to themselves, remain free, independent and happy. Added to this, they now look upon the State of Georgia as severed from the general American Confederacy, and our enemies spare no pains to persuade them, that it will be the same case with the Carolinas, Virginia and Maryland. I have thus given you fully the objections which have been made to the power sent me, that you may take the proper measures to remove them if the State still continues disposed to attempt a loan in Europe.

I am so far removed from the port from whence this is to take its departure, that I cannot send you any new publications, or the public papers; and as the gentleman who will be so good as to take charge of it, is so fully informed of the state of Politics in Europe, tis unnecessary for me to say a word on that subject: I will therefore only add, that next to an honorable, speedy and happy Peace, my most ardent wish is to hear that discord, intrigue, and confusion are totally banished from America, and that Union, harmony, and good order prevail in full vigor. I have the honor &c.

TO ARTHUR LEE.

F——T, 28 September, 1779.

Dear Brother:

Yours of the 18th was so long on the road, that it was too late to consider the Abbé's advice about Anvers, as I was obliged before to give a positive answer about the house of B——lles, which indeed was the only one I saw in the several towns in that country that pleased me in all respects. It is taken for two years certain, and in about 15 daies time I propose to leave this place, so that I may receive a letter from you here, if you write by the 7th or 8th of next month; tho' after I am gone any letters for me will be taken care of. I hope the Abbé has no political reasons relative to the dispositions of the government that make him advise against Bruxelles; if he has, I beg to be inform'd, that every possible precaution may be taken in time: if he has not, you may assure him, that in every respect B. is far preferable for me to Anvers.

I know not any English at B., nor am I likely to know much of any of them, as my design is to be perfectly retir'd, and not to form acquaintances of any kind. My fam'ly and books will employ my whole time, until some business is undertaken, which cannot be done in a hurry, and even then, it will be better to be at some distance from the place of action, since during the war, too much cover or secrecy cannot be used to escape the enemy. You will say what is necessary to the Abbé to prevent his taking offence at his advice not being follow'd, and get his letter to the Banker at Anvers, for tis possible that in time much may be done there, especially if the government is favorable, but it is a very dear place to live in.

I wonder that you have not said one word about the contents of the despatches by Capt. Sampson, on the state of things when he sail'd.

By the Gazettes I see that he arrived the 10th in
Paris and brings papers from Philadelphia to the
19 July, and no doubt letters of a later date. From
the paper you sent I understand that the question
for recalling *Arthur Lee* was lost, the votes being
equal. This was no doubt known at *Passy* in July,
when the other proceedings in April were publish'd, and was omitted or conceal'd with design,
for this seems to have been at the same time. The
same paper must also have been bro't by J.
T[emple]. The conduct of D[ic]k[inso]n may
be accounted for, as he was always violently
against *Independence.* He acted, spoke and voted
against it; therefore, he may have designs of
oversetting *Independence.* But the conduct of M.
S——th * and C. G—f—n, † from Virginia, is to me
utterly unaccountable, unless it is that the first
owes *me* £1400 sterling, which it is fear'd he has
neither capacity or inclination to pay, and the latter has received many favors from *me.* Therefore
by Shakespeare's principles they may have become
enemies. However, I begin to think from a review
of the names and circumstances, that they have
hitherto fail'd in all their plans, and if so, they
must grow more and more feeble and despicable
every day. Can you contrive T. L. to go by the
opportunity by the way of the West Indies that

---

* Meriwither Smith.   † Cyrus Griffin.

you say will go in about a month? He has been very ill for a long time, but I hope both him and Ludwell will now speedily recover as the season is changing.

You seem to have forgot that by matrimony a man is not likely to get any *ready money* in Virginia, which is an article essentially and absolutely necessary to carry on trade; besides, in that country, the cares of a wife and family are amply sufficient to employ a man's whole time. He must however go, and if he could be the bearer of any public despatches, it may be of service to him. At least it may bear the expence of his voyage, which will be as well paid to him as to another.

While Ct. D'Orvilliers kept the sea, the English papers and their partizans on the Continent were crying out for Peace. Now the combin'd fleets are in Port, 8 E. Indiamen safe, 2 F. E. Indiamen, a Manilla and an Havanah ship taken, and the terrors of an invasion blown over, nothing but war and destruction to the House of Bourbon is talk'd of, and if their W. India fleets arrive safe, this insolence will increase and we may expect another year's war. I conceive Ad! Ross and his squadron, are bound to Gibraltar, perhaps to the West Indias; but the first is much more probable, for they conceive in England that the fleet from Brest will not go to sea again this year, and if it does, it will be only to take an airing and practice some new manœuvres.

I see no probability of ending the war speedily, unless measures are taken to prevent the Enemy from looking into Brest and other ports every day, to see what is doing there, which might be easily done; and plans are formed and executed to inter-cept their merchant fleets of convoys.

Our love to you and Ludwell. Farewell.

Portia has continued quite well since her inoculation : 'tis now the 20th day, and not the least symptom of the small pox.

TO PETER HASSENCLEVER.

FRANKFORT, 2 October, 1779.

Sir:

I have had the honor of receiving a letter from you of the 21st. ulto., and have forwarded to Paris the letter you inclosed for Commodore Gillon. As the merchants in your country have not been much accustomed to foreign commerce, 'tis possible that it will take some time to convince them of the ad-vantages that would arise from a trade with Amer-ica, but you who have been in that country may easily open their eyes, especially as I cannot sup-pose there is a man of common sense in all Europe that is so uninformed as not to know now, that it is impossible for G. Britain to succeed in her plan of subjugating America, which must now remain independent. We have been so much distressed with a cruel and ravaging war for near five years, that it cannot be supposed we can furnish great funds to carry on trade with, until we have peace; but in the meantime the Prussian Merchants may reap the whole immense benefits on this commerce both on the exports and imports, if they have but the spirit to make the trial, which might be done with very little risk, by sending moderate cargoes in different vessels, for which purpose I can easily furnish you (if you desire it) with the address of proper houses in the different States, to whom your business may be recommended, and who will conduct it faithfully and well. I know enough of your manufactures and those in your neighborhood which might be easily drawn to be exported from Embden, to convince me that there will be a great trade between the Prussian Dominions and America, as soon as we have peace, and England is obliged to acknowledge our Independence; but those who make the first attempts with you, will certainly share the greatest profits; therefore, I advise you for your own interest to lose no time in advising your friends to begin this commerce. I shall be much obliged to you for giving me a particular description of the Port of Embden, the depth of water, if 'tis a safe port and easy for a stranger to find the way into, if there are many good and substantial mercantile houses there, that are acquainted with business, and if an American

essel, for instance, coming there could find a
eady and good market for her goods, and a suffi-
:ient choice of your manufactures to load with in
·eturn, and any other informations that you may
hink useful and necessary.

TO T. DIGGES.

7 October, 1779.

Dear Sir:
* * * We have the Gazette that shows the
ssue of Sir G. Collier's expedition to Penobscot;
t seems to be of as little importance in itself as the
ɔurning Newark, &c., in Connecticut with respect
o conquest; but 'tis possible the consequences
may be important, as it may be the means of inducing a continuation of the ruinous and hopeless
war. Most political people in this quarter think
that G. B. will certainly seize the opportunity of
the mediation proposed to make the best peace it
can obtain this winter; for if this occasion is trifled
with and peace not made this winter, 'tis most
probable that a storm, from a quarter where it is
least expected will arise, the *fatal consequences* of
which to G. B., all your power, and all the finesse
of your ministry will be employed in vain to prevent. The Independence of America all the great
powers in Europe think, is a thing not only unavoidable, but absolutely necessary; therefore it

will not only be in vain, but the extreme of Foll
for the British Ministry to contend, or even hesi
tate on that point. The withdrawing the troop
from America and relinquishing N. York, as wel
as Rhode Island, will be the wisest step your mir
istry can take, especially as during the Winter
am convinced they will not run the smallest risk o
being interrupted by their enemies in bringin;
them to Europe, or sending them to any island i
the West Indies that they may choose. By thi
time Prevost and Sir James Wright together, mus
be in a deplorable case enough, for I shall b
much mistaken if they had not had enough to d
without thinking of an expedition to Charle
Town. * * *

TO RICHARD HENRY LEE.

FRANKFORT, 14 October, 1779.

*   *   *   *   *   *   *   *

Mr. James Lovell, in the name of the committe
has sent me a short letter just received, saying tha
Congress had recalled me, but that I need not re
pair to America.*

This is all I know, formally.—Had this proceed
ing issued from the divan of Constantinople, o
directly from the cabinet of Versailles, I should no

---

* Printed on p. 721.

ave been surprised; but, that the representatives
f a free people should permit themselves to be
1ade the instruments of a little, contemptible
mmis, to hear an accusation against a confidential
?rvant of the public, most of which their own
?cords prove to *be false;* and without hearing that
?rson's defence, or even letting him know that
e *was accused,* to proceed to judgment and crimi-
al condemnation, is a procedure that future his-
rians will perhaps hardly believe, or at least will
1d much difficulty to account for.—Is it possible
1at the affairs of America can be in such a state
; to make it necessary in order to avoid being
nquered by England to deliver yourselves up
rmally as the voluntary slaves of France?

My heart bleeds at the idea, especially as I could
en to you such deep plans of villiany and de-
ruction that are plotting against you, as would
ake your hair stand up with astonishment.—
our salvation must in my opinion arise from an
1ion more strict than ever with New England.

All Europe has resounded the summer past, with
e invincible strength of the combined fleets and
e numerous army, that was at a mouthfull to
allow up England, Scotland and Ireland; all
1ich has ended in taking the Ardent of 64 guns,
th the loss of above ten thousand men dead in
e Fleets with diseases; above £4,000,000 Sterling
ken from the Spaniards in prizes, 3 French East

Indiamen and other prizes to the value of abou
£2,000,000 Sterling more, while every Englis!
fleet has arrived safe except what has been take:
by the Americans, some of them only convoyed b
a single frigate.—Now the English fleet is full
able to face the combined fleets, and in the sprin
will be much stronger, so that the superiority i
the West Indies will be easily recovered.—Fror
these facts, on the truth of which you may rely, yc
can judge as well as I, what little probability the:
is of peace this winter, especially as from the prize
and the riches of the East Indies, now all the
own, England can raise above £20,000,000 Ster
ing, for the next year supplies, without borrowir
one shilling from foreigners; and the spirit of a
parties, to repel the threatened invasion, has bee
such as to put into the King's hands between .
and 40 thousand new troops exclusive of the militi
which troops I much fear, at least in great par
will be employed next year in America.

The Parliament meets in five weeks, and fro
the speech, we may judge something of their i
tentions. *   *   *   *

---

*Parliament assembled 25 November, 1779. In the spee
from the Throne the King said: "Trusting in the Divine Pro
dence and in the justice of his cause, he was firmly resolved
prosecute the war with vigor."

TO RICHARD HENRY LEE.

BRUXELLES, 30 October, 1779.

My dear Brother:

Inclosed you have a copy of my last, of the 14th inst., to which I beg your attention—Your son, Thom, goes in a vessel to Philadelphia, & I sincerely hope will arrive safe and afford you that satisfaction which you have a right to expect from the attention you have paid and the expense that has been laid out upon his education.

If my abilities enabled me to pay the expense of his continuing longer on this side, (which unhappily for me is not the case) I do not see that there would be the least use in his stay.

He has been long enough in as good a counting house as any in Europe, to get a sufficient knowledge of commerce, especially that of France, where all commerce, except a little to their own islands, is almost annihilated; and your son will tell you how little disposition there is to venture a single livre in the trade to America; therefore, without a capital to begin with, he could do nothing by staying where he is.—In his own country he may find some opportunity of exercising the knowledge he has gained, and I suppose he will be found well qualified to make a good American consul in some of the European ports. Mr Raleigh Colston seems to be a diligent, intelligent gentleman; perhaps they may form some plan together, tho' if Mr Thos.

Jett is in business, he will be a good person for him to be connected with.

It will give me very sincere pleasure to find that you are satisfied with my proceedings; but I must assure you that had he been my own son, I should not have acted otherwise than I have done; for at present I have no possible method of employing him, since the agency for the State of Virginia neither yields profit, or affords occupation at present; and besides I doubt whether my appointment continues, since I have not received any letter from Gov. Henry these 18 months past, which may be imputed to the intrigues of Mr. Deane, who has been always in close correspondence with him, or to some falsehoods of the adventurer Penèt, (of which he is very capable,) and who is, I hear, a very great man with you.   *   *   *

The campaign on sea, in Europe is finished, and nothing done, but an amazing sum of money spent and about 10,000 lives lost by disease. Gibraltar is beseiged, but in England they seem to have little apprehension of its being taken. From the conduct of the British ministry, it would seem as if they wished it should be taken that they may not be embarrassed at the peace, with the demands of Spain relative to it.

The Congress frigate, the Alliance, that brought over the Marquis de la Fayette, has been kept idle in France, ever since her arrival, waiting for some

French privateers * the principal of which, 42 guns, was commanded by Paul Jones, who was formerly in the service of Congress.

Jones was commodore of the fleet, [which] consisted of about 6 ships, including the Alliance of 36 guns. †

How far the dignity of Congress was supported by one of their ships of war sailing under the orders of a Cap.ᵗ of a privateer, you can Judge as well as I; however to leave a loop hold to creep out at, it is supposed these privateers, besides their French commissions, had Congress commissions

---

* To his brother, William wrote that the Alliance was held for the service of Chaumont.

† February 25th Franklin informed Vergennes that he had ordered the *Alliance* to prepare for returning to America, as convoy to a fleet of merchant vessels. Being a swift sailing vessel, it was well fitted for carrying despatches, and the sailing was expected to take place at an early day. Some discontents had arisen between Captain Landais and his officers, and a part of his crew was suspected of being mutinous and disaffected; thirty-eight of the crew had been brought in under confinement, and Landais objected to returning with them. Certain repairs entailed so long a delay that the merchant vessels sailed under the convoy of Lamotte Picquet's fleet from Brest, and soon after, at the request of Sartine, the Alliance was ordered to join Jones' little squadron at L'Orient. Adams, deprived of his expected passage, chafed under the disappointment, while Arthur Lee, under the plea of important dispatches from himself and Izard, insisted upon the Alliance's sailing as proposed, ignorant of the request of the French minister. A full statement is found in Franklin's *Writings*, VII., 210.

given them by Dr Franklin, by whose order it seems the commander of the Alliance acted. This fleet sailed round the north of Scotland, and took several prizes, and in the North sea met a British fleet of seventy sail from the Baltic, laden with naval stores, convoyed by the Serapis of 40 guns and ship of 20 guns.

Jones' ship of 42 guns and the Alliance attacked the Serapis; which after a very hard engagement was taken, Jones' ship being so much damaged, that she was quitted immediately, and sunk. The English 20 gun ship was also taken by the rest of the privateers; but all the merchantmen escaped. The Serapis and 20 gun ship were brought into the Texel in Holland, where it is said they are detained, being claimed by the British ambassador as property of his Master.

The papers also tell us that two prizes made by the privateers, carried into Bergen, in Norway, have been given up at the requisition of the British resident at Copenhagen.* I must tell you that all these vessels, both in Holland and Norway, went into port under American colors. This is one instance that will shew, (if these reports about these vessels prove to be true,) what kind of wisdom directed Congress to determine that ministers were unnecessary anywhere but in France and Spain.

---

* The *Union* was one.

In my opinion, they are more necessary everywhere else. *   *   *   *

I propose to stay here as long as my finances will enable me to do so, or until I hear from America, particularly from you; for there is little prospect of being able to do anything beneficial in the way of trade, while the war continues, and peace seems further off now than it was 20 months ago; for the late proceedings in America have kept up in full vigor, in the King of Great Britain, the thirst of conquering the country by arts or by force; therefore unless some unforseen and unexpectedly favorable occurrence takes place, I can never expect to live to see peace; for as things are conducted it will take a long time before the particular objects of France and Spain can be accomplished,— which being done, if America is not totally ruined and depopulated, she may shift for herself.*—My

---

* "In my opinion unless Dr. Franklin is speedily removed, and an honest, sensible man in his room ; and, on your part, you show more independence in spirit than is to be found in some of your late proceedings, America must be ruined, and become the *prize* of the successful combattant in Europe. This, you may be assured, is the secret butt of the politics on both sides.

"Ireland, in our day, is a lamentable example of a very great and powerful Republic being ruined and losing both its liberty and independence by suffering a powerful foreign state to interfere, by intrigue and cabal, under the mask of friendship, in the appointment, and changing the great officers of the Republic.

"I send you 8 Parliamentary registers, by Mr. Izard, of the

whole family join me in sincerest love to you, our sister and all the children.

Adieu & always believe most affec.^{tly} yours.

P. S. Remember that the political sentiments &c. contained herein, are only for your perusal and Loudon's, but not to be communicated to any one else, as coming from me.

I just hear that the combined fleets are sailed from Brest, and Sir Charles Hardy, with the British fleet, ab.^t 40 sail of the line is sailed from Portsmo: so that your son may possibly carry you the news of an import.^t sea engagement, that may hasten a peace.

---

last session of Parliament, from which you will receive much entertainment, if you have not seen them before. I wish most heartily, that America, by a bold exertion may finish her war before the Spring, for if this is not done, be not surprized to see the better half of Europe in arms against us before 12 months pass over. I this moment see by the English papers what a hopeful pair [Jay and Carmichael] Congress has sent to Spain to complete the business. Gov. Johnstone should be sent in the same capacity to Versailles and Mr Silas Deane as his secretary. How will poor America escape from such hands? Let me hear from you soon. My love to you all." *William Lee to R. H. or F. L. Lee,* 30 November, 1779.

"Digges writes from London that the differences between the Lees and Franklin and Deane were turned against the first from their families being generally in opposition to Washington." *William Lee to Arthur Lee,* 8 December, 1779. Some remarkable letters on these appointments are given in the Works of John Adams, ix., 486, *et seq.*

S. THORPE.

ANTWERP, 1 December, 1779.

I just hear that the packet for England is going, vhich gives me a moment's time to acknowledge he receipt of your favor of the 23d. ulto. It was ever my desire or intention to keep from the good eople of Aldgate Ward that charge which they ntrusted me with, one moment after I knew their vishes on the subject. Therefore it will be per- ctly agreeable to me that you should put the entlemen of the Common Council in possession of he resignation I sent you last year. If you have ny objection to this, let me know it, and tell me hat mode you desire should be adopted, for I all be happier when entirely clear of every public harge than I can be in one, in the present situa- on of things. 'Tis certainly commendable to love ne's country, and I am sure you not only do that, ut you love justice and humanity. * * *

TO WILLIAM LEE.

LONDON, 3 December, 1779.

r:

We have greatly lamented your long absence from s, and the consequent necessary omission of the vari- as duties of this Ward, which you discharged entirely our satisfaction, during your residence here. We close you very unwillingly the resolutions of the ardmote last St. Thomas's Day, for we have till

lately entertained the fond hope of a reconciliation be
tween the mother country and her colonies. From
that flattering expectation, which we entertained ir
common with every good Englishman, we now ar
forced, with much reluctance, to depart: the necessit
of that unhappy circumstance, at present supersedin
every other consideration, the connection between u
must now be dissolved. It is with pain we reflect o
this business, but we shall always retain a grateft
memory of your services as our Alderman. We hav
only farther to desire that your answer to us may ir
close a letter of resignation to the Lord Mayor, an
Court of Aldermen, as Alderman of Aldgate Ward.

We are, sir, &c.

J. BELLET,	J. PARTRIDGE, Deputy,
THOS. HOLDSWORTH,	S. THORPE,
G. HEATH,	CHA. LINCOLN.*

* "A Court of Aldermen is to be held at Guildhall on Tue
day next, when it is expected that the resignation of Alderma
Lee will be accepted; and a day appointed for holding a war
mote for the election of another Alderman in his room. V
cannot help taking notice of the illiberal reflection thrown
that gentleman in a morning paper of yesterday, when it
considered that Mr. Lee is a native of America.

"To a man born and educated in that country, it would be
unpardonable crime to continue to live under and support th
government, who have been attempting to ruin and enslave t
state that gave him birth; he who possesses the liberal sen
ments of an Englishman, will applaud the patriotic virtue o
Lee; but the man that is a stranger to those exalted ideas,
pity rather than condemn." *General Advertiser and Morni
Intelligencer* (London), 11 December, 1779.

The meeting was held on Wednesday (not Tuesday) and t

TO ARTHUR LEE.

FRANKFORT, 24 December, 1779.

I got the Carolina letter safe. You had my answer to Mr. N——. The Guernsey plan is dangerous, and after all might turn out an ignis fatuus, at any rate 'tis more than probable 142 would know the whole from D.

'Tis strange we are kept so much in the dark about their proceedings in America. What Ct. D'Estaing can do in the West Indies, we are at a loss to conjecture, but he will certainly be fortunate if the foggy weather prevents his meeting with Byron who is much stronger.

I beg to know if supplies of clothing, &c., have been sent for the use of the Continental army this winter, and next campaign; without this we must suffer greatly. I suppose you are properly informed of the determinations in England, of which advice should be given to America by various opportunities. The troops now in contemplation to send from England are ye 1 and 2 battalions of Royals, 3, 11, 13, 19, 25, 30, 32, 36 and 39 Regi-

Lord Mayor "informed the Court, that he had received a memorial from several of the inhabitants of the ward of Aldgate, respecting the election of an Alderman of that ward, in the room of William Lee, Esq.; who is gone to reside in America. The court were unanimously of opinion that they had no right to interfere in the business. Mr. Lee must resign his gown, which resignation we hear is every day expected." *Do.*, 16 December.

ments, from Ireland the 18, 66 and 67 Regiments, in all 14 regiments which may make about 5 or 6000 men; tho' the embarkation of these troops is not absolutely decided, as to time and place, yet 'tis very certain that they intend to carry on an offensive war next year against America, from which nothing will prevent them but the Americans taking advantage of Clinton's present weakness, and driving him out of New York or Rhode Island, before he gets reinforced. No new troops will go from this country, and I believe not near the number requisite to recruit the German corps now in America. Some few hundred recruits may possibly be sent.

If France attends to that point and will intercept the troops in their passage from Ireland (for they will most probably set out from Cork with provisions) to America, the next Campaign may finish the war. I have seen a letter here that mentions Mons. Monthieu, Beaumarchais, &c., are sending out 4 frigates, the Fier Roderigue, Drake and two others, with several other vessels loaded with merchandize &c., for America, and that Mr. J. Williams goes Supercargo of the fleet. I do not find that any here will be concerned in this expedition, but I wish to know if any part is on account of Congress or the State of V——a. The Courrier de l'Europe we never see here, so that we have no American accounts of what has passed there in

September and October. There is not the least probability of Peace this winter in Germany, and the politics of the North, I am quite clear have embraced England, which has encouraged the Ministry to go on with the war. If France and Spain proceed on presumption of this, I will answer for it that she will not be deceived. Our love to you all.

Adieu.

TO MR. DEPUTY PARTRIDGE AND THE REST OF THE COMMON COUNCIL OF THE WARD OF ALDGATE, LONDON.

BRUXELLES, 24 December, 1779.

Gentlemen:

On my return from a journey, I had the honor of receiving your favour of the 3d instant, inclosing the proceedings at the Wardmote, in Aldgate Ward, December 21, 1778, and desiring that my answer may inclose a letter of resignation, as Alderman of Aldgate Ward, to the Lord Mayor and Court of Aldermen. The inclosed letter to his Lordship and the Court, will shew you, that above thirteen months ago I sent a letter of resignation to the Lord Mayor, &c., which unfortunately has not come to hand, otherwise the proceedings of the Wardmote would not have taken place, nor would you have had the trouble of again inclosing them to me.

I beg to be assured, and that you will also assure the worthy Freemen of the Ward of Aldgate, that I should have resigned the trust which you and they had the goodness to confer upon me, at a much earlier period, had I not been informed that such a measure was contrary to your and their wishes, which is now confirmed to me by your joint letter.

Nothing but the most irresistible necessity, arising from the implacable vengeance with which the utter destruction of my country is pursued, could have forced me from a post in which your honorable suffrages placed me, and in which I have had the happiness of co-operating with men of the most pure and incorruptible virtue, in defence of public liberty and the constitution, which have been so daringly invaded. But the eagerness with which the savage Indians, and unfeeling mercenaries, have been hired, and excited to the devastations in America, by every species of teachery and barbarity, has made it impossible for me to live any longer under a government, thus capable of employing the vilest means, for the most flagitious purposes.

Such unprincipled and perfidious arts, such inexorable cruelty, such a desperate determination to hazard everything to effect the misery and ruin of a distant, and offending people, never before distinguished the worst of wars. It remained for a combination of them all, to characterize a *Scotish war* under a *Scotish favourite*, waged against the principles of *English liberty*. In such a situation of things, I could not disgrace the name I bear, nor prove myself unworthy of the confidence you have been pleased to place in me, by refusing to lend my feeble aid in so just and necessary a resistance to those who are impiously invading the rights of human nature, and of my country.

I have endeavoured, gentlemen, to execute the office, with which you honoured me, with the strictest fidelity, as long as it was consistent with my principles, and the circumstances already mentioned, for me to remain among you, and I return it, with the highest gratitude for your past favours, and the sincerest wishes for your happiness.

I must particularly request of you, Mr. Deputy, and Gentlemen of the Common Council, to accept my warmest thanks, for the very obliging terms in which you have expressed your entire approbation of my conduct as your Alderman, during my residence among you, which is a most ample reward for my endeavours to serve you, and to defend the rights of the good Freemen of the Ward of Aldgate, in which, however, my efforts would have had very little effect, if they had not been uniformly seconded by so firm and able a Common Council as I had the pleasure of acting with.

I have the honour to be with the highest respect

and consideration, Gentlemen, your much obliged and grateful servant.*

TO ARTHUR LEE.

BRUXELLES, 29 January, 1780.

Dear Brother:

I have received yours of the 22d. with the account of the snuff box presented on the part of his most Xtian Majesty. Your scruples about receiving it were certainly just, but I do not know how you cou'd have refused it, without giving signal offence to his Majesty, which shou'd by all means be avoided, as I think it essentially necessary to cultivate a good understanding and harmony between his Majesty and your constituents by every fair and honorable means in your power. Your judgment cannot easily be deceived, and therefore

---

* Lee's resignation was not laid before the Court till January 19th, when it was at once accepted, and the following Friday fixed for a Ward mote to be held at Ironmongers' Hall. John Burnell was chosen without opposition, and by a majority of twelve, the freemen of the ward gave a vote of thanks to Lee, "the late Alderman."

"There is like to be as warm a contest for the Aldermanship of Aldgate Ward, in the room of William Lee, Esq; (who has resigned) as ever was known. There are no less than seven Candidates which have already started, and were yesterday morning canvassing the ward, all of whom declare they are determined to stand the poll." *London Chronicle*, 15 January, 1780.

you will know how to appreciate civilities; but I suppose some kind of letter will accompany the box, that will show clearly the intention of the giver. I have conversed with our friend here on the subject, and we are both of opinion that you should not write to Congress or anybody in America about it, but carry the box with you and lay it on the table of Congress at your first audience, relating the facts plainly as they are, for without a particular and express resolution of Congress on the subject, I do not conceive that you can with propriety keep it.

Mr. Izard will tell you the state of affairs in Holland, where there is great room for political negotiation, as well as in the courts of the north. Since Mr. I. left us I have not heard anything from the enemy's country. We beg our compliments to all friends with you, and send you our love. Farewell.

P. S. Do you know ye Baron Breteuil, or do you wish to have a letter of introduction to him? He is worthy of every attention in my opinion.*

---

*Addressed, À Monsieur Lee, Hotel Vendome, Rue des petits Augustins, Fauxbg St Germain, Paris.

When taking leave of the French ministry, Arthur Lee was presented by the King, a gold snuff box, bearing his Majesty's picture set with diamonds. "As you may imagine, I was embarrassed about receiving or refusing it. He [Arthur Lee] told the minister that he believed it was contrary to the rules of those he had represented to receive any present. The Count

TO RICHARD HENRY LEE.

BRUXELLES, 15 February, 1780.

My dear Brother:

A few days ago only I received your favor dated 1ˢᵗ Augᵗ from Chantilly, which is all that I have received from you since June 1778, and not one from London since 1777.

This letter came to me from Bilboa, and I suppose was broᵗ by Mʳ John Adams, who arrived in the *Sensible,* French frigate, at Corunna, two months ago from Boston. This gentleman was not got to Paris the 9ᵗʰ inst, tho' he arrived at Bordeaux some time last month.*

The letters you refer me to written from Philadelphia, have never come to my hands, and I can't help supposing that most, if not all my letters, for near two years past, both to Congress and yourself, have been some how or other intercepted or kept back, as well as your letters to me.

Your letter covered Ellis's account current from March to June 1779, balance in my favor £4,126.-11. You say £5408.16 has been paid to our

---

answered that this was a mark of his Majesty's esteem, and was never refused. Upon that it was accepted, with a resolution of leaving it at the disposal of Congress after it had served as a proof to that body of the untruth of what had been reported to them of your friend having given [offence] and being odious to this court." *Arthur Lee to William Lee,* 22 January, 1780.

*Adams with Dana and Thaxter reached Paris on the 9th.

brother F. L. L. for me. This is the only account I have received relative to the estate, since that you sent me from Williamsburg in January 1778.

I fear from a resolution of Congress in July last published in the Gazettes, that the interest on the few dollars lent before March 1778, will no longer be paid in bills on Paris.* If it should be paid in bills, tho' the amount is small, it will be of great service at this time, when the possible means of giving bread to my family is not clear to me, for more than a short time, and it is almost impossible to transport them now to America, where I mean to transport myself as soon as I can find a practicable opportunity, unless some proper employment should occur in Europe, of which I see no prospect at present. Whatever you determine about the estate, whether to sell or not, I hope will turn out for the best; I see no political objection with respect to me personally, because the inclosed Gazette will shew you, that I have made myself more free, than it was in the power of Congress to make me; therefore the only consideration is, which will be the most advantageous, on which I cannot determine, being utterly unacquainted with the actual present situation, and future prospect of things with you.

Copies of the inclosed paper, I dare say, will not easily find their way to America, through France,

---

* *Journals of Congress*, 29 June, 1780.

as the undertrappers of Deane's faction will wish to keep, as long as they can, the only popular subject of making me ungracious to my countrymen.

You remember that Governor Henry, and the council of Virginia in 1777, appointed me agent for the state of Virginia. I have not received any letters from him or anybody else about this business since May 1778, tho' I have written frequently, and so has my brother from Paris. He has requested of you, and so have I, which I do again, to endeavor that remittances be made speedily, to answer the engagements we have made in France, on account of the state; a full state of which has been repeatedly sent to the Governor. This seems now more necessary than ever, for I have just received a letter from one of the first merchants in France, of which the following is an extract.

"Feby 10, 1780. Sundry people of Nantes wrote me that Mr Penet, formerly a West India ship's surgeon, had written that he was appointed agent for the state of Virginia, likewise superintendent of the whole commerce of that state in France. I have found that choice very surprising."

Perhaps others are as much surprised as this gentleman; however, these days are big with wonders. * * * *

TO JOHN ADAMS.

BRUXELLES, 17 March, 1780.

Dear Sir:

I understand that our enemies have now in contemplation the offering of some terms to America, which go no farther than a truce; probably somewhat similar to the propositions made last year by Spain to Great Britain.*

Though I am not informed of the terms of peace with which you are charged, nor whether your powers are discretionary, I trust you will not think it an intrusion in me to offer my sentiments on a proposition as a truce for America, supposing it should be made.

A truce with America must, of course, accom-

---

* "I can never suppose this country so far lost to all ideas of self-importance as to be willing to grant America independence; if that could even be universally adopted, I shall despair of this country being ever preserved from a state of inferiority, and consequently falling into a very low class among the European states. If we do not feel our own consequence, other nations will not treat us above what we esteem ourselves. I hope never to live to see that day, for, however I am treated, I must love this country." *The King to Lord North*, 7 March, 1780.

It is, however, not a little curious that in his "secret" letter ("*pour vous seul*") to Lord North, dated 1 December, 1780, Necker proposed a truce, during which the belligerents in America were each to remain in possession of the territories they then held. George III. rejected the proposal, holding that "independency of the colonies, whether under its apparent name or a truce, is the same in reality."

pany a peace in Europe ; in that case, our enemies, after recovering from their present exhausted state, having their hands clear of European troubles, would have their whole strength to employ against America ; for, I conceive, that with such a prospect before them, there would not be the most distant probability of agreeing on a peace before the expiration of the truce.

In America we must keep up a great military and naval establishment to prevent our being taken by surprise, at nearly as great an expense as we are now at in war, and besides risk the dreadful misfortunes which have almost universally attended standing armies and a heavy load of debt on the state. I cannot suppose it possible that France and Spain would consent to a truce with America while the war is to continue between Great Britain and them ; but if they should, would it be wise in America to accept of a truce on such terms, and to let our allies run the hazard of being destroyed, that we may become an easy prey afterwards?

These are some of the evident objections to a truce in any shape, nor can I see any possible argument in its favor, though I know there are some Americans, though well-intentioned, but visionary geniuses, whose heads run much on the idea of a truce; but I hope nothing will be attended to, unless they are fair, open, and honorable propoitions for a substantial and lasting peace, in which blessed work I most heartily wish you speedy and full success.

The Dutch are in a very disturbed state; as yet there does not seem to be a probability of their taking a decided and open part with us in the war. The influence and power of the Prince of Orange are unfortunately too great to permit them to adopt those measures which their honor and interest direct, and which, I believe, a great majority of the people wish.* The Prince is retained against us by the flattering prospect of marrying his daughter to the Prince of Wales; but in Europe, where every thing is bought and sold, France and Spain may do great things; for the confidant and director of the Prince is as mercenary a wretch as can be found in England, or even in Scotland.

We shall probably see Mr. Laurens here on his way to Holland; but if he does not pass through this town, I shall be much obliged to you for giving me any interesting public intelligence that he brings.

Be pleased to present my respects to Mr. Dana; and if I can be of any service here in promoting

---

* In January 1780 a Dutch fleet, laden with naval stores for France, and convoyed by Count Bylandt, was met by a British squadron under Admiral Fielding. An attempt of the English to search the vessels was resisted, a contest followed, and some of the Dutch ships were taken.

the great work you have in hand, or in rendering
any services to our country, I shall be always
happy in receiving your commands, being with
great esteem &c.

TO WILLIAM LEE.

PARIS, March 21st, 1780.

Dear Sir:

I have just received your favor from Brussels of the
17th of this month, and I thank you for this instance
of your attention to me.

Considering the state of Ireland and the spirit that
seems to be rising in England, which has already
attained such a height as to baffle the Minister and the
East India Company, and to carry many votes in the
House of Commons almost to a balance with him, and
even some against him, I should not be at all surprised, if terms, such as you mention, should be offered
to America; nor should I be surprised if another
rumor, which has propagated at the Palais Royal this
day, should prove true, that a great change is made or
to be made in the Ministry, and that the Lords Shelburne and Rockingham, Burke, &c., are in. Yet I
have no proper accounts of either.

Whatever may be my powers or instructions, or
whether I have any or not, I am very much obliged to
you for your sentiments on such a proposition as a
truce for America, supposing it should be made.
Your arguments are of great weight, and will undoubtedly be attended to by every one, whoever he

may be, who shall be called to give an opinion upon such a question. You will not expect me at present to give, if it is proper for me even to form, any decided opinion upon it. Yet this much I may venture to say, that having had so long an experience of the policy of our enemies, I am persuaded, from the whole of it, if they propose a truce, it will not be with an expectation or desire that America should accept it, but merely to try one experiment more to deceive, divide, and seduce, in order to govern.

You observe that the heads of some well-intentioned, though visionary, Americans run much upon a truce. I have seen and heard enough to be long since convinced that the Americans in Europe are by no means an adequate representation of those on the other side of the water. They neither feel nor reason like them in general. I should, therefore, upon all occasions hear their arguments with attention, weigh them with care, but be sure never to follow them when I knew them to differ from the body of their countrymen at home.

You say the Dutch are disturbed. Do you wonder at it? They have been kicked by the English as no reasonable man would kick a dog. They have been whipped by them as no sober postillion would whip a hackney coach horse. Can they submit to all this upon any principle which would not oblige them to submit if the English were to bombard Amsterdam or cut away their dykes?

I wish I knew the name of the principle confidant and director of the Prince, whom you name.*

---

* Duke of Brunswick, brother to Prince Ferdinand, Field Marshal and commander in chief of the Dutch land forces.

I am very anxious to hear of the arrival of Mr. Laurens, but suspect you will hear it first. Mr. Dana returns his respects to you.

I thank you, sir, for your offers of service; nothing can oblige me more than to communicate to me any intelligence of the designs of our enemies, in politics or war, and their real and pretended forces by sea and land. Pray, what is the foundation of the story of a quintuple alliance between Holland, Sweden, Russia, Prussia, and Denmark?

I am sir, with great esteem, your humble servant,

JOHN ADAMS.

TO SAMUEL W. STOCKTON.

BRUXELLES, 21 March, 1780.

Dear Sir:

I have just received from our mutual friend at Amsterdam your obliging letter of ye 14th November, which gave me very great pleasure, tho' it is very long since y^t I heard of your safe arrival. You will no doubt give me some credit, since you have found things where you are so much like what you know, above 12 months ago, I judged they would be.

Your friend, I hear from various quarters, has been true and steady to the good cause, tho' his name does not appear in my particular favor; but ye part Mr. J. Dickinson has taken, I confess, surprizes me. If you are acquainted with him, I beg

you will give my particular respects to him, and
tell him my esteem for him is not abated, from y⸢e⸣
part he has taken with S. D., because I am convinced y⸢t⸣ he must have been most strangely deceived, otherwise it is incredible that a man of his
good sense, & as I believe goodness of heart, could
have stept forth y⸢e⸣ champion of one of y⸢e⸣ worst
men I ever knew, who has neither Honor, Reputation, or Property to lose, but every thing to gain
by public confusion, the ruin and misery of his
country.*

[†] has been much offended at what has
passed, and was near too fatally showing that he

---

* "I was much concerned to see the Sieur Dickinson, who
some years ago made such a conspicuous figure among the
American patriots, represented in the Gazette of Cologne as being now in Congress, and exerting all his talents and address,
to bring America again under subordination of Great Britain.
Mentioning this yesterday to an intelligent American that has
spent some time in this city, and honors me with his acquaintance, he told me that Mr. Dickinson had exerted himself
against the Declaration of Independence, and that his warmth
on that occasion had rendered him suspected at that time to
his county, and obliged him to quit Congress. But since that,
finding a British party growing strong, headed by Mr. R. Morris, and very imprudently patronized by the first French minister, whom they had most grossly imposed upon, Mr. Dickinson
had returned to Congress, and might very possibly be pursuing
his old system, and endeavoring to get your independency defeated." *William Lee to Arthur Lee*, 15 May, 1780.

†A blank in the original; perhaps the King of Prussia is
meant.

was of importance enough to have some representative to him. But fortunately for us, the prospect of some rupture about P[o]l[an]d has restrained him, which also keeps R[ussi]a quiet, that would otherwise infallibly by this time, have been openly against us; thus it seems, that we shall not have any more European enemies this year than we had before. Mr. J[a]y and his trusty Squire do not seem to have been received with such open arms as they expected; however as they are charged with terms highly beneficial to one, and oppressive to the other, there is no doubt of their being received; and if there is any *stuff* to be fingered, I will answer for both of them sticking like leeches to ye charge. You know that another is to reap the harvest from the seed we sowed at Aix. In Holland they have been for some time in great political fermentation in consequence of ye English taking their fleet of men of war under convoy of a Dutch admiral and merchantmen, in ye channel, and carrying them all into Portsmouth, where ye cargoes of ye merchantmen have been all condemned (tho not contraband), and the men of war permitted to return home. The *States General* have issued some spirited resolutions and 'bove 50 men of war (chiefly frigates) are to be fitted out in the spring; but it will end in smoak, for ye monied men, it is supposed, have ventured above two millions sterling in ye last English loan of 12 millions, where y^e

gain was too great to be refused by a D[utchma]n.
For y⁰ standing interest is near 6 per cent, and y⁰
subscribers already gain 7½ to 7¾ per cent on selling, tho' the loan has not been settled a month.
And, alas! the P. of O. expects to marry his
daughter to the P. of Wales.* * * * * * *

TO JOHN ADAMS.

BRUSSELS, 30 March, 1780.

Dear Sir:

I have had the honor of receiving yours of the
21st. instant. The name of the person you wish to
know, is the Duke of Brunswick, brother to Prince
Ferdinand, Field Marshall and Commander in
Chief of the Dutch land force. He is not liked by
his family, as they conceive he is too much attached to the House of Austria.

The quintuple alliance that you mention, I conceive, is only the conjecture of some politicians; for
there is not in fact any solid appearance of the
Dutch resenting like men or an independent nation

---

* "G. Plater writes to I[zard?], the general purport of
A[dam]s' mission, and says, 'I refer you for particulars to my
friend C[ar]m[ichae]l.' This heavy man is uncle to F. L. L.,
but of an understanding of a right size for C[ar]m[ichae]l or
D[ean]e, to play with, as a cat does with a dead mouse. He
has, however, great property, likes the bottle, and any one that
will laugh or grin." *William Lee to Arthur Lee*, 24 March,
1780.

the cruel injuries and insults (that would be intolerable to any other people) which they have received from the English. The Prince of Orange, the better to deceive, and perhaps reflecting on the fate of DeWitt, pretended to resent highly the insult offered to his flag; but you will agree with me that it must be only a pretence, when you know that Admiral Byland is to be honorably acquitted; and in consequence it is expected that the best Captain in the Dutch navy will resign.

I hope you did not construe my last into any design of drawing from you any of the secrets of your mission, for, believe me, I have no such curiosity, being quite satisfied with that information respecting it, which the world is, and has been a long time, in possession of; and besides, I know too well how extremely necessary circumspection and secrecy are to procure success to a negotiation.*

---

*Adams wished to throw the gage to the English ministry by announcing his powers direct to them; but Vergennes thought it more prudent not to communicate them to any person whatever, and especially to guard against a premature knowledge of them reaching the English government. (24 February, 1780.) Chafing under inaction, Adams urged upon the minister in July, a publication of his powers, but Vergennes was still of opinion that such a measure would be inopportune, and informed him of what the French court had done in aid of America. Still far from being convinced, Adams imprudently undertook to criticise the policy and programme of the French court, and Vergennes abruptly closed his correspondence.

Diffidence and distrust of an enemy are always warrantable, but particularly so when one has had repeated experience of their duplicity and treachery; the fatal experience of the Dutch in the negotiations at Gertruydenberg, as well as many other examples, teach us that distrust and resentment should not be carried to unreasonable length.

A great and good man has wisely observed that the best time to make peace is, when your enemy wishes for it; and I hope that the affairs of Ireland, with vigorous and well-directed operations on our part this campaign, will reduce our enemies to wish for peace in earnest before this year ends; although they seem to be getting the better of the opposition at home, which, it appears, they are determined to do, either by fraud or violence, as the papers will tell you how narrowly the life of Lord Shelburne has escaped one of the Scotch assassins.*

With infinite pleasure, I shall communicate to you what information I may receive in my retirement, of the nature you require; but I apprehend that a few hundred pounds sterling per annum, properly applied, might procure you such intelligence as would be worth millions to America; for, in our enemies' quarters, everything goes by purchase and sale; therefore, it was high time for us to have done with them.

---

* Shelburne was wounded in a duel fought on the 22d March, with a Mr. Fullarton.

We have no intelligence of the arrival of Mr. Laurens, though there are letters which mention his being embarked.

The Spaniards will do well to keep a watchful eye on the buccaneering expedition now preparing in England against their possessions in South America. I have the honor &c.

TO ARTHUR LEE.

ANVERS, 9 April, 1780.

Dear Sir:

I hope this will reach you before your embarkment on the great water, as it conveys to you the fervent wishes of myself and household, for your speedy and happy arrival in your own country, where if your rewards are equal to your merits, they will still not be greater than I wish you, or than I am sure you deserve.

The Gentleman at Madrid cannot meet with many difficulties there, since the Independance of America was publicly proclaimed by beat of drum, at New Orleans the 19th of last August; but I understand that the secretary, Mr Carmichael, has written to Paris, that he went to Madrid first, to prepare the way for Mr Jay, which had occasion'd him an infinite deal of fatigue, in so much that he had not slept for 4 nights; however he had at last surmounted all the difficulties, and Mr Jay was

to make his entry into Madrid the 13th of last
month. *

I send you No. 27 of the Courier de Bas Rhine.
The letter said to be authentic, written from Philadelphia, is said to have been furnished to the
editor of this gazette by a Mr. Dumas, agent for
Doct^{r.} Franklin at the Hague, and who it is reported, expects to be appointed chargé des affaires,
for the United States of America, in Holland.†
An American gentleman here, supposes that the
letter, if 'tis genuine, was written by Mr. Silas
Deane.

The Empress of Russia has declared to the
ambassadors of France, Spain and Great Britain,
that she is determined to keep a strict neutrality
in the present war; and to maintain that neutrality
and the general freedom of commerce, by a great
part of her naval force: that all neutral ships shall
not only sail unmolested on the high seas, but on
the coasts, and into, and out of, the ports of the

---

*There is nothing of this anxiety in Carmichael's letters
printed in the *Diplomatic Correspondence of the Revolution*, V.,
17. Jay's instructions to Carmichael are printed in the same
series, IV., 148. Carmichael did report "a tedious and disagreeable journey." He wrote to Jay on the 18th of February:
"Mr. Arthur Lee corresponded with the Count de Florida
Blanca, but if I am well informed, the correspondence consisted
of American news on the one part, and compliment on the
other."

† See the letter to Arthur Lee, 24 April, 1780, *post*.

parties at war; that free ships shall make free goods, unless in articles of contraband, conformable to the stipulations of her Treaty with Great Britain.*

On these principles she had applied to Sweden, Danemark, Holland and Portugal, publicly to enter into a league with her, which no doubt they will do.

The associations in England, recommended by the meeting of deputies, from the several county committees, seem to be generally approved; but still the Parliament seems to be at the beck of the ministers; tho' we shall be able to form a better judgment on this head, when we know what has been done the 6th of this month, which was fixed for taking the county petitions into consideration.†

In Ireland the people are by no means satisfied with their free trade, notwithstanding the addresses of their two houses of Parliament; they demand a free constitution totally independent of the British Parliament, and this they will have if the war continues.

---

* This declaration was issued 8 March, 1780, (N. S.) In addition to the principles mentioned by Lee, two others were asserted : that contraband are arms and ammunitions of war, and nothing else ; and that no port is blockaded unless the enemy's ships, in adequate number, are near enough to make the entry dangerous.

† See Donne., *George the Third's Letters to Lord North,* II, 292.

Not a word of what has become of Clinton, but it appears by the secret orders on board the transport driven into England, that the general rendezvous was at Tybee.

Walsingham was waiting at St Helena for a fair wind, the 2^d inst with the West India fleet; he will have 6 ships of the line and 6,000 troops; it is given out in England, that he goes first to Africa, and from thence to the West Indies, but some suspect that he goes directly to North America, for he certainly carries out the recruits for the several regiments now in America.* * * *

---

*Signed B^n de Bach, and addressed to Arthur Lee at L'Orient. It was while at L'Orient that Arthur received a copy of Carmichael's statement to Congress. *John Adams' Works*, VII., 133

Carmichael said Lee "sometimes sees things in a different light from any one else. I have not with me a copy of the paper which in consequence of the request of many gentlemen in the house, I laid before Congress, but I recollect the substance of it, viz. that Mr. Lee has rendered himself disagreeable to the Court and individuals of the French nation, and even suspected by the former, and that I derived my knowledge of this from those who were connected with the Court, and named Messrs. Grand on this occasion. This, and much more, M. Gerard and M. Holker confirmed by papers delivered either to Congress, or members of that body, which as well as that written by me are in private journals, or files of Congress." *Carmichael to Franklin*, 27 April, 1780.

"Mr. ? has just bro't me C[armichael]'s *Memoire*, as he would affectedly call it, which, on the whole, is more a panegyric on himself, than a censure on you. You see by his letter

TO JOHN ADAMS.

BRUXELLES, 9 April, 1780.

Dear Sir:

I thank you for your favor of the 2d. instant. The commission you have is certainly very highly important and honorable, and I doubt not of your executing it properly, taking care that the shafts of of envy and malice, which have already begun to show themselves, shall not divert your attention

---

to Mr. G. Grand that he is at his old game, endeavoring to make Jay now appear a cypher, as he did Deane before, by his letters to London. Seriously to reflect on the proceedings in this business, is really distressing : to admit the person as an *evidence*, who stands charged with criminal offences, by the person *now* accused, is subverting every idea of legal evidence that has yet been established in any orderly society. 'Tis not surprising that Bancroft should know of your going to Spain when he was the confidant of Deane and the regular correspondent of C——l. You can't forget that before the date of Ridley's letter, this gentleman had been with Johnson some time in Paris, and had with Williams, lodged in the same hotel with Carmichael, when no doubt he planned the idea of this letter, which poor Ridley does not seem to have executed so well as Jackson did on the same subject after the tutoring he got from C—m—l at Calais, in 1777, when the Public stands charged with about 4 guineas by C. for his expences, under the pretext of going to get a copy of Ct. Maurepas' letter to Lord Mánsfield (see C——l's curious account against Deane).

"Why did he insult Petrie by omitting to honor him in the list of the discontented ? who fortunately for you, make a group of needy adventurers whose main object was to plunder the Public in concert with Deane and Carmichael. The ill-will of the minister, I am satisfied, arose from Beaumarchais and the

from the great object you have in view, which I
have no reason to think at present will be speedily
accomplished. The well-known chicane and duplicity of our enemies will surely well warrant a
fixed determination not to treat on the most trivial
point, unless it is in writing. * * * You say
very truly that, "when a society gets disturbed,
men of great talents and great qualities are always
found or made;" for it is certain that there is

others openly concerned in the plunder of America, now he is
contented with the bills." *William Lee to Arthur Lee*, 24
March, 1780.

"I thank you for your intelligence of the state of affairs at
home, and for the extracts of Mr. Lee's philippics against me.
Such they were intended. But when I consider him as the
most malicious enemy I ever had (tho' without the smallest
cause), that he shews so clearly his abundant Desire to accuse
and defame me, and that all his Charges are so frivolous, so ill
founded, and amount to so little, I esteem them rather as
Panegyrics upon me and Satyrs against himself. . . .

" Mr. Adams is at Paris, with Mr. Dana. We live upon good
terms with each other, but he has never communicated anything of his business to me, and I have made no Enquiries of
him. Nor have I any Letter from Congress explaining it, so
that I am in utter ignorance. . . .

"Messrs Lee and Izard are gone to L'Orient in order to embark in the Alliance together, but they did not travel together
from hence. No Soul regrets their Departure: They separately
came to take leave of me, very respectfully offering their services to carry any dispatches, &c. We parted civilly, for I
have never acquainted them that I knew of their writing
against me to Congress, but I did not give them the Trouble of
my Dispatches." *Franklin to Carmichael*, 31 March, 1780.

always in the world, many more great men than great occasions; but the first architect that ever lived, could not erect a tolerable edifice with rotten straw only. The whole mass of the people in England is too corrupt and putrid to produce anything in the least sound and wholesome, from the trifling fermentation that appears at present. Therefore, in my opinion, the Irish, tho' much debauched and profligate as to politics, are much more worthy of attention and assurances of support than the English. Would it not be good policy in France to have a good stock of muskets and other military stores lodged at Dunkirk, and other sea ports, ready to throw into England at a short warning? * * *

TO RICHARD HENRY LEE.

BRUXELLES, 13 April, 1780.

I have suffered much uneasiness on your account, since our brother A. L. wrote me from L'Orient, that in your letter to him about the middle of August last, you had mentioned your then being very unwell. I know it was a trying season to those who, like you, are subject to bilious complaints, but I trust that as you were then relieved from the infinite care and fatigues that have oppressed you for many years past, you would get reinstated in health and vigor very soon. The enclosed declaration of Russia, which is particularly intended against Great Britain, must give you infinite pleasure, as it must, if anything can, bring our enemies to reason, and a serious desire of peace. For this decisive stroke in our favor from Russia, we are much indebted to the good offices of his Prussian majesty, without whom, that court would not have taken the steps it has done, notwithstanding the seizure of a Dutch fleet, under convoy of Dutch men of war, in the channel by the English in January last, has been the ostensible motive for it. From the terms of the declaration, we must conclude that all neutral trade to America (except articles of contraband) will be protected, as well as into the ports of France, Spain and Great Britain; therefore one would not be surprised to see a Dutch fleet entering into Chesapeake Bay.

I wait impatiently to hear what has been decided about the estate, for until I know that, it is impossible for me to determine on any plan of proceedings for myself. These Virginians have no great spirit of commerce; their former trade having been carried on by British merchants, we were obliged to make great advances to the country. Therefore I do not suppose much would be expected from consignments if a person was to fix with that view in any of the French ports; but the old ideas of our countrymen must change, or the profits on their trade must continue to enrich strange merchants. Maryland seems more enterprising, for there has been a much greater number of vessels at Nantes from Maryland than Virginia; so that Mr. Johnson, agent for Maryland and brother to the late governor, who is established there, seems to be doing very well, and I fancy is looking forward to be consul general for America in France. * * *

There is no saying how far the madness of our enemies will carry them; but if they have one grain of common sense, they must now make peace, as soon as and on the best terms they can; for the whole world seems at present to be leagued against the King of England, 5 or 6 of his confidential ministry, and a few hoards of their honorable and faithful allies the Indians. The people of England have followed the example of America, in adopting Committees of Associations, which may produce another revolution; and Ireland having obtained a free trade, which in time will render her the most formidable rival of Great Britain in commerce, wealth and power, the people now feeling their importance and sure of indemnity from the force of their independent companies, demand a free constitution almost unanimously, and an entire independence of G. B., which two points they will certainly obtain, if the war continues. The two Irish Houses of Parliament have indeed, since gaining a free trade, addressed the King in a most servile manner, but the members of the Patriotic Party, who had been bo't off, that moved and supported those addresses, have fallen into utter contempt and disgrace with their fellow citizens, which proves unquestionably, that the people who have now the sword in their hands, think differently from their Parliament, whose tone must probably change before many months expire. On the whole, of late affairs in Europe have taken a decisive turn in our favor, and I hope they will be as decisively for us in America before this campaign ends.   *   *   *

TO JOHN ADAMS.

BRUXELLES, 25 April, 1780.

Dear Sir:

I thank you for the intelligence contained in your favor of the 13th, and when there are any other arrivals from America, you will greatly oblige me by communicating any intelligence they may bring. I confess I am uneasy to hear from Charleston, for there is no doubt of Clinton having designed his principal force against that Town, as I cannot give any credit to the surmises of some people that the rendezvous was at Tybee, in order to be ready for an attack on some of the Spanish possessions. The infatuation of our enemies is evidently the work of Providence; therefore, I have no expectation of a speedy peace, because the measure of their punishment is not yet full. Their frenzy is turned into raving madness, as you will see by the proclamation against the Dutch, which is tantamount to a declaration of war, and the insulting language used against the Russians in the ministerial papers; therefore, as you say, we need not be, surprised if they were to declare war against the whole world. This would be a favorable minute for Mr. Laurens, if he was in Holland, where no doubt his prudence will direct him to examine well his ground before he moves; for he may meet with characters, both inimical and selfish, who under the garb of patriotic, friendly zeal may endeavor to lead him into error. The Dutch, who are so jealous of any other nation but themselves catching a herring in the open sea, think it not unreasonable or immodest to expect exclusive privileges in some part of American trade, and an equal freedom with others to the fishery on the banks of Newfoundland. * * *

TO ARTHUR LEE.

ANVERS, 24 April, 1780.

If you wait for the Alliance, I am sure this will reach you before you sail; for if what we hear be true, it is probable that her operations this year will be of as little utility to her proprietors, as those of last year were. * It is said that Mr. I[zard] sailed

---

*On the 17 June, Franklin wrote to Jones that he had information that Arthur Lee had advised and promoted the mutiny

the 15th of this month in a frigate, but we hear nothing of you. I sent you some time ago a Bas Rhine Gazette, containing an extract of a letter, said to be furnished by Dr. F—n's agent at the Hague, Mr. D[umas]. On that subject I wrote thus to Mr. D.:

"There has appeared in the Courier de Bas Rhine, No. 27, April 1st, 1780, a piece said to be an extract of an authentic letter written from Philadelphia, which begins thus: *Mons. vous voulez que je vous rende compte de vraie état de nos affaires.* I have been informed that this piece was furnished by you to the Editor of the Bas Rhine Gazette, but as I know these are times in which misinformation is too current, especially in what concerns America, I cannot give implicit faith to such information without it is confirmed by yourself. I therefore presume you will not think it improper in me to request you, that you will candidly tell me whether you did or not furnish the editor of the B. R. with the above mentioned piece."

---

on the *Alliance*, and if that were the case, and the Commodore conceived the peace and good government of the ship during the voyage would be endangered by his presence, he might decline taking him.

"M. Lee has been long at Orient waiting for a passage on board the Alliance. I have yesterday received several letters acquainting me with a mutiny on board that ship which he is supposed to have instigated. I have obtained and sent down orders to apprehend and imprison some of the chiefs, which I hope will produce quiet. That restless genius, wherever he is, must either find or make a quarrel." *Franklin to Carmichael,* 17 June, 1780.

To this Mr. D. replies thus:—

"How a gazettier came at the piece you quote, I
know not. These gentlemen have in this country, as
well as at Paris, at London, and elsewhere, their secret
correspondents, whom they pay for gathering them all
what they can."

You can judge better than me whether this answer is not evasive, and if so, whether it is not an
indirect confession. I think your good sense will
direct you to know well your ground, and consider
with calm and serious attention the situation of
affairs before you take any public step after your
arrival; for I am well convinced that men and
things will be found very different from what we
on this side the water might expect.

You have been before advised of the declaration
of Russia to France, Spain and Great Britain.
This day we receive a proclamation of the present
King of G. B. declaring that all treaties between
the states of the U. Provinces and G. B. are
vacated, and that the Dutch are from henceforth
to be treated as a neutral nation, with whom no
treaties exist, and with all the formality of a declaration of war, particular periods (all short) are
fixed for this proclamation taking place in different
parts of the world. The stocks fell upon this 1½
per cent. The Dutch must now defend themselves
or give up entirely all trade. The alternative will
not set easy on them. However they feel bold or

the declaration of Russia, and Sweden's supplying them with 4000 sailors, and will probably decide on vigorous measures as far as their nature will admit. They are to have twenty ships of the line from Russia, which will be at the Texel in all June; of their own they will have about 15 of the line, and 30 frigates ready at the same time. Therefore they will have strength, if they have but spirit enough, to bring our enemies to reason. Is not this stroke of the foolish mad king and his ministers the last act of desperation? Nothing is now left to compleat his career, and fix him in Hanover, but an insurrection in England and Ireland, which seems to be ripening fast. God send it quickly to give us peace, that we may be forever quit of such desperado pirates; for I think the people have become as infamous and abandoned as their king has ever been.* * * *

---

* "It is said that Mr. R. Morris is now in Congress, at which every body is surprised, as by the confederation no person can serve in Congress more than 3 years out of 6—Mr. Morris having already served more than 3 years. And more particularly does it occasion surprise, as it cannot be supposed that in America they are uninformed of what is publicly spoken in Europe, which is, that Mr. R. Morris is universally considered as the British agent employed by Gov. Johnstone to embarrass, distract and confound the measures of America in her defence, and that he is furnished with the *solid* means of accomplishing those purposes. A young man of his household, only a few months ago, passed from Philadelphia to England by the way of Holland. The object of this voyage may be

TO JOHN ADAMS.

BRUXELLES, 14 June, 1780.

Dear Sir:

I am indebted to you for your favor of the 6th. The American vessels lately arrived in Holland do not, that I hear of, bring any material public news, except the last which came from Boston the beginning of May, and informs us of the Marquis de la Fayette's arrival there, and that they expected there also Mons. de Rochambeau's army, which may be

---

easily conceived, especially as it was immediately after this young man, with some others, had been the defenders of Mr. M. in a house in Philadelphia against the rage of his fellow citizens last year. ['Fort Wilson riot.'] I have myself many reasons for inducing me to believe that Mr. Morris is really the character that most people in Europe that have ever heard of him, suppose him, and I have no doubt that effectual proofs would soon appear against him, if Congress was to adopt the practice, which he used for many years against almost every person in America, viz: of opening all letters to him and from him. Among his brother's papers were found above 150 letters addressed to different persons in Europe and America, that had been opened and detained. Of this fact I have a certificate signed by the King's officer at Nantes. How many more letters had been opened by Mr. Morris (who it must be remembered had learnt his profession under his brother R. M., in Philadelphia), and advantage taken of their contents, every person is left to judge." *William Lee to Richard Henry Lee*, 26 April, 1780.

The charge that Morris was a British agent was apparently based upon an extract from a letter "from a gentleman in high office in America" dated January, 1780, and printed in the English papers.

a means of giving the enemy at N. York sufficient warning to put that place in the best posture of defence their force will admit, and to recall Clinton from Carolina, of whose motions these vessels do not bring any certain intelligence. Nor do I learn that Mr. Laurens has embarked, altho' bills have already appeared drawn upon him in Holland by Congress. This I do not comprehend, nor some other public matters; therefore shall suspend my judgment, sincerely hoping that the party, which have already created so much distraction in Congress and America, will be ultimately disappointed in their dangerous and abominable designs. As to Mr. Deane, I always tho't, and am now convinced, that he was only made use of as a stalking horse, to cover designs and views that his patrons dared not openly to avow.

I cannot say what will probably be the issue of this campaign in the West Indies, where the enemy will be strong. Graves, with 6 ships of the line and 3000 troops, will probably go to Jamaica, where Sir P. Parker has 6 of the line, 2 fifty's, and 4-44 gun ships, besides frigates and about 12 or 1500 soldiers in the island. Walsingham carries to Rodney 3000 troops, and 5 or 6 ships of the line; and 4 others were sent separately, so that Rodney will be very powerful, after providing a convoy for the homeward bound fleet. But we may suppose that Walsingham and the other ships will not get to Rodney before the middle or end of July.

Our last English papers are only to the 6th, but some persons who left London the 8th, on account of the tumults, give a flaming account of the proceedings there on the 7th. and 8th. The people have pulled down and burnt several houses of most of the Roman Catholic places of worship.* The military and citizens have had some rencounters and several lives lost on both sides. 'Tis likely, however, that the ministry and the military will prevail over the people, who do not seem to have provided themselves with the proper instruments of defense, and have the corrupted hands of what is called the opposition, as much against them as the King. This nation appears to me quite lost, and that in fifty years they will be no more considered in the political scale of Europe than the Algerines; but they will die hard, and we must endeavor to let the exertions of their dying agonies be exercised on themselves. The Dutch seem to be feeling some of them, and losing all their ships, while they are differing with each other, whether they should patiently endure or not every thing the English please to do. The language of the English with respect to America is as incomprehensible to me as it is to you, unless they are led

---

*The Gordon riots, which really increased the influence of the ministers by producing a reaction in favor of authority. By a rumor of the day, these outbreaks were attributed to French corruption. See *Franklin's Works*, vii., 87,

by the ministry to give implicit confidence to their partizans that are at large in America, and perhaps permitted to be in Congress and posts of importance.

You ask, will the 22 millions for next year; with the men lost in America and the W. I. by diseases and the chance of war; will seamen be easily found? The 22, or even more, millions will be easily found, as long as the Bank of England can coin with more facility than paper money in America, and while even the French as well as the Dutch, tempted by high interest, will lend them money. Soldiers will be found with more difficulty; but as long as the European powers will permit their sailors to be seized on the high seas, and forced on board the British navy, there can be no fear of their wanting seamen. 'Tis computed by judicious men, that this time full one-half of the British navy is manned by foreigners, impressed in England, or seized on the high seas, and forced on board their ships of war. I sometime since mentioned Portugal to you, and every day proves to me more and more the necessity of treating her as a coadjutor with G. Britain, unless she will shut her ports against the English men of war and privateers. Refusing to admit prizes, is only a pitiful evasion of what she ought to do: which is to refuse admittance to all ships of war, privateers and armed vessels. * * *

TO ARTHUR LEE.

ANVERS, 23 June, 1780.

The above extracts (viz: from General Advertiser and J. A. to W. L.) prove a certain connection, and that if Mr. I. does not effectively succeed, an excuse is ready, and the blame to be laid on another. But if he gains anything, the whole will be attributed to his superior [   ] and abilities. It seems however that the present object of this connection and its adherits on this side the water, is to get *Franklin* removed, as *Adams* has his eye on the place; while the leaders and partisans of the same connection on the other side the water, seem to be playing a bolder game, and levelling their attacks directly against the Independence of America, as may be seen in the following extract from a Philadelphia paper. Dear Sir, the foregoing pieces will show the great necessity for caution and circumspection in *A. Lee* in all his motions. Pray tell him so, and also that *Jenings* is as much, nay more, devoted to *Carmichael* than ever. He is attached to *Adams*, who flatters him,* and from resentment against *Franklin*,† who it is said, has

---

* "A gentleman from Boston tells me he heard there that they were written by one Mr. Jenings. I wish his countrymen knew more than they do about that same Mr. Jenings." *John Adams to Edmund Jenings*, 23 September, 1780.

† "170 seems to have voluntarily undertaken the honorable post of agent for *Adams*, to get all his long-winded and crude

been authorized by *Congress* to appoint to a certain place (which I suspect is *consul general*), and mentioned *Jenings* and the examiner of accounts, as persons either of whom might be proper. But *Franklin* has not tho't so, and very possibly 142 [*Ross?*] stays to exercise that office. You will easily see the management of *R. Morris* in this business, and as 'tis likely 94 will not go to *Holland*, plots will be on foot to get *Deane*—111er [*Courtier?*] there. * * *

TO JOHN ADAMS.

BRUXELLES, 8 July, 1780.

I have been prevented by indisposition, otherwise should have had the honor of writing to you sooner, on a subject which appears to affect the honor of America, of Congress, and of its agents in Europe. The copy of Gen'l Clinton's letter that was intercepted, which you sent here by Mr. Jenings, having afterwards appeared in most of the

---

productions inserted in the London papers. Among this is a history of a voyage from Corun: to P., in which *Adams* speaks of the person at 102 [*Madrid?*] in the highest strains of praise and commendation. I saw the original in the hand-writing of *Adams.*" *William Lee to Arthur Lee*, 16 June, 1780. Adams suggested to Genet some material to be worked into the communication from London. *Works*, vii, 155. And to Digges he wrote a letter probably intended for publication in the English papers. *Works*, vii, 167. So that 170 is presumably Digges.

public papers, there was a formal contradiction of its authenticity, first in the Hague Gazette, and inserted in such a manner as to make the world believe that this contradiction came from Sir Jo: Yorke, the English minister. The Leyden Gazette * confirmed in some measure this contradiction, in which it was followed by the Courier du Bas Rhin, tho' it had before given the letter at length, as having been originally published by order of Congress. But after the intelligence of the surrender of Charleston, this same gazetteer, in No. 51 of June 24, 1780, positively states that letter to have been a forgery, and concludes in these injurious terms:—"donc it vaut mieux se bien defendre et se bien battre, que de supposes des lettres, qui ne peuvent abuser le public qu'un moment."† You must be sensible of the injury it

---

* The editor of this sheet was John Luzac.

† Adams contributed the following to the history of this letter. It "arrived first at L'Orient, in a Philadelphia newspaper which had been sent to Mr. Jay. Mr. Wharton, I think, copied it, and sent it to Dr. Franklin, who communicated it soon after it appeared in Boston(?) and other newspapers, without a hint of its want of authenticity. Within a few days past, I have seen a gentleman from America, who says it was a mere *jeu d'esprit* written by an officer in the army, upon the North River. I have been all along afraid that our countrymen would at length imitate their enemies in this kind of imposition; and I always thought that, whenever they did, they would be ingenious at it. It must be agreed this is ingeniously done, and conveys a great deal of solid truth and important instruction under this fiction.

will bring to America, and the cause of Liberty, if the world is permitted to be impressed with the Idea that Congress, and its agents, are base enough to be guilty of such a mean and pitiful conduct, as to forge and publish the grossest falsehoods as solid truths. Mr. Dumas, who is styled by Dr. Franklin and Mr. Deane the American agent at the Hague, and who is actually paid with the money of America, has a particular connection with the Editor of the Leyden Gazette, and I have reason to believe has a correspondence with the Bas Rhin. Therefore one would naturally imagine, as it was his duty, he would have taken some measures to prevent such a censure on America, &c., from spreading farther than in the small circle in which the Hague Gazette circulates. The Bas Rhin Gazette, as well as that of Berlin, is generally looked on as a Prussian Court Gazette, being printed in the Capital of the Prussian Dominions on the Rhine, and I have no doubt, on the Prussian Minister at Paris being spoke to on the subject, a repetition of such conduct would at least be prevented in the Editor of that Gazette. * * *

Yet, I cannot think the ingenuity of it a justification or excuse. We have no need of such aids as political lies. . . . All that we can do, is to write Congress and beseech them to suppress such practices. The signature of Charles Thomson, hitherto sacred, will no longer be credited, if something is not done to discountenance such abuses." *Adams to William Lee,* 20 July, 1780. Franklin's connection may be seen in his letter to Dumas, 5 June, 1780. *Works,* vii, 72.

TO SAMUEL. W. STOCKTON.

BRUXELLES, 9 July, 1780.

We have no advice yet of old Mr. Laurens, and the young gentleman being a prisoner is no small consolation to the society at Passy, where the conduct of the affairs of America has grown worse and worse, until it has actually become a scandal for any man of the least character to be in any manner concerned with them. The supplies for the American army that should have been in America last fall, are not yet shipped. The league of Sam. Wharton, Jno. Ross, Dr. Bancroft, young and old Jonᵃ Williams, seem to have no other contest, but who shall take to himself the best share of the public money that is intrusted to Dr. Franklin, in which sport they are most eminently assisted by Mr. Chaumont, who has young Moylan of Phila. as his agent at L'Orient, and young Williams at Nantes. The proceedings of these people with Dr. F. and Cap. P. Jones, respecting the Congress Frigate, the Alliance, for near two years past, are really too enormous for me to detail; but I must say that in my opinion, it will be impossible for the American affairs to be properly conducted in France, while Dr. F. continues sole minister, commercial agent, agent for prizes, treasurer, and in short absolute head and proprietor of all American property, dignity, honor and even liberty in France.*

* "July 30. Spent the afternoon, and drank tea with Mr. W.

TO ARTHUR LEE.

ANVERS, 8 October, 1780.

Dear Sir:

I am very sorry to inform you that your intended Minister to Holland, Mr. Henry Laurens, was taken by the English frigates on the Banks of New Foundland and is brought Prisoner to England where by the last accounts he is very ill, at a little place in Devonshire, so as to be unable to be brought to London.

The English papers give out that all his papers, instructions and commission were taken also, but this is not believed by those that know the arts of duplicity of your enemies; however this seems authentic, that General Clinton's dispatches dated the latter end of August demand a re-enforcement of 10,000 men, which if not sent he insisted on being recalled. On this the King and his Council determined that Clinton should be immediately informed that his conduct was in all respects highly approved, that he should have the assistance required as soon as possible. General Fawcitt is to go immediately to Germany to make fresh contracts, if he can, for new bodies of troops, and to hasten the levying recruits for the German corps already in America. If no assistance can be got

---

Lee, Mr. Jenings and his nephew, Mrs. Izard, her two daughters and son, Mrs. Lee and her children, and an agreeable circle of Americans." *John Adams' Diary.*

from Germany, G. B., and Ireland are to be gleaned of all the regular troops to send to Clinton. This is the present determination as all fear of an invasion is over, since the French seem to relinquish any such design; but what may take place if Jamaica should be taken I cannot tell, nor can I say whether the Dutch will defend their possessions in the W. Indies or their trade, both of which have been and continue daily to be attacked by the English.

Portugal has at last driven the English ships of war and Privateers from her Ports and forbid them or their prizes to enter there again. The division which was to have followed Monsieur Ternay has not yet sailed from Brest; it is said that it is to sail the 15th inst. but your enemies are preparing a a large squadron of ships to follow it, either to America or the West Indies. You will hear from me at large by the first sure conveyance. Your friends in this quarter are as well as the times will admit. With high respect I remain,

LE BARON DE BACH.

N. S. Take care of some Marylanders who have been lately sent from England, as it is confidently said, with permission to take the oaths to the present Government, in order the more effectually to create divisions in that State, by means of their connections there, which are said to be among the principal families in that country. Your enemies still dream of unconditional submission only.

TO ARTHUR LEE.

ANVERS, 17 October, 1780.

Dear Sir:

I have before given you notice that your enemies had determined to make a strong push this fall and next spring against North Carolina and Virginia; and that on receiving a late demand from Genl. Clinton, for a reinforcement of 10,000 men, otherwise he insisted on leave to come home, the King and his Council decided to inform Genl. Clinton, that his conduct was in all points highly approved, and that he should have every assistance in their power to send him, and as soon as possible. The vessel with this reply to Clinton, sailed from England the 10ᵗʰ inst, for New York. So far you may rely on to be true. A gentleman from Passy says, that the Alliance was arrived at Boston, as Dʳ F. told him, and that Capt. Landais had been put under an arrest.* We have been highly disappointed

---

* "In the evening [19 August, 1780], M. Gau, commandant of artillery, who arrived from Boston, informed me that the *Alliance*, an American frigate, had just arrived. It had left L'Orient on the 9th of July. The captain, named Landais, born a Frenchman, had left L'Orient without waiting for the King's despatches. He wished to cruise, although laden with powder which he was ordered to bring straight to Boston; his crew,

in finding that the combined fleets in the West Indies have not attempted anything this campaign, but perhaps they will not be idle in the fall and winter.

M.ʳ Laurens, the minister from Congress to the States of Holland, was taken on the Banks of Newfoundland, carried to England, and is committed to the Tower of London, on suspicion of high treason. His material papers were destroyed, but some letters of private correspondence, on mercantile affairs, were taken with M.ʳ Laurens.*

Your minister, M.ʳ J. Adams, has been for some time at Amsterdam, and the other day a member of Congress, a M.ʳ S., passed thro' here, in his way from Paris to Amsterdam, where it is said he is under the guidance of Doct. F. to negotiate the money business that M.ʳ Laurens was to have man-

---

tired of his follies and his vexations, had shut him up in his cabin and had given the command of the frigate to his mate. On board were two French officers, aides-de-camp of M. de la Fayette, and Mr. Lee, who had been a long time in France, a deputy of the Congress. They told us that on the 9th of July the body of troops which they were to send to us, and which they called the second division, had not yet started. Besides this, they gave us no very certain news respecting the affairs of Europe." *Journal of Claude Blanchard*, 56.

* Among the documents taken were copies of letters from Neufville, Commodore Gillon, Mr. Stockton, Col. Derrick, and the treaty made between the city of Amsterdam and William Lee.

aged, and some say he is to be minister in Holland or Portugal. I know not whether he is in any public appointment, but he travels in the style of a public minister.*

M.ʳ Deane lives at Passy with D.ʳ B[ancroft]. These two, it seems, are in the privy council there.

Capt.ⁿ Paul Jones is still at L'Orient, endeavoring to fit out the Ariel, in which he has hitherto found insurmountable difficulties.

The Northern League of Neutrality is acceded to by Holland and Portugal, from which kingdom the British ships of war, privateers and prizes are now excluded.

Ten ships of the line are now about sailing from Brest with about 5000 troops, some say to reinforce Mons.ʳ Ternay, and others that they are for the West Indies.

In Europe the belligerent powers are, on all sides, busily preparing for another campaign; and in England orders are already issued for raising 9 new regiments of foot, & one regiment of horse, to reinforce the British Army in America; since they have little hope of getting a fresh supply of men from Germany. Your spirited countrymen, will, no doubt, be prepared to repel these invaders,

---

*It was James Searle, a member of Congress from Pennsylvania, who reached Paris, 10 September, 1780, with despatches from Congress, and as an agent to negotiate a loan for the State of Pennsylvania.

as triumphantly as they have hitherto done those that preceded them.

LE BARON DE BACH.

TO ARTHUR LEE.

BRUXELLES, 6 November, 1780.

Dear Brother:

I received yours from Boston of Sep.^t 9th, and am well pleased at the determination to withhold your complaints for the present, rather than increase the public embarrassments by expressing them. * * *

The capture of Mr Laurens (who is committed to the tower of London for high treason, and closely kept without the use of pen or ink, or permission to see his friends) was doubly unfortunate, as his papers were taken also; which has occasion'd a memorial from the British Court to the Prince of Orange, relative to what has passed with the regency of Amsterdam, which he laid before the States of Holland. The regency of Amsterdam have avowed their proceedings, and demanded the concurrence of the States of Holland; what turn this business will take time must discover, but nothing effectual can at any rate soon take place in our favor, as there is not any body fully authorized to act for America.

Mr Adams is now and has been for some months at Amsterdam, where he seems decided to stay the winter.

Mr. Searle is gone there; I saw him on his way thro' this town and was surprised at his not bringing me a letter from any one. From some unlucky circumstances I had not an opportunity of getting any material information from him relative to the actual situation of affairs in America. By his style of travelling and proposed manner of living in Amsterdam during the winter, it seems clear that he is on public, and not private business. He, it is said, professes a devoted attachment to *Franklin.*

Russia, Sweden and Danemark have finally ratified their treaty of the armed neutrality, on the original plan of Russia. Portugal has acceded to it. The Emperors of Turkey and Morocco have nearly adopted the same idea. The States of Holland and Friesland have already, and it is expected that the other 5 states of the Netherlands will very soon accede to the Russian system, so Great Britain has not a single ally in this part of the world, but some of the insignificant petty princes in Germany.

The affairs in Ireland still wear a serious aspect, but in England people grow every day more insensible, and are now as contented slaves as any in the world. The new Parliament is not a whit better than the old; and the minister, or rather the King, will be as absolute as ever. Norton goes with a pension to the house of peers.* Cornwall

---

* By too great freedom of speech on financial reform, Sir Fletcher Norton had given offense to the King; and Lord

is Speaker by a majority of 34 votes. Burke, Sawbridge,† Hartley, Temple, Luttrell, Cruger, Lord George Gordon, are left out, but the two first will be brought in by and bye.

The Parliament met the 31 ult? The King in his speech boasts of victories in Carolina; The war must certainly be continued another year, and demands supplies.‡

The reinforcements for America, that are to sail as soon as possible, perhaps about Xmas, are to consist of 9 regiments of foot, and 3 of dragoons dismounted, to be remounted in America. The regiments of foot, by drafts from others are to be complete 9,000 men, and the 3 dragoons are to be 1,000 men, which in the whole is to make 10,000 complete. The great push is to be made first in Virginia and N. Carolina; if success attends them there, they are to advance northwards.

North, without previous notice, set him aside, "lamenting the precarious state of Sir Fletcher's health," although Sir Fletcher protested that he had never been in better health. Charles Wolfram Cornwall was elected Speaker, 203 to 134.

† Sawbridge had been much condemned for his conduct during the Gordon riots, and lost votes for voting in favor of tolerating popery. Burke was defeated at Bristol, but subsequently came in from the borough of Malton. The Parliament contained 113 new members.

‡ The opportune news of the defeat of Gates by Cornwallis, enabled the King to put a better face to the situation than he had hoped. The majority for the government was very large and carried every measure the ministry proposed.

The whole exertions are to be against North America, keeping on the defensive against France and Spain; who are to be amused in the meantime with negotiations, and advantageous *offers* (which are never intended to be complied with,) to induce them to desert America. This, you may be assured, is the enemies plan of operations for the ensuing year.

On our side the Spaniards hear the proposals made to them without giving any reply; which induces the idiot King and his roguish ministers to think they shall succeed in dividing the allies, as they have with their opponents at home.

The division that was to have followed M. Ternay is still at Brest; but reported that it is to sail in 3 or 4 weeks.

The supplies for the American Army, that should have been sent away above 12 months ago, are still in the ports of France; in short the management of your affairs there has gone from bad to worse, and unless the director is speedily changed, the consequences will be severely felt.

The change in the minister of marine in France, it is expected will invigorate their operations. Chaumont has been lately at a stand (it is said) in his payments, but we hear M.r Neckar will countenance him, but this is only rumor. He says his engagements for America have hurt him, when I know his unpaid accepted bills have been travelling thro' Germany for some years past.

America must, as I always said, rely entirely on her own efforts, and then she may be sure of carrying her point. Think not of the conquest of Canada, until the enemy are quite driven from the 13 States. I can't enter into the reasons for this advice, but believe me, they are so important that if the conquest of Canada is attempted, while you have a single enemy within your boundaries, the consequences will be fatal. Monsr Rochambeau and his troops should be *instantly* ordered to Virginia. * * *

TO RICHARD HENRY LEE.

BRUXELLES, 3 Decr 1780.

My dear Brother :

Since mine by your sons, I have not received any letter from you, but have written to you several; indeed since that I have heard but of very few arrivals in any part of Europe, from Virginia, except the fleet that came under convoy of the Fier Roderigue. * * *

No letter has come to me from Mr Ellis since 1778, written a few months after he entered on the estate, and being quite uninformed of the state of affairs in Virginia, and of the money in circulation, or of the actual laws regulating the currency, I cannot advise any particular plan of conducting the business, but must refer to your discretion.

However, if at any time in the next year it becomes practicable to send me some tobacco, either to France or to Holland, I beg it may be done, only have the freight specified in the bills, and let the tobacco be consigned to me, or order. This I much fear will be impracticable, as the London Gazette now tells us in Oct.ʳ Clinton had sent from New York a body of forces to invade Virginia. Orders for this purpose were sent from England last summer, and since the middle of July repeated advice of this plan was sent the present Governor of Virginia, that preparations might be made to give the invaders a proper reception. These savage robbers, that are not to be equalled in iniquity but by their Licenser, who is a more horrid wretch than any one among them, will I apprehend do a great deal of mischief to individuals; everything moveable they will steal, and according to custom, will burn and lay waste what they cannot carry off. Providence however seems to be completing her great work by ridding America of every Tory rascal and traitor that is in her.

Tho' I believe there are very few of this discription among you, yet I shall be happy to hear that the few there are, openly declare themselves; as it is certain, that one concealed traitor is more dangerous to the community than ten open foes.

The councillor has now a valuable and interesting paper on the British navy. The Dutch are arming by sea with spirit, and placing their land forces in their maritime towns, having at last come into the armed neutrality with Russia, Sweden and Denmark.

These powers will have at sea next spring a fleet of 50 sail of the line, and as many frigates to support the plan of free commerce, as published by Russia last spring, which you must have seen, against the insolent pretensions of Great Britain and the piratical robberies of her Royal and private armed vessels.

We are on the eve of a war, all the maritime powers of Europe against Great Britain, who is without a single ally, unless the latter recedes from her ill-founded claims and demands a peace.

France and Spain go on in their system, and maintain a superiority in the European seas,—perhaps before this, if the winds and weather have not prevented, D'Estaing with 42 sail of the line, has given Darby, off Cape Finisterre with 26 sail of the line, a blow that the British navy cannot recover this war.

Your agents in Spain have done nothing but got a little money; some of their old connections from the *Island* have been at Madrid for several months, which the sagacious Spaniard does not like, and consequently fights shy.

The management of your affairs in France seems to grow worse and worse, for the old junto, Silas

Deane in the midst of them, have by some means or other got the whole management uncontrolled into their hands. A reform must take place there, and by the capture of Mr Laurens, your affairs in Holland are not in so good a state as they might be. Mr Laurens with all his letters and papers fell into the enemies hands.

When any person is sent to Europe in a public character, he should at least have good common sense. Surely the several states will now pay more attention than they have done lately, to the respectability of the persons that they send to represent them in Congress; and a little more steadiness in rigidly adhering to fundamental resolutions, will give weight and consequence to their determinations. How an actual member of Congress can do his duty in America, and execute commissions at 3000 miles distance in person, is a problem that we thickheaded people here can't solve. What infatuation induces our country again to employ Genl Stevens? Was not the loss of the battle of Germantown sufficient? but the whole stake must be again lost at Camden. A defeat of Cornwallis there would have ended the war. God bless you all, and believe that we love you and yours sincerely. Adieu.

TO ARTHUR LEE.

ANVERS, 6th Dec^r , 1780.

Dear Sir:

We have heard from you from Boston, and Lebanon, and your two correspondents from this neighborhood have also heard from you. We are happy to hear of your safe arrival, and also of the 6,000 acres of land.

I have written to you frequently since you left us, but as the capture of y^r minister, Mr Laurens, and the *whole* of his papers and letters, shows that the conveyance is not always safe; to show you how many letters miscarry they shall be numbered regularly, beginning with this, no. 1.

Amongst Mr Laurens' papers was found the plan of a treaty between the States of America and the 7 Provinces of the Netherlands, which had been settled between your friend, and an agent of the Pensionary Regency of Amsterdam. This, with a copy of some of the letters, were laid before the Prince of Orange by the British ambassador, Sir J. Yorke, and by the Prince before the States of Holland; expecting, no doubt, that the Regency of Amsterdam would disavow, or apologize to Great Britain for the business.

The Regency on the contrary openly maintain that they had done what was right, and demanded of the States of Holland an approbation of what had been done. This so irritated the British court, that

Sir J. Yorke was ordered, and did present to the States General the most extraordinary memorial that has been seen in Europe in this century. You will see it in the public prints.* No answer has yet been given, for as it sounds like a declaration of war, the Dutch probably wait till the British cannon roar; to which they are prepared to make a proper return. They have formally agreed to enter into the armed neutrality with Russia, Sweden and Denmark, which three have already ratified their treaties, on the plan originally proposed by Russia. These 4 powers will have at sea in the spring a fleet of 50 sail of the line, and as many frigates; and if Great Britain attacks Holland, she attacks the other three, or if she attempts to prevent either of them from supplying France and Spain with naval stores.

Some people think Great Britain will be mad enough to make the attempt, which must prove her ruin, as the enclosed paper must convince every impartial man; but it seems more probable that this armed neutrality will produce a general peace in 1781, especially if Great Britain should receive any check in her plans against America.

This is a critical moment for your country, as it appears very probable that the northern powers, with Holland, might now be easily induced to

*It is printed in *Diplomatic Correspondence of the Revolution*, III., 269. See Adams letter in his *Works*, vii., 329.

acknowledge your independence, if you had proper agents or ministers in Europe to negotiate such an important business; for it is said that the King of Prussia is your friend, and that Austria has no very warm feelings for Great Britain.

But you have no minister in this part of the world; there is a Mʳ Seaʳle at Amsterdam, who is said to be the Consul-General of America in Holland, and at the same time a member of Congress, and a colonel in your militia, which people in general can't believe, because they see the impossibility of one man's performing the duties of those different offices at the same period.

Your minister in Spain [Jay] and his coadjutor [Carmichael] have done nothing but get a little money; indeed your enemies for several months have had two and three agents at Madrid publicly, who have contrived to come at your friends, or to ——, so that your affairs here are no farther advanced than they were twelve months ago.

You have some able and respectable Roman Catholics among you; would not one of them be most proper to send as your representative to Spain?

In France the ministry steadily pursue their old system; tho' Monsʳ Sartine is turned out and the Marquis of Castries is in his place; therefore your political affairs, of course, go on as they did, but the management of your other affairs, we are told, grows worse and worse. S. Deane lives at Passy, and seems to direct and manage in y^r business as formerly.

The supplies for your army, that should have been shipp'd last winter, are most of them still lying in the ports of France, and the famous Paul Jones is now at Brest or L'Orient. The reinforcement that was to have followed Monsr Ternay immediately, is not yet gone; some say your minister is the cause, having hinted that it was not necessary; but this one can hardly believe.

What the cabinet of Versailles has determined (or what seems most probable, that they have not determined anything yet) relative to the operations in America next campaign, the world is not informed.

You will, surely, make a reform at least in France; and confine your minister to politics, and intrust solely to a Consul-General, or mercantile agent, who should be formally introduced to the French ministry, all your monied and mercantile transactions, purchasing and sending out the supplies for your army, and supplying, &c., your ships of war that may enter the ports of France.

You know what the enemy are doing with you. The designs against Virginia the Governor of that state has been frequently advised of, since the middle of July; therefore it is supposed he will not be taken unprepared.

The discovery of Arnold's plot, it is imagined, will lead to the discovery and punishment of his principal associators, so as to deter similar attempts hereafter; for tho' some of the leaders may have by their address got into appointments on this side the water, it is not impracticable to catch and punish them. Curious and attentive observers think you have escaped the greatest danger that has ever threatened you; as the British ministry, on the gaining *one Arnold alone*, are evidently more dejected than if they had lost a whole army. Clinton had before demanded to be recalled, or to send him a reinforcement of 10,000 men to maintain a defensive campaign only. The number has been promised, tho' they know the number is not to be got, perhaps not the half; but this is a plan of Lord North's that Clinton should be obliged to come home, and Cornwallis have the chief command, in order to please the King, with whom Cornwallis has become a mighty favorite, since the insolent cruelties he has exercised in Carolina. The great push is to be made against Virginia and the Carolinas; but if Gen! Leslie's expedition, which is chiefly designed as a diversion to Gen! Gates, thereby to save Cornwallis and Charleston, proves fruitless, you may look on the war with respect to you as ended. The British cabinet are heartily sick of the war, and the only bar to peace, and an acknowledgment of your Independence, is the King; whose will is law in England.

Be steady and true to yourselves, and your enemies can't hurt you ; they will expend at least 25
million sterl^g next year, for which if they get it
they must pay as good as 10 p^r ct. interest.

The English papers tell us that S. Petrie, who
was so confidential at Passy, at the late general
election went over to England, and became a candidate for the borough of Hindon, and is now a
petitioner against that election before the House of
Commons: is it to be credited that he would have
ventured to do all this, unless his proceedings in
Paris and at Passy had been under the directions
and by the permission of the British ministry ?

It is said that the English East India stock has
fallen 10 p^r c^t in consequence of the proceedings
against Holland.

The imprisonment of Mr Trumbull, son to the
Governor of Connecticut, and his examination at
Bow street, you will see an account of in the British papers. 'Tis strange that men of common
sense will accuse themselves, and involve others by
their voluntary confessions, in a country where the
torture is not known to the laws. 'Tis said that a
strict search is making after all those mentioned by
M^r T——ll, but we do not hear that any of them
has been yet apprehended.

The conduct of your enemies seems in every way
to be felo de se. 'Tis evident to every one that
they have received infinitely more advantages from

spies and traitors, that have been permitted to be at large in America, and to mix in your councils, than you have from the unimportant information you get from England ; and by this last measure they set you the example how to act with such characters in America ; especially with those who were dispatched from England to Maryland to work in secret while the British arms were openly in action, as soon as the British cabinet decided on making their great push against Virginia and the Carolinas, that Maryland may be prevented from giving any aid until it is too late. * * *

The 7 ult? D'Estaing with Guichen, his fleet and convoy, left Cadiz to come to Brest, with 45 sail of the line.

The English fleet, of 26 sail of the line, under Darby, was cruising off Cape Finisterre the 16 ult? . Should they join in battle, the English navy must receive an irreparable wound, but the winds have been violent most of the month and chiefly to the East and North, so that I hardly expect they will meet. About 20 of the last Jamaica fleet have been foundered at sea, and the Lyon, a 64 gun ship, is supposed to be foundered also. With the highest esteem, &c.

LE BARON DE BACH.

TO ARTHUR LEE.

ANVERS, 10 December, 1780.

It appears here that your operations have been much embarrassed by the depreciation of your paper currency, which surprises us much, since the effectual remedy seems plain and simple, and within the power of Congress.

Perhaps it is for this very reason that the remedy has been overlooked, or so long neglected. A fund must be established in Europe, to be applied solely and most sacredly to the payment of the interest on your paper currency.

This fund here should be placed under the direction of three persons at least, who should be all men of worth, honor and trustworthy; and not a shilling should be touched without the draft is signed by all the three. These commissioners should every three months balance the accounts, and give several copies to the public ministers residing in the country where the fund is established, to transmit to Congress; and if upon examination of these accounts, he should find that one shilling has been applied to any other purpose than to the payment of drafts drawn from America, for discharging the interest aforesaid; or, if the accounts are not delivered to the minister, within three or six months at farthest, after the expiration of every three months, in either case the minister, with the approbation of any two or more of your public ministers in Europe, should be authorized to suspend one, or all of these commissioners, and appoint others in their place, until the pleasure of Congress is known.

As these commissioners should be men of character, they should have genteel salaries, and if it was £100ᵬ sterᵍ each pʳ anᵐ, the great importance of the business would well warrant it; at the same time they might be employed in other services for Congress.

The interest of your paper should be annually paid at the Continental or public treasuries in each State, by drafts on the fund in Europe; and the interest on bills emitted in any State, according to the last plan published by Congress, should be payable either at the Continental treasury, or any other public treasury of either of the States.

Such a plan regularly executed for a year, would give a credit and currency to your paper equal to the bank notes of England, or Holland; and then you could never be at a loss for the means of supplying your army.

The introduction of specie into America, even of a hundred million, would not answer the purpose of a circulating medium of commerce; because during the war it would be inevitably hoarded up, as what you have now certainly is, for there can be no doubt of there being at this time much more specie in America than at any former period.

This fund, in Europe, must be established and kept up by borrowing until you can support it by remitting your commodities. * * *

Our friend *W. Lee* expects to hear from you soon and fully about what relates to him in *Congress* and *Virginia.*

Your former minister, Mʳ Silas Deane, we are told, since his return to France has been continually employed in invectives against his country; according to him, America is ruined, and must be subjugated by England; therefore all the aid France gives, is so much thrown away. We are surprised at this, as he lives at Passy with your minister, and seems to be his favorite and prime councillor. Mʳ. Deane adds also, that your grand Congress is composed of fools and knaves; we hope he has not experienced them to be so. *

---

*" Soon after my arrival here, which was on the evening of the 23d., I had a visit from *Francisco* [Deane], a long one, during which we went over much political ground, which convinced me every thing we had heard of the very extraordinary conversation of this man, was strictly true. Our country, according to him, was already conquered; the power of Great Britain rising above all control; that of her enemies almost spent; Holland absolutely to be crushed in the course of three months; the armed neutrality in consequence annihilated; the British manifesto extolled for its cogent reasons above all the similar acts of the belligerent powers; all Europe blind to their own interests, which, in fact, were in direct repugnance with those of America, particularly those of Holland and all the northern powers; Congress a mere cipher, having lost all its influence

I wish you every success, but you ought never to forget that your security must depend on your own abilities and exertions, and not on any foreign aid.

everywhere in America; and to crown the whole, an apology for the infamous apostate Arnold." *Francis Dana to John Adams*, January, 1781. A letter printed in Donne (II., 363) would show that Deane either was in the pay of the British court, or was to be approached with an offer, conditioned upon his undertaking to detach individual States from the Confederation. The former relation is the more likely in the light of subsequent events; and that the ministry did not place full confidence in him is shown by the intercepting of his letters for America. "I have only been able to read two of them," wrote the King to North, 19 July, 1781, "on which I form the same opinion of too much appearance of being concerted with this country, and therefore not likely to have the effect as if they bore another aspect." And again (August 7th), "I own I think them too strong in our favor to bear the appearance of his spontaneous opinions, but that, if supposed to be authentic, they will see they have by concert fallen into our hands. The means Mr. Deane should have taken as most conducive of the object he seems now to favor, would have been first to have shown that the hands of France are too full to be able to give any solid assistance to America, and to have pointed out the ruin that must attend a further continuance of the war; and after having given time for these opinions to be digested, then have proposed the giving up all ideas of independency, and have shown that the country is not in a state to subsist without the assistance of some foreign power, and that consequently so mild a government as the British one is the most favorable that America can depend upon."

By October Deane had retired to Ghent, a move that convinced the King of his sincerity; and it was from that place that he wrote the letter to Governor Trumbull, also intercepted by the British, and printed in a garbled and altered version by Rivington.

TO BARON SCHULENBERG.

BRUXELLES, 28 December, 1780.

I have not sooner than this replyed to the Letter your Exc.y did me the honor of writing to me ye 12 of last June, because the events of the War in America, as well as in Europe last season, were so unimportant, that it was not worth while to take up your Exc.y.s time. Our friends, France and Spain, have lost a campaign; but their Navy is unimpair'd, for it is now more powerful than it has been at any former period, while the English have expended in the last Campaign, upwards of 25 Million Sterling, lost above 15,000 Men, and their Navy decaying. In America their situation is critical. Gen.l Clinton confin'd closely to N. Y., which we cannot attack without a Naval Superiority: in South Carolina, notwithstanding the victory at Camden in August, which the English have boasted so much about, it appears by L.d Cornwallis's dispatches dated ye 20 September, that he had not been able to venture into North Carolina, and he says that in South Carolina he was surrounded with Enemies and difficulties. Since that, on the 7th of October, he sustained a heavy loss in the defeat of Col. Ferguson and his Corps; so that 'tis supposed by most people in England that Gen.l Leslie will not be able to extricate L.d Cornwallis from his difficulties in South Carolina.

The treacherous defection of Gen.l Arnold has

been attended with no other consequence but enraging the American Army rather more than they were before against the wickedness of their Enemies. Arnold has been tried by a Court Martial and found guilty of peculation of the public money, and many other bad Practices while he commanded in Philadelphia, for which he was publicly reprimanded at the head of the American Army, where he was become contemptible; but in remembrances of his past services, he was continued in the command of a Post, as he had been rendered incapable of active service by his wounds. On the whole it may be said that we have got clear of one wretch, and the English have added another to their Standard.

In this situation the extravagance of ye British Councils seem to have no bounds, for we now learn that they have already commenced open hostilities against the Dutch, because the States General determined to join the Northern Powers in the League for an Armed Neutrality, in opposition to ye orders and threats of the British Ambassador at ye Hague. By commencing Hostilities at this season of ye year, while all the Northern Ports are frozen up, the English conceived they will strike so heavy a blow on the Dutch Commerce before the Spring that the Northern Powers will not then venture to come to the aid of Holland. In this speculation they will probably be deceived, especially as I suppose the Northern Powers will immediately stop all the British vessels that are in the Baltic and not let them pass the Sound into the North Sea. Some of my countrymen have a desire to make some essays in the Commercial way to the Port of Embden, but they wish to know first what manufactures can be readily got there on reasonable terms to load a vessel without much delay; What American productions, such as Rice, Indigo, Tobacco, furs and Potash would meet with a good market there;—what duties or Imposts they are liable to. A commencement once made, I am satisfied would soon produce a large and beneficial communication between his Majesties Dominions and America; therefore I trust your Excellencies goodness will excuse me for desiring to be informed to whom I can properly apply for the information wanted.

I do not speak from any authority of my Country, but as an individual, I can't help mentioning the indecent and unjust strictures on the conduct of Congress and America that have appeared on several occasions in the Courier de Bas Rhine, printed at Cleves. A different style and conduct in the Editor of that Gazette would certainly tend more to create an individual harmony and good understanding between his Majesties Subjects and my Countrymen.

TO THE PRESIDENT OF CONGRESS.

BRUSSELS, February 10th, 1781.

Sir:

Be pleased to inform Congress that I have received information, which I think is to be depended on, that the British Cabinet has lately determined not to send any more troops for this campaign to North America. I therefore submit to the wisdom of Congress the propriety of making every possible vigorous effort this year to expel the British troops from the continent; for there may be reason to apprehend, if this is not done, and Great Britain can, by any means, extricate herself from the irresistible northern storm she has raised against her by the mad and foolish attack she has made on the Dutch, that her whole force will be employed next year against America, especially if she does not meet with some signal losses there this campaign.

The secret proposals for peace which Great Britain is now making at Versailles and Madrid, are altogether insidious, and only intended to impede the active operations of France and Spain this year, whereby they hope, by getting the start, that they may obtain some decisive advantages in the East and West Indies, for which countries their expeditions are all now on the wing. The King of Prussia has been our steady friend, though wisely so, and has been of much service to us; therefore, from motives of gratitude, as well as of justice and sound policy, he ought not to be much longer neglected; for it is most certain that his wisdom directs greatly the present system of Europe.

I have the honor to be, &c.

TO THE MARQUIS DE CASTRIES.

BRUXELLES, 11 February, 1781.

When your Exc.^{y} is acquainted with the anxious zeal I have always had for the success of the joint cause of France and America against ye common Enemy Great Britain, you will think that I do not stand in need of an Apology for taking up your time with this Letter; for tho' heretofore the advice of those Americans who were only actuated by honest and generous feelings for their Country, and who in the present War, might reasonably have been supposed to know when, where and how, a fatal blow might be given to the common Enemy, has been too much disregarded, I am not discouraged,* but shall proceed.

I am informed, and believe the information true, that the British Cabinet have determined not to send any more Soldiers to America for this Campaign; therefore I would propose, in order to finish the war on our own terms, that 15 or 20 Ships of

---

*This sentence erased, "because I trust that there is not now any of his majesties ministers or their dependants engaged in dirty jobs or plundering schemes of commerce."

the Line with some Frigates should be immediately sent directly to New York, and when they are once within Sandy Hook, they may prevent the whole Navy of Great Britain from coming in to the relief of New York, and may wait there in safety, until the Americans are collected in sufficient Force to take it. Adm! Arbuthnot has with him for the protection of New York about 12 Ships of the Line, which will be chiefly employed in blocking up the French Squadron at Rhode Island, so that their force from Europe may get within Sandy Hook before he has any notice of its coming; but if by chance they should meet at Sea, your Superior force must destroy him. Such a measure will also free the French Squadron now at Rhode Island, and Mons: Rochambeau also, and give him a Liberty of acting where the occasion may be most pressing in order to destroy the common Enemy. Should this plan meet your Excellencies' approbation, and it is accordingly adopted, the squadron should go as straight as possible to New York. It will be advisable that the real destination of the Squadron should not be commuicated to any but the commanding officer, and to deceive the Enemy, it may be proper to have it generally given out that this squadron is destined for the West Indies.

If any measures have been taken to intercept Adm! Darby and his 20 Sail of the Line, now about sailing from Portsmouth with most valuable convoys for the East and West Indias and North America, this expedition to New York will be unnecessary, because the taking or destroying Adm¹ Darby's fleet and Convoys will effectually answer the purpose of bringing the Enemy to our own terms; at the same time I must beg leave to observe that, knowing them so well as I do, I am perfectly convinced they only mean to gain time and advantages in the present campaign by secret propositions of Peace either at Versailles or Madrid.

Tho' contrary to my own opinion of the Emperor's disposition, I could not help being uneasy at various accounts lately of his determination to take part with Great Britain, but I am happy now in being assured that he is not disposed to act in any manner against us.

TO RICHARD HENRY LEE.

BRUXELLES, 20 February, 1781.

My dear Brother:

The last letter I received from you was dated in October 1779. * * * *

I have not heard from Congress, nor received letters from any one relative to discharging the sum due to me for my appointments, while in the public service; but I understand, there are letters on this side which mention, that when Mʳ Izard's appointment was settled, and payment of the balance ordered in Europe, the consideration and settling of mine was postponed; for what reason I cannot conceive.

I hope no one will think it unreasonable, or in any manner derogating from Mr Izard's merit, if I desire only to be put on the same ground with him; for tho' mine was an active, laborious and expensive employment, I make no particular claim for having done my duty to my country and principals, in the best manner I was capable of.

Mr Izard, besides the satisfaction of an unanimous vote of Congress approving his conduct, was allowed for expenses 1,600 Louis d'ors p^r annum; and near 500 Louis d'ors p^r an. for salary.—On the same footing my demand will stand thus: To expenses from the 1st Octr 1777, when my service began as commissioner, to the 13 Jan. 1780, being 3 months after receiving the notification of my recall at 1,600 Louis d'ors p^r an., is in livres £88.000
To salary for the above period. @ 11.-

428 livres p^r an.	26.189
	£114.189
Deduct 3.000 Louis d'ors I rec'd from Com^{rs} at Paris.	72.000

leaves a bal^{ce} due to me from Congress of £42.189

I do not know the name of a single delegate now

in Congress from Virginia, and so many changes
have taken place in that body that I do not know
a single person there, who would be proper and
willing to get the business settled for me; there
fore I must rely entirely on your kindness to get it
negotiated for me, and if possible to get a draft on
some part of Europe remitted to me for the balance. I have written often to Congress on the
subject, but they have either not received or not
answered my letters, that I know of.

I have no doubt you will answer me on this
subject as soon as you can, and by repeated opportunities, which you may do in such a manner as to
be unintelligible to the enemy should your letters
fall into their hands—Our brother Arthur Lee has
a cypher that you can use if necessary. *

---

*"The decision of Congress respecting your letter of April
12th, which came to hand only the 4th of this month, is herewith
transmitted. The period of payment will perhaps be more
distant than you wish; but I am at liberty to assure you from
the Superintendent of our finances, that it is his intention to
take the earliest possible opportunity to close this business."
James Lovell to William Lee, 20 September, 1781.

"*September* 12th, 1781. The committee to whom was referred a letter of the 12th of April last from Mr. William Lee,
report:

"That upon principles admitted by Congress in the settlement of an account similar to that transmitted by Mr. Lee,
there appears to be due to him a balance of 42,189 livres Tournois; whereupon,

"*Ordered*, That the account be referred to the Superinten-

Yourself and Governor Jefferson were frequently advised during the last summer, and I hope not without effect, of the determination of the British cabinet to bend their greatest force against the two Carolinas and Virginia. After the taking of Charleston, and particularly after the battle of Camden, in their usual style of wisdom, they fully expected by Xmas last to be in complete possession of the two Carolinas and part of Virginia as far as the confines of James river at least, and that this campaign would be crowned with the conquest of the remaining part of Virginia, Maryland and Pennsylvania.

At present, however, they have determined not to send any fresh troops to America for this campaign; indeed, we know they have not any to send; therefore it is reasonable to imagine, that weakened as they are, last campaign, the force they have now in America cannot advance much in the way of conquest; but America will be culpable if she does not make a proper use of the favorable moment and by a vigorous exertion drive the enemy entirely off the continent.

A very fine French fleet of 25 sail of the line will sail from Brest in a few days; its true destination is not publickly known; some say to North

---

dent of Finance, to take order for payment of the balance, with interest at the rate of six per cent. per annum from this day, as soon as the state of the public finances will admit."

America and others say to the West Indies; but wherever it goes it ought to fall heavy, and by a deep blow at once finish the war, for the English have no equal force to oppose it.

The grand fleet and whole army of Spain are still amusing themselves with the seige of Gibraltar; where there is only a paltry, sickly garison of about 2000 men.

Your minister at Madrid is no more than a private gentleman; and England has there publicly known agents, Mr. Cumberland, secretary to the Board of Trade, and Mr. Hussey, an Irish priest; who confer with the Spanish ministers and act in the honorable capacity of spies, tho' they are not publicly received as ministers.

The British Declaration of War against the Dutch was the 20th December, since which above 100 Dutch merchantmen have been taken; an expedition is now publicly sailing from Portsmouth against their East India settlements, and orders have been long since sent to attack the West India islands; to all which the Dutch have only replied by a proclamation that they *will* grant letters of marque and reprisals against the English, but as yet there is no manifesto, nor a single Dutch man-of-war or privateer at sea, tho' the winter has been remarkably open, and the coast of England from the Thames quite to the Orkneys, has been totally defenceless.

Be not surprised at this, there are rascals and parricides in other places besides America;—but if I mistake not, before the summer ends the English will sorely repent their attacking the Dutch.

'Tis not known yet whether Russia, Sweden and Denmark will immediately enter into the war against England; but they are well known to express high indignation at her conduct against Holland.

The Emperor is at present determined to remain quite neuter, if the English will let him do so, but they are every day seizing and plundering the vessels of his subjects in the same piratical manner, as they have done those of other nations. The King of Prussia will, I think, as heretofore continue our friend in the cabinet; 'tis therefore to be regretted, that Congress has let him remain so long neglected, especially at this critical moment, when the great advantage is so evident that America might obtain from having ministers at almost every court in Europe, whether they were publicy received as such, or not. On the whole I am clearly of opinion, that a general peace is within this year, unless some unexpected and unforeseen occurrrences in America should happen, that may induce the King of Great Britain to risque every thing elsewhere, in hopes of obtaining his favorite object, the Subjugation of America.— You have the game therefore in your own hands.
* * *

TO RICHARD HENRY LEE.

BRUXELLES, 13 April, 1781.

My dear Brother:

Inclosed you have copies of the two accounts I transmit by this same conveyance to Congress; the reason of my altering the original account No. 1, and new stating it as in No. 2 is mentioned between the two accounts; and I must further observe that the feelings and prevailing sentiments in America, which dictates the resolves of Congress, Sep: 20, 1776, when the appointment to be a commissioner was refused, were very different from those which produced the resolutions of the 6th Aug.ᵗ 1779; when even the President, and other members of Congress were intriguing for such appointments. This however should in justice be considered in rewarding those who undertook the appointments at the different periods.

As I do not know that I have one friend, or acquaintance in Congress to push forward this business for me, I must rely on your kindness to write to some member of your body to bring it to a conclusion; and to take care, that whatever sum Congress may think proper to allow, may be transmitted to me in bills on Europe.

Col. Searle and M.ʳ Dana* passed thro' here

---

*Dana had been appointed to represent Congress at St. Petersburg, and was on his way to that court. His election occurred 19 December, 1780.

yesterday, on their way from Paris to Holland; they both assured me that Bills of Exchange on Europe were plentiful in Virginia, Maryland and Pennsylvania, the exchange 70 for one in the old, and 52 for one in the new paper.—In this state of things I should have hoped to receive some remittances from the estate, but now I can hardly expect any thing this year, as Virginia will be the seat of war.

By repeated conveyances last year I gave the Governors of Virginia and Maryland advice of the determination of the British cabinet to push their chief force last winter & this summer against the Carolinas & Virginia.—Some of those letters must have got to hand, as the vessels they went by arrived safe; but ye warning seems to have had no effect, from the very defenceless and unprepared state that Leslie and the Traitor afterwards found Virginia in.

I am so very feeble, and reduced by a continued and severe illness, ever since Octr last, that I am not able to enter into the large field of European politics, which indeed is somewhat inexplicable.

Heyder Ali, in the East Indies, having made an irruption into the Carnatic, with 80,000 horse, totally defeated and cut to pieces a large British army; has taken the whole country of Arcot; and it is said, had laid seige to Madras, after retaking Pondicherry. This is by far a more sensible blow on our enemies than any they have received *from every* power in Europe, since the commencement of hostilities to this time; or than they are likely to receive this year from them all together, as things appear at present, so very contemptibly are affairs conducted on this quarter of the globe.

The conduct of your affairs in France seems to have grown worse and worse; at last some cloathing is gone, the 29th ult?, in the Marquis de la Fayette, under convoy of the Alliance. The freight paid to this old ship, which will hardly swim to America, they say at Nantes, would have built there, from the stocks, and sent completely fitted to sea, a frigate of 36 guns, and in less time than she has taken to be fitted for this voyage; but Mr Chaumont is said to be a part-owner, which accounts for all. He, and Mr Williams have had the sole management of the ship and her cargo.

Extract of a letter just received from Bourdeaux, dated the 7th April 1781.

"The marquis de la Fayette belonged to a company who purchased her of the old E. I. Co., in which trade she had made some voyages. They sent her to the W. Indies, in which voyage she sunk money to the owners, and being found unprofitable they ordered her to be laid up here.

"Le Ray de Chaumont became proprietor and chartered her to Mr Franklin. Bills to a considerable amount are drawn, by order of the state of Virginia, on

D'Acosta Frères, who have admitted them to be protested. The credit of particular states is in disrepute."

In Great Britain they have this year created a perpetual debt of 21 millions, to borrow 12 million; and they will create besides an unfunded debt of 8 million more over and above their annual income. Thus, the bubble of credit and paper has been carried to a height incredible, and almost inconceivable by the mind of man. But if Heyder Ali pursues his conquests in the East, this bubble will soon burst, and then farewell to British insolence and barbarity forever.

My whole family unite with me in affec^te love to you and all your's; & beg to remember as to all our brothers, sisters & friends. Mr Adams has borrowed for Congress, in Holland, one million florins, upwards of £90.000 ster^lg, which is supposed to be a prelude to a farther and more considerable loan.

TO FRANCIS LIGHTFOOT LEE.

BRUXELLES, 12 February, 1782.

That you may know ye fate of such Letters as you may have written, 'tis proper for me to inform you that it is near four years since I have rec^d a Letter from you of any kind, and above seven years since I have received one about private business; I flatter myself, however, that you have taken care to pay off with paper money all the debts of every kind that I owed in Virginia, or, at least, that you have made legal tenders for y.ᵗ purpose, with the said money, in which I hear the Debts due to me have been discharged; and to prevent any omission or mistake in this business, I again enclose you a List of all the Debts I owed in Virginia in May, 1777;—since which none can have been contracted by me.

You will find also enclosed a Copy of my account against our Father's Estate, the Balance due to me the 5th of Nov.ʳ 1781, being £2,996 . 9 . 7½ Ster.ˡᵍ which account I wish you to get certified and sign'd by the Acting Executors of our late Father's Estate. When this Account is so certified and sign'd, I wish to have it recorded in Westmoreland County Court; and I request of you to let me know by repeated Letters what is done in this business. —In September last Congress ordered that the Superintendant of Finances should pay me 42,189 livres, as soon as the state of y.ᵉ Public Finances would admit. The time and manner of payment being thus left entirely at the discretion of the Superintendant, you will render me a most particular and essential service if you can prevail on the Superintendant to remit me, or pay this money, directly in good Bills on Paris or Amsterdam. I have mentioned this subject to both our brothers A. L. and R. H. L., and of y.ᵉ latter I have desired to be informed particularly, of all y.ᵉ damage that has been done on the Estate at Green Spring during the last Campaign; to have all ye fruit Trees immediately replaced that may have been destroyed; to have promising young Fellows, put apprentices to the different trades necessary for the use of such an Estate; and to have the whole of Powhatan Swamp Converted into a Timothy meadow as fast as possible. This should be the grand object at present, even to ye partial neglect of crops of Tobacco. This Letter being entirely on Private business, I shall conclude with telling you that my family (except myself) are in tolerable good Health; it consists of Mrs. Lee, one Son, William Ludwell, 7 years old; two Daughters, Portia 5 years, and Cornelia 2 years old. The last was born in this Town.

You will readily agree that in times like the present, with a broken Constitution and reduced Fortune, these are enough to provide for, as they ought to be. However, I cannot despair of seeing brighter days, and of once more embracing you in Peace and happiness, when we can, with pleasure, look back on all the dangers we have passed. Heaven bless you and our dear Sister.

TO RICHARD HENRY LEE.

BRUXELLES, 11 March, 1782.

My dear Brother:

I have written to you several long letters lately, one of which will go by the Marquis la Fayette. Since my last a new spirit has arisen in the British House of Commons: General Conway made a motion that the prosecution of an offensive war in America, should be put a stop to. This, after a very long and warm debate, was carried against the ministry by 19 majority. The motion was then modelled into an address to the King, who gave an evasive, and I think rather insolent answer; on this the House of Commons without a division passed another resolve, that he that should advise or attempt to carry on an offensive war in America contrary to the sense of that House, should be deemed an enemy to Great Britain, and punished as such.

Thus for the present, the plundering and burning plans, that have been concerted to be carried into execution this year under Arnold, are put a stop to. The nation at large is really anxious for peace, and it is clear that the ministry will therefore be obliged to make some attempts that way this year; while all the force of Great Britain will be principally employed against the navy of France: but as the King thirsts as much as ever for the blood and devastation of America, unless they suffer some farther losses, so as to render them utterly incapable of going on one moment longer, I fear that peace will hardly take place this year; tho' if America by one vigorous exertion would get possession of New York and Charleston, the business of war would end immediately. * * *

TO THE SECRETARY OF FOREIGN AFFAIRS.

BRUSSELS, 31 March, 1782.

Sir:

Although I have not the honor of a personal acquaintance with you, yet I trust that this letter, being on subjects which concern the interests of our country in general, I shall not stand in need of any apology for writing it.

You will be informed, probably, both by the newspapers and private letters, before this gets to your hands, of the late revolution in the British Ministry; the old set having given place to a new Ministry, composed of the Rockingham, Shelburne, and Grafton parties. This change has been forced on the King, very much against his inclination and that of his secret advisers, Lords Bute and Mansfield, by the general exertion of almost the whole body of the people of England, both in and out of the House of Commons, who ardently wish for a peace, especially with America; and it appears that independence will not be any great impediment, though they will endeavor to barter, as a consideration for acknowledging it for a beneficial treaty of commerce, the Newfoundland fishery, and some other points.

It seems evidently to be the general wish of the nation, that a peace with America should be immediately made almost on any terms, and on that principle it is that they have forced the present Ministry into place; but as I am not quite clear that the principles of Lord Shelburne, or those of his friend, Mr. Dunning, are in any manner friendly to America, and the King's inveteracy continuing as great as ever, it is not possible to say how far the negociations for peace may be traversed and impeded by secret manœuvres and intrigues; therefore, in my opinion it will be wise in America to be well on her guard, and take her present measures as if the war was yet to continue some years. I have not yet heard of his departure, but the 22d instant was fixed for General Carleton to leave Portsmouth in the Ceres, of thirty-two guns, for New York, to take upon him the command in chief in America. The late British Ministry died as they lived, for one of their last official acts was to give the traitor Arnold, by patent, one thousand pounds sterling pension per annum for his and his wife's lives.

It has been mentioned to me by a gentleman in the Government here, that the Emperor is disposed to enter into a commercial treaty with America, and afterwards that a minister or resident from Congress should reside at the Court here, this being the principal commercial country belonging to his Majesty. Though this communication was not official, yet it appears as if it had been made to me from their knowing that I was formerly a Commissioner of Congress at the Court of Vienna; therefore I think it my duty to inform Congress of the circumstance through you, that they may take such measures in it as they think proper.

I will not presume to advise on the propriety or impropriety of appointing a Minister to treat with his Imperial Majesty, because Congress must be sufficiently informed that the capital manufactures of this country in woolen, linen, and cotton, and coarse hats, and the iron and steel manufactures at Leige, will be of great utility at all times in America; and the consumption of tobacco, indigo, rice, furs, skins, and salt fish is not only very considerable in this country but in the adjacent inland ones that always draw their supplies through the ports here. I will only venture to say, in my opinion, fifteen thousand livres Tournois per annum would be a sufficient appointment for an American Minister to reside at this Court, for his salary and expenses together. Should such a Minister be appointed his commission should run thus: "To negociate, agree upon, conclude, and sign a treaty of, &c., &c., &c., between his Imperial and Apostolic Majesty Joseph the Second, Emperor of Germany, King of the Romans, of Hungary, Bohemia, &c., &c., &c., and the Congress of the United States of America, and afterwards to reside as Minister from the said Congress at the Court of Brussels, in the Austrian Netherlands, to transact such affairs as may be given to him in charge." I mention this because there was a capital mistake in the original commission sent me to treat with the Court of Vienna, which I took the liberty of pointing out at the time.

You will find enclosed with this a copy of the London Gazette and sentence of the court-martial on Captain Dundass of the Boneta, which prove pretty explicitly a breach of the articles of capitulation at Yorktown by Lord Cornwallis and Captain Symonds. I do not know that the situation of affairs will render it necessary to take notice of this breach on the part of the enemy, but it appears to me proper that Congress should be informed of the fact.

With the highest consideration and respect, I have the honor to be, &c.

TO SAMUEL THORPE.

BRUXELLES, June 18, 1782.

Dear Sir:

It was not in my power to write to you last Post,

tho' I much wished to give you as early intelligence as possible of what we are confidently assured here; viz, that the Preliminaries of Peace were sign'd last week at Paris; and instead of a *Peace* with America only a *Truce* of 12 years is agreed upon; but if this Truce is not ripened into a *Peace* before ye settlement of ye general business, I am sure it will be attended with very disagreeable consequences, especially to G. B. France always wished to bring the affair to such a conclusion, in order ye more effectually to accomplish her deep lay'd design, of keeping America a perpetual Thorn in ye side of G. B., and she must be now delighted at seeing her adversarys run so easily into the snare. It is much more y^n probable that a War will break out in Europe before ye expiration of 12 years, in which France and England must be Antagonists; in that case, suppose there is now only a Truce with America, she will infallibly take a part with France: but if there is a full peace now, America will then either remain Neuter, or probably take part with G. B. Besides, a Truce will be ye most effectual plan that can be devised to preclude for ever that intercourse and commerce which well disposed [persons] wish should take place immediately between G. B., and America; for you may depend upon it that during the Truce, no British Subjects nor a farthing's worth of British or Irish goods or manufactures, will on any

Account or in any shape, be admitted to enter within any of yᵉ 13 United States of America. Events have so fully confirm'd my presages for 14 years past that I have become confident in my Political Predictions in what concerns G. B. and America; and therefore if you think it will be of any utility, you are at Liberty to communicate what I have here said, where you judge it will be of use. I hope you now understand clearly what I meant by saying some time ago that G. B. for her own sake should take care that yᵉ Independence of America should be Independent.

Now if you please to a little private business. A Flemish Merchant seems to have had very ill usage, from a British Privateer, as the inclosed case will show you, which, at his desire, I am to request that you will get the present Attorney General's opinion as soon as possible; or that of any other councillor learned in the Law, who may be thought to have more learning and skill in such matters than yᵉ Attorney General. You will much oblige me by returning yᵉ case and opinion on it, as soon as you possibly can, marking the expence you are at in the business, which you may charge to my Account.

I am well pleased to see yᵉ Corporation and yᵉ Court on such good terms as they seem to be at present; but I shall be mortified if the people loose the present favorable moment, and do not effectually secure their Liberty against y⁽ᵉ⁾ attempts of such another Administration as y⁽ᵉ⁾ last was, by purifying the House of Commons by means of enlarging the represented body and throwing the decay'd burro's into the neighboring tithings and hundreds, as was done at Cricklade. You have got something in y⁽ᵉ⁾ Contractors and Revenue Officers bill, but you may still be ruined if you stop there.

P. S. Remember that I do not speak of the Preliminaries being sign'd, as a matter of certainty (for I neither am nor desire to be in y⁽ᵉ⁾ secret of any Cabinet), but as a Report in which I think there is some probability; but whether they are sign'd or not, as yet, it will not make any difference in the Argument relative to a Truce or a Peace with America. I cannot pretend to have any Influence; but I have taken no little Pains to dispose the several parties on this side of the channel to a fair and equitable peace, and flatter myself with y⁽ᵉ⁾ hopes that such a one may be accomplish'd, if your present ministers do not follow y⁽ᵉ⁾ example of their predecessors, and suffer themselves to be hurried away by their late good Fortune to make extravagant and silly demands.

TO RICHARD HENRY LEE.

BRUXELLES, 22 June, 1782.

I have to thank you for your letter of the 23^d of last April, tho' am much vexed at the fate of ye Articles sent from Bourdeaux. I have never heard from our B^r. A. what he did with the Dollars you sent by him last year to Phil^a to remit to me, nor a word of the £220.8. Specie you sent to him for the same purpose last March; tho' there are several vessels arrived in France and Holland that left Phil^a and Baltimore late in April. I perceive we have suffered terribly, and are likely to suffer more, from ye invasion of the Enemy last year: but it is in vain to repine at what we could not, nor can not help: therefore rest satisfied with the reflection, that everything was done which could be done to save my property from the ravaging hands, of a cruel and savage Enemy. 'Tis too late in life for me with a debilitated state of health to fix on a plan for ye future happiness of my family without more information on some points than I have at present. I wish therefore to know as soon as possible, what kind of Education can be got for my Son in Virginia; whether any of our houses in Williamsburg or that at Green Spring are in a proper habitable condition for us, and which of the house Servants are still alive and capable of service. On these points I request you will give me the earliest and repeated information by various convey-

864

ances, and your advice on the propriety of going over with my family; which will be a Serious and important measure to me, in point of inconvenience, fatigue, and expence. I should be glad also to know what progress has been made in converting Powhatan Swamp into a Timothy Meadow. I am sure that you will not omit any opportunity of remitting what you possibly can to me, which will be equally necessary, whether I remain some time longer in Europe or go soon to Virginia. You say ye Taxes are heavy this year, and I much fear they will be more so hereafter, as I see that the revenues of Virginia, as well as those of the Continent, are still continued in the same hands, that have already burthened America with a debt that will require half a century to pay off.

TO ARTHUR LEE.

BRUXELLES, 19 July, 1782.

Dear Brother:

In consequence of the information you gave me in your letter of (ye last date of which the 25th of March), I wrote to Dr. Franklin above 10 daies ago desiring to be informed, if he had received orders from ye Superintendent General of Finance to pay me the money due to me from Congress. To this letter I have not received any answer, tho' ye usual time allow'd for receiving an answer from

Paris to a letter written from hence is 4 or 5 daies; therefore, I do not expect any answer from Dr. Franklin, nor do I believe he either has, or ever will receive such order as you Mention, and I can only wonder that you could ever believe such orders were ever given to him. You will much oblige me by procuring and sending to me either a bill of Exchange or an order payable a Month after sight for ye principal debt, and interest thereon till paid, agreeable to ye resolution of Congress in September last, either on Dr. Franklin or Mr John Adams, who has within a few months opened another loan at Amsterdam which, report says, has succeeded better than ye first. You will not forget ye necessity of sending *several duplicates* of either a bill of Exchange or an order for this Money. Our B^r ., R. H. Lee, sent by you last year in April 68,100 Dollars in Loan office certificates to remit to me, from Phil^a ; what did you do with them, and what are they now worth in livres? He also sent to you in March last £220.8. Virginia currency in Specie, to remit to me; of that money you do not mention a word, tho' I hear good Bills on Europe were plenty, and ye Exchange a great deal under par. I have no proofs here of the debt due from De Berdt & Co.; they must, I suppose, have been lodged in ye proper office in Phil^a before ye Attachment was taken out. Anthony Stewart had a full power of attorney and regular proofs of the

debt, with the Account Settled and Signed by
Burkitt & Sayre, the surviving Partners. I believe A. S. appointed Mr. Hill of Phil^a , partner
in ye Madeira House of Hill, Lamar & Bissett, to
act for him in the business. Mr. Hill is now in
Phil^a and I believe A. Stewart is in N. York; from
one or ye other of them you may probably know
where ye papers are, and as soon as I can get a
power of Attorney made out, I will send one to you.
Should you know where Mr. Lotsom now is, pray
inform him that I wrote to him in May last saying
that the principal money he placed in my hands,
was let on Interest to Comte Clonard in Paris, as I
could not fix on any eligible plan of employing it
in trade, having not been able, even at this time,
to get ye former affairs finished in which his money
was adventured. There are some accounts still to
settle, and until they are finally closed 'tis impossible for me to say whether there will be any profit
or not. There has been a great deal of ill Fortune,
as well as bad management in what has been undertaken ; therefore he may think himself in some
measure fortunate that ye principal is not lost ; at
least I think so now, which has determined me not
to be concerned in any adventure, where I cannot
act openly as ye principal Agent, which hitherto
has not been practicable in this Country. But
things seem now to be changing in their Political
aspect. I wish Mr. Lotsom would let me know if

it is agreeable to him that his money should remain in Count Clonard's hands; in y⁰ mean time he may draw on me for Twenty thousand Livres payable three months after sight in Paris. He must always give me advice by Letter of what Bills he draws. Tho' his bills are to be made payable in Paris, they must be directed to me here.

I will send him an exact state of the amount of his money in my hands, as soon as I can get y⁰ former affairs finally settled. Should any opportunity occur of serving me on this side the Atlantic, I suppose you will not neglect it, as you know I am perfectly idle, and I can assure you that my dangerous illness last year arose principally from inactivity and want of employment after upwards of 20 years spent in bustle and continual motion.

TO RICHARD HENRY LEE.

CLEVES, 29 July, 1782.

Dear Sir:

I am sorry to be obliged to confirm now what I have said to you in several letters within 3 months past, viz, that there is no prospect of peace for this year. Since the death of Lord Rockingham, Lord Shelburne is made treasurer, and *ostensible* premier, with an administration of his own composing, on the express convention with the King, to continue the war, and refusing to acknowledge the Independence of America.

An *interior* cabinet is already formed, as in the reign of Lord North, where all schemes are first formed before they are carried to the cabinet council to be confirmed.

General Arnold is again openly at court, high in the King's favor, and frequently closeted with Lord Shelburne.

These are facts, the truth of which you may rely on and make known where you think they are most necessary to be known; as from them you will see as clearly as I that the war in America will be renewed again, unless you take advantage of the enemy's present weakness, and strike another blow.

The time when and the manner how this war will be renewed perhaps is not yet determined; but from Arnold being again in high favor, I suppose the King has revived the plan he had adopted last winter of sending Gen! Frazer,* (who is since dead,) as Commander in Chief, and Arnold as second, to burn and lay waste every part of America that they could come at.

M.ʳ William Pitt, only 22 years old, is Chancellor of Exchequer; Lord Grantham, secretary in the place of Lord Shelburne; Tommy Townsend,

---

* Simon Fraser, sometime Master of Lovat. He died in 1782.

secretary in the room of Mr Fox, and Lord Keppel quits the administration as soon as they can get any body to fill his post; it is to be offered to Lord Howe, as soon as he returns from his present cruize in the channel.

Colonel Barré is paymaster of the forces, and the treasurership of the navy has been offered to the Lord Advocate of Scotland (commonly called Lord Starvation) who is just arrived in London, to advise with the old Scotch Junto, before he accepts it.

On the whole it is thought that England never had so feeble, uninformed in business, and un-connected an administration, as this Lord Shel-burne's will be.

A breath from the King's nostril will dissolve the whole in a moment, and it seems as if the nation would behold their dissolution with great complacency.

Nothing but absolute incapacity to procure men and money, will prevent the enemy from carrying into execution next year the scheme the King and Lord Shelburne have plotted, to carry desolation thro' America; therefore I hope, advantage will be taken of their feebleness this year.

I really do not see how it will be possible for Lord Shelburne to procure money; and as to men, 5,000 from the Irish establishment, 5 or 6,000 British and Irish recruits, and drafts from the

British regulars and guards, and about 2 or 3,000 German recruits, will be all the force they will be able to get, to replace their losses this year and to carry on their operations next year in the West Indies and America.

It seems agreed on all sides that Gibraltar must fall this year. The Dutch fleet are out cruising on their own coast, but without appearing to design any more mischief to the enemy's trade, than they did last year, tho' the English have not a single ship-of-the-line in the North sea; for every one they have, as soon as they can be got ready, are sent to join Lord Howe, who is cruising with 22 sail on the coast of Ireland to meet and protect a large fleet from Jamaica, that is expected every day.

The combined fleet of 27 Spanish and 13 French sail-of-the-line, and about 25 frigates under Don Cordova, have been taking their summer's amusement in cruising, for about 3 weeks, between Scilly and Lizard without taking a single vessel there, tho' Lord Howe passed by them, having remained in their sight for two days, and single ships were going frequently to join Lord Howe on the coast of Ireland.—Don Cordova it is said has now gone back to Cadiz.

A very large and valuable French fleet from St Domingo is arrived safe.

It is reported that Spain has, at length, determined to acknowledge the Independence of America.

Last spring Russia, whose object is to have the war continue as long as possible, to keep the parties nearly equal, threatened the Dutch, if they did not make a separate peace with Great Britain. The Dutch however refused, and since the disaster of the 12th of April in the West Indies was known, Russia has been quiet; for the English have revived their old ideas, and talk of nothing less than totally annihilating the navies of France and Spain.

The English papers tell us that Sir James Jay, since his arrival in London, has had long and frequent conferences with Lord Shelburne, and that he is authorized by Congress to settle the terms of reconciliation between Great Britain and America.

The English affairs in the East Indies are again on the decline; which has made the East India stock fall 15 p^{r.} c^{t.}, and is still falling. At the beginning of the war it was 282 p^{r.} 100 stock, and it is now only 127.

I wish you may get this letter, which goes from Flanders to Chesapeak, as it contains a full tho' concise state of public affairs in Europe.

Mr. Grenville, who was sometime in Paris, under the pretext of negotiating a general peace, has been returned to London about a fortnight, and goes a secretary to his elder brother, Lord Temple, who is to be created Duke of Buckingham, and have Lord Rockingham's blue ribbon, and succeed to the Duke of *

---

* The letter ends here.

TO SAMUEL THORPE.

BRUXELLES, 27 August, 1782.

Last Post bro't me your favor of the 20th instant covering your two notes for £409 S^g due the 10 September next, being the amount of the two bills I remitted to you ye 9th inst. and Col. Faning's note for £89., which you had received for me. For the recovery of this debt from Col. F. I am entirely indebted to your prudent and decisive conduct, and I beg you to accept my sincere acknowledgements for the same. There having been made last sessions an Act of Parliament for laying a stamp Duty on inland bills, I am sure you will excuse me for asking whether notes such as yours come within the Act; for this being a novel device in Finance, the circumstance may easily have escaped your recollection. I have ever tho't it was the best method to be explicit and open, as being the surest way of avoiding misunderstandings between friends; therefore I shall be so now with you. As a proof of the confidence I had in your judgement Integrity and friendship for me, on making my last Will a good while ago, I took the Liberty of naming you as one of my Executors, trusting that your friendship for the Father would be extended to his Infant Children, which charge I must hope you will have the goodness to take upon yourself whenever the Period for its execution may arrive. On recollection lately, I think there are cases and opinions in your law Books that say, all Debts due from an Executor to a deceased Testator are *ipso facto* annul'd and void on the Testator's death unless there is something to show, that the Testator and the Executor understood and intended it shou'd be otherwise.

In this situation of things, as life is precarious, I submit to your consideration whether it may not be proper for you to send me a certificate conceiv'd somewhat in the following terms:

Whereas W. L. Esq, late Merchant and Alderman of London, but now resident in the City of Bruxelles in Brabant, has tho! proper to nominate and appoint me, S. T., of Aldgate, in the said City of London, Haberdasher, an Executor of his last Will and Testament, and whereas I now stand indebted to the said W. L. in certain sums of money had and received from him or for his use, and I may so continue to be indebted at the time of the decease of the said W. L.——now I do hereby declare and make known to all whom it may concern, that whatever sum or sums of money debt or debts may be due and owing from me to ye said W. L., by Bond Bill note or open Account or otherwise, at the time of his decease, whenever and wherever he may happen to depart this Life, shall be equally due, payable and inure to the use and benefit of the Heirs, Assigns, or estate, of the said W. L. as fully and amply to all intents and purposes both in Law and Equity, as if I, the said S. T. had not been so nominated and appointed by the said W. L. an Executor of his last Will and Testament. In witness whereof I have (with the approbation and by the desire of the said W. L.——) hereunto set my name in London aforesaid this —— day of ——.

In 5 or 6 weeks I hope to be able to furnish you with £500—but should that fail I expect to receive £600 in England, when you may be supplied with what part you want. I suppose by two months' notice you mean either by Letter or by a draft payable 2 Months after sight. You have managed the affair of Faning with so much judgment and success, that I could not stand excusable to myself if I did not request you to undertake the following business. The Money for which you have a certain Alderman's draft, was not lent to him, but to Mr. Sam! Brailsford, who was then a Merchant and resident in Bristol, and who, to me, has acted much more reproachfully than the Alderman, however atrocious his conduct has been on other occasions. You have inclosed a letter to Mr. B. which please to read, seal, and forward per Post, and when you get his answer read that also before you forward it, that you may know what passes between us. I have understood that Mr. B. left Bristol some years ago to reside in the Country, where I do not know; but possibly you may get his address from M! Downe in Bartholemew's Lane in the banking house that was Lascelles, Marlar, Pell & Downe, or by writing to M! Thos

Mullitt in Bristol, for whom Mr Alderman Bull will at any time give you a frank, as they are intimate friends.

You have Mr Brailsford guarantee for the payment of W——ge's draft, and if he does not answer my letter properly and put the debt in a way of payment in the course of next month, it will be necessary to commence an action against him to prevent the act of Limitation from taking place until better times, when I can take the trouble off your hands.

Your plan of indorsing the Lottery ticket when you buy one for me is good, for Life you know is precarious; but send me the N^o that I may sing and be merry when I see it announced a £20,000 in the papers. You may see by this that nothing less will satisfy me. Don't forget Banks and the Civilian when you are at leisure.

TO ARTHUR LEE.

BRUXELLES, 30 August, 1782.

Dear Brother :

Some days ago I sent from hence two packets for you to be forwarded from Paris, containing duplicate Proved account and power of Attorney to prosecute the Attachments against the effects of De Berdt & Co, and a protested bill for £300 Sterling to be recovered in Maryland. Yesterday I received a Letter from Dr Franklin, a Copy of which you have on the other side, which cost me some trouble and expence to obtain: you will perceive he does not deny having received my former letter on this subject of the 8th of July, which he never answered, but now when pushed he tells me plainly that I am not to expect the money from him; thus you see what advantage has been taken of the loose wording of ye resolves of Congress to buffet me from Phil.^a to Passy, and from Passy to Phil.^a, and I suppose ye next kick attempted, will be to Madrid or Petersburg. This, you know from my former Letters, was what I expected would be practiced; therefore, 'tis unnecessary to observe on the Doctor's letter, tho' I can't help remarking the Malignant and studied insult of the paragraph beginning—"I hope" &c. You will therefore oblige me much by getting immediate payment of this debt from Mr Morris, either in his own bills of Exchange on Paris or Amsterdam, or in money equal to the value according to the Exchange, for it will be doubly cruel after being curtailed in my Demand and spending my own Money in Europe on the public Account which I was obliged to draw from England at a considerable loss, to compel me to receive the debt in America in a manner that I may loose 15 or 20 p ct more in the Exchange. Should any objection be started that you are not legally authorised to receive the money, I am to inform you that my B.ᵣ F. L. Lee, has an old but ample power of attorney to act in all cases for me; therefore he can easily authorise you to receive the money, if you should find that such an authorization is requisite.

TO RICHARD HENRY LEE.

BRUXELLES, 1 October, 1782.

You ask me in your favor of the 18ᵗʰ of last July whether I have any written or verbal assumption from our late B.ᵣ, Col. P. L. Lee, to pay all our Father's Money Legacies. In reply I must answer that I have not, and for my own part, I never asked, nor would I ever have accepted of any such assumption from him, so as to have made my demand a debt due from him alone. Equal Justice however calls some one to declare, what I shall be always ready to testify on Oath when call'd upon, viz, that I have never applyed to any body for the payment of what was due to me and my Sister agreeable to her regular assignment under the Will of our Father, but to Our B.ᵣ, P. L. Lee, for these reasons—first, he was the Sole acting Executor or Administrator, therefore he was the only regularly legal Person for me to apply to, and from him only did I ever receive any partial payments, a full payment not being made at this day. Secondly— Having had full access for years to, and made repeated examinations of, all the Books, Bonds, Notes and Accounts and papers that my father left at his Death, I always found that there was much more money due to my Father's Estate in G. B. and America than was amply sufficient to pay all the Debts due from the Estate and all the Pecuniary Legacies or Devices in my Father's Will; and of my own personal knowledge, I can declare that our B^r. , P. L. Lee, as Executor to our Father, received almost the whole that was due to him at the time of his Death by Bond, Note, Account, &c, except some very trifling and insignificant sums indeed, and a demand against M^r. Fitzgerald, a merchant in London, who has long since become a Bankrupt, tho' many years after my Father's death; but this demand I never took into Account as a good debt. Thirdly, the produce of the whole of my Father's Estate for the years 1750, 1751, 1752, and I believe, of 1753 also, was received by our B^r. , P. L. Lee, and as to myself I can declare that the whole expended on me for Education and Cloathing from Nov. 1750, when my Father dyed, to Sept. 1758, when I came of Age, did not Amount to 50£ Sterling ; besides that, for the three last years I acted for my Brother, as his Clerk-Steward and principal manager of his whole Estate, for which in Justice he ought to have allowed me a Salary of 30 or 40£ St'g p. annum, exclusive of my maintenance.

For these two last reasons therefore, I always tho't it just that our B^{r}., P. L. Lee, shou'd pay the whole of our Father's Pecuniary Legacies or Devises out of that part of his Estate, which he solely receiv'd and injoy'd. I have only to add, that I earnestly request of you to have the Account I lately transmitted to our B^{r}., F. L. Lee, against my Father's Estate settled and put in a way of payment immediately; otherwise the Duty I owe my Family will compel to institute a Suit directly in order to bring the affair to a conclusion. On this head let me beg for your answer as soon as possible, and by various conveyances.

TO RICHARD HENRY LEE.

BRUXELLES, 1 October, 1782.

I have received and thank you for your letter of y^{e}. 18th. of last July. If M^{r}. Beale does not pay the money you demand for my Tobacco, he will have much outwitted M^{r}. Valentine, and gain'd a considerable advantage of me, for I know he cannot return me better Tobacco, since I know from long experience that there is none so good or so valueable made in Virginia, except by y^{e}. Burwells, near Williamsburg, and y^{e}. famous E. D., near York. However, for the future I now request that no more of my Tobacco made on y^{e}. Estate, may be disposed of in any manner, without particular orders from me. I do not know what your present currency is. How much is a Guinea, or a Dollar in Specie, legally worth ? * * *

The plan you seem to think best to be adopted for my Son, I know is utterly impracticable to any good purpose, therefore you can easily judge of my embarrassment to determine what is best to be done, in my situation. A good Seminary for ye Education of youth being so very essential to ye well being, happiness and prosperity of a Community; I am greatly astonished that your Government permits ye College of William & Mary to be neglected. If some wise and vigorous measures are not taken to remedy this evil, 'tis evident that your State must ever be dependent and inferior to ye Northern and Eastern States. A word or two on Politics. But first, I must Say that your reserve on that head is less warranted now than ever, because you have some body to write a letter for you and no name being signed or place mentioned, no one could tell from whom it came, therefore it could be of no consequence should it miscarry, or fall into ye hands of a Public or Private Enemy. No military operation of ye least importance has happen'd in Europe last Summer. The Dutch have acted worse if possible this year than they did the last: They are a wretched, undone and ruined People forever, beyond redemption; therefore I am sorry that M^r. A[dams] has but ye other day Signed

a Treaty of Commerce between them and America;
by which they have, in my opinion, many advantages and America not one. Gibraltar is not
taken, nor likely to be so, at least as far as we
know; though ye Duke de Crillon has been be-
sieging it upwards of 3 months, with 36,000 men
French and Spaniards. The combined fleet of 50
sail of the Line is moored in ye Bay before it, and
Ld Howe is gone with 35 Sail of the Line to throw
in succors, so that every day we expect to hear of
bloody work. The Negotiations for Peace will be
bro^t to a conclusion, or at least a certainty of a
conclusion, within six weeks from this time—
whether for Peace or War, I will not take upon me
to decide, tho' I may conjecture it will be for
ye former. The only obstacles to a General Peace
for some months past, have certainly been these:
Spain insists on Gibraltar, without giving any
thing in Exchange; France insists on having the
Newfoundland Fishery, agreeable to her Treaty
with America, and some particular advantages in
ye E. Indies. These Demands England has not
yet consented to, and probably will not consent to
them all.   *   *   *   *

TO BENJAMIN FRANKLIN.

BRUXELLES, 7 October, 1782.

I have the honor to send you herewith a copy of

a letter from M^r. Robt. R. Livingston, of the 18th of July last, and of an order of Congress of the 2^d of the same month, to which be pleased to refer. As you informed me in your letter of the 25th of August last, that you had a copy of the order of Congress of the 12th Sept., 1781, ascertaining the balance due to me to be 42,189 livres, with 6 p^r. c^t. per an: interest till paid, I have only to observe, that the interest for 19 months, added to the principal debt, amounts to 46,196 livres, 19 sols, for which sum I have drawn on you the following bills, payable to my own order, the 12th April next, viz—1 for £12.000,—one for £12.000, —1 for £12.000,—and one for £12.196.19^s.

These bills will be presented to you for acceptance, with which I hope you will honor them, as I have drawn them at long date, in order to accommodate you in the most convenient manner; but if you choose to pay the money at a shorter period, be pleased to signify your wishes in a letter to me, sent to the care of Mr Grand in Paris, that I may give him orders to receive it. I have the honor to be &c. &c.

BENJAMIN FRANKLIN TO WILLIAM LEE.

PASSY, 21 October, 1782.

Sir:

I received the letter you did me the honor of writing to me the 7th inst., inclosing a copy of an order of Con-

gress, with a copy of a letter to you from Mr Secretary
Livingston, informing me that you had, in consequence, drawn on me for £46,196.19, payable to your
order, the 12th of April next.—This is to acquaint you
that I have accepted the said bills, hoping to have by
that time funds in hand for payment: But as that is
uncertain, I confide, that you will not hazard the
credit of Congress by indorsing any of them to others,
till you have heard from me that I am likely to be in
cash, of which you shall be informed in the month of
January next.   I have the honor, &c—

B. FRANKLIN.

TO ARTHUR LEE.

BRUXELLES, 25 October, 1782.

Dear Sir:

I have often advised you that the scheme did not
take place in which I had proposed last winter to
employ your money, having luckily discovered
that the principal was a most competent ——, before your agreement was finally settled, and therefore your money was placed at interest in the hands
of Cte De C[lonard]., who unfortunately died a few
daies before his note was due.   How he has left his
affairs, I do not certainly know, but have reason to
think they are somewhat perplexed.   However I
experienced so much uneasiness on ye occasion,
that I am determined not to risk suffering the same
again.   Therefore your money will be placed in

the hands of my banker in Paris, 'till I receive
your farther orders, as I have not any immediate
prospect of employing it to a certain advantage in
commerce, for it will not be prudent to engage in
any enterprize just at the eve of a peace. My
Banker allows only 3 per cent. per annum interest,
unless the money is lodged in his hands for a year
certain, and then he will give 4 per cent. interest ;
but this I cannot agree to, as I don't know when
you will want the money. I have received in part
of Cte de C. note £12,000, and £12,000 are I hope
secured, that is, I have for them a bill on the
French Treasury of Marine for £12,000, accepted
and due the beginning of March next. This bill
being paid, you may reckon in my hands twenty-
eight thousand livres. But there is an old account
of about £15 sterling due from you to Mr. E.
B[rown] which I must pay. You will recollect
also that there still remains two accounts of J. A.
D[urbrick] & Co unsettled, in one of which ye
Company claims about £300 sterling, and in the
other about £7000 levies are claimed from the
Company. The Company's claim of £300 sterling
is clearly a just one, but being complicated and the
partys dispersed, I begin to fear the money will not
be recovered. The demand of £7000 against the
Company is evidently unjust, and therefore will
not be paid unless the law compels it to be so.
When the conveyance is more certain than at

present you shall have an account current; tho'
from this letter you may easily understand the
state of your property in my hands.

P. S. If you have occasion to draw for any part
of this money, you may draw on me at Messrs.
Freres Overman, Bruxelles, but your bills should
be payable in Louis at Paris, and at two or three
months' sight.*

TO ARTHUR LEE.

BRUSSELS, 26 October, 1782.

Dear Brother:

By M^r. Wright and Genl. Du Portail (who I suppose carried Dispatches to Congress from the
American Commissioners at Paris, with advice of
the formal acknowledgment of American Independence by the King and Ministers of G. B.,
and ye negotiations for a General Peace being
seriously commenced at Paris,) sent duplicates of
my proved Accounts against De Berdt & Co., with
a power of attorney to prosecute the Suit, and a
protest for a Bill drawn by —— Hall & Co., in
Maryland, for £300 stg: on West and Hobson in
London, indorsed by Stephen West. I wrote to
you by two conveyances that M^r. Andrew Allen,

---

*Addressed to "Mr. Lotsom;" and on the outer sheet is writ-
ten "Mr. A. Lee is requested to inclose and forward this letter
to Mr. Lotsom."

who was my original Attorney and Councillor in the attachment against ye effects of De Berdt & Co had informed me that an account could not now be necessary, as ye Debt had been ascertain'd by the Verdict of a Jury in ye Court of Com. Pleas, where a interlocutory Judgment had been enter'd; but before final Judgment was entered, M^r R[eed] removed the cause by *certiorari* to the Supreme Court of Pennsylvania. But should it be necessary to have the original Account, &c, if they can't be found in the Prothonotary's office of Pennsylv^a , they must be amongst his papers in New York, for which purpose he has given me the inclosed Letter to Mr And^w Elliot, [who] will deliver y^r order.

I have received your favor of ye 7th of August last, covering a resolve of Congress that I should apply to Dr Franklin for payment of the Debt due to me, and a bill on Messrs Overman for £165.19. Stg. The bill is accepted, but you must be greatly mistaken about the Exchange, which is as high and even higher than before the War. If you are right, Specie Money must be in abundance with you. The order of Congress I had a few daies before received from Mr Secretary Livingston ; and to take away all possibility of excuse from Dr F., I drew on him for the amount of the debt due to me payable in April next; after a fortnight's consideration he accepted my bills, but being satisfied

he will make use of every pitiful chicane to keep
the money from me, I shall not think myself secure until he has paid my bills, the value of which
I am determined now to have of him, if there is
Law or Justice this side the grave. I have already
sent you Duplicates of D^r. F.'s letter wherein he
positively refused last Summer to pay this Money.
M^r J[enin]gs is ye only person here that can prove
that D^r. Franklin knew I have been fixed here for
three years past, and he, in his usual manner,
evades signing any certificate for that purpose.
The motives you can't be at a loss to conceive, as
you know the Man.—The 127 living of *R. Morris*
will be downfall & ruin in ye end. "Give a
Rogue rope enough & he will soon hang himself."
Be quiet and watchful, as *Franklin* is; and the
business will bye and bye fall into your mouth.
Adams finding that 59 is absolute in *Congress* is
mild as a Lamb, and thinks 59 perfectly right in
the prosecution of *A. Lee.* His present object is,
to ingratiate himself that he may be permitted to
be *Minister* in *England.* This opinion of *Adams*
is perfectly just. Mr Adams is just gone to Paris ;
he says you highly approve Mr Jay's conduct.
This I doubt, because you must be greatly misinformed in many respects if you do. Mr Jay and
Dr Franklin, without even consulting Mr Adams
or any Body else, have agreed to appoint young
Mr Temple Franklin, Secretary to the American

Commissioners for making peace. Govr Franklin, with Genl Arnold, are the favorites.

TO BENJAMIN FRANKLIN.

BRUXELLES, 12 November, 1782.

Sir:

I have had the honor of receiving your letter of the 20th of last month, informing me that you had accepted my several bills, amounting to forty-six thousand one hundred and ninety-six livres, nineteen sols, payable the 12th of April next, and you add "I confide, that you will not hazard the credit of Congress by indorsing any of them to others, till you have heard from me that I am likely to be in cash."

This does not surprise me, as coming from Dr Franklin, especially when I have in my hands the following extract from his letter of the 30th of March last, to the Superintendent of Finance, who had ordered him twelve months ago to pay this money, viz: "No demand has been made on me by Mr Wm Lee. I do not know where he is."—At that moment, Doc.^{tr} Franklin knew where I was, as well as any man existing, who had not his eyes on me.

I know, Sir, that the money has been already lodged in your hands, for the specific purpose of paying the debt due to me, which you have hitherto unjustly withheld; consequently the *credit of Congress*, is at present out of the question with respect to me, in this business.

Therefore I am compelled to inform you, that I am not, in any manner, disposed to be trifled with any longer, and that you must take care to pay the bills punctually, which you have accepted.

I have the honor to be, &c.

TO ARTHUR LEE.

BRUXELLES, 20 November, 1782.

Dear Brother:

I have received your letter of the 22nd and 24th September with a note of the 6th of October. The greatest part of its contents have been in fact answer'd by several letters written to you, in the course of 3 months past, and sent by various opportunities.

To guard as much as I can against farther tricks or evasion of Dr Franklin, about paying the bills he has accepted for the debt due me from Congress, I enclose you the correspondence that has passed between us, since I received Mr Secretary Livingston's letter of July last. Mr Geo. Fox, a native of Phila, and has a brother there, spent a part of last winter in Bruxelles, was frequently with me, and in March went from hence to Paris. He was intimate at Passy, and being now on his way home, when he arrives you may possibly from him, get viva voce proof that Dr F. knew where I was the 30th of March last. This is, however, certain, that he almost every day sees Mr Grand or some of his family, and he always knew that Mr Grand was my banker; therefore he could not be at any loss to find out where I was, had he been disposed to pay me.

The trick you will see evidently originates with *R. Morris.* T. Lee can tell you what passed between him and Mr Lovell in Decr last, about this business, who said to my nephew that he had written to me on the subject, and sent 4 copies of his letter, but I neither received original nor any copy, of such letter,—therefore—but enough.

Whenever there is peace, which those out of the circle of the cabinets do not see any kind of certainty of, for this winter, at least, America will do well to rest upon her arms, and not to be in a hurry to form farther European connections.

Her whole attention should be applied to correcting the abuses and disorders, that have arisen from the war. By providing good seminaries of education in each of the states; a steady, wise, and regular system of government and administration, procure the happiness of the present age, as well as of posterity; and by economy in expenditures and judicious imposition of taxes, to pay off its public debt, without injury to Agriculture and population. These are objects well worthy of the whole attention of your wise and virtuous patriots.

Pray present my compliments to D.ʳ Williamson, and when he has a leisure moment to spare, I shall be glad to hear from him.

Col. Gorham, just come from England, asserts that orders have been sent six weeks ago, not to evacuate Chaˢ. Town. The truth of this, you can judge of, from the fact. If it is not evacuated, it will be a decisive proof, that the secret design of renewing the American war is not relinquished in the British cabinet, and of course, you should exert every nerve, to take advantage of the enemy's present weakness, and drive them by force out of the territories of the 13 states next year. L.ᵈ Shelburne and his motley band, seem to be in a very unsteady state. The general opinion in England, is that he cannot keep his ground; but that cannot be ascertained till after the meeting of Parliam.ᵗ the 26ᵗʰ inst. . My opinion of him is not altered, and you know that is, that he is a very great . . . . . . fully equal to D.ʳ F.

We were told last year, that M.ʳ Paradise had lost all his negroes by the invasion of the enemy, and that the lands were confiscated; but he has lately as we are told, received a remittance of between 3 & 400 £ st.ʳ in bills, from his steward, which is double of what I have received.* Pray

---

* February, 1782, Cary Wilkinson, agent for John Paradise,

explain this to me.—Comp⁵. , if you please to Mʳˢ I[zar]d and all friends. Adieu.

TO RICHARD HENRY LEE.

Bruxelles, 22 November, 1782.

My dear Brother:

I received your letter of the 18ᵗʰ of July last, and answered it, via Amsterdam and Boston the, 1ˢᵗ of October. A copy was sent by a Mʳ. Bell, from Ostend to Baltimore or Philadelphia, and another copy was sent to Mʳ. Dobrée at Nantes, to forward from thence. Since that I have received your letter of the 8ᵗʰ October and 15ᵗʰ November, 1781, which my nephew Thom:, your son, was to have forwarded from Philᵃ in Decʳ last; but it did not leave that city till August. I feel myself much oblig'd by the public news you gave me, which would have been very interesting, had your letter come to hand in the reasonable time you had a right to expect. I have not heard of either Colo: Monroe or Parker being arrived in Europe, but you may be always assured that every service and civility in my power, will be rendered to any one that you think worthy of your recommendation.
* * *

---

filed a claim against the French intendant for wood cut from the Ludwell estate. Affidavits were submitted to prove that Paradise was neither a refugee nor a British subject, as had been charged.—*Calendar of Virginia State Papers*, III., 67.

I would cheerfully send you such new publications as I can get here, that are worth your attention, if I could find any method of conveying them to you, but this I cannot do at present. Indeed, I find infinite difficulty in getting a letter to you; for after they reach Philadelphia, as the former practice of a certain great man there,* seems now to have become universal in that city—the letters are either opened and destroyed, or kept there several months.

The public occurrences in Europe last campaign, are hardly worth mentioning.

The Dutch have thrown away two 64 gun ships —lost in the North sea. All attempts against Gibraltar have been fruitless, tho' attended with great loss and infinite expense to Spain.

I have much reason to believe there has been much black work with respect to America, in the negotiations at Paris last summer, which 'tis probable will never be brought fully to light; at least I fear so, from knowing well all those you have had there, to watch over the interest of America.

'Tis unfortunate that Mr Laurens refused at first to act as a commissioner for negotiating a peace; nor do I know yet that he will act, after receiving another call from Congress to take upon him that office; for we hear that he is most deeply affected at the death of his son.

---

* Robert Morris.

Whether we shall have peace or not, this winter, is really more than I can determine at present; but we shall be able to judge better in a few days, for the British parliament meets the 26th of this month. In what state the negotiations are that still go on at Paris, the public are not certainly inform'd; but this the most intelligent assert to be truth, that the terms insisted on by France and Spain, particularly the latter, are such as Great Britain cannot agree to.

American independence is, and has been from the beginning, out of the question with Great Britain. I am however inclined to think we must have peace soon, for both Great Britain and Spain are entirely exhausted both of men and money. The revenues of France are somewhat embarrassed, and there is a cloud hanging over in the north, that will probably break out into a dreadful storm if she continues this war another year. Notwithstanding this the preparations of France and Great Britain are such that it looks as if they intended a warm campaign in the West Indies next year.

Count D'Estaing is gone to Cadiz, to take command of a strong fleet, that is to go as soon as they can be got ready with 10 or 12,000 land forces to the West Indies.

We have had such dreadful weather last summer and fall, that there is a general scarcity of all kinds of grain in Great Britain and Ireland, which has already been productive of great murmurs, and open riots.

Here the frost is now as severe as it was any time last winter, and every appearance looks as if we should have a most severe winter.   *   *

TO WILLIAM DOLMAN.

BRUXELLES, 20 November, 1782.

The difficulty of getting a letter to you for some years past, has prevented me from writing to you so often as I should otherwise have done, relative to your Estate in England, which I formerly had the management of. Since I left London, your Aunt, Mrs Dolman, has dyed, and I hear the little freehold Estate she was in possession of, that you are properly heir at Law to, is now got into the possession of a very artful cunning man, who is determined not to give it up without a Lawsuit. The tenants on the Freehold Estate which I formerly got possession of for you, since my leaving England refuse to pay any rent, and keep possession of the houses as their own property. This they have been able to do f'm a very great omission or Fault in the power of Attorney you sent to me. For you did not give me any authority to empower or authorize any person to act under me; therefore when I left England, there was no body legally impowered to receive ye rents and keep possession of the Estate for you, which ye Tenants have taken ye advantage of, and intend now to keep their several tenements as belonging to themselves. The leases of your Lease-hold Estates in Houses, in Several parts of the suburbs of London, which bro't you the greatest part of your annual rent, have been long since expired, therefore what Estate you have now remaining, that is, to which you have a legal right, consists of between two and three acres of Land, part Freehold and Copyhold, on which there are several little houses and some little gardens as big as the floor of a 40-foot Tobacco house.

In this situation of your affairs I did not imagine that you would ever hereafter receive one shilling benefit from this Estate, and that you would be like several others that I know in Virginia who have a legal right to large Estates in England, but have never been able to get possession of them or one shilling f'm them; however, lately application has been made to me to purchase ye whole of your Estate both Freehold and Copyhold and your right to the little Estate that your Aunt dyed possessed of. This person offers to pay Eight hundred pounds Sterling for the whole as soon as ever he is put into possession—but I think if you choose to sell it, that he will give one thousand pounds Sterling for ye whole; and if you incline to give me full and proper powers, I think I can contrive to get him put into possession, when he must pay down the money. If you were to ask my advice what to do, I should cetainly advise you to accept this offer without a moment's hesitation, for as things are circumstanced, when I leave Europe, which I probably do next year, you will hardly find an opportunity of selling this Estate, and I am satisfied you cannot now get any thing from the rents, as the present tenants will not pay anything and are determined to keep possession as long as they can. I remember upwards of twenty years ago, a poor old planter in your Country, who had a right to an Estate in England that was a very valuable one indeed. Some person wrote to him from England and offer'd him £10,000 Stg. for yᵉ Estate, which his silly Friends in Virgᵃ advised him to refuse; the Consequence was, that the poor old planter in the upper parts of Westmoreland who is since dead, never got one Shilling for the Estate, and the Tenants, who were then in possession, have kept it as their own ever since. Should you be disposed to sell your Estate, you should without loss of time get a full and proper power of attorney drawn up, authorizing and empowering me to get possession of for you as heir-at-Law to Thomas Dolman, late of Virgᵃ, deceased, who was Bʳ and Heir-at-Law to Wᵐ Dolman, late of old Street Road in yᵉ County of

Middlesex in Great Britain, deceased, all ye Estate or Estates whether leasehold Copyhold or Freehold in ye Kingdom of G. B., particularly in ye County of Middlesex in the Kingdom aforesaid, which were in possession of, or were ye property of the said Wm Dolman, and for that purpose to commence prosecute and bring to final conclusion, one or more Action or Actions, Suit or Suits at Law or in Equity, ejectment or ejectments and to take all legal measures that may be requisite for the purposes aforesaid. To ask, demand, and receive or recover, by distress or otherwise, or to make compositions for the same, all rents or dues whatsoever that are or may become due and owing from or on account of any or all of the aforesaid Estates. To rent by lease or otherways any part or ye whole of ye said Estate, or Estates at such yearly rent or conditions as to me may appear most benefitial for your interests; To sell dispose of in perpetuity and for ever, for you and in your name, any part or ye whole of the said Estate or Estates to one or more person or persons for such sum or sums of money as may appear to me a reasonable value for the same. To substitute or appoint one or more attorney or attorneys to act under me, with the same powers and authority that you give me. In short you must get some able and skillful Lawyer to draw up this power of attorney for you, and when you have regularly Signed it, you must

get two or three affidavits that your Father and
Mother were legally married, and that you were
born in proper time after they were so legally
married. The power of attorney and ye affidavits
should be recorded in ye Genl. Court, and you
should send me by two different opportunities
Copies of ye Records with ye State Seal affixed to
them. I will recommend you to Richard Lee,
esq^r., of Lee Hall, to assist you in getting these
papers properly drawn up and to contrive them to
me.

TO ARTHUR LEE.

BRUXELLES, 17 December, 1782.

Dear Sir:

* * * Before this reaches you, no doubt, Congress will receive the provisional articles of peace
between Great Britain and America, signed by the
commissioners on each side the 30th ult^o at Paris;
but as they are not to take effect 'till a peace is
concluded between France and Great Britain, I
know not how to congratulate you at present on
the occasion; for 'tis certain that Lord Shelburne,
the premier in England, and the King's confidant,
and the Duke of Richmond have declared as their
sense of these articles, that they are to be invalid
to all intents and purposes, if the present negotiations with France should not end in a peace; and

it looks very much as if they were determined to have them so construed, as they have hitherto declined to lay them before Parliament, tho' repeatedly called upon so to do by M⸱ Fox and others, that they may be irrevocably ratified.

It is also true, that M⸱ Pitt, Chancellor of the Exchequer, Gen⸱ Conway, and T. Townsend, Secretary of State, have declared in the House of Commons, that they conceive the articles to be irrevocable; however, this contrariety of opinion in the British ministers, is one striking proof of the duplicity and faithlessness of Lord Shelburne, and will no doubt prevent Congress from taking any measures in consequence of their being signed until they are ratified by Parliament, or the event of peace with France takes place, which is to bring them into effect, unless it be to get well supplied with all kind of stores, and be well provided if Great Britain should hereafter either be capable, or desirous of renewing the war in America; tho' indeed I do not conceive this can happen, for I am inclined to think the terms of peace between Great Britain and France are at this moment settled, and agreed upon, or will be so, before the new year begins.

England is totally exhausted, both of men and money, and France wishes much for peace, as she is likely to have very soon work enough on her hands. This I can't venture to explain to you

here, but you may be assured that a great and
terrible conflagration in Europe is nearly on the
point of breaking out; in which France is deeply
concerned.

The old work of stock-jobbing has been carried
on between Paris and London. I have seen a late
letter from a gentleman in London to his friend
here, in which are these words, —

"It is said that several of our countrymen, now at
Paris, and in the confidence of the American negotia-
tors, have made considerable sums, in consequence of
their early intelligence."

However, this moment of universal joy for
peace is not perhaps the proper period for exposing
or bringing to justice either the great or little
rogues, but that salutary work should not be
neglected when the proper season arrives.

In Holland things seem to be coming fast to a
crisis; the Prince's party have begun with raising
riots at the Hague and Amsterdam. All the cities
in Holland, Zealand, Friesland, and Oberyssell have
determined to appoint their own magistrates and
officers, that were before appointed by the Prince of
Orange. This he is determined to oppose *vi et
armis*.

In England, Lord Shelburne seems to have made
up his band of the dependents on the Treasury,
and those insignificant individuals, that did not before belong to any party, such as Lord Abingdon,

Gen! Conway, Geo. Dempster, &c. His Lordship is determined to seize all the patronage and riches of the East Indies, which with the Treasury, he thinks, will bring him dependents and support enough, especially as the Bedfords are kept down by the immense plunder of Rigby.

Lord North, who never had any party or influence but from the Treasury, is silent, and the Rockinghams, somewhat weakened by the desertion of the Duke of Richmond, whose pride and paltry vanity was galled at his not being chosen for the head and leader instead of the Duke of Portland.

These things I know, are totally immaterial to America, but they may be amusing to you and our friend M! Izard, to whom I pray you to present my best respects.

The English papers tell us that D! Franklin has already declared that Congress shall appoint consuls in Dublin, and the other principal ports in Ireland, as soon as there is peace.

'Tis probable that in his sovereign will, he has also, already, fixed on the persons who are to be consuls, not only in Ireland but in England and Holland too.

Our best wishes and love attend you and all friends. Adieu.

TO HENRY LAURENS.

I have just received your favor of the 21st inst., and at the same time that I acknowledge my obligations to you for it, I must confess that I read its contents and that of the anonymous letter accompanying it, with more astonishment than anything I ever read in my life. In answer to the Nefarious accusation bro't against me of being the Writer or Author of the Anonymous Letter, I can only declare to you upon my Honor, which with me has ever been and always shall be as Sacred as the most solemn Oath, that I am not the Author or writer of that Letter, that I do not know who the Author or Writer is, nor anything of its Contents. As I take it for granted that Mr Adams, whom this anonymous Letter writer seems particularly anxious to traduce, has been acquainted with the Affair, I must desire that you will do me the Justice to communicate to him what I have here written. Now Sir, I have a request to make which I am sure you cannot in Justice or Candor refuse to comply with.

It is this, that you will explicitly and by return of Post give me the Name of that person who told you in London that Will Lee of Bruxelles was the Author of that anonymous Letter of which you sent me a copy, and also the name of that third Person whose hand writing was produced in proof the charge. I have Charity enough to suppose that there may be a mistake somewhere in this business, for I am unwilling to believe that there is one among your friends in England, or elsewhere, so much my Enemy, and so infamously wicked, as designedly and Wittingly to charge me so untruly, with such a mean, base and horrible deed. I shall expect your answer with much impatience and the mean time with great regard and Respect I remain, &c.

TO HENRY LAURENS.

BRUXELLES, 25 December, 1782.

I had received and answered yesterday your favor of the 21 inst. directing to you at the Hotel De York, Rue Jacob. Since which I have received a copy of your Letter, which came here under cover to Messrs Fréres Overmann, and as you add in a Postscript that "*the subject treated of is now become very important,*" I subjoin hereto a copy of my Letter of yesterday's date, and shall put this under cover to Mr Grand, desiring him to send it to you immediately, as you have not pointed out any mode for me to direct to you.

I am utterly at a loss to conceive how this affair can have *become very important* to any one but myself; but as you say so, I am sure you must agree with me in opinion, that I am now warranted in

Insisting on the Name of the Person who charges me with the fact and the name of the third person whose hand writing was produced in support of the charge, being immediately communicated to me. I shall not say one word more on the subject at present, least passion (for I am naturally warm on such occasions,) shou'd hurry me beyond the bounds of temper. Mrs Lee unites with me in best Compliments to yourself and your worthy Son, and with great Esteem and Respect, I am, Dear Sir. &c.

TO WILLIAM BRIDGEN.

BRUXELLES, 3 January, 1783.

I receiv'd lately a letter from Henry Laurens Esq., dated in Paris the 21st of last month, wherein he says, "On the 1st June last at Antwerp I rec^{d} from a friend in London Copy of an Anonymous Letter which he said, *he had receiv'd in a disguised hand from, as he guessed, a most worthy American Gentleman who was honor and truth itself.*" A copy of that Copy of the anonymous Letter sent to me by Mr Laurens you will find annex'd hereto. Mr Laurens adds thus,

"When I returned to London, I made a point of interrogating my friend respecting the supposed author of that wicked performance; he told me Mr Lee, or in his own words, Will Lee of Bruxelles is the man." It wou'd not be easy for me to express

the indignation I felt on finding myself thus unjustly accused of a most infamous and wicked
action; however I wrote instantly to M.ʳ Laurens in
the most positive terms, denying that I was either
the Author or writer of that base Letter, adding
that I did not know who the Author or writer was,
nor anything about its contents, and at the same
time desired that M.ʳ Laurens wou'd communicate
to me directly the Name of his friend in London,
who had asserted to him that Will Lee of Bruxelles was the Author of the Anonymous Letter in
question.   In reply M.ʳ Laurens, with that Candor
and Honor which marks all his Conduct, immediately writes to me thus the 28ᵗʰ ult.º —"It was late
last Evening when your favor of the 24ᵗʰ appear'd.
There happen'd to be a friend in the house who
was just on the point of departure for London.   I
embraced the favorable opportunity and write to
M.ʳ Bridgen, from whom I had receiv'd the information which you so anxiously and so very naturally wish to develope."   M.ʳ Laurens also auth-
orises me to send you a copy of his whole letter,
which does not at present seem to me necessary to
be done.   Thus, Sir, the Charge is bro't home to
you in the first instance of accusing me of a most
base wicked and infamous action, but I will not
suppose at this time that the accusation originated
with you, therefore must now insist that you will
immediately, and in the most explicit terms, let

me know, on what authority, you have made this accusation against me. I shall expect Chapter and verse, that is, precision in dates, words, names, &c., if you have any written authority to ground your accusation upon. This, Sir, your Justice and your own Honor call upon you to comply with instantly and a due regard to my wounded reputation compels me to demand of you. I shall expect your answer by the first mail, which you will please to put under a Cover addressed thus Á. M. Fréres Overman, Neg^{ts}, Bruxelles.

I have the Honor to be Sir &c.

TO HENRY LAURENS.

BRUXELLES, 3 January, 1783.

I duly received your two favors both dated the 28th Ult^o and have written to Mr Bridgen (a copy of which you will have herewith), by this day's Mail, which, is the first for England since your Letters came to hand. Tho' I was astonished beyond description at the contents of your first Letter on this subject, yet I must confess that your subsequent ones have really plunged me into a Labyrinth of amazement. Had not the fact really happen'd one wou'd have conceiv'd it to be incredible that a person so perfectly retired as I have been for above three years past, and two thirds of the time in such a miserable state of health, as to call for more meditation on another world, than concern with what passes in this wicked one in which we live, shou'd be dragged in neck and shoulders, as the principal Agent in a dark and villainous Plot.

By *whom* this has been done, I must expect to learn in a short time from M.̇ Bridgen; but I can't delay conveying to you my sincerest thanks for the Manly and candid manner you have acted in the whole affair, which has my warmest approbation, and I shall ever hold myself your debtor, for affording me the opportunity of vindicating my attainted character, and bringing the Assassin forth to view.

M.̇ Adams is totally mistaken in *one* part at least of his *mights*, for I solemnly declare that the Anonymous letter in question never was in my hands in any manner or form whatever, therefore No Person without a Lye direct, "*might say he had it from me.*"

If there is no impropriety in answering me, I shall be obliged to you for telling me when you intend to leave Paris, and when you do, if you propose to go to America.

TO THOMAS BARCLAY.

BRUXELLES, 9 January, 1783.

Dear Sir:

I have received your letter of y.ᵉ 20.ᵗʰ Ult.°̣, cover-

ing an advertisement informing y.ᵉ Public that you
are now the sole agent for the State of Virginia,
which you desire me to have inserted in y.ᵉ Bruxelles Gazette and any other that I may think proper.
In consequence I have had it inserted in y.ᵉ Bruxelles Gazette of this day, as you will see by the inclosed, and have taken measures to have it inserted
in two others in this Country, and two in Germany,
that are extensively circulating and commercial
papers. The whole expence shall be conveyed to
you as soon as I know it. You say,

"That some time ago y.ᵉ State of Virg.ᵃ had appointed
you agent to complete some engagements which were
begun with yᵉ court of France." And that "You
had received a letter from the Governor in Council, expressing a great deal of uneasiness least y.ᵉ Person who
was formerly agent for y.ᵉ State might have made, or
should make, an Improper use of the Power with which
he was invested; and directing you to take such measures to prevent the evil Consequences, as to you should
seem most proper."

But you do not mention, *who* this former agent
was; therefore for very particular and cogent
Reasons, which you may know if you desire it, I
must request you will be so good as to give me the
Name of the former Agent, that y.ᵉ Gov.ʳ in council
in Virginia has expressed much uneasiness least he
should have, or may abuse his Trust. I am happy
in returning you my congratulations on y.ᵉ prospect

of Peace which I believe and hope is not far distant. The Inclosed letter to my Brother, I beg you will be kind enough to inclose to your Correspondent in Phil^a, and forward it by the first vessel that sails for America.

P. S.   I shall be obliged to you for ye American Papers, whenever you can meet with any private hand coming this way.

TO HENRY LAURENS.

BRUXELLES, 14 January, 1783.

Dear Sir:

I have received your two favors of ye 7 and 8th instant, the first of which I should have acknowedged sooner had I not been reattacked by my old Companion the Rheumatism, which I verily believe has been brought on by the vexation I have suffered about ye dirty business that has been ye subject of our late Correspondence. I felt not a little for you, who at such an unhappy period, should be compelled to take an active part in such an odious business. The Original Author is a base, mean and wicked creature, and the intermediate medling Characters, if not as wicked, or more so, as they hereafter appear, must at least be stamp'd as impertinently officious Blockheads, similar to those busy, medling Fools. that we have often seen depicted on ye Stage. I have known frequent instances where Men, who have been said by y.e World, to have *good hearts*, and to be *mighty good sort of men*, do much more mischief by their ridiculous folly and officiousness, than the artful and designing, by their wicked Intrigues. It is some consolation to me that *you* did not from y.e beginning give any credit to y.e base accusation that has been brought against me; and tho' I have reason to believe yet various insidious attempts have been made to prejudice me in y.e opinion of M.r Adams, I think he must know me too well, ever to have entertained y.e least supicion of my being the Author of y.e Anonymous Letter. If that Gentleman conceives me to be his Enemy, he is mistaken; for if I was, I should not hesitate to declare my opinion openly. I am not of a temper, nor accustomed to fear or flatter either Princes or Kings, whose conduct appears to me reprehensible; that occupation I leave to the servile and narrow Geniuses who are born to be despicable tools in the hands of intriguing, vicious characters. The Accuser whoever he is seems to have satisfied you yet he was not the Author of y.e original letter; but I do not find yet he has in any manner Vindicated himself from having brought, or insinuated, a most unjustifiable accusation against me; I must however wait for M.r Bridgen's answer, to obtain a full eclaircissement of this mysterious intrigue.

Do not, my Dear Sir, say with Woolsey, that

"in your Age, your Country has left you naked to your Enemies." For as to *Enemies* I do not know or believe yet you have any. *Envyers*, you may have, for the Poet justly says, "Envy, will merit as its Shade pursue, and like the Shadow, prove the substance true," and I am convinced, that your Country has placed you where you are from a double motive: To obtain for itself ye Benefit of your able and disinterested Services on a most important occasion; and to do you Honor, in the face of ye World. I am extremely concern'd to hear that your health still continues so bad, but if I am not mistaken in my peep into the political World from my cave, ye Active occupation has now, or will very shortly commence, when full employment may procure some relief to your mind and consequently be of service to your health. It would make me extremely happy if my health and other circumstances should permit me to cross ye Atlantic with you in ye Spring, but ye old Gentleman at Passy, confines me till April, before I can possibly take any decided resolution about my future movements.

P. S. The above was written and just going to ye Post, when I received your favor of the 9th, which made its course properly to the West, instead of the South, in order that it should reach you safely and it is lucky yet it was not sealed as I have this moment (Jan^r 14.) received a letter from M^r

Bridgen of the—(for it has no date), which is so candid that it must be satisfactory to me, tho' I can't help feeling a little, that any person who ever knew y.º least of me should ever conjecture that on such an occasion, I could commit such an act. When I have time perhaps, I may send you a copy of Mr.B's Letter. Give me leave now to express my concern that your health should make it necessary for you to go to Bath, as well as at y.º public appearances that ye Dreadful Demon of War is still to be gluted, with carnage, murder and Devastation.

TO EDWARD BRIDGEN.

BRUXELLES, 17 January, 1783.

Last mail bro't me a letter from you without any date, the contents of which are so honest and candid an acknowledgement of your error in charging me with being the Author of a certain anonymous Letter, that I shou'd put myself in the wrong, if I was not to express my entire satisfaction on that head. You have said what every Man of Honor would say in a similar situation, and you have said as much as any Gentleman could require.

I think it will be more consistent for your own reputation, as well as mine, that you should yourself communicate to Mr Laurens, what you have written to me, rather than that I should send him a copy of your letter; which I shall decline doing, in confidence that in this point you will coincide with my opinion and act conformably. I hope to obtain your belief, when I assure you that my only motive for observing on the reasons you give for supposing me to be the Author of the Letter, is to prevent you on future occasions from forming false conclusions from mistaken premises. You say as reasons for your first conjecture. "First, I knew of no 3ᵈ person in Flanders who was inform'd of my intimacy with Mʳ Laurens; 2ᵈˡʸ, I knew that its being sent without a Post Mark must be by the connivance of a Postmaster, and that you were acquainted with the Postmaster at Ostend; and lastly, that there were strokes in that letter which resembled your hand writing as well as your former Clerk, Mʳ Brown." Now I mean to show you that every one of those positions which you took for granted, are *every one* of them mistakes. First, I know of a certainty that there were at that time *more* than *three* Persons in Flanders, or at least in the Low Countries, who knew of your intimacy with Mʳ Laurens. 2ᵈˡʸ, the omission of the Post Mark might happen *without any connivance with a Postmaster*, since in certain cases it is a common routine of Office: nor do I know the Postmaster at Ostend, nor have I ever seen him, nor wrote to him in my Life, nor do I know his name, and tho' the Letter came to you by the Flanders Mail, it might as well have been sent from Paris,

Ghent, Spa or Antwerp, as from Bruxelles. Lastly, how far the Characters may resemble my hand writing or that of Mʳ Browne, I can not tell; but this is certain, that they cannot resemble both—for I hardly know two persons whose hand writing are more easily distinguish'd from each other than those of Mʳ B and mine. You do not mention the name of your Friend with whom you originally corresponded on the subject of the letter; but whoever he is, he seems to me to be little entitled to the sacred appelation of *Friend* from you, and still less so from me, for he certainly acted in a very unjustifiable manner to us both in keeping a profound silence, after he had artfully drawn from you the name of the person you suspected, by an express and positive promise, that if you did mention the name "*he wou'd tell you whether you both had the same Idea of the Man;*" for by his silence he evidently confirm'd you in your Error, and convey'd an insidious tho' indirect Slander against me. These are my sentiments, and it will require very convincing reasons and facts to make me alter them.

TO SAMUEL THORPE.

BRUXELLES, 17 January, 1783.

* * * I observe that Dʳ F. has given a Certificate in vindication of Silas Deane, relative to the charge against him about the Magazine of Old

Firelocks. Was I in London, I would make the following reply in the Public papers:

"A correspondent, who has read Dr B. Franklin's Certificate, published in the London Papers, in vindication of Mr Silas Deane, from a charge bro't against him, the said S. D., for a gross imposition on the Congress of the United States of America, in the purchase of a Magazine of old Iron and old useless musquets, says, it puts him in mind of an Associate appearing at the old Bailey, in support of the character and honesty of his fellow Laborer in the same vocation, who stood arraign'd for a high Way Robbery; for he has seen a publication in America, wherein Dr B. Franklin is publicly charged with being as Deep in the Mud as Mr Silas Deane is in the Mire, about this same Magazine of old Rusty Iron; and to this public Charge Dr B. Franklin has never yet found it expedient to make any reply."

W. Woodfall would probably be glad of such an Article. The Doctor is however protected, for Reasons obvious, by the Court of Versailles, and until there is full Peace, he can't be bro't to the punishment he has too deeply merited. But I have more than one written proof even under his own hand writing, that he carried his hand to a direct falsehood. * * *

Your minister here, *pro tempore*, from ye authority of Mr Fitzherbert, has openly assured several Gentlemen, that a General Peace is as good as signed. I hope he is not mistaken, as I would not willingly believe that L.^d S[helbur]ne would thus palpably deceive ye world; for the present therefore, I have only to repeat my assurances y.^t I am, &c.

TO SAMUEL THORPE.

BRUXELLES, 24 January, 1783.

Most joyfully and heartily do I congratulate you on ye long wish'd for Peace being at last concluded. 'Tis indeed more than I once expected ever to see. God grant it may be perpetual between Great Britain and America. I am too much pleased, or I should certainly growl at your not dropping me a line by your last Friday's Mail, which we received here on Monday; for we are told that the Preliminaries of Peace arrived at Versailles on Sunday night, already sign'd by George the 3.^d, and were sign'd by Lewis the 16.th at 7 o'Clock on Monday morning. I have not asked about the terms, because I still adhere to my old position, which is as easily proved as that 3 and 2 make 5—that Peace on *any terms* is for Great Britain infinitely preferable to a continuation of the War. But should the terms be in any respect not agreeable to the National Palate, the Nation can only blame itself for embarrassing the Minister, by so greedily and stupidly swallowing the insidious and absurd Language of Lord North, who, in his usual knavish manner and with uncommon effrontery, dared to assert in the House of Commons that you were now in a situation to *demand* and obtain the most advantageous terms of peace. I will now have done with Ministers. America is Free; Ireland is as much so as she ought to be; and England is in a better constitutional State than she was 10 years ago, and may be soon quite secure from Despotism, if there is Virtue enough in the Nation, to finish the great work of purifying the House of Commons.

TO THOMAS BARCLAY.

BRUXELLES, 2 February, 1783.

I have received your esteem'd favor of ye 20 Ult^o, and promise myself great entertainment from the American papers that you were so good as to send me by Mess. Steward and Mr Meyers, when they arrive here, and I beg you to accept my thanks for your kindness.

It is with infinite pleasure that I can with confidence congratulate you on the near approach of a general cessation of hostilities, which I hope and trust will be of long Duration; at least with respect to America. The Gazette here is entirely under the direction of Government—your original advertisement was given to the Censor of the Gazette, and he chose to have it inserted in the manner you saw it was; his reason for so doing I cou'd not obtain, and by this time you will know, that in such cases the only reason you can get is, *Car tel est mon plaisir.* I can't yet learn, whether it has been inserted in the other gazettes as I order'd, nor have I seen it in those you mention'd, tho' indeed the Courier de L'Europe is seldom seen here. The publication may be of service, for it has lately been reported here that some little time ago a Person was at Leipsic, Frankfort, and other parts of Germany, endeavoring to obtain Money and goods as an American Agent. He pass'd by the name *in some places* of Montague, but the description of his person and manners resembled those of M^r. Penet. I have not heard that this person did obtain either money or goods, but such attempts should always be prevented as far as it can be done with propriety, for they really injure the credit of America. Can you send me the act of Congress, prohibiting the importation of British Manufactures into America? Or can you tell me if this prohibition will continue in force any longer than the War continues? I took the liberty of inclosing in my last a letter to my Brother, which I hope was in time to go by the Washington Packet; and when you favor me with another Letter, you will much oblige me by mentioning what Vessels there may be at your Port bound in the course of this and next month, either to Philadelphia or Virginia.

TO SAMUEL THORPE.

BRUXELLES, 11 February, 1783.

* * * * Your Senatorial madness seems to be rising higher than ever, for on all sides of ye House, not content with striving who shall be foremost in unnecessarily throwing all the Power, Dignity, and Trade that G. B. has left into the lap of Ireland, they are running full Tilt at the Navigation Act, which has been the Grand foundation of all your Naval Glory. My clear opinion is, that this Act should be now adher'd to more strictly than ever, in all cases, except with respect to America, whose Vessels and Citizens should be legally esteem'd in G. B. just as they were before the War. This Policy would Unite the two Countries in one common Interest, and might be done by one single Act of Parliament. I look on Mr Alderman T[ownsen]d not only as a Senator, but a friend of the Ministers; therefore if you think proper and find a suitable occasion, you may communicate to him this idea of mine as that of a private individual, and should he think it worth attention, and be desirous of my reasons at large for such opinions, I will readily communicate them to him.* * *

P. S. Pray who are now these mighty and Clamorous Quebec Merchants? When I left London they were chiefly a parcel of insignificant Scotch

Adventurers, that knew no more of Geography or
the proper Limits of Canada than the Pump at
Aldgate. In short I have not seen in your papers
a single Objection to ye Peace, that has the Shadow
of Reason or plausibility in it.

TO SAMUEL W. STOCKTON.

BRUXELLES, 10 February, 1783.

My Dear Sir:

You ask what has become of me? I answer that
for 18 months I was at Death's Door with a horrid
Rheumatism, ye foundation of which was layed in
that dreadful Journey we had together, when we
built the foundation of ye present Union of the
Twenty Provinces, which our old Friend De Neufville so anxiously wish'd for. You will believe
easily, that it is with no small degree of pleasure I
congratulate you on the happy restoration of Peace,
on such terms too, as no true American will find
fault with; I trust however that your Joy on ye occasion will be tempered with a manly Prudence,
and that free from intemperate distraction and dissipation, America will calmly set about ye weighty
work of reforming the abuses and disorders, that
naturally flowed from a state of War, and the
License that such an astonishing Revolution necessarily produced. Digesting a proper system for
liquidating ye Public Debt: providing for ye Army

that has so nobly Shed its blood for ye general cause; putting ye Finances of every state on a proper footing, will require infinite wisdom and patriotism; but it is absolutely necessary that they should be settled, that ye future Peace and Prosperity of America may be fixed on a Durable Basis, and I trust that they will be settled, before any more public Money is thrown away on the most Romantic of all romantic Schemes, that of raising at this time an American Navy.

Accept my congratulations on your Brother in Law's filling ye most exalted Post in America. I have not ye honor of his acquaintance, or I would request of you to make my Comp^ts to him on ye occasion; but when you see our old friend Dr Williamson, please to present my Comp^ts to him, and when he has a leisure moment, I should be glad to hear from him. You say that M^r D[eane']s Credit is very low. It is to be hoped that his great Patrons, who I perceive are still in ye highest Posts of Trust, Honor, and Profit, have repented of ye Injury they did their Country and of their injustice to Individuals, by Patronizing that Man in his wicked attempts: but if you see the English papers you will perceive that D^r F—n has very lately step'd forth as ye Public Champion and Advocate for M^r D . . 's Integrity. (Par Nobili Fratrum.) I wrote to you several times last year, none of which it seems had reached you, as appears by your last favor of Novr 30 per Mr Myers.

The cessation of War has created great Confusion amongst the mercantile World in Europe, as their crys resound from N., W., E. and South; and tho' the Negotiations for Peace have been so long in hand y.ᵉ general Idea was, that it would not take place till y.ᵉ very moment of its conclusion, and after all, we are greatly indebted to the Emperor for it. A Historian that is well informed, may give the World some curious Anecdotes respecting y.ᵉ negotiation; but this you may be assured of, that America is not indebted to y.ᵉ *kindness* or *Good will* of any other Power for the Peace. When we meet, which I hope will be before this year ends, I may explain myself more fully, but least any thing should prevent my putting my intended plan into Execution I hope you will continue to write to me either by England, France, or Holland, directing as before.

TO ARTHUR LEE.

BRUXELLES, 10 February, 1783.

My dear Brother:

Tho' my congratulations on y.ᵉ happy restoration of Peace will reach you late, they are not y.ᵉ less sincere and heartfelt. The conditions you will of course have from your Minister, and may also see them in all y.ᵉ public papers. I gave you information that this event would take place, as soon as I could with any degree of certainty. I hope Amer-

ica will be temperately discreet in her expressions
of Joy on this occasion, especially as I can assure
you with confidence, that she is not indebted to the
Good will or kindness of any Power in Europe for
what she has obtained. The Parisians have already
broached the Idea that a Statute of L . . . XVI. is
to be erected in Phil^a, with an inscription in which
he is to be called *Liberator* of ye Americans—This
word I wholly object to, or any other that conveys
a false Idea, or that express ye least subserviency or
dependence. I hope the Peace between America
and Great Britain will be of long duration; indeed
I see no reason why it should not be perpetual,
which it may be if America is wise and keeps clear
from the baneful influence of foreign Intrigue.

This will go by Mrs Izard; therefore I send you,
as you desired it, pretty authentic Proof that D^r F.
did know where M^r. W. L. was in March last; and
ye enclosed London paper will show that I was
not mistaken in saying some time ago to you or
Mr Izard that I had reason to think, the old connection between S. D. and his former associates
and correspondents was not broken off; but the
known apostacy of S. D. from the cause of his
country, and the universal indignation with which
he was looked upon in America, had made them a
little more cautious and circumspect than formerly
in their connection and correspondence with him.
We are told that your ministers in France, Spain,

and Holland, have each Started for yᵉ place of M[iniste]r in England. Therefore, Dʳ F. has twice written of late for leave to resign his present appointment and has plann'd to get W. T. F., his grandson, in his present place. Since this, it is said that Messʳˢ Adams and Jay have compounded, and agreed as formerly to join interests, to get the former appointed minister to England, and the latter to France. All this however I do not speak of with certainty, as yᵉ Parties have with sedulous attention conceal'd yᵉ whole Intrigue from me, as much as they could. I will endeavor to be with you in yᵉ Course of next Summer, but you will not look upon it as certain until I write again. Therefore continue to write to me as before, and any bills you may draw on me will be duly taken care of, if you direct them to me at Messʳˢ Overman's, in Bruxelles.

172 is gone to England—he has been a principal here in a very dirty business which is fully known to *Izard* who may possibly tell you of it when you meet. 192 has devoted himself soul and Body to *Adams* being flatter'd by him with the hopes that by his influence he will be taken notice of by *Congress*, in some Shape or other. I do not yet hear of any one who is talked of as in 51.

The Political System of Europe does not as yet seem to be much affected by yᵉ Peace, but there will be a great revolution in the Diplomatique

Corps. Y.^r acquaintance the Cte D. Mouthere* goes
to England as Minister 'till all the Treaties are ratified,—when he is to be succeeded by ye Duke
Vauguyon, and Adhemar from this Court takes his
place at the Hague. Fitzherbert goes to Russia,
Carmarthen to Paris, and Mont Stewart to Spain.

The Earl of Surrey is at present talked of to go to
America. This however will depend on the State
of Power in ye House of Commons, where L.^d
North has been hitherto playing a double game between ye Shelburnites and Foxites, sometimes with
one, and sometimes with the other: but unless the
King cheats Ld Shelburne, he will keep his Post.
By this time I suppose that Mr Dana has been publickly received as American Minister at Petersburg,
and I have been assured, tho' not Ministerially,
yet by the minister himself, that ye Emperor would
be very glad to see an American Minister authorized to enter into a commercial Treaty between
him and ye United States, on terms of perfect
equality, and he added *ye sooner the better.* I
should like to see Mr Rutledge at Vienna and M.^r
Izard at Paris, and our best friend, you know who,
should be Secretary for Foreign Affairs, Paris. P.
O. Bulletin, Dr F. going to America to form a code
of Laws. Congress owes the King of France 80
Millions, to be paid at 6 or 7 Millions per Annum.

---

* Moustier.

Writer in pay of D.ʳ F. either directly or indirectly.
Treaty sign'd with Sweden. Adhemar to Eng-
land, Vauguyon to Spain, Fitzherbert to the
Hague, Torrington here.

TO RICHARD HENRY LEE.

BRUXELLES, 11 February, 1783.

My dear Brother:

The happy and long wished for Period of Peace
is at length arrived, on which Event I most cordially congratulate you and our Country whose
Liberty you have had so great a share in securing.
Most sincerely do I pray that the Peace may be a
lasting one, and I am sure it will be between G. B.
and America if the latter continues to act with Prudence and manly sense, and care is taken to guard
against foreign intrigue and Insolent interference
in your Councils, whereby she may save herself
from being involved in any future European Broils;
for it is more than probable, that this Continent
will be in flames before seven years expire. Attend
to your Revenue and expenditure, and take care,
in Virginia especially of being again yᵉ Dupes of
every foreign adventurer who puts on a fine coat.
Reform your Constitution, attend to your Seminaries of Learning, and above all, let no Man Whatever, *without* yᵉ State, presume to meddle or advise
about your Government in any Respect.   *   *   *

TO ARTHUR LEE.

My dear Brother:

I wrote to you a few daies ago, to go by Mrs. I[zar]d, who intends to embark for Philadelphia from L'Orient the latter end of next month.

I intend to embark myself for Virginia the last of April or early in May, leaving my family here; but this you will not look upon as certain, because many things may intervene to prevent me, tho' I wish you on receipt of this write to Mr. Valentine at G. S.* to expect and prepare for my coming in the month of June, and in the meantime let no opportunity be missed of remitting any money to me, directing as usual, or of shipping my tobacco to London, Amsterdam or Ostend (@ two or three pounds sterling per hhd freight, and consign'd p^r. bill of loading to be delivered to me or my order at the port where the vessel that brings it may arrive. He should also pick up all the good goose feathers that are to be sold in the neighborhood to the amount of 4 or 500 lbs. If he can, at a reasonable price, get 3 or 4 carriage or two good saddle horses, he will do well. Write this to R. H. L. and to Loudoun.

The 17th inst^t a motion was made in the House of Lords for an address to ye King on the preliminary articles of peace; an amendment was proposed

---

* Green Spring.

and debated 'till ¼ after 4 o'clo. in the morning, when on a division 55 and 4 proxies were for the amendment, and 69 and 3 proxies were against it. Majority in favor of the address only 13. Lord Carlisle violent against America; Lord Germaine also; Lord Gower against the Peace, but voted for the address; Richmond and Keppel both spoke against the peace; so did Wedderburne, and pledged himself to the House to prove that the King had no power or authority to declare America independent. The Lord Chancellor took up the challenge and pledged himself to prove the King's legal and constitutional right to do it. The same motion for an address was made in the House of Commons the same day by Tho: Pitt. An amendment was proposed by Lord G. Cavendish, seconded by Mr. St. John, full of compliment to the King, but not one word of approbation of the peace. This amendment was debated 'till ½ after 7 o'clo. in the morning of the 18th, when on division 224 were for the amendment, and 208 against it, so that there was a majority of 16 for the amendment, and against the Minister and consequently against the peace. This majority was obtained by the extraordinary union of the Northites, Fox, Burke, all the Cavendishes and Rockinghamites, a large share of the Bedfords, and some of the dirty Scotch, and the intrigues of the C\ of V.,* who hate Lord S. as much for mak-

---

* Court of Versailles.

ing the peace with America as it stands, as for anything else, and want to get Lord North and his
myrmidons again in place. Lord S.* was greatly
faulty in political wisdom in bringing the different
Peacifications with F. S. and A.† together into deliberation; for had the peace with America been
first decided on, Fox, Burke, Richmond, Keppel
and all the Rockinghams must have been with the
Minister, and the Northites, Bedfords, &c. would
have been with him on the peace with France and
Spain. As it is, I can't tell how things will be
settled, but I imagine the Corporation of London
will address on the peace, and others may follow.
If this is done Lord S. will keep his place. If it is
not, possibly Lord North and all the old troop will
come in again. I wish it may not appear that a
great deal of noise against the American peace has
arisen from the extreme folly of 172,‡ to whom
Adams has made many improper communications;
for 172 hates Lord S. because Lord S. despises him,
and looks upon him as a silly, busy, meddling
blockhead. Whether we are to have a continental
war in Europe this year, I believe is not yet entirely decided. The Emperor and Russia wish to
be upon the Turks, which France cannot permit,
nor ought England to enforce it, if she wishes to
save herself; but really that unhappy nation seems

---

* Shelburne.   † France, Spain and America.
‡ I think 172 is Edmund Jenings.

to be as mad as ever. We hear that a treaty is signed between America and Sweden, but of what nature, or by whom it was signed on the part of America, I do not hear. I can with authority assure you that the Emperor is very desirous of entering into a Commercial treaty with America, on terms of equality and mutual advantage, but that Court never makes the first *official* advances of this kind to any other power. You will soon have a Dutch minister in America.

You have every good wish that we can send you. Remember me to all friends, and believe me, affectionately yours ——. Adieu.

P. S. Any bills you may draw on me on account of Mr. Lotsom, and directed as before desired, will be duly honored whether I am here or not.

TO JOHN ADAMS.

BRUXELLES, 9 March, 1783.

Dear Sir:

Having been lately on a Journey I could not sooner thank you for your obliging favor of ye 23d Ult^o , which I found here on my return home. In consequence of what you tell me, I shall refer the Emperor's Agents to Mr Dana. At the same time I perfectly coincide with your opinion, that we ought not to be in a hurry, now we have Peace, to enter into commercial Treaties. I see no reason for changing ye opinion I long since entertained, that while the War continued, America should have had Ministers or Agents in all ye principal Courts in Europe to endeavor to obtain an acknowledgment of our Independence, which might have greatly operated in prevailing on G. B. to make Peace with us; but if that point could not be obtained, she might be prevented from getting any assistance either in men or Money to carry on ye War. When we have Peace we ought to be on the reserve and let the Powers of Europe court us, for they will certainly receive more benefit from a Commerce with us, than we shall. Congress, however, has hitherto pursued a line of conduct directly opposite to my Ideas, possibly induced to do so from Versailles or Passy, where it was wished to confine everything that related to America; which in my opinion was one great leading cause of the War continuing so long as it has done; and I shall not be surprised if a reverse of conduct takes place now, when we see American Ministers and Treaties as plenty as Blackberries. A wise Administration will however first consider how ye expence is to be furnished; and whether ye Benefits likely to accrue to America from such Treaties will be equivalent to the expence of making them, and of keeping a Watch to see that they are maintained. At all Events, I hope and Trust that no engagements whatever will be entered into on ye part of America, that can in any manner involve us in the disputes that may arise in Europe. If M.r Dana enters into Negotiations with y.e Emperor, I suppose he will be well inform'd of y.e nature of commerce in this country, for in many respects a Treaty with the Emperor to be beneficial to America, must differ from that of France. We are told here that Congress sent to D.r Franklin a particular Commission to make a Treaty with Sweden at y.e express desire of his Swedish Majesty. Is this true? I have y.e Honor to be, &c.

TO WILLIAM PITT, CHANCELLOR OF THE EXCHEQUER.

BRUXELLES, 14th March, 1783.

I observe in the London Newspapers, an Abstract of a bill you have bro't into Parliament for y.e Establishment, &c, of Trade and Commerce between the Subjects of G. B. and those of the U. S. of Am.a ; wherein it is among other things recited, that whilst y.e aforesaid Provinces were annex'd to G. B. the inhabitants of the said Provinces *enjoyed all rights, franchises, &c, of British Subjects*, &c— And that it is highly expedient y.e intercourse between G. B. and y.e said states should be established on y.e most enlarged principles of reciprocal benefit to both Countries, &c, &c. Then it proceeds to Enact that y.e Ships and vessels of y.e *Subjects* of

America, with the merchandise on board the same, shall be admitted into all the Ports of G. B. in the same manner as vessels of the Subjects of other Independent States; *but the Merchandise and goods on board such vessels*, being of the produce of the said States, shall be liable to the same duties only, as y.e said Merchandizes would be subject to, if they were the property of British Subjects, &c, &c, &c.* Now Sir, if it is the serious wish of the British Governm.t to revive and consolidate the former intercourse and friendship that subsisted between the two Countries, it appears to me that this Bill is very inadequate to the purpose; since it does not give America the same privileges in G. B. that she enjoys by Treaty in France. Why are the American Ships put on a different footing from the American productions? You can as easily consider American Ships on the same footing in y.e British Ports, as those of British Subjects, as you can exempt the American productions from the payment of Alien's Duties. The continuation of the former bounties and Drawbacks are demonstrably for the benefit of G. B. alone, and therefore cannot ever be consider'd as a Grace or Favor to America. In my poor apprehension, in order to make the inhabitants of both Countries feel themselves mutually interested in the prosperity of their different Gov-

---

*Printed in full in *Trade of Great Britain with the United States*, 1791.

ernments, it would be politically Wise to Enact in
this Bill that the Citizens of ye United States of
America should, from henceforth, enjoy in G. B.
and all its dependencies the same privileges, Franchises, &c, which the inhabitants of the said States
formerly enjoyed, and were entitled to when they
were consider'd and deem'd to be British Subjects.
It is very natural to immagine that America, now
sore and even bleeding with the wounds that she
has so lately received from G. Britain, cannot be
easily reclaim'd to her wonted feelings and Affection, but by the most unbounded Liberality on
your part, without any Stipulation expressed or
even hinted at, for an equivalent return. Leave
that to the feelings of a generous People, the descendants of Englishmen, in which you cannot be
injured materially; since whatever regulations you
now make, can be hereafter reform'd if you do not
find they answer your wishes; but surely it will be
wise to do whatever is done, with the appearance
at least, of the utmost Liberality on your part,
rather than as if the whole was extorted from you.
I am sure also that it will be much more acceptable
in America to make use in the Bill of the Word,
Citizens, instead of *Subjects*, of the United States
of America.

You have here a few hints from an Individual
who does not pretend to penetrate so far into political subjects as very many of his Countrymen, but

should they meet the concurrence of your superior, inlighten'd Judgment he will feel himself singularly happy in having communicated them; and as this goes by the first Mail from hence, since the paper containing the abstract prepar'd came to hand, he hopes it may not be too late to enlarge the system that is the object of your Bill. I propose to embark in the course of next Month for America, And should be particularly pleased if I cou'd conscientiously assure the good People there that the Government of G. B. was sincerely and generously disposed to do every thing that can be as reasonably expected or wish'd for, to bind the two Countries forever together in an indissoluble Bond of Mutual Interest. Your time I know is precious, and every moment of it occupied in most important affairs, therefore I cannot expect an answer; but should you think proper to Honor me with a line it will readily come to hand by the common mail, if directed to me here, or sent to Mess. Welch & Rogers, Bankers in Cornhill, London, to forward.

TO JOHN ADAMS.

BRUXELLES, 27 March, 1783.

Your obliging favor of the 15th inst. did not reach me 'till ye 8th day after its date, but it did not appear to have been open'd, tho' the directions was in a handwriting that I am not acquainted with.

I can readily subscribe to the truth of every thing you have said in your Letter, and from my own experience and to prevent Dr Franklin from repeating the same unwarrantable practice with the Emperor (which from some expressions drop't I have reason to think was in agitation) as with the King of Spain, I have plainly inform'd the Government here, that no person in Europe is authorized by Congress to treat with the Emperor but Mr Dana, who is now at Petersburg; and was I in Paris, I would make a point of giving the same explicit information to ye Imperial Ambassador there. I know it has always been the creed at Passy that Congress ought not to presume to make any appointments for Europe, which Dr F. was not at the head of, or commanded to be done; upon this principle I suppose it is that he has had the effrontery, as I am told, to nominate Mr W. T. Franklin to Congress to be appointed American Minister at the Court of Versailles, it having been settled between the D.^r and Count De Vergennes, that the D.^r himself, as being the most trusty person, shou'd be sent as American Minister to London. Dr F. I see has the superlative *Modesty*, by his Agent in London, to style himself in the English Papers— The Founder of the New American Empire; but I have long look'd upon him to have been born to be a scourge to America; therefore considering the penetrating and sagacious Judgment of your particular Countrymen, it has surprised me to see him blazon'd out in the Boston Papers, in nearly as fulsome terms as in the Bulletins that are sent from the General Post Office in Paris to most of y.ᵉ Gazettes in Europe. The contending Parties there seem to place a great deal of their merit in the share they enjoy in his good graces—(See the writings about M.ʳ Jn.º Temple, &c). It would give me most sincere pleasure, if our Country would learn Wisdom from Experience; in that case I shall think it fortunate that we have received such Imperious and iniquitous treatment from a certain quarter, as they ought to convince every American that there is nothing due from us on the score of Gratitude, which may prevent us from hereafter being intrigued into schemes, that can only produce Injury and disgrace to us. A plot seems already form'd to get General Washington to Paris, which I trust Am.ᵃ will have wisdom enough to prevent the execution of, for I can never forget from what Source the King of Spain drew the Idea, nor by whose assistance he carried into execution the Nefarious plan of depriving his Country of its Liberties which he had sworn to maintain, and immediately afterwards impiously attempted to cloath his Sacrilege with the cloak of Religion, by going to Church, taking a prayerbook out of his pocket, and singing psalms, thus making a mockery both of God and Man. What a Pity it is, that the

Genius of Sweeden did not at that moment produce a Brutus or a Cassius.

Please to give me a safe direction to Mr Dana, that I may write to him, tho' I am much employed at present in preparing for my voyage to America, which may take place in the course of next month, and shall be happy to be the Bearer of your commands. Pray tell me if you think British Manufactures will now be admitted, as I shall be almost obliged to take some of them for my own private use. Intelligence from London mention, that great Intrigue and exertion was used from a certain quarter, to prevent the bill for opening a commerciai Intercourse between G. B. and the U. S. from passing in the original form as introduced by Mr Pitt, and they have pretty well succeeded; but all this may be cured by a judicious Treaty. Have you heard lately from my B.^r, and do you know if he is still in Congress? Who has succeeded Mr Livingston as Secretary?

TO ARTHUR LEE.

BRUXELLES, 2 April, 1783.

My dear Brother:

I have not heard from or of you since the 6th of Oct. last, nor from any one in Virginia for 11 months past. Mrs. I[zar]d has since Xmas reeeived several letters from her husband, in none of which are you mentioned.

Knowing as you do the people in England, you will not be surprized to see by the public papers that in February the House of Commons by a majority of 17 voted that the peace with F., S. and the U. S. of Am?. , was an inadequate and inglorious one. This vote was carried by a Union of the Rockinghams or Portlands with Lord North and all the rankest Tories in England against Lord Shelburne. The Nation, however, at large, approves of the peace, and addresses consequently to the throne on the occasion are numerous; but this union has so decided a majority in the House of Commons that Lord S. has been obliged to resign, and his friends go out also. But for 3 weeks past there has been such a scuffle for the loaves and fishes between the nefarious and ill combined union, that they had not been able the 28th ult? to agree about dividing the spoil, consequently there was no ministry, which kept all public business at a stand, particularly the peace with Holland, a definitive one with F., S., and the U. S., and settling a plan of commerce between G. B. and America. The heavy clouds that have been for some time hanging over Europe, are not yet entirely gone; but at this moment everything stands still, for all the world is occupied in gazing on the madness of England. We are told that a certain Cabinet has been combined with Dr. F. in a plot to get him appointed by Congress American Minister, and his *double refin'd Progeny*, W. T. F. to be American Minister at Versailles. I feel so much indignation over this impudent attempt, that I cannot suppose Congress will permit it to be mentioned in their assembly. Another deep plot is also layed to get to [blank]. This should by all means be defeated. My present intention is to embark for Virginia as soon as I can meet with an agreeable conveyance; but as this is yet uncertain, you may continue to write to me as usual. We are all impatient to hear what you think of the peace in America, and what you have been doing in consequence of it. The Emperor, I am told from high authority, is very desirous of entering into a commercial treaty with the U. S. Our love to all with you. Every blessing attend you. Farewell (in haste.)

TO SAMUEL THORPE.

BRUXELLES, 11 April, 1783.

* * * The ministerial arrangement seems to please you, and as it is your affairs not mine, I have no right to complain; therefore shall only say, the like was never seen before. But to make the whole complete Wedderburne must be Sole Chancellor; and then you will have at the head of your Councils one young Scotsman who is esteem'd not three degrees remov'd from Idiotism in all the Courts of

Europe, where he has resided, and he has nearly made the Tour, tho' bursting with pride and impudence; and the disposal of all the property in the Kingdom in the hands of another young Scotsman, who is too Notorious to need a Comment.

Oh halcyon daies for the *North*, and all these blessings you owe to the *Man of the People*, thrice, thrice happy and virtuous Isle! On the whole, Dear Sir, if this monstrous conjunction does *any* good, or if it subsists twelve months, I shall be very greatly disappointed. You have added to my other obligations to you, by offering to answer for my personal security with you, if I come over, which you think it my interest to do; but as I never cou'd make my feelings yield Bend to my Interest, and am not fond of forcing myself into a Man's house that I despise, and who of course must hate me, I do not at present feel any great propensity to trouble with my Company the Domains where N. S., W., M., E., &c, &c, wield the Sceptre. That this is the case with you now—a little time will convince all the World that Mess. F., B. and their party think, or pretend to think what they please. Besides I am at this time really in a hospital, my poor boy is yet in a vary precarious state, and yᵉ Girls beginning to prepare for inoculation; so that yᵉ real pleasure I should have in seeing you must be defer'd for some time. I do not see now any more likelyhood of a vessel from hence to em-

bark in for Virginia than when I saw you. If
y⁰ horses can't be sent at a reasonable freight directly to Virginia, they must be let alone. M⁰ˢ
Lee is happy to hear that the ruffles pleased.
When y⁰ Carriage is ship'd there must be a case for
y⁰ Body in w⁰ʰˡ y⁰ Harness & other light articles
may be put & also in y⁰ Trunk.

TO JOHN ADAMS.

BRUXELLES, 24 April, 1783.

Above ten daies after its date I was honor'd with
your favor of the 10ᵗʰ instᵗ., and indeed am apprehensive with you that America has lost the favorable moment for establishing a desirable commercial connection with G. B.; but this is not y⁰ only
nor the greatest mischief that has flowed upon us
from y⁰ same source.

You will by this time be able to judge of the dispositions of the new British Ministry and y⁰ Nego-
tiator; therefore it is needless for me to say any
thing with respect to them, especially as you are so
well acquainted with their Character; I will only
observe that self important Men are generally
pleased when they are allow'd to think that other
Men have as high an Idea of their Abilities and consequence as they have themselves. It appears unnecessary now to trouble Mᵣ. Dana with any observations on y⁰ subject of a Treaty with the Emperor,

as I am told that his Majesty has already nam'd
a Minister to go to Congress, and I believe that
some conversation has been already or will be soon
held with you Gentlemen at Paris on the Subject;
and as I conjecture that it will be communicated to
Cte de N. you may easily imagine into what Channel he will endeavor to turn the business. You
can't have a higher opinion of M^r. Saml. Adams
than I have, for he was long before I left Eng^d my
constant Toast as ye American Aristides. As to
D^r. F. I am convinced that with all his Art* he
would soon sink into total oblivion like his friend
Sil. Deane if the expenditure of the Public money
was taken out of his hands, and his adversaries
were to cease talking of him, unless they mean to
bring him to Public Tryal for his enormous mis-
deeds. I know him too well to suppose for a moment that he would pay a Livre of his own money
to any little insignificant French Novelist for rank-
ing him with ye Gods. I propose to embark for
Virg^a in three weeks from this time, but in order
to make my passage convenient I have been obliged
to purchase a Ship. Will you therefore be so good
as to inform me whether an American passport will
be necessary or useful, and if it is, can I request the
favor of you to send me a blank one? I cou'd wish
to know whether American Vessels will now be

---

*And *wickedness* stricken out.

admitted into the Havannah, or any other Spanish port in the West Indies—Should the definitive treaty of Peace, between G. B. and America be sign'd before I go, you will greatly oblige me by a communication of the Event, if there is no political reason that forbids your doing so.

TO ARTHUR LEE.

OSTENDE, 22 June, 1783.

My dear Brother:

I have been here with my son ten daies waiting to embark in the Virginia, Cap.t Robertson, p.r James River in Virginia. We shall sail in two daies certainly if the wind permits, but as we are to call at Madeira this is sent by a vessel from this port to Baltimore; and if she has a quick passage this may reach you some time before we arrive. Therefore wish you to write immediately to R. H. L. to prepare to come down to Green Spring, with his son Thom, to meet me, for I shall have great occasion to see them and our brother Loudoun immediately on my arrival. Therefore shall send an express to them for that purpose the moment I get on shore. Can I get 3 or 4 carriage horses in Virginia, or are they to be got cheaper or better at Philadelphia? If they are, can you purchase two good ones for me, and contrive them to Green Spring by the middle of September at farthest? If you can, I shall be obliged to you for doing so, but remember I cant afford to give above 30 or 35£ Virginia currency a piece for stout, good, and young carriage horses from 4 to 6 years old. In In August last I sent you some important papers. They were directed under cover to the President of Congress, then by Mrs. Izard put up in a packet with her own letters, directed to her husband, and delivered into the hands of Gen'l DuPortail.

If you have not received these letters, may inquire of Mr. Izard and Gen!. Du P. about them.

English and French news you will have more authentic and fresh from England and France than this could carry to you. It seems pretty certain that war is by this time commenced between Russia and the Turks. The Emperor will certainly join Russia, and in this case many think that France and even England will assist the Turks. If so, the war will be general in Europe.

I have just received your favor of the 19th April from Alexandria with its inclosures, for which I greatly thank you.

Adieu till I see you.*

---

*Mr. Lee sailed from Ostende on the last day of June, and arrived at Green Spring, after a tedious passage, on September 25th.

ROBERT MORRIS.*

M^r. Robt. Morris seems to be a most dangerous man in Am^a., from the particular attention that is paid to every creature, dependent and connection of his that appears in Europe, by Franklin and Jno. Adams, two Men that are Rivals, in all the low cunning and . . . tricks of Politicks—This conduct puts one in mind of the Theology of the native Indians of N^o. Am^a., on the first discovery of that Continent. They never worship'd an all powerfull, good and gracious Divinity, but they paid their adorations and erected Temples, to a wick'd, malignant, Artfull, and malicious Being, such as the Devil is painted to be by the Europeans; because, they said, that a good being wou'd not, nor cou'd he from his nature, do them any harm; but it was necessary by adoration, sacrifices, &c, to appease the malignant spirit of the wicked Dæmon.

In this principle of their conduct, no doubt Messrs Franklin and Jno. Adams have been directed by observing that M^r. Morris, long before the War between Am^a. & G. Britain, tho' supported by the large property and still larger credit of his partner M^r. Willing, had bro't the house of Willing, Morris & Co. to a State that is call'd Bankruptcy, in every commercial Country in Europe; and when the

---

* From a Memorandum in Lee's Letter-book.

Am^n War commenced, he had the address to get the direction of the expenditure of the greatest part of the paper money issued by Congress, 'till at length he bro't the United States of Am^a to a Public Bankruptcy, while he at the same time amassed an immense fortune for himself; and even after this, when the Congress paper money was driven out of Circulation for the want of payment, M^r. Morris had influence enough in Congress to get himself appointed Financier General of the United States of Am^a., when nothing but Gold and Silver were allowed to be Current, by which manœuvre M^r. Morris cou'd secure to himself the payment of the immense quantity of the former Congress paper money that he had collected while it was current at 1000 & 1200 p^{ct} under value. *

---

*"Robert Morris (since you ask me my opinion of him) was a frank, generous, and manly mortal. He rose from nothing but a naked boy, by his industry, ingenuity, and fidelity, to great business and credit as a merchant. At the beginning of our revolution, his commerce was stagnated, and as he had overtraded, he was much embarrassed. He took advantage of the times, united with the Whigs, came into Congress, and united his credit, supported by my loans in Holland, and resources of the United States. By this means he supported his credit for many years; but at last grew extravagant, as all conquerors and extraordinary characters do, and died as he had lived, as I believe, all his days, worth very little solid capital." *John Adams to Benjamin Rush*, 16 February, 1809. Prof. William G. Sumner is preparing a biography of Morris.

WILL OF WILLIAM LEE.

In the name of God, Amen. I, William Lee, of Virginia, late alderman of London, being of sound disposing sense and memory, do make, publish and declare this instrument, or written paper, to be and contain my last will and Testament, hereby revoking annulling and rendering void, to all intents and purposes, all former wills or testaments by me heretofore made. First, my soul I commit to our Gracious God and Heavenly father, stedfastly hoping, that through his infinite mercy and the precious merits of our blessed redeemer Jesus Christ, it will enter into eternal salvation. Amen. Item. I desire that my body may be committed to the earth wherever I may chance to die, without any pomp or parade, or any unnecessary expense whatever. Item. My will and desire is that my executor hereinafter named, do pay as soon after my decease as may be consistent with the good of my estate, all my just debts ; that is to say all demands not debarr'd by any act or acts of limitation, and which shall be supported by indifferent testimony, and no others. The various affairs in which I have been concerned ; the variety of Countries in which my transactions have been, and the circumstances of the late Revolution, which have necessarily occasioned the loss of many material papers and vouchers ; together with the misfortune of loosing my eyesight, which has caused my accounts to be more imperfect than they otherwise would have been, render this precaution absolutely necessary. Item. I give and devise and bequeath to my dearly beloved Son, William Ludwell Lee, and his heirs forever, all that estate real, personal and mixed, lying, being and situate in James City county, James Town, and the City of Williamsburg, which descended to his mother, my late dear wife, Hannah Philippa Lee, as coheiress and legatee of her late father, the Honorable Philip Ludwell, and as coheiress to her late sister, Frances Ludwell,* with all the Horses, Mares, colts, Mules, asses, Horn'd cattle, sheep, Hogs, and stocks of every kind, and all the plantation utensils, that may be on the said estate at the time of my decease, and also all my Books, plate and furniture, that may be in my house at Greenspring, or in the hands of any other persons or person, at the time of my decease, except such particular Books and pieces of plate or furniture which I shall hereinafter bequeath to either of my two dear daughters, Portia and Cornelia.† Item. I give and bequeath unto my dear daughter, Portia Lee, and her heirs forever, all that tract or parcel of Land lying and being on the waters of Bull run, and in the County of Prince William or Loudoun, which I purchased of John Page Esq., of Rosewell, in the County of Gloucester, containing by estimation twelve hundred and fifty acres more or less, which tract of land was conveyed to me and my heirs

---

*Frances Ludwell died 14 September, 1768.

†Portia married William Hodgson, of White Haven, England, and died at Alexandria, Va., 19 February, 1840. Cornelia married John Hopkins, and died in 1817 or 1818.

forever by the said John Page, by deed bearing date on
the twelfth day of October in the year one thousand
seven hundred and eighty seven, and by him acknowledged in the General Court on the twenty sixth day
of the said October, in the said year, and then and
there ordered to be recorded ; together with all houses,
improvements, advantages, and hereditaments and appurtenances to the said tract of land, in any wise belonging, when she shall arrive to the age of twenty one
years, or on her day of marriage ; provided she doth
not marry without the consent of a majority of her
Guardians herein after appointed, who shall act in that
capacity, to be obtained in writing, and not before she
shall arrive to the age of sixteen years. My will and
meaning is, that if she shall marry before she shall be
of the age of sixteen years, or after that, before she
shall be of the age of twenty-one years, without the
consent in writing previously obtained of a majority of
her guardians aforesaid, as aforesaid, in either of the
above cases the devise herein made of the land aforesaid, shall be void and of no effect ; but the said land
shall pass and go to my son, William Ludwell Lee, and
his heirs forever. Item. I give and bequeath to my
said daughter, Portia Lee, twelve hundred and fifty
pounds sterling money of Great Britain, to be paid to
her at the age of twenty one years or on her day of
marriage, but upon the same condition and provision
which hath been herein before annexed to the devise
of the land herein before given to her. And in the
meantime my will and desire is, that the profits of the

land herein before devised to her and the interest of the legacy of twelve hundred and fifty pounds sterling aforesaid, shall be applied, from the time of my decease, to her maintenance and education, or so much thereof as my executors think proper, and the overplus, if any there be, shall be paid as before mentioned with regard to the said money legacy to my said daughter, Portia Lee. Item. I give and bequeath unto my said dear daughter, Portia Lee, a Mahogany desk and bookcase, which stands in my chamber, and was used always by her late dear Mother, together with all the printed and manuscript Books therein at the time of my decease. Item. I give and bequeath to my dear daughter, Cornelia Lee, two thousand pounds sterling money of Great Britain to be paid to her when she shall arrive to the age of twenty one years, or on the day of her marriage, provided she doth not marry without the consent of a majority of her Guardians herein after appointed, who shall act in that capacity, to be obtained in writing, and not before she shall arrive to the age of sixteen years. For my will and meaning is, that if she shall marry before she shall be of the age of sixteen years, or, after that, before she shall be of the age of twenty one years, without the consent in writing previously obtained of a majority of her Guardians aforesaid, as aforesaid, in either of the above cases the bequest herein made to her shall be void and of no effect, but the said legacy shall pass and go to my son, William Ludwell Lee, forever, and in the mean time, until the said legacy shall be payable to her, my Will

and desire is, that the profits or interest of the said two
thousand pounds sterling from the time of my decease,
shall be applied to her maintenance and education, or
so much thereof as my Executors herein after mentioned, or a majority of them, shall think proper ; and
the overplus, if any there be, shall be paid as before
mentioned with regard to the legacy itself to my said
dear daughter, Cornelia Lee. Item. My will and desire is that my property in the British Funds which is
placed there in the names of Thomas Rogers and
George Welch, Bankers in London, shall not be applied either to payment of debts due from me, or or
any of the legacies herein bequeathed until after my
other personal Estate not herein before given shall have
been applied and found insufficient. Item. I hereby
nominate, constitute and appoint, the Honorable John
Blair of the City of Williamsburg, Benjamin Harrison
Esq:, of Brandon, in Prince George County, and my
two dear Brothers, Francis Lightfoot Lee, and Arthur
Lee, Esq. to be executors of this my last Will and Testament, and g rardians to my children; and I also appoint my dear Sister Rebecca Lee,* of Menokin, guar-
dian to my two dear daughters, Portia and Cornelia Lee,
particularly desiring, that they may be under her sole
care and discretion respecting their education. Item. I
give to each of my above mentioned executors a mourning ring of five guineas value, as a testimony of my esteem, and in full of every claim that they might or may

---

*Rebecca [Tayloe] Lee, wife of Francis Lightfoot Lee.

have against my estate as being executors thereof ; and my meaning is that my executors, or any of them, shall not be discharged by virtue of this will or any clause thereof, from the payment of any debt or debts that they, or any of them, now owe, or at the time of my decease, may be owing to me. Item. I give to my dear sister, Rebecca Lee of Menokin, a mourning ring of ten guineas value. Item. My Will and desire is, that my son William Ludwell Lee may henceforth omit the name of Lee and take and bear the name of William Ludwell only, that the family name of Ludwell, so ancient and honorable, both in England and America, from which he is lineally descended, may be revived. Item. It is my will and desire, and earnest request to my executors, that they take special care that no woodland be cleared, and that no timber or other trees be cut down on any part of my estate in James City County, on any pretext whatsoever, except for the necessary purposes of my said estate ; that is to say for firewood to be used on my plantations, for the necessary building and repairing of the houses, for making and repairing the fences on my lands, for tobacco Hogsheads and tight casks for the use of my plantations, and for wheelwright timber to be worked by my own people, and for coal for my blacksmiths shop. Item. I desire that my Executors may have two women servants at least to be occupied in and about my house, Greenspring, and a man and a boy to work in the gardens, to take care of the fruit trees on my several plantations and to take [care] of my stables.

Lastly I give, devise and bequeath to my Son, William Ludwell Lee, and his heirs forever, all the rest and residue of my Estate not herein before devised, whether the same be real, personal or mixed.

In Witness whereof I have this twenty fourth day of February, in the year one thousand seven hundred and eighty nine, subscribed my name and fixed my seal.

W. LEE. [SEAL.]

Signed, sealed, published and declared,
   by the said William Lee in our presence, as his last Will and Testament;
   at whose request and in whose presence, and in the presence of each
   other, we have hereunto subscribed
   our names as witness thereto.
     ANNE LEE.
     THEODORICK LEE.
     CHARLES LEE.

I, William Lee, of Greenspring, in the Parish and county of James City, and Commonwealth of Virginia, do make, publish and declare this writing to be a codicil to my last Will and testament dated (I think) in February, 1789, which is now in the possession of my Brother Francis Lightfoot Lee Esq. of Menokin, in the County of Richmond, and Commonwealth aforesaid: Whereas in my said last Will and Testament I have given and devised to my only son William Ludwell and his heirs forever, all my lands both freeholds and leese hold in the said County of James City, all my Houses and lots in Williamsburg and James Town, which I hold in right of his late dear Mother Hannah Philippa, oldest daughter and coheiress of the late Honorable Philip Ludwell, also all my lands in Loudoun or Prince William County, which I purchased of John Page, Esq., of Rosewell, in the County of Gloucester, also all my negro slaves, horses, horn'd cattle, sheep, goats, hogs, asses, mules and stock of every kind, with all my plantation utensils which may be on my said lands; and furthermore have made him, my said Son, my residuary legatee, whereby he will be entitled to and inherit all that Tract or parcel of Land adjoining to Green Spring, being part of the Land commonly called and known by the name of the Main or Governor's Land, which I have lately bargained for with the Professors of William and Mary Colledge, and with the approbation of the Visitors of said Colledge. Now I do hereby declare and make known, that my intention by the before mentioned legacies and devises was and is to give and bequeath all the said before mentioned lands, houses, lots, negro slaves, with their increase, and all the other property therein mentioned to my said son, William Ludwell, and his heirs forever, when he shall arrive at the age of twenty-one years; and in the meantime so much of the produce or profits thereof as my Executors shall think proper, shall be applied to his Maintenance and education, and the remainder of such profits or produce, if any there be, to go and descend to him with the other real and personal Estate. But if my said Son, William Ludwell, should depart

this life before she arrives at the age of twenty one
years, then and in that case, I give and bequeath to my
oldest daughter Portia, and her heirs forever, when she
shall arrive at the age of twenty one years, if she then
be unmarried, or at the age of eighteen years if she be
then married, or at any time thereafter when she shall
be married, before she arrives at the age of twenty one
years, provided always that she marries agreeably to
the restrictions pointed out in my said last Will and
Testament, all that tract or parcel of land lying and
being in the said Parish and County of James City,
commonly called and known by the name of Green
spring, whereon are the plantations called Green
Spring, Scotland, and Verneys, and several tenements,
also all that tract or parcel of Land adjoining Greenspring, being part or parcel of that tract of land commonly called and known by the name of the Main or
Governor's land, which I lately bargained for with the
professors of William and Mary Colledge and with the
approbation of the Visitors of the said Colledge, also all
my Lots in James Town, also half of my Negroe slaves,
respecting quantity and quality, in which half all the
tradesmen are to be included, together with one half
of all my Horses, horn'd Cattle, sheep, Hogs, and
stocks of every kind, and all the plantation utensils,
that may be on the said lands, and the produce and
profits of the said lands and personal estate from the
time of my decease or that of my said son William Ludwell, whichever shall last happen, shall go and descend
to my said daughter Portia, together with the real and

personal estate herein given to her. Item. In case my
said son Wm. Ludwell departs this life before he arrives at the age of twenty one years, then and in that
case, I give and devise to my daughter Cornelia and
her heirs forever, when she shall arrive at the age of
twenty one years, if she be then unmarried, or at the
age of eighteen years, if she shall be then married, or
at any time thereafter before she arrives at the age of
twenty one years, when she shall be married, provided
she marries agreeably to the restrictions mentioned in
my said last Will and Testament, all these two tracts
or parcels of land, lying and being in the said county
of James City, commonly called and known by the
names of Hotwater, and New Quarter, all my Houses
and lots in the City of Williamsburg, and all my Lands
in Loudoun or Prince William County, which I purchased of John Page, Esq. of Gloucester County, and
also the remaining one half of all my negro slaves, of
all my horses, Horn'd Cattle, sheep, Hogs, and Stocks
of every kind, and all the plantation Utensils that may
be on the lands herein given to her, the produce and
profits of the said real and personal estate from the time
of my decease, or that of my son William Ludwell,
which ever shall last happen, shall go and descend to
my said daughter Cornelia, together with the real and
personal estate herein before given to her. Item. I
hereby nominate and appoint Mr. Robert Andrews of
the City of Williamsburg, Mr. William Wilkinson Jun.
of the Main, executors of this codicil and of my last
Will and Testament jointly with those gentlemen men-

ioned as my executors in my said last will and Testament. Item. I give to the said Robert Andrews and
William Wilkinson, Jun., to each of them, a mourning
ing of five guineas value as a mark of my esteem and
ompensation for their trouble in acting as my Execu-
ors. Item. I desire that this codicil may be proved
nd recorded in the same Court with my said last Will
nd testament. Given under my hand at Green Spring,
his twenty first day of April, in the year of our Lord
ne thousand seven hundred and ninety.

W. LEE.

ign'd, published and declared by William Lee, being of perfect sense and
memory, to be a codicil to his last
Will and Testament, and, at his request and in the presence of each
other, we have subscribed our names
hereto as witness.

JOHN D. WILKINSON of the Main.
WILLIAM MOODY, York County.
RICHD. MOOR, Overseer at present
at Greenspring.

Know all men, that I William Lee of Greenspring
n James City County, and Commonwealth of Virginia,
being of sound disposing sense and memory, do make,
ordain, publish and declare this to be a codicil to my
last Will and Testament, to which I shall subscribe my
name at the bottom, this fourth day of February in the
year of our Lord Jesus Christ seventeen hundred and
ninety five. Whereas I did on the sixth day of Octo-

ber last, at a public sale of the lands and other pro-
erty of John Warburton deceased, purchase of h
Ex'ors one tract of land in the Main, containing by
late survey three hundred acres, whereon the late Jol
Harriss some time since lived and dyed, and one oth-
tract of land lying in the pine woods between the lar
of William Wilkinson Jun. and John D. Wilkins
containing between fifty and sixty acres more or les
for which two tracts or parcels of land the said Exec
tors of John Warburton deceased have made an
passed deeds of conveyance to me, which are recorde
in the County Court of James City. Now I do by th
codicil give and bequeath the said two above men
tioned tracts or parcels of land with all their appurte-
ances to my son William Ludwell, and his heirs fo-
ever, exactly in the same manner that I have give
to him my other lands in James City County, with th
further condition, that he is, in consideration of th
devise, to pay to my two daughters Portia and Corne
lia, the sum of seven hundred pounds current mone
to be equally divided between them, their respectiv
portions or moieties of the said seven hundred pound
to be paid to each of them, when they shall arrive a
the age of twenty one years, or be married, which eve
event shall first take place. But in case my said so
William Ludwell should depart this life before he a
rives at the age of twenty one years, then I give an
bequeath the said two before mentioned tracts or par
cels of land with all their appurtenances, to my daugh
ter Portia Lee and her heirs forever, she or they i

onsideration of this devise paying to my daughter
Cornelia Lee, the sum of five hundred pounds current
Money when she, the said Cornelia Lee, shall arrive
at the age of twenty one years or be married, which
ver event shall first take place. In Witness whereof
I have hereunto set and subscribed my name the day
and year above written.   W. LEE.

Signed published and declared in our
    presence by William Lee, of Green-
    spring, in the County of James City,
    to be a codicil to his last Will and
    Testament, and at his request we
    have hereunto subscribed our names
    as Witness.
        JOHN D. WILKINSON.
        LEON'D HENLEY.
        JOHN NETTLES.

Virginia to Wit;
    At a General Court held at the Capitol, in the
        City of Richmond, the 11th day of June 1796.
A writing, bearing date the twenty-first day of April
1790, purporting to be a codicil to this will was proved
by the oaths of John D. Wilkinson and Richard Moor,
Witnesses thereto, who being further sworn deposed,
that they saw William Moody the other witness thereto,
who is now dead, subscribe his name to the same in the
presence and at the request of the Testator; and another writing, bearing date the fourth day of February
1795, also purporting to be a codicil to the said Will
was proved by the oaths of John D. Wilkinson, Leonard Henley and John Nettles witnesses thereto, on the

seventeenth day of the same Month the said Will wa
proved by the oaths of Ann Lee and Charles Lee wit
nesses thereto, and together with the said Codicils or
dered to be recorded; and thereupon for reason appear
ing to the Court, and because the Executors therei
named had not attended to qualify as such, On th
motion of William Ludwell Lee, who made oath, an
together with Charles Lee and Robert Gamble his se
curity, entered into and acknowledged their Bond i
the penalty of eighteen thousand pounds conditione
according to Law, he was appointed to collect an
preserve the goods and chattels of the Testator
until the Executors in the said will and codicil
named should appear and qualify, until the furthe
order of the Court. And at a General Court hel
at the Capitol aforesaid the thirteenth day of Jun
1797, John Blair, Benjamin Harrison, William Wilkinson, Robert Andrews, and Francis Lightfoot Lee, th
surviving Executors named in the said will and th
codicils thereto, having severally renounced the Ex-
ecutorship of the said will, on the motion of William
Ludwell Lee, Son of the Testator, who made oath and,
together with Theodorick Lee and Robert Gamble his
securities (who severally justified as to their respective
sufficiency,) entered into and acknowledged their Bond
in the penalty of Thirty thousand pounds, conditioned
as the law directs, certificate was granted him for obtaining letters of Administration of the Estate of the
said Testator with his said Will annexed in due form.

A copy,   Teste   J. Brown, Cl. Cur.

       Teste.   Peyton Drew c. g. c.

LORD CHATHAM TO WILLIAM LEE.

HAYES, Sept. 24, 1774.

Lord Chatham presents his compliments to High Sheriff Lee, and desires to express many thanks to him for the favor of his very obliging attention in communicating the instructions from Philadelphia. A true friend and affectionate well-wisher to America cannot but lament extremely that zeal overheated by persecution has carried a suffering people much as I conceive beyond the mark. To be restored to their Charters, and give as they judge proper their own money were it was thought the essential objects. Declining as they now do to recognize the Supreme authority of the Parliament of Great Britain to bind America by *laws of trade & Navigation*, must if persevered in disarm their friends here, while it multiplies and strengthens their enemies. Overstrained authority on this side has united America in one common cause. Pretensions & Claims pushed to excess on the part of the Americans may dispose and unite England to resist even their most just demands. The cause of America, which I have sincerely at heart, will I fear lose ground apace on this side of the Atlantic as soon as their unadvised instructions come to be more publicly known.

INDEXES.

LETTERS WRITTEN BY WILLIAM LEE TO INDIVIDUALS AND COMMITTEES, PRINTED IN THESE VOLUMES.

GENERAL INDEX.

ERRATA.

Page 58, 6th line from top, for *Dana*, read *Deane*.

" 195, 14th line from bottom, for *Edward* read *Edmund*.

" 208, 16th line from top, for *S——r* read *S[chweighause]r*.

" 327, 15th line from bottom, for *Jennings* read *Jenings*.

" 368, 6th line from top, for *L——t C——t* read *L[amber]t C[our]t.*

" 387, 6th line from bottom, for *vice* read *rice*.

" 390, Heading of letter, for *Scuhlenberg* read *Schulenberg*.

" 428, 16th line from bottom, for *Thoronton* read *Thornton*

" 825, 6th line from bottom, for *Stevens* read *Stephen*.

" 905, Heading of letter, for *William* read *Edward*.